T0189086

Lecture Notes in Computer Science　13443

More information about this series at https://link.springer.com/bookseries/558

Nadia Magnenat-Thalmann · Jian Zhang ·
Jinman Kim · George Papagiannakis ·
Bin Sheng · Daniel Thalmann ·
Marina Gavrilova (Eds.)

Advances in Computer Graphics

39th Computer Graphics International Conference, CGI 2022
Virtual Event, September 12–16, 2022
Proceedings

 Springer

Editors
Nadia Magnenat-Thalmann (iD)
University of Geneva
Geneva, Switzerland

Jinman Kim (iD)
University of Sydney
Sydney, NSW, Australia

Bin Sheng
Shanghai Jiao Tong University
Shanghai, China

Marina Gavrilova (iD)
University of Calgary
Calgary, AB, Canada

Jian Zhang (iD)
Bournemouth University
Poole, UK

George Papagiannakis
University of Crete
Heraklion, Greece

Daniel Thalmann
Swiss Federal Institute of Technology
Lausanne, Switzerland

ISSN 0302-9743   ISSN 1611-3349 (electronic)
Lecture Notes in Computer Science
ISBN 978-3-031-23472-9   ISBN 978-3-031-23473-6 (eBook)
https://doi.org/10.1007/978-3-031-23473-6

Preface

Welcome to the Lecture Notes in Computer Science (LNCS) proceedings of the 39th Computer Graphics International conference (CGI 2022). CGI is one of the oldest international conferences in computer graphics in the world. It is the official conference of the Computer Graphics Society (CGS), a long-standing international computer graphics organization. The CGI conference has been held annually in many different countries across the world and gained a reputation as one of the key conferences for researchers and practitioners to share their achievements and discover the latest advances in computer graphics.

This year, the CGI conference was again held virtually due to the ongoing COVID-19 pandemic that is still affecting travel and other activities in many countries around the world. CGI 2022 was organized online by MIRALab, University of Geneva, and took place during September 12–16, 2022. All presentations from CGI 2022 are available on the conference YouTube channel.

This CGI 2022 LNCS proceedings is composed of 45 papers. We accepted 21 papers that were reviewed highly in the Visual Computer (TVC) track from over 100 submissions. We further accepted 24 papers for the LNCS track from approximately 60 additional submissions. To ensure the high-quality of the proceedings, each paper was reviewed by at least three experts in the field (all reviews were double blind) and the authors of accepted papers were asked to revise their papers according to the review comments prior to publication.

The proceedings also feature papers from the ENGAGE 2022 workshop (10 full papers), focused specifically on important aspects of geometric algebra including surface construction, robotics, encryption, qubits, and expression optimization. This workshop has been part of the CGI conference since 2016.

We would like to express our deepest gratitude to all the Program Committee members and external reviewers who provided timely high-quality reviews. We would also like to thank all the authors for contributing to the conference by submitting their work.

September 2022

Nadia Magnenat-Thalmann
Jian Zhang
Jinman Kim
George Papagiannakis
Bin Sheng
Daniel Thalmann
Marina Gavrilova

Organization

Conference Chairs

Nadia Magnenat Thalmann   University of Geneva, Switzerland
Jian Zhang   Bournemouth University, UK

Program Chairs

Jinman Kim   The University of Sydney, Australia
George Papagiannakis   University of Crete, Greece
Bin Sheng   Shanghai Jia Tong University, China
Daniel Thalmann   EPFL, Switzerland

Publication LNCS Chair

Marina Gavrilova   University of Calgary, Canada

Program Committee

Antonio Agudo   Universitat Politècnica de Catalunya, Spain
Kamel Aouaidjia   Algerian Space Agency, Algeria
Nantheera Anantrasirichai   University of Bristol, UK
Andreas Aristidou   University of Cyprus, Cyprus
Selim Balcisoy   Sabanci University, Turkey
Loic Barthe   IRIT – Université de Toulouse, France
Jan Bender   RWTH Aachen University, Germany
Bedrich Benes   Purdue University, USA
Lei Bi   The University of Sydney, Australia
Yiyu Cai   Nanyang Technological University, Singapore
Tolga Capin   TED University, Turkey
Jian Chang   Bournemouth University, UK
Muhammad Nadeem Cheema   COMSATS University Islamabad, Pakistan
Falai Chen   University of Science and Technology of China, China
Jie Chen   Hong Kong Baptist University, Hong Kong, China
Jie Chen   University of Oulu, Finland
Frederic Cordier   Université de Haute-Alsace, France
Etienne Corman   CNRS, France

Ligang Liu	University of Science and Technology of China, China
Luca Magri	Politecnico di Milano, Italy
Marcelo Malheiros	Federal University of Rio Grande, Brazil
Nadia Magnenat Thalmann	University of Geneva, Switzerland
Xiaoyang Mao	University of Yamanashi, Japan
Anum Masood	NTNU, Norway
Saleha Masood	COMSATS University Islamabad, Pakistan
Stefano Mattoccia	University of Bologna, Italy
Fanman Meng	University of Electronic Science and Technology, China
Bochang Moon	GIST, South Korea
Shigeo Morishima	Waseda University, Japan
Soraia Musse	Pontificia Universidade Catolica do Rio Grande do Sul, Brazil
Ahmad Nasri	Fahad Bin Sultan University, Saudi Arabia
Anam Nazir	COMSATS University Islamabad, Pakistan
Luciana Nedel	UFRGS, Brazil
Junyong Noh	Korea Advanced Institute of Science and Technology, South Korea
Jinshan Pan	Nanjing University of Science and Technology, China
George Papagiannakis	University of Crete, Greece
Giuseppe Patanè	CNR-IMATI, Italy
Xi Peng	A*STAR, Singapore
Konrad Polthier	Freie Universität Berlin, Germany
Nicolas Pronost	Université Claude Bernard Lyon 1, France
Jianjun Qian	Nanjing University of Science and Technology, China
Beatriz Remeseiro	University of Oviedo, Spain
Remi Ronfard	Inria, France
Robert Sablatnig	TU Wien, Austria
Filip Sadlo	Heidelberg University, Germany
Yusuf Sahillioglu	METU, Turkey
Gerik Scheuermann	University of Leipzig, Germany
Hyewon Seo	ICube – University of Strasbourg, France
Bin Sheng	Shanghai Jiao Tong University, China
Yun Sheng	Liverpool John Moores University, UK
Oh-Young Song	Sejong University, South Korea
Alexei Sourin	Nanyang Technological University, Singapore
Constantine Stephanidis	ICS – FORTH, Greece
Daniel Thalmann	Ecole Polytechnique Fédérale de Lausanne, Switzerland

Contents

Image Analysis and Processing

Multi-granularity Feature Attention Fusion Network for Image-Text
Sentiment Analysis 3
   Tao Sun, Shuang Wang, and Shenjie Zhong

Toward Efficient Image Denoising: A Lightweight Network
with Retargeting Supervision Driven Knowledge Distillation 15
   Beiji Zou, Yue Zhang, Min Wang, and Shu Liu

A Pig Pose Estimation Model for Measuring Pig's Body Size 28
   Yukun Yang, Wenhu Qin, Libo Sun, and Weipeng Shi

Topology-Aware Learning for Semi-supervised Cross-domain Retinal
Artery/Vein Classification 41
   *Hanlin Liu, Jianyang Xie, Yonghuai Liu, Huaying Hao, Lijun Guo,
   Jiong Zhang, and Yitian Zhao*

Face Super-Resolution with Better Semantics and More Efficient Guidance 53
   *Jin Chen, Jun Chen, Zheng Wang, Chao Liang, Zhen Han,
   and Chia-Wen Lin*

Graphs and Networks

Layout and Display of Network Graphs on a Sphere 67
   Anshul Guha and Eliot Feibush

Joint Matrix Factorization and Structure Preserving for Domain Adaptation 79
   Wenhao Shao, Hui Chen, Min Meng, and Jigang Wu

Graph Adversarial Network with Bottleneck Adapter Tuning for Sign
Language Production 92
   Chunpeng Yu, Jiajia Liang, Yihui Liao, Zhifeng Xie, and Bin Sheng

Estimation and Feature Matching

Facial Landmarks Based Region-Level Data Augmentation for Gaze
Estimation 107
   Zhuo Yang, Luqian Ren, Jian Zhu, Wenyan Wu, and Rui Wang

An Efficient Dense Depth Map Estimation Algorithm Using Direct Stereo
Matching for Ultra-Wide-Angle Images 117
  Xiuxiu Gui and Xinyu Zhang

Ad-RMS: Adaptive Regional Motion Statistics for Feature Matching
Filtering 129
  Bin Nan, Yinghui Wang, Yanxing Liang, Min Wu, Pengjiang Qian,
  and Gang Lin

3D Reconstruction

Visual Indoor Navigation Using Mobile Augmented Reality 145
  Han Zhang, Mengsi Guo, Wenqing Zhao, Jin Huang, Ziyao Meng,
  Ping Lu, Liu Sen, and Bin Sheng

Cost Volume Pyramid Network with Multi-strategies Range Searching
for Multi-view Stereo 157
  Shiyu Gao, Zhaoxin Li, and Zhaoqi Wang

Reconstructing the Surface Mesh Representation for Single Neuron 170
  Ivar Ekeland and Roger Temam

WEmap: Weakness-Enhancement Mapping for 3D Reconstruction
with Sparse Image Sequences 183
  Kun Zhang, Chunying Song, Jingzhao Wang, Kai Wang, and Nan Yun

Rendering and Animation

Comparing Traditional Rendering Techniques to Deep Learning Based
Super-Resolution in Fire and Smoke Animations 199
  Anton Suta and Helmut Hlavacs

Real-Time Light Field Path Tracing 211
  Markku Mäkitalo, Erwan Leria, Julius Ikkala, and Pekka Jääskeläinen

Crowd Simulation with Detailed Body Motion and Interaction 227
  Xinran Yao, Shuning Wang, Wenxin Sun, He Wang, Yangjun Wang,
  and Xiaogang Jin

Towards Rendering the Style of 20th Century Cartoon Line Art in 3D
Real-Time 239
  Peisen Xu and Davide Benvenuti

Detection and Recognition

Face Detection Algorithm in Classroom Scene Based on Deep Learning 255
  Yi Zhang and Chongwen Wang

GRVT: Toward Effective Grocery Recognition via Vision Transformer 266
  Shu Liu, Xiaoyu Wang, Chengzhang Zhu, and Beiji Zou

A Transformer-Based Cloth-Irrelevant Patches Feature Extracting Method
for Long-Term Cloth-Changing Person Re-identification 278
  Zepeng Wang, Xinghao Jiang, Ke Xu, and Tanfeng Sun

Learning Unified Binary Feature Codes for Cross-Illumination Palmprint
Recognition 290
  *Jianxiong Wei, Lunke Fei, Shuping Zhao, Shuyi Li, Jie Wen,
  and Jinrong Cui*

Colors, Paintings and Layout

SemiPainter: Learning to Draw Semi-realistic Paintings from the Manga
Line Drawings and Flat Shadow 305
  Keyue Fan, Shiguang Liu, and Wenhuan Lu

Hierarchical Bayesian Network Modeling and Layout of Huizhou
Traditional Villages in Geographic Environment 318
  Zude Zheng, Lin Li, Xiang Wang, and Xiaoping Liu

AE-GAN: Attention Embedded GAN for Irregular and Large-Area Mask
Face Image Inpainting 330
  Yongtang Bao, Xinfei Xiao, and Yue Qi

Synthesis and Generation

Procedural Generation of Landscapes with Water Bodies Using Artificial
Drainage Basins 345
  Roland Fischer, Judith Boeckers, and Gabriel Zachmann

High-Fidelity Dynamic Human Synthesis via UV-Guided NeRF
with Sparse Views 357
  Zhifeng Xie, Zhaosheng Wang, Sen Wang, Yuzhou Sun, and Lizhuang Ma

Rec2Real: Semantics-Guided Photo-Realistic Image Synthesis Using
Rough Urban Reconstruction Models 369
  Hui Miao, Feixiang Lu, Tiancheng Xu, Liangjun Zhang, and Bin Zhou

3D Digital City Structure Model Based on Image Modeling Technology 381
Zhen Wang, Xiaoxuan Li, and Hengshuo Xu

AR and User Interfaces

Augmented Reality-Based Home Interaction Layout and Evaluation 395
*Ningxin Chen, Zheng Lu, Xinhui Yu, Liuming Yang, Pengfei Xu,
and Yachun Fan*

LiteAR: A Framework to Estimate Lighting for Mixed Reality Sessions
for Enhanced Realism 407
*Chinmay Raut, Anamitra Mani, Lakshmi Priya Muraleedharan,
and Raghavan Velappan*

Personalized User Interface Elements Recommendation System 424
*Hao Liu, Xiangxian Li, Wei Gai, Yu Huang, Jingbo Zhou,
and Chenglei Yang*

Medical Imaging

A Feature Point Extraction Method for Capsule Endoscope Localization 439
Jiaxing Ma, Yinghui Wang, Pengjiang Qian, and Gang Lin

Automated Diagnosis of Retinal Neovascularization Pathologies
from Color Retinal Fundus Images 451
*Rahma Boukadida, Yaroub Elloumi, Rostom Kachouri,
Asma Ben Abdallah, and Mohamed Hedi Bedoui*

Segmentation

DDCNet: A Lightweight Network with Variable Receptive Field
for Real-Time Portrait Segmentation in Complex Environment 465
Dongjin Huang, Di Wu, Jinhua Liu, and Yushan Lv

A Chromosome Segmentation Method Based on Corner Detection
and Watershed Algorithm 477
*Zhifeng Zhang, Jinhui Kuang, Xiao Cui, Xiaohui Ji, Junxia Ma,
Jinghan Cai, and Zhe Zhao*

Voxel-Based 3D Shape Segmentation Using Deep Volumetric
Convolutional Neural Networks 489
Yuqi Liu, Wei Long, Zhenyu Shu, Shun Yi, and Shiqing Xin

Object Detection

Few-Shot Detection Based on an Enhanced Prototype for Outdoor Small
Forbidden Objects 503
  Jia Chen, Xinzhou Chen, Jin Huang, Xinrong Hu, and Tao Peng

Research on Real-Time Forestry Pest Detection Based on Improved
YOLOv5 515
  Jipeng Yu, Taizhe Tan, and Yaoyu Deng

Power Line Detection Based on Feature Fusion Deep Learning Network 527
  Kuansheng Zou, Zhenbang Jiang, and Shuaiqiang Zhao

Image Attention and Perception

Wider and Higher: Intensive Integration and Global Foreground Perception
for Image Matting 541
  *Yu Qiao, Ziqi Wei, Yuhao Liu, Yuxin Wang, Dongsheng Zhou,
  Qiang Zhang, and Xin Yang*

Authenticity Identification of Qi Baishi's Shrimp Painting with Dynamic
Token Enhanced Visual Transformer 554
  Wenjie Chen, Xiaoting Huang, Xueting Liu, Huisi Wu, and Fu Qi

Modeling and Simulation

An Optimized Material Point Method for Soil-Water Coupled Simulation 569
  Zhaoyu Xiong, Hao Zhang, Haipeng Li, and Dan Xu

SlimFliud-Net: Fast Fluid Simulation Using Admm Pruning 582
  *Hao Xiang, Songyang Yu, Ping Li, Weiguang Li, Enhua Wu,
  and Bin Sheng*

Author Index 595

Image Analysis and Processing

Multi-granularity Feature Attention Fusion Network for Image-Text Sentiment Analysis

Tao Sun, Shuang Wang$^{(\boxtimes)}$, and Shenjie Zhong

Qilu University of Technology, Shandong, China
wangang_2021@163.com

Abstract. Multi-modal sentiment analysis of images and texts in social media has surpassed traditional text-based analysis and attracted more and more attention from researchers. Existing studies on multi-modal sentiment analysis of texts and images focus on learning each modal feature independently, which ignores the correlation between images and texts. In the field of social media, such correlation is often multi-granularity, that is, image areas are often associated with text (words, phrases, sentences) with multiple granularity. In this paper, a multi-granularity feature attention fusion network is proposed to model the correlation between image content and multi-granularity text content for multi-modal sentiment analysis. Specifically, the model proposed in this paper includes feature learning layer, interactive information fusion layer and classification layer. Image features and text features of multi-granularity can be learned in feature learning layer. In the interactive information fusion layer, multi-granularity text features and image features are interacted and fused, and the last classification layer uses the features learned last time to complete classification. The proposed model is validated on two public multimodal data sets of graphs and texts, and the experimental results show that the model is effective.

Keywords: Multi-modal sentiment analysis · Multi-granularity feature · Feature fusion · Attention

1 Introduction

Nowadays, more and more people are willing to share information and express their opinions on social media. Social media has become an important platform for us to exchange information. For example, in Sina Weibo and Twitter posts and tweets with text and images. Sentiment analysis of these multimodal data is of great significance in the analysis and prediction of user behavior. Some practical applications, for example, personalized recommendation [1], stock prediction [2] and health care [3]. Therefore, images and text analyses emotional multimodal data has very important practical significance.

Sentiment analysis originally refers to the task of detecting and analyzing the attitudes and emotions contained in text data [4, 5], which is a branch of natural language processing. In view of the fact that single modal information is prone to information loss and interference from other factors, images data and text data are complementary to some extent, emotion analysis based on the fusion of images mode and text mode has gradually become a hotspot of current research. In the process of graphic data of emotional analysis, although most of the research considers the image data and text data, but most of these studies did not take into account the image and text of the internal interaction relationship. More importantly, the interaction between images and text in social media tends to be multi-granular. For example, words "trah" and "debris" associated with picture information in can better express negative emotional information in Fig. 1 (A). The phrase "beautiful butterflies" associated with the picture is more likely to express positive emotions in Fig. 1 (B). The words "flower" and the phrase "excited tears" associated with the picture cannot accurately express the correct emotions in Fig. 1 (C).

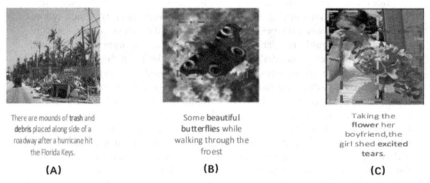

There are mounds of trash and debris placed along side of a roadway after a hurricane hit the Florida Keys.

(A)

Some beautiful butterflies while walking through the froest

(B)

Taking the flower her boyfriend,the girl shed excited tears.

(C)

Fig. 1. Example of association between images and text of different granularity

To solve the above problems, this paper proposes a multi-granularity feature attention fusion network (MGFAFN) for multi-modal sentiment analysis to mine complex associations between images and their text descriptions.Specifically, the multi-granularity feature attention fusion network proposed in this paper includes feature learning layer, interactive information fusion layer and classification layer. In the feature learning layer, natural language processing and deep learning techniques are used to obtain text multi-granularity features (word-level features, word-level features, sentence-level features), and deep learning techniques are used to obtain image features. In the interactive information fusion layer, the interactive relationship between multi-granularity text features and image features is learned and fused into joint features. The final classification layer classifies the combined features of text images learned from the previous layer to obtain the final emotional polarity. The main work of this paper is summarized as follows:

- The multi-granularity feature attention fusion network (MGFAF) proposed in this paper parses text from multiple granularity levels and obtains text semantic features of different granularity levels for mining the association relationship with image features.
- This paper analyzes the internal relation between image and text and excavates the complex relation between image features and text features.

- The proposed model is tested on two public datasets, MVSA-Single and MVSA-Multiple. Experimental results show that the proposed multi-granularity feature attention fusion network (MGFAF) has better performance than other baseline methods. The validity of the proposed model is proved.

2 Related Work

2.1 Text Sentiment Analysis

As a relatively active research direction in the field of natural language processing, traditional sentiment analysis research methods can be divided into two categories: sentiment dictionary-based method and machine learning based method. Dictionary-based methods identify the emotional polarity of texts by artificially constructed emotional dictionaries. Literature [6] uses a grammar analyzer and an emotion dictionary to achieve a relatively high accuracy in emotion recognition of web news. Machine learning methods input the effective features extracted from the text to the pre-trained machine learning classifier to achieve emotion classification. The common methods mainly include Support Vector Machine (SVM), Random Forest(RF), Naive Bayesian Model(NBM)and Logistic Regression. Feng et al. [7] used continuous bayesian to conduct sentiment analysis of e-commerce comments, which greatly improved the classification accuracy With the development of deep learning in the field of vision, methods based on deep learning have also been widely applied in the field of text emotion analysis. Severyn et al. [8] used unsupervised neuro-linguistic model to train word embedding, adjusted it on supervised corpus, and finally used pre-training parameters to initialize the model.

The development of text sentiment analysis has experienced dictionary-based methods, machine learn-based methods and deep learn-based methods. At present, the research has become relatively mature. However, due to the development of technology, the field of social media is no longer a single text data, so sentiment analysis research is developing towards multi-modal data.

2.2 Image Sentiment Analysis

Image sentiment expression than text sentiment expression is more abstract and subjective, so images sentiment analysis compared to text sentiment analysis is more challenging. Traditional image sentiment analysis mainly uses machine learning methods to carry out sentiment on the underlying objective features of image. Siersdorfer et al. [9] proposed a model based on the visual word bag to predict the sentiment polarity of images based on the low-level features and color distribution of images obtained. Borth [10] et al. used the method based on intermediate features of images to extract 1200 adjectival-noun pairs (ANP) to establish a middle-level representation, so as to carry out sentiment analysis of images. With the development of deep learning, many researchers began to apply neural network technology to image sentiment analysis. You et al. [11] proposed a deep neural network based on convolutional neural network step-by-step training and domain migration, which improved the classification accuracy of weakly labeled data with noise.

Image emotion analysis has also achieved some research results, but with the combination of multiple modes of emotion analysis is increasingly important. Multimodal sentiment analysis, which makes up for the loss of single modal information and the interference of other factors, has become a research hotspot.

2.3 Multimodal Sentiment Analysis

The importance of sentiment analysis by combining multiple modes is increasing. Make up a single modal information easy to loss and vulnerable to the interference of other factors of multimodal sentiment analysis become the research hot spot. Current research on multi-mode fusion technologies can be divided into three categories: feature layer fusion [12, 13], decision layer fusion [14, 15] and hybrid fusion [16, 17]. The feature layer fusion will integrate the different modal features immediately after the completion of the extraction and input them into the sentiment classifier. For example, Poria et al. [12] integrated the text features and visual features extracted by convolutional neural network into the multi-kernel learning classifier for fusion analysis. Xu et al. [13] proposed a collaborative memory network, which extracted mutually promoting features of text and image through mutual iterative modeling between text words and visual content, and carried out image classification based on feature fusion. After extracting the features from each mode, the decision layer immediately input them to each mode classifier for training, and finally aggregate the classification results of each mode. For example, Cao [14] et al. conducted sentiment analysis on texts and pictures in microblog posts respectively, and then integrated the results of text analysis and picture analysis. Kumar et al. [15] proposed a hybrid deep learning model that uses convolutional neural network (CNN) and support vector machine (SVM) to process text and image respectively, and then uses decision fusion method. The accuracy of this model has been improved. Hybrid fusion combines the advantages of feature layer fusion and decision layer fusion and fuses the result of feature layer fusion with the result of each single mode to get the final prediction result. For example, Xu et al. [16] proposed a multi-interaction memory network model using recursive neural network to learn not only the modal interaction information of pictures and texts, but also the information of each single mode. Zhao et al. [17] used the traditional SentiBank method to extract middle-level features, integrate other text features and social features, and train the two modal sentiment classifiers according to the consistency of text and text, so as to effectively utilize the correlation between images and text.

Although most of the existing multi-modal sentiment analysis of text and image considers the correlation between different modal data, most of them analyze content from a single granularity and capture attention from a single granularity, which cannot make full use of the comprehensive complementary correlation between text and text modes for sentiment analysis. Therefore, we propose a multi-granularity feature attention fusion network for image-text sentiment analysis.

3   Our Proposed Model

In this part, we will introduce in detail our proposed multi-granularity feature attention fusion network for multi-modal sentiment analysis of image-texts. We first introduced our overall framework and then walked through each part of the framework step by step.

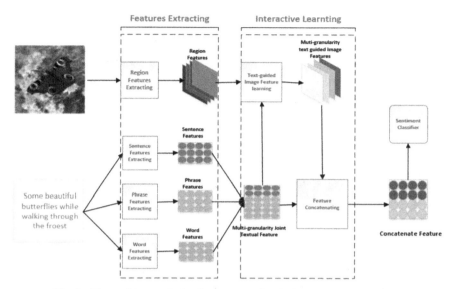

Fig. 2. The multi-granularity feature attention fusion network (MGFAF)

3.1   Model Overview

In social media, picture data and text data often appear at the same time. In social media, picture data and text data often appear at the same time. In this paper, $I^i - T^i$ is set to represent the image-text pair, where $I^1, I^2...I^i$ represents the image set and $T^1, T^2...T^i$ represents the text description set. Our goal is to predict the emotional polarity tag *positive, netural, negative* of picture-text pairs by considering both text and image modes.

The multi-granularity feature attention fusion network proposed in this paper consists of three layers: feature learning layer, interactive information fusion layer and classification layer. The network structure is shown in Fig. 2. Feature learning layer learns to extract multi-granularity text features and image features. The interactive information fusion layer learns the multi-granularity correlation between images and texts. This layer associates the emotional image region with the corresponding multi-granularity text description, that is, the multi-granularity text pays attention to the image, makes the image region features interact with the multi-granularity text of words, phrases and sentences, and obtains the visual region features concerned by the text features of different granularity. Image features and text features with association information are fused to obtain joint features. The last classification layer classifies the joint features of the pictures obtained from the interactive information fusion layer to obtain the emotional polarity.

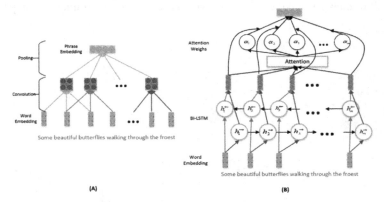

Fig. 3. Multi granularity text feature extraction

3.2 Feature Learning Layer

Multi-granularity Text Features. In the case of a given image-text pair $I^i - T^i$. The text description $T_i = w_1, w_2, w_j, w_m$ with M words is used as the input of the multi-granularity text feature extraction network. The entire multi-granularity text feature extraction network is shown in Fig. 3. Firstly, the Word Embedding vector is obtained by inputting text description into Word Embedding model:

$$x_{w,j} = G_{glove} w_j, j \in [1, m], x_{w,j} \in R^{d_w} \tag{1}$$

where G_{glove} is the pre-trained word embedding matrix [18], which is fine-tuned in subsequent training, m is the total number of words in the text description, and d_w is the dimension of word embedding.

When matching with the image region, there is the phrase level information corresponding to the image region. Compared with a single word, phrases can provide richer semantic information, so this paper uses phrases composed of three adjacent words to embed the word embedding vector. Specifically, this paper adopts a convolution layer and a pooling layer to obtain phrase features:

$$x_{p,j} = \tanh\left(W_p x_{w,j:j+2}\right) \tag{2}$$

$$x_p = max\left(x_{p,j}\right) \tag{3}$$

where $x_{p,j} \in R^d$ is the phrase feature output of the JTH word position, and W_p is the weight parameter. The extraction process is shown in Fig. 3 (A).

In the process of sentence feature extraction, the Bi-directional Long Short-Term Memory (BiLSTM) is used to obtain vector representation with context sequence information. The BiLSTM takes word embedding vector $x_{w,j}$ as input and outputs new hidden vector $h_j = \{h_j^{\rightarrow}, h_j^{\leftarrow}\}$, where $h_j^{\rightarrow}$ is obtained by the forward BiLSTM and $h_j^{\leftarrow}$ is obtained by the reverse BiLSTM:

$$h_j^{\rightarrow} = Bi - \text{LSTM}\left(h_{j-1}^{\rightarrow}, w_{w,j}\right) \tag{4}$$

$$h_j^{\leftarrow} = Bi - \text{LSTM}\left(h_{j+1}^{\leftarrow}, x_{w,j}\right) \tag{5}$$

where $h_{j-1}^{\rightarrow}$ is the output of the last neural unit of forward long short-term memory, and $h_{j+1}^{\leftarrow}$ is the output of the last neural unit of reverse long short-term memory.

The effect of all words in the whole sentence on sentiment prediction is not equal, and some words have more sentiment information. Therefore, the influence of some words should be increased in the process of extracting sentence feature vectors. Therefore, Attention is introduced into the construction of the sentence feature extraction network to assign an influence weight to each word in the corresponding sentence representation. The output of the BiLSMN was weighted to highlight the influence of key words and obtain more accurate representation of sentence features.

$$e_j = \tanh\left(W_h h_j + b_h\right) \tag{6}$$

$$\alpha_j = \frac{\exp(e_j)}{\sum_{j=1}^{m} \exp(e_j)} \tag{7}$$

$$y_s = \sum_{j=1}^{m} h_j \alpha_j \tag{8}$$

where, e_j is the unstandardized attention score, indicating the degree of emotional meaning of the word h_j. Where W_h is the weight matrix and b_h is the offset matrix, both of which will be modified in subsequent learning. The unstandardized attention score e_j is normalized by layer *soft* max to obtain the standard attention score. The sentence feature representation is weighted by the total word representation h_j and its attention score α_j. The process of obtaining sentence feature representation is shown in Fig. 3 (B).

Image Features. Convolutional Neural Networks (CNN) have good performance in many image recognition tasks. Therefore, the most advanced convolutional neural network-Residual network (ResNet) model was used in this paper to extract image features of different visual blocks from input image set $I = \{I^1, I^2, \ldots, I^i, \ldots, I^n\}$. Firstly, the input image I^i is adjusted to 224×224 pixel, and then the adjusted image is input to the pre-trained residual network ResNet152 [19] model and the last convolutional layer is taken as the output of the model to obtain image feature representation. The process can be described as follows:

$$y_i = \text{ResNet}(I^i) \tag{9}$$

where, $y_i \in R^{n \times d_v}$ is the image feature representation of image I^i. Where n is the number of eigenmatrix graphs, and d_v is the size of the eigenmatrix.

3.3 Interactive Information Fusion Layer

This section uses the Attention mechanism to realize the interaction between the above multi-granularity features and image features. Considering the input of two modes, the image mode is set as the target mode input, and the multi-granularity text mode is set as the auxiliary mode input to obtain the output of the target mode. We first splice the multi-granularity text features to obtain the joint text features, and then map the multi-granularity text joint features and image features to the same dimensional space. The mapping process is described as follows:

$$T = T_w \| T_p \| T_s \tag{10}$$

$$T_i = \tanh(W_t T + b_t) \tag{11}$$

$$V_i = \tanh(W_v y_i + b_v) \tag{12}$$

where $W_t \in R^{d_h \times d_t}$, $W_v \in R^{d_h \times d_v}$ are weight matrices; b_t, b_v is the offset matrix.

The attention weight is assigned to each regional feature based on the correlation between image feature A and multi-granularity joint text feature B. Visual features with textual attention are weighted by all regional features and their attention scores:

$$g_i = \tanh\left(T^T W V_i + b\right) \tag{13}$$

$$\beta_i = \frac{\exp(g_i)}{\sum_{i=1}^{n} \exp(g_i)} \tag{14}$$

$$V^i = \sum_{i=1}^{n} V_i \beta_i \tag{15}$$

At present, many advanced methods use simple concatenation to integrate features from different modes, but this paper argues that simple concatenation will inevitably ignore higher-order interactions between different modes. Therefore, this paper adopts the widely used multi-layer Perceptron (MLP) to learn the combined features of images and texts:

$$H^i = \left(\tanh\left(W_v V^i\right) \circ \tanh\left(W_T T^i\right)\right) + b \tag{16}$$

where, H^i is the joint feature of the image and text, W_v, W_t are the weight matrix, and b is the offset matrix, which will be obtained in later learning.

3.4 Interactive Information Fusion Layer

The joint future of image and text input to the classification of *soft*max layer for Sentiment label $F \in \{positive, netural, negative\}$:

$$p(H^i) = soft\text{max}(W_h H^i) \tag{17}$$

In the model training stage, the multi-classification Cross Entropy is used as the objective function of a-layer to calculate the loss:

$$\tau = -\sum_{f=1}^{k} F_f \log(p_f(H^i)) \tag{18}$$

4 Experimental Results

4.1 Dataset Description

The multimodal dataset of text-image used in the experiment in this paper are two datasets, MVSA-Single and MVSA-Multi, which are made public by MCRLab [20]. Two datasets of each sample of tweets from Twitter's collection of text-images. MVSA-Single contains 5129 text-image pairs, and MVSA-Multi contains 19,600 text-image pairs. After noise removal data processing, the datasets are shown in Table 1.

Table 1. The number of instances of each sentiment tag in the dataset.

Dateset	Positive	Neutral	Negative	All
MVSA-Single	2683	470	1385	4511
MVSA-Multi	11318	4408	1298	17024

4.2 Baselines

Compare the proposed method with the following methods. The following methods have been proven to be superior to traditional single mode sentiment analysis methods:

– SentiBank+SentiStrength [10]: Extract 1200 adjective - noun analysis of image futures and style of English grammar and spelling is used to calculate the emotion scores.
– CNN-Multi [21]: Convolutional neural network is used to learn text features and visual features, and the learned text features and visual features are input into another convolutional neural network for classification.
– DNN-LR [22]: Convolutional neural network is used to learn text features and visual features, and the learned text features and visual features are input into logistic regression for classification.
– HSAN [23]: A multi-layer semantic attention network based on image title is proposed for multimodal sentiment analysis. The network uses image titles as visual features and layers of text semantics.
– MultiSentiNet [24]: Think of objects in the image and scene plays an important factor in the sentiment analysis, put forward using a visual object futures and futures of the visual scene guide attention length memory neural network to extract more important to the tweets of emotional words, and the visual guide the semantic futures of the emotional classification and object and scene features integration.

4.3 Experimental Results and Analysis

Accuracy and F1-score were selected as experimental evaluation indexes in this paper. Table 2 shows the experimental results of other baseline approaches compared with our approach on both the MVSA-Single and MVSA-Multi datasets.

It can be seen from Table 2 that the performance of SentiBank+SentiStrength model is the worst among all models, which indicates that the sentiment information of images and texts cannot be well understood only by using traditional manual extraction features and statistical features. With the development of technology, machine learning and deep learning are becoming more and more popular among researchers. CNN-Multi model uses Convolutional Neural Network technology to process image data and text data respectively, and inputs the features of the two modes into another neural network for classification, achieving better performance. DNN-LR model is similar to CNN-Multi model. Text and image are input into their respective convolutional neural networks respectively to extract features, and the extracted features are input into logistic regression together for classification, and better results are obtained. This shows that machine learning and deep learning techniques are superior to traditional statistical feature methods in the field of multi-modal sentiment analysis of texts and images. The HSAN model uses the Recurrent Neural Network in the process of extracting text features, which improves the performance compared with the convolutional neural network, indicating the effectiveness of the Recurrent Neural Network in the processing of text data. The MultiSentiNet model has the best performance of all the baseline models because it not only uses recurrent neural networks to process text data, but also takes into account modal relationships.

Table 2. The number of instances of each sentiment tag in the dataset.

Model	MVSA-single		MVSA-multi	
	Accuracy	F1 Score	Accuracy	F1 Score
SentiBank+SentiStrength	52.05%	50.08%	65.62%	55.36%
CNN-Multi	61.20%	58.37%	66.30%	64.19%
DNN-LR	61.42%	61.03%	67.86%	66.33%
HSAN	66.83%	66.90%	68.16%	67.76%
MultiSentiNet	69.84%	69.63%	68.86%	68.11%
Proposed Model	70.76%	69.86%	70.46%	69.34%

Furthermore, we can see that the performance of the model proposed in this paper is better than all the baseline models. Compared with the best MultiSentiNet model, the accuracy of our model is improved by 0.94% and 1.66% respectively in the two data sets, and there are also varying degrees of improvement in F1-core. Although MultiSentiNet model takes into account the influence between modes, it adopts coarse-grained attention mechanism and only considers the interaction between text word-level features and images, which may lead to partial information loss. Compared with the proposed model in the feature layer not only learning the word granularity characteristics, also learned phrases and sentences both granularity characteristics, in the interactive information fusion layer with different particle size of text feature and image feature interaction fusion can be more comprehensive considering the relationship between different granularity between images and text. Therefore, the model proposed in this paper achieves more advanced effects than the baseline model.

To further verify the effectiveness of the proposed multi-granularity text feature for sentiment analysis, a set of ablation experiments were performed on the MVSA-Signal dataset. Specifically, only word features will be used as text features, represented by W; Only phrase features are used as text features, represented by P; Only sentence features are used as text features, represented by S (Table 3).

Table 3. Ablation test.

Model	Accuracy	F1 Score
w	62.42%	61.03%
p	65.83%	64.90%
s	66.83%	66.90%
MGFAF	70.76%	69.86%

Regardless of the granularity of text features used alone, the model will be adversely affected and will not achieve the best performance. The full version of MGMLFF model can achieve the best performance, which indicates that the combination of text features with three granularity in text features can indeed help improve the performance of sentiment analysis. Therefore, it can be concluded that there is indeed multi-granularity correlation between image and text, and using these correlations is conducive to more effective fusion of image and text so as to improve the performance of text-text fusion sentiment analysis.

5   Conclusions

This paper proposes a sentiment analysis method for image text multimodal social media. Compared with previous work, this paper adopts multi-granularity text features to guide image attention and effectively extracts multi-granularity matching relations between text and image. Experimental results on two open data sets show that the proposed model has better performance than the most advanced models available.

References

1. Pan, Y., Desheng, W.: Personalized Online-toOffline (O2O) service recommendation based on a novel frequent service-set network. IEEE Syst. J. **13**(2), 1599–1607 (2019)
2. Xu, S., et al.: Venue2Vec: an efficient embedding model for fine-grained user location prediction in geo-social networks. IEEE Syst. J. **14**(2), 1740–1751 (2019)
3. Yadav, S., et al.: Medical sentiment analysis using social media: towards building a patient assisted system. In: Proceedings of the Eleventh International Conference on Language Resources and Evaluation (LREC 2018) (2018)

4. Dashtipour, K., et al.: Multilingual sentiment analysis: state of the art and independent comparison of techniques. Cogn. Comput. **8**(4), 757–771 (2016)
5. Preoiuc-Pietro, D., et al.: Beyond binary labels: political ideology prediction of Twitter users. In: Proceedings of the 55th Annual Meeting of the Association for Computational Linguistics (Volume 1: Long Papers) (2017)
6. Nasukawa, T., Yi, J.: Sentiment analysis: capturing favorability using natural language processing. In: International Conference on Knowledge Capture DBLP (2003)
7. Feng, X.A., Rui, X.B.: E-commerce product review sentiment classification based on a nave Bayes continuous learning framework. Inf. Process. Manag. **57**, 5 (2020)
8. Dragoni, M., Petrucci, G.: A neural word embeddings approach for multi-domain sentiment analysis. IEEE Trans. Affect. Comput. 1 (2017)
9. Siersdorfer, S., et al.: Analyzing and predicting sentiment of images on the social web. In: ACM Multimedia 2010. ACM (2010)
10. Borth, D., et al.: Large-scale visual sentiment ontology and detectors using adjective noun pairs. In: ACM International Conference on Multimedia ACM (2013)
11. Misra, A.: Image sentiment analysis using deep learning. In: 2018 IEEE/WIC/ACM International Conference on Web Intelligence (WI) IEEE (2018)
12. Poria, S., et al.: Convolutional MKL based multimodal emotion recognition and sentiment analysis. In: 2016 IEEE 16th International Conference on Data Mining (ICDM). IEEE (2017)
13. Nan, X., Mao, W., Chen, G.: A co-memory network for multimodal sentiment analysis. In: The 41st International ACM SIGIR Conference on Research and Development in Information Retrieval. ACM (2018)
14. Cao, D., et al.: A cross-media public sentiment analysis system for microblog. Multimedia Syst. **22**(4), 479–486 (2016)
15. Kumar, A., et al.: Hybrid context enriched deep learning model for fine-grained sentiment analysis in textual and visual semiotic modality social data. Inf. Process. Manag. **57**(1), 102141.1–102141.25 (2020)
16. Xu, N., Mao, W., Chen, G.: Multi-interactive memory network for aspect based multimodal sentiment analysis. In: The Thirty-Third AAAI Conference on Artificial Intelligence (AAAI 2019) (2019)
17. Zhao, Z., et al.: An image-text consistency driven multimodal sentiment analysis approach for social media. Inf. Process. Manag. **56**(6) (2019)
18. Pennington, J., Socher, R., Manning, C.: Glove: global vectors for word representation. In: Conference on Empirical Methods in Natural Language Processing (2014)
19. He, K., et al.: Deep Residual Learning for Image Recognition. IEEE (2016)
20. Teng, N., et al.: Sentiment analysis on multi-view social data. In: International Conference on Multimedia Modeling Springer International Publishing (2016)
21. Cai, G., Xia, B.: Convolutional Neural Networks for Multimedia Sentiment Analysis. In: Li, J., Ji, H., Zhao, D., Feng, Y. (eds) Natural Language Processing and Chinese Computing. NLPCC 2015 2015. Lecture Notes in Computer Science, vol 9362. Springer, Cham (2015). https://doi.org/10.1007/978-3-319-25207-0_14
22. Yu, Y., et al.: Visual and textual sentiment analysis of a microblog using deep convolutional neural networks. Algorithms **9**(2), 41(2016)
23. Xu, N.: Analyzing multimodal public sentiment based on hierarchical semantic attentional network. In: IEEE International Conference on Intelligence Security Informatics. IEEE, 152–154 (2017)
24. Nan, X., Mao, W.: MultiSentiNet: a deep semantic network for multimodal sentiment analysis. In: The 26th ACM International Conference on Information and Knowledge Management (CIKM) ACM (2017)

Toward Efficient Image Denoising: A Lightweight Network with Retargeting Supervision Driven Knowledge Distillation

Beiji Zou[1,2], Yue Zhang[1,2], Min Wang[1,2], and Shu Liu[1,2(✉)]

[1] School of Computer Science and Engineering, Central South University, Changsha 410083, China
sliu35@csu.edu.cn
[2] Hunan Engineering Research Center of Machine Vision and Intelligent Medicine, Changsha 410083, China

Abstract. Image denoising is a fundamental but critical task. Previous works based on deep networks have made great progress, but suffer from the problem of computational overload. This paper addresses the demands by (1) a lightweight denoising network and (2) a novel knowledge distillation algorithm. The experimental results show the usefulness of the RS-KD on the proposed lightweight network and consistent gains that can be obtained on both synthetic and real-world datasets. Especially, benefiting from the retargeting supervision, our proposed distillation framework allows for arbitrary high-performance teacher networks.

Keywords: Efficient image denoising · Retargeting supervision · Arbitrary teacher · Knowledge distillation

1 Introduction

Image denoising, restoring the latent clean images from the observed noisy images, is a classic and long-lasting task in image processing. With the wide application of cameras, manufacturers such as smartphones and industrial cameras are desperately trying to upgrade their products with efficient denoising models. As a result, it is an urgent and challenging matter to implement efficient image denoising on resource-constrained devices.

In recent years, deep-learning based image denoising approaches have shown considerable success [1–4]. In contrast, to design sophisticated handcrafts, DnCNN [1] achieves impressive performance by stacking multiple convolutional layers. To take sufficient advantage of the image priors, NLRN [2] and NBNet [4] incorporates the non-local modules. Besides, the attention mechanisms have also been incorporated into the current network architecture design [3]. However, these methods are still computationally intensive and even more impractical to integrate into practice than some traditional methods. Fortunately, some techniques are proposed to overcome the computing problem, typically knowledge distillation (KD) [5]. They accomplish the model compression and computational cost reduction through the

N. Magnenat-Thalmann et al. (Eds.): CGI 2022, LNCS 13443, pp. 15–27, 2022.
https://doi.org/10.1007/978-3-031-23473-6_2

teaching paradigm between high-performance teacher networks usually with massive computational costs and lightweight student networks. However, these distillation methods are specifically designed for high-level tasks, and they bring no performance gains when applied to image denoising.

In this paper, we address the foregoing concerns by a lightweight network and a novel distillation algorithm with the retargeting supervision for efficient image denoising. Considering the absence of a lightweight network for RGB image denoising, we establish a lightweight deep denoising network, LUNet, by carefully considering the challenging trade-off between denoising performance and efficiency, resulting in a 14× reduction in computation cost and 10× fewer parameters. We further propose a novel distillation algorithm to improve LUNet. We first present a theoretical analysis of the image-level distillation algorithm in image denoising by modeling the distillation process as a probabilistic model. Then, we propose the retargeting supervision-driven knowledge distillation (RS-KD) algorithm to pick up the missing randomness. Specifically, we find that since the naive distillation algorithm assumes that the restored images by the teacher network are completely trustworthy, they discard randomness in the real distillation process inducing distillation failure. To overcome the deficiency, we propose the RS-KD algorithm for student networks. In contrast, to directly utilize the output of teacher networks as the supervision, we construct a multivariate Gaussian distribution with a data-adaptive variance for the prediction of teacher networks. It is tough to enable the network to learn complex distributions directly. To address this issue, we simplify the complex distribution with sampling operation. In this way, the samples shall keep moving closer to the real complex distribution as the iterations increase, hence maintaining the validity of distillation. We conduct extensive experiments to demonstrate the effectiveness of our proposed distillation methods on multiple synthetic and realistic datasets. Especially, benefiting from the retargeting supervision, our proposed distillation framework allows for arbitrary high-performance teacher networks.

In summary, our main contributions are as follows:

(1) We design a lightweight image denoising network (LUNet) for RGB image denoising, providing a baseline for the next distillation algorithm.
(2) We analyze the distillation process via a probabilistic model, theoretically uncovering the essence of the image distillation.
(3) We present a novel and flexible distillation algorithm with retargeting supervision for efficient image denoising.
(4) Extensive experiments on multiple synthetic and real-world datasets demonstrate the effectiveness of our distillation algorithm for the single image denoising task.

2   Proposed Method

2.1   Lightweight U-shaped Denoising Network: LUNet

Since a lightweight model is still absent for RGB image denoising, we present a lightweight U-shaped network, LUNet. It will also serve as a baseline model for

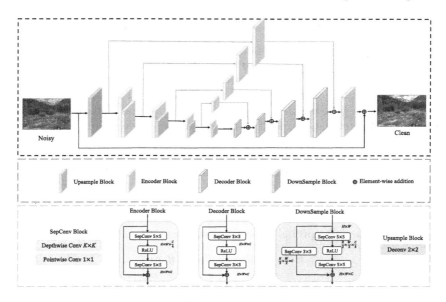

Fig. 1. Overall architecture of LUNet and structure of key building blocks. LUNet is based on UNet architecture with a depth of 4 and depth-wise separable convolutions. LUNet takes only 1.08 GMAC to process 256×256 inputs.

the subsequent distillation algorithm. LUNet has an encoder-decoder structure, where the input image is a noisy image and the output image is a clean image. As shown in Fig. 1, LUNet has four encoding stages and corresponding decoding stages. Given an input noisy image $\mathbf{I} \in \mathbb{R}^{W \times H \times 3}$, the network first applies a 3×3 convolutional layer with step size 1 to project the input image into the feature space. Then, the subsequent encoders encode the projected features. In the latter step of each encoding stage, the downsample block subsamples the feature maps to reduce the memory consumption. Specifically, the input feature $\mathbf{X} \in \mathbb{R}^{W \times H \times C}$ of each encoder is downsampled to $\mathbf{X} \in \mathbb{R}^{\frac{1}{2}W \times \frac{1}{2}H \times 2C}$. After encoding, the feature map with the smallest spatial size feature is gradually decoded to the original size. The input feature map is up-sampled by a 2×2 deconvolutional layer, which up-samples the spatial resolution by a factor of 2, and then compresses the number of channels of the feature map. The input and output of the downsampling operation are exactly opposite to the input and output of the upsampling operation so that the upsampled feature map at the decoder shall be decoded together with the input feature map from the encoder. After decoding, we obtain a feature map of the same size as the input map. Finally, the feature map is projected into the pixel space using a 3×3 convolutional kernel layer with step size 1 and output by adding the input noise image. Practically, for 256×256 inputs, LUNet only takes 1.08 GMAC, which is $14\times$ lesser than the original UNet [6].

2.2   Retargeting Supervision Driven Knowledge Distillation

Analysis. Given an image pair, (x, y), where x is the corrupted image with noise and y is the ground truth, $x, y \in \mathbb{R}^{W \times H \times 3}$. Here, we denote the restored images of the student and teacher networks as $\hat{y}, \bar{y}$, respectively.

The naive distillation algorithm usually take the L1 loss for the teaching process, *i.e.*, $||\hat{y} - \bar{y}||_1$, which is based on the assumption that the teacher can perfectly reconstruct the degraded image. However, image denoising is a typical ill-posed task, which means that the optimal solution is not singular. Therefore, it is too ideal and intuitive to use only a single image as the optimal recovery. In contrast, we leave this assumption behind and turn to the probabilistic approach to explore the real principle.

From a statistical viewpoint, the images recovered by both the teacher network and the student network are typically random variables. The primary goal is to maximize the joint probability distribution:

$$P(\hat{y}, \bar{y}|x) = P(\hat{y}|\bar{y})P(\hat{y}|x) \tag{1}$$

where $\bar{y}$ serves as the given knowledge and plays a crucial role in (1). It was noted that the naive knowledge distillation algorithm supposes that we have got a perfect image restored by the teacher network. In other words, the images recovered by the teacher network subject to a probability $P(\bar{y}|x)) = 1$. The desperation they strive for is merely a matter of simplification *i.e.*, $\max P(\hat{y}|\bar{y})$. As we have discussed above, it is unreasonable and also is the essential explanation for the failure of naive knowledge distillation.

In contrast, we consider the recovered image of the teacher network as a true random variable with probability density $P(\hat{y}|\bar{x})$. According to the central limit theorem, we shall model the image restored by the teach-er network as a multivariate Gaussian distribution:

$$P(\bar{y}|x) \sim \mathcal{N}(\mu, \Sigma) \tag{2}$$

where μ is the mean value, which is equivalent to the output of the teacher output. Σ is the variance term and it needs to be set delicately. It is worth noting that the distribution of $P(\bar{y}|\bar{x})$ is not required to be Gaussian. Actually, it is more close to Laplace. Fortunately, the Laplace distribution might be re-parameterized as $\bar{y} - \Sigma * \text{sgn}(z) * \ln(1 - 2|z|)$, where $z \sim \mathcal{N}(0, 1)$. For ease of illustration, we use the Gasussian distribution as a typical example.

Our goal is to allow the student network to learn from this distribution of teachers. According to [7,8], $P(\hat{y}|\bar{y})$ can be modeled as Boltzmann distribution:

$$p(\hat{y}|\bar{y}) \propto exp(-\frac{|\hat{y} - \bar{y}|}{kT}) \tag{3}$$

where the kT is a constant, and it is the product of Boltzmann's constant k and thermodynamic temperature T.

Therefore, we have obtained the explicit probability densities of all the demanded distributions, $P(\bar{y}|x)$ and $P(\hat{y}|\bar{y})$, in Eq. 1. It would be quite preferable to optimize the above joint probability density distribution directly, however it is still intractable to enable the network to learn the probability density function. To solve this problem, we propose a simplified method to ease the learning process. In each iteration, we approximate the conditional probability distribution $P(\bar{y}|x)$ by some instances in it. Specifically, we first sample some variables in the distribution $P(\bar{y}|x)$, replacing the whole distribution in $P(\hat{y}, \overline{(y)})$. Fortunately, with the increasing number of training iterations, this approximation would be safe because this approximation keeps getting closer to the real distribution. Thus, we shall use the sampled joint probability density function, $P(\hat{y}|\bar{y})$, as supervision for the student network. It should be emphasized that the $\bar{y}$ here is randomly sampled, which is intrinsically dissimilar to the one in naive KD. Finally, we apply the negative log-likelihood as our optimization goal:

$$\min \mathbb{E}_{\bar{y} \sim \mathcal{N}(\mu, \Sigma)}[\|\hat{y} - \bar{y}\|_1] \qquad (4)$$

We shall denote Eq. 4 as $\mathcal{L}_{distil}$ for notation convenience. In addition, according to the Jensen's inequality, we have $\mathbb{E}[f(x)] \geq f(\mathbb{E}[x])$ for any convex function $f(\cdot)$. Because the p-norm is convex and thus we shall get

$$\mathbb{E}_{\bar{y}}[\|\hat{y} - \bar{y}\|_1] \geq \|\mathbb{E}_{\bar{y}}[\hat{y} - \bar{y}]\|_1 = \|\hat{y} - \bar{y}\|_1 \qquad (5)$$

which suggests that our optimization objective is an upper bound for naive knowledge distillation. In other words, naive knowledge distillation suffers from a degraded problem. It loses the randomness during training and the supervision of the student network is unfortunately restricted to the output of the teacher network. Therefore, to solve this problem, we take the sampled joint probability distribution described in the last section as a new learning objective for the student network.

The Retargeting Supervision. The analysis demonstrates an probabilistic model for Knowledge distillation. The prior distribution $P(\bar{y})$ determines the supervision quality of the students' network, especially the variance term. An intuitive idea is to set the Σ as a small constant value, kI, only for introducing randomness. I is the identity matrix. However, such an operation is equivalent to adding a small random noise $z \sim \mathcal{N}(0, kI)$ to the output of the teacher network, which leads to worse results. In contrast, we introduce retargeting supervision to help the student network learning efficiently. Especially, we propose a data-adaptive Σ to acquire randomness.

$$\Sigma = |\bar{y} - y| \qquad (6)$$

where $|\cdot|$ refers to element-wise absolute function. In particular, as shown in Fig. 2. We introduce an auxiliary network branch attached to the student network to learn the variance. This would allow the student network to capture the distribution completely. Especially, Eq. 6 may introduce a denoising bias. However, the sampling of multivariate Gaussian distributions can alleviate the problem to some extent. We use L1 loss to enable the auxiliary network to capture the data-adaptive variance

$$\mathcal{L}_{aux} = \||\bar{y} - y| - \sigma\|_1 \qquad (7)$$

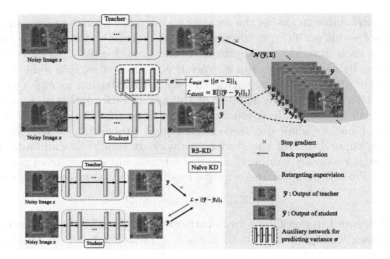

Fig. 2. The pipeline of our proposed Retargeting Supervisionis driven Knowledge Distillation (RS-KD) framework. During training, RS-KD distills the student network via retargeting supervision with the assistance of an auxiliary network. For testing, the only required network is the original student network, leaving no auxiliary network.

where σ is the output of the auxiliary network. Incorporating Eq. 4 and Eq. 7, the final loss function is formulated as:

$$\min \; \mathcal{L}_{total} = \mathcal{L}_{distil} + \alpha \mathcal{L}_{aux} \tag{8}$$

where α is the hyper-parameter to balance different aspects of loss. As a result, the multivariate Gaussian distribution composed by the output of the teacher network and the data-dependent variance term forms the new retargeting supervision.

Note that, in Eq. 8, we do not directly apply the given ground truth as the supervision. This brings an advantage in that we do not have to carefully weigh the ground truth and the output of the teacher while training the student network. In addition, since $|\bar{y} - y|$ contains the information passed by both ground truth and the teacher, the supervision from teachers dominates Eq. 8. This enables an arbitrary high-performance teacher network to be selected in our distillation framework. This paper uses MIRNet [9] as the teacher. After training, we only need to keep the original student network, LUNet, for testing. Therefore, we do not introduce additional computation in the student network.

3   Experimental Results

3.1   Experimental Settings

Implementation Details. We train all the models with the Adam optimizer with momentum terms (0.9, 0.999). During training, we crop images into 256 × 256 patches and training networks with a batch size of 32 for 400, 000 iterations. The initial learning rate is 2×10^{-4}, and it steps at 240, 000 and 360, 000 iterations with scale 0.1. We apply random rotation and flipping to augment the training data. For distillation experiments, we do not perform a pretraining process on LUNet. We perform all experiments on Nvidia 2080Ti GPUs. Specifically, we take PSNR and SSIM as the metrics.

Datasets. For synthetic datasets, the training dataset are consisted of 432 images from BSD [10], 400 images from the validation set of ImageNet [11] and 4,774 images from the Waterloo dataset [12]. We follow the same setting in [13] to generate non-i.i.d Gaussian noise as following,

$$n = M * n^1, n_{ij}^1 \sim \mathcal{N}(0, 1) \tag{9}$$

where M is a spatially variant mask with the same size as the clean image. In this paper, we choose a Gaussian window function with a variance being 10. We utilize the above generated data as training data and test models with regular Gaussian noise. While testing, we consider three noise levels, namely $sigma = 15, 25, 50$. Then we evaluate on Set5 [14], LIVE1 [15] and BSD68 [16].

For real-world datasets, we conduct experiments on Smartphone Image Denoising Dataset (SIDD) [17]. SIDD is composed of about 30,000 noisy images from 10 scenes under different lighting conditions. It employs five representative smartphone cameras and generates their gro-und truth images through a systematic procedure. SIDD is available to measure the denoising performance of smartphone cameras. As a benchmark, SIDD splits 1280 color images for validation.

3.2   Quantitative and Qualitative Results

Comparisons of Efficient Denoising. We report the quantitative results on both synthetic and real-world datasets. The real-world denoising performance on SIDD presents in Table 1. We also compare the computational complexity of the latest methods, including the model parameters as well as the practical running time. FAN is chosen as the efficient baseline model. It is worth noting that our LUNet has a higher performance, nearly 2 dB. Our LUNet effectively weighs computational cost and performance. In comparison with the original UNet [6], LUNet has comparable performance with less computation.

Table 1. Quantitative results on real-world dataset SIDD [17]. LUNet† is the LUNet trained in the standard fashion. LUNet* means the LUNet is trained with our distillation scheme. The time tests perform on all performed on a single Nvidia 2080Ti GPU.

Method	MAC(G) ↓	Param(G) ↓	Runtime(ms) ↓	PSNR ↑	SSIM ↑
DnCNN [1]	68.15	0.56	21.69	23.66	0.583
BM3D [18]	-	-	41.56	25.65	0.685
WNNM [19]	-	-	-	25.78	0.809
NLM [20]	-	-	-	26.76	0.699
KSVD [21]	-	-	-	26.88	0.842
CBDNet [22]	40.38	4.37	80.76	30.78	0.754
RIDNet [23]	40.34	1.49	98.13	38.71	0.914
VDN [13]	41.88	7.70	99.00	39.28	0.909
DANet+ [24]	14.85	9.15	65.62	39.47	0.918
MIRNet [9]	786.43	31.79	192.61	39.72	0.959
MPRNet [3]	588.14	15.74	180.00	39.71	0.958
NBNet [4]	354.80	13.3	37.44	**39.75**	**0.973**
UNet [6]	14.85	9.15	4.1	36.71	0.913
FAN [25]	2.67	0.26	3.6	34.59	0.901
LUNet†	1.08	0.95	3.6	36.39	0.912
LUNet*	**1.08**	**0.95**	**3.6**	36.56	0.914

Table 2. Quantitative results PSNR on synthetic datasets with i.i.d Gaussian noise. LUNet† is the LUNet trained in the standard fashion. LUNet* means the LUNet is trained with our distillation scheme.

Dataset	sigma	CBM3D [26]	WNNM [19]	DnCNN [1]	MemNet [27]	FFDNet [28]	UDNet [29]	VDN [13]	**NBNet** [4]	UNet [6]	FAN [25]	LUNet† [25]	LUNet* ours
Set5 [14]	15	33.42	32.92	34.04	34.18	34.30	34.19	34.34	**34.64**	32.30	30.28	30.27	31.52
	25	30.92	30.61	31.88	31.98	32.10	31.82	32.24	**32.51**	27.43	26.24	26.34	28.40
	50	28.16	27.58	28.95	29.10	29.25	28.87	29.47	**29.70**	23.60	21.06	21.02	21.50
LIVE1 [15]	15	32.85	31.70	33.72	33.84	33.96	33.74	33.94	**34.25**	31.12	30.87	30.93	31.42
	25	30.05	29.15	31.23	31.26	31.37	31.09	31.50	**31.73**	27.38	27.50	27.43	27.85
	50	26.98	26.07	27.95	27.99	28.10	27.82	28.36	**28.55**	23.44	20.90	20.99	21.85
BSD68 [16]	15	32.67	31.27	33.87	33.76	33.85	33.76	33.90	**34.15**	31.74	31.16	31.07	31.97
	25	29.83	28.62	31.22	31.17	31.21	31.02	31.35	**31.54**	28.62	27.15	27.27	27.79
	50	26.81	25.86	27.91	27.91	27.95	27.76	28.19	**28.35**	22.64	21.85	21.68	22.48
Average	-	30.18	29.30	31.19	31.24	31.34	31.11	31.47	**31.71**	27.58	26.34	26.33	27.19

The Effectiveness of RS-KD. Our distillation algorithm can enhance the performance of LUNet on both synthetic and real-world datasets. As shown in Table 1, the distilled LUNet has a higher SSIM value compared to the original UNet, which means that the proposed optimization introduces a trade-off between quality and speed. We suppose that the introduced randomness allows

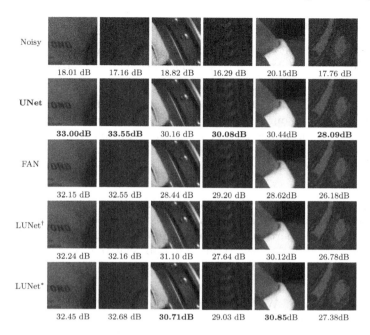

Fig. 3. Qualitative results on SIDD [17]. Our distillation algorithm enables LUNet to produce visual-pleasing denoised images. Please enlarge the screen for more detailed information.

Table 3. Ablation study of the KD methods. Naive KD is shown in the bottom left in Fig. 2. RS means our proposed retargeting supervision driven KD.

KD methods	Loss	PSNR	SSIM
Naive	L1	36.41(+0.02)	0.9120(+0.0001)
RS	Eq. 8	36.56(**+0.17**)	0.9141(**+0.0022**)

the student network to capture more probable textures in the learning process. This further demonstrates the effectiveness of our proposed distillation algorithm. As shown in Table 2, our RS-KD algorithm an average gain of 0.85 dB to LUNet for synthetic experiments on Gaussian noise. This further demonstrates the superior performance of our method for simple noise.

Qualitative Results. We show the visual comparisons in Fig. 3. Compared with the results of FAN, LUNet can produce favorable recovery results. Moreover, our distillation algorithm makes the original LUNet more effective in recovering texture information without color distortion.

3.3   Ablation Studies

We present the ablation studies to analyze the contribution of each component of our model. The evaluations are performed on the intractable SIDD dataset.

Comparison with the KD Methods. As shown in Table 3, compared to the naive KD supervision, our retargeting supervision drive KD design can provide effective enhancement to the baseline. This phenomenon is consistent with that in the classification task, meaning that naive KD do not convey the knowledge of teachers properly.

The Hyperparameter α. We explore the importance of the information in the retargeting supervision. As shown in Table 4, when $\alpha = 0.0001$, the performance is optimal. In particular, when $\alpha = 0$, *i.e.*, using only the naive KD for the distillation supervision, the results are also relatively poor. This shows the necessity of the existence of the auxiliary network.

The Variance Term. We further explore the different choices of the variance item. We generate them in two ways, *i.e.*, $|y - \bar{y}|$ and $|y - \hat{y}|$ respectively. As shown in Table 5, $|y - \bar{y}|$ performs better for PSNR. We suppose that this approach enables the student network to identify the shortcomings of the teacher network and thereby learn the teacher network thoroughly. Besides, both of them have higher SSIM than that of the original UNet. This may means that our approach can effectively leverage the knowledge of the teacher network to enhance the performance of the student network.

Table 4. Ablation study of the hyperparameter α.

α	0.01	0.005	0.001	0.0001	0.00001	0
PSNR	36.39	36.5	36.51	**36.56**	36.46	36.45
SSIM	0.9097	0.9119	0.9137	**0.9141**	0.9109	0.9119

Table 5. Ablation study of the variance item.

Variance	α	PSNR	SSIM
$\Sigma = \|y - \bar{y}\|$	0.0001	**36.56**	**0.9141**
$\Sigma = \|y - \hat{y}\|$	0.0001	36.50	0.9138

The Teacher Network. We explore the contribution of different teacher networks in the proposed distillation framework as shown in Table 6. In contrast to previous studies [30, 31], our distillation algorithm has no restrictions on the teacher network, offering considerable flexibility.

Table 6. Ablation study of the teacher model.

Teacher model	Student model	Baseline	Distilled
VDN [13]	LUNet	36.39	36.52(**+0.13**)
DANet+ [24]	LUNet	36.39	36.51(**+0.12**)
MPRNet [3]	LUNet	36.39	36.49(**+0.10**)
MIRNet [9]	LUNet	36.39	36.56(**+0.17**)

4   Conclusions

In this paper, we make contributions for efficient image denoising from two aspects, efficient network structure and distillation algorithm respectively. We first design a lightweight U-shaped network, LUNet, which has $14\times$ lower computation cost and $10\times$ fewer parameters than the original UNet. Then, we propose a novel distillation algorithm to improve the performance of LUNet. Finally, supported by the RS-KD algorithm, LUNet accomplishes efficient image denoising. We expect that our work will encourage further research on the knowledge distillation algorithms for other low-level vision tasks.

Acknowledgements. This work was supported by the National Science and Technology Major Project under Grant 2018AAA0102100, and the National Natural Science Foundation of China under Grant 61902435. We are grateful for resources from the High Performance Computing Center of Central South University.

References

1. Zhang, K., Zuo, W., Chen, Y., Meng, D., Zhang, L.: Beyond a gaussian denoiser: residual learning of deep CNN for image denoising. IEEE Trans. Image Process. **26**(7), 3142–3155 (2017)
2. Liu, D., Wen, B., Fan, Y., Loy, C.C., Huang, T.S.: Non-local recurrent network for image restoration. arXiv preprint arXiv:1806.02919 (2018)
3. Zamir, S.W., et al.: Multi-stage progressive image restoration. In: Proceedings of the IEEE/CVF Conference on Computer Vision and Pattern Recognition, pp. 14821–14831 (2021)
4. Cheng, S., Wang, Y., Huang, H., Liu, D., Fan, H., Liu, S.: NBNet: noise basis learning for image denoising with subspace projection. In: Proceedings of the IEEE/CVF Conference on Computer Vision and Pattern Recognition, pp. 4896–4906 (2021)

5. Hinton, G., Vinyals, O., Dean, J.: Distilling the knowledge in a neural network. arXiv preprint arXiv:1503.02531 (2015)
6. Ronneberger, O., Fischer, P., Brox, T.: U-Net: convolutional networks for biomedical image segmentation. In: Navab, N., Hornegger, J., Wells, W.M., Frangi, A.F. (eds.) MICCAI 2015. LNCS, vol. 9351, pp. 234–241. Springer, Cham (2015). https://doi.org/10.1007/978-3-319-24574-4_28
7. Bruna, J., Sprechmann, P., LeCun, Y.: Super-resolution with deep convolutional sufficient statistics. arXiv preprint arXiv:1511.05666 (2015)
8. He, X., Cheng, J.: Revisiting L1 loss in super-resolution: a probabilistic view and beyond. arXiv preprint arXiv:2201.10084 (2022)
9. Zamir, S.W., et al.: Learning enriched features for real image restoration and enhancement. In: Vedaldi, A., Bischof, H., Brox, T., Frahm, J.-M. (eds.) ECCV 2020. LNCS, vol. 12370, pp. 492–511. Springer, Cham (2020). https://doi.org/10.1007/978-3-030-58595-2_30
10. Arbelaez, P., Maire, M., Fowlkes, C., Malik, J.: Contour detection and hierarchical image segmentation. IEEE Trans. Pattern Anal. Mach. Intell. 33(5), 898–916 (2010)
11. Deng, J., Russakovsky, O., Krause, J., Bernstein, M.S., Berg, A., Fei-Fei, L.: Scalable multi-label annotation. In: Proceedings of the SIGCHI Conference on Human Factors in Computing Systems, pp. 3099–3102 (2014)
12. Ma, K., et al.: Waterloo exploration database: new challenges for image quality assessment models. IEEE Trans. Image Process. 26(2), 1004–1016 (2016)
13. Yue, Z., Yong, H., Zhao, Q., Zhang, L., Meng, D.: Variational denoising network: Toward blind noise modeling and removal. arXiv preprint arXiv:1908.11314 (2019)
14. Kim, J., Lee, J.K., Lee, K.M.: Accurate image super-resolution using very deep convolutional networks. In: Proceedings of the IEEE Conference on Computer Vision and Pattern Recognition, pp. 1646–1654 (2016)
15. Sheikh, H.R., Sabir, M.F., Bovik, A.C.: A statistical evaluation of recent full reference image quality assessment algorithms. IEEE Trans. Image Process. 15(11), 3440–3451 (2006)
16. Martin, D., Fowlkes, C., Tal, D., Malik, J.: A database of human segmented natural images and its application to evaluating segmentation algorithms and measuring ecological statistics. In: Proceedings Eighth IEEE International Conference on Computer Vision, ICCV 2001, vol. 2, pp. 416–423. IEEE (2001)
17. Abdelhamed, A., Lin, S., Brown, M.S.: A high-quality denoising dataset for smartphone cameras. In: Proceedings of the IEEE Conference on Computer Vision and Pattern Recognition, pp. 1692–1700 (2018)
18. Dabov, K., Foi, A., Katkovnik, V., Egiazarian, K.: Image denoising with block-matching and 3D filtering. In: Image Processing: Algorithms and Systems, Neural Networks, and Machine Learning, vol. 6064, p. 606414 (2006)
19. Gu, S., Zhang, L., Zuo, W., Feng, X.: Weighted nuclear norm minimization with application to image denoising. In: Proceedings of the IEEE Conference on Computer Vision and Pattern Recognition, pp. 2862–2869 (2014)
20. Buades, A., Coll, B., Morel, J.M.: A non-local algorithm for image denoising. In: 2005 IEEE Computer Society Conference on Computer Vision and Pattern Recognition (CVPR 2005), vol. 2, pp. 60–65. IEEE (2005)
21. Aharon, M., Elad, M., Bruckstein, A.: K-SVD: an algorithm for designing overcomplete dictionaries for sparse representation. IEEE Trans. Signal Process. 54(11), 4311–4322 (2006)
22. Shi, G., Zifei, Y., Kai, Z., Wangmeng, Z., Lei, Z.: Toward convolutional blind denoising of real photographs. arXiv preprint arXiv:1807.04686 (2018)

23. Anwar, S., Barnes, N.: Real image denoising with feature attention. In: Proceedings of the IEEE/CVF International Conference on Computer Vision, pp. 3155–3164 (2019)
24. Yue, Z., Zhao, Q., Zhang, L., Meng, D.: Dual adversarial network: toward real-world noise removal and noise generation. In: Vedaldi, A., Bischof, H., Brox, T., Frahm, J.-M. (eds.) ECCV 2020. LNCS, vol. 12355, pp. 41–58. Springer, Cham (2020). https://doi.org/10.1007/978-3-030-58607-2_3
25. Young, L.D., et al.: Feature-align network with knowledge distillation for efficient denoising. In: Proceedings of the IEEE/CVF Winter Conference on Applications of Computer Vision, pp. 709–718 (2022)
26. Guo, S., Yan, Z., Zhang, K., Zuo, W., Zhang, L.: Toward convolutional blind denoising of real photographs. In: Proceedings of the IEEE/CVF Conference on Computer Vision and Pattern Recognition, pp. 1712–1722 (2019)
27. Tai, Y., Yang, J., Liu, X., Xu, C.: Memnet: a persistent memory network for image restoration. In: Proceedings of the IEEE International Conference on Computer Vision, pp. 4539–4547 (2017)
28. Zhang, K., Zuo, W., Zhang, L.: FFDNet: toward a fast and flexible solution for CNN-based image denoising. IEEE Trans. Image Process. 27(9), 4608–4622 (2018)
29. Lefkimmiatis, S.: Universal denoising networks: a novel CNN architecture for image denoising. In: Proceedings of the IEEE Conference on Computer Vision and Pattern Recognition, pp. 3204–3213 (2018)
30. Tung, F., Mori, G.: Similarity-preserving knowledge distillation. In: Proceedings of the IEEE/CVF International Conference on Computer Vision, pp. 1365–1374 (2019)
31. Guo, Q., et al.: Online knowledge distillation via collaborative learning. In: Proceedings of the IEEE/CVF Conference on Computer Vision and Pattern Recognition, pp. 11020–11029 (2020)

A Pig Pose Estimation Model for Measuring Pig's Body Size

Yukun Yang🆔, Wenhu Qin$^{(\boxtimes)}$🆔, Libo Sun$^{(\boxtimes)}$🆔, and Weipeng Shi🆔

School of Instrument Science and Engineering, Southeast University, Nanjing 210096, China
{qinwenhu,sunlibo}@seu.edu.cn

Abstract. In this paper, we present a pig pose estimation model to solve the non-contact measurement of body size. The model includes the network header, down-sampling module, and up-sampling module. The network header includes the integration of image and image edge information. The original edge information in the image can be effectively used in the network, and the Canny operator calculates the edge information. The down-sampling module comprises residual structure and Triplet attention mechanism, which can effectively preserve the network context information while extracting image features. In the up-sampling module, the deconvolution method obtains the heat map containing the key point information. We also constructed a pig key point dataset to map pig key points with body size information. We can achieve 93.4% average precision by verifying our pig key point dataset. Compared with the 84.2% average precision of the baseline model, we achieved a 9.2% improvement.

Keywords: Triplet · Attention mechanism · Canny · Network header

1 Introduction

The large-scale and intelligent modern management mode is a way to improve production efficiency and reduce the cost of livestock breeding. In the production process of the existing breeding, the evaluation of the body size of livestock mainly depends on manual work, which is inefficient and difficult to measure. The non-contact automatic measurement method can reduce the difficulty of animal body measurement. Compared with manual measurement, automatic measurement is more normative. Pigs are essential livestock, so it is of great significance to improve the level of pig breeding to realize the automatic measurement of body size in pig breeding.

The automatic measurement of pig body size mainly bases on computer vision. With the development of computer vision and depth neural networks, there are two mainstream methods for pig body size automatic measurement. The first method is to extract the outline of livestock, then uses envelope or other methods to extract the body size [1]. However, this kind of method requires a specific shooting angle and the pigs need to

Supplementary Information The online version contains supplementary material available at https://doi.org/10.1007/978-3-031-23473-6_3.

maintain a specific posture. The other method is to use depth camera or other equipment to extract the point cloud of pig, then adopts point cloud rotation normalization or other methods to calculates the body size [2]. However, this method also has limitations, such as requiring pigs should not be too dense and have high requirements for devices. The core of these automatic measurements of pig body size is to find the key point of pig to calculate the body size.

In recent years, deep learning has developed rapidly, we found that algorithms based on deep learning can achieve a good performance on human pose estimation. Considering that pigs have similar bones and limbs as humans, we can also identify pig's key points. After obtaining a pig's key points, we can measure pig's body size. Therefore, we adopt deep learning algorithms to measure pigs' body size. We first proposed a set of key points suitable for pig body size measurement and constructed a dataset. Then we used the top-down detection method for identifying pig key points [3]. When we recognize the key points, we need crop the pig from the image. However, there may be many other pigs in the cropped image, and some other problems, such as single-color and unclear edge information. Consequently, we add the Triplet attention module [4] to the algorithm and propose a network header fused with the Canny operator to solve these problems. The integration of an attention mechanism can enhance the features extracted. Adding our network header can increase the representation of edge information. Our contributions can be summarized as follows:

(1) We build a pig key point dataset, and we propose a set of key points suitable for pig body size measurement.
(2) We propose a network header structure integrating Canny operator, and add the Triplet attention module to the down-sampling module of the algorithm.
(3) We achieve 93.4% average precision on our dataset. Compared with the baseline model, we achieved a 9.2% improvement.

2 Related Work

2.1 Measuring Animal Body Size

With the development of technologies, there are some researches about automatic measurement of animal body size. The synthetic image is obtained using CAD animal models, and the prediction of animal bones in the actual image is realized using a semi-supervised learning method [5]. Employing semantic segmentation and the envelope, the body size of croaker can be extracted from side image [6]. The cow's body size can be measured using semantic segmentation and envelope lines in images from upper and lateral angles [7]. The depth camera obtains the three-dimensional point cloud information of pigs [1]. The body size information of pigs can be extracted by point cloud rotation normalization or clustering segmentation. The pig contour is extracted from the image by threshold segmentation, and then the pig scale can be measured by using the idea of the envelope. Using the depth camera to extract the pig contour, then using the difference method to obtain the key points can also calculate the pig body size [8]. By designing the narrow lane, reading the sheep's position information according to RFID, and then obtaining the image through the camera in three directions, the sheep's body size can be measured using image segmentation and other technologies [9].

2.2 Key Point Identification

The research of key point recognition technology is mainly used for human pose estimation. These studies identify human joints in images to represent human structure. With the excellent performance of deep learning in various fields recent years, there have also been many key point recognition studies based on animals.

Newell et al. proposed a stacked hourglass network for human posture estimation, achieved good results on FLIC and MPII datasets [10]. Wei et al. used a sequential convolution structure to represent spatial texture information for human posture key point detection based on the CNN network [11]. Xiao et al. proposed the Simple Baselines algorithm [12], which uses the residual network and three-layer deconvolution to detect the human posture. Based on the Simple Baselines algorithm, sun et al. proposed a detection model HRNet [13]. The feature layer is not reduced in the convolution layers. Psota et al. proposed a key point dataset including 24,842 pigs, each pig has four key points and realized the key point detection of pigs [14]. Li et al. proposed a regression-based pose recognition method using cascade Transformers, which fused human body recognition and key point detection into one algorithm [15]. Liu et al. Studied multi-frame human posture estimation in a complex environment and proposed a model that integrates posture, time, and residual into the network [16]. Lee proposed a pig posture recognition model, which uses Mask R-CNN to extract the pig contour, then uses the stacked hourglass network to detect the pig key points [17]. Chen et al. designed an unsupervised adaptation channel for animal posture estimation [18]. The channel includes a multi-scale adaptation module, a self-distillation module, and a mean-teacher network. Hans et al. proposed that Combining Raw Hip-Worn Accelerometry can reach 2D Pose Estimation of child [19]. Zhang et al. proposed a relative pose estimation algorithm for light field cameras by matching LF-point pairs [20]. Vladimir et al. propose a method that estimates the scale factor β used in the pose error functions and get a better effect than PoseNet [21].

Among the methods mentioned above, Simple Baselines is a simple and effective method. It uses RESNET for feature extraction. It only adds three layers of deconvolution to get heatmaps and carries out coordinate transformation to identify key points. By that way, we use this model as the baseline in this paper.

2.3 Attention Mechanism

In recent years, the attention mechanism has been one of the hotspots in deep learning. It gives different weights to different parts of the model. This strategy is beneficial to preserve the context of perceptual information during network computing. Many research proposed different attention mechanisms in the past few years. Combining attention mechanisms networks can improve the effectiveness of visual tasks. Next, we summarize some attention mechanisms that have emerged in recent years.

Residual attention network proposes an attention module including mask branch and trunk branch, which plays an essential role in target classification [22]. SENet pointed out that many previous studies improved the network performance from the spatial dimension [23]. This study proposed an attention module that focuses on channel relationships. CBAM (Convolutional Block Attention Module) includes spatial and channel domain, which improved the effect of the attention mechanism by combining the maximum pool feature in the channel domain and spatial attention component [24]. After CBAM, Park et al. focused on the effect of attention in general deep neural networks [25]. They proposed a simple and effective attention module named Bottleneck Attention Module (BAM). Selective Kernel unit was proposed in SKNet, in which multiple branches with different kernel sizes are fused using softmax attention guided by the information in these branches [26]. A new attention mechanism was proposed in A2-Net [27]. It integrates all the critical features of the input image and then calculates the weight of each feature. GSoP-Net adds a second-order pool in the structure to collect essential features from the entire input space to facilitate the identification and propagation of other layers [28]. The Triplet attention module adopts the crossed latitude interaction that was not considered in the past research and combines three dimensions of image interaction [4].

3 Our Approach

This paper focuses on identifies pig key points on a deep convolution neural network. Due to the dense pig population, the background of the cropped pig image often contains other pigs, it is difficult to distinguish the key points between the current pig and other pigs in the background. In addition, due to the single and dim color of the breeding environment, we find that the points maybe outside the pig body while identifying. Based on these problems, firstly, the network should be able to better retain the perceptual information transmitted between the network layers. Therefore, we combine the residual block in the down-sampling module with the Triplet attention module to ensure the model can obtain more affluent and characteristic perceptual information. Secondly, the network should distinguish pig from the background. Therefore, we use the Canny operator to fuse the input image and the edge information in the network header to further improve the network's ability.

Fig. 1. The framework of our algorithm

The framework of our method is shown in Fig. 1, composed of a header, a down-sampling module, and an up-sampling module. Our header consists of an image and a Canny channel. The image channel comprises a 64-layer convolution. The Canny module comprises a 32-layer and a 64-layer convolution, whish input is the edge information calculated by the Canny operator. The down-sampling module comprises residual and Triplet attention modules responsible for feature extraction. The up-sampling module comprises three deconvolution layers, which is responsible for outputting heatmaps containing key point information. The following article will describe our network header and down-sampling module in detail.

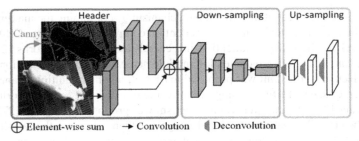

Fig. 2. The structure of our algorithm

As shown in Fig. 2, a model for pig key point recognition is constructed in this paper. The orange and purple branches of the network represent our header structure, and the blue module in the network represents the residual module [29] added with the attention mechanism. The grey trapezoid represents deconvolution.

3.1 Our Network Header

Our network header includes two branches: the image module and the Canny module. We add the Canny module into our header. In that way, the network can obtain adequate edge information and better identify key points, as Fig. 2 shows. After two convolution calculation branches extract edge information and image, the two tensors are added and input into the down-sampling module to extract features.

The canny operator is used to calculate the image edge, which includes four steps: Firstly, using a Gaussian filter to smooth the image; Secondly, the gradient amplitude and direction are calculated by the first-order partial derivative finite difference method; Thirdly, the gradient amplitude is suppressed by non-maximum value; Finally, using a double threshold algorithm to detect and connect edges. Our network header structure can be expressed by Eq. (1):

$$Header(X) = \psi(X) + \psi_2(\psi_1(Canny(X, th_1, th_2))) \tag{1}$$

where ψ represents convolution calculation, Canny represents the input images use Canny operator to calculate the edge information. th_1 and th_2 represents the two thresholds in the Canny operator, which are taken as 60 and 160 according to the empirical method in this paper. We took these values because we made several experiments, and we found the edges can be most clearly extracted under these values.

3.2 Down-Sampling Module

The structure of the down-sampling module is mainly realized by the residual network. In order to better preserve the context information when the network extracts the feature information, we add an attention mechanism to the residual unit of the residual network. Based on the effect of the added attention mechanism in the experiment, we use the triplet attention module to add the down sampling module.

In the Triplet attention module, the input tensor is calculated by three branches to obtain the output. Take an input tensor T with a size of C × H × W as an example. In the first branch, we permute T to obtain T_1, then after Z pooling and convolution, we get T_1' with size of 1 × H × C. Then T_1 is multiplied by the collocated elements of T_1', finally we permute the tensor to obtain out_1; In the second branch, T does not rotate, and the operations are the same as those in the first branch to obtain out_2; In the third branch, we permute T to obtain T_3, and the operations are the same as those in the first branch to obtain out_3. Finally, the tensors of the three branch outputs are averaged to the output. The Triplet module can be represented by Eq. (2), and the calculation of three branches in the module can be represented by Eqs. (3)–(5).

$$output = (out_1 + out_2 + out_3)/3 \tag{2}$$

$$out_1 = T_1 \odot \sigma(\psi(Z(T_1))) \tag{3}$$

$$out_2 = T \odot \sigma(\psi(Z(T))) \tag{4}$$

$$out_3 = T_3 \odot \sigma(\psi(Z(T_3))) \tag{5}$$

where ψ represents convolution operation; $\odot$ represents the multiplication of homologous elements; Z indicates Z pooling, which is achieved by concatenating tensor after maximum pooling and average pooling, as shown in Eq. (6).

$$Z(X) = \left[MAX_{pool}(X), AVG_{pool}(X)\right] \tag{6}$$

As shown in Fig. 3, we add Triplet attention module to each residual unit of the model. Similarly, the CBAM attention module used in the follow-up experiment was added to the baseline model in the same way as the Triplet module.

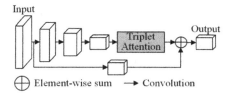

Fig. 3. Residual unit with Triplet attention module

3.3 Selection of Key Points

In this study, we selected a set of key points to measure the body size. Pig body size includes width and length. Body width refers to the width between two front legs, body length refers to the distance from the midpoint of ears to the root of tail. In past research, scholars mainly used the envelope to extract key points from pig contour. Using this method, we can only get five key points. That is impossible to measure the body size when a pig is bending. As shown in Fig. 4, we use the Canny operator to extract the edge information in images. Figure 4 (a) shows that edges exist at the scapula when pig is standing. Figure 4 (b) shows inevitable dents exist at the outline of the pig at its scapula when pig is side-lying. We choose this point as a new key point. We can measure the body size when pig is bending after adding this new key point.

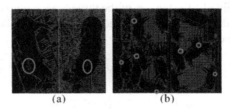

(a)   (b)

Fig. 4. Pig edge information image

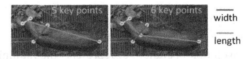

Fig. 5. Comparison of key point groups

The pig's body size before and after adding the center of the scapula as the key point is shown in Fig. 5. The figure shows that when the pig's body is bent, increasing this key point can get a more reasonable pig's body length.

4   Experiments

The experiments are implemented in the system of Ubuntu 16.04 using the Pytorch framework. The algorithm's server processor is intelcorei7-5930K@3.50 GHz with twelve cores, 64 GB memory, and NVIDIA TITAN XP graphics card with 12 GB video memory. The batch size of each experiment was 32; the model's iteration times (epoch) are all 150 generations; The initial learning rate of the model is 0.001, which decreases to 0.0001 after the 90th iteration and 0.00001 after the 120th iteration, then remains unchanged. Before the header of the network, we process pig images to 256×192 size. The output tensor of all models in the experiment is $64 \times 48 \times 6$. Each 64×48 size heat map defines the coordinates of a feature point.

4.1   Dataset

One part of the images was collected from Shangdang oasis pig farm, Dantu District, Zhenjiang City, Jiangsu Province, China. The other part came from the images in the pig data set provided on the website http://psrg.unl.edu/Projects/Details/12-Animal-Tra

cking. We used a camera with a focal length of 4 mm to collect images. The image acquisition time is from April 2021 to March 2022. We collected pig image data when the camera was at an angle of 45 degrees and 90 degrees to the ground. The size of the collected images is 3840 × 2160. The size of the pig image obtained from website is 1920 × 1080. The image formats are all JPG. The pig key point data set built in this paper has 1000 images. The data set contains 5236 labeled pigs. Our models train on the training set with 800 labeled images and 4097 labeled pigs. We validate our models on the testing set with 200 labeled images and 1139 labeled pigs. Figure 6 shows the live pig image collection site. The figure shows our data collection device, including patrol inspection equipment, camera, and infrared camera.

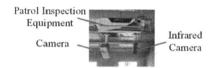

Fig. 6. Image acquisition device

4.2 Results on Image and Video

We also verified our results on pig images and pig videos. As shown in Fig. 7, the results of our method compared with the baseline algorithm and the baseline algorithm with CBAM or Triplet attention module.

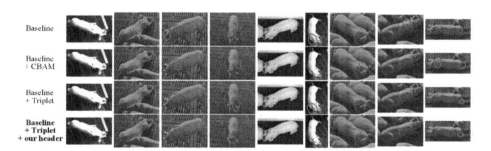

Fig. 7. Comparison results

The pictures we used to compare the key point recognition effect have different light intensities, pig densities, and pig postures. In the figure, we used red circles to mark several methods' inaccuracy of key point detection in pig images. As for the baseline algorithm, there are many errors detection in the recognition results. As for the baseline algorithm combined with CBAM or Triplet attention mechanism, there are relatively few errors in the recognition results, but there are still some problems, such as key point deviation and key points are not on pigs' bodies. As for the algorithm which header is replaced by the structure proposed in this paper. Through comparison, its result is better than the previous three algorithms, and the number of error detection and apparent detection deviation is significantly reduced. Moreover, we can find that our algorithm has a better recognition effect when the lighting conditions are dark, the pigs are dense, and the pigs are in a bending angle posture.

In the attachment, we show the recognition results of pig key points in the video by the external algorithm, and we find that the algorithm's performance is still good. We trained a YOLOv4 [30] model to detect pigs in video, then we used the output information about pigs' location and frames of video to recognize key points of pigs.

4.3 Results on Combining Attention Mechanism

Table 1 reports the algorithm results on the pig key point data set before and after adds the attention mechanism. AP refers to the average value of average accuracy when IOU is between 0.5 and 0.95, mainly reflecting the accuracy of prediction results. AP50 and AP75 represent the average accuracy when IOU is 0.5 and 0.75. AR refers to the ratio of the number of correct identifications to the sum of the number of correct identifications and errors, mainly reflecting the missed detection rate in identification. It is worth noting that we used the baseline method and CBAM attention mechanism as comparative experiments to verify the effect of the Triplet attention mechanism. The three groups of experiments all started from scratch without using the pre-training model of the residual network.

Table 1. Comparison of results on testing set from baseline and baseline with attention mechanisms.

Model	AP	AP50	AP75	AR
Baseline	84.2%	89.2%	86.2%	87.1%
Baseline + CBAM	91.6%	95.4%	93.4%	93.2%
Baseline + Triplet	**92.8%**	**95.6%**	**95.6%**	**94.8%**

The results show that the AP reached 92.8% with the Triplet attention module and 91.6% with the CBAM attention module. Compared with the baseline model, it increased by 8.6% and 7.4%. Since the model's performance is better when the Triplet attention module is added, we have added the Triplet attention module to our model.

Figure 8 (a) shows AP curves of three methods in training process, and Fig. 8 (b) shows loss curves. After smoothing the curve data, the figure shows that the convergence speed and detection accuracy of the model is greatly improved after adding the attention module. The Triplet module can get better results than the CBAM module.

4.4 Results on Using Our Network Header

We also change the network header structure of the algorithm to our proposed structure which integrates the Canny operator and carries out comparative experiments to verify the

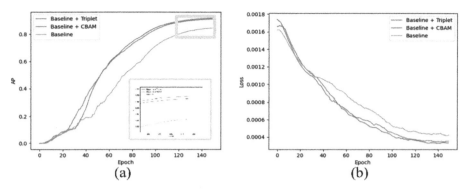

Fig. 8 Comparison of baseline and baseline with CBAM or Triplet attention module

effect of this structure. Table 2 shows results after adding the Triplet attention mechanism and after replacing the headers of models by our proposed header. The results show that our network header can achieve better results. After using our network header in the baseline model, the AP and AR scores increased by 2% and 1.8%. Using our header in the baseline model with the Triplet attention module, we also achieved 0.6% and 0.2% improvement in AP and AR.

Table 2. Comparison of results on our testing set from baseline and baseline with Triplet attention module and header proposed by us.

Model	AP	AP50	AP75	AR
Baseline	84.2%	89.2%	86.2%	87.1%
Baseline + our header	86.2%	90.5%	88.5%	88.7%
Baseline + Triplet	92.8%	95.6%	**95.6%**	94.8%
Baseline + Triplet + our header	**93.4%**	**96.5%**	95.5%	**95.0%**

Figure 9 (a) and (b) show the AP and loss curves of the four models. We also smoothed the data when drawing the curves. The figure shows that after using our network header structure, the average precision of the model is improved, and the convergence speed of the model is also improved. The model using our network header and adding the Triplet attention module achieved the best results.

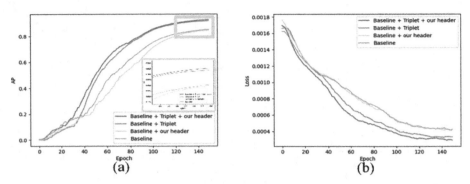

Fig. 9. Comparison of baseline before and after adding Triplet attention module or our header

5 Conclusion

This paper proposes a network header structure integrating the Canny operator. This structure inputs part of the edge information in the picture and the picture into the backbone network, so that the network can more easily identify the key points through the edge information in the image. At the same time, this paper adds Triplet attention module to the network, so that the network can enhance the extracted features. The experimental results show that both the attention mechanism and the network header structure proposed in this paper can improve the model's accuracy on the self-built pig key point data set, and model's AP can achieve 93.4%.

Acknowledgements. This work was supported by Jiangsu Modern Agricultural Industry Key Technology Innovation Project under Grant CX(20)2013, the Key R&D Program of Jiangsu Province under Grant BE2019311 and National Key Research and Development Program under Grant 2020YFB160070301.

References

1. Liu, T., Teng, G., Fu, W., Li, Z.: Extraction algorithms and applications of pig body size measurement points based on computer vision. Trans. Chin. Soc. Agric. Eng. **29**, 161–168 (2013)
2. Wang, K., Guo, H., Liu, W., Ma, Q., Su, W., Zhu, D.: Extraction method of pig body size measurement points based on rotation normalization of point cloud. Trans. Chin. Soc. Agric. Eng. **33**, 253–259 (2017)
3. Toshev, A., Szegedy, C.: Deeppose: human pose estimation via deep neural networks. In: Proceedings of the IEEE Conference on Computer Vision and Pattern Recognition, pp. 1653–1660 (2014)
4. Misra, D., Nalamada, T., Arasanipalai, A.U., Hou, Q.: Rotate to attend: convolutional triplet attention module. In: Proceedings of the IEEE/CVF Winter Conference on Applications of Computer Vision, pp. 3139–3148 (2021)
5. Mu, J., Qiu, W., Hager, G.D., Yuille, A.L.: Learning from synthetic animals. In: Proceedings of the IEEE/CVF Conference on Computer Vision and Pattern Recognition, pp. 12386–12395 (2020)

6. Yang, J., Xu, J., Lu, W., Zeng, D.: Computer vision-based body size measurement and weight estimation of large yellow croaker. J. Chin. Agric. Mech. **39**, 70–74 (2018)
7. Guo, H., Zhang, S., Ma, Q., Wang, P., Su, W., Zhu, D., Qi, B.: Cow body measurement based on Xtion. Trans. Chin. Soc. Agric. Eng. **30**, 116–122 (2014)
8. Yongsheng, S., Lulu, A., Gang, L., Baocheng, L.: Ideal posture detection and body size measurement of pig based on Kinect. Nongye Jixie Xuebao/Trans. Chin. Soc. Agric. Mach. **50** (2019)
9. Zhang, A.L.N., Wu, B.P., Jiang, C.X.H., Xuan, D.C.Z., Ma, E.Y.H., Zhang, F.Y.A.: Development and validation of a visual image analysis for monitoring the body size of sheep. J. Appl. Anim. Res. **46**, 1004–1015 (2018)
10. Newell, A., Yang, K., Deng, J.: Stacked hourglass networks for human pose estimation. In: Leibe, B., Matas, J., Sebe, N., Welling, M. (eds.) Computer Vision – ECCV 2016. ECCV. Lecture Notes in Computer Science, vol. 9912, pp. 483–499. Springer, Cham (2016). https://doi.org/10.1007/978-3-319-46484-8_29
11. Wei, S.-E., Ramakrishna, V., Kanade, T., Sheikh, Y.: Convolutional pose machines. In: Proceedings of the IEEE Conference on Computer Vision and Pattern Recognition, pp. 4724–4732 (2016)
12. Xiao, B., Wu, H., Wei, Y.: Simple baselines for human pose estimation and tracking. In: Ferrari, V., Hebert, M., Sminchisescu, C., Weiss, Y. (eds) Computer Vision – ECCV 2018. ECCV 2018. Lecture Notes in Computer Science, vol. 11210, pp. 466–481. Springer, Cham(2018). https://doi.org/10.1007/978-3-030-01231-1_29
13. Sun, K., Xiao, B., Liu, D., Wang, J.: Deep high-resolution representation learning for human pose estimation. In: Proceedings of the IEEE/CVF Conference on Computer Vision and Pattern Recognition, pp. 5693–5703 (2019)
14. Psota, E.T., Mittek, M., Pérez, L.C., Schmidt, T., Mote, B.: Multi-pig part detection and association with a fully-convolutional network. Sensors **19**, 852 (2019)
15. Li, K., Wang, S., Zhang, X., Xu, Y., Xu, W., Tu, Z.: Pose recognition with cascade transformers. In: Proceedings of the IEEE/CVF Conference on Computer Vision and Pattern Recognition, pp. 1944–1953 (2021)
16. Liu, Z., et al.: Deep dual consecutive network for human pose estimation. In: Proceedings of the IEEE/CVF Conference on Computer Vision and Pattern Recognition, pp. 525–534 (2021)
17. Lee, S.K.: Pig pose estimation based on extracted data of mask R-CNN with VGG neural network for classifications. South Dakota State University (2020)
18. Li, C., Lee, G.H.: From synthetic to real: unsupervised domain adaptation for animal pose estimation. In: Proceedings of the IEEE/CVF Conference on Computer Vision and Pattern Recognition, pp. 1482–1491 (2021)
19. Hõrak, H., Jermakovs, K., Haamer, R.E.: Modeling physical activity in children by combining raw hip-worn accelerometry, 2D pose estimation, and direct observation. IEEE Access **10**, 39986–40000 (2022)
20. Zhang, S., Jin, D., Dai, Y., Yang, F.: Relative Pose Estimation for Light Field Cameras Based on LF-Point-LF-Point Correspondence Model. IEEE Transactions on Image Processing **31**, 1641–1656 (2022)
21. Ocegueda-Hernández, V., Román-Godínez, I., Mendizabal-Ruiz, G.: A lightweight convolutional neural network for pose estimation of a planar model. Mach. Vis. Appl. **33**, 1–21 (2022)
22. Wang, F., et al..: Residual attention network for image classification. In: Proceedings of the IEEE Conference on Computer Vision and Pattern Recognition, pp. 3156–3164 (2017)
23. Hu, J., Shen, L., Sun, G.: Squeeze-and-excitation networks. In: Proceedings of the IEEE Conference on Computer Vision and Pattern Recognition, pp. 7132–7141 (2018)

24. Woo, S., Park, J., Lee, J.-Y., Kweon, I.S.: Cbam: convolutional block attention module. In: Ferrari, V., Hebert, M., Sminchisescu, C., Weiss, Y. (eds) Computer Vision – ECCV 2018. ECCV 2018. Lecture Notes in Computer Science, vol. 11211, pp. 3–19. Springer, Cham. https://doi.org/10.1007/978-3-030-01234-2_1

25. Park, J., Woo, S., Lee, J.-Y., Kweon, I.S.: Bam: bottleneck attention module. arXiv preprint arXiv:1807.06514 (2018)

26. Li, X., Wang, W., Hu, X., Yang, J.: Selective kernel networks. In: Proceedings of the IEEE/CVF Conference on Computer Vision and Pattern Recognition, pp. 510–519 (2019)

27. Chen, Y., Kalantidis, Y., Li, J., Yan, S., Feng, J.: A^ 2-nets: double attention networks. Advances in Neural Information Processing Systems, vol. 31 (2018)

28. Gao, Z., Xie, J., Wang, Q., Li, P.: Global second-order pooling convolutional networks. In: Proceedings of the IEEE/CVF Conference on Computer Vision and Pattern Recognition, pp. 3024–3033 (2019)

29. He, K., Zhang, X., Ren, S., Sun, J.: Deep residual learning for image recognition. In: Proceedings of the IEEE Conference on Computer Vision and Pattern Recognition, pp. 770–778. (2016)

30. Bochkovskiy, A., Wang, C.-Y., Liao, H.-Y.M.: Yolov4: optimal speed and accuracy of object detection. arXiv preprint arXiv:2004.10934 (2020)

Topology-Aware Learning for Semi-supervised Cross-domain Retinal Artery/Vein Classification

Hanlin Liu[1], Jianyang Xie[2], Yonghuai Liu[3], Huaying Hao[2], Lijun Guo[1], Jiong Zhang[2(✉)], and Yitian Zhao[2(✉)]

[1] Faculty of Electrical Engineering and Computer Science, Ningbo University, Ningbo, China
[2] Cixi Institute of Biomedical Engineering, Ningbo Institute of Materials Technology and Engineering, Chinese Academy of Sciences, Ningbo, China
{zhangjiong,yitian.zhao}@nimte.ac.cn
[3] Department of Computer Science, Edge Hill University, Ormskirk L39 4QP, UK

Abstract. Pixel-level Artery/Vein (A/V) classification of retinal blood vessels is important in diagnosing and understanding a wide spectrum of diseases. Deep learning-based methods have achieved promising results, but manual image annotation is a labor-intensive and time-consuming process and annotations between different datasets cannot be fully utilized. The model performance might be significantly decreased when training on one dataset but testing on another. Some unsupervised domain adaptation (UDA) methods can alleviate this problem. However, annotating a few target samples is usually very manageable and worthwhile especially if it improves the adaptation performance substantially. Consequently, we propose a novel semi-supervised retinal A/V classification method where a few labeled target samples and the labeled publicly-accessible source dataset are available. We first employ the teacher-student framework to achieve semi-supervised learning. Then, a new regional mixing method is proposed to reduce the domain gap at the region level, which takes into account the topological features of retinal vasculature. Furthermore, we combine spatial transformation with regional mixing to generate additional synthetic images, thus improving the generalization ability of the model. We evaluate the proposed method on a publicly accessible (DRIVE-AV) dataset and a private dataset, and the results show that the proposed method achieves state-of-the-art performance for A/V classification.

Keywords: A/V classification · Domain-shift · Semi-supervision

1 Introduction

Several studies have shown that the morphological changes of retinal vasculature are associated with many eye-related and systemic diseases [1–5]. For example, retinal venular widening is closely related to the development and progression of diabetic retinopathy [1] and the risk of stroke [3]. In particular, the Arteriolar-to-Venular diameter Ratio (AVR) is an important metric for the performance

© The Author(s), under exclusive license to Springer Nature Switzerland AG 2022
N. Magnenat-Thalmann et al. (Eds.): CGI 2022, LNCS 13443, pp. 41–52, 2022.
https://doi.org/10.1007/978-3-031-23473-6_4

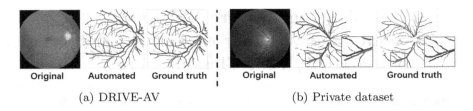

Original   Automated   Ground truth   │   Original   Automated   Ground truth

(a) DRIVE-AV   (b) Private dataset

Fig. 1. Illustrations of the domain-shift issue. Both were obtained using U-Net trained on the DRIVE-AV dataset. (a) Result of source domain (DRIVE-AV); (b) Result of target domain (private dataset). Blue indicates veins and red indicates arteries. (Color figure online)

of the methods that usually degrades when directly taking a trained model of one dataset to process another dataset, caused by data discrepancy of different imaging devices. In clinical practice, the arteries and veins are usually manually annotated by ophthalmologists. However, this process is time-consuming and prone to human errors [6]. Therefore, it is indispensable to develop fully automatic and accurate retinal arteries and veins (A/V) classification method.

In the last decade, several A/V classification methods have been proposed and can be categorised into two types: graph-based [7–11] and learning-based approaches [12–15]. The former uses vessel topology to reconstruct the vessel tree and classify them into artery and vein. However, they require vessel segmentation as a primary step. The latter, especially the deep learning models, has achieved state-of-the-art classification performance.

However, there are still two main problems: 1) It is unrealistic to label all the images. 2) Labeled samples can only improve the performance on images with similar characteristics because of domain shift [16]. For the first problem, manual labeling is very expensive. We hope to make full use of existing annotations even if they come from different datasets. However, it may lead to the second problem. More specifically, different characteristics between datasets will result in reduced performance. It may be caused by the physical properties of different imaging devices [17]. Figure 1 shows that the model trained on a publicly-accessible dataset (DRIVE-AV [18]) performs poorly on a private dataset. As mentioned above, we focus on training a model that performs well on the new dataset by using only a few annotations of the new dataset and full annotations of other datasets.

The semi-supervised learning is a strategy to alleviate the domain-shift and over-fitting problems based on limited labeled data with the aid of unlabeled data [19–21]. For example, Li *et al.* [16] introduced a semi-supervised learning method for the cross-domain A/V classification. They regularized a model to deal with the data perturbations of the mixed image inputs from two different retinal fundus devices, by imposing consistent posterior distributions of arteries and veins. However, this method ignores the vessel topological features, and vessels are frequently disconnected at the edge of the mixed areas.

In this paper, we focus on minimizing the inter-domain discrepancy for the A/V classification task through the training on a source dataset with complete annotation and a target dataset with a small number of annotations. The proposed method mainly consists of a spatial transformation module and a regional mixing module, where the former aims to address the lack of sufficient manual annotation in the new dataset, and the latter regularizes the model to give topological consistency in vessel-mixing samples. The underlying topology helps the mixing module produce vessel-mixing samples with consistent posterior distribution, and preserves the overlooked topology in the existing mixup method [16].

We summarise our contributions as follows: 1) We develop semi-supervised cross-domain A/V classification with consistency regularization. We make full use of the existing labeled data and unlabeled data, and solve the inconsistency introduced between the two streams of the teacher-student model from spatial transformation with different parameters. 2) A regional mixing method is proposed to ensure the integrity of vessels by considering the topological characteristics of vessels in the mixed images, thus improving the cross-domain generalization ability for pixel-wise classification.

2   Method

2.1   Overview

In this paper, we use a fully annotated dataset and a new dataset with a few annotations to train a semi-supervised model that fits the new data. Unlike unsupervised domain adaptation, which focuses on using as little annotation as possible, we are more concerned with fully using the existing annotations to improve performance on new data. Considering the domain shift between the datasets, we define the fully annotated dataset as the source domain x_s, and the new dataset with a few annotations as target domain x_t. To make full use of the existing label, we introduce a semi-supervised framework based on a teacher-student network, which contains two regularization modules: the spatial transformation module and the regional mixing module. Then we train the proposed model by using the target domain images x_t and the source domain images x_s to improve the cross-domain classification performance. In this paper, the Mean-teacher framework [19] is applied as the backbone. The teacher and student models are defined as $f(x, \theta)$ and $f(x, \theta')$, respectively, where x is the input data and θ is the parameters of the model to be learned. The architecture of the proposed method is shown in Fig. 2.

2.2   Spatial Transformation Module

A/V classification can be considered as a pixel-level multi-class classification task. The data augmentation techniques have been shown to be useful in semi-supervised image-level classification [4]. However, they are not always suitable for dense outputs in semi-supervised learning [22]. In pixel-wise classification tasks, spatial transformation such as flipping, rotation, scaling, and cropping may result in alterations in both images and labels [22]. As a result, the transformed inputs

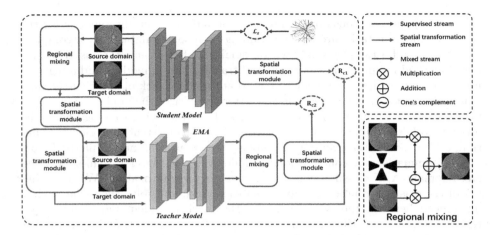

Fig. 2. The architecture of the proposed method. The spatial transformation contains flip, rotation, scale, and crop, the exponential moving average (EMA) of the student model's weights are transferred to the teacher model's weights [19].

of the student and teacher models may correspond to different labels, which is undesirable in semi-supervised learning. For example, if we cut out a blood vessel in the input of the student model, the same operation will be applied only on the student label without affecting the teacher label. Different student and teacher labels will make it impossible to carry out consistency constraint.

To solve this issue, a spatial transformation module $g(x; \phi)$ is proposed in this work, where x is the input data and ϕ is the parameters of the transformation. Transformation includes random scaling, rotation, flip, crop, and color jitter. Specifically, a random image transformation is applied to the input images of the teacher model and the prediction of the student model, respectively. Then, the two outputs that come from the student and teacher models are supposed to be similar pixel by pixel. To this end, the mean-squared error (MSE) loss is applied to minimize the distribution distance between these two streams, which can be formulated as:

$$\mathcal{R}_{C1} = \mathcal{L}_{mse}(g(f(x; \theta'), \phi)), f(g(x; \phi); \theta)). \tag{1}$$

2.3   Regional Mixing Module

Cutmix shows great potential in semi-supervised pixel-wise A/V classification [23]. This method generates a new training sample $(\widetilde{x}, \widetilde{y})$ by mixing the regions of two training samples (x_A, y_A) and (x_B, y_B) according to a random mask M. The combining operation is defined as:

$$\begin{aligned}
\widetilde{x} &= M \odot x_A + (1 - M) \odot x_B \\
\widetilde{y} &= M \odot y_A + (1 - M) \odot y_B
\end{aligned} \tag{2}$$

where $M \in \{0, 1\}^{W \times H}$ denotes a binary mask indicating which sample is selected to fill the pixels of the new sample.

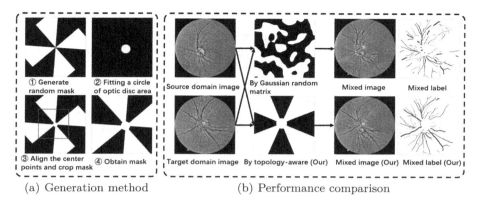

(a) Generation method   (b) Performance comparison

Fig. 3. The description of the mixing strategy. (a) Generation method of topology-aware mask; (b) Mixing performance comparison with the method proposed in [16];

Mask generated by Gaussian random matrix causes frequent vessel interruptions in the mixed images, as shown in Fig. 3(b). This may disrupt the topology of the vessel. Even worse, the topology of images can affect the result of the segmentation. For example, TA-Net [24] completes the gland segmentation task using the topology of the gland. ClDice [25] proposes a topology-preserving loss function. They all demonstrate that the topology in images plays an important role in the segmentation task. Therefore, the topology of the data should be preserved as much as possible when using data augmentation.

Algorithm 1 Regional mixing

Input: The image to be mixed and the prediction of the teacher model from the source domain $D_s = (x_i^s, y_i^s)_{i=1}^N$ and the target domain $D_t = (x_i^t, y_i^t)_{i=1}^N$, where N is the batch size. Optic disc segmentation model $f_{Seg}()$.

1: **for** i = 1, 2, ..., N **do**
2:      generate a random fan mask M_{fan}
3:      segment optic disc area by model $f_{Seg}(x_i^s), f_{Seg}(x_i^t)$
4:      circle^s = cv2.minEnclosingCircle($f_{Seg}(x_i^s)$)
5:      circle^t = cv2.minEnclosingCircle($f_{Seg}(x_i^s)$)
6:      align circle^s.center and M$_{fan}$.center to circle^t.center
7:      crop all images according to the boundary of x_i^t
8:      $X_i^{Mixed} = x_i^t \times M_{fan} + x_i^s \times (1 - M_{fan})$
9:      $Y_i^{Mixed} = y_i^t \times M_{fan} + y_i^s \times (1 - M_{fan})$
10: **end for**
11: **return** $(X_i^{Mixed}, Y_i^{Mixed})_{i=1}^N$

In this section, we consider fully the fact that vessel flows start at the optic cup and thus propose a new mask generation method to preserve the topology of retinal vessels. The flow of mask generation can be divided into four steps, as shown in Fig. 3(a). Firstly, a random fan mask is generated (① in Fig. 3(a)), whose size is two times the fundus image. Then, the optic disc (OD) is segmented by applying the open source method [26,27], which achieves 95% dice on multiple datasets. Then we find a circle of the minimum area enclosing optic disc area by OpenCV minEnclosingCircle function (② in Fig. 3(a)). Next, we align the center of the circles of the two samples with the center of the mask (③ in Fig. 3(a)). Finally, the mask is obtained by cropping one of the fundus image windows from the standard fan shape (④ in Fig. 3(a)). As shown in Fig. 3(b), mixing the source domain image x_s and target domain image x_t before spatial transformation, the mixed image can be obtained by:

$$X_{mixed}(x_s, x_t, M, \phi) = g(M \odot x_s + (\mathbb{1} - M) \odot x_t; \phi). \tag{3}$$

Similarly, the mixed prediction Y_{mixed} can be formulated as:

$$Y_{mixed}(x_s, x_t, M, \phi, \theta) = g(M \odot f(x_s; \theta) + (\mathbb{1} - M) \odot f(x_t; \theta); \phi), \tag{4}$$

where $\odot$ represents Hadamard product. By minimizing the MSE loss among the mixture of the prediction $Y_{mixed}(x_s, x_t, M, \phi, \theta)$ of the origin input images, and the prediction of their mixed variant $X_{mixed}(x_s, x_t, M, \phi)$, the topology-aware regional mixing regularization can be formulated as:

$$\mathcal{R}_{C2} = \mathcal{L}_{mse}(f(X_{mix}(x_s, x_t, M, \phi), \theta')), Y_{mix}(x_s, x_t, M, \phi, \theta)). \tag{5}$$

2.4 Loss Function

For this specific task, binary cross-entropy (BCE) loss is applied to calculate the supervised A/V classification loss $\mathcal{L}_S$, which can be formulated as:

$$\mathcal{L}_S = \mathcal{L}_{bce}^a(f(x_s), y_s, w_{pos^a}) + \mathcal{L}_{bce}^v(f(x_s), y_s, w_{pos^v}) + \mathcal{L}_{bce}^b(f(x_s), y_s, w_{pos^b}), \tag{6}$$

where a, v and b represent arteries, veins and background. The w_{pos} is the positive weight to mitigate class imbalances, and are set as 1, 1, 0.1 for arteries, veins and background, respectively. As a result, The total loss in our proposed framework can be represented as:

$$\mathcal{L} = \mathcal{L}_S + \lambda_1 \mathcal{R}_{C1} + \lambda_2 \mathcal{R}_{C2}, \tag{7}$$

where λ_1 and λ_2 are weights that control the proportion of regularization terms defined above.

3 Experimental Results

3.1 Datasets

Two retinal color fundus image datasets acquired by two different devices were used in our experiments. DRIVE-AV [18] is a publicly-accessible dataset with A/V manual annotations. It contains 40 images with a resolution of 584×565 pixels. All images were acquired by Canon CR5 nonmydriatic 3CCD camera. The images of our in-house dataset were collected from a local hospital, and it contains 5,336 color fundus with a resolution of 3608×3608 pixels. All images were captured by a Zeiss camera. Three clinicians were invited to label all the vessels into arteries and veins manually from 98 images, and their consensus was finally used as ground truth.

3.2 Implementation Details

U-Net [28] was applied as the backbone in the mean teacher framework, the parameters of the teacher model were updated from the student model by using the exponential moving average (EMA). In our experiments, we set the EMA decay α to 0.99 in the first 50 epochs and 0.999 in the subsequent epochs. All the images were scaled and cropped to 512×512 pixels. The pre-processing method proposed in [29] was utilized to enhance image contrast, and the non-signal area was masked out. The batch size of both source and target domain inputs was set to 2. The initial weights λ_1 and λ_2 in the total loss were set to 0.8 and 0.7, respectively. A sigmoid ramp-up [19], formulated as $\lambda = \beta e^{-5(1-m)^2}$, was utilized to update the weights λ_1 and λ_2, where β is the initial weight and m represents the ratio between the current epoch and the total ramp-up epochs which were set to 80 empirically.

3.3 Artery/Vein Classification Performance

In this subsection, we evaluate the artery/vein classification performance on the DRIVE-AV and private datasets. To show the superiority of the proposed method, the following methods were compared: (1) Semi-superivised segmentation methods: cross-pseudo supervision (CPS) [30] and uncertainty-aware self-ensembling mean teacher (UA-MT) [31]; (2) Unsupervised domain adaptation segmentation method: spatial transformation based consistency regularization (ST-CR) [32]; (3) Semi-superivised domain adaptation segmentation method: VM-CR [16]. The ablation study was also performed to evaluate the proposed two components. Following the standard performance assessment protocol for Artey/Vein classification, the accuracy (Acc), sensitivity (Se), specificity (Sp), G-mean score (G-mean) [33], Dice coefficient (Dice) [34], Kappa [35] and False Discovery Rate (FDR) [36] were utilized for quantitative evaluation.

Comparison with the State-of-the-art Methods. In DRIVE-AV $\rightarrow$ Private dataset experiment, the DRIVE-AV dataset was considered as the *source* domain, and the private dataset was defined as the *target* domain. 40 labeled images from DRIVE-AV, 4,950 unlabeled and 10 labeled images from the private datasets were involved in the training phase. The rest of the labeled images (88 images) in the private dataset were utilized for testing.

Figure 4 shows the classification results of different methods for training. Compared to other methods, the proposed model shows better performance in

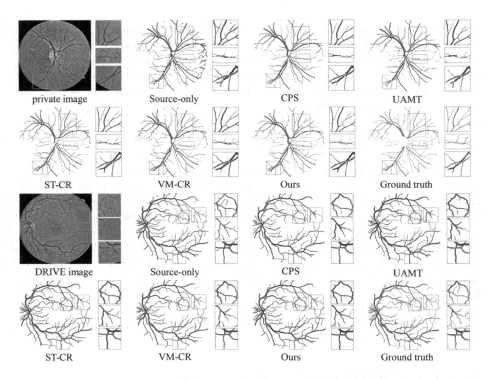

Fig. 4. The results of different methods in A/V classification tasks on two datasets.

preserving vessel continuity. To further prove the effectiveness of our method, we report the quantitative results in Table 1. We can observe that the proposed method achieves the best performance. More specifically, the classification performance of *source-only* is severely degraded compared to our method. There are significant decreases in ACC (88.98% to 82.72%), Se (86.54% to 80.36%), Sp (90.96% to 84.64%), G-mean (88.72% to 82.47%), Dice (87.57% to 80.66%), Kappa (86.29% to 78.41%) and FDR (11.37% to 19.02%) between *source-only* and the proposed method. It is worth noting that when compared with ST-CR, our method outperforms it in all metrics. Meanwhile, ACC improves by 2.12%, Se improves by 0.15%, Sp improves by 3.71%, G-mean improves by 1.9%, Dice improves by 2.06%, Kappa improves by 2.82% and FDR improves by 3.98%, respectively. This confirms our argument that the model can have significant improvement by adding a few target domain information. Compared with VM-CR, our method achieves significant improvements in all metrics, with 3.47% higher on ACC, 2.32% higher on Se, 4.4% higher on Sp, 3.34% higher on G-mean, 3.66% higher on Dice, 4.46% higher on Kappa and 5.03% higher on FDR, respectively. This is because the regional mixing module plays a key role. Compared to the crude mixing method, the proposed module preserves the topological information of the vessels and can enhance the generalization performance of the A/V classification model.

Table 1. Performance comparison of A/V classification using different approaches on two datasets. Source-only indicates only the source-domain dataset was applied to train the model.

Methods	DRIVE-AV → Private dataset						
	Acc	Se	Sp	G-mean	Dice	Kappa	FDR
Source-only	82.72	80.36	84.64	82.47	80.66	78.41	19.02
UA-MT [31]	81.28	79.89	82.42	81.15	79.29	76.48	21.29
CPS [30]	85.52	84.24	86.57	85.39	83.92	81.84	16.38
VM-CR [16]	85.51	84.22	86.56	85.38	83.91	81.83	16.40
ST-CR [32]	86.86	86.39	87.25	86.82	85.51	83.47	15.35
Ours	**88.98**	**86.54**	**90.96**	**88.72**	**87.57**	**86.29**	**11.37**
Methods	Private dataset → DRIVE-AV						
	Acc	Se	Sp	G-mean	Dice	Kappa	FDR
Source-only	70.44	68.91	71.74	70.31	68.11	62.36	32.67
UA-MT [31]	74.42	69.05	78.96	73.84	71.21	68.14	26.49
CPS [30]	73.87	70.57	76.66	73.55	71.21	67.09	28.12
VM-CR [16]	73.35	68.54	77.41	72.84	70.20	66.69	28.05
ST-CR [32]	76.41	71.33	**80.70**	75.87	73.48	70.60	**24.24**
Ours	**77.19**	**74.52**	79.44	**76.94**	**74.95**	**71.22**	24.60

Table 2. Ablation study of different modules in the proposed method.

ST	Mixing	A/V classification					
		Acc	Se	Sp	Dice	Kappa	FDR
		81.25	82.75	80.03	79.83	76.09	22.88
✓		85.86	83.29	87.94	84.08	82.38	15.10
	✓	85.90	**86.58**	85.34	84.64	82.14	17.22
✓	✓	**88.98**	86.54	**90.96**	**87.57**	**86.29**	**11.37**

Similarly, we evaluated our method in the Private dataset → DRIVE-AV experiments, where 98 labeled images in the private dataset, 20 unlabeled and 10 labeled images in the DRIVE-AV dataset were used for training. The rest (10 images) were utilized for testing. The result also shows that the proposed method has great success in semi-supervised A/V classification.

Ablation Study. To better reveal the contribution of two modules in our network, the ablation experiments were added to the DRIVE-AV → Private dataset experiment. We removed each module to verify the effectiveness of utilizing all the proposed modules and compared their results in Table 2. Compared to the backbone, our method achieves higher performance, where the Acc increases from 81.25% to 88.98%, Dice from 79.83% to 87.57%, Kappa from 76.09% to 86.29%, FDR from 22.88% to 11.37%. The performance of the model improves significantly when we integrate all the modules together. These results further confirm that every module in our proposed method is essential for the semi-supervised cross-domain A/V classification.

4 Conclusion

In this paper, we proposed a novel topology-aware artery/vein classification method, which contains two novel modules: the spatial transformation and the topology-aware regional mixing, to mitigate the data discrepancy problem in semi-supervised cross-domain artery/vein classification. The advantages of our method can be summarized in two parts. Firstly, it uses a mean teacher framework to train a semi-supervised domain adaptation model where a target dataset with few annotations and a labeled public dataset are available. Second, the proposed method takes into account the vessel topology and generates a more realistic mixed vessel structure for learning. The experimental results and ablation study show that the proposed framework is effective in improving the A/V classification performance. In our future work, other medical images will be used for validation. In particular, image segmentation with structural topology information, such as OCTA A/V classification or vessel segmentation.

Acknowledgement. This work was supported in part by the National Science Foundation Program of China (62103398 and 61906181), Zhejiang Provincial Natural Science Foundation of China (LR22F020008), in part by the Youth Innovation Promotion Association CAS (2021298), in part by the Ningbo major science and technology task project (2021Z054, 2019B10033 and 2019B10061) and in part by the AME Programmatic Fund (A20H4b0141).

References

1. Nguyen, T.T., Wong, T.Y.: Retinal vascular changes and diabetic retinopathy. Curr. Diabetes Rep. **9**(4), 277–283 (2009)
2. Abràmoff, M.D., Garvin, M.K., Sonka, M.: Retinal imaging and image analysis. IEEE Rev. Biomed. Eng. **3**, 169–208 (2010)
3. Yatsuya, H., Folsom, A.R., Wong, T.Y., Klein, R., Klein, B.E., Sharrett, A.R.: Retinal microvascular abnormalities and risk of lacunar stroke: atherosclerosis risk in communities study. Stroke **41**(7), 1349–1355 (2010)
4. Liu, R., et al.: Deepdrid: diabetic retinopathy-grading and image quality estimation challenge. Patterns 100512 (2022)
5. Dai, L., et al.: A deep learning system for detecting diabetic retinopathy across the disease spectrum. Nat. Commun. **12**(1), 1–11 (2021)
6. Estrada, R., Allingham, M.J., Mettu, P.S., Cousins, S.W., Tomasi, C., Farsiu, S.: Retinal artery-vein classification via topology estimation. IEEE Trans. Med. Imaging **34**(12), 2518–2534 (2015)

7. Dashtbozorg, B., Mendonça, A.M., Campilho, A.: An automatic graph-based approach for artery/vein classification in retinal images. IEEE Trans. Image Process. **23**(3), 1073–1083 (2013)

8. Relan, D., MacGillivray, T., Ballerini, L., Trucco, E.: Retinal vessel classification: sorting arteries and veins. In: 2013 35th Annual International Conference of the IEEE Engineering in Medicine and Biology Society (EMBC), pp. 7396–7399. IEEE (2013)

9. Relan, D., MacGillivray, T., Ballerini, L., Trucco, E.: Automatic retinal vessel classification using a least square-support vector machine in vampire. In: 2014 36th Annual International Conference of the IEEE Engineering in Medicine and Biology Society, pp. 142–145. IEEE (2014)

10. Yin, B., et al.: Vessel extraction from non-fluorescein fundus images using orientation-aware detector. Med. Image Analy. **26**(1), 232–242 (2015)

11. Sheng, B., et al.: Retinal vessel segmentation using minimum spanning superpixel tree detector. IEEE Trans. Cybern. **49**(7), 2707–2719 (2018)

12. Ma, W., Yu, S., Ma, K., Wang, J., Ding, X., Zheng, Y.: Multi-task neural networks with spatial activation for retinal vessel segmentation and artery/vein classification. In: MICCAI 2019. LNCS, vol. 11764, pp. 769–778. Springer, Cham (2019). https://doi.org/10.1007/978-3-030-32239-7_85

13. Kang, H., Gao, Y., Guo, S., Xu, X., Li, T., Wang, K.: Avnet: a retinal artery/vein classification network with category-attention weighted fusion. Comput. Meth. Prog. Biomed. **195**, 105629 (2020)

14. Hu, J., et al.: Automatic artery/vein classification using a vessel-constraint network for multicenter fundus images. Front. Cell Dev. Biol. 1194 (2021)

15. Karlsson, R.A., Hardarson, S.H.: Artery vein classification in fundus images using serially connected u-nets. Comput. Meth. Prog. Biomed. **216**, 106650 (2022)

16. Li, C., Zhang, Y., Liang, Z., Ma, W., Huang, Y., Ding, X.: Consistent posterior distributions under vessel-mixing: a regularization for cross-domain retinal artery/vein classification. In: International Conference on Image, pp. 61–65 (2021)

17. Galdran, A., Meyer, M., Costa, P., Campilho, A., et al.: Uncertainty-aware artery/vein classification on retinal images. In: 2019 IEEE 16th International Symposium on Biomedical Imaging (ISBI 2019), pp. 556–560. IEEE (2019)

18. Hu, Q., Abràmoff, M.D., Garvin, M.K.: Automated separation of binary overlapping trees in low-contrast color retinal images. In: Mori, K., Sakuma, I., Sato, Y., Barillot, C., Navab, N. (eds.) MICCAI 2013. LNCS, vol. 8150, pp. 436–443. Springer, Heidelberg (2013). https://doi.org/10.1007/978-3-642-40763-5_54

19. Tarvainen, A., Valpola, H.: Mean teachers are better role models: weight-averaged consistency targets improve semi-supervised deep learning results. Adv. Neural Inf. Process. Syst. **30** (2017)

20. Lee, D.H., et al.: Pseudo-label: the simple and efficient semi-supervised learning method for deep neural networks. In: Workshop on Challenges in Representation Learning, ICML, vol. 3, p. 896 (2013)

21. Li, C., et al.: Hierarchical deep network with uncertainty-aware semi-supervised learning for vessel segmentation. Neural Comput. Appl. **34**(4), 3151–3164 (2022)

22. Ke, Z., Qiu, D., Li, K., Yan, Q., Lau, R.W.H.: Guided collaborative training for pixel-wise semi-supervised learning. In: Vedaldi, A., Bischof, H., Brox, T., Frahm, J.-M. (eds.) ECCV 2020. LNCS, vol. 12358, pp. 429–445. Springer, Cham (2020). https://doi.org/10.1007/978-3-030-58601-0_26

23. Yun, S., Han, D., Oh, S.J., Chun, S., Choe, J., Yoo, Y.: Cutmix: regularization strategy to train strong classifiers with localizable features. In: Proceedings of the IEEE/CVF International Conference on Computer Vision, pp. 6023–6032 (2019)

24. Hu, X., Li, F., Samaras, D., Chen, C.: Topology-preserving deep image segmentation. Adv. Neural Inf. Process. Syst. **32** (2019)
25. Shit, S., et al.: cldice-a novel topology-preserving loss function for tubular structure segmentation. In: Proceedings of the IEEE/CVF Conference on Computer Vision and Pattern Recognition, pp. 16560–16569 (2021)
26. Lei, H., Liu, W., Xie, H., Zhao, B., Yue, G., Lei, B.: Unsupervised domain adaptation based image synthesis and feature alignment for joint optic disc and cup segmentation. IEEE J. Biomed. Health Inform. **26**(1), 90–102 (2021)
27. Wang, R., et al.: Retinal optic disc localization using convergence tracking of blood vessels. Multimedia Tools Appl. **76**(22), 23309–23331 (2017)
28. Ronneberger, O., Fischer, P., Brox, T.: U-Net: convolutional networks for biomedical image segmentation. In: Navab, N., Hornegger, J., Wells, W.M., Frangi, A.F. (eds.) MICCAI 2015. LNCS, vol. 9351, pp. 234–241. Springer, Cham (2015). https://doi.org/10.1007/978-3-319-24574-4_28
29. Van Grinsven, M.J., van Ginneken, B., Hoyng, C.B., Theelen, T., Sánchez, C.I.: Fast convolutional neural network training using selective data sampling: application to hemorrhage detection in color fundus images. IEEE Trans. Med. Imaging **35**(5), 1273–1284 (2016)
30. Chen, X., Yuan, Y., Zeng, G., Wang, J.: Semi-supervised semantic segmentation with cross pseudo supervision. In: Proceedings of the IEEE/CVF Conference on Computer Vision and Pattern Recognition, pp. 2613–2622 (2021)
31. Yu, L., Wang, S., Li, X., Fu, C.-W., Heng, P.-A.: Uncertainty-aware self-ensembling model for semi-supervised 3D left atrium segmentation. In: Shen, D., et al. (eds.) MICCAI 2019. LNCS, vol. 11765, pp. 605–613. Springer, Cham (2019). https://doi.org/10.1007/978-3-030-32245-8_67
32. Perone, C.S., Ballester, P., Barros, R.C., Cohen-Adad, J.: Unsupervised domain adaptation for medical imaging segmentation with self-ensembling. NeuroImage **194**, 1–11 (2019)
33. Espíndola, R.P., Ebecken, N.F.: On extending f-measure and g-mean metrics to multi-class problems. WIT Trans. Inf. Commun. Technol. **35** (2005)
34. Guindon, B., Zhang, Y.: Application of the dice coefficient to accuracy assessment of object-based image classification. Can. J. Rem. Sens. **43**(1), 48–61 (2017)
35. Chmura Kraemer, H., Periyakoil, V.S., Noda, A.: Kappa coefficients in medical research. Stat. Med. **21**(14), 2109–2129 (2002)
36. Benjamini, Y., Hochberg, Y.: Controlling the false discovery rate: a practical and powerful approach to multiple testing. J. R. Stat. Soc. Ser. (Method.) **57**(1), 289–300 (1995)

Face Super-Resolution with Better Semantics and More Efficient Guidance

Jin Chen[1,2], Jun Chen[1,2(✉)], Zheng Wang[1,2], Chao Liang[1,2], Zhen Han[1,2], and Chia-Wen Lin[3]

[1] National Engineering Research Center for Multimedia Software,
School of Computer, Wuhan University, Wuhan, China
`chenj.whu@gmail.com`
[2] Hubei Key Laboratory of Multimedia and Network Communication Engineering,
Wuhan University, Wuhan, China
[3] Department of Electrical Engineering, National Tsinghua University,
Hsinchu 30013, Taiwan

Abstract. Recently, facial priors have been widely used to improve the quality of super-resolution (SR) facial images, but it is underutilized in existing methods. On the one hand, facial priors such as semantic maps may be inaccurately estimated on low-resolution (LR) images or low-scale feature maps with L_1 loss. On the other hand, it is inefficient to guide SR features with constant prior knowledge via concatenation at only one intermediate layer of the guidance network. In this paper, we focus on face super-resolution (FSR) based on semantic maps guidance and propose two simple and efficient designs to address the above two limitations respectively. In particular, to address the first limitation, we propose a novel one-hot supervision strategy to pursue accurate semantic maps, which focuses more on penalizing misclassified pixels by relaxing the regression constraint. In addition, a semantic progressive guidance network (SPGN) is proposed that uses semantic maps to learn modulation parameters in normalization layers to efficiently guide SR features layer by layer. Extensive experiments on two benchmark datasets show that the proposed method improves the state-of-the-art in both quantitative and qualitative results at ×8 scale.

Keywords: Face super-resolution · One-hot supervision strategy · Semantic progressive guidance

1 Introduction

Face super-resolution aims to generate high-resolution (HR) facial images from low-resolution observations, which is a challenging problem since it is highly ill-posed due to the ambiguity of the super-resolved pixels. It is a fundamental problem in face analysis and can make a significant contribution to face-related work [1–9].

In contrast to Single Image Super-Resolution (SISR), FSR only focuses on the recovery of facial images. Since different faces share the same components, these

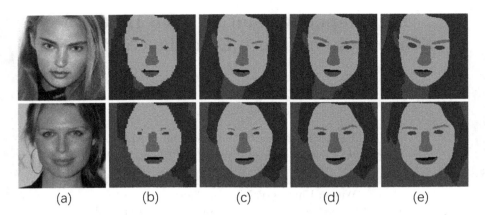

Fig. 1. (a) shows ground truth image, (b) and (c) are parsing maps with resolution of 64 and 128 pixel predicted by L1 loss supervision, (d) shows the predicted parsing map of the SPN via the proposed supervision strategy, (e) shows a ground truth parsing map.

specific facial configurations are a strong prior knowledge that is very useful for FSR. Many FSR methods based on facial priors have been proposed and achieved impressive performance [10–20]. CBN [10] estimates dense correspondence fields as structure prior to guide FSR. Facial component heatmaps are predicted in [11] to provide structure prior to improve the SR quality. SuperFAN [12] uses facial component heatmaps as structure prior to supervise SR network training. In addition, PFSR [13] improves the quality of SR images via a progressive training strategy and multi-scale heatmaps supervision. FSRNet [14] simultaneously estimates landmark heatmaps and semantic maps to improve the details of SR images. JASRNet [17] makes the two mutually reinforcing by jointly learning the SR task and the face alignment task, and using a shared encoder to extract complementary features.

To fully utilize semantic prior knowledge to assist FSR, there exist two key challenges: how to extract accurate semantic prior knowledge and how to effectively use semantic prior knowledge to guide FSR. However, most existing FSR methods do not fully address these issues. On the one hand, previous approaches [14,15] used L_1 loss to supervise the estimation of semantic maps on LR images or low-scale feature maps. However, the semantic maps are difficult to be estimated accurately at the LR level using L_1 loss directly. As shown in Fig. 1(b), when the resolution of the output of semantic maps is 64, the semantic prior network pays more attention to large semantic components (e.g., skin, hair) while small semantic components (e.g., eyes, eyebrows) are easily ignored in the estimation due to the averaging effect of L_1 loss. Therefore, the estimated semantic maps are not accurate enough. On the other hand, in terms of guidance, the semantic maps are simply concatenated with SR features at an intermediate layer of the guidance network and then followed by a convolution layer in [14]. Due to the domain gap effect between SR features and semantic maps, it is inefficient to capture collaborative knowledge using single-layer guidance. Therefore, it weakens the role of semantic maps in guiding SR features.

In this paper, we propose two simple and efficient designs to address the above two limitations respectively. First, we propose a novel one-hot supervision strategy to pursue accurate semantic maps. Unlike previous approaches that directly use L_1 loss to accurately regress all dimensions of semantic label, the proposed supervision strategy relaxes this constraint by only guaranteeing that the corresponding dimension of the true semantic label has the maximum prediction output. With this relaxation, the semantic prior network can focus more on penalizing misclassified pixels to improve the accuracy of the predicted semantic maps. Second, considering the inadequacy of single-layer guidance, we design a progressive guidance strategy. Also, since different feature layers in the guidance network have different characteristics, different layers should be guided by layer-adaptive semantic prior. Based on these two considerations, we design a semantic progressive guidance network that makes full use of the semantic maps to guide SR features adaptively layer by layer.

In summary, the main contributions of the proposed method are as follows: (i) We propose a novel one-hot supervision strategy to pursue accurate semantic maps by relaxing the regression constraint and focusing more on penalizing misclassified pixels; (ii) We design a semantic progressive guidance network to guide SR features by adaptively learning the modulation parameters of different layers of SR features with semantic maps.

2   Method

2.1   Overview of the Proposed Framework

As shown in Fig. 2, the proposed framework consists of three parts: the Coarse SR Network (CSN), the Semantic Prior Network (SPN), and the Semantic Progressive Guidance Network (SPGN). Given an LR input I_{lr}, we first use the CSN to produce a rough SR facial image I_c to recover the facial structure. Then, the I_c is sent to the SPN to extract semantic maps $\hat{M}$. Finally, both $\hat{M}$ and I_c are sent to the SPGN to progressively guide SR features and recover the final SR facial image I_{sr}.

2.2   Better Semantic Prior

It is crucial to extract accurate semantic maps to guide SR features in the following process. To extract semantic maps, the L_1 loss is usually used to supervise the learning of SPN [14,15]. Due to the averaging effect of L_1 loss, the large semantic components with more pixels seem to dominate the training resulting in small semantic components that are easily ignored in the estimation. As a result, the extracted semantic maps are inaccurate, especially for small semantic components shown in Fig. 1(b)–(c).

Since the L_1 loss aims at regressing all dimensions of semantic label accurately. Given a pixel with semantic label $M_{gt} \in R^N$, and the predicted semantic

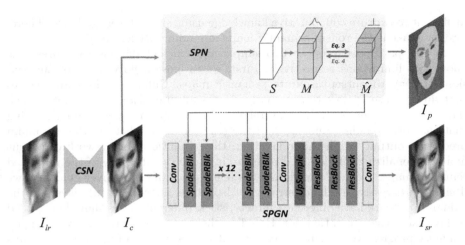

Fig. 2. Overview of the proposed framework. The framework consists of three parts: the CSN is used to recover the coarse SR facial image I_c. The SPN aims at pursuing accurate semantic maps $\hat{M}$. The SPGN focuses on guiding SR features progressively with semantic maps and recovering the final SR facial image I_{sr}.

label is $M_p \in R^N$, and N is the number of semantic class. The L_1 loss of the pixel can be calculated as:

$$L_1 = \sum_{i=1}^{N} |\hat{M}_{i,p} - M_{i,gt}|, \tag{1}$$

If the true semantic class dimension of a pixel is the j-th dimension, the L_1 loss can be further decomposed into two parts: the loss of semantic-related dimension and other semantic-uncorrelated dimensions. Then the L_1 loss can be further represented as:

$$L_1 = \underbrace{|M_{j,p} - M_{j,gt}|_1}_{semantic-related} + \underbrace{\sum_{i=1,i \neq j}^{N} |M_{i,p} - M_{i,gt}|_1}_{semantic-unrelated}, \tag{2}$$

If we directly use L_1 loss to supervise SPN, there are two drawbacks. On the one hand, it increases the difficulty of network optimization. The result is that when the predicted semantic label has sufficient semantic information, but semantic-unrelated part still causes a loss that cannot be ignored. For example, the true semantic label of a pixel is [0, 0, 1, 0], and when the predicted semantic label is [0.1, 0.1, 0.8, 0.0], we can easily achieve the correct semantic label via *argmax* operation. However, the loss of semantic-unrelated part still brings about 0.2 cost (0.2 = 0.1 + 0.1). We argue that the loss of semantic-unrelated part is unnecessary when the true semantic class dimension has the maximum predicted value. On the other hand, due to the exclusiveness of semantic class definitions, if we try to regress all semantic dimensions accurately, we will ignore the correlation between different semantic classes. For example, the texture of the skin is closer to the texture of the nose than to the texture of the hair. If we treat the semantic class of hair and nose's equally, it also confuses the network training to some extent.

To alleviate the learning difficulty of SPN and achieve accurate semantic maps, we propose a novel one-hot supervision strategy that relaxes the constraint of regressing all dimensions of semantic label accurately and only guarantees that the corresponding dimension of the true semantic label has the maximum prediction output. An intuitive solution is to transform the predicted semantic maps into one-hot semantic maps using the $argmax$ operation before computing the loss. Let's look at the above example again. When the true semantic class dimension of the predicted label has the maximum output, the predicted label [0.1, 0.1, 0.8, 0.0] is first transformed into a one-hot label [0, 0, 1, 0] via $argmax$ operation, and since the transformed one-hot label is the same as the true label, there is no loss in updating the network, thus reducing the focus of the SPN on pixels with correctly predicted semantic class. When the predicted label [0.1, 0.5, 0.4, 0.0] has no maximum output for the true semantic dimension. After it is converted to a one-hot label [0, 1, 0, 0], the loss of semantic-related part increases from 0.6 to 1 cost, and it forces the SPN to focus more on penalizing misclassified pixels (*e.g.*, small semantic components), resulting in a more accurate semantic maps.

Due to the $argmax$ operation is not differentiable, to achieve one-hot maps while enabling the SPN to be optimized end-to-end, we introduce the Gumbel Softmax trick [31] for this purpose. As shown at the top of Fig. 2, **in the forward process**, the SPN first extracts semantic maps $M \in R^{N \times H \times W}$ with an input I_c, then the M is transformed to one-hot semantic maps $\hat{M} \in R^{N \times H \times W}$, N is the number of semantic class. The one-hot semantic maps $\hat{M}$ can be computed as:

$$\hat{M} = one\_hot(\underset{n}{argmax}\, M_n),\tag{3}$$

Then, we use one-hot semantic maps $\hat{M}$ to compute L_1 loss. **In the backward process**, we compute the gradient of $\hat{M}$ by the following formula:

$$\hat{M} = \frac{exp((M + g)/\tau)}{\sum_{n=1}^{N} exp((M_n + g_n)/\tau)},\tag{4}$$

where g is drawn from $Gumbel(0,1)$, τ is a temperature value and set as 1 in our experiments. And the optimization process of the one-hot semantic maps $\hat{M}$ in the training stage can be summarized as follows:

$$\hat{M} = \begin{cases} (3), & forward, \\ (4), & backward. \end{cases}\tag{5}$$

2.3   More Efficient Guidance

After extracting accurate semantic maps, the key here is how to exploit the semantic maps to guide SR features and further improve the quality of SR images. To make full use of semantic maps for SR guidance, we design an SPGN. Different from single-layer guidance in previous works [14, 15], the SPGN guides SR features at each intermediate layer in the guidance network. Also, since different layers in the guidance network have different characteristics, so SR features of different intermediate layers should be guided by layer-adaptive semantic prior. Motivated by the success of SPADE [25] in the semantic image synthesis task by learning to adaptively modulate the normalization layer, we employ the SpadeRBlk as a unit module to adaptively guide SR features.

As shown at the bottom of Fig. 2, the SPGN starts with a convolution layer (Conv) of stride 2, and followed by twelve SpadeRBlk blocks to progressively guide SR features with semantic maps adaptively, then a Conv, an Upsample block of factor 2, three ResBlock blocks and a Conv to reconstruct the final facial image. A SpadeRBlk [25] block stacks two SPADE blocks and two Conv together and ends with a skip connection. In SPADE, given an SR features $f^i \in R^{C^i \times H^i \times W^i}$, the activation value at site $(c \in C^i, y \in H^i, x \in W^i)$ is given by,

$$\hat{f}^i_{c,y,x} = \gamma^i_{c,y,x} \frac{f^i_{c,y,x} - \mu^i_c}{\sigma^i_c} + \beta^i_{c,y,x}, \tag{6}$$

where $f^i_{c,y,x}$ and $\hat{f}^i_{c,y,x}$ are the input and modulated activation at site (c,y,x), respectively. μ^i_c and σ^i_c are the mean and standard deviation of $f^i_{c,y,x}$ in channel c. The variables $\gamma^i_{c,y,x}$ and $\beta^i_{c,y,x}$ are the learned modulation parameters of the normalization layer using a two-layer convolutional network with semantic maps as input. All convolutions in the SPGN are 3×3 kernel size with 64 channels. The UpSample block and the ResBlock block are described in [14].

2.4   Loss Functions

To make the recovered facial images are of similar visual quality as the origin HR versions, we use L_1 loss as the content loss. The total loss for training can be defined as:

$$L_{total} = \|I_{hr} - I_{sr}\|_1 + \alpha \|I_{hr} - I_c\|_1 + \lambda \left\| M_{gt} - \hat{M} \right\|_1, \tag{7}$$

where $I_c, I_{sr}, I_{hr}, \hat{M}, M_{gt}$ are the coarse SR facial image, the final SR facial image, the origin HR image, the predicted semantic maps and the ground truth semantic maps respectively. α and λ are weights of individual loss terms and we set $\alpha = 0.5, \lambda = 1.0$ in our experiments empirically.

3   Experiments

3.1   Implementation Details

The proposed method is based on the framework of FSRNet [14], but our Coarse SR Network contains more ResBlock blocks. And the Semantic Prior Network can be replaced by a state-of-the-art parsing network.

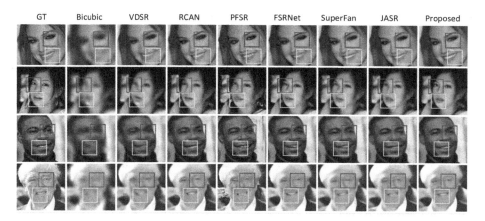

Fig. 3. Visual comparison with state-of-the-art methods. The resolution of input is 16 × 16 and the upscale factor is 8. Other SISR or FSR methods may either produce structural distortions on key facial parts or present undesirable artifacts. The qualitative comparison indicated the proposed method outperforms other SISR or FSR methods.

We conduct experiments on both CelebA [26] and Helen [27]. For both datasets, we use the face parsing model based on EHANet [28] to parse semantic labels as ground truth. For a fair comparison with FSRNet, we merge 19 classes of semantic labels into 11 classes to be consistent with the setup in [14]. Following the experimental setup in [19], we use about 169k images for training and 1k images for testing on the CelebA dataset. For the Helen dataset, we use about 2k images for training and 50 images for testing. All face images in the training and testing stages are resized to 128 × 128 pixels as HR ground truth. The LR faces are obtained by downsampling the HR images to 16 × 16 pixels by bicubic interpolation. To avoid over-fitting, we perform data augmentation on training images with random rotation (90°, 180°, 270°), horizontal flipping and image rescaling in [0.7, 1.3]. PSNR and SSIM [29] are used to quantitatively evaluate SR results. They are computed on the Y channel of transformed YCbCr space. For the quantitative evaluation of semantic maps, the mean of class-wise intersection over union (mIoU) is applied to investigate the accuracy.

For optimization, we set the batch size to 16 and use Adam [30] to optimize the network with $\beta_1 = 0.9$ and $\beta_2 = 0.999$. We first train the SPN separately with the learning rate of 1e–4 on HR facial images for 80 epochs, then we jointly train other networks and fine-tune the SPN with fixed learning rate of 1e–5. For CelebA, we train the whole network for 30 epochs with the initial learning rate of 2e–4, divided by 2 at the epoch of [5, 15, 20, 25]. For Helen, we train the whole network for 250 epochs with the learning rate of 2e–4, divided by 2 at the epoch of [40, 120, 200, 220].

3.2   Comparisons with the State-of-the-Arts

We compare our method with state-of-the-art methods general image SR methods, including SRResNet [21], VSDR [22] and RCAN [23], and FSR methods,

Table 1. Comparison of PSNR and SSIM performance with state-of-the-art general SR methods and FSR methods on CelebA and Helen.

Method	CelebA ×8		Helen ×8		Params(M)
	PSNR↑	SSIM↑	PSNR↑	SSIM↑	
Bicubic	23.58	0.6285	23.89	0.6751	–
VDSR [22]	25.68	0.7219	25.24	0.7253	0.67
SRResNet [21]	25.82	0.7369	25.30	0.7297	0.88
RCAN [23]	26.90	0.7779	26.10	0.7599	15.74
URDGN [24]	24.63	0.6851	24.22	0.6909	1.05
SuperFAN [12]	26.69	0.7679	25.61	0.7545	1.49
FSRNet [14]	26.48	0.7718	25.90	0.7759	3.42
FSRGAN [14]	25.06	0.7311	24.99	0.7424	3.42
PFSR [13]	24.43	0.6991	24.73	0.7323	8.97
JASRNet [17]	27.04	0.7833	25.96	0.7565	19.88
Baseline	26.77	0.7740	25.82	0.7555	1.9
Map×64	26.98	0.7836	26.32	0.7779	5.63
Map×128	27.06	0.7860	26.41	0.7815	6.07
Proposed	**27.16**	**0.7904**	**26.49**	**0.7858**	6.07

including URDGN [24], FSRNet [14], SuperFAN [12], PFSR [13] and JASR-Net [17]. As shown in Table 1, these general image SR methods improve performance by optimizing the network architecture or introducing attention design, however, those methods which not fully exploit facial prior knowledge result in sub-optimal performance. Compared with FSRNet, our method improves PSNR performance from 26.48 dB to 27.16 dB. Compared with JASRNet, our method has a 0.53 dB improvement is achieved on the small-scale dataset (Helen). And our method achieves the best PSNR and SSIM performance on both datasets. Unlike some previous FSR methods are guided via concatenation, the proposed method uses semantic maps to adaptively learn the modulation parameters of different semantic components in different feature layers of the guidance network to better represent the characteristics of different semantic components and thus better recover the details of semantic components(*e.g.*, eyes, mouth). Figure 3 shows the visual comparison at scale ×8, and we observe that the proposed method recovers the best quality in fine details.

3.3 Ablation Study

To verify the effectiveness of each module in our method, we further implement a series of ablation studies.

Effect of Semantic Maps. We remove the SPN and replace all SpadeRBIk blocks with ResBlock blocks in the SPGN while keeping the CSN unchanged, denoted by Baseline. As shown in Table 1, compared with Baseline, the proposed method is superior in SR performance on both test sets, which proves that semantic maps are beneficial for FSR.

Table 2. Ablation study of the parsing performance of different parsing strategies on Celeba dataset.

Method	x64	x128	one-hot	mIoU
Map×64	✓			52.42
Map×128		✓		53.85
Proposed		✓	✓	**57.31**

Scale of the Predicted Semantic Maps. We predict semantic maps at 64 pixels and 128 pixels, denoted by Map×64 and Map×128 respectively. And we study the effect of the scale of the predicted semantic maps on parsing performance and SR performance. As shown in Table 2, compared with Map×64, Map×128 achieves a better parsing performance. As shown in Fig. 1(c), Map×128 achieves a more accurate parsing result. It indicates that it is easier to predict accurate semantic maps in HR level. Furthermore, as shown in Table 1, compared with Map×64, Map×128 achieves a better SR performance on both datasets, which suggests that semantic maps are more accurate and more beneficial for FSR.

Efficiency of the One-Hot Supervision Strategy. We evaluate the effect of the one_hot supervision strategy on parsing performance and SR performance further. As shown in Table 2, compared with Map×128, the proposed strategy can achieve a 3.46 mIoU performance improvement. As shown in Fig. 1(d), it achieves a more accurate parsing result, especially on small components like eyes and brows. In Table 1, we show that the SR performance is further improved as well. These performance improvements demonstrate the effectiveness of the proposed one_hot supervision strategy.

Table 3. Ablation study of different semantic prior on Helen dataset.

Prior	S	$\hat{M}$
PSNR/SSIM	26.24/0.7768	**26.49/0.7858**

Choice of Semantic Prior. We define the output and the last convolution layer of the SPN as two types of semantic prior, denoted by $\hat{M}$ and S, and study the efficiency of different semantic prior. As shown in Table 3, it achieves a better SR performance by guidance with $\hat{M}$, which indicates that the one-hot semantic maps $\hat{M}$ is more suitable for semantic guidance here.

Table 4. Ablation study of the progressive guidance on Helen dataset.

Num	0	1	2	4	8	Proposed
PSNR	25.82	26.06	26.28	26.38	26.44	**26.49**
SSIM	0.7555	0.7659	0.7764	0.7787	0.7845	**0.7858**

Progressive Guidance Strategy. To evaluate the effectiveness of progressive guidance strategy in the SPGN, we keep the depth of the SPGN constant, replace SpadeRBIk block with ResBlock block, and gradually increasing the number of SpadeRBIk blocks from the backend. As shown in Table 4, the SR performance gradually improves as the number of SpadeRBIk blocks increases. Compared with single-layer guidance, the proposed progressive guidance strategy achieves a 0.33dB SR performance improvement. It indicates that the progressive guidance strategy is more effective.

Table 5. Ablation study of the adaptive guidance on Helen dataset.

Strategy	SPGN-SHARED	**SPGN**
PSNR/SSIM	26.22/0.7730	**26.49/0.7858**

Adaptive Guidance Strategy. To evaluate the effectiveness of adaptive guidance strategy in each SPADE, we design a new guidance network, denoted by SPGN-SHARED. Different from SPGN which adaptively learns modulation parameters in all SPADE blocks independently, the SPGN-SHARED uses a shared modulation parameters in all SPADE blocks. As shown in Table 5, The SPGN achieves a higher SR performance, which indicates that the adaptive guidance strategy that learns to modulate SR features each layer independently is more effective.

Limitations. Although semantic prior knowledge improves the quality of super-resolution face images, the parameters of the semantic prior network and the semantic guidance network are large. As shown in Table 1, compared with Baseline, the parameters of the proposed method are increased more than three times. So, how to design lightweight semantic prior network and semantic guidance network is the direction of our future research.

4   Conclusion

In this letter, we propose two simple and efficient designs to improve the quality of SR facial images. Specifically, we propose a novel one-hot supervision strategy to pursue accurate semantic maps and design a semantic progressive guidance network to more efficiently guide SR features. Quantitative and qualitative results of FSR on two benchmark datasets demonstrate the effectiveness of the proposed method.

Acknowledgement. This research was supported partially by National Nature Science Foundation of China (U1903214, 62072347, 62071338, 61876135), in part by the Nature Science Foundation of Hubei under Grant (2018CFA024, 2019CFB472), in part by Hubei Province Technological Innovation Major Project (No. 2018AAA062).

References

1. Bai, Y., Zhang, Y., Ding, M., Ghanem, B.: Finding tiny faces in the wild with generative adversarial network. In: Proceedings of the IEEE Computer Vision and Pattern Recognition, pp. 21–30 (2018)
2. Chen, L., Su, H., Ji, Q.: Face alignment with kernel density deep neural network. In: Proceedings of the IEEE International Conference on Computer Vision, pp. 6992–7002 (2019)
3. Kumar, A., et al.: LUVLi Face alignment: estimating landmarks location, uncertainty, and visibility likelihood. In: Proceedings of the IEEE Conference on Computer Vision and Pattern Recognition, pp. 8236–8246 (2020)
4. Masi, I., Mathai, J., AbdAlmageed, W.: Towards learning structure via consensus for face segmentation and parsing. In: Proceedings of the IEEE Conference on Computer Vision and Pattern Recognition, pp. 5508–5518 (2020)
5. Pan, J., Ren, W., Hu, Z., Yang, M.H.: Learning to deblur images with exemplars. IEEE Trans. Patt. Anal. Mach. Intell **41**(6), 1412–1425 (2019)
6. Ge, S., Zhao, S., Li, C., Zhang, Y., Li, J.: Efficient low-resolution face recognition via bridge distillation. IEEE Trans. Image Process. **29**, 6898–6908 (2020)
7. Ge, S., Zhao, S., Gao, X., Li, J.: Fewer-shots and lower-resolutions: towards ultrafast face recognition in the wild. In: Proceedings of the 27th ACM International Conference on Multimedia, pp. 229–237 (2019)
8. Hsu, C.C., Lin, C.W., Su, W.T., Cheung, G.: Sigan: siamese generative adversarial network for identity-preserving face hallucination. IEEE Trans. Image Process. **28**, 6225–6236 (2019)
9. Hong, S., Ryu, J.: Unsupervised face domain transfer for low-resolution face recognition. IEEE Signal Process. Lett. **27**, 156–160 (2019)
10. Zhu, S., Liu, S., Loy, C.C., Tang, X.: Deep cascaded Bi-network for face hallucination. In: Leibe, B., Matas, J., Sebe, N., Welling, M. (eds.) ECCV 2016. LNCS, vol. 9909, pp. 614–630. Springer, Cham (2016). https://doi.org/10.1007/978-3-319-46454-1_37
11. Yu, X., Fernando, B., Ghanem, B., Porikli, F., Hartley, R.: Face super-resolution guided by facial component heatmaps. In: Proceedings of the European Conference on Computer Vision, pp. 217–233 (2018)
12. Bulat, A., Tzimiropoulos, G.: Super-fan: integrated facial landmark localization and super-resolution of real-world low resolution faces in arbitrary poses with gans. In: Proceedings of the IEEE Conference on Computer Vision and Pattern Recognition, pp. 109–117 (2018)
13. Kim, D., Kim, M., Kwon, G., Kim, D.S.: Progressive face super-resolution via attention to facial landmark. arXiv preprint arXiv:1908.08239 (2019)
14. Chen, Y., Tai, Y., Liu, X., Shen, C., Yang, J.: Fsrnet: end-to-end learning face super-resolution with facial priors. In: Proceedings of the IEEE Conference on Computer Vision and Pattern Recognition, pp. 2492–2501 (2018)
15. Wang, C., Zhong, Z., Jiang, J., Zhai, D., Liu, X.: Parsing map guided multi-scale attention network for face hallucination. In: Proceedings of the IEEE International Conference on Acoustics, Speech and Signal Processing, pp. 2518–2522 (2020)

16. Hu, X., et al.: Face super-resolution guided by 3D facial priors. In: Vedaldi, A., Bischof, H., Brox, T., Frahm, J.-M. (eds.) ECCV 2020. LNCS, vol. 12349, pp. 763–780. Springer, Cham (2020). https://doi.org/10.1007/978-3-030-58548-8_44
17. Yin, Y., Robinson, J., Zhang, Y., Fu, Y.: Joint super-resolution and alignment of tiny faces. In: Proceedings of the AAAI Conference on Artificial Intelligence, vol. 34, pp. 12693–12700 (2020)
18. Xin, J., Wang, N., Gao, X., Li, J.: Residual attribute attention network for face image super-resolution. In: Proceedings of the AAAI Conference on Artificial Intelligence, vol. 33, pp. 9054–9061 (2019)
19. Ma, C., Jiang, Z., Rao, Y., Lu, J., Zhou, J.: Deep face super-resolution with iterative collaboration between attentive recovery and landmark estimation. In: Proceedings of the IEEE Computer Vision and Pattern Recognition, pp. 5569–5578 (2020)
20. Shen, Z., Lai, W. S., Xu, T., Kautz, J., Yang, M.H.: Deep semantic face deblurring. In: Proceedings of the IEEE Computer Vision and Pattern Recognition, pp. 8260–8269 (2018)
21. Ledig, C., et al.: Photo-realistic single image super-resolution using a generative adversarial network. In: Proceedings of the IEEE Computer Vision and Pattern Recognition, pp. 4681–4690 (2017)
22. Kim, J., Lee, J. K., Lee, K.M.: Accurate image super-resolution using very deep convolutional networks. In: Proceedings of the IEEE Computer Vision and Pattern Recognition, pp. 1646–1654 (2016)
23. Zhang, Y., Li, K., Li, K., Wang, L., Zhong, B., Fu, Y.: Image super-resolution using very deep residual channel attention networks. In: Proceedings of the European Conference on Computer Vision, pp. 286–301 (2018)
24. Yu, X., Porikli, F.: Ultra-resolving face images by discriminative generative networks. In: Leibe, B., Matas, J., Sebe, N., Welling, M. (eds.) ECCV 2016. LNCS, vol. 9909, pp. 318–333. Springer, Cham (2016). https://doi.org/10.1007/978-3-319-46454-1_20
25. Park, T., Liu, M.Y., Wang, T.C., Zhu, J.Y.: Semantic image synthesis with spatially-adaptive normalization. In: Proceedings of the IEEE Computer Vision and Pattern Recognition, pp. 2337–2346 (2019)
26. Liu, Z., Luo, P., Wang, X., Tang, X.: Deep learning face attributes in the wild. In: Proceedings of the IEEE Conference on Computer Vision, pp. 3730–3738 (2015)
27. Le, V., Brandt, J., Lin, Z., Bourdev, L., Huang, T.S.: Interactive facial feature localization. In: Fitzgibbon, A., Lazebnik, S., Perona, P., Sato, Y., Schmid, C. (eds.) ECCV 2012. LNCS, vol. 7574, pp. 679–692. Springer, Heidelberg (2012). https://doi.org/10.1007/978-3-642-33712-3_49
28. Luo, L., Xue, D., Feng, X.: Ehanet: an effective hierarchical aggregation network for face parsing. Appl. Sci. 10(9), 3135 (2020)
29. Wang, Z., Bovik, A.C., Sheikh, H.R., Simoncelli, E.P.: Image quality assessment: from error visibility to structural similarity. IEEE Trans. Image Process. 13(4), 600–612 (2004)
30. Kingma, D.P., Ba, J.: Adam: A method for stochastic optimization. arXiv preprint arXiv:1412.6980 (2014)
31. Jang, E., Gu, S., Poole, B.: Categorical reparameterization with gumbel-softmax. arXiv preprint arXiv:1611.01144 (2016)
32. Liu, Z.S., Siu, W.C., Chan, Y.L.: Reference based face super-resolution. IEEE. Access 7, 129112–129126 (2019)

Graphs and Networks

Layout and Display of Network Graphs on a Sphere

Anshul Guha[1] and Eliot Feibush[2(⊠)]

[1] Yale University, New Haven, USA
[2] Princeton Plasma Physics Laboratory, Princeton, NJ, USA
`efeibush@pppl.gov`

Abstract. There are many advantages to displaying a network graph on a sphere instead of on a plane. For instance, 3D models can be rotated so that any node is in the center of the user's field of view. Moreover, an opaque sphere provides a natural filtering mechanism for selecting a small subset of data to display. However, the spherical geometry presents some challenges to modeling and displaying a graph, and the literature for 3D layout algorithms is not as rich as that of 2D layout algorithms. We developed a Visualization Pipeline to parse input data and visualize it on a 3D sphere. Within this pipeline, we have developed a 3D version of the Fruchterman-Reingold Layout Algorithm, and also present a method for creating 3D arcs that connect the nodes on a sphere. We created four modified force-directed algorithms, and determined which of their objective functions produced graphs with more evenly-distributed nodes. Our implementation functions in readily available 3D visualization programs and our browser-based display functions on all common operating systems and devices.

Keyword: 3D force directed graph algorithm

1 Introduction

Graphs are formally defined as an ordered pair (V, E), where V is a set of vertices and E is a set of edges that connect pairs of vertices. Node-link diagrams, which display vertices as points and edges as straight lines connecting vertices, are the most common method for visualizing graphs. Currently, most graph visualization research assumes that:

1. All vertices lie on a plane.
2. All edges are straight or curved lines in the same plane as the vertices.

These assumptions are quite reasonable since they ensure that the graphs can be printed on a flat 2D surface (paper) without distortion. Furthermore, research into 3D graphs has often focused on graphs where vertices are arbitrarily allowed

Supplementary Information The online version contains supplementary material available at https://doi.org/10.1007/978-3-031-23473-6_6.

to lie anywhere in the 3D space. Although some graphs are better visualized in higher dimensions, or in non-euclidean geometries. This research is motivated by the need to show the influence of one research paper on subsequent papers. Even a modest 2D graph with 50 nodes and 200 edges can be cluttered so it is difficult to follow the connections. Modeling the graph in three dimensions significantly expands the space for locating nodes. Positioning the nodes on a sphere provides a strong visual context that is very familiar to people exploring a graph.

We developed a Visualization Pipeline to parse raw data and display the graphs on a sphere. Within this visualization pipeline we explore a variety of algorithms to display graphs on a sphere.

We implement four different force-directed algorithms for displaying graphs, all of which are inspired by the original Fruchterman-Reingold algorithm [6]. These algorithms have been adapted to address several problems which arise when force-directed diagrams are carried over to convex surfaces (like the sphere). For example, ·

1. Unlike planes, vectors which lie in a tangent plane to a sphere and have a head on the sphere do not have a tail on the sphere.
2. If two vertices repel each other with too much force, they can actually end up closer to each other on the other side of the sphere.

In this paper we analyze citation maps - graphs where each node corresponds to a separate scientific paper and each edge represents the event of one paper citing another - as our input data. However, the algorithms and software written apply generally to all graphs. Modeling graphs on a sphere requires connecting the nodes in each edge pair using curves that lie on the 3D sphere. As a simplifying assumption, we chose to connect these nodes with a 3D arc along the unique great circle path that connects them, since the great circle path is the shortest distance between any two points on the sphere. However connecting nodes with non-great-circle curves is possible, particularly if these paths are uniquely suited to avoid node and edge crossings.

The rest of the paper proceeds as follows: In Sect. 2 we give an overview of related work on force-directed algorithms and spherical graph visualization. Section 3 provides a high-level overview of the pipeline that transforms raw data into a spherical visualization in either Paraview or a browser. In Sect. 4 we describe the force-directed algorithms that calculate the final locations of the nodes on the sphere and provide the mathematical basis for drawing arcs on a sphere. Section 5 has an overview of the implementation of the browser-based visualization, followed by conclusions in Sect. 6.

2   Related Work

Force-directed algorithms were first explored by Tutte [14], whose algorithm relied on the barycentric representations of vertices on a 2D plane. His idea was revisited in 1984 by Eades [5] and in 1991 by Fruchterman and Reingold [6]. Both of these papers define attractive and repulsive forces, modeling the interactions between every pair of vertices by Hooke's Law. These papers paved the way for more force-directed layout algorithms to be proposed. For instance, ForceAtlas and ForceAtlas2 were published by the creators of the 2D graph visualization software Gephi [2].

Spherical graph visualization has been most recently studied by Perry, Yin, Gray, and Kobourov [10]. They propose two algorithms for spherical visualization; one which computes a 2D visualization and another which uses spherical multi-dimensional scaling. In addition, they have also constructed a pipeline to parse data and create an in-browser spherical visualization.

Some other authors have also experimented with spherical visualization. For example, Munzner [9] has constructed many spherical and hyperbolic tree visualizations, and Sprenger [7] has used concentric spheres in graph visualization in the past.

Additionally, Brath and MacMurchy [3] have conducted a user study on how individuals (stock brokers) react to graph visualizations on a sphere. Moreover, in [12], Schulz presents a spherical graph layout algorithm for graphs with large numbers of nodes. He applies his layout algorithm to a citation map of Web of Science sociology papers. Similar papers have largely concluded that while spherical visualization has some drawbacks (such as being harder to implement), it also have many advantages, such as being able to rotate any vertex to the center of the screen.

Finally, some research has been conducted into 3D force-directed algorithms as well. For instance, Lu and Si [8] propose four clustering-based graph layout algorithms which are successful in reducing edge crossings in 3D graphs.

3   Visualization Pipeline

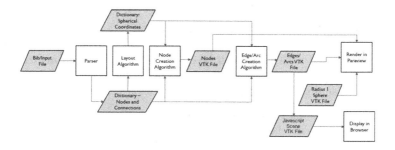

Fig. 1. A flowchart of the steps to convert input data into three separate VTK files representing a spherical graph layout: one to model the unit sphere, another to describe a small sphere for each node, and the third file that models each great circle arc that connects two nodes.

The first step of the pipeline is to run the data through a parser that stores the vertex and edge data as lists. (In our specific implementation, we wrote a

Parser that reads and interprets Bibtex files, so that the nodes of the graph are individual papers and the edges represent instances of papers referencing each other.) Call these lists V and E. Then V and E are passed into the Layout Algorithm, which returns a dictionary S of spherical coordinates - one for each node of the graph (Fig. 1).

S is then passed into a function called CreateNodes. CreateNodes generates a Nodes file containing instructions for the 3D visualization software to create a polygonal mesh approximating a sphere with radius 0.02 around each element of S, thereby creating a set of $3D$ spheres that represent each node in the final graph G. The points and polygonal mesh associated with these $3D$ spheres are written out to Nodes.

Next, S and E are passed into the CreateEdges algorithm. Each edge is actually an arc of a great circle of G. Because VTK has no function to automatically create arcs of spheres, each edge between two nodes at points A and B is approximated by equally spaced points along the arc connecting A and B. In typical views, connecting these points with short line segments renders curved arcs along the surface of the unit sphere.

Finally, a polygonal mesh is generated to model the unit sphere. Separating the components of the graph enables controlling the display and applying selection filters to the data.

Our implementation produces data sets that can be displayed in scientific visualization tools such as Paraview [1] and VisIt [4] which are both based on the Visualization Toolkit software [11]. These programs provide 3D viewing techniques and operators for filtering the nodes and edges in the graph. Both programs are freely available for Windows, Mac OS, and Linux. This approach to interoperability handles 3D viewing across platforms.

For added portability, our implementation generates Javascript files that can be displayed interactively in a browser.

4   Graph Visualization Algorithms

Our overarching goal with the graph layouts was to develop an algorithm that created evenly-distributed nodes with no node overlaps and minimal "dense" edge crossing. Usually, this meant some combination of:

1. Nodes are equally distributed across the sphere.
2. High-degree nodes are far away from each other.

4.1   Layout - Adaptation of Fruchterman-Reingold Algorithm

The Fruchterman-Reingold algorithm (FR) is a well-known layout algorithm which produces high-quality $2D$ graph layouts. To study the effectiveness of an FR-like algorithm on spheres, we developed four different algorithms for spherical graph visualization, each of which is modeled after the original 2-dimensional FR-algorithm. These spherical algorithms have not been previously studied.

The Spherical-FR-Layout Algorithm can be described as follows:

1. Define a static constant $k = \frac{4\pi}{\text{number of nodes}}$
2. Assign a random Cartesian coordinate to every node in V.
3. Run the Update Algorithm until the coordinates converge. (We ran the update algorithm for 50 iterations.)

(Note: Within the code, all rotations are performed by converting Cartesian coordinates to Spherical coordinates, carrying out the necessary rotation, and then converting back to Cartesian coordinates. Cartesian coordinates are used primarily to simplify the vector addition operations, and also because Paraview and THREE.js require Cartesian input.)

The Update-Algorithm can be described as follows:

1. For each node N in V, let $N.pos$ be the the original Cartesian coordinates of the point N. Additionally, for each N, create a vector called $N.update$ with an initial value of $[0, 0, 0]$.
2. Iterate through every pair of nodes (N_1, N_2), where both N_1 and N_2 are in V. Both N_1 and N_2 are modeled as positive electric charges which repel each other with a force proportional to the distance between them. $N_1.update$ and $N_2.update$ are modified so that the coordinates $N_1.pos + N_1.update$ and $N_2.pos + N_2.update$ move apart from each other.
3. Iterate through every pair of nodes (N_3, N_4), where both N_3 and N_4 are in V. N_3 and N_4 can be imagined to be connected by a spring with an equilibrium length of 0, so that the attractive force is directly proportional to the distance between them. Again, $N_1.update$ and $N_2.update$ are modified to move the $N_1.pos + N_1.update$ and $N_2.pos + N_2.update$ coordinates closer to each other.

The difference between the standard FR algorithm and our modified FR algorithm is encapsulated in two details. First, how is the distance between any two nodes calculated? There are two options:

1. The distance between two nodes can be defined to be equal to the Euclidean distance between them.
2. The distance between two nodes can be defined to be equal to the length of the shortest (great-circle) arc on the sphere that connects them.

Another important detail to consider is that if $N.pos$ is on a sphere of radius 1, then $N.pos + N.update$ may no longer be on the sphere of radius 1. There are two ways to correct this:

1. Move $N.pos + N.update$ along the 'true' update vector and then to scale N up or down so that its coordinates once again have a radius of 1.
2. Move the point $N.pos$ along the unit sphere in the same direction as $N.update$ and for the same distance as the length of $N.update$.

After implementing all four variations on the FR algorithm, we judged that the graphs that were produced when we defined distance as the minimal arc length and strictly moved the nodes along the unit sphere itself were the most aesthetically pleasing. A quantitative evaluation of this graph algorithm is provided in Sect. 4.2. These graphs tended to be the most evenly distributed and also contained the least number of node overlaps.

We have created an animation of the movement of nodes showing 50 steps of the Spherical-FR Layout Algorithm. It is available in the supplemental file. In the animation the nodes are initially arranged along lines of latitude and longitude, compared to the random starting locations in Fig. 2a. Both starting arrangements converge to the same final layout shown in Fig. 2b. After varying the relative strength of the attractive and repulsive forces, we found that the vertices always converge to some final location, unlike the $2D$ Fruchterman-Reingold algorithm, where the locations of the nodes sometimes oscillate or enter a chaotic state after many iterations.

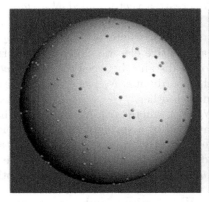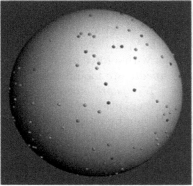

(a) A Random Starting configuration for the Spherical-FR-Layout Algorithm.

(b) Final positions of the nodes after 50 iterations. At this point, the node positions have converged to their final locations.

Fig. 2. The movement of nodes in Spherical-FR-Layout Algorithm. This particular dataset contains 186 nodes and 791 edges. The edges are omitted from this example for the sake of clarity.

The 2D Fruchterman-Reingold Algorithm described in [6] differs in one key respect from our 3D adaptation. In particular, the 2D algorithm relies on a "cooling" function that limits the maximum displacement of every node after each iteration of the Update algorithm. This cooling function approaches zero as the number of iterations increases, which effectively forces the convergence of the 2D Fruchterman-Reingold algorithm. Without the cooling function the 2D Fruchterman-Reingold algorithm can lead to oscillating or chaotic behavior, depending on the relative strength of the attractive and repulsive forces. Our algorithm does not depend on a cooling function to ensure that all the nodes converge to a final location. This is because repeated testing with different parameters for the strength of the attractive and repulsive forces in our algorithms all resulted in the vertices of the graph converging to a stable position. A theoretical explanation of this phenomenon (which is not true in the 2-dimensional case) is a potential avenue for future research.

4.2   Quantitative Evaluation

A quantitative consideration for graph quality is the length of the edges between the nodes. The goal is to eliminate long edges and increase the uniformity of edge length. We calculated the arc length of each edge in the citation graph and plotted histograms of the lengths in Fig. 4. The histogram at an early iteration of the algorithm shows some very long arcs greater than 5 rad. In the final iteration the very long arcs have been eliminated and a larger number of arcs are less than 1 rad. This indicates the progress of the Update Algorithm as it iterates through each pair of nodes.

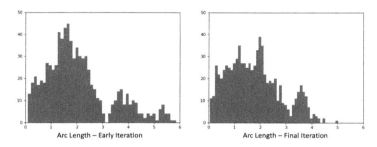

Fig. 3. Histogram of arc lengths (edges between nodes) at early and late iterations of the Update Algorithm.

4.3   Visualizing Spheres in Paraview

VTK files do not have a built-in specification for spheres but a polygonal mesh can be created to model our unit sphere. The points of the polygonal mesh are located at all spherical coordinates of the following forms:

1. $(\varphi, \theta) = \left(\frac{\pi m}{16}, \frac{\pi n}{8}\right)$ with $1 \le m \le 15$, $0 \le n \le 15$.
2. $(\varphi, \theta) = (0, 0)$ or $(0, \pi)$.

After generating this list of 242 vertices, the UnitSphere.vtk file also defines which coordinates to connect in order to create the 256 polygons of the mesh. For typical visualizations at 1920×1080 resolution, the resulting discrete polygonal mesh is visually indistinguishable from a continuous sphere representation.

Each node in the Nodes file is also created using a modified version of this method, where the spherical coordinates are converted to Cartesian coordinates, scaled down by a factor of 50, and then translated to their correct position. Ideally the spheres in the nodes file would be instances of a single master definition. Unfortunately VTK files do not have this capability. This approach can be implemented through Paraview's Python programming interface in a future version of our visualization pipeline.

4.4   Mathematical Basis for Visualizing Arcs in Paraview

Our method relies on spherical coordinates and rotation matrices to simplify the problem of drawing great-circle arcs on a sphere. To our knowledge, this method has not been described in the previous literature. However, we note that an alternate method for spherical interpolation can be derived by using quaternions to express rotations, as mentioned by Ken Shoemake in [13].

In order to model an arc between any two points A and B on a unit sphere, the key step is to calculate the coordinates of N equidistant points along the arc from A to B. We achieved good results with 64 points per arc.

Let the spherical coordinates of A and B be (φ_1, θ_1) and (φ_2, θ_2). The Cartesian coordinates (a_1, a_2, a_3) and (b_1, b_2, b_3) for A and B respectively can be calculated by the well-known equations, where $i \in \{1, 2\}$:

$$
\begin{aligned}
x_i &= \cos \varphi_i \sin \theta_i \\
y_i &= \sin \varphi_i \sin \theta_i \\
z_i &= \cos \theta_i
\end{aligned}
\tag{1}
$$

Given the points $A = (a_1, a_2, a_3)$ and $B = (b_1, b_2, b_3)$, the shortest arc A on a unit sphere that connects A and B will be contained entirely in the great circle S that passes through both A and B. S, in turn, will be contained entirely within the plane P passing through A, B, and $O = (0, 0, 0)$.

Notice that the cross product

$$
\begin{aligned}
\vec{C} = \vec{OA} \times \vec{OB} &= \begin{bmatrix} \hat{i} & \hat{j} & \hat{k} \\ a_1 & a_2 & a_3 \\ b_1 & b_2 & b_3 \end{bmatrix} \\
&= (a_2 b_3 - a_3 b_2)\hat{i} + (a_3 b_1 - b_3 a_1)\hat{j} \\
&\quad + (a_1 b_2 - a_2 b_1)\hat{k}
\end{aligned}
\tag{2}
$$

is perpendicular to P. So, P can be characterized as the set of all points (x, y, z) such that

$$
\begin{aligned}
0 &= \langle a_2 b_3 - a_3 b_2, a_3 b_1 \\
&\quad - b_3 a_1, a_1 b_2 - a_2 b_1 \rangle \cdot \langle x, y, z \rangle \\
\implies 0 &= (a_2 b_3 - a_3 b_2)x + (a_3 b_1 - a_1 b_3)y \\
&\quad + (a_1 b_2 - a_2 b_1)z
\end{aligned}
\tag{3}
$$

We now attempt to rotate the plane OAB so that it coincides with the xy-plane, in order to eliminate the z-coordinate and simplify the problem. This is equivalent to rotating $\vec{C}$ until it becomes parallel to the z-axis. Therefore we can let $C = (c_1, c_2, c_3) = (a_2 b_3 - a_3 b_2, a_3 b_1 - b_3 a_1, a_1 b_2 - a_2 b_1)$.

Now, applying the equations

$$
\begin{aligned}
\theta_C &= \arccos \left(\frac{c_3}{\sqrt{c_1{}^2 + c_2{}^2 + c_3{}^2}} \right) \\
\varphi_C &= \operatorname{atan2}(c_2, c_1)
\end{aligned}
\tag{4}
$$

yields the spherical coordinates (φ_C, θ_C) of C. Let $R_{y,-\theta_C}$ and $R_{z,-\varphi_C}$ be the rotation matrices that rotate vectors by $-\theta_C$ degrees clockwise around the y-axis and by $-\varphi_C$ clockwise around the z-axis respectively. Then $C' = R_{y,-\theta_C} R_{z,-\varphi_C} C^T$ will have x and y-coordinates of 0. Similarly, $A' = R_{y,-\theta_C} R_{z,-\varphi_C} A^T$ and $B' = R_{y,-\theta_C} R_{z,-\varphi_C} B^T$ have z-coordinates of 0. Let

$$
A' = \begin{bmatrix} a'_1 \\ a'_2 \\ 0 \end{bmatrix} \text{ and } B' = \begin{bmatrix} b'_1 \\ b'_2 \\ 0 \end{bmatrix} \tag{5}
$$

Then one can define $\theta_A = \text{atan2}(a'_2, a'_1)$ and $\theta_B = \text{atan2}(b'_2, b'_1)$. The coordinates of N evenly spaced points from A' to B' are now much easier to parameterize:

1. In the case where $\theta_1 < \theta_2$ and $\theta_1 + \pi > \theta_2$, the points are of the form

$$
S_i = \begin{bmatrix} \cos\left(\theta_1 + \frac{(\theta_2 - \theta_1)i}{N}\right) \\ \sin\left(\theta_1 + \frac{(\theta_2 - \theta_1)i}{N}\right) \\ 0 \end{bmatrix} \text{ with } 0 \le i < N \tag{6}
$$

2. In the case where $\theta_1 < \theta_2$ and $\theta_1 + \pi < \theta_2$, let $\theta_3 = \theta_1 + 2\pi$. Then the points are of the form

$$
S_i = \begin{bmatrix} \cos\left(\theta_2 + \frac{(\theta_3 - \theta_2)i}{N}\right) \\ \sin\left(\theta_2 + \frac{(\theta_3 - \theta_2)i}{N}\right) \\ 0 \end{bmatrix} \text{ with } 0 \le i < N \tag{7}
$$

3. In the case where $\theta_1 > \theta_2$ and $\theta_2 + \pi < \theta_2$, the points are of the form

$$
S_i = \begin{bmatrix} \cos\left(\theta_2 + \frac{(\theta_1 - \theta_2)i}{N}\right) \\ \sin\left(\theta_2 + \frac{(\theta_1 - \theta_2)i}{N}\right) \\ 0 \end{bmatrix} \text{ with } 0 \le i < N \tag{8}
$$

4. In the case where $\theta_1 > \theta_2$ and $\theta_2 + \pi > \theta_1$, let $\theta_3 = \theta_2 * 2\pi$. Then the points are of the form

$$
S_i = \begin{bmatrix} \cos\left(\theta_1 + \frac{(\theta_3 - \theta_1)i}{N}\right) \\ \sin\left(\theta_1 + \frac{(\theta_3 - \theta_1)i}{N}\right) \\ 0 \end{bmatrix} \text{ with } 0 \le i < N \tag{9}
$$

The final step is to rotate A' and B' back to A and B. Notice that $A = R_{y,\varphi_C} R_{x,\theta_C} A'$, and $B = R_{y,\varphi_C} R_{x,\theta_C} B'$, as well as all points of the form S_i for $0 \le i < 64$. Let $S'_i = R_{y,\varphi_C} R_{x,\theta_C} S_i$. Then the set of S'_i are the coordinates of N equidistant points on the shortest arc from A to B. Adding S'_i to the list of points in ArcEdges.txt allows these points to be rendered by Paraview, giving the appearance of a solid spherical arc connecting A and B, as in Fig. 4.

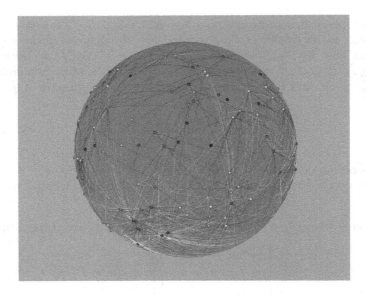

Fig. 4. A network graph created using the variant of the Fruchterman-Reingold algorithm described in Sect. 4.1. This particular graph is a directed citation graph of a set of research papers in gyrokinetics. The arc lines are shaded from blue to white. The node at the white end of the arc is the paper being referenced. (Color figure online)

5   Browser-Based Visualization

Displaying the visualization in a browser increases access and portability for researchers, as mentioned in [6]. We provide some implementation details. We used THREE.js, a JavaScript 3D library that is freely available online. (All imports linked to websites at www.unpkg.com, so our programs are not

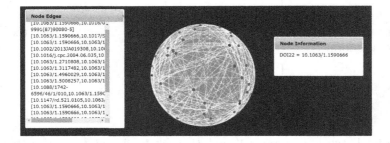

Fig. 5. To increase understanding we programmed two dialog boxes that were not present in the original Paraview visualization. When a node on the graph is clicked, it changes from red to green, and its name is displayed in the dialog box titled "Node Information". Furthermore, all edges containing the green node are also displayed in the dialog box titled "Node Edges". (Color figure online)

dependent on the host computer's local version of THREE.js.) Furthermore, using THREE.js (a wrapper for WEBGL) as well as Javascript allows displaying our visualizations on any device with a Javascript-enabled browser. The source code and a sample dataset are available at https://github.com/Bhombal/NGV.

6   Conclusion

In our research we created a visualization pipeline to parse raw data and display graphs on a 3D sphere. We built on the work of [10] and [6] by developing new versions of the Fruchterman-Reingold Algorithm for layout on a 3D sphere. Defining node distance as the minimal arc length and moving nodes along the unit sphere succeeded in producing graphs with reduced edge length. Our implementation enables the graphs to be viewed and manipulated within the Paraview application or within a web browser.

In the future, the possibility of connecting nodes with non-great-circle edges is vital to explore reduced edge crossings. Additionally, a theoretical explanation for why the modified Fruchterman-Reingold algorithm seems to always converge regardless of the relative strengths of the attractive and repulsive forces (instead of settling into an oscillating or chaotic pattern) will be informative.

References

1. Ahrens, J., Geveci, B., Law, C.: Paraview: an end-user tool for large-data visualization. Vis. Handb. **717**(8) (2005)
2. Bastian, M., Heymann, S., Jacomy, M.: Gephi: an open source software for exploring and manipulating networks. In: Proceedings of the International AAAI Conference on Web and Social Media, vol. 3, no. 1, pp. 361–362 (2009)
3. Brath, R., Macmurchy, P.: Sphere-based information visualization: challenges and benefits. In: 2012 16th International Conference on Information Visualisation, pp. 1–6 (2012)
4. Childs, H.: Visit: an end-user tool for visualizing and analyzing very large data. In: High Performance Visualization-Enabling Extreme-Scale Scientific Insight, pp. 357–372 (2012)
5. Eades, P.: A heuristic for graph drawing (1984)
6. Fruchterman, T.M., Reingold, E.M.: Graph drawing by force-directed placement. Softw. Pract. Exper. **21**(11), 1129–1164 (1991)
7. Gross, M.H., Sprenger, T.C., Finger, J.: Visualizing information on a sphere. In: Proceedings of VIZ 1997: Visualization Conference, Information Visualization Symposium and Parallel Rendering Symposium, pp. 11–16 (1997)
8. Jiawei Lu and Yain Whar Si: Clustering-based force-directed algorithms for 3D graph visualization. J. Supercomput. **76**, 12 (2020)
9. Munzner, T.: Exploring large graphs in 3D hyperbolic space. IEEE Comput. Graph. Appl. **18**(4), 18–23 (1998)
10. Perry, S., Yin, M.S., Gray, K., Kobourov, S.: Drawing Graphs on the Sphere. Association for Computing Machinery, New York, NY, USA (2020)
11. Schroeder, W., Martin, K., Lorensen, B.: The Visualization Toolkit. Kitware (2006)
12. Schulz, C.: Visualizing Spreading Phenomena on Complex Networks (2018)

13. Shoemake, K.: Animating rotation with quaternion curves. In: SIGGRAPH 1885, (1985)
14. Tutte, W.T.: How to draw a graph. Proc. London Math. Soc. s3–13(1), 743–767 (1963)

Joint Matrix Factorization and Structure Preserving for Domain Adaptation

Wenhao Shao, Hui Chen, Min Meng$^{(\boxtimes)}$, and Jigang Wu

School of Computer Science and Technology, Guangdong University of Technology, Guangzhou, China
mengmin1985@gmail.com

Abstract. Domain adaptation aims to learn robust classifiers for the target domain by transferring knowledge from the labeled source domain. However, most of the existing studies emphasize learning domain-invariant feature representations by employing distribution alignment on the feature space, which ignores the influence of data noise and structure knowledge. To address these issues, we propose a new domain adaptation approach, which can effectively reduce the impact of data noise and simultaneously thoroughly exploit the manifold data structures to transfer discriminative knowledge. Specifically, we jointly model matrix factorization, maximum entropy, distribution alignment in a unified framework, which can effectively alleviate the negative transfer of the outliers. Furthermore, we devise graph dual regularization to thoroughly explore the intrinsic manifold data structures, which can significantly reduce structure discrepancy across domains. Experimental results on various domain adaptation tasks demonstrate the superiority of the proposed method.

Keywords: Domain adaptation · Matrix factorization · Maximum entropy · Graph dual regularization

1 Introduction

Due to the rapid increase in the number of images, it is very expensive or impossible to classify images manually [16]. Domain adaptation is a technique for solving the problem of insufficient label data.

However, the performance of domain adaptation methods may be poor due to the distribution discrepancy across domains. To solve this problem, considerable researches are devoted to domain adaptation. Most existing researches are mainly based on distribution alignment to reduce the differences across domains [6,8,13,14,25]. JDA [13] performs marginal and conditional distribution alignment by the **MMD** criteria. DICD [8] aims to learn discriminative features with important properties preserved. Recently, deep learning methods are widely used [3,10,11,15,17,23]. DAN [10] can learn transferable features. JAN [15] proposes to align the joint distributions of multiple domain-specific layers. Although existing methods attempt to address the problem of distribution discrepancy, there still exist limitations, one is that they still suffer from the influence of data noise, and the other is that they ignore the manifold structure of the data.

© The Author(s), under exclusive license to Springer Nature Switzerland AG 2022
N. Magnenat-Thalmann et al. (Eds.): CGI 2022, LNCS 13443, pp. 79–91, 2022.
https://doi.org/10.1007/978-3-031-23473-6_7

To tackle these challenges, in this paper, we propose a novel domain adaptation approach, termed as joint Matrix Factorization and Structure Preserving (MFSP) for domain adaptation, which can build a robust model by integrating matrix factorization, distribution alignment and graph dual regularization into a unified learning framework. Specifically, we employ matrix factorization techniques to learn the discriminative features of the data, and use maximum entropy to alleviate the impact of data noise on the extracted features. Meanwhile, our proposed method jointly aligns the marginal and conditional probability distributions and introduces the label information to reduce the distribution discrepancy between the source and target domains. Furthermore, to take advantage of the useful information contained in the decomposed matrices, we adopt graph dual regularization to accurately capture the intrinsic manifold structures of data. The main contributions of this work can be summarized as follows:

1. We propose a novel domain adaptation method to perform joint matrix factorization and structure preserving, which can alleviate the impact of data noise on feature discrimination via maximum entropy and capture the intrinsic manifold structures of data through graph dual regularization.
2. We employ matrix factorization to learn discriminative and domain-invariant features, which was aligned by **MMD** criteria and label information.
3. Extensive experiments are conducted on several benchmark data sets, which validates the superior performance of our method.

2   Related Work

In this section, we review some previous works related to this work. First, we review some feature based domain adaptation methods. Then, we briefly review the works related to matrix factorization.

Domain adaptation aims to help the classification model transfer knowledge from source domain to target domain. According to the survey [16,26], most of the existing works are feature-based. For instance, [13] aligns the marginal distribution and conditional distribution by **MMD** criteria. Based on this work, several novel approaches are proposed, such as jointly matching the features and re-weights the instances between domains [14], considering the landmark selection to enhance the robustness of the model [7], aligning the distributions in Grassmann manifold to learn a domain invariant classifier [22]. In addition, [24] uses the low-rank framework to extract features, which introduces linear regression and label matrix to learn a discriminative subspace, and the label relaxation matrix can enlarge the margins between different classes.

Meanwhile, some works introduce matrix factorization techniques into domain adaptation [12,18,19]. Long et al. [12] proposes to learn the potential factors by nonnegative matrix factorization (NMF), which considers simultaneous optimization of empirical likelihood and geometric structures. The work of [19] performs graph dual regularization in the NMF framework with label constraints to learn the domain-invariant features. Although these methods have achieved good performance, there still exists a common deficiency. Typically,

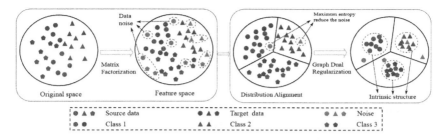

Fig. 1. Illustration of the proposed approach, which integrates matrix factorization, domain alignment and graph dual regularization into a unified model.

feature-based methods perform distribution alignment to address the negative effect of domain shift, which neglects the influence of data noise. Our work also belongs to the feature-based method. Different from the previous works, we adopt matrix factorization to learn domain-invariant features, and use maximum entropy to eliminate the influence of noise. Meanwhile, we consider the manifold structure of the data by employing graph dual Laplacian so that local structure information can be preserved as much as possible.

3 Proposed Method

3.1 Notations

In this paper, vectors and matrices are denoted by bold lowercase letters and bold uppercase letters, respectively. Assume we have a labeled source domain $\mathcal{D}_s = \{(\mathbf{x}_{s_i}, \mathbf{y}_{s_i})\}_{i=1}^{n_s}$ with n_s data samples and a unlabeled target domain $\mathcal{D}_t = \{\mathbf{x}_{t_i}\}_{i=1}^{n_t}$ with n_t data samples. $\mathbf{x}_{s_i}$ and $\mathbf{x}_{t_i}$ belong to the same data space $\mathcal{X}$ with dimensionality m, $\mathbf{y}_{s_i} \in \mathcal{Y}_s = \{1, \cdots, k\}$ is the label vector associated to $\mathbf{x}_{s_i}$. For simplicity, we denote $\mathbf{X}_s = [\mathbf{x}_{s_1}, \cdots, \mathbf{x}_{s_{n_s}}] \in \mathbb{R}^{m \times n_s}$ and $\mathbf{Y}_s = [\mathbf{y}_{s_1}, \cdots, \mathbf{y}_{s_{n_s}}] \in \mathbb{R}^{k \times n_s}$ as the source data matrix and the corresponding label matrix, respectively. Likewise, $\mathbf{X}_t = [\mathbf{x}_{t_1}, \cdots, \mathbf{x}_{t_{n_t}}] \in \mathbb{R}^{m \times n_t}$ denotes the target data matrix. We assume that the source and target domains share the same label space $\mathcal{Y}_s = \mathcal{Y}_t$. Let $P_s(\mathbf{X}_s)$ and $P_t(\mathbf{X}_t)$ denote the marginal distributions of $\mathbf{X}_s$ and $\mathbf{X}_t$, $Q_s(\mathbf{Y}_s|\mathbf{X}_s)$ and $Q_t(\mathbf{Y}_t|\mathbf{X_t})$ denote the conditional distributions. In general, the marginal distribution and conditional distribution across domains are different: $P_s(\mathbf{X}_s) \neq P_t(\mathbf{X}_t)$ and $Q_s(\mathbf{Y}_s|\mathbf{X}_s) \neq Q_t(\mathbf{Y}_t|\mathbf{X_t})$.

3.2 Problem Formulation

The key to domain adaptation is to reduce the distribution difference across domains. To this end, we propose a novel domain adaptation approach, which can build a robust model with three properties: 1) learn the discriminative features of data, 2) alleviate the impact of data noise, 3) capture the intrinsic manifold structures of data. Figure 1 gives an illustration of the proposed framework, which integrates three learning objectives into a unified optimization model:

$$\min_{\mathbf{W},\mathbf{U},\mathbf{V}} \Psi_{MF}(\mathbf{W},\mathbf{U},\mathbf{V}) + \Psi_{DA}(\mathbf{V}) + \Psi_{GDR}(\mathbf{U},\mathbf{V}), \tag{1}$$

where $\mathbf{U}$ and $\mathbf{V}$ are two low rank matrices for matrix factorization, and $\mathbf{W}$ is a weight matrix to reduce the influence of data noise. $\Psi_{MF}(\mathbf{W},\mathbf{U},\mathbf{V})$ employs matrix factorization and maximum entropy techniques to learn the common latent features and reduce the negative effect of data noise. $\Psi_{DA}(\mathbf{V})$ is used to minimize the distribution divergence between the source and target domains. $\Psi_{GDR}(\mathbf{U},\mathbf{V})$ adopts the graph dual regularization to preserve geometrical structures of data in each domain. We will describe the details from three perspectives.

Matrix Factorization. We employ matrix factorization to extract the common latent features and adopt maximum entropy technology to minimize the impact of data noise or irrelevant features. We aim to reduce the negative effects of noise or irrelevant features on knowledge transfer. In our method, we treat source data matrix $\mathbf{X_s}$ and target data matrix $\mathbf{X_t}$ as a whole data matrix $\mathbf{X} = [\mathbf{X}_s, \mathbf{X}_t] \in \mathbb{R}^{m \times n}$, where $n = n_s + n_t$. The data matrix $\mathbf{X}$ is decomposed into two low rank matrices $\mathbf{U} \in \mathbb{R}^{m \times k}$ and $\mathbf{V} \in \mathbb{R}^{k \times n}$, which can provide a good approximation to the data matrix $\mathbf{X}$. We can obtain the following optimization problem:

$$\Psi_{MF}(\mathbf{U},\mathbf{V}) = \|\mathbf{X} - \mathbf{UV}\|_F^2 \tag{2}$$

where $\| \cdot \|_F$ is the Frobenius norm, $\mathbf{U}$ and $\mathbf{V}$ are treated as the indicator and feature matrices, respectively. However, the real world data is always noisy. Maximum entropy technique can be used to alleviate the influence of data noise [5]:

$$\Psi_{MF}(\mathbf{W},\mathbf{U},\mathbf{V}) = \frac{1}{2}\|\sqrt{\mathbf{W}} \odot (\mathbf{X} - \mathbf{UV})\|_F^2 + \beta\|\overline{\mathbf{W}}\|_1$$
$$+ \gamma \sum_{i,j} (w_{ij} \log w_{ij} + \bar{w}_{ij} \log \bar{w}_{ij}) \tag{3}$$
$$\text{s.t. } \mathbf{W} + \overline{\mathbf{W}} = \mathbf{1}; \quad \mathbf{W} \text{ and } \overline{\mathbf{W}} \in [0,1]^{m \times n}$$

where $\| \cdot \|_1$ is the l_1 norm, $\odot$ represents the Hadamard product operator, $\mathbf{W}$ is a weight matrix which is used to reduce the influence of data noise. β and γ are two weight coefficients to the corresponding terms. The elements indicated by $\mathbf{W}$ are slightly polluted, while those indicated by $\overline{\mathbf{W}}$ are severely polluted.

Distribution Alignment. Distribution shift between different domains is essentially an obstacle to domain adaptation. Therefore, we employ the distribution alignment to reduce the distribution divergences across domains. Inspired by [13], we adopt **MMD** criteria to reduce the marginal and conditional distribution discrepancies. First, we use **MMD** to compute the marginal distribution distance between source and target domain in the k-th dimension subspace $\mathbf{V}$:

$$\Psi_{DA}^m(\mathbf{V}) = \|\frac{1}{n_s}\sum_{i=1}^{n_s}\mathbf{v}_i - \frac{1}{n_t}\sum_{j=n_s+1}^{n_s+n_t}\mathbf{v}_j\|_F^2$$

$$= Tr(\mathbf{V}\mathbf{M}_0\mathbf{V}^T) \tag{4}$$

where $\mathbf{M}_0$ is the **MMD** matrix [13].

Then, we minimize the divergence between conditional distributions:

$$\Psi_{DA}^c(\mathbf{V}) = \|\frac{1}{n_s^{(c)}}\sum_{\mathbf{v}_i \in \mathbf{V}_s^{(c)}}\mathbf{v}_i - \frac{1}{n_t^{(c)}}\sum_{\mathbf{v}_j \in \mathbf{V}_t^{(c)}}\mathbf{v}_j\|_F^2$$

$$= Tr(\mathbf{V}\mathbf{M}_c\mathbf{V}^T) \tag{5}$$

where $n_s^{(c)} = |\mathbf{V}_s^{(c)}|$, and $\mathbf{V}_s^{(c)} = \{\mathbf{v}_i : \mathbf{v}_i \in \mathbf{V}_s \wedge y(\mathbf{v}_i) = c\}$. $y(\mathbf{v}_i)$ is the true label of $\mathbf{v}_i$. Similarly, $n_t^{(c)} = |\mathbf{V}_t^{(c)}|$, and $\mathbf{V}_t^{(c)} = \{\mathbf{v}_j : \mathbf{v}_j \in \mathbf{V}_t \wedge \hat{y}(\mathbf{v}_j) = c\}$. $\hat{y}(\mathbf{v}_j)$ is the predicted label of $\mathbf{v}_j$. The **MMD** matrix $\mathbf{M}_c$ can be calculated like [13].

Finally, we minimize both marginal and conditional distribution differences:

$$\Psi_{DA}^m(\mathbf{V}) + \Psi_{DA}^c(\mathbf{V}) = \sum_{c=0}^{k} Tr(\mathbf{V}\mathbf{M}_c\mathbf{V}^T)$$

$$= Tr(\mathbf{V}\mathbf{M}\mathbf{V}^T) \tag{6}$$

where $c \in \{0, 1, ..., k\}$ is the distinct class.

To enhance the discrimination of subspace, we introduce linear regression to make full use of label information [24].

$$\Psi_{DA}(\mathbf{V}) = Tr(\mathbf{V}\mathbf{M}\mathbf{V}^T) + \lambda\|\mathbf{Y} - \mathbf{V}\|_F^2 \tag{7}$$

where λ is parameter, $\mathbf{Y} = [\mathbf{Y}_s, \hat{\mathbf{Y}}_t]$ and $\hat{\mathbf{Y}}_t$ is the pseudo label matrix for target domain. However, the binary label matrix is too rigid. Inspired by [24], we relax the strict binary label matrix into a slack variable matrix $\mathbf{Y} = [\mathbf{Y}_s + \mathbf{B} \odot \mathbf{N}, \hat{\mathbf{Y}}_t]$, where $\mathbf{B}$ and $\mathbf{N}$ is constructed like [24].

Graph Dual Regularization. Furthermore, we use graph dual regularization to accurately capture the intrinsic local manifold structures of data. The instances and features lie on nonlinear low-dimensional manifolds embedded in high-dimensional spaces, respectively. Preserving the structure of manifolds allows the learning models to respect domain-specific data distributions [19]. Therefore, we use two graphs to explore the structures of instance and feature manifolds, respectively. We have the following equation:

$$\Psi_{GDR}(\mathbf{U}, \mathbf{V}) = \frac{1}{2}\sum_{i,j=1}^{n}\|\mathbf{v}_i - \mathbf{v}_j\|^2\mathbf{S}_{i,j}^v + \frac{1}{2}\sum_{i,j=1}^{m}\|\mathbf{u}_i - \mathbf{u}_j\|^2\mathbf{S}_{i,j}^u$$

$$= \eta_1 tr(\mathbf{V}\mathbf{L}^v\mathbf{V}^T) + \eta_2 tr(\mathbf{U}^T\mathbf{L}^u\mathbf{U}) \tag{8}$$

where η_1, η_2 are the trade-off parameters, $\mathbf{S}^v$ and $\mathbf{S}^u$ are the affinity matrices which can be learned from the data matrix $\mathbf{X}$, $\mathbf{L}^v$ and $\mathbf{L}^u$ are the graph Laplacian matrices of the corresponding graphs.

Overall Objective Function. By integrating the matrix factorization, distribution alignment and graph dual regularization into a unified framework, where the influence of data noise can be minimized and the structure of instance and feature manifolds can be preserved. Therefore, our model can well transfer knowledge from source domain to target domain. We obtain the final equation:

$$
\min_{\mathbf{U},\mathbf{V},\mathbf{W}} \frac{1}{2}\|\sqrt{\mathbf{W}} \odot (\mathbf{X} - \mathbf{UV})\|_F^2 + \beta\|\overline{\mathbf{W}}\|_1 + \gamma \sum_{i,j} (w_{ij} \log w_{ij} + \bar{w}_{ij} \log \bar{w}_{ij})
$$
$$
+ \lambda\|\mathbf{Y} - \mathbf{V}\|_F^2 + \eta_1 Tr(\mathbf{V}(\mathbf{L}^v + \mathbf{M})\mathbf{V}^T) + \eta_2 Tr(\mathbf{U}^T\mathbf{L}^u\mathbf{U}) \tag{9}
$$
$$
\text{s.t.} \quad \mathbf{W} + \overline{\mathbf{W}} = 1; \quad \mathbf{W} \text{ and } \overline{\mathbf{W}} \in [0,1]^{m \times n}
$$

3.3 Optimization

In this subsection, we show how to solve the poblem using the *alternating direction method of multiplers* (ADMM) scheme [9]. We propose to introduce an auxiliary variable $\mathbf{J}$ tp represent $\mathbf{UV}$. Accordingly, $\mathbf{J} = \mathbf{UV}$ acts as a constraint. Thus, the problem (9) can be rewritten as:

$$
\min_{\mathbf{U},\mathbf{V},\mathbf{J},\mathbf{W}} \frac{1}{2}\|\sqrt{\mathbf{W}} \odot (\mathbf{X} - \mathbf{J})\|_F^2 + \beta\|\overline{\mathbf{W}}\|_1 + \gamma \sum_{i,j} (w_{ij} \log w_{ij} + \bar{w}_{ij} \log \bar{w}_{ij})
$$
$$
+ \lambda\|\mathbf{Y} - \mathbf{V}\|_F^2 + \eta_1 Tr(\mathbf{V}(\mathbf{L}^v + \mathbf{M})\mathbf{V}^T) + \eta_2 Tr(\mathbf{U}^T\mathbf{L}^u\mathbf{U}) \tag{10}
$$
$$
\text{s.t. } \mathbf{J} = \mathbf{UV} \quad \mathbf{W} + \overline{\mathbf{W}} = 1 \quad \mathbf{W} \text{ and } \overline{\mathbf{W}} \in [0,1]^{m \times n}
$$

We solve the problem (10) by minimizing its augmented Lagrangian function:

$$
\zeta = \frac{1}{2}\|\sqrt{\mathbf{W}} \odot (\mathbf{X} - \mathbf{J})\|_F^2 + \beta\|\overline{\mathbf{W}}\|_1 + \gamma \sum_{i,j} (w_{ij} \log w_{ij} + \bar{w}_{ij} \log \bar{w}_{ij})
$$
$$
+ \lambda\|\mathbf{Y} - \mathbf{V}\|_F^2 + \eta_1 Tr(\mathbf{V}^T(\mathbf{L}^v + \mathbf{M})\mathbf{V}) + \eta_2 Tr(\mathbf{U}^T\mathbf{L}^u\mathbf{U}) \tag{11}
$$
$$
+ \langle \mathbf{Z}, \mathbf{J} - \mathbf{UV} \rangle + \frac{\mu}{2}\|\mathbf{J} - \mathbf{UV}\|_F^2
$$

where $\mathbf{Z}$ is the Lagrange multiplier matrix, and μ is the penalty parameter. The constrains on $\mathbf{W}$ and $\overline{\mathbf{W}}$ are enforced as hard constrains.

Update U: while fixing $\mathbf{V},\mathbf{J},\mathbf{W}$ to update $\mathbf{U}$, the problem (11) reduces to:

$$
\eta_2 Tr(\mathbf{U}^T\mathbf{L}^u\mathbf{U}) + \langle \mathbf{Z}, \mathbf{J} - \mathbf{UV} \rangle + \frac{\mu}{2}\|\mathbf{J} - \mathbf{UV}\|_F^2 \tag{12}
$$

By setting the derivative of (12) to zero, we have:

$$
\eta_2(\mathbf{L}^u + (\mathbf{L}^u)^T)\mathbf{U} + \mathbf{U}(\mu\mathbf{VV}^T) = (\mu\mathbf{J} + \mathbf{Z})\mathbf{V}^T \tag{13}
$$

This is a sylvester linear matrix equation $\mathbf{AX} + \mathbf{XB} = \mathbf{C}$ that can be solved efficiently using the Bartels-Stewart algorithm [2].

Update V: while fixing $\mathbf{U}, \mathbf{J}, \mathbf{W}$ to update $\mathbf{V}$, the problem (11) reduces to:

$$\lambda||\mathbf{Y} - \mathbf{V}||_F^2 + \eta_1 Tr(\mathbf{V}^T(\mathbf{L}^v + \mathbf{M})\mathbf{V}) + \langle \mathbf{Z}, \mathbf{J} - \mathbf{UV} \rangle + \frac{\mu}{2}||\mathbf{J} - \mathbf{UV}||_F^2 \quad (14)$$

By setting the derivative of (14) to zero, we have:

$$\mu(\mathbf{U}^T\mathbf{U})\mathbf{V} + \eta_2\mathbf{V}(\mathbf{L}^v + (\mathbf{L}^v)^T + \mathbf{M} + \mathbf{M}^T) = \mathbf{U}^T(\mu\mathbf{J} + \mathbf{Z}) + \lambda\mathbf{Y} \quad (15)$$

Like (13), we can solve it by Bartels-Stewart algorithm.

Update J: while fixing $\mathbf{U}, \mathbf{V}, \mathbf{W}$ to update $\mathbf{J}$, the problem (11) reduces to:

$$\frac{1}{2}||\sqrt{\mathbf{W}} \odot (\mathbf{X} - \mathbf{J})||_F^2 + \langle \mathbf{Z}, \mathbf{J} - \mathbf{UV} \rangle + \frac{\mu}{2}||\mathbf{J} - \mathbf{UV}||_F^2 \quad (16)$$

This problem can be solved by:

$$\mathbf{J} = \frac{\mathbf{W} \odot \mathbf{X} + \mu\mathbf{UV} - \mathbf{Z}}{\mathbf{W} + \mu\mathbf{1}} \quad (17)$$

where the division is element-wise.

Update W: while fixing $\mathbf{U}, \mathbf{V}, \mathbf{J}$ to update $\mathbf{W}$, the problem (11) reduces to:

$$\frac{1}{2}||\sqrt{\mathbf{W}} \odot (\mathbf{X} - \mathbf{J})||_F^2 + \beta||\overline{\mathbf{W}}||_1$$
$$+ \gamma\sum_{i,j}(w_{ij}\log w_{ij} + \bar{w}_{ij}\log\bar{w}_{ij}) \quad (18)$$
$$\text{s.t. } \mathbf{W} + \overline{\mathbf{W}} = \mathbf{1} \quad \mathbf{W} \text{ and } \overline{\mathbf{W}} \in [0,1]^{m \times n}$$

The closed form solution is:

$$w_{ij} = \frac{1}{1 + \exp(([\mathbf{X} - \mathbf{J}]_{ij}^2/2 - \beta)/\gamma)} \quad (19)$$

Update the Other Parameters: Penalty parameter μ and Lagrange multiplier $\mathbf{Z}$ can be updated as follows:

$$\begin{aligned} \mathbf{Z} &:= \mathbf{Z} + \mu(\mathbf{J} - \mathbf{UV}) \\ \mu &:= \mu\rho, \quad \rho \geq 1 \end{aligned} \quad (20)$$

The detailed procedures are outlined in Algorithm 1.

4 Experiments

4.1 Datasets Description

We conduct experiments on three benchmark datasets. The statistics of these datasets are listed in Table 1. *Office-Caltech10* dataset [4] contains 2533 images in 10 shared classes from four domains. We conducted experiments on the two features of the datasets. Then, the following 12 tasks were performed: A → C,

---

Algorithm 1 The Proposed MFSP Method

Input: Source data $\{\mathbf{X}_s, \mathbf{Y}_s\}$; Target data $\mathbf{X}_t$; Parameters $\beta, \gamma, \lambda, \eta_1, \eta_2$.
  Initialization:$\mu = 1, \rho = 1.1$; label matrix $\mathbf{Y}$, $\mathbf{Z} = 0, \mathbf{V} = \mathbf{Y}$.
while not converged **do**
    1. Update $\mathbf{U}$ by using (13);
    2. Update $\mathbf{V}$ by using (15);
    3. Update $\mathbf{J}$ by using (17);
    4. Update $\mathbf{W}$ by using (19);
    5. Update $\mathbf{Z}, \mu$ by using (20);
end while
Output: $\mathbf{U}, \mathbf{V}, \mathbf{J}, \mathbf{W}$.

Table 1. Description of the datasets

Dataset	Subsets	Samples	Feature	Classes
Office-Caltech10	Amazon (A)	958	800/4096	10
	Caltech (C)	1123		
	DSLR (D)	157		
	Webcam (W)	295		
Office-Home	Art (Ar)	2421	2048	65
	Clipart (Cl)	4379		
	Product (Pr)	4428		
	RealWorld (Re)	4357		
Image-CLEF	Caltech-256 (C)	600	2048	12
	ImageNet ILSVRC 2012 (I)	600		
	Pascal VOC 2012 (P)	600		

A → D, ... , W → D. *Office-Home* dataset [20] contains 4 domains. And each domain contains 65 categories. We construct 12 different cross domain tasks: Ar → Cl, ..., Re → Pr. *ImageCLEF-DA* dataset [1] contains 12 categories of images belonging to 3 domains. By choosing different domains for the cross-domain recognition tasks, we have 6 cross-domain tasks: C → I, C → P, ..., P → I.

We compare our method with 10 state-of-the-art traditional methods: 1-NN, GFK [4], JDA [13], TJM [14], TGNMF [18], JGSA [25], DICD [8], EasyTL [21], LPJT [6], GPDA [19]. Further, six recent deep methods are used for comparison: DAN [10], DANN [3], JAN [15], CDAN [11], DWT-MEC [17] and AFN [23].

We set $\beta = 1$ for all datasets. We set $\gamma = 0.01, \lambda = 2, \eta_1 = 0.001, \eta_2 = 0.002$ for *Office-Caltech10* with SURF feature, $\gamma = 0.1, \lambda = 0.1, \eta_1 = 0.1, \eta_2 = 1$ for for *Office-Caltech10* with DeCAF6 feature, $\gamma = 0.1, \lambda = 10, \eta_1 = 1, \eta_2 = 0.1$ for *Office-Home* and $\gamma = 0.1, \lambda = 10, \eta_1 = 1, \eta_2 = 0.3$ for *ImageCLEF-DA*.

4.2 Results

The classification accuracy are shown in Table 2–Table 5.

Table 2. Accuracy (%) on Office-Caltech10 datasets with SURF features

Tasks	A→C	A→D	A→W	C→A	C→D	C→W	D→A	D→C	D→W	W→A	W→C	W→D	Avg.
1NN	26.0	25.5	29.8	23.7	25.5	25.8	28.5	26.3	63.4	23.0	19.9	59.2	31.4
GFK	43.6	44.6	45.1	51.6	43.3	44.1	39.1	31.7	85.4	31.8	34.3	87.9	48.5
JDA	39.4	39.5	38.0	44.8	45.2	41.7	33.1	31.5	89.5	32.8	31.2	89.2	46.3
TJM	39.5	45.2	42.0	46.8	44.6	39.0	32.8	31.4	85.4	30.0	30.2	89.2	46.3
TGNMF	39.4	38.9	37.6	42.9	48.4	40.7	34.6	31.7	79.5	34.0	31.4	77.1	44.7
JGSA	41.5	47.1	45.8	51.5	45.9	45.4	38.0	29.9	**91.9**	**39.9**	33.2	**90.5**	50.0
DICD	42.4	38.9	45.1	47.3	49.7	46.4	34.5	34.6	91.2	34.1	33.6	89.8	49.0
EasyTL	42.3	**48.4**	43.1	52.6	50.6	**53.9**	38.3	36.1	86.1	38.2	35.4	79.6	50.5
LPJT	**44.7**	43.7	**46.5**	41.1	48.1	39.4	31.4	**40.9**	82.2	33.8	35.7	82.0	47.5
GPDA	40.8	40.1	41.4	43.7	**52.2**	42.4	35.7	32.5	84.8	35.6	31.9	87.3	47.4
MFSP	44.1	**48.4**	46.4	**58.4**	49.0	53.4	**42.2**	34.5	86.1	39.6	**37.6**	87.3	**52.3**

Table 3. Accuracy (%) on Office-Caltech10 datasets with DeCAF6 features

Tasks	A→C	A→D	A→W	C→A	C→D	C→W	D→A	D→C	D→W	W→A	W→C	W→D	Avg.
1NN	71.7	73.9	68.1	87.3	79.6	72.5	49.9	42.0	91.5	62.5	55.3	98.1	71.0
GFK	77.3	84.7	81.0	88.5	86.0	80.3	85.8	76.0	97.3	81.8	73.9	100.0	83.2
JDA	83.2	86.6	80.3	88.7	91.1	87.8	91.8	85.5	99.3	90.2	84.2	100.0	89.1
TJM	82.4	86.0	80.7	89.7	89.8	80.7	90.6	79.9	98.0	89.5	80.4	98.1	87.2
TGNMF	87.2	**91.7**	84.1	91.6	89.8	89.5	92.0	86.7	99.7	90.5	86.8	100.0	90.8
JGSA	84.9	88.5	81.0	91.4	**93.6**	86.8	92.0	86.2	99.7	90.7	85.0	100.0	90.0
DICD	86.0	83.4	81.4	91.0	**93.6**	**92.2**	92.2	86.1	99.0	89.7	84.0	100.0	89.9
EasyTL	86.5	91.7	85.8	**93.0**	89.2	82.7	91.3	84.5	98.0	89.8	**90.8**	99.4	89.4
LPJT	85.3	86.0	79.7	91.4	89.2	84.4	92.4	86.5	100.0	88.9	84.0	100.0	89.0
MFSP	**87.7**	89.8	**90.9**	92.9	89.2	89.2	**92.8**	**88.1**	99.7	**93.7**	87.3	100.0	**91.8**

The results on *Office-Caltech10*: Table 2 and Table 3 respectively summarized the results of two features. We can observe that our proposed method achieves the best average performance in both datasets, with a 1.8% improvement over the optimal competitor in SURF feature. The reason is that our method can effectively reduce the impact of data noise, enabling alleviate the negative transfer during adaptation.

The results on *Office-Home*: From Table 4, our method outperforms all other traditional and deep comparison methods in average performance. The performances of distribution alignment methods [8,14] are generally worse than our method. This indicates the advantages of our method in reducing the influence of noise while coping with the distribution discrepancy.

The results on *ImageCLEF-DA*: As shown in Table 5, our method achieves the best performance among all comparison methods. To be specific, our method outperforms all comparison methods in 4 out of 6 tasks, which indicates our method can effectively improve the classification accuracy in exploring the inherent manifold data structure.

Table 4. Accuracy (%) on Office-Home datasets with Resnet-50 featrues

Tasks	Traditional methods										Deep methods					
	1-NN	GFK	JDA	TJM	JGSA	DICD	EasyTL	LPJT	GPDA	MFSP	DAN	DANN	JAN	CDAN	DWT_MEC	AFN
Ar→Cl	43.2	46.9	51.1	48.6	51.1	53.0	49.8	52.9	52.9	**56.2**	43.6	45.6	45.9	49.0	50.3	50.2
Ar→Pr	61.2	62.9	67.4	65.4	71.0	71.0	72.5	73.3	73.4	**76.7**	57.0	59.3	61.2	69.3	72.1	70.1
Ar→Re	67.8	68.4	70.9	70.4	74.3	72.7	75.8	75.6	77.1	**78.0**	67.9	70.1	68.9	74.5	77.0	76.6
Cl→Ar	47.1	47.6	51.3	49.4	53.1	55.1	60.7	54.8	52.9	59.6	45.8	47.0	50.4	54.4	59.6	**61.1**
Cl→Pr	58.9	58.9	64.1	64.5	68.8	66.7	69.5	66.7	66.1	**71.1**	56.5	58.5	59.7	66.0	69.3	68.0
Cl→Re	60.9	61.2	64.3	63.2	68.8	66.4	71.2	69.4	65.6	**71.6**	60.4	60.9	61.0	68.4	70.2	70.7
Pr→Ar	50.1	50.7	54.4	53.4	56.4	58.4	59.0	54.8	52.9	58.8	44.0	46.1	45.8	55.6	58.3	**59.5**
Pr→Cl	42.3	44.4	47.7	46.7	48.0	51.1	47.1	49.9	44.9	50.9	43.6	43.7	43.4	48.3	48.1	48.4
Pr→Re	69.9	70.1	73.4	73.0	76.3	75.0	76.4	75.8	76.1	77.0	67.7	68.5	70.3	75.9	**77.3**	77.3
Re→Ar	61.6	62.8	68.2	62.9	65.1	67.2	64.8	65.8	65.6	68.1	63.1	63.2	63.9	68.4	69.3	**69.4**
Re→Cl	47.7	50.9	53.7	53.2	52.9	**55.9**	51.1	55.2	49.7	55.6	51.5	51.8	52.4	55.4	53.6	53.0
Re→Pr	75.2	75.7	78.7	78.1	78.9	79.5	77.3	80.5	79.2	81.4	74.3	76.8	76.8	80.5	**82.0**	80.2
Avg	57.2	58.4	61.8	60.7	63.7	64.3	64.6	64.6	63.0	**67.1**	56.3	57.6	58.3	63.8	65.6	65.4

Table 5. Accuracy (%) on Image-CLEF datasets with Resnet-50 featrues

Tasks	Traditional methods										Deep methods					
	1-NN	GFK	JDA	TJM	TGNMF	JGSA	DICD	EasyTL	LPJT	MFSP	DAN	DANN	JAN	CDAN	DWT_MEC	AFN
C→I	80.4	87.0	90.8	**92.0**	89.3	91.7	90.8	91.5	91.3	91.2	86.3	87.0	89.5	90.5	87.5	89.6
C→P	67.8	74.5	75.0	77.8	74.5	77.2	77.7	77.7	77.0	**78.0**	69.2	74.3	74.2	74.5	73.4	74.9
I→C	90.8	92.8	93.2	95.0	93.2	84.5	95.5	96.0	94.7	95.5	92.8	96.2	94.7	**97.0**	94.3	94.4
I→P	75.2	75.7	76.5	78.0	77.5	76.8	77.7	78.7	77.8	**79.2**	74.5	75.0	76.8	76.7	77.7	76.9
P→C	82.2	82.2	87.3	84.2	84.3	89.2	88.2	95.0	91.0	**96.0**	89.8	91.5	91.7	93.5	94.5	92.9
P→I	79.2	77.7	78.2	81.0	81.2	84.0	83.5	90.3	85.3	**91.5**	82.2	86.0	88.0	90.6	89.7	89.0
Avg	79.9	81.6	83.5	84.7	83.3	85.7	85.4	88.2	86.2	**88.6**	82.5	85.0	85.8	87.1	86.2	86.3

4.3 Parameter Sensitivity and Ablation Study

We conduct extensive parameter sensitivity tests to validate that the proposed method can achieve optimal performance in a wide range of parameter value. We vary one parameter and fix the others as the optimal values. The result are reported in Fig. 2 (a)–(e). It can be observed that our method is robust for a wide range of parameter values.

We further conduct experiments to verify the effectiveness of the components of our method. MFSP$_{MD}$ considers matrix factorization and distribution alignment, MFSP$_{MG}$ considers matrix factorization and graph dual regularization. We choose JDA [13] as the baseline, which is based on distribution alignment. The average accuracies of all tasks on three datasets are shown in Fig. 2 (f). By comparing MFSP with MFSP$_{MD}$, we notice that the classification accuracy can be effectively improved by considering the effect of noise reduction. By comparing MFSP and MFSP$_{MG}$, we infer that exploration of retaining data manifold structure can better promote knowledge transfer. The proposed MFSP method achieves the best performance, which indicates that all three terms are essential to our method.

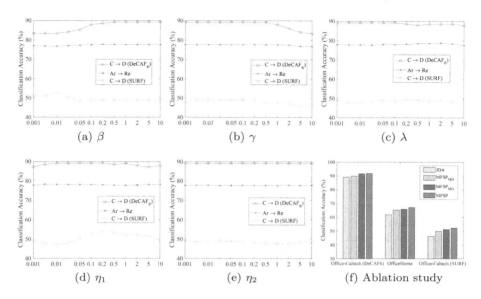

Fig. 2. Parameter sensitivity analysis with respect to $\beta, \gamma, \lambda, \eta_1, \eta_2$ and ablation study.

5 Conclusion

In this paper, we present a novel domain adaptation approach. Specifically, our method is designed to reduce the negative impacts of noisy by using maximum entropy, as well as jointly enforce distribution alignment with label information, and capture the intrinsic manifold structures via graph dual regularization. Experiments on several benchmarks have demonstrated our proposed method can obtain superior performance than other state-of-the-art algorithms.

Acknowledgements. This work was supported in part by the National Natural Science Foundation of China under Grant 62172109 and Grant 62072118, in part by the Natural Science Foundation of Guangdong Province under Grant 2022A1515010322, in part by the High-Level Talents Programme of Guangdong Province under Grant 2017GC010556, and in part by the Guangdong Basic and Applied Basic Research Foundation under Grant 2021B1515120010.

References

1. Caputo, B., et al.: ImageCLEF 2014: overview and analysis of the results. In: Kanoulas, E., et al. (eds.) CLEF 2014. LNCS, vol. 8685, pp. 192–211. Springer, Cham (2014). https://doi.org/10.1007/978-3-319-11382-1_18
2. Csurka, G., Chidlowskii, B., Clinchant, S., Michel, S.: Unsupervised domain adaptation with regularized domain instance denoising. In: Hua, G., Jégou, H. (eds.) ECCV 2016. LNCS, vol. 9915, pp. 458–466. Springer, Cham (2016). https://doi.org/10.1007/978-3-319-49409-8_37

3. Ganin, Y., et al.: Domain-adversarial training of neural networks. J. Mach. Learn. Res. **17**, 59:1–59:35 (2016)
4. Gong, B., Shi, Y., Sha, F., Grauman, K.: Geodesic flow kernel for unsupervised domain adaptation. In: CVPR, pp. 2066–2073. IEEE Computer Society (2012)
5. Guo, X., Lin, Z.: Low-rank matrix recovery via robust outlier estimation. IEEE Trans. Image Process. **27**(11), 5316–5327 (2018)
6. Li, J., Jing, M., Lu, K., Zhu, L., Shen, H.T.: Locality preserving joint transfer for domain adaptation. IEEE Trans. Image Process. **28**(12), 6103–6115 (2019)
7. Li, J., Lu, K., Huang, Z., Zhu, L., Shen, H.T.: Transfer independently together: a generalized framework for domain adaptation. IEEE Trans. Cybern. **49**(6), 2144–2155 (2019)
8. Li, S., Song, S., Huang, G., Ding, Z., Wu, C.: Domain invariant and class discriminative feature learning for visual domain adaptation. IEEE Trans. Image Process. **27**(9), 4260–4273 (2018)
9. Lin, Z., Liu, R., Su, Z.: Linearized alternating direction method with adaptive penalty for low-rank representation. In: NIPS, pp. 612–620 (2011)
10. Long, M., Cao, Y., Wang, J., Jordan, M.I.: Learning transferable features with deep adaptation networks. In: ICML. JMLR Workshop and Conference Proceedings, vol. 37, pp. 97–105. JMLR.org (2015)
11. Long, M., Cao, Z., Wang, J., Jordan, M.I.: Conditional adversarial domain adaptation. In: NeurIPS, pp. 1647–1657 (2018)
12. Long, M., Wang, J., Ding, G., Shen, D., Yang, Q.: Transfer learning with graph co-regularization. IEEE Trans. Knowl. Data Eng. **26**(7), 1805–1818 (2014)
13. Long, M., Wang, J., Ding, G., Sun, J., Yu, P.S.: Transfer feature learning with joint distribution adaptation. In: ICCV, pp. 2200–2207. IEEE Computer Society (2013)
14. Long, M., Wang, J., Ding, G., Sun, J., Yu, P.S.: Transfer joint matching for unsupervised domain adaptation. In: CVPR, pp. 1410–1417. IEEE Computer Society (2014)
15. Long, M., Zhu, H., Wang, J., Jordan, M.I.: Deep transfer learning with joint adaptation networks. In: ICML. Proceedings of Machine Learning Research, vol. 70, pp. 2208–2217. PMLR (2017)
16. Pan, S.J., Yang, Q.: A survey on transfer learning. IEEE Trans. Knowl. Data Eng. **22**(10), 1345–1359 (2010)
17. Roy, S., Siarohin, A., Sangineto, E., Bulò, S.R., Sebe, N., Ricci, E.: Unsupervised domain adaptation using feature-whitening and consensus loss. In: CVPR, pp. 9471–9480. Computer Vision Foundation/IEEE (2019)
18. Song, P., Ou, S., Zheng, W., Jin, Y., Zhao, L.: Speech emotion recognition using transfer non-negative matrix factorization. In: ICASSP, pp. 5180–5184. IEEE (2016)
19. Sun, J., Wang, Z., Wang, W., Li, H., Sun, F.: Domain adaptation with geometrical preservation and distribution alignment. Neurocomputing **454**, 152–167 (2021)
20. Venkateswara, H., Eusebio, J., Chakraborty, S., Panchanathan, S.: Deep hashing network for unsupervised domain adaptation. In: CVPR, pp. 5385–5394. IEEE Computer Society (2017)
21. Wang, J., Chen, Y., Yu, H., Huang, M., Yang, Q.: Easy transfer learning by exploiting intra-domain structures. In: ICME, pp. 1210–1215. IEEE (2019)
22. Wang, J., Feng, W., Chen, Y., Yu, H., Huang, M., Yu, P.S.: Visual domain adaptation with manifold embedded distribution alignment. In: ACM Multimedia, pp. 402–410. ACM (2018)

23. Xu, R., Li, G., Yang, J., Lin, L.: Larger norm more transferable: an adaptive feature norm approach for unsupervised domain adaptation. In: ICCV, pp. 1426–1435. IEEE (2019)
24. Xu, Y., Fang, X., Wu, J., Li, X., Zhang, D.: Discriminative transfer subspace learning via low-rank and sparse representation. IEEE Trans. Image Process. **25**(2), 850–863 (2016)
25. Zhang, J., Li, W., Ogunbona, P.: Joint geometrical and statistical alignment for visual domain adaptation. In: CVPR, pp. 5150–5158. IEEE Computer Society (2017)
26. Zhang, L.: Transfer adaptation learning: A decade survey. CoRR abs/1903.04687 (2019)

Graph Adversarial Network with Bottleneck Adapter Tuning for Sign Language Production

Chunpeng Yu[1], Jiajia Liang[1], Yihui Liao[1], Zhifeng Xie[1(✉)], and Bin Sheng[2]

[1] Shanghai University, Shanghai, China
{zjycp,jjl,yihui_l,zhifeng_xie}@shu.edu.cn
[2] Shanghai Jiao Tong University, Shanghai, China
shengbin@cs.sjtu.edu.cn

Abstract. Sign language production (SLP) task aims to convert spoken language sentences into corresponding sign language expressions such as sign pose sequences, animations or videos. Previous deep learning based SLP solutions mostly utilize encoder-decoder structure and lack the ability to obtain the contextual representation of sentences, resulting poor performance on unseen data. In order to tackle the problem, we propose a method called graph adversarial network with bottleneck adapter tuning (BatGANet). Specifically, we present a generalizable and parameter-efficient bottleneck adapter structure, to fine-tune a pre-trained language model and extract the contextual representation of spoken language text. Furthermore, we develop an adversarial training scheme based on spatial-temporal graph convolutional networks, which enables to captures the motion patterns of sign poses, and facilitates natural and realistic sign motion generation.

Keywords: Sign language production · Transfer learning · Graph neural network · Generative adversarial network

1 Introduction

Sign language, as a visual language, is the primary communication medium in deaf community, which also has the same linguistic properties like spoken language. Establishing an outstanding communication approach between deaf and hearing people is an urgent issue needed to be solved. Sign language production (SLP) aims to convert spoken language text into its corresponding sign language expression such as sign pose sequences, sign animations or videos.

Traditional works on SLP were mostly based on avatar animation [5,9], which needed to design isolated sign motions artificially. In recent years, researchers tried to take advantage of deep neural network to generate sign language conditioned by text or speech, which choose to concatenate isolated sign sequences [18,26] or leverage neural machine translation mechanism to regress the sign pose [14,20,27]. However, since these work trained the models on a small dataset from scratch, they lacked the ability to obtain the contextual representation, which made them generalize poorly on unseen data.

N. Magnenat-Thalmann et al. (Eds.): CGI 2022, LNCS 13443, pp. 92–103, 2022.
https://doi.org/10.1007/978-3-031-23473-6_8

In this paper, we propose graph adversarial network with bottleneck adapter tuning (BatGANet) to produce sign pose with high expressiveness and generalizability. As shown in Fig. 1, our method mainly consists of four modules: Adapter-based Contextual Representation module (ACR), Channel-wise Target Length Predictor (CTLP), Cross-modal Sige Pose Generator (CMSPG) and Spatial-Temporal Graph Convolutional Discriminator (STGCD). ACR enables to learn the contextual representation of source text, where we integrate pre-trained language model and bottleneck adapter layer. CTLP aims to predict the corresponding sign pose sequence length given the sentence representation, which is different to the counter embedding that was commonly used in previous work. CMSPG leverages cross-modal attention mechanisms to produce the sign frame in an auto-regressive manner. In addition, we devise STGCD to distinguish real sign pose from the data created by the CMSPG.

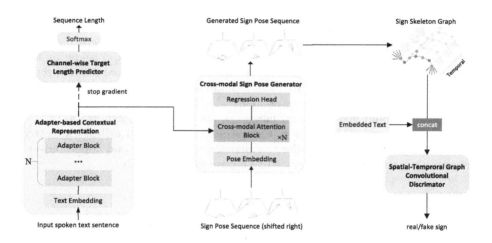

Fig. 1. The structure of BatGANet, which consists of Adapter-based Contextual Represent (ACR), Channel-wise Target Length Predictor (CTLP), Cross-modal Sign Pose Generator (CMSPG) and Spatial-Temporal Graph Convolutional Discriminator (STGCD).

We evaluate our method on the public PHOENIX14T dataset. The result shows that we achieve state-of-the-art SLP back translation score both on the *gloss2pose* and *text2pose* task. Glosses are shortened approximation of spoken language. The main contributions of our work can be summarized as follows:

1) We propose an unified end-to-end SLP method named BatGANet to generate more realistic and expressive sign pose conditioned by spoken language text.
2) we develop bottleneck adapter structure to fine-tune pre-trained language model, extracting contextual representation with parameter-efficiency and generalizability.

3) we aggregate skeleton nodes in spatial and temporal respectively by graph convolution operation, promoting to better capture joint motion patterns and enhance the ability of discriminator.

2   Related Work

2.1   Sign Language Production

Early research on sign language production focused on statistical models and avatar-based approaches [5,9]. These methods usually synthesized sign language videos by modeling the isolated sign language clips and then matching the phrases or words in the sentences. Building avatar sign language data needs expert knowledge and is time-consuming as well as laborious. Recently, deep learning based generation models have made significant advances. In 2020, Stoll et al. proposed Progressive Transformers [14] using Neural Machine Translation, which is the first end-to-end sign language production model. In order to cope with the low efficiency of auto-regressive model, Huang et al. [8] proposed a Non-AuToregressive model with a parallel decoding scheme. Besides, considering the sign language is a combination of manual feature and non-manual feature, some works [13,16,20] expand SLP to include non-manual features, producing the head motion and mouthing patterns alongside the hands and body. Although previous work could generate sign language, they are low generalizability and the results were under-articulation. Comparably, our method utilize the better contextual representations in order to enhance generalization and applies adversarial training to make the generated sign pose more expressive.

2.2   Transfer Learning

Transfer learning is used to improve a learner from one domain by transferring information from another domain [21]. Adapter, as a parameter-efficient transfer learning method, was first proposed in computer vision [12] then explored for text classification task in NLP [6]. Adapter layers [17] are usually inserted between the layer of a pre-trained model like BERT, BART whose parameters are fixed. Transfer learning has previously been used to improve model performance in sign language recognition and translation [3]. Since transfer learning makes the model has better generalization performance and require less data, we aim to leverage language models pre-trained on large datasets with bottleneck adapter layers for encoding the spoken language sentences, in order to gain the more precise contextual representations. To the best of our knowledge, we are the first to leveraged transfer learning in sign language production directly.

2.3   Graph Convolutional Network

Graph Convolutional Network (GCN) is suitable for non-Euclidean and graph-structural data like point cloud, social network and human skeleton [22]. Since graph convolution is more inclined to capture spatial information, several graph-based models have been employed for skeleton action recognition [2], motion prediction [25] and 3D pose estimation [24] task. Besides, Plizzari et al. demonstrated Spatial-Temporal Graph Convolutional Networks (ST-GCN) [11] that was effective in learning both spatial and temporal dependencies on non-grid data. In addition, Saunders et al. proposed SGSA [15], which is a graphical attention layer that embeds a skeleton inductive bias into SLP model. Our method aggregates skeleton nodes in multi-scales and treats GCN to be an adversarial network, which enables to better capture the sign pose motion features and promotes to obtain a more precise discrimination.

3 Method

Sign language production task can be defined as a sequence to sequence problem. In detail, given a spoken language sentence with S words, $X = \{x^1, x^2, ..., x^S\}$, the model aims to translate it to the sign pose sequence, $Y = \{y^1, y^2, ..., y^T\}$ where y^i is i-th pose frame and T is the sequence length.

3.1 Adapter-Based Contextual Representation

As shown in Fig. 1, Adapter-based Contextual Representation module accepts raw text as input and aims to obtain the corresponding contextual representation. Firstly, we convert the spoken language word x_i into numerical representation using tokenizer and word embedding layers. An position embedding layer is also applied in order to incorporate the order of the words. The embedded text is defined as $X_{emb} \in \mathbb{R}^{S \times d_k}$ where d_k is embedding dimension.

Then a stack of N Adapter Blocks follows after word embedding. As shown in Fig. 2(a), each block is mainly organized by multi-head self-attention (MHA) and Bottleneck Adapter layers. We use self-attention to learn token dependencies and contextual information from embedded text, which can be described as:

$$Q = X_{emb}W^Q, K = X_{emb}W^K, V = X_{emb}W^V \tag{1}$$

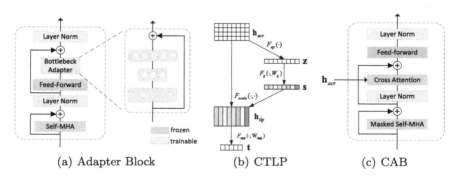

(a) Adapter Block   (b) CTLP   (c) CAB

Fig. 2. The architecture of Adapter Block, Channel-wise Target Length Predictor (CTLP) and Cross-modal Attention Block (CAB).

$$H = softmax(\frac{QK^T}{\sqrt{d_k}})V \tag{2}$$

where $\{Q, K, V\} \in \mathbb{R}^{N \times d_k}$, $\{W^Q, W^K, W^V\} \in \mathbb{R}^{d_k \times d_k}$. The output from all attention heads are concatenated and combined with a linear layer as: $\boldsymbol{h}_{att} = [H_1, ..., H_h]W^o$ where $W^o \in \mathbb{R}^{h \cdot d_k \times d_k}$, $[\cdot]$ means concatenation, and h is the number of attention heads. Then a residual connect with layer norm and feed forward network are employed to the $\boldsymbol{h}_{att}$ and output the result $\boldsymbol{h}_{ffn}$.

The bottleneck adapter is composed of two fully connected (FC) layers with a residual connection, which can be defined as:

$$adapter(\boldsymbol{h}_{ffn}) = \sigma(\boldsymbol{h}_{ffn}W_{down})W_{up} + \boldsymbol{h}_{ffn} \tag{3}$$

where $W_{down} \in \mathbb{R}^{d_k \times b}$ and $W_{up} \in \mathbb{R}^{b \times d_k}$ are the weight of FC layers. The first FC layer encodes the input to a bottleneck dimension b, and the second one projects the output back to the initial dimension. The output of bottleneck adapter layer is then passed into the layer normalization with a residual connection. Finally, the ACR module output the contextual representation $\boldsymbol{h}_{acr} \in \mathbb{R}^{S \times d_k}$ of the text. In our method, we apply an pre-trained mBART-50 model to initialize the ACR module since it achieves better performance. The weight of MHA and FFN are fixed while the adapters and the norm layers are updated during adapter tuning.

3.2   Channel-Wise Target Length Predictor

As shown in Fig. 2(b), Channel-wise Target Length Predictor takes the sentence contextual representation as input and predicts the length of corresponding pose sequence. Inspired by SENet [7], we use 1D average pooling F_{ap} to generate channel-wise statistics $\boldsymbol{z} \in \mathbb{R}^{d_k}$. The c-th element of $\boldsymbol{z}$ is calculated by:

$$\boldsymbol{z}_c = F_{ap}(\boldsymbol{h}_{acr}(\cdot, c)) = \frac{1}{S}\sum_{i=1}^{S}\boldsymbol{h}_{acr}(i, c) \tag{4}$$

where $\boldsymbol{h}_{acr}(\cdot, c)$ is the c-th dimensions of contextual representation $\boldsymbol{h}_{acr} \in \mathbb{R}^{S \times d_k}$. The channel-wise statistics $\boldsymbol{z}$ can be interpreted as a collection of whole contextual representation. Then we opt to employ a simple gating mechanism F_g as:

$$\boldsymbol{s} = F_g(\boldsymbol{z}, W_g) = \sigma(\delta(\boldsymbol{z}W_{g,1})W_{g,2}) \tag{5}$$

where δ refers to the ReLU function, σ is sigmoid activation, $W_{g,1} \in \mathbb{R}^{d_k \times d_h}$ and $W_{g,2} \in \mathbb{R}^{d_h \times d_k}$ are the weight of FC layer. We parameterize the gating mechanism by forming two fully-connected layers with hidden dimension d_h, which aims to fully capture channel-wise dependencies. We utilize scale function F_{scale} to combine $\boldsymbol{h}_{acr}$ and $\boldsymbol{s}$, as:

$$\boldsymbol{h}_{tlp} = F_{scale}(\boldsymbol{h}_{acr}, \boldsymbol{s}) = \boldsymbol{h}_{acr}\boldsymbol{s} \tag{6}$$

where $\boldsymbol{h}_{tlp}$ is the scaled contextual representation. Finally, we aggregate the $\boldsymbol{h}_{tlp}$ by sum operation and shrink it through one fully-connected layer, as:

$$\boldsymbol{t} = F_{agg}(\boldsymbol{h}_{tlp}, W_{agg}) = sum(\boldsymbol{h}_{tlp})W_{agg} \tag{7}$$

where $W_{agg} \in \mathbb{R}^{L \times d_k}$ is the weight of FC layer, $sum(\cdot)$ is sum operation over hidden dimension and L is the pre-defined max sequence length. The result $t \in \mathbb{R}^{L \times 1}$ represents the probability of each length after applying softmax function.

3.3   Cross-modal Sign Pose Generator

Cross-modal Sign Pose Generator (CMSPG) aims to generate sign pose sequence, which works in an autoregressive mode. In the i-th time step, the predicted output of CMSPG can be described by:

$$\hat{y}_{i+1} = CMSPG(\hat{y}_i | \hat{y}_{1:i-1}, h_{acr}) \tag{8}$$

where $\hat{y}_i$ is the generated pose frame, h_{acr} is the contextual representation.

In detail, the pose embedding layers convert pose sequence Y into a dense space Y_{emb}. The cross-modal attention block (CAB) learns the relationship between contextual representation and sign pose, which is similar with the vanilla Transformer [19]. As shown in Fig. 2(c), a masked multi-head self-attention with skip-connection and layer norm are first applied to Y_{emb}. Mask enables to prevent from attending to future sign pose. The cross attention is similar with self-attention while we take the contextual representation h_{acr} as the query to produce Q in Formula 1. Feed forward network and layer norm are located at the end of cross-modal attention block. Finally, given the output of cross-modal attention block Y_c, the sign pose $\hat{Y}$ are synthesized by an regression head.

3.4   Spatial-Temporal Graph Convolutional Discriminator

As shown in Fig. 1, Spatial-Temporal Graph Convolutional Discriminator is developed to distinguish the generated sign pose $\hat{Y}$ from ground truth Y of the dataset. We consider the skeleton joints as the graph vertex V and the connection between joints as graph edge E, creating the sign skeleton graph $G(V, E)$. Inspired by [4], STGCD is mainly composed of three types of layers: temporal downsampling, spatial downsampling and graph convolutions layers. In detail, the temporal downsampling layers consists of 2D convolutions that reduces the time dimension and aggregate the temporal information. The spatial downsampling layer using an aggregation function defined by an adjacency matrix A^ω that maps a graph G to a smaller graph $G'(V', E')$. For the vertex feature f in the graph G, the aggregation operation can be given by:

$$f'_i = \sum_{k,j} A^\omega_{kij} f_j \tag{9}$$

where f'_i is the features of vertex i in the new graph G' and $k \in \{0, 1\}$ indicates distance between each vertex in G. After applying the temporal and spatial downsampling operations, the discriminator uses the graph convolutional layers defined by Yan et al. [23]. In STGCD, the feature vectors are assigned to each vertex as follows: the first layer contains a graph of 50 vertex, representing 50 skeleton joints, where their feature vectors are composed of the (x, y, z) coordinates. The embedded text is concatenated with the pose sequence over the time dimension. In the subsequent layers, the features of each node are computed by the operations of downsampling and aggregation. The last layer contains only one node that output the probability of input sign pose sequence being real.

3.5 Loss Function

Our framework is optimized under the weighted summation of pose reconstruction loss $\mathcal{L}_{REC}$ and GAN loss $\mathcal{L}_{GAN}(G, D)$. The pose reconstruction loss applied L_2 distance in all K skeleton joints over T frames as follows:

$$\mathcal{L}_{REC} = \frac{1}{KT} \sum_{i=0}^{K-1} \sum_{j=0}^{T-1} \sqrt{(\hat{y}_j^i - y_j^i)^2} \tag{10}$$

where y_j^i is the coordinates of i-th joint in j-th frame and $\hat{y}$ is the corresponding ground truth. Besides, considering the STGCD as D and CMSPG with ACR module as G, the GAN loss is formulated as:

$$\mathcal{L}_{GAN}(G, D) = \mathbb{E}[\log D(\hat{Y}|X)] + \mathbb{E}[\log(1 - D(G(X)|X))] \tag{11}$$

where X is the spoken language sentence, $\hat{Y}$ is the ground truth sign pose. The total loss function $\mathcal{L}_{total}$ can be formed as:

$$\mathcal{L}_{total} = \lambda_{REC}\mathcal{L}_{rec} + \lambda_{gan}\mathcal{L}_{GAN}^G \tag{12}$$

where the λ_{gan} and λ_{rec} are the weight of each loss. For the CTLP module, we utilize an individual cross entropy loss as follows:

$$\mathcal{L}_{ctlp} = -\frac{1}{L} \sum_{i=1}^{L} I(T = i)\log\left(\frac{e^{t_i}}{\sum_{j=1}^{L} e^{t_j}}\right) \tag{13}$$

where L is the pre-defined max target length, t is the output of CTLP module, $I(\cdot)$ is the indicator function.

4 Experiments

4.1 Datasets

We train and test our framework on the public sign language dataset RWTH-PHOENIX-Weather 2014 T [10], which includes 8257 continuous sign language samples for weather forecasts from 9 different signers. The dataset contains parallel sign language videos, gloss annotations and the translation sequences. Following the preprocessing pipeline in [14], we use OpenPose [1] to extract 2D joint positions from videos. Then we leverage the skeletal model estimation method [26] to lifted the joint positions into 3D as x, y and z coordinates.

Table 1. Back translation results on the PHOENIX14T dataset for G2P task.

Approach	Dev set					Test set				
	BLEU1	BLEU2	BLEU3	BLEU4	ROUGE	BLEU1	BLEU2	BLEU3	BLEU4	ROUGE
PT (base) [14]	12.03	5.32	3.02	1.87	9.72	11.21	4.64	2.36	1.35	9.29
PT (F&G) [14]	27.79	17.71	12.98	10.22	27.76	26.4	16.99	12.16	9.44	26.51
Mert's [27]	29.80	19.16	13.86	10.88	29.92	28.68	19.12	13.93	10.86	28.75
Ours	**32.37**	**21.87**	**16.19**	**12.79**	**32.23**	**30.12**	**20.51**	**15.12**	**11.87**	**30.1**

Table 2. Back translation results on the PHOENIX14T dataset for T2P task

Approach	Dev set					Test set				
	BLEU1	BLEU2	BLEU3	BLEU4	ROUGE	BLEU1	BLEU2	BLEU3	BLEU4	ROUGE
PT (base) [14]	10.80	4.49	2.40	1.56	10.21	10.51	4.24	2.16	1.29	9.81
PT (F&G) [14]	13.70	7.34	5.31	4.25	13.62	13.87	7.72	5.65	4.56	13.61
Ours	**32.65**	**23.28**	**18.03**	**14.59**	**32.76**	**31.12**	**21.17**	**15.83**	**12.53**	**31.34**

4.2 Training Settings

We build the ACR module and CMSPG module with $N = 2$ identical block, $h = 4$ attention heads and embedding size of 1024. We set $\lambda_{gan} = 0.01$ and $\lambda_{reg} = 1$ for the loss function and train the model using the Adam optimizer with plateau learning schedule. Our model is implemented by PyTorch and trained on NVIDIA RTX 3090 GPUs.

4.3 Evaluation Metrics

We use back translation [14] to evaluate performance of our method. We leverage an state-of-the-art sign language translation model [3] and modify it to suit the PHOENIX14T dataset. The back translation translates the sign language pose sequence to its corresponding text and computes BLEU and ROUGE score which manifest the similarity between translation result and reference sentence.

4.4 Quantitative Evaluation

We conduct experiments on the Gloss2Pose (G2P) task and Text2Pose (T2P) task. We compare our BatGANet with the Progressive Transformer (PT) [14], and with its data augmentation approaches (F&G) as well as Mert's work [27] that only tackles the G2P problem. Table 1 shows the back translation scores on G2P task. We can see that our BatGANet achieves the best performance on the overall measuring metrics. The result demonstrates that the generated sign pose of our method are more understandable, showing the effectiveness of the contextual representation and graph adversarial network. Table 2 shows the back translation scores on T2P task. The score in T2P task is also higher than others, showing that BatGANet is effective for the raw form of spoken language. We believe that our method has a better awareness of natural spoken language because BatGANet leverage knowledge from other language model by transfer learning and the bottleneck adapter tuning avoids the overfitting.

Table 3. Ablation study on the PHOENIX14T dataset for G2P task

Approach	Dev set					Test set				
	BLEU1	BLEU2	BLEU3	BLEU4	ROUGE	BLEU1	BLEU2	BLEU3	BLEU4	ROUGE
w/o STGCD	29.96	19.89	14.57	11.36	30.2	29.34	19.34	14.15	11.05	28.47
w/o Apater	30.13	20.14	14.87	11.8	30.61	27.4	18.21	13.2	10.28	27.51
w/o both	27.94	18.26	13.22	10.35	27.51	27.02	17.31	12.75	10.08	27.25
w/t 1D-CNN	27.90	18.31	13.33	10.41	28.21	26.95	17.57	12.62	9.68	26.96
BatGANet	**32.37**	**21.87**	**16.19**	**12.79**	**32.23**	**30.12**	**20.51**	**15.12**	**11.87**	**30.1**

4.5 Visual Comparison

Visual results of the generated sign pose sequences are illustrated in Fig. 3 and Fig. 4. The results are all generated by taking the gloss text as input for fair comparison. We can find that the hand shape, orientation and body movement of BatGANet are closer to the ground truth pose. As highlighted in the Fig. 3, the left hand of BatGANet in the fourth column is open like the ground truth, however the other two methods generate fingers that close together and point upwards. In the last column, our BatGANet produce the hands that putted on the chest as the ground truth but the hands of other methods are all far apart. Besides, Fig. 4 shows the result of taking the long sentence as input. We can see that the pose frames of PT and Mert's regress to a mean pose without obvious movement, while our method still generates exact pose. We believe that the BatGANet could produce stable and continuous sign pose due to the effect of our spatial-temporal graph adversarial training.

4.6 Ablation Study

In this section, we conduct the ablation study to verify the effectiveness of our model design. In detail, we remove the bottleneck adapter and train the ACR module from scratch, which is termed as w/o Adapter. We also remove the STGCD, which is termed as w/o STGCD. Beside, we use 1D convolution as the discriminator rather than our STGCD (w/t 1D-CNN), which is similar to [13]. The results are presented in Table 3. We can find that with the help of ACR module, the score improves a lot, showing that the adapter-based transfer learning generalizes well on unseen data. Furthermore, it proves that a better contextual representation helps the sign language production. As for the STGCD, it also improves on the test dataset, which shows that the graph adversarial training could promote the network generate more realistic sign pose. In addition, comparing with the 1D-CNN, STGCD achieves a higher score. We believe that spatial-temporal graph convolution enables to capture the movement pattern of sign pose.

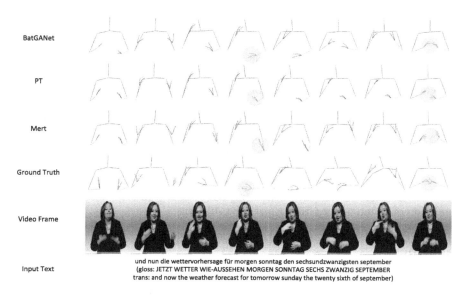

Fig. 3. Visual comparison. The left hand of BatGANet in the fourth column is like the ground truth, while PT [14] and Mert's [27] generate the hand that points upwards. In the last column, the hands of BatGANet are same as ground truth that positioned at the front of chest but the other two are at the wrong position and far apart.

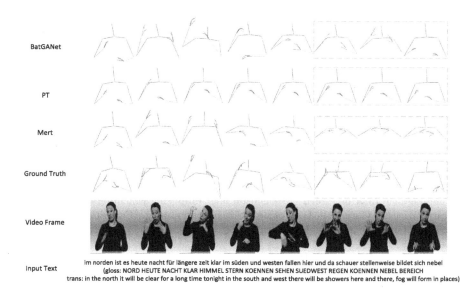

Fig. 4. Visual comparison for a long sentence. The result shows that the pose of PT [14] and Mert's [27] method regresses to a mean pose without obvious movement as the time goes by, while BatGANet could still generate exact and expressive pose.

5 Conclusion

In this paper, we propose graph adversarial network with bottleneck adapter tuning (BatGANet), a method for sign language production. We present ACR module to extracting contextual representation with parameter-efficiency as well as STGCD module to enhance the ability of discriminator and promote generating expressive pose. Experiments result demonstrates that the proposed method achieves state-of-the-art performance. Since our work is based on skeleton data, the keypoint-based visualizations is less understandable than synthesized realistic videos. As for future work, we would like to generate images-based realistic human signer and try to adopt non-autoregressive approach for high efficiency.

Acknowledgements. This work was supported by the Shanghai Natural Science Foundation of China under Grant No. 19ZR1419100.

References

1. Cao, Z., Hidalgo, G., Simon, T., Wei, S.E., Sheikh, Y.: OpenPose: realtime multi-person 2D Pose estimation using part affinity fields. IEEE Trans. Pattern Anal. Mach. Intell. **43**(1), 172–186 (2021)
2. Chen, Y., Zhang, Z., Yuan, C., Li, B., Deng, Y., Hu, W.: Channel-wise topology refinement graph convolution for skeleton-based action recognition. In: Proceedings of the IEEE/CVF International Conference on Computer Vision, pp. 13359–13368 (2021)
3. De Coster, M., et al.: Frozen pretrained transformers for neural sign language translation. In: Proceedings of the 1st International Workshop on Automatic Translation for Signed and Spoken Languages (AT4SSL), pp. 88–97 (2021)
4. Ferreira, J.P., et al.: Learning to dance: a graph convolutional adversarial network to generate realistic dance motions from audio. Comput. Graph. **94**, 11–21 (2021)
5. Glauerta, J.R., Elliott, R., Cox, S.J., Sheard, M.: VANESSA - a system for communication between deaf and hearing people. Technol. Disabil. **18**(4), 207–216 (2006)
6. Houlsby, N., et al.: Parameter-efficient transfer learning for NLP. In: International Conference on Machine Learning, pp. 2790–2799. PMLR (2019)
7. Hu, J., Shen, L., Sun, G.: Squeeze-and-excitation networks. In: Proceedings of the IEEE Conference on Computer Vision and Pattern Recognition, pp. 7132–7141 (2018)
8. Huang, W., Pan, W., Zhao, Z., Tian, Q.: Towards Fast and High-Quality Sign Language Production, vol. 1. Association for Computing Machinery (2021)
9. Karpouzis, K., Caridakis, G., Fotinea, S.E., Efthimiou, E.: Educational resources and implementation of a Greek sign language synthesis architecture. Comput. Educ. **49**(1), 54–74 (2007)
10. Koller, O., Forster, J., Ney, H.: Continuous sign language recognition: towards large vocabulary statistical recognition systems handling multiple signers. Comput. Vis. Image Underst. **141**, 108–125 (2015)
11. Plizzari, C., Cannici, M., Matteucci, M.: Skeleton-based action recognition via spatial and temporal transformer networks. Comput. Vis. Image Underst. **208–209**, 103219 (2021)

12. Rebuffi, S.A., Bilen, H., Vedaldi, A.: Learning multiple visual domains with residual adapters. In: Advances in Neural Information Processing Systems, pp. 507–517, December 2017
13. Saunders, B., Camgoz, N.C., Bowden, R.: Adversarial training for multi-channel sign language production. arXiv (2020). http://arxiv.org/abs/2008.12405
14. Saunders, B., Camgoz, N.C., Bowden, R.: Progressive transformers for end-to-end sign language production. In: Vedaldi, A., Bischof, H., Brox, T., Frahm, J.-M. (eds.) ECCV 2020. LNCS, vol. 12356, pp. 687–705. Springer, Cham (2020). https://doi.org/10.1007/978-3-030-58621-8_40
15. Saunders, B., Camgoz, N.C., Bowden, R.: Skeletal graph self-attention: embedding a skeleton inductive bias into sign language production (2021). http://arxiv.org/abs/2112.05277
16. Saunders, B., Camgoz, N.C., Bowden, R.: Signing at scale: learning to co-articulate signs for large-scale photo-realistic sign language production (2022). https://arxiv.org/abs/2203.15354
17. Stickland, A.C., Murray, I.: BERT and PALs: projected attention layers for efficient adaptation in multi-task learning. In: Proceedings of the 36th International Conference on Machine Learning, vol. 97, pp. 5986–5995 (2019)
18. Stoll, S., Camgoz, N.C., Hadfield, S., Bowden, R.: Sign language production using neural machine translation and generative adversarial networks. In: British Machine Vision Conference 2018, pp. 1–12 (2019)
19. Vaswani, A., et al.: Attention is all you need. In: Advances in Neural Information Processing Systems, pp. 5999–6009, December 2017
20. Viegas, C., İnan, M., Quandt, L., Alikhani, M.: Including facial expressions in contextual embeddings for sign language generation (2022). http://arxiv.org/abs/2202.05383
21. Weiss, K., Khoshgoftaar, T.M., Wang, D.D.: A survey of transfer learning. J. Big Data 3(1), 1–40 (2016). https://doi.org/10.1186/s40537-016-0043-6
22. Xie, Z., Zhang, W., Sheng, B., Li, P., Chen, C.L.P.: BaGFN: broad attentive graph fusion network for high-order feature interactions. IEEE Trans. Neural Netw. Learn. Syst., 1–15 (2021)
23. Yan, S., Xiong, Y., Lin, D.: Spatial temporal graph convolutional networks for skeleton-based action recognition. In: 32nd AAAI Conference on Artificial Intelligence, AAAI 2018, pp. 7444–7452, January 2018
24. Yang, Y., Ren, Z., Li, H., Zhou, C., Wang, X., Hua, G.: Learning dynamics via graph neural networks for human pose estimation and tracking. In: Proceedings of the IEEE/CVF Conference on Computer Vision and Pattern Recognition (CVPR), pp. 8074–8084 (2021)
25. Yin, W., Yin, H., Kragic, D., Björkman, M.: Graph-based normalizing flow for human motion generation and reconstruction, pp. 1–8 (2021). http://arxiv.org/abs/2104.03020
26. Zelinka, J., Kanis, J.: Neural sign language synthesis: words are our glosses. In: Proceedings - 2020 IEEE Winter Conference on Applications of Computer Vision, WACV 2020, pp. 3384–3392 (2020)
27. İnan, M., Zhong, Y., Hassan, S., Quandt, L., Alikhani, M.: Modeling intensification for sign language generation: a computational approach (2022). http://arxiv.org/abs/2203.09679

Estimation and Feature Matching

Facial Landmarks Based Region-Level Data Augmentation for Gaze Estimation

Zhuo Yang[1], Luqian Ren[1], Jian Zhu[1(✉)], Wenyan Wu[1], and Rui Wang[2]

[1] School of Computer Science and Technology, Guangdong University of Technology, Guangzhou, China
dr.zhuj@gmail.com
[2] State Key Lab of CAD&CG, Zhejiang University, Hangzhou, Zhejiang, China

Abstract. Data augmentation (DA) is an effective technique and is widely used in various deep learning tasks (including gaze estimation). Appearance-based gaze estimation aims to directly learn a mapping from face images to gaze directions. Since subtle changes in eye regions are important for gaze estimation, direct data augmentation on faces is likely to damage key features in the eye region. We propose a facial landmarks based region-level data augmentation method. The method use facial landmarks to divide the face into eye regions and non-eye regions. Then we generate face images under different data augmentation methods by augmenting non-eye regions. We preserve the key features of eye regions. And the features of non-eye regions are augmented. We conduct experiments on the largest 2D dataset – GazeCapture. Comprehensive experiments show that the proposed method achieves promising results. Wide range of gaze estimation based application will be aspired from this work.

Keywords: Gaze estimation · Data augmentation · Facial landmarks · Human-computer interaction

1 Introduction

Gaze estimation is an important task and has wide-spread applications in many fields. For example, gaze estimation techniques are widely used in human attention diagnosis, especially fatigue driving [12], saliency detection [7,21], etc. Gaze has also became a newly developing human-computer interaction method [15,16]. To enable such applications, accurate gaze estimation methods are important.

Up to now, many gaze estimation methods have been proposed including model-based and appearance-based methods. Model-based methods aim to fit a 3D eye model to the image and calculate gaze via specific geometric constrains [22]. They usually require some dedicate devices like high resolution cameras, RGB-D cameras [1,18]and infrared cameras [26]. Appearance-based methods do not require dedicated devices and use web cameras to capture human eye appearance and regress gaze from the appearance. Appearance-based methods which directly map gaze from appearance have made great progress [23]. Some appearance-based methods using convolutional neural networks (CNNs) [2,5,10,

13, 24] have been proposed and show convincing results. This also benefits from the powerful feature extraction capability of CNN.

With the further research on gaze estimation, it is found that face images contain rich information [13]. Data augmentation has been proved to be an essential technique for increasing the effective data size and promoting the diversity of training examples [8, 25]. We can use data augmentation to augment facial information [14]. Subtle changes in eye regions are important for the gaze estimation [3]. However, direct data augmentation on faces is likely to damage key features in the eye region. Besides, data augmentation methods such as flipping and affine transformation can reduce the performance of gaze estimation. Because these methods change the implicit features of face images such as head pose [24]. Gong et al. [8] propose a simple yet highly effective approach called KeepAugment. This method is first to use the saliency map to detect important regions on the original images and then preserve these informative regions during augmentation. This information preserving strategy allows us to generate more faithful training examples.

So, we propose a facial landmarks based region-level data augmentation method for gaze estimation. Firstly, we use landmarks to divide the face into eye regions and non-eye regions. Then, we generate face images under different data augmentation methods (illumination conditions, random occlusion and Gaussian blur) by augmenting non-eye regions. Finally, we fuse the augmented non-eye regions with eye regions to generate the final augmented image. As with most data augmentation methods, our region-level data augmentation method allows our model to show better generalization ability.

In summary, the contributions of this paper are as follow:

1. We propose a facial landmarks based region-level data augmentation method for gaze estimation.
2. We comprehensively consider the influence of illumination conditions, random occlusions and Gaussian blur on images to generate the facial image in different data augmentation methods.
3. We conduct experiments on the largest popular dataset – GazeCapture. The result show that the proposed method is close to the state of the art (SOTA) on tablets and outperforms the SOTA on mobile phones.

2   Related Works

2.1   Gaze Estimation

As an active research topic, many different methods have been proposed to address gaze estimation problem. In particular, appearance-based gaze estimation methods achieve excellent results. Cheng et al. [4] present a comprehensive overview of deep learning-based gaze estimation methods.

Appearance-based methods aim to find the direct mapping function from image appearance to gaze location. 2D Gaze estimation assumed a fixed head pose of the target person [20] and consequently focused on the 2D gaze estimation task where the estimator is trained to output on screen gaze locations. Krafka et al. [13] propose a multi-region 2D gaze estimation architecture— iTracker that takes individual eye images, the face image and a face grid as input. In particular, this work provides a large scale public dataset— GazeCapture. Junfeng et al. [10] present an on-device few-shot personalization method for 2D gaze estimation. The method reduces the number of calibration points required by the user. Guo et al. [9] propose a new tolerant and talented (TAT) training scheme, which is an iterative random knowledge distillation framework enhanced with cosine similarity pruning and aligned orthogonal initialization. Recently, Bao et al. [2] propose an accurate appearance-based gaze estimation method named AFF-Net. The proposed AFF-Net improves gaze tracking accuracy by adaptively fusing two eye features and face appearance characteristics guided eye feature extraction. And the AFF-Net achieved SOTA on the GazeCapture dataset at that time.

2.2   Data Augmentation

Data augmentation is a widely used technique to artificially enlarge the training dataset from existing data using various transformations. Two classes of augmentation techniques are widely used for achieving SOTA results on computer vision tasks:

Image-Level Augmentation apply label invariant transformations on the whole image such as solarization, sharpness, posterization, color normalization and illumination [14]. Sun et al. [19] present a learning-based technique for single image portrait relighting: taking a single RGB image of a human subject in an unconstrained environment and modifying it to appear as though it were illuminated by a different environment. Image-level transformations are often manually designed and heuristically chosen.

Region-Level Augmentation transform a specific area of an image. Some classical image transformation methods are also widely used in model training [11,17] such as, translation, rotation, flipping, cropping. These classic techniques are fundamental to obtain highly generalized deep models. It is shown in some literature that abandoning certain information in training images is also an effective approach to augment the training data. Cutout [6] and random erasing [25] work by randomly masking out or modifying rectangular regions of the input images and creating partially occluded data examples outside the span of the training data. However, both two methods may mask or even damage key features of eye regions. Therefore, it is important to select an appropriate region for data augmentation.

3   Proposed Method

The proposed method consists of two steps–facial landmarks based region mask and non-eye regions data augmentation. The following is a detailed description of two steps.

3.1   Facial Landmarks Based Region Mask

Firstly, as shown in Fig. 1, we extract the 2D facial landmarks. Landmark is a method of facial feature point extraction. This method uses the ERT (Ensemble of regression trees) cascaded regression algorithm and uses a series of calibrated face images for training and then generates a model.

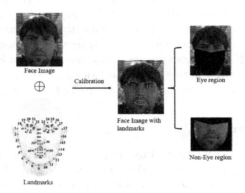

Fig. 1. The process of dividing face image into eye regions and non-eye regions.

To explain the method more theoretically, we introduce some notations. Let $X_i \in \mathbb{R}^2$ be the x, y coordinates of the ith facial landmark in an image I. Then the vector $\mathbf{Z} = \left(X_1^T, X_2^T, ..., X_i^T \right) \in \mathbb{R}^{2p}$ denotes the coordinates of all the i facial landmarks in I. We refer to the vector $\mathbf{Z}$ as the shape. As shown in Eq. (1), we use $\hat{\mathbf{Z}}^{(t)}$ to denote our current estimate of $\mathbf{Z}$. Each regressor, $r_t (.,.)$, in the cascade predicts an update vector from the image and $\hat{\mathbf{Z}}^{(t)}$ that is added to the current shape estimate $\hat{\mathbf{Z}}^{(t)}$ to improve the estimate.

$$\hat{\mathbf{Z}}^{(t+1)} = \hat{\mathbf{Z}}^{(t)} + r_t \left(I, \hat{\mathbf{Z}}^{(t)} \right) \tag{1}$$

The keypoint of the cascade is that the regressor r_t makes its predictions based on features such as pixel intensity values computed from I and indexed relative to the current shape estimate $\hat{\mathbf{Z}}^{(t)}$.

3.2   Non-eye Regions Data Augmentation

This section describes the data augmentation method for non-eye regions, as shown in Fig. 2, including illumination conditions, random occlusion and Gaussian blur.

Random Erasing. In training, we randomly erase with a certain probability. In this process, non-eye region images with various levels of occlusion are generated. For a non-eye region image I in a mini-batch, the probability of it undergoing

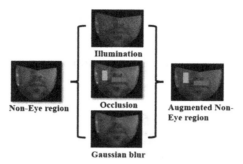

Fig. 2. The augmentation process of the non-eye region.

random erasing is p and the probability of it being kept unchanged is 1-p. Firstly, this method randomly selects a rectangle region $I_e \subseteq I$ in the non-eye region and erases its pixels with random values. Assume that the size of the non-eye region is $S = W \times H$. W and H refer to the width and height of the farthest border of the non-eye region. S refer to the area of the non-eye region.

Then, we randomly initialize the area of erasing rectangle region to S_e, where $\frac{S_e}{S}$ is in range specified by minimum S_l and maximum S_h. The aspect ratio of erasing rectangle region is randomly initialized between r_1 and r_2. We set it to r_e. The size of I_e is $W_e = \sqrt{\frac{S_e}{r_e}}$ and $H_e = \sqrt{S_e \times r_e}$.

Finally, this method randomly initialize a point $p^* = (x_e, y_e)$ in I. If $x_e + W_e \leq W$ and $y_e + H_e \leq H$, as shown in Eq. (2), the selected rectangle region is:

$$I_e = (x_e, y_e, x_e + W_e, y_e + H_e) \tag{2}$$

Otherwise repeat the above process until an appropriate I_e is selected. And erased regions are filled with random color patches.

Gaussian Blur. Gaussian blur is an image processing method based on Gaussian function shown in Eq. (3).

$$f(x) = \frac{1}{\sigma\sqrt{2\pi}} e^{-(x-\mu)^2/2\sigma^2} \tag{3}$$

where μ is the mean of x and σ is the standard deviation of x.

In the normal distribution curve, the farther to the "center point", the smaller the value. So, we take the "center point" as the origin and assign weights to other points according to their positions on the normal curve. And then a weighted average can be obtained. That is shown in Eq. (4):

$$G(x, y) = \frac{1}{2\pi\sigma^2} e^{-(x^2+y^2)/2\sigma^2} \tag{4}$$

In this way, we can reduce the influence of gaze irrelevant features in non-eye regions on the gaze estimation.

Simulate Illumination Conditions. Illumination is one of the important factors that affect the facial features. Due to the changes in illumination conditions, the same face appears differently [14]. In our illumination synthesis process, as shown in Fig. 3, we generate face images by adjusting brightness, contrast and saturation.

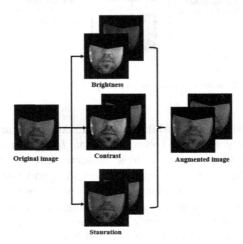

Fig. 3. Non-eye region images under different illumination conditions.

Finally, as shown in Fig. 4, we compare images augmented directly on the face and images augmented with the proposed method. If we augment the face image directly, it is likely to damage the key features of eye regions such as the eye regions are erased. Hence, our data augmentation method only works on the non-eye region and the key features of the eye region are fully preserved. The proposed method can effectively augment facial data and reduce the influence of gaze irrelevant features on gaze estimation.

4   Experiments

4.1   Experimental Setup

Datasets. GazeCapture is the largest 2D gaze dataset with more than 2M images from more than 1,400 subjects. The dataset is captured by mobile phones or tablets in different orientations. There are 1,490,959 frames have both face and eye detections, which are further divided into 1,251,983 training images, 59,480 validation images and 179,496 test images. For training, each of the samples is treated independently. For testing, we average the predictions of the samples to obtain the prediction on the original test sample.

Original Images

Images augmented
directly on the face

Images augmented
with our method

Fig. 4. Comparison of two data augmentation methods. The 1st row shows original face images and the 2nd row shows images augmented directly on the face. The 3rd row shows images augmented with the proposed method.

Training Details. The experiments are implemented using PyTorch. We use the ResNet-50 as experimental model. Network parameters are initialized by the default initialization of PyTorch. The model is trained for 18 epochs on the GazeCapture. The batch size is set to 32. The initial learning rate is set to 0.001 and it becomes 0.0001 after 8 epochs. The optimizer uses SGD. Further, we use a momentum of 0.9 and a weight decay of 0.0005 throughout the training procedure.

Evaluation Metrics. For gaze point estimation on GazeCapture dataset, we use the Euclidean distance shown in Eq. (5) to measure the error between the predicted and the ground truth gaze points.

$$d_e = \frac{1}{M} \sum_i^M \left\| p^i - \hat{p}^i \right\|_2 \tag{5}$$

where M is the total number of images in GazeCapture. p^i and $\hat{p}^i$ are the ground truth and the predicted gaze point, for the ith image.

4.2   Performance Comparison

We conduct two experiments test different methods on the GazeCapture dataset. We choose four methods for comparison on GazeCapture, which are iTracker [13], SAGE [10], TAT [9] and AFF-Net [2]. The results are shown in Tables 1. To the best of our knowledge, AFF-Net shows the SOTA performance on GazeCapture.

The proposed method achieves 1.58 cm error on mobile phones and 2.36 cm error on tablets which outperforms SOTA methods on mobile phones. For the mobile phone image test, the iTracker has the highest error as 1.86 cm. SAGE and TAT have similar performance around 1.77 cm, improve about 5% from iTracker. AFF-Net achieves 1.62 cm error which outperforms both two methods significantly. The proposed method achieves 1.58 cm that outperforms AFF-Net and improves about 15% from iTracker. For the more challenging tablet image

Table 1. Gaze estimation error in centimeters compares with sota methods on the gazecapture dataset.

Methods	Phone error (cm)	Tablet error (cm)
iTracker [13]	1.86	2.81
SAGE [10]	1.78	2.72
TAT [9]	1.77	2.66
AFF-Net [2]	1.62	2.3
Proposed method	**1.58**	2.36

test, the error of iTracker is 2.81 cm. SAGE and TAT has similar performance around 2.69 cm. AFF-Net achieves 2.3 cm error which is almost 0.39 cm lower than SAGE and TAT. The proposed method achieves similar results to AFF-Net and the error is 2.36 cm which is 12.3% lower than SAGE and TAT. The proposed method can improve the performance of gaze estimation on tablets than most previous methods. These experiment results show that the proposed method has clear advantages over other methods, especially on mobile phone.

Limitations. For the more challenging tablet test, the error of the proposed method is 2.36 cm which is 2.6% higher than AFF-Net. The reason is that the tablet image is less than the phone image in the dataset. The proposed method has great room for improvement on the tablet.

4.3   Ablation Studies

In this section, we conduct experiments to demonstrate the effectiveness of the proposed method. First, we test the error of the model without using data augmentation. Then, we directly augment faces and test error. We compare both two experimental results with the result obtained by training with the proposed method. The results are shown in Table 2.

Table 2. Full face v.s. non-eye region DA comparison.

Full face	Non-eye region	Phone error (cm)	Tablet error (cm)
×	×	1.68	2.59
✓	×	1.73 ↑	2.82 ↑
×	✓	**1.58**	**2.36**

The results are shown in Table 2. Without data augmentation, the error of mobile phones and tablets is 1.68 cm and 2.59 cm. Data augmentation methods on full face reduce the performance of the model. The error of mobile phone and tablet is 1.73 cm and 2.82 cm which increase by 0.05 cm and 0.23 cm. Because data augmentation methods apply directly on full face (including the eye region) reducing the availability of key features in eye regions. For example, the eye region may be completely erased, as shown in Fig. 4 (row 2). With non-eye regions data augmentation, the error of mobile phone and tablet is 1.58 cm and 2.36 cm. The error is reduced by 6% and 9% for mobile phones and tablets.

5 Conclusions

In this work, we propose a facial landmarks based region-level data augmentation method for gaze estimation. The face are divided into eye regions and non-eye regions. Then, we generate face images under different data augmentation methods by augmenting non-eye regions. The proposed method achieves excellent performance on the largest 2D gaze dataset—GazeCapture dataset. On tablets the proposed method is close to the current SOTA methods and on mobile phones outperforms the SOTA methods. These results prove the effectiveness of the proposed method. In the future, we will study more appropriate data augmentation methods for tablet devices. Gaze estimation and its applications are promising research topics. We believe researchers will be inspired from this work.

Acknowledgments. This research is supported by National Natural Science Foundation of China (No. 61907009, No. 61872319) and Science and Technology Planning Project of Guangdong Province (No. 2019B010150002).

References

1. Alberto Funes Mora, K., Odobez, J.M.: Geometric generative gaze estimation (G3E) for remote RGB-D cameras. In: Proceedings of the IEEE Conference on Computer Vision and Pattern Recognition, pp. 1773–1780 (2014)
2. Bao, Y., Cheng, Y., Liu, Y., Lu, F.: Adaptive feature fusion network for gaze tracking in mobile tablets. In: 25th International Conference on Pattern Recognition, pp. 9936–9943. IEEE (2021)
3. Cheng, Y., Bao, Y., Lu, F.: PureGaze: purifying gaze feature for generalizable gaze estimation. CoRR abs/2103.13173 (2021)
4. Cheng, Y., Wang, H., Bao, Y., Lu, F.: Appearance-based gaze estimation with deep learning: a review and benchmark. arXiv preprint arXiv:2104.12668 (2021)
5. Cheng, Y., Zhang, X., Lu, F., Sato, Y.: Gaze estimation by exploring two-eye asymmetry. IEEE Trans. Image Process. **29**, 5259–5272 (2020)
6. Devries, T., Taylor, W.G.: Improved regularization of convolutional neural networks with cutout. CoRR abs/1708.04552 (2017)
7. Fan, D.-P., Cheng, M.-M., Liu, J.-J., Gao, S.-H., Hou, Q., Borji, A.: Salient objects in clutter: bringing salient object detection to the foreground. In: Ferrari, V., Hebert, M., Sminchisescu, C., Weiss, Y. (eds.) ECCV 2018. LNCS, vol. 11219, pp. 196–212. Springer, Cham (2018). https://doi.org/10.1007/978-3-030-01267-0_12
8. Gong, C., Wang, D., Li, M., Chandra, V., Liu, Q.: KeepAugment: a simple information-preserving data augmentation approach. In: Proceedings of the IEEE/CVF Conference on Computer Vision and Pattern Recognition, pp. 1055–1064 (2021)

9. Guo, T., et al.: A generalized and robust method towards practical gaze estimation on smart phone. In: Proceedings of the IEEE/CVF International Conference on Computer Vision Workshops, pp. 1131–1139 (2019)
10. He, J., et al.: On-device few-shot personalization for real-time gaze estimation. In: IEEE/CVF International Conference on Computer Vision Workshops, pp. 1149–1158 (2019)
11. He, K., Zhang, X., Ren, S., Sun, J.: Deep residual learning for image recognition. In: Proceedings of the IEEE Conference on Computer Vision and Pattern Recognition, pp. 770–778 (2016)
12. Ji, Q., Yang, X.: Real-time eye, gaze, and face pose tracking for monitoring driver vigilance. Real Time Imaging **8**, 357–377 (2002)
13. Krafka, K., et al.: Eye tracking for everyone. In: Proceedings of the IEEE Conference on Computer Vision and Pattern Recognition, pp. 2176–2184 (2016)
14. Lv, J.J., Shao, X.H., Huang, J.S., Zhou, X.D., Zhou, X.: Data augmentation for face recognition. Neurocomputing **230**, 184–196 (2017)
15. Piumsomboon, T., Lee, G., Lindeman, R.W., Billinghurst, M.: Exploring natural eye-gaze-based interaction for immersive virtual reality. In: IEEE Symposium on 3D User Interfaces, pp. 36–39. IEEE (2017)
16. Ren, L., Huang, H., Wang, H., Yang, Z.: Gazegrid: a novel interaction method based on gaze estimation. In: IEEE International Conference on Automatic Face and Gesture Recognition, pp. 1–5. IEEE (2021)
17. Srivastava, K.R., Greff, K., Schmidhuber, J.: Training very deep networks. In: Annual Conference on Neural Information Processing Systems, pp. 2377–2385 (2015)
18. Sun, L., Liu, Z., Sun, M.T.: Real time gaze estimation with a consumer depth camera. Inf. Sci. **320**, 346–360 (2015)
19. Sun, T., et al.: Single image portrait relighting. ACM Trans. Graph. **38**(4), 79:1–79:12 (2019)
20. Valenti, R., Sebe, N., Gevers, T.: Combining head pose and eye location information for gaze estimation. IEEE Trans. Image Process. **21**(2), 802–815 (2011)
21. Wang, W., Shen, J., Dong, X., Borji, A., Yang, R.: Inferring salient objects from human fixations. IEEE Trans. Pattern Anal. Mach. Intell. **42**(8), 1913–1927 (2019)
22. Xiong, X., Liu, Z., Cai, Q., Zhang, Z.: Eye gaze tracking using an RGBD camera: a comparison with a RGB solution. In: Proceedings of the ACM International Joint Conference on Pervasive and Ubiquitous Computing: Adjunct Publication, pp. 1113–1121 (2014)
23. Zhang, X., Park, S., Beeler, T., Bradley, D., Tang, S., Hilliges, O.: ETH-XGaze: a large scale dataset for gaze estimation under extreme head pose and gaze variation. In: Vedaldi, A., Bischof, H., Brox, T., Frahm, J.-M. (eds.) ECCV 2020. LNCS, vol. 12350, pp. 365–381. Springer, Cham (2020). https://doi.org/10.1007/978-3-030-58558-7_22
24. Zhang, X., Sugano, Y., Fritz, M., Bulling, A.: It's written all over your face: full-face appearance-based gaze estimation. In: Proceedings of the IEEE Conference on Computer Vision and Pattern Recognition Workshops, pp. 51–60 (2017)
25. Zhong, Z., Zheng, L., Kang, G., Li, S., Yang, Y.: Random erasing data augmentation. In: Proceedings of the AAAI Conference on Artificial Intelligence, vol. 34, pp. 13001–13008 (2020)
26. Zhu, Z., Ji, Q.: Novel eye gaze tracking techniques under natural head movement. IEEE Trans. Biomed. Eng. **54**(12), 2246–2260 (2007)

An Efficient Dense Depth Map Estimation Algorithm Using Direct Stereo Matching for Ultra-Wide-Angle Images

Xiuxiu Gui and Xinyu Zhang[✉]

Shanghai Key Laboratory of Trustworthy Computing, Engineering Research Center of Software/Hardware Co-design Tech and Application, East China Normal University, Shanghai, China
xyzhang@sei.ecnu.edu.cn

Abstract. We present an efficient dense depth map estimation algorithm using patch-based direct stereo matching for ultra-wide-angle images. Our algorithm takes account of the fact that the neighboring pixels inside a local patch are likely to lie on the same plane. Our algorithm propagates the "good" initial guesses to the neighboring pixels by spatial propagation, followed by a random refinement process. Therefore, this allows finding precise depth value for each point in an infinite space using a random search strategy. Our algorithm can be used to perform 3D reconstruction using the dense depth maps directly generated from ultra-wide-angle images, especially from stereo camera pairs.

Keywords: Ultra-wide-angle camera · Depth map · Patch-based stereo matching

1 Introduction

To understand and reconstruct surrounding environments, cameras play a crucial role in many applications due to the rich and comprehensive information in images [1–3]. Among various cameras, ultra-wide-angle lenses capture the large views of a surrounding environment and expect to benefit many applications like augmented reality and robotics [4,5]. For example, in virtual/augmented reality, panoramic cameras often use a combination of multiple ultra-wide-angle lenses to capture immersive environments [6]. Mounting ultra-wide-angle cameras on the vehicle also becomes a standard option for environmental perception in autonomous driving [7] and mobile robots [8]. Depth cues of the capturing scene can benefit many computer vision tasks, such as post-processing approaches of depth-of-field rendering [2,9] and image deblurring [10].

Unlike the image features generated using sparse depth cues [11,12], dense depth map estimation aims at leveraging the large field of view to perform 3D reconstruction for the entire surrounding environment. Estimating depth from a monocular ultra-wide-angle camera is considered as a challenging and ill-posed problem. Therefore, in virtual/augmented reality, multiple ultra-wide-angle lenses are often used to perform stereo matching to generate immersive depth maps. There still exhibit a few challenges for stereo matching using ultra-wide-angle lenses. First, ultra-wide-angle cameras have severe geometric distortions. Many standard stereo matching algorithms like image rectification may undergo perspective projection [13], spherical model projection [14] or equirectangular projection [15]. These projections exhibit severe distortions in the resulting depth maps and therefore this may significantly reduce the view coverage provided by the ultra-wide-angle cameras. Second, estimating correct depth values is non-trivial especially for ultra-wide-angle cameras. For example, plane sweeping [16] searches pre-defined plane hypotheses for depth values of each pixel and often leads to inaccurate depth values for pixels located at the planes that are not included in the pre-defined plane set. Note that the pre-defined possible planes are limited, though the number of candidate planes is infinite. Third, many studies can only handle ultra-wide-angle stereo pairs undergoing small displacements [17], but they may not suit for rapid movement.

Main Result: In this paper, we present a new efficient patch-based stereo matching algorithm for the ultra-wide-angle lens. We introduce the PatchMatch randomized searching method [18], which is proved to be efficient on searching the matching patch in image domain [2, 19]. Patch matching stereo allows finding accurate depth values for each point in an infinite space with a random search strategy. Intuitively, patch match stereo efficiently traverses the infinite candidate planes and performs a one-shot optimization in which the planes and pixel assignments to corresponding planes are determined at the same time. This avoids the problem of missing correct planes. Our algorithm has the following novel aspects.

- The algorithm can be directly applied to ultra-wide-angle image pairs without rectification, thus providing dense depth maps for the entire environment captured by cameras.
- Using patch-based stereo matching, our algorithm can locate correct planes for each pixel with a random search strategy, which avoids missing the accurate depth values.
- Our algorithm deals with stereo pairs with an arbitrary baseline. This allows handle the rapid camera movement and perform reconstruction from stereo pairs with large displacements.
- Our algorithm is applicable for any camera projection model, as long as it has a closed-form inverse.

2   Patch Matching Stereo

In this section, we first introduce the double sphere camera projection model for ultra-wide-angle lenses. Then we demonstrate adopting the double sphere camera model in patch-based stereo matching.

2.1   Camera Projection Model

In this paper, we demonstrate the proposed algorithm with the double sphere camera model [20] since it has a closed-form inversion (unprojection) and can avoid high computational costs. Note that our algorithm works for any ultra-wide-angle lens model that has a closed-form inversion. As shown in Sect. 3, we demonstrate some results under the unified camera model.

In the double sphere model, a point in the world space are projected onto two unit spheres consecutively. We assume that the distance between the centers of the two unit spheres is ξ. Then the point is projected onto the image plane shifted by $\frac{\alpha}{1-\alpha}$ under perspective projection. Let the camera intrinsic parameters be $\mathbf{K} = [f_x, f_y, c_x, c_y, \xi, \alpha]^T$, where $[f_x, f_y]$ are focal lengths and $[c_x, c_y]$ is the principal point given in a perspective projection. They can be typically estimated using camera calibration.

For a 3D point $\mathbf{x}$ and its corresponding image pixel $\mathbf{u}$, the function $\mathbf{u} = \pi(\mathbf{x}, \mathbf{K})$ represents the map from a 3D point onto the corresponding image plane. The unprojection function $\mathbf{x} = \pi^{-1}(\mathbf{u}, \mathbf{K})$ maps an image pixel to its corresponding viewing ray. Here, we omit the details of the double sphere camera model. We refer the readers to [20] for more explanation.

2.2   Patch Matching Stereo for Ultra-Wide-Angle Images

Patch matching stereo has been proven efficient and accurate for 3D reconstruction under perspective projection [21,22]. Here, we propose adopting an ultra-wide-angle lens projection model on patch-based stereo matching.

The proposed algorithm aims at estimating depth value based on the ultra-wide-angle stereo pair. The patch matching stereo algorithm takes input image pairs $\mathbf{I} = \{I_i, I_j\}$, together with the associating camera parameters $\{\mathbf{K}_i, \mathbf{R}_i, \mathbf{C}_i\}$ and $\{\mathbf{K}_j, \mathbf{R}_j, \mathbf{C}_j\}$, where $\mathbf{K}$ stands for camera intrinsics and $[\mathbf{R}, \mathbf{C}]$ are camera pose parameters. For a given pixel, its support plane is denoted as $[\mathbf{x}_i, \mathbf{n}_i]$, where $\mathbf{x}_i$ is a 3D point on the plane and $\mathbf{n}_i$ is the plane normal.

To generate the depth map for image I_i, we first perform a random initialization by assigning a random plane to each pixel in I_i. From the probability point of view, there must be some pixels assigned a plane very close to the correct one. Later, these good guesses will be able to propagate to the neighboring pixels by spatial propagation. The 3D point $\mathbf{x}_i$ on the random plane is defined by the scale factor of the viewing ray and can be obtained from inverse projection function given in Eq. (1).

$$\mathbf{x}_i = d_i \pi_i^{-1}(\mathbf{u}_i, \mathbf{K}_i). \tag{1}$$

We assign a random depth value d_i for $\mathbf{x}_i$, and the plane normal is defined in spherical coordinates

$$\mathbf{n}_i = \begin{bmatrix} cos\theta sin\phi \\ sin\theta sin\phi \\ cos\phi \end{bmatrix}. \tag{2}$$

where $\theta \in [0, 360°]$ is the angle between the plane's normal and the x axis. $\phi \in [0, 180°]$ is the angle between $\mathbf{n}_i$ and the z axis.

After initializing the random candidate plane to each pixel, we propagate initial guesses to neighboring pixels and add random perturbations. Here, we aim to find the support plane with the minimal aggregated matching cost for each pixel. We first map a pixel to other view to find its corresponding patch using the assigned plane parameter. Then the matching cost is evaluated between two corresponding patches.

More specifically, for an input image I_i, each pixel $\mathbf{u}_i$ is mapped to a random plane and then is rendered onto the other view I_j^i. We use homography to perform planar mapping [23] defined in Eq. (3) with the plane parameters. To find the corresponding pixel in the other image I_j^i, we apply the projection function and transformation homography $\mathbf{H}_{ji}$ to each pixel's homogeneous coordinates $\mathbf{u_i}(u_i, v_i, 1)$ as Eq. (4). To obtain the direct dense matching on wide-angle images, we use the double sphere camera model given in Eqs. (3) and (4).

$$\mathbf{H}_{ji} = \mathbf{R}_j^T \mathbf{R}_i + \frac{1}{\mathbf{n}_i^T \mathbf{x}_i} \mathbf{R}_j^T (\mathbf{C}_j - \mathbf{C}_i) \mathbf{n}_i^T \tag{3}$$

$$[u_j^i, v_j^i, 1] = \pi_j \mathbf{H}_{ji} \pi_i^{-1} [u_i, v_i, 1] \tag{4}$$

Using the above equation, we locate the corresponding patch on I_j. We check the image variance between the corresponding patches centered at the given pixel. For a pixel $\mathbf{u}(u, v)$ in I_i, we select a correlation window $\mathcal{W}$ centered on that pixel position (u, v) and warp all the pixels in $\mathcal{W}$ to reference image I_j in order to find its corresponding patch I_j^i using Eq. 4. To evaluate image variance, we compute negative zero mean normalized cross correlation (ZNCC) over the window $\mathcal{W}$. A negative ZNCC between two corresponding patches at a given pixel position can be written as Eq. (5).

$$\mathcal{M}(\mathbf{u}, f) = \frac{- \sum_{(x,y) \in \mathcal{W}} \{I_i(x,y) - \overline{I_i}(x,y)\}\{I_j^i(x,y) - \overline{I_j^i}(x,y)\}}{\sqrt{\sum_{(x,y) \in \mathcal{W}} \{I_i(x,y) - \overline{I_i}(x,y)\}^2 \sum_{(x,y) \in \mathcal{W}} \{I_j^i(x,y) - \overline{I_j^i}(x,y)\}^2}} \tag{5}$$

We traverse the given image in a row-wise order and optimize the parameters for each pixel. Then we perform propagation and random refinement. This optimization process is performed in many iterations for a single image. In the odd-numbered iterations, we start at the top left corner of the image and end at the bottom right corner. In the even-numbered iterations, we start at the bottom right corner until we reach the top left corner.

We examine whether the plane parameters of four neighboring pixels are better choices for the given pixel in spatial propagation. Here, we take the fact that neighboring pixels are more likely to lie on the same plane. In an odd-numbered iteration, we check the left pixel and the top pixel in spatial propagation. In an even-numbered iteration, we check the right pixel and the bottom pixel. Let the current pixel denoted by $\mathbf{p}$ and its plane denoted by f_p. We assign its neighboring pixel $\mathbf{q}$'s plane f_q to $\mathbf{p}$. We check the condition $\mathcal{M}(\mathbf{p}, f_q) < \mathcal{M}(\mathbf{p}, f_p)$, and if it holds, update $\mathbf{p}$ with $f_p = f_q$.

The random refinement searches for the plane parameters exhibiting a smaller matching cost. In this step, we alter the plane parameters within a wide range in the early stage. It is reasonable if the current parameters are completely wrong. Then we reduce the search region, so the planes are close to the optimal one. Let the plane at point $\mathbf{p}$ be defined by the depth value d and the normal vector $\mathbf{n}$. We set the maximum change for the plane's depth Δd_{max} and the normal $\Delta\mathbf{n}(\Delta\theta_{max}, \Delta\phi_{max})$. Then we randomly choose values Δd from $[-\Delta d_{max}, \Delta d_{max}]$, and $\Delta\mathbf{n}(\Delta\theta, \Delta\phi)$. We can generate a new plane by adding those random values to $\mathbf{p}$'s plane $f'_p = [d + \Delta d, \mathbf{n} + \Delta\mathbf{n}]$. In our work, the variation range is set $\Delta d_{max} = \frac{1}{4}(d_{max} - d_{min})$, $\Delta\theta \in [0, 180°]$, $\Delta\phi \in [0, 90°]$. If the condition $\mathcal{M}(\mathbf{p}, f'_p) < \mathcal{M}(\mathbf{p}, f_p)$ holds, we update the plane in $\mathbf{p}$.

We perform the random refinement for a few iterations (e.g. 4) at each pixel and decrease the variation range by half in each iteration. This strategy effectively narrows the search space. It is essential to search a wide range in the early optimization stages, for there might be a false plane assignment. In later iterations, a compact variation range leads to precise exploration and allows accurate depth values for points on a smooth surface.

3   Experimental Results

We implemented our patch-based stereo algorithm using CUDA. Our algorithm can run effectively both on Windows and Linux. The performance of our algorithm was evaluated on a PC with NVIDIA GeForce GTX 2080Ti and 32GB main memory. We perform quantitative and qualitative comparisons against the state of the art fisheye stereo matching methods on public datasets. We perform the evaluations on two datasets: the TUM VI Benchmark [24] and the Oxford RobotCar dataset [25–27].

3.1   The TUM VI Benchmark

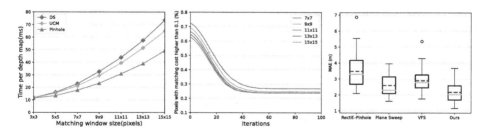

Fig. 1. Left: The average computational time per depth map under three camera models and various matching window. Middle: The pixel percentage of matching cost (<0.1) in terms of the number of iterations under various matching window. Right: MAE of four methods for the Oxford RobotCar dataset. The orange lines indicate the median values of the depth difference between the estimation and the LiDAR data. The purple dash lines highlight the mean values.

Fig. 2. Top Row: Input ultra-wide-angle images; Bottom Row: The corresponding ultra-wide-angle depth maps generated using our algorithm using double sphere camera model. Depth maps of the first and second columns are computed with the double sphere camera model, and the third and fourth columns use the unified camera model.

Fig. 3. The first and third images are input images, and the second and fourth images show the 3D point clouds constructed from our depth maps. Pay attention to the highlighted regions.

We tested our algorithm using the TUM VI Benchmark [24]. The benchmark contains an ultra-wide-angle stereo camera pair and provides calibration sequences. We first perform calibration to obtain the cameras intrinsics and extrinsics using Kalibr calibration toolbox [28]. In this experiment, the images have 512×512 pixels and $195°$ FOV. The matching window has 9×9 pixels. A larger window results in fewer noises (errors) in the resulting depth map. We first generate the depth map for one image and then take the output depth map as the initial guess for another. This greatly reduces the computational costs compared with random initialization for both images.

Figure 1-(Left) shows the computational time of generating a depth map under various matching window sizes. We implemented our patch-based stereo matching algorithm under three camera models: double sphere (DS), unified camera model (UCM) and pinhole camera model. Note that we refer to the algorithm in [22] for rectified fisheye image under the pinhole camera model. In Fig. 1-(Middle), we also evaluated the matching cost in terms of the number of iterations. A larger matching window has a lower matching cost while taking more computational time.

In our experiment, the first image takes 60–80 iterations, while the second only takes 5–10 iterations. In addition, the depth result in successive frames can also be used as the initial guess for acceleration. Figure 2 show our experimental results. Our algorithm can generate continuous depth maps with clear object boundaries. Note that those images were taken in various lighting conditions. Our algorithm is less sensitive to illumination changes. In Fig. 3, we also show a few dense point clouds constructed from our depth maps. Moreover, our algorithm can work for any camera projection model, as long as it has a closed-form inverse. We tested our algorithm using the unified camera model. The third and fourth columns of Fig. 2 show some promising depth maps.

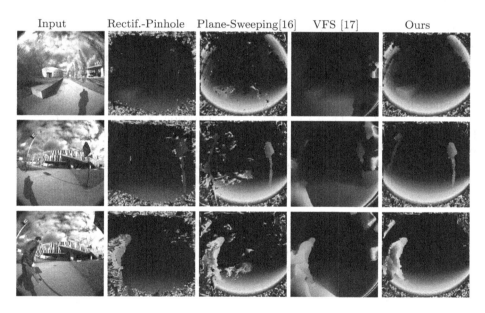

Fig. 4. Comparisons under the TUM VI dataset. Each row shows from left to right: input image, patch match stereo under the pinhole camera model [22], plane-sweeping [16], VFS [17] and our algorithm.

3.2   Comparisons

In Fig. 4, we compare our algorithm against the related work, including rectified wide-angle images under the pinhole camera model [22] (2nd column), plane-sweeping stereo[1] [16] (3rd column), variational fisheye stereo (VFS)[2] [17] (fourth column). Plane-sweeping stereo and VFS directly perform stereo matching on wide-angle images. Plane-sweeping stereo searches for depth value from pre-defined hypotheses, and VFS searches for the correspondence along the epipolar curve using a trajectory field induced by camera motion. Note that the Kannala-Brandt camera model was used in VFS [29]. The last column in Fig. 4 shows the results using our algorithm. In these comparisons, the number of candidate planes is 256 in plane-sweeping. The number of iterations in the patch matching algorithm is 60. The matching window is 11 × 11. The computational performance and comparison are shown in Table 1.

Patch matching using the rectified images under the pinhole camera model exhibits clear noises near image boundaries. These boundary areas have to be cropped and therefore significantly reduce the valid coverage. Plane sweeping also generates a large number of inaccurate (noisy) depth values in the resulting depth maps. Besides the comparison results shown in Fig. 4, Fig. 5 shows another comparison against VFS. VFS generates depth maps with fewer noises, but the objects near the boundary are blended with the background. Our algorithm generates high-quality depth maps with clear and sharp object boundaries. Due to a large matching window, the objects may expand slightly along their boundaries.

We also perform quantitative comparison in terms of matching accuracy. For each pixel $\mathbf{u}$ in image I_i, we project the pixel into the world space $\mathbf{x}$ using the obtained depth d_i. Then, we map the pixel $\mathbf{u}$ onto the other image I_j to get its corresponding point $\mathbf{u}_j^i$, and project the point $\mathbf{u}_j^i$ into the space $\mathbf{x}'$ according to the depth map of I_j. Then we check if the condition $|\mathbf{x} - \mathbf{x}'| > \epsilon$ holds. If it holds, the depth value at $\mathbf{u}$ is considered invalid. We set $\epsilon = 2$. Table 1 shows the percentage of pixels that have depth errors less than $\epsilon = 2$. We also evaluate the matching cost in Eq. 5 for the resulting depth map. Our algorithm outperforms other algorithms in terms of depth error and matching cost (see Table 1).

Table 1. Performance and accuracy comparison

–	TUM VI			Oxford RobotCar	
	Time (ms)	Depth error <2(%)	Matching cost <0.2(%)	MAE	σ
Rectif.	28.5	63.12	85.88	3.483	2.923
Plane sweeping [16]	38.6	74.59	90.59	2.593	2.933
VFS [17]	207.8	80.92	40.68	2.962	2.763
Ours	39.4	83.56	92.49	2.169	2.552

---

[1] https://www.cvg.ethz.ch/research/planeSweepLib/.

[2] https://github.com/menandro/vfs.

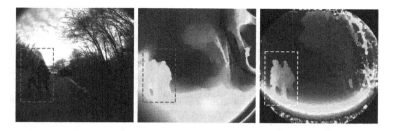

Fig. 5. Left: input images; Middle: depth maps generated using VFS; Right: our results. Pay attention to the rectangular areas. Our algorithm shows a clear object boundary compared with VFS.

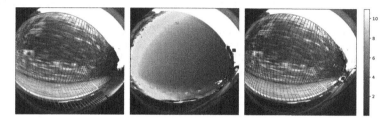

Fig. 6. Left: input image with LiDAR data projected; Middle: The resulting depth map computed by our algorithm. Right: The depth error per pixel where the LiDAR data are available.

3.3 The Oxford RobotCar Dataset

We further evaluated our algorithm using the Oxford RobotCar dataset with LiDAR, GPS and INS ground truth. The wide-angle image sequences are collected from three wide-angle cameras mounted on the left, the right and the rear. We use the left-mounted global shutter camera images with a 180° FOV. We calibrate the camera with the Kalibr toolbox to obtain the intrinsic parameters. For the extrinsic of each image, we apply the unified camera model to ORB-SLAM2 [30] to get the keyframe poses. Then we compute the depth maps

Fig. 7. The point cloud generated using our algorithm.

Input   Rectif.-Pinhole   Plane-Sweeping[16]   VFS [17]   Ours

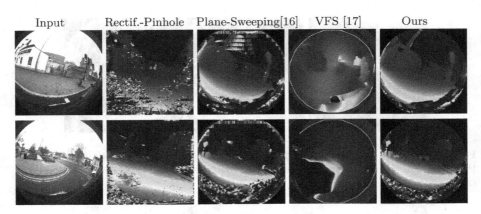

Fig. 8. Depth maps generated using four methods. The patch match stereo on rectified wide-angle images generated noise(inaccurate depth values), and the plane sweeping fails at the background sky area. VFS does not work well on images with significant displacement. Our method can generate high-quality depth maps with clear object boundaries.

for these keyframes. All the stereo matching algorithms are performed for two consecutive images. We compare our algorithm with point clouds scanned using LiDAR, as shown in Fig. 6. We observe that the depth maps generated using our algorithm are close to the depth resulted from the LiDAR. Figure 7 shows the point clouds generated by the proposed algorithm.

We also performed a comparison against other algorithms using the Oxford Radar RobotCar Dataset. The comparison results are given in Fig. 8. The matching window is 9×9 and 11×11 for evaluating the matching cost. The maximum number of iterations for patch match stereo is 60. The number of candidate planes for plane sweeping is 256.

We also compare the depth maps using the Velodyne HDL-32E LiDAR scans on the dataset. We evaluate the mean absolute error (MAE) on every depth map for the pixels whose depth is less than 20 m. We calculate the scale factor for every depth map. We take 50 keyframes and evaluate the dense stereo matching algorithms. The comparison result is shown in Table 1 and Fig. 1-(Right). The experimental results indicate that our algorithm has the best performance in comparison.

4   Conclusion

In this paper, we demonstrate that patch-based stereo matching can be directly applied to ultra-wide-angle images. Our algorithm can directly estimate depth values at each pixel for the given ultra-wide-angle images and generates high-quality depth maps with clear object boundaries. We further accelerate our algorithm using GPUs.

Our work has some limitations. For texture-less or shining surfaces, there exhibit false matches due to insufficient local evidence. This may cause obvious noises in the resulting depth maps.

In future, we would like to investigate the patch-based stereo matching algorithm in the stereoscopic 360 camera rig in order to generate a full range of depth maps for the surrounding environment. In addition, we would like to consider mounting stereo ultra-wide-angle cameras onto our mobile robot platform. Robot path planning is expected to greatly benefit from the resulting depth maps.

Acknowledgement. This work is supported by the National Key R&D Program of China under grant 2021ZD0114501.

References

1. Tao, Y., Shen, Y., Sheng, B., Li, P., Lau, R.W.H.: Video decolorization using visual proximity coherence optimization. IEEE Trans. Cybern. **48**(5), 1406–1419 (2018)
2. Zhang, B., Sheng, B., Li, P., Lee, T.Y.: Depth of field rendering using multilayer-neighborhood optimization. IEEE Trans. Vis. Comput. Graph. **26**(8), 2546–2559 (2020)
3. Guo, H., Sheng, B., Li, P., Chen, C.L.P.: Multiview high dynamic range image synthesis using fuzzy broad learning system. IEEE Trans. Cybern. **51**(5), 2735–2747 (2021)
4. Courbon, J., Mezouar, Y., Eckt, L., Martinet, P.: A generic fisheye camera model for robotic applications. In: IEEE/RSJ International Conference on Intelligent Robots and Systems, pp. 1683–1688 (2007)
5. Gu, Z., Liu, H., Zhang, G.: Real-time indoor localization of service robots using fisheye camera and laser pointers. In: IEEE International Conference on Robotics and Biomimetics, pp. 1410–1414 (2014)
6. Zhang, X., Zhao, Y., Mitchell, N., Li, W.: A new 360 camera design for multi format VR experiences. In: IEEE Conference on Virtual Reality and 3D User Interfaces, pp. 1273–1274 (2019)
7. Häne, C., et al.: 3D visual perception for self-driving cars using a multi-camera system: calibration, mapping, localization, and obstacle detection. Image Vis. Comput. **68**, 14–27 (2017)
8. Kumar, V.R., Klingner, M., Yogamani, S., Milz, S., Fingscheidt, T., Mader, P.: SynDistNet: self-supervised monocular fisheye camera distance estimation synergized with semantic segmentation for autonomous driving. In: IEEE/CVF Winter Conference on Applications of Computer Vision, pp. 61–71 (2021)
9. Lee, S., Kim, G.J., Choi, S.: Real-time depth-of-field rendering using anisotropically filtered mipmap interpolation. IEEE Trans. Vis. Comput. Graph. **15**(3), 453–464 (2009)
10. Wen, Y., et al.: Structure-aware motion deblurring using multi-adversarial optimized CycleGAN. IEEE Trans. Image Process. **30**, 6142–6155 (2021)
11. Liu, S., Guo, P., Feng, L., Yang, A.: Accurate and robust monocular SLAM with omnidirectional cameras. Sensors **19**(20), 4494 (2019)
12. Wang, Y., et al.: CubemapSLAM: a piecewise-pinhole monocular fisheye SLAM system. In: Jawahar, C.V., Li, H., Mori, G., Schindler, K. (eds.) ACCV 2018. LNCS, vol. 11366, pp. 34–49. Springer, Cham (2019). https://doi.org/10.1007/978-3-030-20876-9_3

13. Shah, S., Aggarwal, J.: Depth estimation using stereo fish-eye lenses. In: IEEE International Conference on Image Processing, vol. 2, pp. 740–744 (1994)
14. Li, S.: Real-time spherical stereo. In: IEEE International Conference on Pattern Recognition, vol. 3, pp. 1046–1049 (2006)
15. Li, J., Xu, W., Zhang, Z., Zhang, M., Wang, Z.: Fisheye image rectification for efficient large-scale stereo. In: International Conference on Systems and Informatics, pp. 881–885 (2016)
16. Häne, C., Heng, L., Lee, G.H., Sizov, A., Pollefeys, M.: Real-time direct dense matching on fisheye images using plane-sweeping stereo. In: IEEE International Conference on 3D Vision, p. 57–64 (2014)
17. Roxas, M., Oishi, T.: Variational fisheye stereo. IEEE Robot. Autom. Lett. **5**(2), 1303–1310 (2020)
18. Barnes, C., Shechtman, E., Finkelstein, A., Goldman, D.B.: PatchMatch: a randomized correspondence algorithm for structural image editing. ACM Trans. Graph. **28**(3), 24 (2009)
19. Sheng, B., Li, P., Gao, C., Ma, K.L.: Deep neural representation guided face sketch synthesis. IEEE Trans. Vis. Comput. Graph. **25**(12), 3216–3230 (2019)
20. Usenko, V., Demmel, N., Cremers, D.: The double sphere camera model. In: International Conference on 3D Vision, pp. 552–560 (2018)
21. Bleyer, M., Rhemann, C., Rother, C.: PatchMatch stereo-stereo matching with slanted support windows. In: British Machine Vision Conference, vol. 11, pp. 1–11 (2011)
22. Shen, S.: Accurate multiple view 3D reconstruction using patch-based stereo for large-scale scenes. IEEE Trans. Image Process. **22**(5), 1901–1914 (2013)
23. Hartley, R.I., Zisserman, A.: Multiple View Geometry in Computer Vision. Cambridge University Press, Cambridge (2004)
24. Schubert, D., Goll, T., Demmel, N., Usenko, V., Stueckler, J., Cremers, D.: The TUM VI benchmark for evaluating visual-inertial odometry. In: International Conference on Intelligent Robots and Systems, pp. 1680–1687 (2018)
25. Barnes, D., Gadd, M., Murcutt, P., Newman, P., Posner, I.: The Oxford radar robotcar dataset: a radar extension to the Oxford robotcar dataset. In: Proceedings of the IEEE International Conference on Robotics and Automation, pp. 6433–6438 (2020)
26. Maddern, W., Pascoe, G., Gadd, M., Barnes, D., Yeomans, B., Newman, P.: Real-time kinematic ground truth for the Oxford robotcar dataset. arXiv preprint arXiv: 2002.10152 (2020)
27. Maddern, W., Pascoe, G., Linegar, C., Newman, P.: 1 year, 1000km: the Oxford RobotCar dataset. The Int. J. Robot. Res. **36**(1), 3–15 (2017)
28. Furgale, P., Rehder, J., Siegwart, R.: Unified temporal and spatial calibration for multi-sensor systems. In: IEEE/RSJ International Conference on Intelligent Robots and Systems, pp. 1280–1286 (2013)
29. Kannala, J., Brandt, S.S.: A generic camera model and calibration method for conventional, wide-angle, and fish-eye lenses. IEEE Trans. Pattern Anal. Mach. Intell. **28**(8), 1335–1340 (2006)
30. Mur-Artal, R., Tardós, J.D.: ORB-SLAM2: an open-source SLAM system for monocular, stereo, and RGB-D cameras. IEEE Trans. Robot. **33**(5), 1255–1262 (2017)

Ad-RMS: Adaptive Regional Motion Statistics for Feature Matching Filtering

Bin Nan[1]([✉]), Yinghui Wang[1]([✉]), Yanxing Liang[1], Min Wu[2], Pengjiang Qian[1], and Gang Lin[3]

[1] School of Artificial Intelligence and Computer Science, Jiangnan University, Wuxi 214122, China
6201613037@stu.jiangnan.edu.cn, wangyh@jiangnan.edu.cn
[2] School of Internet of Things Engineering, Jiangnan University, Wuxi 214122, China
[3] Gastroenterology Department, Affiliated Hospital of Jiangnan University, Wuxi 214122, China

Abstract. The Grid-based Motion Statistics (GMS) is a popular feature matching filtering method, and can effectively support 3D reconstruction systems such as ORB-SLAM and has been used effectively in many fields. However, the GMS divides the image into a certain number of grids with a fixed size, which cannot better reflect the feature information of the region. So that when large affine changes occur in the images, the grids cannot delineate a reasonable consistent region. Such a region division leads to errors and even failures in the subsequent process using the grid to reject error feature matching. As a consequence, this paper proposes an adaptive regional motion statistics method based on adaptive region division for region detection to replace the fixed grid division, which enhances the affine invariance of the feature matching filtering algorithm, and verifies the effectiveness of this paper's method through the precision experiments of feature matching and homography matrix.

Keywords: Adaptive region · Regional motion statistics · Feature matching filtering · Affine invariance

1 Introduction

Feature matching is a fundamental part of computer vision research and is indispensable in applications such as image stitching [1], copy-move forgery detection [2], and 3D reconstruction. The main task of feature matching is to find correspondences between feature points in two images based on their descriptors, and it has always been a challenge to reject incorrect correspondences. The common methods of rejecting false matches are computationally complex and prone to global non-smoothness, which affects the accuracy of the rejected false matches [3].

The proposal of the GMS (Grid-based Motion Statistics) algorithm [4] effectively alleviates this problem to some extent, that is, GMS assumes that motion consistency will prevent random mismatches in a certain region from gathering in a certain region of another image. Through this assumption, the GMS algorithm is urged to achieve more universal feature matching filtering without strict geometric constraints, and the matching precision is not lower than that of other algorithms in a shorter running time.

However, the GMS algorithm does not work as well with the more complex affine transform, which includes not only rotation and scale transformations but also shear transformation. which cause more types of deformations in the image and make it more difficult to filter feature matching. Liu [5] adding the LK optical flow constraint before using the GMS algorithm makes the algorithm more robust to rotation, illumination and blur changes, but does not solve the problem of affine transformation. Specifically, if the affine transformation occurs in the images, the GMS algorithm will have the problem of feature matching filtering as shown in Fig. 1. The reason for the problem is that the affine transformation makes the dissimilar local patterns similar, resulting in more feature matching in the more similar regions, and only less feature matching corresponds to the correct regions. When using the GMS algorithm to find a better corresponding relationship for feature matching, the adaptability to affine transformation first depends on the way of grids dividing, and then on the way of determining the correct correspondence of grids. Due to the fixed size grids of the original algorithm, there are several grids containing similar regional features in the image, and the correct grid correspondence and feature matching is filtered in the grid-based motion statistics judgment. The region features include grey scale, texture, geometry, etc. Thus, these problems encountered by the GMS algorithm are improved if the features in the regions divided by the same image are all distinguishable from other regions, that is, the regions are not similar.

From the above analysis, one of the reasons why the GMS algorithm cannot work well in the case of affine transformations of images is that the grids division does not have affine invariance. Therefore, in this paper, a new adaptive regional motion statistics method (Ad-RMS) is proposed based on the GMS algorithm. Specifically, we use the Maximally Stable Extremal Regions (MSER) algorithm [24], based on region detection by image scale to perform adaptive region division of the image instead of the uniform grid division in the GMS algorithm. And the constraints on the GMS are adjusted in detail to make them more suitable for the algorithms in this paper.

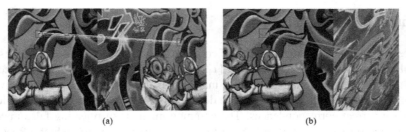

(a)   (b)

Fig. 1. The effect of the GMS algorithm on the affine transformation images. In Fig. 1(a), when the degree of affine transformation is small, the GMS filtered features are matched accurately, as shown in the grid area boxed in red; however, in Fig. 1(b), when the degree of affine transformation is large, the GMS algorithm assumes that the green grid is the correct counterpart, but the actual correct counterpart is the red grid. (Color figure online)

2 Related Works

In this paper, we focus on the improvement of feature matching precision by filtering out incorrect matching and retaining more correct feature point correspondences, and by constructing algorithms that can accommodate feature matching screening of affine transformed image pairs. At the same time, the constructed algorithm can adapt to the feature matching filtering of affine transformed image pairs. Typical feature extraction and description algorithms with some adaptability to the affine transform are SIFT [6], Harris-Affine, Hessian-Affine [7] and ASIFT [8]. The similarity comparison of the obtained feature descriptors in the above session is generally done using the nearest neighbor distance ratio, such as KNN (K-Nearest Neighbor) [9] and FLANN (Fast Library for Approximate Nearest Neighbors) [10], which in turn determine the distance from the measurement space to establish a preliminary correspondence of feature points.

The next step is the removal of incorrect matches, i.e. using local or global consistency constraints to filter the initial correspondence from the feature matching to get the correct correspondence. The most commonly used algorithm for the removal of false matches is based on resampling, represented by the classical method RANSAC [11]. It sets the correspondence algorithm of the feature matches as a parametric geometric relation such as using a fundamental matrix or a homography matrix. Later scholars made a series of improvements to RANSAC, such as LO-RANSAC [12], PROSAC [13], MAGSAC++ [14], and so on. However, this kind of method of rejecting incorrect feature matching is greatly affected by outliers. If the proportion of outliers is relatively large, it is very easy to reject the correct feature matching.

At the same time, some algorithms relax the geometric constraint and combine it with other constraints to achieve a good rejection of mis-matching in the face of affine transformations. For example, in recent years, there are the methods proposed by Jiang et al. [15] to make the corresponding algorithm for feature matching into spatial clustering with outliers. Lee et al. [16] define this type of problem as a Markov random field. Maier et al. [17] propose a guided matching algorithm based on statistical optical flow (GMbSOF). Lipman et al. [18] propose methods such as the Twisted Boundary Algorithm for solving feature point sets. However, the GMS algorithm has simpler constraints, lower computational cost, and better algorithm performance than the above algorithms.

The GMS algorithm divides the regions by a certain number of grids. This method is more general and the division is not affected by the image, but it lacks region information and consistency of the regions. Besides the grid-based region dividing methods, adaptive region dividing methods can also be used. The adaptive region method divides the image based on features such as grey scale, texture and geometry, and the resulting regions are non-intersecting and have distinctly different features. The advantage of the adaptive region division method is the consistency of the regions, i.e. when the images are transformed, the corresponding region can still be detected by this type of division. Traditional algorithms commonly used are the seeded region growing algorithm [19], region splitting and merging algorithm [20], and watershed algorithm [21]. The seeded region growing algorithm requires a homogeneous image pixel feature and a long computation time. The region splitting and merging algorithm is computationally large and region boundaries are easily lost. Compared with the two former algorithms, the watershed algorithm can better preserve the boundaries of regions, and the MSER algorithm [22] implemented based on the watershed idea can extract stable regions in the image, even if the image undergoes various types of transformation, it has better adaptability.

In addition to the above three classical algorithmic concepts, other algorithms can achieve adaptive division of regions, such as detection algorithms based on feature space clustering [23]. There are various methods derived from clustering and numerous application scenarios, but the results of clustering algorithms are greatly influenced by parameters and more factors need to be considered, such as the number of clusters, initial parameters and operational complexity.

3   Method

In this paper, we propose a feature matching filtering algorithm with adaptive regional motion statistics. With the core idea of local support matching of the GMS algorithm, we combine the method of dividing adaptive regions with regional motion statistics to constitute the Ad-RMS algorithm, and the specific algorithm framework diagram is shown in Fig. 2.

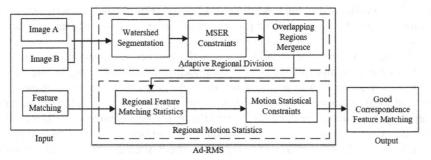

Fig. 2. Framework of our method.

The Fig. 2 shows the basic framework of the Ad-RMS algorithm in this paper. The algorithm is mainly divided into two modules: adaptive region division and regional motion statistics. The grey-scale maps of image A and image B are input to the adaptive regional division module individually. The images are divided into connected regions under different thresholds by the watershed algorithm. And the stable adaptive regions are obtained by the maximum stable extreme value region constraint in the MSER algorithm, and the overlapping parts of the adaptive region are merged to obtain the region division result of the two images. The above division results and feature point matches are input to the regional motion statistics module, where the corresponding feature matches for each region are counted and filtered by the motion statistics constraints to produce the corresponding region and the filtered feature point matches.

3.1 Adaptive Regional Division

This algorithm uses an adaptive regional division method for the input image, using Nister David's modified watershed method to implement the MSER algorithm [24]. The core idea of the watershed approach is to fill the current basin with water at any place and then spread it around until the whole image is submerged, obtaining a connected area at each level as the water level rises.

This is achieved by starting from a point in the image and using the 4-neighborhood lookup to create a set of pixel points related to the grey level threshold of the current point. And during the lookup process, the set of points is manipulated according to the change in the threshold of the lookup point to obtain connected regions with different grey level thresholds. The core process of the watershed algorithm is shown in Algorithm 1.

When Algorithm 1 is finished, the regions under various thresholds can be judged to be maximum stable extreme value regions using Eq. (1), $q(i)$ is the rate of change of region Q_i at threshold i. When it is less than the set maximum rate of change, the connected region is considered to be a maximum stable extreme value region.

$$q(i) = \frac{|Q_i - Q_{i-\text{delta}}|}{|Q_{i-\text{delta}}|} \tag{1}$$

Based on the algorithm's idea and process, it is known that the region of a certain threshold is gradually expanded by smaller regions within the region than its threshold, so the list of regions obtained can be labeled in reverse order, and if a pixel has been labeled, the region containing that pixel has been labeled. The Fig. 3 shows the results of using adaptive region delineation.

Algorithm 1: Watershed division	**Algorithm 2: Regional Motion Statistics**

Algorithm 1: Watershed division

Input: Gray scale image matrix M;
Initialize: region pixel stack C; border pixel heap H; regions R; current = (0,0);

1: C.push(new block())
2: **for** c_i ∈ fourNeighbor(current) **do**
3: │ **if** c_i is accessible **then**
4: │ │ H.push(c_i)
5: │ │ **if** c_i.grayValue < current.grayValue **then**
6: │ │ │ current← c_i; **GOTO** label 2
7: │ │ **end if**
8: │ **end if**
9: **end for**
10: CT ← C. getTopStack(); CT.push(current)
11: h ← H.pop()
12: **if** h is NULL **then**
13: │ exit function
14: **end if**
15: **if** h.grayValue == CT.grayValue **then**
16: │ current ← h; **GOTO** label 3
17: **else**
18: │ CT2 ← C.getSecondTopStack();
19: │ **if** h.grayValue < CT2.grayValue **then**
20: │ │ CT.grayValue ← h.grayValue;
21: │ │ **GOTO** label 3
22: │ **else**
23: │ │ R.push(CT); merge(CT,CT2);
24: │ │ CT ← C.getTopStack(); **GOTO** label 20
25: │ **end if**
26: **end if**
Output: regions R

Algorithm 2: Regional Motion Statistics

Input: the region of two images R_a, R_b;
   the original feature matching m
Initialize: feature matching to each region
   between the two images M_{ij};
   the number of M_{ij} is N_{ij}

1: **for** $i = 0$ to R_a **do**
2: │ $j = 0$, flag=1
3: │ **for** $k = 0$ to R_b **do**
4: │ │ **if** $N_{ik} > N_{ij}$ **then**
5: │ │ │ $j = k$
6: │ │ **end if**
7: │ **end for**
8: │ **for** $t = 0$ to R_a **do**
9: │ │ **if** $N_{tj} > N_{ij}$ **then**
10: │ │ │ flag = 0
11: │ │ │ **break**
12: │ │ **end if**
13: │ **end for**
14: │ **if** $N_{ij} > τ$ and flag == 1 **then**
15: │ │ $goodMatches$.push(M_{ij})
16: │ **end if**
17: **end for**
Output: $goodMatches$

(a)   (b)

Fig. 3. Results of using adaptive regional delineation. Figure 3(a) shows that the region delimitation boundaries are obvious, and one color represents a region and the presence of white undetected regions is identified as an unstable region. Figure 3(b) shows that this method can still delineate the corresponding regions when the image is transformed.

3.2   Regional Motion Statistics

After the adaptive region division in Subsect. 3.1, the filtering of feature matches is carried out using the region motion statistical algorithm after the image has been divided into different regions. The algorithm uses the core idea in the GMS algorithm: the consistency of motion will make other matches.in the same region have similar motion if they are correctly matched. The motion consistency can be represented by the statistical algorithm, where feature points within a region of the image correspond to another image, and will cluster together if the correspondence is correct, and not vice versa.

When filtering feature matches by the motion statistics method, it can be simply assumed that the idea is more reliable when the total number of matches is higher. It is also possible to derive this idea from the following reduction.

Definition: the number of feature points in the left image I_l is L and the number of feature points in the right image I_r is R. The regions to be matched in the two images are P_l and P_r, and the number of feature points contained in both are l and r. Assume that the matching algorithm is accurate, using as $f_l^t = t$.

From this, we deduce that when regions P_l, P_r are the corresponding regions, the probability that the feature points of region P_l corresponding to the nearest neighbor match in region P_r is denoted as p_t, as shown in Eq. (2). And $p_f=(1 - t)r/R$.

$$p_t = p\left(f_l^r|T_l^r\right) = t + (1 - t)\frac{r}{R} \tag{2}$$

The matching of each feature point is independent and the probability of the number of feature points γ_i in the region corresponding to a common region with a feature point can be approximated by a binomial distribution.

$$\gamma_i \sim \begin{cases} B(l, p_t), & \text{the correct region corresponds} \\ B(l, p_f), & \text{the wrong region corresponds} \end{cases} \tag{3}$$

The probability mass function of this binomial distribution can be drawn based on the above equation, as shown in Fig. 4. The values are set to $t = 0.6$ and $r/R = 0.1$. Only when the number of features in the two corresponding regions reaches the threshold, the correct event for the region will occur. By comparing the two plots in Fig. 4, it is confirmed that the greater the distinguishability of the incorrect and correct regional correspondence when there is more feature matching. In turn, this reflects the more reliable constraint on the regional motion statistics at this moment.

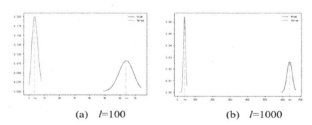

(a) l=100   (b) l=1000

Fig. 4. Corresponding probability mass functions for correct/incorrect regions. Fig. (a) sets $l = 100$ and Fig. (b) sets $l = 1000$. The orange curves are correspondence of the wrong region and the blue curves are correspondence of the correct region. (Color figure online)

The GMS algorithm evaluates the distinction between correct and incorrect region correspondence in the same probability distribution described by P as expressed in

Eq. (4), considering that the larger P is the more significant the distinction. Since P increases as l increases, Eq. (4) is approximated $P \propto \sqrt{l}$. It can be that the more matching points a region contains, the more distinguishable the correct and incorrect matches are.

$$P = \frac{m_t - m_f}{s_t + s_f} = \frac{lp_t - lp_f}{\sqrt{lp_t(1 - p_t)} + \sqrt{lp_f(1 - p_f)}} \propto \sqrt{l} \qquad (4)$$

In implementing the algorithm, the method of region division makes regions covering the same grey scale feature information, so that the correspondence of such regions in an image pair can only be one-to-one. This is different from the GMS algorithm where grid pairs should allow many-to-one. The core algorithm for regional motion statistics is shown in Algorithm 2.

The GMS algorithm is to judge the grid as corresponds to the threshold value of $\tau = \alpha\sqrt{l}$, where the α parameter is empirical and is generally set to 6. However, the regional motion statistics method proposed in this paper does not divide the image uniformly into a certain number. Set the threshold $\tau + \alpha l$, where l is the number of feature matching in the region and α takes values from 0 to 1. The algorithm in this paper sets the empirical value α according to the number of feature matching contained in a region. It is necessary to adopt a suitable threshold design, set the threshold as shown in Eq. (5), where the average number of feature points contained in the grid is called *average_count*. The threshold setting of Eq. (5) is based on the previous conclusion: the more number of feature matches in a region, the more obvious distinction between correct and incorrect regions. In this case, a more relaxed threshold can be set to ensure both the correct rate and feature matching of the large region is not easily filtered. On the contrary, setting strict thresholds for small regions only ensure precision.

$$\tau = \begin{cases} 0.98l \; l \in (0, average\_count/4) \\ 0.85l \; l \in (average\_count/4, 4 * average\_count) \\ 0.6l \; l \in (a * average\_count, +\infty) \end{cases} \qquad (5)$$

4 Experiment

4.1 Evaluation

The algorithm evaluation metric used in this experiment is based on Mikolajczyk [25] using a precision rate evaluation algorithm. Define image A is transformed into image B by the homography matrix H_1, and feature point a in image A transformed by H_1 and its corresponding coordinates of feature point b in image B. If the distance is less than the threshold ε, the correspondence is considered correct, as shown in Eq. (6). In this paper, the threshold value is set to 1.

$$\varepsilon < dist(H_1 a, b) \qquad (6)$$

Building on the idea that evaluation metrics mentioned by Jin [26] should focus on algorithm performance in the downstream task. We also use the precision of calculating the homography matrix after feature matching, which is measured by the precision ratio of the feature matching after the homography matrix transformation.

4.2 Dataset and Input Data

Our algorithm responds to situations where the scene is affine transformed images, mainly using the Graffiti image set from the VGG dataset [25]. This part of image set from the low to a high degree of affine transformation.

In tests of the affine transform images, data from both ASIFT and Harris-Affine feature detection and KNN matching are used as input data for the filtering algorithm. The Ad-RMS algorithm is compared without the use of the false feature matching removal algorithm and the GMS algorithm. The data obtained without using of the false feature matching removal algorithm represents the original matching data that has not been filtered.

Also to measure the performance of the Ad-RMS algorithm in this paper on other datasets, i.e. bikes, boats, leuven. The bikes dataset is blur variation. The boats dataset is rotation with scale variation. The leuven dataset is illumination variation. In this part of the dataset, the common feature extraction algorithms, i.e. SIFT, SURF and ORB, were used as the input data for the algorithm after matching. Using the same three algorithms as above.

4.3 Parameters

By analysing the algorithm processes, the main parameters of this experiment are the *delta* of Eq. (1), the threshold of q(i) (the maximum rate of change of the allowed regions) and the threshold of the percentage of regional features matching set in Eq. (5). Through the above parameter adjustment, the main parameters that have an impact on the results of the algorithm are delta, and α for case 2 in Eq. (5). The results of the influence of the two parameters are shown in Fig. 5.

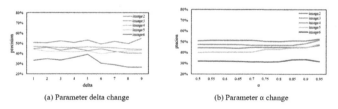

(a) Parameter delta change   (b) Parameter α change

Fig. 5. The main parameters influence

The Fig. 5(a) shows how the algorithm precision varies for the parameter *delta* in the range [1, 9]. The average of precision over the same pair of images is calculated to be close to the accuracy when *delta* is 1. And it can be inferred from the formula that when *delta* is 1, the constraint on the region is smaller and the image region can be preserved as much as possible. Therefore, the parameter of *delta* is generally set to 1.

The Fig. 5(b) shows the variation of the algorithm precision for the threshold α adjustment range of [0.5, 0.95] for the condition 2 in Eq. (5). The higher the threshold value, the higher the precision. But the number of filtered feature matches decreases sharply. And the threshold value of 0.85 is considered to be an appropriate value.

4.4 Comparative Analysis of Results

The Fig. 6 show the results of the initial matching data obtained by the ASIFT and Harris-Affine algorithms under the Graffiti dataset when input to different filtering algorithms. The feature matching results of ASIFT are better input data for the affine transform. The filtering performed on this basis better reflects the performance of the algorithm. In terms of the precision of the algorithm, the Ad-RMS algorithm has improved over the GMS algorithm. And the homography precision of the Ad-RMS algorithm is significantly higher than that of the GMS algorithm in the case of large affine transformations. The Harris-Affine algorithm shows that the GMS and Ad-RMS algorithm can still improve the matching precision of feature matching in the case of poor input data. And the Ad-RMS algorithm in this paper is more effective.

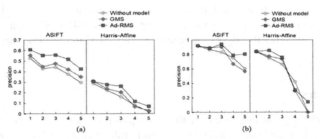

Fig. 6. Experimental comparison of the Graffiti dataset. Where each image contains the variation of the precision rate in Fig. (a) and the variation of the homography precision in Fig. (b).

The Fig. 7 show the comparison results of the different filtering algorithms under the three datasets bikes, boats and leuven. In most experiments, our algorithm is better than the GMS algorithm. However, only when the illuminated scenes, our algorithm is affected by the limitations of the made region division which causes its results to be poor under the SIFT input data. For other input data in this scene, our algorithm is still better than the GMS algorithm.

5   Summary

The advantage of grid-based motion statistics is to correlate the motion consistency of feature matching with its statistical distribution. This allows for faster and more stable rejection of incorrect feature matching. But in the case of large image affine transformations, dividing the image into equal rectangular regions is not good enough for filtering false feature matching. Therefore, this paper proposes the Ad-RMS algorithm based on the GMS algorithm. Our algorithm adaptively divides regions based on image greyscale values, then uses regions that do not intersect each other and have consistent image information for regional motion statistics, improving the adaptability and robustness of filtering feature matching in the case of affine transformation of the images. In a normal scene dataset, the feature matching data obtained by different feature extraction algorithms are filtered, and our algorithm has an advantage over the GMS algorithm in more

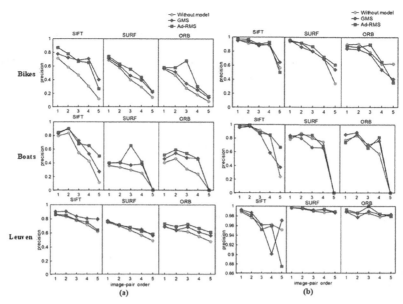

Fig. 7. Test results for other image set. Each image contains the variation of the precision in Fig. (a) and the homography precision in Fig. (b).

scenes. It is also verified that our algorithm provides good support for the application of various methods for multi-view 3D reconstruction such as SLAM, SFM, etc.

Acknowledgements. This work was supported by the National Natural Science Foun-dation of China [grant numbers 61872291, 62172190], and The Innovation & Entre-preneurship Plan of Jiangsu Province (JSSCRC2021532).

References

1. Liu, Q., Xi, X., Zhang, W., Yang, L., Hanajima, N.: Improved image matching algorithm based on LK optical flow and grid motion statistics. Int. J. Comput. Appl. T. **68**(1), 49–57 (2022)
2. Shi, Z., Wang, P., Cao, Q., Ding, C., Luo, T.: Misalignment-eliminated warping image stitching method with grid-based motion statistics matching. Multimed. Tools Appl. **81**(8), 10723–10742 (2022)
3. Lin, W.Y.D., Cheng, M., Lu, J., Yang, H., Do, M.N., Torr, P.: Bilateral functions for global motion modeling. In: Fleet, D., Pajdla, T., Schiele, B., Tuytelaars, T. (eds.) Computer Vision – ECCV 2014. ECCV 2014. Lecture Notes in Computer Science, vol. 8692, pp. 341–356. Springer, Cham (2014). https://doi.org/10.1007/978-3-319-10593-2_23
4. Bian, J.W., Lin, W.Y., Matsushita, Y., Yeung, S.K., Nguyen, T.D., Cheng, M.M.: GMS: grid-based motion statistics for fast, ultra-robust feature correspondence. In: Proceedings of the IEEE Conference on Computer Vision and Pattern Recognition, CVPR 2017, pp. 4181–4190. IEEE, Honolulu (2017)

5. Gan, Y., Zhong, J., Vong, C., Gan, Y., Zhong, J., Vong, C.: A novel copy-move forgery detection algorithm via feature label matching and hierarchical segmentation filtering. Inf. Process. Manag. **59**(1), 102783 (2022)

6. Lowe, D.G.: Distinctive image features from scale-invariant keypoints. Int. J. Comput. Vis. **60**, 91–110 (2004)

7. Mikolajczyk, K., Schmid, C.: Scale & affine invariant interest point detectors. Int. J. Comput. Vis. **60**, 63–86 (2004)

8. Yu, G., Morel, J.M.: ASIFT: an algorithm for fully affine anvariant comparison. Image Process. Line **1**, 11–38 (2011)

9. Altman, N.S.: An introduction to kernel and nearest-neighbor nonparametric regression. Am. Stat. **46**(3), 175–185 (1992)

10. Muja, M., Lowe, D.G.: Fast approximate nearest neighbors with automatic algorithm configuration. In: Proceedings of the Fourth International Conference on Computer Vision Theory and Applications, VISAPP 2009, pp. 331–340. SciTePress, Lisboa (2009)

11. Fischler, M.A., Bolles, R.C.: Random sample consensus: a paradigm for model fitting with applications to image analysis and automated cartography. Commun. ACM **24**(6), 381–395 (1981)

12. Chum, O., Matas, J., Kittler, J.: Locally optimized RANSAC. In: Michaelis, B., Krell, G. (eds.) Pattern Recognition. DAGM 2003. Lecture Notes in Computer Science, vol. 2781, pp. 236–243. Springer, Heidelberg (2003). https://doi.org/10.1007/978-3-540-45243-0_31

13. Chum, O., Matas, J.: Matching with PROSAC-progressive sample consensus. In: Proceedings of Computer Society Conference on Computer Vision and Pattern Recognition. CVPR 2005, pp. 220–226. IEEE, Washington (2005)

14. Barath, D., Noskova, J., Ivashechkin, M., Matas, J.: MAGSAC++, a fast, reliable and accurate robust estimator. In: Proceedings of the IEEE/CVF Conference on Computer Vision and Pattern Recognition. CVPR 2020, pp. 1304–1312. IEEE, Seattle (2020)

15. Jiang, X., Ma, J., Jiang, J., Guo, X.: Robust feature matching using spatial clustering with heavy outliers. IEEE Trans. Image Process. **29**, 736–746 (2019)

16. Lee, S., Lim, J., Suh, I.H.: Progressive feature matching: incremental graph construction and optimization. IEEE Trans. Image Process. **29**, 6992–7005 (2020)

17. Maier, J., Humenberger, M., Murschitz, M., Zendel, O., Vincze, M.: Guided matching based on statistical optical flow for fast and robust correspondence analysis. In: Leibe, B., Matas, J., Sebe, N., Welling, M. (eds.) Computer Vision – ECCV 2016. ECCV 2016. Lecture Notes in Computer Science, vol. 9911, pp. 101–117. Springer, Cham (2016). https://doi.org/10.1007/978-3-319-46478-7_7

18. Lipman, Y., Yagev, S., Poranne, R., Jacobs, D.W., Basri, R.: Feature matching with bounded distortion. ACM Trans. Graph **33**(3), 1–14 (2014)

19. Adams, R., Bischof, L.: Seeded region growing. IEEE Trans. Pattern Anal. Mach. Intell. **16**(6), 641–647 (1994)

20. Li, Y., Li, L.: A split and merge EM algorithm for color image segmentation. In: Proceedings of International Conference on Intelligent Computing and Intelligent Systems, ICIS 2009, pp. 395–399. IEEE, Shanghai (2009)

21. Vincent, L., Soille, P.: Watersheds in digital spaces: an efficient algorithm based on immersion simulations. IEEE Trans. Pattern Anal. Mach. Intell. **13**(6), 583–598 (1991)

22. Matas, J., Chum, O., Urban, M., Pajdla, T.: Robust wide-baseline stereo from maximally stable extremal regions. Image Vis. Comput. **22**(10), 761–767 (2004)

23. Carevic, D., Caelli, T.: Region-based coding of color images using Karhunen-Loeve transform. Graph. Models Image Process. **59**(1), 27–38 (1997)

24. Nistér, D., Stewénius, H.: Linear time maximally stable extremal regions. In: Forsyth, D., Torr, P., Zisserman, A. (eds.) Computer Vision – ECCV 2008. ECCV 2008. Lecture Notes in

Computer Science, vol. 5303, pp. 183–196. Springer, Berlin, Heidelberg (2008). https://doi. org/10.1007/978-3-540-88688-4_14

25. Mikolajczyk, K., Schmid, C.: A performance evaluation of local descriptors. IEEE Trans. Pattern Anal. Mach. Intell. **27**(10), 1615–1630 (2005)

26. Jin, Y., Mishkin, D., Mishchuk, A., Matas, J., Fua, P., Yi, K.M., Trulls, E.: Image matching across wide baselines: from paper to practice. Int. J. Comput. Vis. **129**(2), 517–547 (2021)

3D Reconstruction

Visual Indoor Navigation Using Mobile Augmented Reality

Han Zhang[1], Mengsi Guo[2], Wenqing Zhao[2(✉)], Jin Huang[2(✉)], Ziyao Meng[3],
Ping Lu[4], Liu Sen[2], and Bin Sheng[3(✉)]

[1] Southeast University, Nanjing, China
[2] School of Computer Science and Artificial Intelligence, Wuhan Textile University, Wuhan,
China
[3] Department of Computer Science and Engineering, Shanghai Jiao Tong University, Shanghai,
China
shengbin@cs.sjtu.edu.cn
[4] State Key Laboratory of Mobile Network and Mobile Multimedia Technology, ZTE
Corporation, Shenzhen, China

Abstract. Navigation in complex indoor environments is often difficult, and many
of the current navigation applications on the market are not yet mature enough for
indoor use. To address this issue, this project developed an application based on
Unity's ARCore extension for AR Foundation and Google Cloud Anchor Service,
combined with the real-time database, to identify, record the location of key points
indoors, and to provide self-localization, path planning and navigation functions
for users. The application is divided into two sections: Administrator and User. In
the administrator interface, the device camera scans the environment to record the
posture of key points and the characteristics of the area where they are located,
generates anchor points, and uploads them to the cloud platform database. In
the user interface, the user can choose to download the data, after which the
environmental features scanned by the camera will be matched with the anchor
point features in the database, and the anchor point in the current environment
will be identified and displayed on the screen for the purpose of self-localization,
after the user selects the destination, the path planning algorithm will be invoked
and the planned navigation route will be displayed on the screen.

Keywords: Indoor navigation · Localization · Augmented reality · Mobile

1 Introduction

In complex large indoor scenes, it is often difficult for people to quickly and accurately
find the destination they need to reach. There are two major problems in the indoor navigation services provided by popular navigation software. First, the accuracy of indoor
positioning is insufficient, and the second is that the display of 2D maps for navigation
routes is not intuitive and clear.

In order to achieve the function of navigation, first realize high-precision positioning. For outdoor scenes, we usually use GPS for positioning, but for indoor navigation,

the accuracy of GPS positioning is not ideal due to the blocking of satellite signals by buildings. At present, the popular indoor positioning methods are Bluetooth positioning [1], Wi-Fi [4] positioning etc., but Bluetooth positioning generally requires the installation of multiple devices, and Wi-Fi positioning needs to access a dense network, Both improve accuracy over GPS positioning, but also require more complex infrastructure. Augmented reality (AR) technology [8, 9] achieves positioning by matching the image information collected by the camera with the pre-recorded feature anchor information. This method is accurate in positioning, without the need for redundant hardware facilities, and can intuitively present the positioning information and subsequent navigation routes to the user in a way that is integrated with the environment.

For the display of navigation routes, AR [8] technology is clearer than traditional 2D maps, and the images acquired by the camera can be used to naturally transform the display content with the movement of the user's perspective, guiding the user to the destination.

The project aims to use AR technology to build an Android application in Unity [25] combined with the ARCore [26] extension of Unity's AR Foundation. For the application background administrator can easily add keys and upload them to the cloud platform, so that all users and administrators can share the key path points of the map; For the user to be able to scan the surrounding environment to match.

the visual features in the created map, so as to locate, and the anchor as the starting point of the path, and then independently select the destination, the application will provide the shortest path through the path planning algorithm and display the path in the screen, the user follows the path points displayed one by one, and finally can reach the destination. The overall framework of the system is shown in Fig. 1.

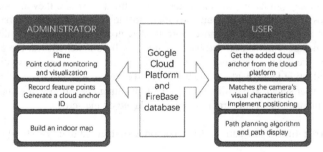

Fig. 1. Overall framework for system implementation.

2   Related Work

2.1   Indoor Navigation System

Due to the blocking of satellite signals by different buildings, it is difficult to construct an indoor navigation system with a solution similar to the outdoor Global Navigation Satellite System (CNSS) that is fully adaptable. Xiao et al. [19] used common objects as references to locate users by detecting static objects in a large indoor space to calculate the smartphone's position that saves a significant amount of cost. There are also many systems that focus on improving indoor localization accuracy using various approaches, Jamil et al. [21] used artificial neural network based learning module and Kalman filter as prediction algorithm for system position estimation, Feng et al. [28] used the extended Kalman filter (EKF) and unscented Kalman filter (UKF) combining the Inertial measurement unit (IMU) and ultrawideband (UWB) to improve the robustness and accuracy of the system, and the accuracy of the indoor navigation system can be improved by training a decision tree that is the data in the true measurement and using the decision tree as a rejection gate in the Kalman filter [29]. Cabral et al. [17] pro-posed an Acoustic Localization System (ALOS) in an indoor architecture system for multiple UAV localization, using ultrasound to calculate the distance between receiver modules. An approach using edge computing [18] was proposed for an indoor navigation system with enhanced vision. By implementing the localization function on hardware devices such as smartphones [16, 19], it can be used in large multi-story indoor areas such as hospitals and shopping plazas for guiding visitors.

Improving the accuracy of indoor localization must be combined with accurate labeled floor plans, which are costly to obtain, and for these problems, some crowdsourcing-based context-aware methods [20] have been proposed for automatic generation of labeled floor plans. Simultaneous localization and mapping (SLAM) is a fundamental technology fast for indoor navigation systems, but the performance of tracking feature points in environments that lack texture such as blank walls is difficult to provide reliable localization, [22] analyzed and compared LiDAR SLAM-based indoor navigation methods, and Nakagawa et al. [23] proposed a method to automatically generate geometric network models for indoor navigation using point clouds that represents the changing indoor environment to improve accuracy, while there are challenges in directly mapping 3D data acquisition to indoor GML coding, Yang et al. [24] proposed a semantic guidance method to reconstruct indoor navigation elements from 3D coloring points.

2.2 Positioning and Navigation Technology

Since GPS signals are affected by the indoor environment and cannot achieve accurate indoor positioning, some indoor positioning techniques have emerged. Satan [1] et al. introduced the development of a Blue-tooth beacon-based indoor navigation system for Android. Considering the range, security, and privacy issues, Singh, Amit, et al. [2] proposed an indoor navigation system using low-energy beacons, and Blue-tooth low-energy was also applied to localize for the visually impaired [3]. Bluetooth technology has the advantages of high security, low cost, and low power consumption, but the Bluetooth devices required for indoor systems are more expensive and are susceptible to interference from noise during positioning. Wi-Fi-based localization [4] approaches connect terminals such as computers and handheld devices together via radio to provide indoor localization techniques. Wang, Fei, et al. [5] proposed a novel deep learning framework that unites Wi-Fi channel state information (CSI) fingerprinting with activity recognition and indoor localization tasks for activity recognition and indoor localization. Poulose et al. [6] used pedestrian dead reckoning (PDR) and Wi-Fi signal received signal strength indication (RSSI) for localization to improve indoor localization accuracy, and Ghantous et al. [15] based on existing Wi-Fi access point indoor localization method, combined with the trilateration method, an augmented reality solution was proposed. But its still requires complex infrastructure. Deep learning-based wireless localization methods [7] allow off-the-shelf Wi-Fi devices such as smartphones to access a map of the environment and estimate the location relative to that map with some utility. Accurate wireless localization is necessary to achieve indoor navigation but its coverage is limited, [27] enhances indoor navigation by augmenting the fusion of advanced ultrawideband localization, monocular simultaneous localization and mapping to enable UAV flight in uncovered areas.

Augmented Reality (AR) technology [8, 9, 10] achieves localization by matching image information captured by a camera with pre-recorded feature anchor information. This method does not require extra hardware facilities and visualizes the positioning information and navigation routes in a way that blends with the environment, using augmented reality to guide people in complex indoor environments [11]. Some augmented reality based applications [12, 13] can illustrate the usefulness of augmented reality technology in various fields. Dosaya et al. [14] proposed a low cost model using augmented reality to place anchor points pro and with-out using GPS technology on the structure, in this method the placed anchor points are ubiquitous throughout the indoor environment to achieve smooth navigation.

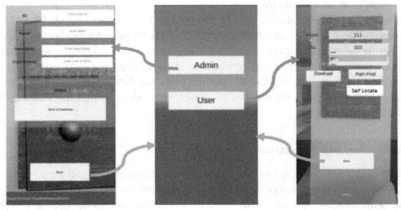

Fig. 2. Overall framework of UI interface(Click on the screen to generate a key point cloud anchor, customize the in-formation entered, the SendToDatabase button is used to upload to Google Cloud and the database, the Back button is used to return to the menu screen. The Download button in the user interface is used to download data from the cloud and database, and the SelfLocate button is used for self-location. To FindPath button for path planning. Back button for returning to the menu screen.)

3   Research Content and Methodology

This project uses the AR Foundation's ARCore extension to visualize the detected point clouds and planes, and use camera scanning to record feature points to form a 3D map of the indoor environment. The overall frame-work of the UI interface is shown in Fig. 2.

3.1   Plane and Point Cloud Detection and Visualization

A process called simultaneous localization and mapping (SLAM) is used to understand the location of the phone relative to its surroundings. Visually distinctive features, called feature points, are detected in the captured camera images. These points are used to calculate the change in its position. The visual information is combined with inertial measurements from the device's IMU to estimate the camera's pose (position and orientation) with respect to the world, enabling the function of motion tracking. Its understanding of the real environment is continuously improved by detecting feature points and planes.

3.2   Indoor Map Construction

By recording feature points by camera scans, we chose areas that are more inclined to have visual features that are easy to distinguish as the location to place anchor points. Then click on the device plane to get the coordinate position of the key point cloud anchor relative to the camera initialized coordinate system by colliding with the detected plane. The device camera is then pointed at the location of the key point that needs to be recorded, and the area around it. While keeping the camera in the center of focus and roughly maintaining the physical distance between the device and the center of focus, the mobile device draws a map of the environment from different perspectives and locations for up to 30 s. Moving around in space while keeping the device camera in the center of attention position, this will capture the visual features of the area of interest from all angles, thus making the parsing more robust.

Initiate hosting requests to the cloud server to upload visual data, device poses and anchor poses to the platform. Create a 3D feature map of the space and return a unique cloud anchor ID for the device's anchor. Cloud Anchor (Cloud Anchor) can achieve multi-user AR interaction, and form an anchor point, first need an SLAM system to provide the position of the camera, scan the real location through the camera, click the screen, and place the anchor point at the intersection of the identified environmental plane, which includes a physical location and a bunch of visual features.

The user first uploads the visual feature information of the anchor point and its surrounding parts to the cloud, which processes and generates the three-dimensional point cloud information, generates the cloud anchor point, and returns its corresponding ID, which can be shared with other users. Other users access the existing cloud anchor point through the ID, ARCore uploads the local visual information to the cloud server, and the cloud server tries to align the received visual information with the three-dimensional point cloud corresponding to the cloud anchor, so as to unify the position and posture of multiple users under the same coordinate system. It can realize the separation of the administrator side and the user side, and support multi-user simultaneous use. A larger area, the characteristics are generally not particularly dense, usually only a cloud anchor is required for storage. The generated cloud anchor ID and the data such as the key point ID, name, neighbor, distance from the neighbor point are used as the data structure of the key point, and uploaded to the database. The information in the database is shown in Fig. 3.

3.3   Map Download and Self-positioning

Download all the key point information from the database to the local, add it to the list, and the cloud anchor ID is the visual feature of the indoor environment map. Click on the self-positioning button, change the app status to "Wait for self-positioning", the phone camera scans the environmental features, iterates over the stored map, converts the cloud anchor ID into a visual feature.

When the user points the device camera at the area of the key point, the cloud server is requested to periodically compare the visual features in the scene with the 3D feature map. Once created, use this location to pin-point the user's position and orientation relative to the key point cloud anchor. The visual features of the key point cloud anchor are queried sequentially every 10 frames to match the visual features.

Gets the name of the current location, implements the positioning, and uses it as the initial point for path planning.

Fig. 3.   Data information in the database.

3.4   Path Planning and Display

The user selects the destination, clicks the Look For button, changes the application status to "Waiting to generate a path", and performs path planning. Common shortest path programming algorithms are Dijkstra[] algorithm and A*[] algorithm, which is a classic problem of graph theory, its purpose is to find the shortest path between nodes in a graph, this method requires both finding the optimal path and minimizing the time complexity and spatial complexity of the algorithm itself in the search process. Dijkstra's algorithm solves the problem of finding the shortest path from a single source with non-negative weights, the algorithm is simple in thinking, can find the shortest path between vertices, and is continuously optimized [32], so in this article, we use the algorithmic to find the shortest path.

The Dijkstra algorithm divides all nodes into two sets: one is the node set that has determined the shortest path, represented by the letter S, and the other node set that has not determined the shortest path, represented by the letter U, when initialized, there is only one source point v in the collection S, the rest of the nodes are in the collection U, if the shortest path from the source point to the node is found during the search process, the node is moved to the collection where the shortest path has been determined. The algorithm terminates until all nodes are added to collection S. In the process of each iteration, the node closest to the source point v is selected from the node set where the shortest path is not determined, and in the process of joining, it is always necessary to ensure that the path length of the source point v to other nodes in the collection S is less than the path length of the source point v to the other nodes in the collection U.

The steps to find the shortest path from source point v to other vertices using the Dijkstra algorithm are as follows:

First, contains only the source point v, i.e. S = {v}, when the set S is initialized, and the distance from v is 0. The set U contains other nodes besides v, i.e. U = {the rest of the node}, if the node u in U is an adjacent point directly connected to v, then node v and u have normal weights, if u is not a directly connected adjacent point of v, then the weights of node v and u are positive infinity.

Second, in the set U, select a node k with the smallest weight directly connected to the source point v, and add k to the set S (the selected weight is the shortest path from v to k).

Third, then use k as the middle point for reconsideration, and modify the distance of each node in U; If the distance from source point v to node u (through node k) is shorter than the original distance (without node k), the distance value of node u is modified, and the distance value from source point v to node u is the distance from source point v to node k plus the weight of node v and node u.

Fourth, repeat steps Step2 and Step3 until all nodes are contained in collection S.

After finding the shortest path, the system scans the environment to match the visual features stored at the key points on the path with the visual features in the camera. Prefab instantiation of key points is displayed in the environment as path points in turn, and the user follows the generated path points one by one, and finally reaches the destination (i.e. the path is displayed on the screen).

4   Experiment

In GPS navigation, although it is possible to receive satellite signals by placing them in a window, in practice, not everywhere is possible. In this paper, we use the technique of AR SLAM for path orientation and compare the above techniques, as shown in Table 1.

Table 1. Technology comparison.

Waypoint v/s technology	GPS	AR SLAM
Waypoint 1:0 m	0 m	0 m
Waypoint 2:0.45 m	0.14 m	0.035 m
Waypoint 3:1.5 m	0.21 m	0.013 m
Waypoint 4:2.05 m	0.17 m	0.011 m
Total variation	0.52 m	0.059 m

From the above table, it is obvious that AR SLAM is accurate because its total variance is 0.059, while the total variance of GPS is 0.52.

In addition, to test the effectiveness of the indoor navigation software, we chose to conduct an experiment on navigation in a real-world scenario. Start by adding a key point process to your environment in administrator mode. As shown in Fig. 4, after entering the administrator interface, click the screen at the location where the key point needs to be added, and then the instantiated key point will appear at the intersection with the identified environment plane, and the window that requires the administrator to enter the KEY point ID, name, adjacent node and path length will pop up. After the relevant information is entered, click the button to upload the data to the cloud server and database together with the cloud anchor ID of the generated key point.

Fig. 4. Administrator interface to add key point cloud anchor.

The user interface function is shown in Fig. 5, we set multiple anchor points near the two bookshelves and in an area between them in the administrator mode, and add information such as their neighbors and path length, where the anchor points near the two bookshelves are set to the start(start) and end(end) respectively, while the rest are the midpoints that show the path. When we enter the user mode, first click the Download Data button to select the download anchor related data from the cloud, and then click the self-positioning button, the system begins to scan the current environment and match the key point data, and quickly successfully locates the cur-rent start3 key point (Fig. 5).

 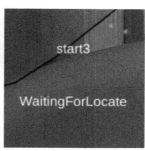

a. Scan the environment   b. Gets the location

Fig. 5. User scans the environment for self-positioning.

After that, select the destination in the Select Endpoint drop-down box, where we selected the endpoint end (Fig. 6).

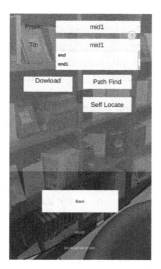

Fig. 6. Drop-down checkbox to select a destination.

The application calculates the shortest path through the path planning algorithm and displays the current shortest path from start to end in the form of instantiation of key points on the screen (Fig. 7).

Fig. 7. The planned shortest path is displayed in the screen.

5   Analysis of Results

In this article, our mobile indoor navigation application based on augmented reality implements functions such as self-positioning, destination selection, planning path, navigation path display, etc. When performing self-positioning operations, if the self-positioning fails or runs slowly, in addition to choosing to restart self-positioning, the user can still successfully complete the navigation function by selecting the location of the starting point and the end point in the drop-down menu of the starting point. In addition, through the use of cloud anchors, the separation of the administrator side and the user side can be realized, and multi-user simultaneous use can be supported.

At present, our indoor navigation system still has some shortcomings, the display of the planning path is not clear enough, and the current implementation of the way to show the path by instantiating the key points is very dependent on the density of the key points. For the user, when the two key points generated are too far apart, it may be difficult to find the location of the next point; For administrators, a large number of key points need to be added manually. In addition, when the application scenario is large, too much key point data will lead to a large amount of data in the background data inventory, which will affect the speed of user download, path planning algorithm, and occupy a large number of storage resources of user devices. A more feasible optimization method is to connect the adjacent key points, and the path displayed in the form of a line will be able to more intuitively guide the user to the destination, and this does not require adding too many intermediate nodes, which requires further research.

Finally, for a system put into practical application, exquisite and beautiful UI interface is very important, in the subsequent optimization, you can consider redesigning the layout of the interface and other content, the initial development version of the gradual iterative packaging into a mature product that can be loved by users.

Acknowledgements. This work was supported in part by the National Natural Science Foundation of China under Grants 62272298, 61872241 and 62077037, in part by Shanghai Municipal Science and Technology Major Project under Grant 2021SHZDZX0102.

References

1. Satan, A.: Bluetooth-based indoor navigation mobile system. In: 2018 19th International Carpathian Control Conference (ICCC). IEEE, pp. 332–337 (2018).
2. Singh, A., Shreshthi, Y., Waghchoure, N., et al.: Indoor navigation system using bluetooth low energy beacons. In: 2018 Fourth International Conference on Computing Communication Control and Automation (ICCUBEA). IEEE, pp. 1–5 (2018)
3. Nagarajan, B., Shanmugam, V., Ananthanarayanan, V., et al.: Localization and indoor navigation for visually impaired using Bluetooth low energy. In: Somani, A.K., Shekhawat, R.S., Mundra, A., Srivastava, S., Verma, V.K. (eds.) Smart Systems and IoT: Innovations in Computing. Smart Innovation, Systems and Technologies, vol. 141, pp. 249-259. Springer, Singapore. https://doi.org/10.1007/978-981-13-8406-6_25
4. Yang, C., Shao, H.R.: Wi-Fi-based indoor positioning. IEEE Commun. Mag. **53**(3), 150–157 (2015)
5. Wang, F., Feng, J., Zhao, Y., et al.: Joint activity recognition and indoor localization with Wi-Fi fingerprints. IEEE Access **7**, 80058–80068 (2019)
6. Poulose, A., Han, D.S.: Indoor localization using PDR with Wi-Fi weighted path loss algorithm. In: 2019 International Conference on Information and Communication Technology Convergence (ICTC). IEEE, pp. 689–693 (2019)
7. Ayyalasomayajula, R., Arun, A., Wu, C., et al.: Deep learning based wireless localization for indoor navigation. In: Proceedings of the 26th Annual International Conference on Mobile Computing and Networking, pp. 1–14 (2020)
8. Joshi, R., Hiwale, A., Birajdar, S., et al.: Indoor navigation with augmented reality. In: Kumar, A., Mozar, S. (eds.) ICCCE 2019. Lecture Notes in Electrical Engineering, vol. 570, pp. 159–165. Springer, Singapore. https://doi.org/10.1007/978-981-13-8715-9_20
9. Saha, J., Pal, T., Mukherjee, D.: Indoor Navigation System using Augmented Reality. Applications of Machine Intelligence in Engineering. CRC Press, pp. 109–115 (2022)
10. Huang, B.C., Hsu, J., Chu, E.T.H., et al.: Arbin: augmented reality based indoor navigation system. Sensors **20**(20), 5890 (2020)
11. Gerstweiler, G.: Guiding people in complex indoor environments using augmented reality. In: 2018 IEEE Conference on Virtual Reality and 3D User Interfaces (VR). IEEE, 801–802 (2018)
12. Rajeev, S., Wan, Q., Yau, K., et al.: Augmented reality-based vision-aid indoor navigation system in GPS denied environment. In: Mobile Multimedia/Image Processing, Security, and Applications 2019. SPIE 2019, vol. 10993, pp. 143–152 (2019)
13. Yoon, C., Louie, R., Ryan, J., et al.: Leveraging augmented reality to create apps for people with visual disabilities: A case study in indoor navigation. In: The 21st International ACM SIGACCESS Conference on Computers and Accessibility, pp. 210–221 (2019)
14. Dosaya, V., Varshney, S., Parameshwarappa, V.K., et al.: A low cost augmented reality system for wide area indoor navigation. In: 2020 International Conference on Decision Aid Sciences and Application (DASA). IEEE, pp. 190–195 (2020)
15. Ghantous, M., Shami, H., Taha, R.: Augmented reality indoor navigation based on Wi-Fi trilateration. Int. J. Eng. Res. Technol. (IJERT) **7**(07), 396–404 (2018)
16. Bao, Q., Papachristou, C., Wolff, F.: An indoor navigation and localization system. In: 2019 IEEE National Aerospace and Electronics Conference (NAECON). IEEE, pp. 533–540 (2019)

17. Cabral, K.M., dos Santos, S.R.B., Nascimento, C.L., et al.: ALOS: Acoustic localization system applied to indoor navigation of UAVs. In: 2019 International Conference on Communications, Signal Processing, and their Applications (ICCSPA). IEEE, pp. 1–6 (2019)
18. Zhao, W., Xu, L., Qi, B., et al.: Vivid: augmenting vision-based indoor navigation system with edge computing. IEEE Access **8**, 42909–42923 (2020)
19. Xiao, A., Chen, R., Li, D., et al.: An indoor positioning system based on static objects in large indoor scenes by using smartphone cameras. Sensors **18**(7), 2229 (2018)
20. Li, T., Han, D., Chen, Y., et al.: IndoorWaze: a crowdsourcing-based context-aware indoor navigation system. IEEE Trans. Wirel. Commun. **19**(8), 5461–5472 (2020)
21. Jamil, F., Iqbal, N., Ahmad, S., et al.: Toward accurate position estimation using learning to prediction algorithm in indoor navigation. Sensors **20**(16), 4410 (2020)
22. Zou, Q., Sun, Q., Chen, L., et al.: A comparative analysis of LiDAR SLAM-based indoor navigation for autonomous vehicles. IEEE Trans. Intell. Transp. Syst. (2021)
23. Nakagawa, M., Nozaki, R.: Geometrical network model generation using point cloud data for indoor navigation. ISPRS Ann. Photogramm. Remote Sens. Spat. Inf. Sci. **4**(4) (2018)
24. Yang, J., Kang, Z., Zeng, L., et al.: Semantics-guided reconstruction of indoor navigation elements from 3D colorized points. ISPRS J. Photogramm. Remote Sens. **173**, 238–261 (2021)
25. Mihajlovna, K.E.: Developing an indoor navigation application in the unity engine (2021)
26. Zhang, X., Yao, X., Zhu, Y., et al.: An ARCore based user centric assistive navigation system for visually impaired people. Appl. Sci. **9**(5), 989 (2019)
27. Tiemann J, Ramsey A, Wietfeld C. Enhanced UAV indoor navigation through SLAM-augmented UWB localization. In: 2018 IEEE International Conference on Communications Workshops (ICC Workshops). IEEE, pp. 1–6 (2018)
28. Feng, D., Wang, C., He, C., et al.: Kalman-filter-based integration of IMU and UWB for high-accuracy indoor positioning and navigation. IEEE Int. Things J. **7**(4), 3133–3146 (2020)
29. Hu, G., Zhang, W., Wan, H., et al.: Improving the heading accuracy in indoor pedestrian navigation based on a decision tree and Kalman filter. Sensors **20**(6), 1578 (2020)
30. Xu, Y., Wen, Z., Zhang, X.: Indoor optimal path planning based on Dijkstra Algorithm. In: International Conference on Materials Engineering and Information Technology Applications (MEITA 2015). Atlantis Press, pp. 309–313 (2015)
31. Bell, M.G.H.: Hyperstar: a multi-path Astar algorithm for risk averse vehicle navigation. Transp. Res. Part B: Methodol. **43**(1), 97–107 (2009)
32. Deshmukh, D., Gonte, B., Khachane, N., et al.: Self-deployable indoor navigation system using Dijkstra's-AES-Apriory Algorithm (2019)

Cost Volume Pyramid Network with Multi-strategies Range Searching for Multi-view Stereo

Shiyu Gao$^{(\boxtimes)}$, Zhaoxin Li$^{(\boxtimes)}$ (ID), and Zhaoqi Wang

Institute of Computing Technology, Chinese Academy of Sciences, Beijing, China
{gaoshiyu,zqwang}@ict.ac.cn, cszli@hotmail.com

Abstract. Multi-view stereo is an important research task in computer vision while still keeping challenging. In recent years, deep learning-based methods have shown superior performance on this task. Cost volume pyramid network-based methods which progressively refine depth map in coarse-to-fine manner, have yielded promising results while consuming less memory. However, these methods fail to take fully consideration of the characteristics of the cost volumes in each stage, leading to adopt similar range search strategies for each cost volume stage. In this work, we present a novel cost volume pyramid based network with different searching strategies for multi-view stereo. By choosing different depth range sampling strategies and applying adaptive unimodal filtering, we are able to obtain more accurate depth estimation in low resolution stages and iteratively upsample depth map to arbitrary resolution. We conducted extensive experiments on both DTU and BlendedMVS datasets, and results show that our method outperforms most state-of-the-art methods. Code is available at: https://github.com/SibylGao/MSCVP-MVSNet.git.

Keywords: Multi-view stereo · 3D reconstruction · Cost volume · Coarse-to-fine

1 Introduction

Multi-view stereo is one of the fundamental computer vision tasks which is widely used in augmented reality, 3D modeling and autonomous driving. In deep learning era, deep CNNs used for cost regularization and extracting representative image features have achieved promising performance. Yao et al. [2] first proposed an end-to-end MVS pipeline that constructs cost volume based on plane sweeping algorithm and aggregates different views by minimizing differential variance. However, this method consumes huge memory because that 3D CNN used for regularization is cubically proportional to image resolution. As a result, subsequent methods like [2,3] downsample high resolution images to regularize cost

---

Supported by National Natural Science Foundation of China Under Grants (Nos. 62172392 and 61702482).

volume in a smaller resolution. To this end, methods designed in coarse-to-fine manner [7–10] are put forward, which iteratively refine depth map based on cost volume pyramid and consume less memory.

However, current coarse-to-fine methods suffer from two limitations. First, the accuracy of the predicted depth map is highly dependent on the initial low-resolution depth map, since it is difficult to correct the depth of ill-posed and occluded pixels in the following narrow range. Second, current coarse-to-fine methods use same searching strategies in refinement stages after gaining initial depth map, which, however, not fully considered the characteristics of the cost volumes in each stage.

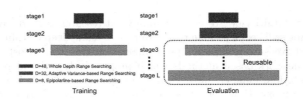

Fig. 1. Our method during training and evaluation.

In this work, we propose a multi-strategies cost volume pyramid multi-view stereo network (MSCVP-MVSNet). Instead of single depth range searching strategy, we utilize multi-dimensional information to calculate depth searching range for each layer. To further utilize the information contained in the cost volume, we introduce unimodal distribution as a training label at second stage during the training process.

Our main contributions can be summarized as follows:

We present multiple depth range searching methods in different stages of pyramid structure, leveraging multi-dimension information. On the second stage, variance-based strategy is applied to exploit previous predicted probabilities for each pixel. For the succeeding refinement stage, we employ parameter-free method to propagate neighboring information to an arbitrary resolution during upsampling.

To further exploit information in cost volume of deep MVS and obtain more accurate predictions in low-resolution stage before refinement, we propose unimodal assumption as a training label in second stage.

Quantitative results show that our method obtains SOTA results on DTU dataset and satisfactory qualitative results on BlendedMVS.

2   Related Work

2.1   Coarse-to-Fine MVS Methods

Deep MVS methods [3,4] based on pipeline of MVSNet [2] build cost volume at the resolution of output images, which usually occupy large memory dealing with high resolution dataset such as DTU [5] or Tanks and Temples [6]. In order to save memory and computation consumption, coarse-to-fine methods [8–10]are put forward. For example, CVP-MVSNet [9] and Cascade-MVSNet [10] build cost volume across the entire depth range in the coarsest resolution, after that, a narrowed sampling range is calculated based on previous depth predictions. Based on these works [9,10], Yu et al. [11] propose AACVP-MVSNet, which introduces attention mechanism to CVP-MVSNet [9] framework. Zhang et al. [12] took into account the visibility between different views based on Cascade-MVSNet [10].

2.2   Depth Sampling Range

Coarse-to-fine pyramid networks uniformly sample the entire depth range in the first stage. In the following stage, they iteratively narrow depth searching range by various strategies. CVP-MVSNet [9] determines the local sampling range around the current depth by back projecting the corresponding pixels along epipolar line in source views. Cas-MVSNet [10] narrows sampling range of each stage by hand-crafted range with specific decay ratio. For the first time, Cheng et al. [16] utilized variance of probability distribution to describe the uncertainty of depth estimation.

All these methods mentioned above employ identical sampling range searching strategies in each stage of three- or four-layer pyramid. In order to leverage both variance and neighbouring contextual information without adding complicated neural network modules, we apply different sampling range calculation strategies in different stage of coarse-to-fine MVS framework.

2.3   Cost Volume

Recently, cost volume is widely used in MVS and stereo matching methods. MVSNet [2] first introduces cost volume for end-to-end MVS pipeline by calculating photometric matching cost of each pixel in different fronto-parallel planes hypothesis. A standard cost volume has a resolution of $H \times W \times D \times F$, where H, W, D, F are height, width, number of plane hypothesis and feature channels, respectively. While cost volume indicates matching cost of each depth hypothesis of each pixel intuitively, it is regularized by 3D UNet to generate an estimated probability value and indirectly supervised as an intermediate layer. In order to integrate multi-scale information of cost volume, Shen et al. [18] proposed cost volume fusion module to obtain better initial disparity map. Like CFNet [18], we further utilize cost volume to obtain better initial depth map before refinement.

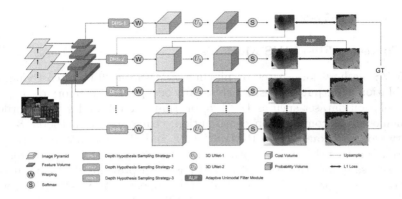

Fig. 2. The network structure of MSCVP-MVSNet.

3   Methods

3.1   Overview

In this section, we introduce our multi-strategies cost volume pyramid network for high-resolution MVS reconstruction in details. The overview of the network is shown in Fig. 2. We assume the input reference image denoted by $I_0 \in \mathbb{R}^{H \times W}$, and source images represented by $\{I_i\}_{i=1}^{N-1}$. To build a pyramidal structure, we downsample input images L times to obtain images pyramid $\{I_i^j\}_{j=1}^L$, where $i \in \{0, 1, \cdots, N\}$. Feature pyramid $\{F_i^j\}_{j=1}^L$ are build by weights-shared feature extraction module.

As shown in Fig. 2, three different sampling strategies and two separated UNets are employed in our framework.

Inspired by GwcNet [14], we build cost volume by group-wise correlation instead of calculating feature volume variance over all views proposed by Yao et al. [2].

3.2   Depth Sampling Range Estimation

As introduced in related work [9,11,18], previous methods employ single strategy in each stage to calculate depth range, which either ignore statistical properties of each pixel or neighbouring information. To solve this, we fuse multi-dimensional information by simply combine different uncertainty estimation strategies in different stage without any additional neural network modules and achieve satisfactory results.

In this section, we present our depth hypothesis sampling strategies in details. As shown in Fig. 1, the number of pyramid layers in our framework is flexible, we train 3 different layers while evaluate with arbitrary number of stages.

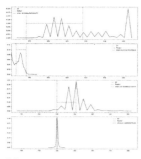

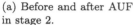

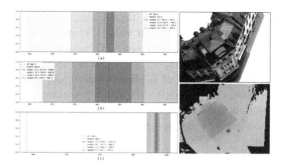

(a) Before and after AUF   (b) Depth searching range in each stage
in stage 2.

Fig. 3. Depth searching range visualization.

In the first stage, we uniformly sampled depth hypothesis over the entire range to obtain a coarsest initial depth map. Due to the large sampling range, we sampled more depth hypothesis ($D^1 = 48$) in this stage.

For second stage, we take advantage of probability distributions to calculate specific depth sampling range of each pixel. Previous methods [13,18] indicate that texture-less and occluded pixels tend to have multiple or wrong matches, as a result, the expectation of the per-pixel distributions can not depict the properties of multimodality and dispersion. To solve this issue, we leverage the variance of the probability distribution as well as adaptive unimodal constraints (Sect. 3.3) to estimate per-pixel uncertainty and reduce local maxima of probabilities. We set the number of depth hypothesis, $D^2 = 32$ in this stage. For stage l, the variance at pixel i is defined as:

$$\hat{V}_i^l = \sum_{j=1}^{D^l} P_{i,j}^l (d_{i,j}^l - \hat{d}_i^l)^2, \tag{1}$$

where $P_{i,j}^l$ is the probability of pixel i at sampled depth j, $d_{i,j}^l$ is the depth of sampled plane j, $\hat{d}_i^l$ is the estimated depth of pixel i at current stage.

Different from UCSNet [16], we adopt the idea of CFNet [18] that originally proposed in stereo matching task, which use learned instead of hand-crafted scale parameters to determine confidence interval:

$$\begin{aligned} d_{max}^{l+1}(i) &= \hat{d}_i^l + \alpha^l \sqrt{\hat{V}_i^l} + \beta^l, \\ d_{min}^{l+1}(i) &= \hat{d}_i^l - \alpha^l \sqrt{\hat{V}_i^l} - \beta^l, \end{aligned} \tag{2}$$

where α^l and β^l are learned parameters in stage l. Same as CFNet [18], we initial α^l and β^l as 0 at the beginning of training. In texture-less regions with multimodal distributions, the variances tend to be large, and adaptive uncertainty range estimation algorithm adjust depth hypothesis to a larger range so as not to miss the truth depth value before small-range refinement. Depth searching ranges in Fig. 3 show the effectiveness of our variance-based method in 2nd stage.

Our first two layers have yielded fair results at the low resolution stage, and the depth values of high-resolution depth maps are obtained via upsampling operation. Specifically, we apply parameters-free method to determine sampling range, which takes advantage of contextual information provided by neighboring pixels along epipolar line [9].

3.3 Supervise on Cost Volume

As shown in Fig. 3, it is hard to correct misestimated depth in refinement stages. To attain better predictions before neighboring-based refinement, we further utilize the information in cost volume at 2nd stage.

Cost volume is defined to reflect the similarity between different views, where the true depth value should have the lowest cost, which means the probability distribution should be unimodal and peaked at the true depth hypothesis under ideal circumstances. Based on this assumption, we construct unimodal distributions as reference distributions which directly constraint on the cost volume to reduce errors introduced by multi-modal distributions. Following [13], we defined reference unimodal distribution as:

$$P^l(i) = softmax(-\frac{|d^l(i) - d^l_{gt}(i)|}{\sigma_i}), \tag{3}$$

where σ_i is variance of reference distribution for pixel i, which controls the sharpness of peak and it is defined as:

$$\sigma^l_i = \alpha^l_c(1 - f^l_i) + \beta^l_c, \tag{4}$$

where f^l_i is confidence value of pixel i in stage l. We estimate confidence value for each pixel by a 2D confidence estimation network. α^l_c and β^l_c are scale factor and lower bound, respectively. Different from [13], we use learned neural network parameters instead of hand-crafted factors to adapt different properties of probability distributions for different datasets. Large σ indicates low confidence of pixel, which usually caused by mismatch in textureless regions.

We leverage stereo focal loss proposed by AcfNet [13] to guide network to generate unimodal distributions for each pixel. The stereo focal loss is defined as:

$$\mathcal{L}_{SF} = \frac{1}{|\mathcal{P}|} \sum_{i \in \mathcal{P}} (\sum_{d=0}^{D-1} (1 - P_i(d))^{-\gamma} \cdot (-P_i(d) \cdot \log \hat{P}_i(d))), \tag{5}$$

where $P_i(d)$ is probability value of reference unimodal distribution at depth d of pixel i, and $\hat{P}_i(d)$ is estimated probability of pixel i at depth d given by our UNet. Instead of simple cross entropy loss, we set $\gamma \geq 0$ to force unimodal guidance to focus on high-confidence regions.

After adaptive unimodal filtering (AUF), some local maximas are eliminated, and the errors in stage 2 are decreased. Figure 3(left) presents depth searching range of our method with and without AUF, respectively. The depth sampling range in 2nd stage indicates that AUF narrows down the sampling range and contributes to a more accurate initial depth map before refinement.

3.4   Loss Function

Our total loss consists of three parts: regression loss in each stage, stereo focal loss and confidence loss, which is denoted as:

$$\mathcal{L} = \lambda_{SF}\mathcal{L}_{SF} + \lambda_C\mathcal{L}_C + \sum_{l=1}^{L}\omega^l\mathcal{L}_{regression}^l \tag{6}$$

where λ_{SF} and λ_C are two factors to balance stereo focal loss and confidence loss on second stage. The confidence loss $\mathcal{L}_C$ is defined as:

$$\mathcal{L}_C = \frac{1}{|\mathcal{P}|}\sum_{i \in \mathcal{P}} -\log f_i \tag{7}$$

We apply negative log-likelihood function as confidence loss to encourage confidence estimation network to predict high confidence values for each pixel.

Regression loss $\mathcal{L}_{regression}^l$ is defined to reflect the difference between the predicted depth map and ground-truth at stage l. We use hand-crafted weight ω at each stage. For stage l, the $L1$ norm is defined as:

$$\mathcal{L}_{regression}^l = \sum_{i \in \mathcal{P}}\|d_i^l - \hat{d}_i^l\|_1 \tag{8}$$

4   Experiment

4.1   Dataset

DTU Dataset. We train and evaluate our network on DTU dataset [5] to obtain quantitative results. DTU dataset [5] consists of 124 large scale of scenes in 49 or 64 different views and 7 different light conditions, with the evaluation reference obtained by a structured light scanner. We use the same splited training and evaluation sets with [3,9,11]. While the original size of evaluation image is 1600×1200, we crop it to 1600×1184 to fit the upsample process.

BlendedMVS. BlendedMVS [22] is a collection of images captured from different views of 113 various scenarios. It contains 17K training samples in low-resolution (768×576) as well as high-resolution (2048×1536). Following the official training and validation list given by the released dataset files, we divided 106 scenes for training and the other 7 for validation in low-resolution Blended-MVS. We train our model on low-resolution BlendedMVS and evaluate on both low-resolution and high-resolution.

Table 1. Quantitative results on DTU

Methods	acc.	comp.	overall
MVSNet [2]	0.396	0.527	0.462
R-MVSNet [3]	0.383	0.452	0.418
MVSCRF [4]	0.371	0.426	0.398
PointMVSNet [7]	0.361	0.421	0.391
CVP-MVSNet [9]	**0.296**	0.406	0.351
AACVP-MVSNet [11]	0.357	0.326	0.341
Vis-MVSNet [12]	0.369	0.361	0.365
USCNet [16]	0.338	0.349	0.344
PVSNet [21]	0.337	0.315	**0.326**
Ours	0.379	**0.278**	0.328

Table 2. Different strategies

Strategies	acc.	comp.	overall
DHS1	0.444	0.361	0.402
DHS1+DHS2	**0.338**	0.349	0.344
DHS1+DHS3	0.404	0.321	0.362
DHS1+DHS2+DHS3	0.389	**0.279**	**0.334**

Note: DHS1 denotes uniformly sampling the whole range, DHS2 denotes variance-based method, and DHS3 back-projects pixels along epipolar line to calculate depth searching range.

4.2   Implementation Details

Training. We train and evaluate our model on DTU dataset and low-resolution BlendedMVS. For first stage, we uniformly sample the whole depth range $[425, 1065]$ with $D^1 = 48$, while for 2nd and 3rd stage, we choose $D^2 = 32$ and $D^3 = 8$, respectively. As the training process with high-resolution inputs is memory and time consuming, we downsample the training set into a size of 320×256, and the coarsest resolution is 40×32 in the first stage. We set hyper-parameters $\lambda_{SF} = 10$, $\lambda_C = 80$ in equation (6) and choose $\omega^1 = 0.5$, $\omega^2 = 1$, $\omega^3 = 2$ to balance $L1$ loss in each stage. As for the reference unimodal distribution, the scale factors are initialized as $\alpha_c^2 = 13$ and $\beta_c^2 = 9$, respectively, based on empirical evidence from [13]. We use 3 different views as inputs and Adam [19] as optimizer in the training stage of the proposed network. We set batch size as 16 and train our model on 2 Nvidia GeForce RTX 3090 for 40 epoches with initial learning rate 0.001 multiplied by 0.5 at 10th, 12th, 14th, 20th epoch.

Evaluation. For DTU dataset, we crop the original images to 1600×1184 for evaluation. We set $L = 5$ for image feature pyramid to maintain a similar size with training stage at the coarsest stage (50×37). Similar to [2,3,9], we choose 5 views in evaluation for fair comparison. The depth sampling numbers D in each stage the same as training process. As for BlendedMVS, we evaluate our proposed method on both low-resolution and high-resolution dataset.

Post processing and Metrics. After estimating the depth map, we fuse all views into a dense point cloud model for each scene. For fair comparison, we follow the common post processing method used by [2,3,9], which is a fusion method provided by Galliani et al. [20]. We run the official evaluation code provided by DTU dataset [5] to obtain quantitative results of mean accuracy (acc.), mean completeness (com.) and overall score (overall). The evaluation results are listed in Table 1.

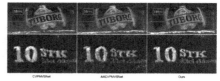

Fig. 4. Reconstruction results on DTU dataset.

4.3   Results on DTU Dataset

We train and evaluate our method on DTU dataset to conduct quantitative results in comparison with other learning based methods. As shown in Table 1, our method achieves state-of-the-art results in overall score, which is comparable to PVSNet [21]. Especially, our method outperforms all methods in Table 1 in terms of completeness. As shown in Fig. 4, We visualize several reconstructed 3D models constructed by CVP-MVSNet [9], AACVP-MVSNet [11] and our proposed method.

4.4   Results on BlendedMVS

As BlendedMVS dataset does not provide any reference point clouds for quantitative evaluation, we conduct the visual comparison with CVP-MVSNet [9]. $L = 3$ in training process, while for evaluation, we set $L = 5$ and $L = 6$ for low and high resolution evaluation sets, respectively. In the same way, we compare our method with CVP-MVSNet [9] and the results of low- and high-resolution dataset are shown in Fig. 5. On high-resolution data sets, the superiority of our method in terms of completeness is even more evident.

4.5   Effectiveness of Multi-strategies

As shown in Table 2, we compare our proposed multi-strategies with other combinations of strategies. For strategy "DHS1", we apply DHS1 and uniformly sample at each stage with handcrafted searching range $[40, 20, 10, 5]$ from 2nd to 5th stage (range 1 corresponds to stage 2). "DHS1+DHS2" and "DHS1+DHS3" perform results of single strategy DHS2 and DHS3 from 2nd to 5th stage, respectively.

As shown in Fig. 3, CVPMVSNet [9] applies DHS3 in each stage and fails to locate an interval which contains true depth value from 2nd to the last stage. Its single and inflexible range searching strategy makes it hard to jump out of the pattern and rectify mismatch in previous stage. We believe that DHS2 which is based on the variance of previous prediction is more accurate and effective to locate true depth value (see (b) range 1 in Fig. 3), but proper scale factors are needed in each specific stage. Our proposed multi-strategies method combines both DHS2 and DHS3, in the second stage, DHS2 gives a reasonable searching range based on previous predicted probabilities, while for the rest stages, DHS3 which is parameter-free provides an effective way to propagate depth of neighboring pixels along epipolar line to an arbitrary resolution during upsampling refinement. Noteworthy, multi-strategies method works better when it combines with two separated UNets (see CVP-MS and CVP-MS-U^2Net in Table 2).

Fig. 5. Reconstruction results on BlendedMVS dataset.

4.6   Ablation Study

In this section, we perform ablation experiments on DTU dataset to validate the effectiveness of each component of our proposed network. Results are shown in Table 3. Below we analyse each component in details.

Table 3. Ablation study on DTU dataset

Methods	Variance	Epipolar line	U^2Net	Auf	acc.	comp.	overall
CVP (baseline)	✗	✓	✗	✗	**0.313**	0.394	0.354
CVP-MS	✓	✓	✗	✗	0.343	0.439	0.391
CVP-U^2Net	✗	✓	✓	✗	0.330	0.379	0.355
CVP-MS-Auf	✓	✓	✗	✓	0.321	0.398	0.360
CVP-MS-U^2Net	✓	✓	✓	✗	0.389	0.279	0.334
Ours	✓	✓	✓	✓	0.379	**0.278**	**0.328**

- **Non-parameter-sharing UNet.** 3D UNet is designed for cost volume regularisation and explore cost volume information in three dimensions. Quantitative results on DTU dataset show that our two parameter-separating UNets gain better results (0.328 vs.0.360) than parameter-sharing UNet. The huge gap indicates that former stages which search in a wider range have different characteristics with refinement stages in the cost volume regularization process.
- **Supervise on cost volume.** While multi-strategies with two non-parameter-sharing UNet framework has achieve promising results (see CVP-MS-U^2Net in Table 3), we obtain even better results when further adding adaptive unimodal filtering (AUF) on 2nd stage. As shown in Fig. 3, the depth sampling range in 2nd stage is narrowed after adding AUF module. Interestingly, quantitative results of CVP-MS-Auf and CVP-MS in Table 3 show that

adaptive unimodal filtering gives a greater boost when parameter-sharing UNet is adopted.

- **Image resolution during training and evaluation.** Table 4 shows that the performance of the model trained with higher resolution input is better than that with lower resolution input. To discover the relationship between pyramid levels and quality of output depth map, we also evaluate our method with different pyramid levels on DTU dataset. As shown in Table 4, coarse-to-fine network with 5 pyramid stages achieves the best overall score.

Table 4. Quantitative results on DTU dataset with different training and evaluation resolution.

Coarsest Res_T	Coarsest Res_E	$Levels_E$	mem. (M)	runtime (s)	acc.	comp.	overall
40 × 32	25 × 18	6	**6809**	2.543	0.372	0.292	0.332
20 × 16	25 × 18	6			0.382	0.324	0.353
40 × 32	50 × 37	5	7863	2.550	0.379	**0.278**	**0.328**
20 × 16	50 × 37	5			0.371	0.328	0.349
40 × 32	100 × 74	4	6935	2.483	0.360	0.311	0.335
20 × 16	100 × 74	4			**0.349**	0.478	0.413
40 × 32	200 × 148	3	7861	**2.366**	0.375	0.530	0.452
20 × 16	200 × 148	3			0.531	1.959	1.245

5 Conclusion

In this paper, we present an efficient deep-learning based cost volume pyramid network for MVS. By combining different sampling range estimation strategies for each stage, we integrate multi-dimensional information without additional neural network modules. Then, we apply adaptive unimodal filters to further improve the low-resolution depth map before refinement. Results on different datasets show the effectiveness and generalisability of our method.

Acknowledgements. This work was supported by National Natural Science Foundation of China under Grants (Nos. 62172392 and 61702482).

References

1. Ji, M., Gall, J., Zheng, H., Liu, Y., Fang, L.: SurfaceNet: an end-to-end 3D neural network for multiview stereopsis. In: Proceedings of the IEEE International Conference on Computer Vision, pp. 2307–2315 (2017)
2. Yao, Y., Luo, Z., Li, S., Fang, T., Quan, L.: MVSNet: depth inference for unstructured multi-view stereo. In: Ferrari, V., Hebert, M., Sminchisescu, C., Weiss, Y. (eds.) ECCV 2018. LNCS, vol. 11212, pp. 785–801. Springer, Cham (2018). https://doi.org/10.1007/978-3-030-01237-3_47

3. Yao, Y., Luo, Z., Li, S., Shen, T., Fang, T., Quan, L.: Recurrent MVSNet for high-resolution multi-view stereo depth inference. In: Proceedings of the IEEE/CVF Conference on Computer Vision and Pattern Recognition, pp. 5525–5534 (2019)

4. Xue, Y., et al.: MVSCRF: learning multi-view stereo with conditional random fields. In: Proceedings of the IEEE/CVF International Conference on Computer Vision, pp. 4312–4321 (2019)

5. Aanas, H., Jensen, R.R., Vogiatzis, G., Tola, E., Dahl, A.B.: Large-scale data for multiple-view stereopsis. Int. J. Comput. Vis. **120**(2), 153–168 (2016)

6. Knapitsch, A., Park, J., Zhou, Q.Y., Koltun, V.: Tanks and temples: benchmarking large-scale scene reconstruction. ACM Trans. Graph. (ToG) **36**(4), 1–13 (2017)

7. Chen, R., Han, S., Xu, J., Su, H.: Point-based multi-view stereo network. In: Proceedings of the IEEE/CVF International Conference on Computer Vision, pp. 1538–1547 (2019)

8. Yu, Z., Gao, S.: Fast-MVSNet: sparse-to-dense multi-view stereo with learned propagation and gauss-newton refinement. In: Proceedings of the IEEE/CVF Conference on Computer Vision and Pattern Recognition, pp. 1949–1958 (2020)

9. Yang, J., Mao, W., Alvarez, J.M., Liu, M.: Cost volume pyramid based depth inference for multi-view stereo. In: Proceedings of the IEEE/CVF Conference on Computer Vision and Pattern Recognition, pp. 4877–4886 (2020)

10. Gu, X., et al.: Cascade cost volume for high-resolution multi-view stereo and stereo matching. In: Proceedings of the IEEE/CVF Conference on Computer Vision and Pattern Recognition, pp. 2495–2504 (2020)

11. Yu, A., et al.: Attention aware cost volume pyramid based multi-view stereo network for 3D reconstruction. ISPRS J. Photogramm. Remote Sens. **175**, 448–460 (2021)

12. Zhang, J., Yao, Y., Li, S., Luo, Z., Fang, T.: Visibility-aware multi-view stereo network. arXiv:2008.07928, August 2020. https://arxiv.org/abs/2008.07928

13. Zhang, Y., et al.: Adaptive unimodal cost volume filtering for deep stereo matching. In: Proceedings of the AAAI Conference on Artificial Intelligence, vol. 34, no. 07, pp. 12926–12934, April 2020

14. Guo, X., Yang, K., Yang, W., Wang, X., Li, H.: Group-wise correlation stereo network. In: Proceedings of the IEEE/CVF Conference on Computer Vision and Pattern Recognition, pp. 3273–3282 (2019)

15. Chang, J. R., Chen, Y.S.: Pyramid stereo matching network. In: Proceedings of the IEEE Conference on Computer Vision and Pattern Recognition, pp. 5410–5418 (2018)

16. Cheng, S., et al.: Deep stereo using adaptive thin volume representation with uncertainty awareness. In: Proceedings of the IEEE/CVF Conference on Computer Vision and Pattern Recognition, pp. 2524–2534 (2020)

17. Mao, Y., et al.: UASNet: uncertainty adaptive sampling network for deep stereo matching. In: Proceedings of the IEEE/CVF International Conference on Computer Vision, pp. 6311–6319 (2021)

18. Shen, Z., Dai, Y., Rao, Z.: CFNet: cascade and fused cost volume for robust stereo matching. In: Proceedings of the IEEE/CVF Conference on Computer Vision and Pattern Recognition, pp. 13906–13915 (2021)

19. Kingma, D.P., Ba, J.: Adam: a method for stochastic optimization. arXiv preprint arXiv:1412.6980 (2014)

20. Galliani, S., Lasinger, K., Schindler, K.: Massively parallel multiview stereopsis by surface normal diffusion. In: Proceedings of the IEEE International Conference on Computer Vision, pp. 873–881 (2015)

21. Xu, Q., Tao, W.: PVSNet: pixelwise visibility-aware multi-view stereo network. arXiv preprint arXiv:2007.07714 (2020)
22. Yao, Y., et al.: BlendedMVS: a large-scale dataset for generalized multi-view stereo networks. In: Proceedings of the IEEE/CVF Conference on Computer Vision and Pattern Recognition, pp. 1790–1799 (2020)

Reconstructing the Surface Mesh Representation for Single Neuron

Ivar Ekeland[1(✉)] and Roger Temam[2]

[1] Princeton University, Princeton, NJ 08544, USA
I.Ekeland@princeton.edu
[2] Université de Paris-Sud, Laboratoire d'Analyse Numérique,
Bâtiment 425, Orsay, France

Abstract. In this paper, we present a pipeline to reconstruct the membrane surface of single neuron. Based on the abstract skeleton described by points with diameter information, a surface mesh representation is generated to approximate the neuronal membrane. The neuron has multi-branches (called neurites) connected together. Using a pushing-forward way, the algorithm computes a series of non-parallel contour lines along the extension direction of each neurite. These contours are self-adaptive to the neurite's cross-sectional shape size and then be connected sequentially to form the surface. The soma is a unique part for the nerve cell but is usually detached to the neurites when reconstructed previously. The algorithm creates a suitable point set and obtains its surface mesh by triangulation, which can be combined with the surface of different neurite branches exactly to get the whole mesh model. Compared with the measurements, experiments show that our method is conducive to reconstruct high quality and density surface for single neuron.

Keywords: Triangle mesh · Surface reconstruction · Neuron

1 Introduction

Individual neuron is the starting point during the exploration of the brain in modern neuroscience [1]. It is recognized to be the basic functional unit of nervous system. The immediate study for single neuron is its morphological structure, which mainly consists of a cell body (also called soma) and the neurites. However, the neuron is hard to be observed directly by human eyes because it is microscale, having tiny geometry, and is semitransparent. Visualizing the neuron is therefore not trivial.

Modern electron microscope can clearly observe biological specimens and save them as images, while state of the art laser microscope even can directly image living brain tissue with super-resolution. Forming the images achieves persistent preservation of neuronal structure. An advanced computer technology, known as neuron tracing [2,3], allows researchers to extract the neuron from microscopy images. The tracing actually converts the image data sets into a much more parsimonious representation of neuronal topology and geometry, described as a

N. Magnenat-Thalmann et al. (Eds.): CGI 2022, LNCS 13443, pp. 170–182, 2022.
https://doi.org/10.1007/978-3-031-23473-6_14

set of sample points. These points with their intrinsic connectivity express the morphology of single neuron as 3D skeleton, i.e. the medial axis lines generated by inward contraction of the neurites.

The skeleton representation keeps a well-behaved abstraction of neuronal structure, but the lack of neurite's thickness brings some limitations. The most drawback is that the skeleton does not provide a continuous surface representation. Nevertheless, the neuron is the cell with smooth and continuous membrane surface. The membrane separates both inside and outside of the neuron, which gives a particular 3D appearance of the nerve cell. Reconstructing the corresponding surface allows perceiving the neurite thickness (and therefore volume) immediately. Here we describe a simple and general method to provide a surface reconstruction pipeline of neuronal membrane. This approach results in a surface mesh representation, which is made up of triangles with high quality and density. For one thing, the reconstruction in this paper can further improve the visual presentation power of the neuron and be a supplement to the ball-and-stick model in some visualization software [4]. For another, the 3D representation may benefit neuroscience researches, such as helping the computational neuroscientists to build brain function model, simulating electrophysiological experiments of voltage dynamics [5] and so on.

The rest of the paper is structured as follows. Section 2 reviews some related works. In Sect. 3, we describe our method in detail and Sect. 4 shows the experimental results. The paper ends with a conclusion.

2   Related Work

Creating an accurate closed surface based on a skeleton is a significant research topic in computer graphics. It has been applied in various modeling domains, such as trees [6–8] and blood vessels [9–11]. The relevant techniques usually are divided into implicit and explicit, corresponding to implicit surface and explicit surface [12].

An implicit surface is defined as an isosurface that all of the points have the same given scalar field, satisfying a specific implicit field function [13]. The implicit surface-based modeling is able to reconstruct surfaces for any objects theoretically. However, its modeling potential is limited by the exact definition of an implicit function, which is closely related the shape of the object. Yet neurons are diverse and it is impossible to find one or several functions to describe all neurons. Additional, an implicit surface needs to be polygonized through isosurface extraction algorithms (like marching cube [14]) for visualizing and rendering. In contrast, the explicit surface is rendered directly in computer's graphic system. The basic explicit element is isolated point. For example, point clouds obtained by 3D scanning can be observed immediately as long as they are input. They are regarded the original data in many cases as well for surface reconstruction [15]. The surface for explicit form is represented by polygonal mesh, which is widely applied to approximate geometric objects in computer graphics.

In recent years, there are a few research studies creating surface meshes from neuronal skeleton. Lasserre et al. [16] used mesh extrusion starting from a fixed soma to obtain a coarse mesh with quadrilateral faces and refined it by subdivision for a detailed mesh. Carcia-Cantero et al. [17] also extruded the meshes of neurites but applied an improved Finite Element Method [18] to the fixed soma, making it more realistic. Abdellah et al. [19] developed a tool named Skin Modifiers for high fidelity neuronal meshes but they even need to complete reconstruction in Blender software.

However, in this current work, the method inputs the skeleton and directly outputs a refined surface mesh with high quality. It is simple and intuitive, without subdivision operation or other software.

3   Method

The main goal of the method presented here is reconstructing a 3D polygonal model that represents the neuronal membrane surface approximately. The first step takes as input a single neuron and divides it into individual neurite branches. The second step computes adaptive contours and connects them sequentially to form the surface mesh for each branch, together with saving the connectivity information that makes for the surface of different branches to be spliced subsequently. As for the soma, the algorithm constructs a suitable point set used to triangulate and the triangulation result can be combined exactly to the branches' surface. The following sections describe above steps in detail.

3.1   Branch Identification

The source of neuronal morphologies is from a public and online database NeuroMorpho.Org [20]. Each digital neuron in this repository is stored in text file with SWC format (Fig. 1(a)), which contains a hierarchical morphology skeleton described as a set of connected sample points (Fig. 1(b)). Each point provides several components, including its sample number (id), type (t), coordinates (x, y, z), local thickness (r) and connectivity information (p) which links this point to a parent one.

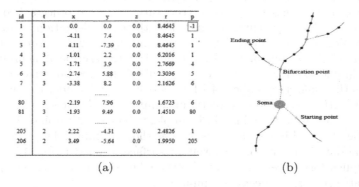

id	t	x	y	z	r	p
1	1	0.0	0.0	0.0	8.4645	-1
2	1	-4.11	7.4	0.0	8.4645	1
3	1	4.11	-7.39	0.0	8.4645	1
4	3	-1.01	2.2	0.0	6.2016	1
5	3	-1.71	3.9	0.0	2.7669	4
6	3	-2.74	5.88	0.0	2.3036	5
7	3	-3.38	8.2	0.0	2.1626	6
......						
80	3	-2.19	7.96	0.0	1.6723	6
81	3	-1.93	9.49	0.0	1.4510	80
......						
205	2	2.22	-4.31	0.0	2.4826	1
206	2	3.49	-5.64	0.0	1.9950	205
......						

(a)   (b)

Fig. 1. a Example of a SWC file. b The skeleton abstraction of single neuron

In Fig. 1(b), the abstract skeleton shows that the neuronal morphology is multi-branches structure. Here a branch is defined as successive samples from a starting point to an ending point. However, the bifurcation point will bring ambiguous during dividing different branches, because there are two child points connected to it in most cases. Thus, the process of branch identification need to determine which child point is the best successor of the bifurcation point.

The selection of the best successor is in light of the potential that brings convenience to the contour connection between the bifurcation point and its child. There are two constraints to be considered. First, the algorithm priorities the largest angle condition. For instance, point **B** in Fig. 2(a) is selected due to $\alpha_1 < \alpha_2$. If the difference value between those two angles is less than a given threshold t, the algorithm considers the selected child whose r-component is closer to the bifurcation point (see point **D** in Fig. 2(b)). Unselected child as a starting point radiates a new branch.

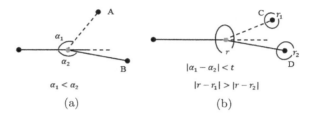

Fig. 2. Selection of the best successor. α and r represent the angle and the local thickness, respectively

Currently the neuronal morphology can be regarded as a collection of individual branches. For convenience of description later, the primary branch is used to signify a branch that includes the bifurcation point, while the secondary branch means a new branch starting from a child point. The concept of those two categories is relatively changing, especially during the process of mesh splicing. That is, a primary branch in one case may be a secondary branch in another case. In addition, the soma branch is used to signify a branch that radiates from the soma.

3.2   Surface Reconstruction of Neurites

This section describes that how to obtain the surface mesh for individual neurite branch and splice different branches, including four subsections in the following.

Resampling. Original sample points of each branch are lower density and cannot meet the requirements of surface reconstruction in this article. This leads to resampling operation for original data. The resampling utilizes the thoughts of interpolation curve fitting. It not only increases the data's density while preserving the old points but also maintains the consistency of neuronal shape before and later.

The Catmull-Rom [21] fitting method is adopted to construct a spline curve for every branch. This method is piecewise fitting, so it is necessary to calculate the interpolation precision (i.e., the number of resampling points) for each two original adjacent points. Assuming that an individual branch is denoted as $\mathbf{B} = \{(P_i, r_i)|i = 1, 2, \ldots, n\}$, where $P_i = (x_i, y_i, z_i)$. The interpolation precision δ between P_i and P_{i+1} is calculated as follows:

$$\delta_{(P_i, P_{i+1})} = \frac{D(P_i, P_{i+1})}{r_{avg}} + k_1, i \in [1, n) \tag{1}$$

In formula 1, $D(P_i, P_{i+1})$ represents the Euclidean distance and r_{avg} represents the average value of r-component of n points on branch $\mathbf{B}$. A control parameter k_1 is used due to the Catmull-Rom method needs to consider end-point condition during piecewise calculation. If P_i is the starting point of $\mathbf{B}$, the value of k_1 equals to number 2; otherwise, it equals to number 1.

Besides, the tangent vector is calculated by the first-order derivative of the fitting curve, determining the contour's orientation of each sampling point.

Contour Generation. The contour characterizes the cross-sectional shape of a neurite branch at some local position. At point P_i, it is defined as an inscribed polygon of the circle whose center is P_i and radius is r_i. The contour's vertices are the sampling points on the circle so that the contour approximates gradually to the circle as the number of vertices growing. This is consistent with the cognition that neurites are tubular branches with circular cross-section. The plane in which the contour lies is stated by $P_i \cdot o_i$, where o_i represents the orientation vector of P_i's contour.

A pushing-forward way is used to calculate the contour for each point on the same branch and every contour is self-adaptive to its own radius and orientation. A contour at point P_i with m_i vertices can be written as $C_i = \{C_i^j | j = 1, 2, \ldots, m_i\}$, where C_i^1 is the first vertex on it. Then, the corresponding vertex C_{i+1}^1 on the contour at P_{i+1} can be obtained according to the following steps (see Fig. 3(a)).

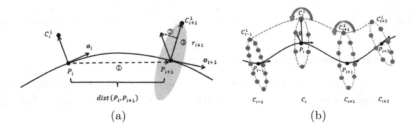

(a)   (b)

Fig. 3. a The computation of the first sample vertex on each contour. b The schematic view of contour generation using the pushing-forward way

Step 1 Vector $\boldsymbol{P_i C_i^1}$ from point P_i to its contour's vertex C_i^1 is translated to point P_{i+1} along the direction of $\boldsymbol{P_i P_{i+1}}$;
Step 2 The vector after translation is projected onto the plane $P_{i+1} \cdot o_{i+1}$;

Step 3 The vector after projection is normalized, and then is multiplied by the radius of point P_{i+1} to obtain the vector $\boldsymbol{P}_{i+1}\boldsymbol{C}_{i+1}^1$.

Similarly, the first vertex of the other contours can be obtained in the same manner. The rest vertices on the same contour can be calculated using the Rodrigues rotation formula [22].

$$\boldsymbol{v}_{rot} = \boldsymbol{v}\cos\theta + (\boldsymbol{k} \times \boldsymbol{v})\sin\theta + \boldsymbol{k}(\boldsymbol{k} \cdot \boldsymbol{v})(1 - \cos\theta) \tag{2}$$

Given a vector $\boldsymbol{v}$ in R^3, formula 2 rotates it with a specific angle θ around a fixed rotation axis $\boldsymbol{k}$ to get a new vector $\boldsymbol{v}_{rot}$. For P_i's contour C_i, the vector $\boldsymbol{P}_i\boldsymbol{C}_i^1$ is regarded as $\boldsymbol{v}$ and C_i's orientation vector $\boldsymbol{o}_i$ is regarded as $\boldsymbol{k}$. The angle θ starts from zero and increases $\frac{2\pi}{m_i}$ for each rotation. Figure 3(b) depicts the pushing-forward way and rotation process.

The contour adheres that the bigger the point's r-component is, the more the number of vertices is. The vertices' number of P_i's contour is calculated as follows:

$$m_i = ceil(\frac{2\pi}{\arccos\frac{1-r_{avg}^2}{2r_i^2}}) + k_2, k_2 = 0, 1 \tag{3}$$

where $ceil()$ is a rounding function to obtain an integer and k_2 is another control parameter to ensure that the number m_i keeps an even all the time.

Adjacent contour may intersect with each other causing self-intersection in the resulting mesh. The algorithm marks and ignores these intersected contours when contour connection. Additionally, each contour keeps track of its center point so that associated information (like orientation) can be accessed in the following stage conveniently.

Contour Connection. The surface of an individual branch is reconstructed by contour connection. This technique sequentially connects the vertices on adjacent contours of a branch. The contours obtained above are non-parallel in 3D space and have different number of vertices. The algorithm converts adjacent contours from non-parallel to parallel state temporarily before connecting them. For adjacent contours C_i and C_{i+1}, the former is projected on to the plane $P_i \cdot o_{i+1}$. Now the connection process between C_i and C_{i+1} is converted to C_{i_pro} and C_{i+1}.

The connection here belongs to one-to-one case [23], which needs to select a vertex on adjacent contours respectively as initial condition for starting the generation process of mesh triangle. Traditional method selects arbitrary vertex on one contour and uses "shortest distance" principle to select the other on another contour [24]. They may make mistakes for 3D contours (Fig. 4). In contrast, our pushing-forward way to calculate contours makes the 1–1 correspondence among contour's first vertex, avoiding the potential errors.

The first vertex $C_{i\_pro}^1$ on contour C_{i_pro} and C_{i+1}^1 on contour C_{i+1} can be regarded as the initial condition directly for constructing the first triangular

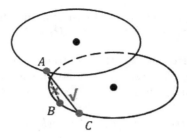

Fig. 4. Point a should correspond to point C, but may to point B

patch. There are two choices to select the third vertex of this triangle. The "minimum included-angle" criterion is used to determine whether the third vertex is $C^2_{i\_pro}$ or C^2_{i+1}. If the included angle formed by $C^1_{i\_pro}C^2_{i+1}$ and P_iP_{i+1} is smaller than the angle formed by $C^2_{i\_pro}C^1_{i+1}$ and P_iP_{i+1}, the third vertex is C^2_{i+1}; otherwise, it is $C^2_{i\_pro}$. Then, the vertices $C^1_{i\_pro}$ and C^2_{i+1} or $C^2_{i\_pro}$ and C^1_{i+1} are regarded as new initial condition to construct the next triangular patch. The local surface mesh between two contours is reconstructed by traversing the vertices in the same winding order and connecting them. Finally, the vertex coordinates of the projected contour C_{i_pro} are replaced back to the coordinates of the contour C_i correspondingly.

Following the same procedure, the algorithm processes all of the adaptive contours in sequence to complete the surface reconstruction for individual branch.

Mesh Splicing. The transition surface between different branches is formed by mesh splicing. But the surface of a secondary branch may intersect with the surface of the corresponding primary branch near the bifurcation area (Fig. 5(a)). This problem is handled before the real surface generation of the secondary branch. If any vertex of a contour of the secondary branch is situated in the

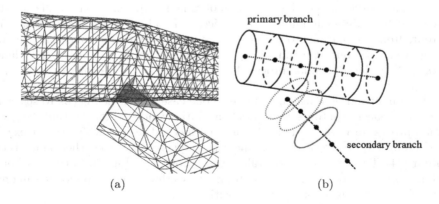

(a)   (b)

Fig. 5. Preprocessing intersection. **a** Mesh intersection. **b** Excluding dashed contours

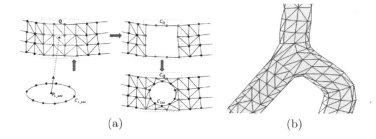

(a)   (b)

Fig. 6. a Splicing area determination. **b** Splicing example

volume of the primary branch, the algorithm does not deal with this contour when performing contour connection for the secondary branch (Fig. 5(b)).

The algorithm selects from the surface of the primary branch a suitable area $\mathbf{Q}$, which orients toward to the starting point's contour of the secondary branch. As shown in Fig. 6(a), a ray is emitted from the starting point P_{1_sec} of the secondary branch to the bifurcation point. Along the ray path, there exists some intersection points on the surface of the primary branch. The triangle where the closest intersection to point P_{1_sec} is marked as target. The algorithm finds other triangles around the target to form the area $\mathbf{Q}$. The splicing in this part is hence to form the transition mesh between the border of $\mathbf{Q}$ (denoted as $C_{\mathbf{Q}}$) and the contour of P_{1_sec} (denoted as C_{1_sec}). The distance from $C_{\mathbf{Q}}$ to C_{1_sec} may be so large that directly connecting them may cause lower quality mesh. Therefore, the algorithm inserts some middle contours between $C_{\mathbf{Q}}$ to C_{1_sec}.

To begin with, the algorithm determines a middle contour for locating, denoted as C_{loc} whose center P_{loc} and orientation $\mathbf{o}_{loc}$ are same with the barycenter and normal of the marked triangle. The center of each middle contour is positioned on the line from P_{loc} to P_{1_sec}, and the vertices are obtained by performing vector operations (such as projection, multiplication) for C_{1_sec}'s vertices. Secondly, the algorithm computes the distance of each pair of vertices on contours C_{loc} and C_{1_sec} separately and records the minimum value. This value is used to make modulus operation with E_{ave} to get the number of middle contours (denoted as N_{mids}). The E_{ave} represents an average edge-length of the polygon $C_{\mathbf{Q}}$. The plane in which each middle contour lies is represented by $P_t \cdot \mathbf{o}_t$, where P_t is this contour's center ($P_t = P_{t-1} + \frac{1}{N_{mids}} \cdot |\boldsymbol{P}_{loc}\boldsymbol{P}_{1\_sec}|$) and $\mathbf{o}_t$ is the orientation vector ($\mathbf{o}_t = \frac{\mathbf{o}_{t-1} + \boldsymbol{P}_{loc}\boldsymbol{P}_{1\_sec}}{2}$). The parameter t is from 0 to $N_{mids} - 1$ and when $t = 0$, $P_0 = P_{loc}$, $\mathbf{o}_0 = \mathbf{o}_{loc}$. Finally, $C_{\mathbf{Q}}$ and those middle contours as well as C_{1_sec} are connected to each other based on the contour connection algorithm described in previous subsection. Figure 6(b) gives an example of mesh splicing between two branches.

3.3   Surface Reconstruction of the Soma

The soma is only a point in original SWC data, without other more detailed information to describe its geometry. For generating its surface, the solution presented here constructs a suitable point set to be the input of Delaunay triangulation.

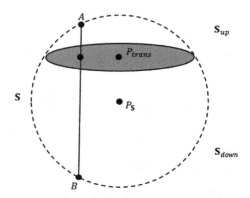

Fig. 7. Both A and B have the same projection on the plane in which C_{trans} lies. Point A is removed because of $A \in \mathbf{S}_{up}$

In the beginning, a collection of discrete points sampled uniformly on a sphere is as the initial point set, denoted as $\mathbf{S}$ with its center $P_\mathbf{s}$. For a soma branch, the first contour C_{1_sec} and its orientation vector $\boldsymbol{o}_{1\_sec}$ as well as center point P_{1_sec} are known. A copy (denoted as C_{trans} with its center P_{trans}) of contour C_{1_sec} is translated along the direction of vector $\boldsymbol{P}_{1\_sec}\boldsymbol{P}_\mathbf{S}$ until the copy is equivalent to a small circle on the sphere. The plane in which the C_{trans} lies divides $\mathbf{S}$ into two subsets ($\mathbf{S}_{up}$ and $\mathbf{S}_{down}$). Then, the algorithm removes from $\mathbf{S}$ the points that belong to $\mathbf{S}_{up}$ (Fig. 7) and inserts to $\mathbf{S}$ the points of the copy.

The planes in which the translated copies of different soma branches lies may lead to intersection. The algorithm removes the vertices in $\mathbf{S}_{up}$ of them respectively. After that, the algorithm removes the vertices after projection that belong to the common area formed by the intersected copies and inserts the remaining vertices.

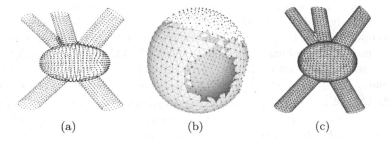

(a)   (b)   (c)

Fig. 8. The basic idea for updating the $\mathbf{S}$ set and the triangulation

For achieving a better appearance after triangulation, point interpolation is used to add extra points between the vertices of the first contour of each soma branch and the vertices of its translated copy. Finally, the vertices of every soma branch's first contour and those extra points are inserted to update the $\mathbf{S}$ set (Fig. 8(a)). Furthermore, the vertices of the first contours and of their copies have a new attribute to signify that they are boundary points. During Triangulation, no triangles are formed inside the area enclosed by the boundary points (Fig. 8(b)). Figure 8(c) shows the triangulation result, which can be merge exactly into the surface mesh of the branches.

4   Experiments and Results

The experiments are implemented by C++ language in this paper and the results are exported as OBJ format to visualize and render through a famous visualization software MeshLab [25]. Figure 9 shows part of a neurite branch, from the discrete points to its surface mesh representation, including the original points in (a), the spline curve in (b), the resampling in (c) and their adaptive contours in (d) as well as the surface mesh in (e).

Figure 10 shows the whole reconstructions of three neurons, which belong to the brain stem of the mouse. We evaluate the quality and validity of the reconstructed mesh through comparing with the provided measurement information. The measurements from NeuroMorpho.Org are the Soma Surface, the Total Surface and the Total Volume. The comparison results are listed in Table 1. It is obvious that there are some errors between our computations and the measurements. As approximated representations, the mesh model allows these errors. But performing some extra-processing operations like smooth on the mesh may help to improve and reduce these errors probably.

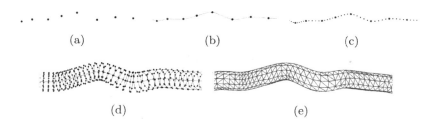

Fig. 9. Surface reconstruction of a neurite branch

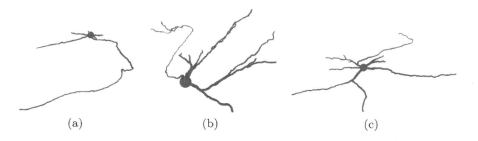

Fig. 10. Examples. a NMO_45929. b NMO_45928. c NMO_45927

Table 1. Comparing with the measurements. M (measurement); O (ours); E (error)

ID	Soma surface			Total surface			Total volume		
	M	O	E	M	O	E	M	O	E
NMO_45927	899.92	849.44	5.61%	8310.37	8766.53	5.49%	6398.93	7211.06	12.69%
NMO_45928	1287.75	1246.71	3.18%	13449.30	13299.55	1.11%	10517.60	11142.51	5.94%
NMO_45929	1256.04	1207.07	3.90%	8659.32	9379.83	8.32%	8080.25	8923.37	10.43%
Average	–	–	4.23%	–	–	4.97%	–	–	9.69%

5   Conclusion

In this paper, we have proposed a surface reconstruction pipeline to generate a mesh representation, which approximates the membrane of single neuron. The method converts the discrete points with radius and position information into a manifold mesh model with high density and good quality. For one thing, considering the differences of each points, our method uses a pushing-forward way to calculate adaptive contours for those points so that simplifying the branch's mesh generation based on contour connection. However, the splicing does not involve the uncommon case where there are more than two children point at the bifurcation point. For another, the surface reconstruction for complex topology near the soma is solved to a certain extent. This is accomplished by constructing a suitable point set and then performing the 3D triangulation directly. Nevertheless, the construction relies on the assumption that the soma is a sphere. In fact, the real shape of the soma is diverse, like star, cone or pear, etc. Additionally, original SWC data lacks detailed information about the soma. As a result, how to represent the soma precisely is a challenge task all the time.

When reviewing relevant literatures, we found that the convolution surfaces have great potential for modelling objects with complex geometries and are well suited to surface reconstruction of neuronal soma consequently. But we need to solve the problem that the convolution surface are not easily control as a kind of implicit surface. Even if it solved, we still have to consider how the convolution surface merges with the surface mesh of neurites. All these questions are the main directions in our future work.

References

1. Bear, M.F., Connors, B.W., Paradiso, M.A.: Neuroscience: Exploring the Brain, 4th edn. Wolters Kluwer (2015). https://doi.org/10.1007/BF02234670
2. Merjering, E.: Neuron tracing in perspective. J. Cytimetry Part A **77**(7), 693–704 (2010). https://doi.org/10.1002/cyto.a.20895
3. Donohue, D.E., Ascoli, G.A.: Automated reconstruction of neuronal morphology: an overview. J. Brain Res. Rev. **67**, 94–102 (2010). https://doi.org/10.1016/j.brainresrev.2010.11.003
4. Peng, H.C., Bria, A., Zhou, Z., Iannello, G., Long, F.H.: Extensible visualization and analysis for multidimensional images using Vaa3D. J. Nat. Protoc. **9**(1), 193–208 (2014). https://doi.org/10.1038/nprot.2014.011

5. Glesson, P., Steuber, V., Sliver, R.A.: neuroConstruct: a tool for modeling networks of neurons in 3D space. J. Neuron **54**(2), 219–235 (2007). https://doi.org/10.1016/j.neuron.2007.03.025

6. Livny, Y., Yan, F.L., Olson, M., Zhang, H., Chen, B.Q., EI-Sana J.: Automatic reconstruction of tree skeletal structures from point clouds. J. ACM Trans. Graph. **29**(6), 1–8 (2010). https://doi.org/10.1145/1882261.1866177

7. Zhu, X.Q., Guo, X.K., Jin, X.G.: Efficient polygonization of tree trunks modeled by convolution surfaces. J. Sci. China Inf. Sci. **56**, 1–12 (2013). https://doi.org/10.1007/s11432-013-4790-0

8. Xie, K., Yan, F.L., Sharf, A., Oliver, D., Huang, H., Chen, B.Q.: Tree modeling with real tree-parts examples. J. IEEE Trans. Vis. Comput. Graph. **22**(12), 2608–2618 (2016). https://doi.org/10.1109/TVCG.2015.2513409

9. Luboz, V., et al.: A segmentation and reconstruction technique for 3D vascular structures. In: Duncan, J.S., Gerig, G. (eds.) MICCAI 2005. LNCS, vol. 3749, pp. 43–50. Springer, Heidelberg (2005). https://doi.org/10.1007/11566465_6

10. Wu, X.L., Luoz, V., Krissian, K., Cotin, S., Dawson, S.: Segmentation and reconstruction of vascular structures for 3D real-time simulation. J. Med. Image. Anal. **15**(1), 22-34 (2015). https://doi.org/10.1016/j.media.2010.06.006

11. Yu, S., Wu, S.B., Zhang, Z.C., Chen, Y.L., Xie, Y.Q.: Explicit vascular reconstruction based on adjacent vector projection. J. Bioeng. Bugs **7**, 365–371 (2016). https://doi.org/10.1080/21655979.2016.1226667

12. De-Araújo, B.R., Lopes, D.S., Jepp, P., Jorge, J.A., Wyvill, B.: An survey on implicit surface polygonization. J. ACM Comput. Surv. **47**(4), 1–39 (2015). https://doi.org/10.1145/2732197

13. Wyvill, B., Wyvill, G.: Field functions for implicit surfaces. J. Vis. Comput. **5**(1), 75–82 (1989). https://doi.org/10.1007/BF01901483

14. Newman, T.S., Yi, H.: A survey of the marching cubes algorithm. J. Comput. Graph. **30**(5), 854–879 (2006). https://doi.org/10.1016/j.cag.2006.07.021

15. Yin, K.X., Huang, H., Zhang, H., Gong, M.L., Cohen-Or, D., Chen, B.Q.: Morfit: interactive surface reconstruction from incomplete point clouds with curve-driven topology and geometry control. J. ACM Trans. Graph. **33**(6) (2014). https://doi.org/10.1145/2661229.2661241

16. Lasserre, S., Hernando, J., Hill, S., Schümann, F., de Miguel Anasagati, P., Jaoudé, G.A., Markram, H.: A neuron membrane mesh representation for visualization of electrophysiological simulations. J. IEEE Trans. Vis. Comput. Graph. **18**(2), 214–227(2011). https://doi.org/10.1109/TVCG.2011.55

17. Carcia-Cantero, J.J., Brito, J.P., Mata, S., Pastor, L.: NeuroTessMesh: a tool for the generation and visualization of neuron meshes and adaptive on-the-fly refinement. J. Front. Neuroinform. **11** (2017). https://doi.org/10.3389/fninf.2017.00038

18. Brito, J.P., Mata, S., Bayona, S., Pastor, L., DeFelipe, J., Benavides-Piccione, R.: Neuronize: a tool for building realistic neuronal cell morphologies. J. Front. Neuroanat. **7**(15) (2013). https://doi.org/10.3389/fnana.2013.00015

19. Abdellah, M., Favreau, C., Hernando, J., Lapere, S., Schürmann, F.: Generating high fidelity surface meshes of neocortical neuronss using Skin Modifiers. In: Tam, G.K.L., Roberts, J.C. (eds.) Computer Graphics & Visual Computing(CGVC) 2019 (2019). https://doi.org/10.2312/cgvc.20191257

20. Ascoli, G.A., Donohue, D.E., Halavi, M.: NeuroMorpho.Org: a central resource for neuronal morphologies. J. Neurosci. **27**(35), 9247–9251 (2007). https://doi.org/10.1523/jneurosci.2055-07.2007

21. Eyiyurekli, M., Breen, D.E.: Localized editing of Catmull-rom splines. J. Comput. Aided Des. Appl. **6**(3), 307–316 (2009). https://doi.org/10.3722/cadaps.2009.307-316

22. Liang, K.K.: Efficient conversion from rotating matrix to rotation axis and angle by extending Rodrigues' formula. J. Comput. Sci. (2018). https://doi.org/10.48550/arXiv.1810.02999

23. He, J.G.: The correspondence and branching problem in medical contour reconstruction. In: 2008 IEEE International Conference on Systems, Man and Cybernetics, pp. 1591–1595. IEEE (2008). https://doi.org/10.1109/ICSMC.2008.4811514

24. Ekoule, A.B., Peyrin, F.C., Odet, C.L.: A triangulation algorithm from arbitrary shaped multiple planar contours. J. ACM Trans. Graph. **10**(2), 182–199 (1991). https://doi.org/10.1145/108360.108363

25. Cignoni, P, Callieri, M, Corsini, M, Dellepiane, M, Ganovelli, F, Ranzuglia, G.: MeshLab: an open-source mesh processing tool. In: Eurographics Italian Chapter Conference, vol. 2008, pp. 129–136 (2008). https://doi.org/10.2312/LocalChapterEvents/ItalChap/ItalianChapConf2008/129-136

WEmap: Weakness-Enhancement Mapping for 3D Reconstruction with Sparse Image Sequences

Kun Zhang[1], Chunying Song[1], Jingzhao Wang[1], Kai Wang[1(✉)], and Nan Yun[2]

[1] College of Computer Science, Nankai University, Tianjin, China
wangk@nankai.edu.cn
[2] Tianjin Zero Carbon Co., Ltd., Tianjin, China

Abstract. Previous studies assume that a dense image sequence can be used for 3D reconstruction because the images are easily captured by mobile devices. However, mobile devices are not applicable in some cases, such as smart factories, which require real-time monitoring and site safety. Therefore, conducting 3D reconstruction with sparse image sequences is important to reduce the number of used devices, and thus, lower the cost of image acquisition. In this study, we propose weakness-enhancement mapping (WEmap) to improve the results of 3D reconstruction based on sparse image sequences. After the initial reconstruction, the contribution of each image is evaluated by mapping the 3D point cloud to 2D images. The low-contribution images and corresponding matching images are weighted to enhance the weaknesses of the initial reconstruction. To the best of our knowledge, this is the first study on 3D reconstruction with sparse image sequences. Experimental results on the sparse DTU [1] and sparse Tanks & Temples [3] datasets demonstrate that WEmap can effectively enhance a reconstructed structure.

Keywords: 3D reconstruction · Monocular camera · Sparse image sequence

1 Introduction

3D scenario reconstruction is gradually being used in fields such as autonomous driving [22], industrial manufacturing [17] and medicine [4]. Ali et al. [2] utilized 3D reconstruction for the diagnosis of glaucoma. An efficient technique [5] for liver surface reconstruction has been proposed, which can assist surgeons to visualize liver surface more efficiently with better depth perception. Depending on the type of input sample, there are different reconstruction methods, such as monocular camera-based [15], binocular camera-based [23], and RGBD image-based methods [20]. Owing to its low cost and fewer restrictions on application scenarios, the monocular camera-based method has been the most widely used method for 3D reconstruction, which only requires RGB images without any depth information.

The basic steps for 3D reconstruction include feature extraction, feature matching, camera pose estimation, sparse point cloud reconstruction, and point

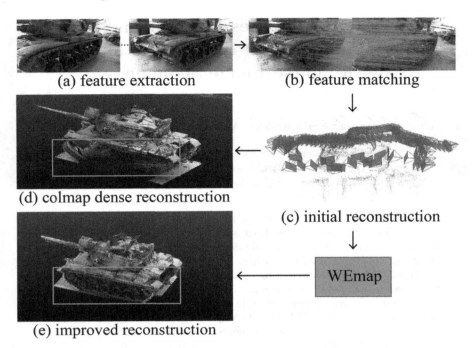

(a) feature extraction   (b) feature matching

(d) colmap dense reconstruction

(c) initial reconstruction

(e) improved reconstruction

Fig. 1. 3D reconstruction results of colmap (d) and our WEmap (e) using the sparse image sequence sampled from the Tanks & Temples dataset. As can be seen from the region in the green bounding box, the colmap loses some structural information, whereas WEmap can retain this information.

cloud densification. Previous research [7,8] focused on the development of each step, assuming that a dense image sequence can be easily captured by mobile devices for 3D reconstruction. However, because of real-time monitoring requirements and site safety considerations, mobile devices are not allowed in some scenarios, such as smart factories. Thus, the cameras must be set up at some fixed points to support 3D reconstruction. Obviously, conducting 3D reconstruction from dense image sequences requires numerous fixed cameras [13], which is difficult to implement in practice owing to the high setup and maintenance costs of these devices.

As an alternative, conducting 3D reconstruction from sparse image sequences requires fewer devices, thus lowering the cost. However, the performance of existing methods decreases significantly with increasing image sequence sparsity. For example, among open-source monocular 3D reconstruction methods [10,21], colmap [18], proposed by Schonberger et al. in 2016, is the most popular method currently available because it provides the fastest speed and highest accuracy on dense image sequences. Moreover, it does not require prior camera information, such as focal length. As shown in Fig. 1(d), when we apply colmap on a sparse image sequence, the result is not satisfactory, and some structural information is lost.

To improve the 3D reconstruction using sparse image sequences, we propose weakness-enhancement mapping (WEmap). After the initial reconstruction, an enhanced subset of the original images is dynamically determined based on the correspondence between 3D points in the point cloud and 2D points in the image, which correspond to the weak regions in the initial point cloud. Then, the 3D reconstruction is performed once again, where the weights of the images in the enhanced set are increased to compensate for the weakness in the initial point cloud to obtain a more complete point cloud structure. Using this method, we can use fewer images to achieve a reconstruction effect similar to that achieved using dense images. As shown in Fig. 1, compared to the result obtained by colmap (d), WEmap can maintain a more complete structure (e).

Our contributions are summarized as follows:

1) We introduce a new task for the monocular camera-based 3D reconstruction, which compensates for the restrictions on using mobile devices in certain applications. To the best of our knowledge, this is the first study on 3D reconstruction from sparse image sequences.
2) We propose WEmap to improve the 3D reconstruction using sparse image sequences, which can dynamically compensate for the lost structure by considering the contribution of each image.
3) Experimental results on the DTU and the Tanks & Temples datasets demonstrate that the proposed WEmap can enhance the reconstructed structure completeness.

2   Related Work

At present, 3D reconstruction methods can be divided into traditional [16,18] and deep learning-based [6,14,24] methods. Deep learning-based methods utilize the concept of cost volume for depth estimation, which uses the initial matching performed by traditional methods as input. Traditional methods utilize the principle of multi-visual geometry for 3D reconstruction from motion, which calculates 3D information from 2D images. Here, we briefly review these two methods.

3D Reconstruction Based on Deep Learning. Deep learning-based 3D reconstruction methods have gained popularity; however, they are still not ideal for practical applications. For example, MVSNet [24] takes a reference image and multiple source images as input, utilizing the concept of cost volume to predict the depth information for the reconstruction of the 3D point cloud. FAST MVS-Net [25], USCNet [6], and cascaded-MVSNet [12] improve the performance of MVSNet [24] to achieve better reconstruction results. However, when using MVS-Net and its variants to reconstruct scenarios, processing by traditional methods is required for image undistortion, which includes the matching of image pairs and internal/external parameter estimation of cameras. Moreover, the training process of the model is supervised, thus requiring additional annotation information, which inevitably introduces domain migration issues.

3D Reconstruction Based on Traditional Methods. Structure from motion (SFM) is a popular algorithm using monocular cameras. To date, the incremental SFM algorithm is the most widely used for unordered images, and the mainstream frameworks for 3D reconstruction include colmap [18], bundler [21], pmvs [10], and open multiple view geometry (openMVG) [16]. They follow the same reconstruction process, including feature extraction, feature matching, camera pose estimation, sparse point cloud reconstruction, and point cloud densification. Bundler [21] is one of the earliest SFM frameworks proposed by Snavely et al., and its results can be processed using pmvs [10] to obtain a dense point cloud. However, bundler needs the camera parameters contained in the image exif information. Compared to bundler [21] and pmvs [10], colmap [18] contains the complete process for 3D reconstruction, which can recover the scenario structure faster and more accurately. Therefore, despite the popularity of deep learning-based methods, it remains important to improve traditional methods such as colmap. However, most current studies are aimed at improving the speed or completeness of the reconstruction assuming that a dense image sequence can be easily collected; there is no study that aims to improve the 3D reconstruction from sparse image sequences in difficult sampling scenarios. In this study, we propose WEmap to improve 3D reconstruction from sparse image sequences. As shown in Fig. 1, WEmap (e) generates a more complete structure compared to colmap (d).

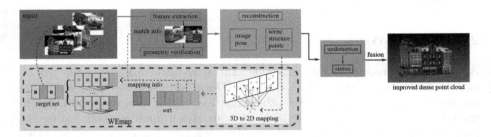

Fig. 2. Overview of our WEmap. WEmap reconstructs 3D scenarios from sparse image sequences. After the initial reconstruction based on colmap, the contribution of each image is calculated by mapping the 3D point cloud to 2D images. The weights of the low-contribution images and corresponding strongest matched images in the input set are enhanced to obtain a more complete scenario structure.

3   Method

Current methods use the same weights for all images to calculate a point cloud, followed by the reconstruction of the 3D scenarios. In fact, the contribution of each image to the point cloud is different. Some image pairs with weak feature matching contribute less to the point cloud, which generates sparse regions in the point cloud. As a result, the sparse regions may cause some local structures in the reconstructed result to be incomplete. To improve the reconstructed result, our WEmap enhances these weak regions in the point cloud.

As shown in Fig. 2, we map the 3D points in the initial point cloud generated by the sparse reconstruction to the feature points of the corresponding 2D images. Then, the number of feature points in an image corresponding to the points in the initial point cloud is counted and used to measure the contribution of the image. Images with fewer feature points correspond to the weak regions in the initial point cloud; therefore, they are regarded as low-contribution and should be added to the enhanced set. Moreover, a point cloud is generated by the feature matching between images instead of feature points in a single image. Therefore, we should add an image pair to the enhanced set rather than a single image. As a result, according to the feature matching information from the initial reconstruction, we add both the low-contribution images and their strongest matched images to the enhanced set. Finally, we increase the image weights in the enhanced set to repair the weak regions in the initial point cloud and obtain a more complete point cloud structure.

3.1 Initial Reconstruction

Monocular-based 3D reconstruction takes a set of 2D images $I = \{I_1, I_2, .., I_N\}$ as input and generates a dense point set $P = \{P_1, P_2, ..., P_M\}$ in 3D space to reconstruct the real scenario structure. The features of the input images are extracted using the SIFT algorithm to obtain the feature set $F = \{F_1, F_2, ..., F_N\}$. Each $F_i(i = 1, 2, ..., N)$ is represented by a triplet set $\{F_{ij} = (x_{ij}, y_{ij}, f_{ij})|j = 1, 2, ..., N_i\}$, where N_i is the number of feature points in the i-th input image, x_{ij} and y_{ij} denote the axes of the j-th feature point, and f_{ij} is the corresponding local feature descriptor. When image matching is performed, local feature descriptors are used to compute the similarity between two feature points from different images. In addition, a set of feature point pairs $M_{ab} = \{(F_{ai'}, F_{bj'})|i' \in [1, N_a], j' \in [1, N_b]\}$ can be generated for any two images I_a and I_b according to the principle of most similarity, where $a < b$ to avoid repeated calculations. Obviously, M_{ab} is an empty set ϕ if I_a and I_b do not overlap. For each image pair (I_a, I_b), we can measure the strength of matching via the number of feature correspondences between these two images, that is,

$$S(I_a, I_b) = |M_{ab}| \tag{1}$$

where $|.|$ denotes the number of elements present in the set.

Then, incremental reconstruction can be performed after geometric verification of the matching results, where the image pose information Z_i and initial point cloud set $P_{initial}$ are calculated. According to colmap [18], densification is directly conducted on the initial point cloud set $P_{initial}$ to generate the final dense point cloud set P. However, as shown in Fig. 1(d), the result obtained by colmap loses some structural information that corresponds to the weak regions in the point cloud. In our WEmap, these weak regions need to be enhanced before the densification operation on $P_{initial}$ so that a more complete structure can be reconstructed. After obtaining the initial sparse point cloud set $P_{initial}$ and matching information, the low-contribution images that correspond to the weak regions in the point cloud are determined. The initial reconstruction is a process of mapping feature points in 2D images to the points in the 3D point cloud $P_{initial}$. We represent the mapping from the 2D feature point set F to 3D point cloud set $P_{initial}$ as follows:

$$f_{map} : F \rightarrow P_{initial} \tag{2}$$

One 2D feature point corresponds to a unique 3D point, whereas a 3D point corresponds to multiple 2D feature points. To determine the contribution of each image, we need a backward mapping from points in the 3D point cloud $P_{initial}$ to the feature points in the input 2D images, that is,

$$f'_{map} : F \leftarrow P_{initial} \tag{3}$$

The corresponding feature points can be found in multiple input images. For each input image $I_i \in I$, we denote the feature point set generated by backward mapping from the 3D point cloud as follows:

$$F_i^{map} = \{f'_{map}(p_j) | f'_{map}(p_j) \in F_i, p_j \in P_{initial}\} \tag{4}$$

Note that not all feature points in an image correspond to the 3D point cloud. Therefore, F_i^{map} is a subset of F_i, that is, $F_i^{map} \subseteq F_i$.

After all points in $P_{initial}$ are mapped to the 2D space, we need to determine which images in I correspond to weak regions in $P_{initial}$. If an image contains more feature points mapped from the initial point cloud $P_{initial}$, the image has a larger contribution to the 3D point cloud, which corresponds to a more complete initial point cloud region. Conversely, if an image contains fewer feature points mapped from $P_{initial}$, the contribution of the image is lower, which more likely corresponds to weak regions in $P_{initial}$. Based on the above analysis, we propose a contribution metric function for the initial reconstruction for all $I_i \in I$.

$$f_{metric}(I_i) = |F_i^{map}| \tag{5}$$

where $|.|$ denotes the number of elements present in the set.

3.2   Generation of the Enhanced Set

According to the metric function defined in (5), the fewer the mapped feature points in an image, the lower is the contribution of the image. Therefore, we sort the images according to their value of $f_{metric}(.)$ for each I_i. Then, the images with lower contributions are selected to form an image set I_{weak}, which corresponds to the weak region in the initial point cloud $P_{initial}$ that should be further enhanced.

Note that during the initial point cloud generation, the input is the feature correspondence between two images instead of a single feature point in one image.

Therefore, when we enhance the weak regions in the initial point cloud, we should increase the weight of the feature correspondence rather than the weight of the feature point. Based on the above analysis, the enhanced set not only includes the images in I_{weak} that directly correspond to the weak regions in the initial point cloud $P_{initial}$ but also includes the images used to generate the feature correspondence with the images in I_{weak}. Therefore, we generate another image set I_{link} that satisfies:

$$I_{link} = \{\arg\max_{I_j} S(I_i, I_j) | I_i \in I_{weak}, I_j \in I, j \neq i\} \qquad (6)$$

Finally, we obtain the enhanced set $I_{enhanced} = I_{link} \cup I_{weak}$, which is used to expand the input data for a more complete point cloud.

3.3   Reconstruction with Weighted Samples

The weights of the input images are dynamically adjusted by introducing the enhanced set $I_{enhanced}$. Then, the weighted samples are utilized to conduct the 3D reconstruction. Finally, the result with a more complete structure can be reconstructed on the sparse image sequence, as shown in Fig. 1(e). We demonstrate the effectiveness of WEmap through the subsequent experiments.

4   Experiments

We demonstrate the effectiveness of our WEmap on the DTU and Tanks & Temples datasets.

4.1   Datasets

DTU Dataset [1]: DTU is a dataset dedicated to 3D reconstruction, which contains 80 indoor scenarios. Each scenario was captured by 49 or 64 cameras under seven different lighting conditions. As with other methods, we use the testing set in our experiments, which consists of 22 scans. Each scan contains RGB images of 49 views.

Tanks & Temples Dataset [3]: Compared to DTU, the Tanks & Temples dataset contains larger outdoor scenarios, which are more suitable for practical applications. There are eight scenarios in the intermediate set, and each scenario contains images ranging in number from 151 to 307. There are 2149 images in total.

Note that these two datasets are both shot at dense angles for data acquisition. To simulate a sparse image sequence, we subtract approximately one-third of the images from each scenario, generating a sparse version of the DTU and Tanks & Temples datasets. Then, we use these two sparse datasets to demonstrate the effectiveness of WEmap.

Experimental Settings: WEmap only introduces one additional hyperparameter R that represents the number of images in I_{weak}. Considering the computational cost, we set $R = 0.2 * N$, where N is the number of images used for 3D reconstruction.

Evaluation Protocols: To quantitatively evaluate the effectiveness of our proposed method, we used colmap to reconstruct the original DTU and Tanks & Temples datasets, which are regarded as experimental baselines. Then, we conducted the reconstruction using colmap and our WEmap on the sparse datasets. Finally, we compared the point clouds reconstructed from the sparse datasets with the baseline point clouds reconstructed from the original datasets.

Cloudcompare software [11] that implements the cloud-to-cloud method [9, 19] was used to calculate the distance between two point clouds. We used two local models, the least square plane and quadric, to obtain the corresponding mean distance and standard deviation, respectively.

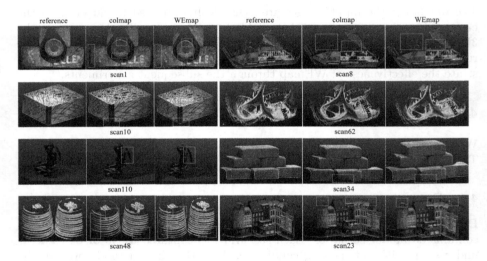

Fig. 3. Visualization results on the sparse DTU dataset. The reference reconstructed by colmap on the original dense data, the point cloud reconstructed by colmap on the sparse data, and the point cloud reconstructed by WEmap on the sparse data are displayed from left to right, respectively. The green bounding boxes indicate the regions in which colmap loses some detailed structures, whereas WEmap retains more complete structures. (Color figure online)

4.2   Experiments on the Sparse DTU Dataset

Here, we provide the visualization and numerical results on the sparse DTU dataset, followed by a discussion.

Results Visualization. Figure 3 shows the comparative results on the sparse DTU dataset. For each scan, the point cloud reconstructed by colmap on the original dense image sequence, that by colmap on the sparse image sequence, and that by WEmap on the same sparse image sequence are displayed from left to right, respectively. It can be observed from the regions in the green bounding boxes that there are many missing details in the results reconstructed by colmap, whereas our WEmap can preserve these details.

Numerical Evaluation. Table 1 reports the evaluation results on the sparse DTU dataset. Here, colmap denotes the mean distance between the reference generated on the original dense data and the point cloud generated by colmap on the sparse data. WEmap denotes the mean distance between the reference generated by colmap on the dense data and the point cloud generated by WEmap on the sparse data. All results were calculated using the quadric model.

Discussion. From the visualization results, we can observe that WEmap retains more detailed structures compared to colmap, as depicted in the regions marked by the green bounding boxes in Fig. 3. For numerical evaluation, a smaller mean distance indicates that the point cloud is more similar to the reference, and a smaller standard deviation indicates that the results are more stable. From the

Table 1. Comparison of mean distances between colmap and WEmap on the sparse DTU dataset. The smaller the mean distance, the more similar are the reconstructed point cloud and the reference.

Methods	Scan1	Scan4	Scan8	Scan10	Scan11	Scan12	Scan13	Scan15
Colmap	0.0157	0.0463	0.0080	0.0234	0.0123	0.0552	**0.0117**	**0.0163**
WEmap	**0.0143**	**0.0385**	**0.0049**	**0.0199**	**0.0107**	**0.0448**	0.0127	0.0169
Methods	scan23	scan24	scan29	scan32	scan33	scan34	scan48	scan49
Colmap	0.0053	0.0141	0.0728	0.0062	0.0116	0.0294	0.0268	0.0245
WEmap	**0.0057**	**0.0121**	**0.0496**	**0.0048**	**0.0107**	**0.0205**	**0.0095**	**0.0125**
Methods	scan62	scan75	scan77	scan110	scan114	scan118		
Colmap	**0.0180**	0.0643	0.1712	0.0359	0.1275	0.0131		
WEmap	0.0210	**0.0386**	**0.1287**	**0.0147**	**0.1075**	**0.0128**		

Table 2. Average mean distance and standard deviation values for 22 scans in the sparse DTU dataset. The results calculated with both quadric and least square models are compared. WEmap performs better overall than colmap.

Local models	Mean distance		Std deviation	
	Colmap	WEmap	Colmap	WEmap
Quadric	0.2499	**0.2121**	0.0368	**0.0278**
Least square	0.2873	**0.2500**	0.0545	**0.0457**

results reported in Table 1, we can observe that WEmap achieves a smaller mean distance and smaller standard deviation compared to colmap in most scans. The average results listed in Table 2 show that WEmap performs better than colmap overall.

These results demonstrate the effectiveness of WEmap on the sparse DTU dataset. However, we observed there are more noise points in the point clouds reconstructed by WEmap on scans 62 and 23, which results in a larger distance from the reference. One of our future studies will be aimed at filtering these noise points for better reconstruction results.

4.3   Experiments on the Sparse Tanks and Temples Dataset

To demonstrate that WEmap performs well in larger scenarios as well, we conducted experiments on the sparse Tanks & Temples dataset that contains eight scans. The visualization and numerical results are presented in Fig. 4 and Table 3, respectively.

Discussion. From Fig. 4, it can be observed that WEmap reconstructs more complete structures than those of colmap, as shown in the regions marked by the green bounding boxes. Moreover, as shown in Table 3, similar to the results on the sparse DTU dataset, the mean distance and standard deviation of WEmap are smaller than those of colmap in most scans. The average results demonstrate that WEmap performs better than colmap overall on the sparse Tanks & Temples dataset.

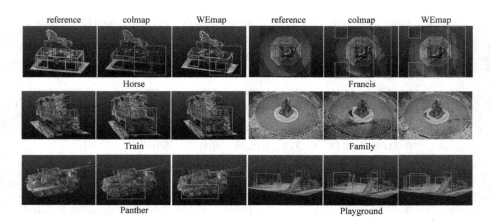

Fig. 4. Visualization results on the sparse Tanks & Temples dataset. For each scenario, the point cloud reconstructed by colmap on the original dense image sequence, that by colmap on the sparse image sequence, and that by WEmap on the same sparse image sequence are displayed from left to right, respectively. The regions in the green bounding boxes indicate that there are many missing details in the results reconstructed by colmap. The regions in the red bounding boxes indicate that there are some noise points in the results reconstructed by WEmap.

Table 3. Evaluation results on the sparse Tanks & Temples dataset. Similar to the results on the sparse DTU dataset, WEmap performs better than colmap in most scans.

Scans	Mean distance		Std deviation	
	Colmap	WEmap	Colmap	WEmap
Family	0.0118	**0.0063**	0.0115	**0.0090**
Horse	0.240	**0.0070**	0.0585	**0.0091**
M60	0.0113	**0.0038**	0.0185	**0.0048**
Francis	0.0091	**0.0035**	0.0055	**0.0033**
Lighthouse	0.0117	**0.0054**	0.0140	**0.0096**
Panther	**0.0058**	0.0082	0.0064	**0.0057**
Playground	0.0157	**0.0043**	0.0116	**0.0054**
Train	**0.0143**	0.0183	**0.0120**	0.0156
Average	0.0130	**0.0069**	0.0176	**0.0078**

Note that on the Panther and Train scans, the mean distance for WEmap is larger than that for colmap. For the Train scan, the standard deviation for WEmap is larger than that for colmap. From the regions marked by the red bounding boxes in Fig. 4, we can see that the reason here is the same as that for scans 62 and 23; some additional noise points are generated by WEmap.

5   Conclusion

In this study, we proposed a new task for the monocular camera-based 3D reconstruction with a sparse image sequence, which compensates for the restrictions on using mobile devices in certain applications, such as smart factories. Moreover, to maintain more complete reconstructed structures, we proposed WEmap that can enhance the weak regions in the point clouds generated by the previously developed method on the sparse data. Experiments on the sparse DTU and Tanks & Temples datasets demonstrate the effectiveness of WEmap.

Acknowledgments. This work was supported in part by the Natural Science Foundation of Tianjin of China under Grant No. 21JCZDJC00740.

References

1. Aans, H., Jensen, R., Vogiatzis, G., Tola, E., Dahl, A.: Large-scale data for multiple-view stereopsis. Int. J. Comput. Vis. (IJCV) **120**(2), 153–168 (2016)
2. Ali, S.G., et al.: Cost-effective broad learning-based ultrasound biomicroscopy with 3D reconstruction for ocular anterior segmentation. Multimedia Tools Appl. **80**(28), 35105–35122 (2021)
3. Angelova, A., Long, P.M.: Benchmarking large-scale fine-grained categorization. In: IEEE Winter Conference on Applications of Computer Vision, pp. 532–539 (2014)

4. Cheema, M.N., Nazir, A., Sheng, B., Li, P., Qin, J., Feng, D.D.: Liver extraction using residual convolution neural networks from low-dose CT images. IEEE Trans. Biomed. Eng. **66**(9), 2641–2650 (2019)

5. Cheema, M.N., et al.: Image-aligned dynamic liver reconstruction using intra-operative field of views for minimal invasive surgery. IEEE Trans. Biomed. Eng. **66**(8), 2163–2173 (2018)

6. Cheng, S., et al.: Deep stereo using adaptive thin volume representation with uncertainty awareness. In: Proceedings of the IEEE/CVF Conference on Computer Vision and Pattern Recognition (CVPR), June 2020

7. DeGol, J., Bretl, T., Hoiem, D.: Improved structure from motion using fiducial marker matching. In: Ferrari, V., Hebert, M., Sminchisescu, C., Weiss, Y. (eds.) ECCV 2018. LNCS, vol. 11207, pp. 281–296. Springer, Cham (2018). https://doi.org/10.1007/978-3-030-01219-9_17

8. Fischler, M.A., Bolles, R.C.: Random sample consensus: a paradigm for model fitting with applications to image analysis and automated cartography. Commun. ACM **24**(6), 381–395 (1981)

9. Ahmad Fuad, N., Yusoff, A.R., Ismail, Z., Majid, Z.: Comparing the performance of point cloud registration methods for landslide monitoring using mobile laser scanning data. ISPRS Int. Arch. Photogramm. Remote Sens. Spat. Inf. Sci. **4249**, 11–21 (2018)

10. Furukawa, Y., Ponce, J.: Accurate, dense, and robust multiview stereopsis. IEEE Trans. Pattern Anal. Mach. Intell. **32**(8), 1362–1376 (2010)

11. Girardeau-Montaut, D.: Cloudcompare. http://www.cloudcompare.org

12. Gu, X., Fan, Z., Zhu, S., Dai, Z., Tan, F., Tan, P.: Cascade cost volume for high-resolution multi-view stereo and stereo matching. In: Proceedings of the IEEE/CVF Conference on Computer Vision and Pattern Recognition (CVPR), June 2020

13. Guo, H., Sheng, B., Li, P., Philip Chen, C.L.: Multiview high dynamic range image synthesis using fuzzy broad learning system. IEEE Trans. Cybern. **51**(5), 2735–2747 (2019)

14. Liu, F., Tran, L., Liu, X.: Fully understanding generic objects: Modeling, segmentation, and reconstruction. In: Proceedings of the IEEE/CVF Conference on Computer Vision and Pattern Recognition (CVPR), pp. 7423–7433, June 2021

15. Locher, A., Havlena, M., Van Gool, L.: Progressive structure from motion. In: Ferrari, V., Hebert, M., Sminchisescu, C., Weiss, Y. (eds.) ECCV 2018. LNCS, vol. 11208, pp. 22–38. Springer, Cham (2018). https://doi.org/10.1007/978-3-030-01225-0_2

16. Moulon, P., Monasse, P., Perrot, R., Marlet, R.: OpenMVG: open multiple view geometry. In: International Workshop on Reproducible Research in Pattern Recognition (2017)

17. Muthukrishnan, S., Ramakrishnan, S., Sanjayan, J.: Technologies for improving buildability in 3D concrete printing. Cem. Concr. Compos., 104144 (2021)

18. Schonberger, J.L., Frahm, J.-M.: Structure-from-motion revisited. In: Proceedings of the IEEE Conference on Computer Vision and Pattern Recognition (CVPR), June 2016

19. Shen, Y., Lindenbergh, R., Wang, J.: Change analysis in structural laser scanning point clouds: the baseline method. Sensors **17**(1), 26 (2017)

20. Sheng, B., Li, P., Fang, X., Tan, P., Enhua, W.: Depth-aware motion deblurring using loopy belief propagation. IEEE Trans. Circuits Syst. Video Technol. **30**(4), 955–969 (2019)

21. Snavely, N., Seitz, S.M., Szeliski, R.: Modeling the world from internet photo collections. Int. J. Comput. Vis. **80**(2), 189–210 (2008)

22. Song, S., Chandraker, M.: Robust scale estimation in real-time monocular SFM for autonomous driving. In: Proceedings of the IEEE Conference on Computer Vision and Pattern Recognition (CVPR), June 2014

23. Tian, X., Liu, R., Wang, Z., Ma, J.: High quality 3D reconstruction based on fusion of polarization imaging and binocular stereo vision. Inf. Fus. **77**, 19–28 (2022)

24. Yao, Y., Luo, Z., Li, S., Fang, T., Quan, L.: MVSNet: depth inference for unstructured multi-view stereo. In: Ferrari, V., Hebert, M., Sminchisescu, C., Weiss, Y. (eds.) ECCV 2018. LNCS, vol. 11212, pp. 785–801. Springer, Cham (2018). https://doi.org/10.1007/978-3-030-01237-3_47

25. Yu, Z., Gao, S.: Fast-MVSNet: sparse-to-dense multi-view stereo with learned propagation and gauss-newton refinement. In: Proceedings of the IEEE/CVF Conference on Computer Vision and Pattern Recognition (CVPR), June 2020

Rendering and Animation

Comparing Traditional Rendering Techniques to Deep Learning Based Super-Resolution in Fire and Smoke Animations

Anton Suta and Helmut Hlavacs[✉]

Entertainment Computing, University of Vienna, Vienna, Austria
helmut.hlavacs@univie.ac.at

Abstract. The following work explores and compares the differences between rendering fire and smoke simulations in high resolution vs rendering these same simulations in low resolution and using deep learning based neural networks to up-scale the output via super-resolution. Several simulations are created at different levels of detail, both with and without post-processing noise added to them. The simulations are then rendered in both high and low resolutions, the lower of which is used for the super-resolution step. The results are then compared in terms of quality and time cost, to determine whether such a computationally expensive task can be improved with deep learning methods. The evaluation shows that using low resolution inputs does not create comparable results to classic high resolution renders, however using a high resolution render of a lower detail simulation creates similar results to high resolution renders of more detailed simulations.

1   Introduction

Creating physically realistic, detail rich fire and smoke animations has been a long standing challenge in the field of computer graphics. To create physically realistic simulations we rely on the Navier-Stokes equations to help us describe the flow of incompressible fluids. Attempting to model every particle in a smoke plume would achieve the desired physical realism, but is computationally unfeasible, and as such, fluid solvers such as the one proposed by Stam et al. [20] work with density grids.

Such solvers can function in real-time on modern hardware, given a reasonable grid size, and provide reasonable physical characteristics, however the computational resources necessary skyrocket as grid sizes increase. The trade-off therefore is physical realism at the expense of computational resources or time.

To combat this explosion of necessary resources a variety of methods have been developed, such as improving the accuracy of the advection step [11], adding noise to a coarse base simulation [13], or speeding up the pressure projection step [1].

All of the above-mentioned techniques use an understanding of fluid mechanics and advanced mathematics to both create basic fluid simulations, and improve upon their quality and speed. The approach of this paper is not to provide an alternative method for improving the computation time of fire and smoke simulations but rather to compare traditional rendering techniques to the more novel approaches of using Machine Learning (ML). Specifically the focus will be on comparing normal rendering to using Deep Learning (DL)-based super-resolution.

In our method the fire and smoke simulations are created using the 3D creation suite Blender [2] and the built-in fluid solver Mantaflow [17]. Using these tools, multiple models are generated at different resolutions and grid sizes. To make the models as realistic as possible, post-processing noise and external forces are applied to each model. The post-processing steps help mimic real-life scenarios such as the wind blowing the smoke in a particular direction. Lower quality renders serve as the input for the resolution enhancing Generative Adversarial Network (GAN) TecoGAN [5]. The output of TecoGAN is then compared to a traditional higher resolution render to assess the results both in terms of quality, and time it took to produce each result.

To summarize, the contributions of this work are:

- Application of a pre-trained Artificial Intelligence (AI) model to enhance low resolution renders of fire and smoke simulations.
- Comparison and evaluation of the efficacy of using DL to enhance low resolution renders as opposed to traditional high resolution renders.

In combination the contributions of this work answer the question of the efficacy and benefits of using DL to enhance a low resolution render, rather than creating a higher resolution render and forgoing the enhancement step. The enhanced output is compared to a traditional high resolution render of the same scene, in terms of the time it took to produce both videos and the quality of the result.

2   Related Work

Works such as Jiang et al. [8] and Zhu et al. [23] have approached the problem of animating complex physical systems by coming up with better and more efficient algorithms. Using different ML techniques we can attempt to solve such problems without the need to improve on already existing algorithms.

Convolutional Neural Networks (CNNs) have shown great promise in image recognition [18], predicting image similarity [16] and even super-resoltion [22]. Chu et al. [4] used CNNs to generate high detail volumetric smoke by teaching the network to correlate high and low resolution patches.

Work by Goodfellow et al. [7] has shown that by pitting two neural networks against each other, one as the generator, tasked with creating as convincing a fake image as it possibly can, and the other as the discriminator, tasked with identifying the fake images the generator produces, we can create very convincing fake images of almost anything [3]. This is known as an adversarial training method and the entire Neural Network (NN) is called a Generative Adversarial

Network (GAN). Over time both the generator and discriminator get better at their respective jobs, to the point where the output becomes almost indistinguishable from reality [10,21]. The concept of a GAN can also be used to infer a high-resolution image from a low-resolution input [14,15], a process known as super-resolution.

In the case of fire and smoke simulations however, it is not enough to increase the resolution of static images, we are interested in simulations and videos of simulations. Such a task commissions the NN on two fronts, firstly to improve the resolution of each individual frame of an input video, and secondly to maintain the spacio-temporal coherence between the frames. As such the network must accommodate content that changes naturally over time [12].

Created specifically for video super-resolution and Unpaired Video Translation (UVT) is TecoGAN [5]. TecoGAN bases its approach on already existing GAN-based image generation techniques, while adding a frame-recurrent generator alongside a spacio-temporal discriminator. Due to the promising nature of the output generated when using its super-resolution network, TecoGAN is used in this paper to evaluate the efficacy of using GANs for creating super-resolution videos of fire and smoke simulations. The UVT aspects of the project are disregarded.

3   TecoGAN

TecoGAN [5] introduces the concept of temporal self-supervision as part of its solutions for video super-resolution and UVT. It uses existing GAN-based image generation approaches and integrates spatio-temporal learning by using a frame-recurrent generator in unison with a spatio-temporal discriminator.

The central approach of this project of this project is its use of the spatio-temporal discriminator (Fig. 1c) which receives frame triplets. Typically, spatial discriminators only supervise a single image. By concatenating adjacent frames along the channel dimension they provide the networks with short-term temporal information and gradient information in regard to spacial structures.

3.1   Network Architecture for Video Super-Resolution

For super-resolution problems there exists an input domain, made up for low resolution frames that then needs to be mapped to a higher resolution output domain. The output domain contains more complex details and motion than the input domain does, and since multiple patterns in high resolution could be mapped to the same low resolution pattern, video super-resolution represents a multimodal problem.

The discriminator (Fig. 2) guides the generator to learn correlation between low and high resolution frames, by using three low resolution frames as conditional input. The frame triples are concatenated together so that the discriminator will penalize the generator if it contains less details or creates artifacts in its frames, compared to the real inputs given.

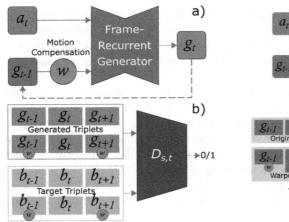

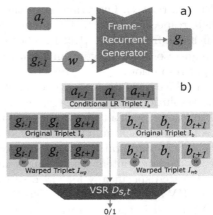

Fig. 1. a) Frame-recurrent generator. b) Spatio-temporal discriminator. *Image Source and Caption:* Chu et al. [5]

Fig. 2. a) Frame-recurrent VSR Generator. b) Conditional VSR Discriminator *Image Source and Caption:* Chu et al. [5]

3.2 Usage

We chose to use TecoGAN due to its proven results for super-resolution video generation tasks. The original paper goes into detail about the project's competence in comparison to other neural networks and manages to show the efficacy of their approach.

For the super-resolution tasks in the following chapters, we used a pre-trained version of TecoGAN, courtesy of Sony's nnabla-examples GitHub [19]. The trained model runs inside a Jupyter Notebook [9] in a virtual environment inside the Google Colab ecosystem. This allows the pre-trained model to take advantage of the available GPUs and computational resources to deliver results in a timely manner. This approach was also chosen due to the ease of sharing that comes with using Google Colab, as well as the lack of cross-compatibility issues that come with attempting to run the same file on different machines.

The time costs measured in Table 3 can vary based on which physical machine is available to support the virtual environment in which the Juypter Notebook will run at the time of execution. This means that the data in this table will be different when if the notebook is run several times. The important takeaway from Table 3 is that the time cost varies very little between simulations at the same resolution.

4 Dataset Generation

As this paper focuses on the comparison between traditional rendering techniques and TecoGAN's [5] super-resolution it is important to create a varied set of simulations at different levels of quality, to better judge the effect of the base simulation on the final render output in both cases. In the interest of reproducibility, all of the different fire and smoke simulations were created and rendered on the same machine, using Blender version 2.91.0.

The hardware specifications are as follows:

- **CPU:** Intel Core i5 3570 (3.40 GHz)
- **RAM:** 16,0 GB Dual-Channel DDR3 (655 MHz)
- **Motherboard:** Dell Inc. 0KRC95
- **Graphics:** NVIDIA GeForce GTX 1050 (2047 MB)

4.1 Creating a Smoke Simulation

Creating a basic smoke animation in Blender is actually quite straightforward as the built-in fluid solver Mantafow offers the option of creating a "quick smoke" simulation. This simulation is however very basic and only offers a puff of smoke, as can be seen in Fig. 3, and is therefore not as interesting when trying to simulate something physically realistic (Fig. 4).

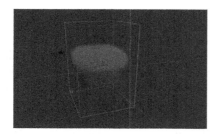
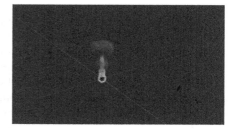

Fig. 3. a) Smoke emitter (inner cube) b) Smoke domain (outer cube). The emitter creating a single puff of low detail smoke at a single point in time. The puff is constrained to the space of the domain.

Fig. 4. The emitter is now continuously creating smoke for as long as the animation runs, and is deformed via random noise to generate a realistic flame.

To make the simulation more realistic we need to add fire to the emitter, to simulate a physical flame that will produce continuous smoke. As the behaviour of fire seems random to human intuition, we can also subdivide the emitter into multiple, smaller emitters that we can deform using random noise. This creates a more natural feel of the fire's behaviour over time.

Lastly, we would like the simulation to react to external forces the same way a bonfire would when the wind blows. To achieve this we can add some external forces and turbulances that change position and intensity throughout the animation to simulate a wind-like force affecting the flame (Fig. 5).

Fig. 5. Simulation reacting to external forces.

Table 1. Time cost of creating fire and smoke simulations at different qualities on the aforementioned hardware.

Resolution divisions	Base simulation	Noise	Full simulation
32	55 s	1 m 31 s	2 m 26 s
64	3 m 29 s	5 m 53 s	9 m 22 s
96	14 m 13 s	18 m 12 s	32 m 25 s
128	31 m 43 s	35 m 11 s	1 h 6 m 54 s
192	1 h 14 m 55 s	1 h 12 m 37 s	2 h 17 m 32 s
256	2 h 42 m 32 s	2 h 21 m 15 s	5 h 3 m 47 s

With this general setup, the base animation is established. We can now tweak some parameters such as the resolution divisions (can be thought of as 3D pixels) and the post-processing level of noise to create vastly different qualities in the simulation, the renders of which can then be used in the evaluation stage.

4.2 Multiple Simulations

To best judge the effect that super-resolution has on the final output render, it is important to create multiple simulations with different levels of detail and see if that same level can be maintained when using DL. Another aspect to be considered is the fact that the more detail a simulation has, the longer it will take to compute for a given amount of frames. It is therefore not unreasonable to check if we can achieve a high level of detail by providing TecoGAN [5] with a render of a less detailed simulation, to investigate if it can infer and add details that are not part of the base simulation (as opposed to providing it a low resolution render of a high detail simulation, where the details are present in the simulation, but not the render). If this is the case, such a method could be used to save valuable computational resources and time.

For this paper, each simulation has exactly the same length, 210 frames, played at 24 frames per second. This results in around 7 s of animation. To create simulations with different levels of detail, we created 12 different simulations, all rendered on the hardware mentioned at the beginning of this chapter. There are 6 different levels of resolution division, ranging from 32 to 256, and two types of groups, base simulation (without post-processing noise), and full simulation, which is identical to the base simulation, but has post-processing noise added to it. Noise was applied using wavelet turbulence [13] at an up-res factor of two.

The time cost to create each simulation, their respective resolution divisions and the application of noise can be found in Table 1 (Fig. 6).

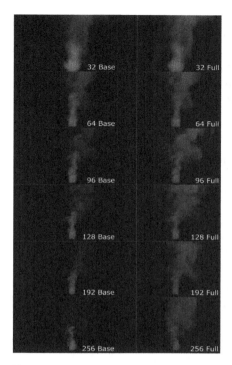 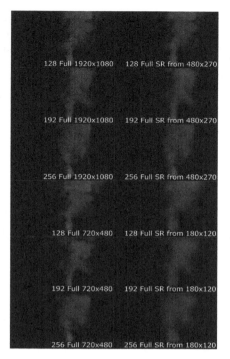

Fig. 6. Side by side comparison of the different simulations.

Fig. 7. Side by side comparison of high resolution renders vs super-resolution created by TecoGAN

5   Evaluation

The most straightforward approach to evaluating the usefulness of super-resolution using TecoGAN [5] would be to time the process and see how long it takes compared to just normally rendering a higher resolution version. This is a somewhat naive approach as it does not take into account the quality of the final render, much less base this on the underlying level of detail of the simulation we are trying to up-scale.

To best judge the efficacy of super-resolution, time will be a an important factor, but it will be looked at while also considering the resolution divisions of the simulation, because as can be seen from Table 1, if we have more resolution divisions in a simulation, it takes significantly longer to compute, but the level of detail increases.

5.1   Creating Different Renders

TecoGAN's super-resolution scales an input up video by a factor of four [5]. A good way to evaluate the time constraint therefore is to render the same video twice, once in the desired resolution, such as 1920×1080, and once in a resolution four times as small, in this case 480×270. We can then pass the lower resolution render to TecoGAN which then scales it up to the level of the higher resolution render, making a side by side comparison straightforward. Timing both approaches gives us the first evaluation metric. The time cost to render each simulation at each respective resolution can be found in the table below (Table 2):

Table 2. Time cost of renders at different resolutions

Table 3. Time cost for super-resolution.

Resolution divisions	1920×1080	480×270	720×480	180×120
32 Base	3 m 7 s	1 m 32 s	1 m 37 s	1 m 18 s
32 Full	3 m 9 s	1 m 34 s	1 m 45 s	1 m 27 s
64 Base	3 m 12 s	1 m 48 s	1 m 40 s	1 m 26 s
64 Full	3 m 27 s	1 m 56 s	2 m 1 s	1 m 55 s
96 Base	3 m 57 s	1 m 55 s	2 m 5 s	1 m 41 s
96 Full	5 m 8 s	3 m 21 s	3 m 2 s	3 m 8 s
128 Base	4 m 36 s	2 m 18 s	2 m 30 s	2 m 10 s
128 Full	6 m 27 s	4 m 21 s	4 m 37 s	4 m 7 s
192 Base	5 m 35 s	3 m 29 s	3 m 41 s	3 m 33 s
192 Full	9 m 26 s	7 m 44 s	7 m 54 s	7 m 52 s
256 Base	7 m 24 s	5 m 39 s	6 m 30 s	6 m 1 s
256 Full	14 m 16 s	13 m 24 s	14 m 8 s	15 m 22 s

Resolution divisions	480×270	180×120
32 Base	2 m 33 s	29 s
32 Full	2 m 31 s	26 s
64 Base	2 m 29 s	26 s
64 Full	2 m 30 s	26 s
96 Base	2 m 29 s	26 s
96 Full	2 m 31 s	27 s
128 Base	2 m 28 s	26 s
128 Full	2 m 31 s	27 s
192 Base	2 m 27 s	26 s
192 Full	2 m 29 s	26 s
256 Base	2 m 27 s	26 s
256 Full	2 m 29 s	26 s

From Table 2 we can see that, while it is slightly cheaper to render simulations in lower resolution, the amount of time we save, especially at higher resolution divisions of the simulation, becomes negligible, it is however cheaper to render a simulation with less detail. This is likely due to the fact that the majority of costs when rendering lie not within the render itself, but with advancing the fire and smoke simulation one time step forward. These results do not speak for a great amount of time saved, if any at all, as super-resolution also takes a certain amount of time to compute. The time cost to up-scale each lower resolution render can be found in the table below (Table 3):

Table 3 shows that the level of detail in a simulation is irrelevant and that the main factor in the time it takes for the super-resolution to work is the resolution of the video we pass in as input. This is an expected result, because when working with a GAN, the most time invested is in training the NN, but using it is cheaper. The likely reason for it taking longer at higher resolutions is the large amount of memory needed and the larger space of possible motions over time.

Given the data in Tables 2 and 3 we can see that trying to use super-resolution to upscale either lower resolution video is not more time efficient when looking at data across the same simulation, as the base render costs are already extremely high compared to simply creating a high resolution render. Unfortunately this means that using super-resolution to cut down render time for the same simulation is not feasible. Time could be saved if the quality of a simulation with lower resolution divisions can be brought to the level of a simulation with more resolution divisions. Should this be the case, time could be saved on two fronts, both in the costs of creating the initial simulation, and in the render time itself.

5.2 Comparing Video Quality

Quality is an important metric, as super-resolution would not be particularly useful if the video we are trying to up-scale decreases in caliber. To measure this aspect, each lower resolution render is used as input to TecoGAN [5] which will then increase the size of the video by a factor of four, allowing for a side by side comparison with the higher resolution render.

Figure 7 shows that TecoGAN's super resolution comes nowhere near the traditional high resolution render in terms of quality. The images show that the generic shape of the flame and smoke plume are there, however none of the finer details can be seen. This is the case when using both high and low detail input images.

So far, using super-resolution would not be worth it when it comes to saving render time. Now we can also see that using a low resolution render as the input to be up-scaled does not create high quality images. A possible reason for such a lackluster output is the possibility that we have provided TecoGAN with a type of input that in itself contains little detail. The AI cannot infer details for an input that never had any in the first place, as is the case in such low resolution renders. We might therefore achieve better results by creating a high resolution render of a simulation that has less resolution divisions, downsize that, and use the downsized version to compare it to a high resolution render of a simulation with more resolution divisions.

5.3 Cross Simulation Comparison

To compare across simulations, we render a high resolution video of a simulation with less resolution divisions, downsize this using ffmpeg [6] to a quarter size, and use this now smaller video as input to TecoGAN. Since reducing the scale of a video takes very little time, the actual time cost for performing this step will be discarded, as it is insignificant compared to all other steps.

To perform cross simulation comparison the 1920×1080 resolution render of the 192 resolution division with noise was taken as the base. The resolution was re-scaled to 480×270 using ffmpeg and used as the input for the super-resolution step. The results of this can be seen in the figure below (Fig. 8).

Fig. 8. Cross simulation comparison

While the position of the smoke plume and flame do not line up perfectly, the remarkably better results can still be seen. The output has more detail than the downscaled input, and is very similar in quality to the ground truth high resolution render. The better results can be explained by the fact that TecoGAN can now infer details since they are actually part of the input, since we started out with a lot of detail in the first place. Having a high detail input leads to a higher detail output, but if little to no details are present, none will be added. There is no clear winner between the super-resolution output and the high resolution render of the 256 resolution division simulation, but the two are similar in quality.

6   Conclusion

Creating a simulation of a physically realistic flame that produces smoke is a challenging task, made only more challenging the closer one tries to get to the real world ideal. Attempting to model that physical ideal would take a fluid solver [20] with an infinitely large grid size, which is simply a computational impossibility. Because of this limitation, different methods have been proposed to combat it, such as improving the accuracy of the advection step [11], adding post-processing noise to a coarse base simulation [13] or speeding up the pressure projection step [1].

In the age of Machine Learning and AI it only makes sense to use these novel techniques to improve this computationally challenging task. Chu et al.'s TecoGAN [5] was used to enhance low resolution renders of several fire and smoke simulations, all of which had different grid sizes, and therefore different levels of detail.

Rendering and timing a 210 frame video of each simulation (Table 2) showed that there was very little to be gained by rendering a lower resolution version instead of directly rendering in a resolution four times as great. The main time cost benefit was in rendering simulations with less resolution divisions, a result which can be explained by the fact that advancing the simulation one time step forward is more computationally expensive than producing an image of it after the fact.

The quality of the video used as input did not have much effect on the time it took TecoGAN to create a super-resolution version (Table 3), only the video's resolution mattered. As rendering in lower resolution and using super-resolution was shown to take a similar amount of time as directly rendering in high resolution, it can be concluded that there is little to no time cost benefit to this approach.

The results generated by TecoGAN in terms of image quality were also not very promising, as Fig. 7 has shown. The AI simply cannot infer any of the details of the simulation from a low resolution render, likely because of the low amount of detail in the input video. As such the output ends up just being a substandard version of a traditional high resolution render, with the general shape being present, but lacking any significant details.

To achieve good super-resolution results, the NN needs a high detail input, so that it can improve on these preexisting details. The best results were achieved when providing TecoGAN with a downsized version of a high resolution render. Figure 8 shows that when using the aforementioned method, the super-resolution output not only adds significant details to the input video provided, it is also comparable to a high resolution render of a more detailed simulation.

Using this method, saves us not only render time after the simulation has already been computed, but allows a lower detail simulation to be computed in the first place, saving significantly more time than if we simply reduced render time. Being able to save on simulation costs cuts down on the most expensive process, allowing us to inch ever closer to real time applications.

References

1. Ando, R., Thürey, N., Wojtan, C.: A Dimension-reduced Pressure Solver for Liquid Simulations (2015)
2. Blender Foundation. https://www.blender.org/. Accessed 08 Feb 2022
3. Brock, A., Donahue, J., Simonyan, K.: Large Scale GAN Training for High Fidelity Natural Image Synthesis (2019)
4. Chu, M., Thuerey, N.: Data-Driven Synthesis of Smoke Flows with CNN-based Feature Descriptors (2017)
5. Chu, M., et al.: Learning temporal coherence via self-supervision for GAN-based video generation (TecoGAN). ACM Trans. Graph. (TOG) **39**(4), 75 (2020)
6. FFmpeg Team. https://www.ffmpeg.org/. Accessed 14 Feb 2022
7. Goodfellow, I.J., et al.: Generative adversarial networks (2014)
8. Jiang, J., et al.: Real-time hair simulation with heptadiagonal decomposition on mass spring system. Graph. Models **111**, 101077 (2020). ISSN 1524-0703
9. Jupyter Project. https://jupyter.org/. Accessed 15 Feb 2022
10. Karras, T., Laine, S., Aila, T.: A Style-Based Generator Architecture for Generative Adversarial Networks (2019)

11. Kim, B.M., et al.: FlowFixer: Using BFECC for Fluid Simulation (2005)
12. Kim, B., et al.: Transport-based neural style transfer for smoke simulations. ACM Trans. Graph. (TOG) **38**(6), 188 (2019)
13. Kim, T., et al.: Wavelet Turbulence for Fluid Simulation (2008)
14. Ledig, C., et al.: Photo-Realistic Single Image Super-Resolution Using a Generative Adversarial Network (2017)
15. Li, L., et al.: Unsupervised face super-resolution via gradient enhancement and semantic guidance. Vis. Comput. **37**(9–11), 2855–2867 (2021). ISSN 0178-2789
16. Mobahi, H., Collobert, R., Weston, J.: Deep Learning from Temporal Coherence in Video (2009)
17. Pfaff, T., Thuerey, N.: http://mantaflow.com/index.html. Accessed 08 Feb 2022
18. Simonyan, K., Zisserman, A.: Very Deep Convolutional Networks for Large-Scale Image Recognition (2015)
19. Sony. https://github.com/sony/nnabla. Accessed 15 Feb 2022
20. Stam, J.: Real-Time Fluid Dynamics for Games (2003)
21. SYNCED. GAN 2.0: NVIDIA's Hyperrealistic Face Generator (2018). Accessed 09 Feb 2022. https://syncedreview.com/2018/12/14/gan-2-0-nvidias-hyperrealistic-face-generator/
22. Wen, Y., et al.: Deep color guided coarse-to-fine convolutional network cascade for depth image super-resolution. IEEE Trans. Image Process. **28**(2), 994–1006 (2019). ISSN 1057-7149
23. Zhu, J., et al.: Animating turbulent fluid with a robust and efficient high-order advection method. Comput. Animat. Virtual Worlds **31**(4–5), e1951 (2020). ISSN 1546-4261

Real-Time Light Field Path Tracing

Markku Mäkitalo$^{(\boxtimes)}$, Erwan Leria, Julius Ikkala, and Pekka Jääskeläinen

Tampere University, P.O. Box 553, 33014 Tampere, Finland
`markku.makitalo@tuni.fi`

Abstract. Light field rendering and displays are emerging technologies that produce more immersive visual 3D experiences than the conventional stereoscopic 3D technologies, as well as provide a more comfortable virtual or augmented reality (VR/AR) experience by mitigating the vergence–accommodation conflict. Path tracing photorealistic synthetic light fields in real time is extremely challenging, since it involves rendering a large amount of viewpoints for each frame. However, these viewpoints are often spatially very close to each other, especially in light field AR glasses or other near-eye light field displays. In this paper, we propose a practical real-time light field path tracing pipeline and demonstrate it by rendering a 6×6 grid of 720p viewpoints at 18 frames per second on a single GPU, through utilizing denoising filters and spatiotemporal sample reprojection. In addition, we discuss how the pipeline can be scaled to yield higher-quality results if more parallel computing resources are available. We also show that our approach can be used to simultaneously serve multiple clients with varying light field grid sizes, with the quality remaining constant across clients.

Keywords: Ray tracing · Image-based rendering · Virtual/augmented reality · Image processing

1 Introduction

Photorealistic rendering has a wide variety of applications ranging from entertainment, telepresence and other remote communications, medical industry, architecture, industrial design, and many other virtual and augmented reality applications. With steadily growing interest towards more interactivity and an ultra-realistic immersive user experience, there are significant challenges in rendering such content in real time with high resolutions and high frame rates. The currently available stereoscopic displays lack in providing all the necessary visual cues for an immersive 3D experience, and often cause visual discomfort due to the vergence–accommodation conflict [6, 7]. A light field can be used to describe a 3D scene from multiple viewing angles simultaneously, thus also providing more accurate visual cues. However, this comes at the cost of a vast increase in computational complexity, since we need to process data for all the different viewpoints.

Supplementary Information The online version contains supplementary material available at https://doi.org/10.1007/978-3-031-23473-6_17.

Specifically, the light field can be characterized with a 5D vector function called the plenoptic function. Further, assuming it is in unobstructed space, it can be reduced to a 4D function, with individual viewpoints being different 2D slices of this 4D function [15]. These 2D slices, or perspective images, typically exhibit significant redundancy, as they are representing the same scene from slightly varying viewpoints. Hence, especially in real-time rendering applications, exploiting this redundancy is crucial in order to reduce the amount of data to be rendered. This can be done for example by reprojecting already rendered samples, both spatially between the viewpoints and temporally between frames.

Path tracing is a ubiquitously used algorithm for photorealistic rendering, which models how the light physically travels and interacts with the world. It is a progressive process, yielding higher-quality results as more samples (paths) per pixel are traced. This is computationally very expensive even for traditional monoscopic applications, and much more so with the challenging goal of photorealistic real-time light field rendering. Given the strict computational constraints of real-time rendering, we can currently afford to trace only a few samples per pixel (spp), even when rendering just a single viewpoint and using hardware-accelerated tracing.

In this paper, we propose and demonstrate a practical pipeline capable of real-time light field path tracing. Its basic principle is to path trace a subset of the pixels, and improve and synthesize the full data through an effective combination of denoising and spatiotemporal sample reprojection. In particular, we consider a light field represented by a grid of regularly spaced virtual cameras with small horizontal and vertical translations between the adjacent viewpoints, producing a grid of 2D perspective images. In our experiments, we focus on a 6×6 grid in order to match a prototype near-eye light field display; it is also close to what other similar devices, such as Huang et al. [8], use. In addition, we demonstrate that our approach can be used to simultaneously serve multiple clients with varying light field grid sizes, at a comparable quality for each client.

Our main contributions in this paper are:

- We propose a general pipeline that is suitable for real-time light field path tracing, and flexible for scaling the performance according to the available parallel resources.
- We demonstrate that a simple viewpoint-based practical implementation of the pipeline can render a light field in real time on a single GPU (a 6×6 grid of 720p viewpoints at 18 frames per second) with acceptable quality, by path tracing and denoising only a single full viewpoint in the middle of the grid, and using it to synthesize the other 35 viewpoints.
- We show that the rendered data can be used to simultaneously serve multiple light field clients, with the quality remaining constant across different grid sizes.

The rest of the paper is structured as follows: Sect. 2 reviews the related work on sample reprojection, denoising, and view synthesis. Section 3 introduces the proposed pipeline and discusses our specific implementation details. Section 4 describes our experiments, Sect. 5 presents the runtime and quality results obtained with our implementation, and finally, Sect. 6 concludes the paper.

2   Related Work

In image-based rendering (IBR), a collection of 2D images is used in order to reconstruct the 3D scene or to synthesize novel viewpoints. This reuse of rendered data can be done even from a single 2D image, by warping, or reprojecting, the existing samples from one viewpoint onto another, based on the depth information and knowledge about the camera parameters and transformations between the two viewpoints. For natural images, these need to be estimated, but for synthetic rendering, the information is readily available, simplifying the process.

The IBR problem can also be modelled as a plenoptic sampling problem [18], hence considering the existing viewpoints as sparsely sampled data from the full (i.e., densely sampled) light field. Then, reconstructing the densely sampled light field, also enabling novel view synthesis, is often approached in the epipolar plane image (EPI) domain [23] or in Fourier domain [21]. Due to anisotropy in the light field, samples can also be reused to reconstruct a more dense temporal or indirect light field from a sparse input, thus increasing the effective sampling rate significantly [13,14]. However, these approaches are generally targeting high-quality reconstruction, and are currently not suitable for real-time view synthesis.

On the other hand, sample reprojection is straightforward and computationally cheap, so it is commonly used even in monoscopic real-time rendering applications in order to utilize the temporal coherence between successive frames. For example, most of the state-of-the-art real-time and interactive path tracing denoising filters, such as [10,11,17,19,20], incorporate temporal reprojection in their reconstruction pipeline. Out of these denoising filters, we identify BMFR [11] and SVGF [19] as particularly suitable candidates for improving the quality of real-time light field path tracing: it takes only about 1 ms to denoise a single 1280 × 720 pixel viewpoint with either of the two filters.

Besides temporal reprojection, in stereoscopic rendering the samples can also be reprojected between the two viewpoints, and this approach can be further generalized for multi-view rendering. In particular, Andersson et al. [1] accelerate multi-view ray tracing through multi-dimensional adaptive sampling and edge detection. Fraboni et al. [3] accelerate multi-view path tracing by progressively generating the traced paths in a way that facilitates sharing a significant portion of their contributions between different viewpoints. Nevertheless, neither of these multi-view methods target real-time applications, and are rather costly to compute. A light field display, such as the one by Lanman and Luebke [12] or Huang et al. [8], typically requires dozens of viewpoints to be rendered for a single frame, so the benefit of reprojection quickly becomes very significant, if only a few viewpoints need to be rendered and the rest can be synthesized based on the existing data. This is crucial especially for multi-view applications striving for real-time rendering.

Neural networks have also been employed for multi-view reprojection [2,5,25]. However, they consider the reprojection part to be straightforward enough, so that it is left to be done outside of the network; the networks only perform the final blending of the novel viewpoint, given the multiple existing viewpoint inputs. They produce high-quality results, but are computationally too expensive for real-time frame rates or require hours of preprocessing.

Sample reprojection is used by Hansen et al. [4] for accelerating rasterized light field rendering for head-mounted displays. They consider a 15 × 8 grid of perspective viewpoints, in which they only render the four corner viewpoints, and reproject all the remaining viewpoints. Although they reach an interactive performance of about 5 FPS, filling the missing data in places where the reprojection fails is difficult with their method. In contrast, with path tracing, the missing pixels can easily be traced after the reprojection step.

Mäkitalo et al. [16] present a systematic evaluation of the quality of reprojected path traced samples for the stereoscopic case. They report that spatiotemporal reprojection brings an almost 25-fold quality increase for 1 spp input data in terms of the effective spp, with having to path trace only 2–6 % of the samples in the target frame. We are not aware of such work existing for light fields.

Finally, Xie et al. [24] demonstrate production-quality real-time cluster path tracing rendering that scales linearly with the number of RTX cluster nodes used. However, they focus on single-view rendering and increasing the spp count by adding more nodes, instead of attempting to reduce the computational effort through reusing data.

3   General Pipeline and Our Implementation

3.1   General Pipeline

Figure 1 visualizes the proposed general pipeline for real-time light field path tracing. First, a number of independent *source regions* are path traced, where the number of regions can be decided based on the amount of parallel resources available for real-time path tracing; the figure uses two regions for the purposes of visualization. These regions can correspond to the viewpoints in the light field grid, but they can also be smaller or larger regions. They can even be sparse discontinuous sets of pixels, although that will likely present additional challenges for the denoising filters, for optimizing the memory accesses, and for data transfers between different computing nodes.

Next, temporal reprojection is applied for each path traced source region, in order to blend the current data for the region with the corresponding data in the previous frame, thus increasing the effective quality.

Alternative steps in the pipeline are marked with dashed blue and red routes. In particular, the denoising filter can be applied either to the path traced source regions (regions 1 and 2 in the example graph) after temporal blending, or at a later stage after all the missing *target regions* (3..n) have been synthesized through spatial reprojection. The former option (shown with the blue route) is particularly useful if the amount of parallel resources is limited, as the denoising improvement can be propagated from the few source regions into all the target regions without expending too much computational effort on the denoising. On the other hand, the latter option (red route) likely produces a higher-quality

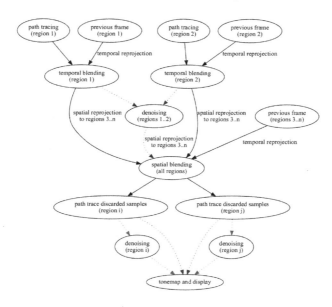

Fig. 1. A high-level task graph of the proposed general pipeline. The blue route can be replaced by the red route, if there are enough resources to denoise all regions in parallel in real time. The choice of two independently path traced regions is only for the visualization; the number is not dictated by the pipeline. (Color figure online)

result. However, it requires enough resources to denoise all n regions in parallel in real time, and ensuring that the separately denoised regions do not cause distracting artifacts at the region boundaries; irregularly shaped regions or additional lightweight deblocking filters could be used to alleviate that. In either case, the temporally blended source regions (denoised or not), are used to synthesize the remaining regions $3..n$ through spatial reprojection.

Backward reprojection is commonly used for both temporal and spatial reprojection, starting from the target region, and finding for each pixel, which pixel in the source region maps to it. Not all pixels can be reprojected, due to data being out of the viewing frustum or occluded in one of the regions, for example. Having multiple source regions in different parts of the light field grid brings better coverage for those areas, but at the cost of having to path trace more source regions, which is expensive.

The discarded pixels in the synthesized target regions now need to be filled by path tracing. As this step does not depend on the previously chosen region division, a different set of regions can be used for the remainder of the pipeline (regions i and j in the graph), if it is deemed more optimal in terms of the currently available parallel resources. If there were a lot of discarded pixels, denoising after the missing pixels have been path traced (red route) will reduce the visible differences between the reprojected higher-quality areas and the newly path traced areas. Finally, all the regions will be combined for tonemapping and displaying the result.

3.2 Our Implementation

For this paper, we implement a version of the pipeline that targets real-time light field path tracing on a single GPU. More specifically, we assume for simplicity that each region corresponds to a full viewpoint in the light field grid, and that denoising is applied only on the source viewpoint(s) before spatial reprojection, not on the target viewpoints. In other words, we adhere to the blue route shown in Fig. 1.

We use backward reprojection in all of our experiments. For each sample, we look at the difference in both world positions and shading normals of the source and target pixel locations, and the instance IDs of the objects. The sample is reprojected to the target location if the instance IDs match and both differences stay below specified thresholds. The thresholds are chosen manually for each scene based on the scale of the scene. If either threshold is exceeded, or if the instance IDs do not match, or if the target pixel is otherwise not visible in the source viewpoint (out-of-frustum data), we discard that pixel. The discarded pixels will then be path traced after spatial reprojection. Note that the reprojection requires us to render the G-buffers for the non-rendered target viewpoints as well. This comes with a modest additional cost, as our runtime experiments will indicate. Furthermore, we specifically opt to use a relatively simple reprojection strategy in order to demonstrate the feasibility of reprojection in general as a part of a real-time light field path tracing pipeline; it utilizes only the world positions, shading normals, and instance IDs, but is very fast to evaluate. However, more accurate reprojection could be achieved by leveraging more information, such as material properties, or anisotropy in the light field.

The reprojection in general is not a 1:1 pixel mapping, so it involves a resampling step in order to pick the closest pixel(s) from the source viewpoint to reproject. For example, using bilinear interpolation between the closest existing samples acts as a simple blurring kernel, which improves the quality of the noisy data. Moreover, when multiple source viewpoints have candidate pixels for the reprojection, their contributions can be combined, blending the final pixel value. In such cases, in order to minimize the computational overhead, we simply pick the source pixel with the smallest depth value, instead of blending multiple values together.

In addition, temporal reprojection usually includes accumulation, which increases temporal stability and the effective spp count. We accumulate the pixel data temporally with a blending factor of 0.2, as is commonly done [11,19].

Our implementation considers only fully path traced individual viewpoints. However, the proposed pipeline also allows for sparsely and adaptively distributed samples irrespective of the viewpoint boundaries, although that is likely to present additional challenges both for the denoising algorithms and for distributing the computations. Specifically, denoising algorithms typically rely on spatially neighbouring samples to be present, which would not necessarily be the case with sparse sampling. For example BMFR operates in a blockwise fashion, and SVGF estimates the variance in a spatial neighbourhood when only one sample per pixel is available.

4   Experiments

We consider four test scenes: Sponza, Eternal Valley, Warehouse, and Bistro Interior. Each scene consists of 30 frames, each frame having a 6×6 grid of 1280×720 pixel viewpoints. The camera paths range from a simple forward dolly tracking in Sponza to a very rapid nonlinear fly-through in Bistro Interior. The difference between adjacent viewpoints is approximately 7 pixels for Sponza, 9 pixels for Eternal Valley, and 8 pixels for both Warehouse and Bistro Interior. An example 4096 spp reference frame for each scene is shown in Fig. 2.

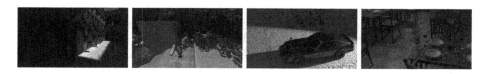

Fig. 2. Example 4096 spp reference viewpoints of the datasets used in the experiments. Each frame has a 6×6 grid of 1280×720 pixel viewpoints. From left to right: Sponza, Eternal Valley, Warehouse, Bistro Interior.

In Sect. 5.1 (**"Runtime"**), we measure the real-time performance of our implementation described in Sect. 3.2, both as a whole and by looking at the individual stages of the pipeline. Our implementation is built on top of our own Vulkan-based real-time path tracer, running on a high-end desktop with an NVIDIA RTX 3090 GPU. By default, we path trace 1 spp both for the source viewpoint(s) and when filling the discarded pixels later, using a maximum of 8 bounces, and *next event estimation* (NEE) on.

In order to identify the most suitable source viewpoint configuration for single-GPU rendering, we also look at the runtimes and spatial discard percentages for five different configurations with 1–4 path traced source viewpoints; each additional path traced viewpoint requires a significant amount of additional computations, but can improve the reprojection, as the scene is covered from multiple angles. Specifically, we have two single-camera setups, with the rendered viewpoint either in the middle of the 6×6 grid, or at the top left corner. In our dual-camera setup we render the top left and bottom right viewpoints; in the three-camera setup, the rendered viewpoints form a triangular shape; and in the four-camera setup, all four corner viewpoints are rendered. These locations are depicted with camera icons in Fig. 5 (Appendix A).

In Sect. 5.2 (**"Quality"**), we evaluate the quality of the rendering, focusing on evaluating the most efficient setup identified in the previous experiment, which turns out to be to path trace only the middle viewpoint. That is, we start with a 1 spp path traced input in the middle viewpoint, denoise it, and then spatiotemporally reproject it onto the other 35 viewpoints. For the denoising filter, we use a state-of-the-art real-time filter, specifically either BMFR [11] or SVGF [19]. By denoising before reprojection, we aim to propagate the benefits of the denoising filter onto all viewpoints without incurring the extra computational cost of having to denoise all viewpoints. BMFR and SVGF were chosen for their good balance between speed and quality: it takes only about 1 ms to denoise a single 1280×720 pixel viewpoint with either of them. We measure the average results in terms of root mean squared error (RMSE) and SSIM [22] against the 4096 spp reference, both for spatiotemporal reprojection on its own, and for the combination of denoising and reprojection.

Finally, we consider a scenario where a rendering server is providing data for multiple light field clients, whose display configurations may vary. For example, the clients' display grids may vary between 3×3 and 6×6 viewpoints. However, with the proposed configuration, the path traced middle viewpoint can be used as the basis for all clients, with the amount of reprojected viewpoints around it determined by the client. Depending on the rendering capabilities and data transfer requirements, the server can then perform the reprojection and send the desired subset of viewpoints to a client; or if the client is also able to apply reprojection and do lightweight path tracing for the samples discarded by the reprojection algorithm, the server can only transfer the path traced middle viewpoint. To corroborate the validity of the multi-client approach, we evaluate the quality after denoising and reprojection as in the earlier quality experiments, but now for grid sizes of 3×3, 4×4, 5×5, and 6×6. A representative selection of these results is shown at the end of Sect. 5.2.

5   Results

This section presents our results for the runtime and quality experiments described in Sect. 4.

5.1   Runtime

The runtime differences of spatial reprojection for the five viewpoint configurations are fairly minor: Spatial reprojection takes 0.07–0.08 ms per target viewpoint for both single-camera setups, and 0.09–0.14 ms for the multi-camera setups, with the average time being close to the lower end of the range in each case. Hence, spatial reprojection to 35 viewpoints, for example with the path traced middle viewpoint, takes about 2.45 ms per frame in total. Temporal reprojection also takes 0.07–0.08 ms per viewpoint, resulting in about 2.52 ms per frame when reprojecting all 36 viewpoints.

Figure 3 shows the execution time of the different pipeline stages when rendering Sponza. Generating the G-buffers takes 0.28 ms per viewpoint, so about 10 ms in total for the 36 viewpoints. Path tracing the middle viewpoint of a 6×6 grid of 720p viewpoints (1 spp, 8 bounces, next event estimation on) takes 22 ms.

Then, that viewpoint is denoised with BMFR or SVGF, taking about 1 ms. After the temporal and spatial reprojection stages, which take about 2.5 ms each as described above, path tracing is used to fill in the discards in the 35 target viewpoints, in this case 2.08 % of the pixels (see Table 1). This takes 16 ms, yielding a total execution time of 54 ms, or about 18 FPS. With the other viewpoint configurations, the corresponding numbers are about 16 FPS (path traced top left viewpoint), 15 FPS (top left + bottom right), 11 FPS (triangle), and 9 FPS (corners).

Appendix A further illustrates the relationship of the viewpoint-wise average discard percentages and the camera locations in different configurations. In summary, we conclude that in terms of our target of achieving real-time frame rates, rendering a single viewpoint in the middle of the grid offers the best trade-off between the reprojection benefits and the amount of path tracing required. Hence, in the quality experiments, we focus on evaluating the middle-viewpoint single-camera configuration.

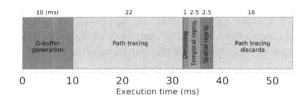

Fig. 3. Execution time breakdown of our implementation, rendering the Sponza light field (6×6 grid of 720p viewpoints) on RTX 3090 in 54 ms.

Overall, path tracing dominates the total execution time. This further validates our choice of minimizing the number of path traced viewpoints, as our implementation aims to achieve real-time frame rates. Specifically, NEE takes up most of the path tracing time. Disabling it reduces the path tracing time per viewpoint from 22 ms to 6 ms, so it would boost the performance from 18 FPS to 36 FPS, albeit yielding a somewhat lower visual quality. Similarly, the number of bounces could be reduced at the cost of sampling complex light transport less accurately: for example, with 3 bounces instead of 8, path tracing a viewpoint takes 7.5 ms instead of 22 ms, yielding 33 FPS (with NEE still on).

5.2   Quality

The RMSE and SSIM results for all four test scenes are presented in Table 1. Each value is an average taken over all 30 frames and over all the viewpoints. First, we see that even when spatiotemporal reprojection is applied on its own without a denoising filter before it, the quality increase compared to the 1 spp input is significant. However, the combination of denoising and reprojection is able to provide much larger overall improvements, especially on the more difficult Eternal Valley, Warehouse and Bistro Interior scenes.

On the other hand, a large area of Sponza is under direct illumination, so the 1 spp input is already of relatively high quality. Interestingly, the RMSE improvements obtained for Sponza with a denoiser included are smaller than those obtained with the spatiotemporal reprojection on its own. We suspect this is due to the denoising filters causing some additional blurring, which RMSE appears to consider unfavourable, as opposed to SSIM. This scene-specific deficiency could be addressed by fine-tuning the temporal accumulation parameters, or by using a denoising filter with more advanced adaptive capabilities, such as A-SVGF [20].

Table 1 also shows the spatiotemporal discard percentages for each scene, averaged over all frames and viewpoints. For Sponza, Eternal Valley and Warehouse, only 2.1–3.7 % of the samples in the 35 synthesized viewpoints need to be filled by path tracing. In Bistro Interior, the discard percentage is much higher at 11.5 %, but this is expected due to the rapid camera motion and a large amount of disocclusions, especially near the chairs, tables and glasses. Hence, the RMSE and SSIM results are also clearly lower than in the other scenes, as the larger disoccluded areas do not benefit from reprojection or temporal accumulation.

Example result frames are presented in Appendix B, where the subjective visual quality and temporal stability are also discussed. Moreover, example results for all scenes are presented in the supplementary video.

Table 1. RMSE and SSIM of the denoised and spatiotemporally reprojected frames compared to the 4096 spp reference, averaged over 30 frames and over all the viewpoints. Similarly averaged spatiotemporal reprojection discard percentages are also presented.

		Discard %	RMSE	SSIM
Sponza	1 spp input	2.08	0.1014	0.2631
	Spatiotemporally reprojected		0.0393	0.6384
	BMFR + reprojected		0.0512	0.7953
	SVGF + reprojected		0.0425	0.8046
Eternal Valley	1 spp input	3.69	0.2732	0.0704
	Spatiotemporally reprojected		0.1447	0.2960
	BMFR + reprojected		0.0756	0.6002
	SVGF + reprojected		0.0913	0.5728
Warehouse	1 spp input	2.30	0.1546	0.1520
	Spatiotemporally reprojected		0.1196	0.2489
	BMFR + reprojected		0.0582	0.7595
	SVGF + reprojected		0.0671	0.6671
Bistro Interior	1 spp input	11.53	0.2519	0.0435
	Spatiotemporally reprojected		0.2155	0.1073
	BMFR + reprojected		0.1252	0.4905
	SVGF + reprojected		0.1468	0.3904

For the multiple-client setup with grid sizes of 3×3, 4×4, 5×5, and 6×6, the SSIM results after denoising and spatiotemporally reprojecting the 1 spp input are illustrated in Fig. 4 for Sponza and Eternal Valley. For both scenes, the quality is fairly constant for all grid sizes. Since the discard percentages for the viewpoints furthest away from the middle are higher in Eternal Valley than in Sponza, there is a slight drop in SSIM for the largest grid sizes, but the effect is still very minor. These results indicate that the described setup can be used to serve different light field displays with comparable quality across all of them.

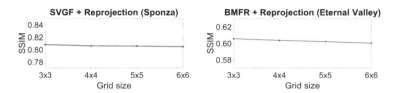

Fig. 4. SSIM of the denoised and spatiotemporally reprojected 1 spp frames for varying grid sizes.

6   Conclusions

We proposed a real-time pipeline for photorealistic light field path tracing, and demonstrated it with a practical implementation that renders a 6×6 grid of 1280×720 viewpoints at 18 frames per second on a single GPU. The real-time performance is achieved by path tracing a viewpoint in the middle of the grid at 1 spp, denoising it, and constructing the 35 other viewpoints around it through spatiotemporal reprojection. We also showed that this pipeline could be used for simultaneously serving multiple light field clients with different display grid sizes, with the quality remaining constant across clients.

Our implementation works best for scenes with slow or moderate movement; rendering fast-paced content proves more challenging, due to the compromises made in order to achieve real-time performance on a single GPU. However, if more distributed resources are available, all viewpoints can be denoised in parallel after reprojection, instead of only denoising the path traced viewpoint(s) before reprojection. With more resources available, path tracing multiple viewpoints also becomes a more feasible option, and is expected to improve the quality for fast-paced content. The additional resources could also be used to improve the input spp, in which case more lightweight denoising may be sufficient.

Acknowledgements. This project is supported by the Academy of Finland under Grant 325530.

Appendix A: Discard Percentages

Figure 5 illustrates the average discard percentages per viewpoint after spatial reprojection in Sponza, for the five tested viewpoint configurations. Overall, the average discard percentages confirm the intuition that rendering a middle viewpoint is slightly better in terms of spatially discarded pixels than rendering the top left viewpoint, specifically for the furthest reprojected viewpoints in the corners. Adding a second rendered viewpoint clearly lowers the amount of discarded pixels compared to the single-camera setups. However, path tracing more viewpoints means much more computational effort compared to rendering only a single viewpoint, so Fig. 5 indicates that the reduction in the discard percentages is simply not enough to justify path tracing an additional viewpoint when striving for real-time performance.

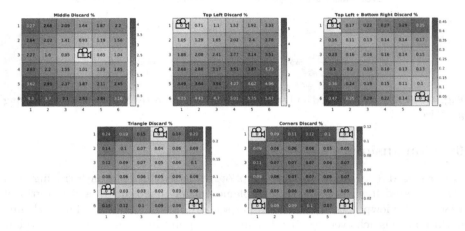

Fig. 5. Viewpoint-wise spatial discard percentage heatmaps for Sponza, for the different tested configurations. The path traced viewpoints are marked with camera icons. Note that each heatmap has a different range.

Appendix B: Comparison Images

Figures 6 and 7 illustrate the results for all scenes, showing the original 1 spp input for the middle viewpoint, the denoised + reprojected results for the synthesized top left viewpoint, and the reference 4096 spp top left viewpoint. Overall, the visual quality is high enough to be usable in various real-time applications; the most visible denoising artifacts are the oversmoothing of shadows, and a moderate amount of blur. Moreover, the blockwise nature of BMFR can still be seen in the Eternal Valley result (Fig. 6d), as temporal accumulation has not yet had time to fully compensate for it. Similarly, temporal accumulation has not yet removed some of the residual noise in Figs. 7c–f.

In general, narrow strips along the top and left borders exhibit a higher amount of noise, as they were not visible in the middle viewpoint, and thus did not benefit from the denoising. The effect of discards due to the fast camera motion is also evident in the disoccluded areas of Bistro Interior (Figs. 7d and 7f). These are further visualized in Fig. 8, which shows a selection of the results in Figs. 6 and 7 before the discarded areas have been filled in, and with the discards shown in red. These artifacts could be mitigated for example by path tracing more samples at the affected locations, or by leveraging the denoise-after-

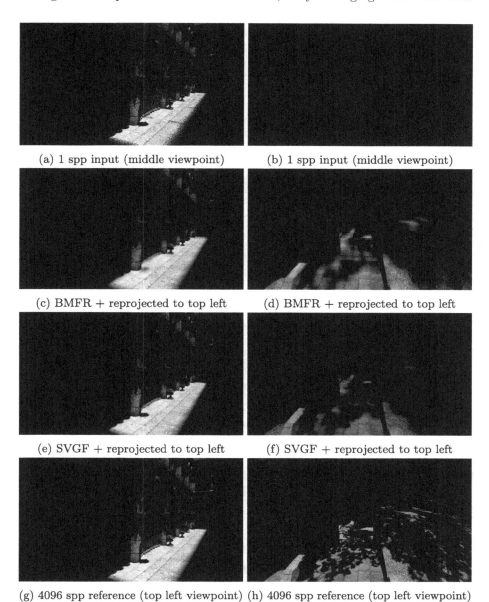

(a) 1 spp input (middle viewpoint)   (b) 1 spp input (middle viewpoint)

(c) BMFR + reprojected to top left   (d) BMFR + reprojected to top left

(e) SVGF + reprojected to top left   (f) SVGF + reprojected to top left

(g) 4096 spp reference (top left viewpoint) (h) 4096 spp reference (top left viewpoint)

Fig. 6. Results for frame 15 of Sponza (left column) and Eternal Valley (right column) after denoising and reprojecting the middle viewpoint onto the top left viewpoint of the 6 × 6 grid.

reprojection pipeline option if parallel resources are available. Applying deep learning based temporal rendering techniques (see [9]) can also be an attractive option in that case.

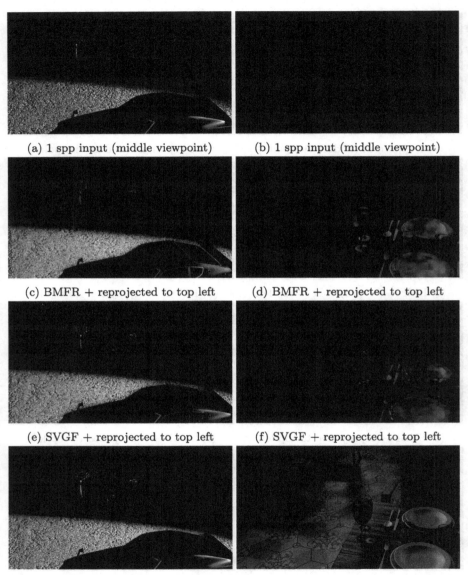

(a) 1 spp input (middle viewpoint)   (b) 1 spp input (middle viewpoint)

(c) BMFR + reprojected to top left   (d) BMFR + reprojected to top left

(e) SVGF + reprojected to top left   (f) SVGF + reprojected to top left

(g) 4096 spp reference (top left viewpoint) (h) 4096 spp reference (top left viewpoint)

Fig. 7. Results for frame 6 of Warehouse (left column) and frame 8 of Bistro Interior (right column) after denoising and reprojecting the middle viewpoint onto the top left viewpoint of the 6 × 6 grid.

The temporal quality of the results can be seen in the supplementary video, which features all four test scenes. Overall, the temporal behaviour is relatively stable, thanks to the temporal accumulation. However, the accumulation does also involve a tradeoff between introducing ghosting (too much reuse) and not being able to suppress fireflies (too little reuse), as highlighted in the video for Eternal Valley. As for the quality in the disoccluded areas, the single-frame examples discussed above are also representative of the full video sequences.

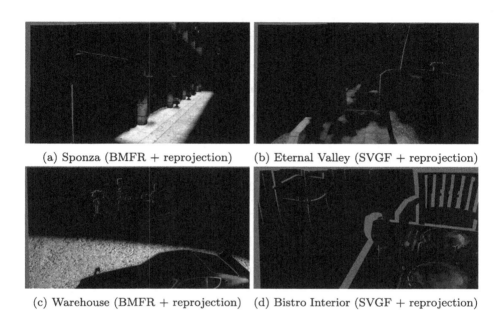

(a) Sponza (BMFR + reprojection)   (b) Eternal Valley (SVGF + reprojection)

(c) Warehouse (BMFR + reprojection)   (d) Bistro Interior (SVGF + reprojection)

Fig. 8. The denoising + reprojection results corresponding to Fig. 6c, Fig. 6f, Fig. 7c and Fig. 7f, before the discarded reprojection locations (visualized in red) have been filled in with path tracing. (Color figure online)

References

1. Andersson, M., Johnsson, B., Munkberg, J., Clarberg, P., Hasselgren, J., Akenine-Möller, T.: Efficient multi-view ray tracing using edge detection and shader reuse. Vis. Comput. **27**(6–8), 665–676 (2011)
2. Flynn, J., Neulander, I., Philbin, J., Snavely, N.: Deepstereo: learning to predict new views from the world's imagery. In: Proceedings of IEEE Conference on Computer Vision and Pattern Recognition (2016)
3. Fraboni, B., Iehl, J.C., Nivoliers, V., Bouchard, G.: Adaptive multi-view path tracing. In: Proceedings of 30th Eurographics Symposium on Rendering (2019)
4. Hansen, A.J., Klein, J., Kraus, M.: Light field rendering for head mounted displays using pixel reprojection. In: VISIGRAPP (1: GRAPP) (2017)

5. Hedman, P., Philip, J., Price, T., Frahm, J.M., Drettakis, G., Brostow, G.: Deep blending for free-viewpoint image-based rendering. ACM Trans. Graph. **37**(6), 1–15 (2018)

6. Hoffman, D.M., Girshick, A.R., Akeley, K., Banks, M.S.: Vergence-accommodation conflicts hinder visual performance and cause visual fatigue. J. Vis. **8**(3), 33 (2008)

7. Hua, H.: Enabling focus cues in head-mounted displays. Proc. IEEE **105**(5), 805–824 (2017)

8. Huang, F.C., Luebke, D., Wetzstein, G.: The light field stereoscope. In: ACM SIGGRAPH 2015 Emerging Technologies. ACM, New York (2015)

9. Huo, Y., Yoon, S.E.: A survey on deep learning-based Monte Carlo denoising. Comput. Vis. Media **7**(2), 169–185 (2021)

10. Işik, M., Mullia, K., Fisher, M., Eisenmann, J., Gharbi, M.: Interactive Monte Carlo denoising using affinity of neural features. ACM Trans. Graph. **40**(4), 1–13 (2021)

11. Koskela, M., et al.: Blockwise multi-order feature regression for real-time path-tracing reconstruction. ACM Trans. Graph. **38**(5), 1–14 (2019)

12. Lanman, D., Luebke, D.: Near-eye light field displays. ACM Trans. Graph. **32**(6), 1–10 (2013)

13. Lehtinen, J., Aila, T., Chen, J., Laine, S., Durand, F.: Temporal light field reconstruction for rendering distribution effects. In: ACM SIGGRAPH 2011 Papers (2011)

14. Lehtinen, J., Aila, T., Laine, S., Durand, F.: Reconstructing the indirect light field for global illumination. ACM Trans. Graph. **31**(4), 1–10 (2012)

15. Levoy, M., Hanrahan, P.: Light field rendering. In: Proceedings of 23rd Annual Conference on Computer Graphics and Interactive Techniques (1996)

16. Mäkitalo, M.J., Kivi, P.E., Jääskeläinen, P.O.: Systematic evaluation of the quality benefits of spatiotemporal sample reprojection in real-time stereoscopic path tracing. IEEE Access **8**, 133514–133526 (2020)

17. Meng, X., Zheng, Q., Varshney, A., Singh, G., Zwicker, M.: Real-time Monte Carlo denoising with the neural bilateral grid. In: EGSR (DL) (2020)

18. Pearson, J., Brookes, M., Dragotti, P.L.: Plenoptic layer-based modeling for image based rendering. IEEE Trans. Image Process. **22**(9), 3405–3419 (2013)

19. Schied, C., et al.: Spatiotemporal variance-guided filtering: real-time reconstruction for path-traced global illumination. In: Proceedings of High Performance Graphics (2017)

20. Schied, C., Peters, C., Dachsbacher, C.: Gradient estimation for real-time adaptive temporal filtering. Proc. ACM Comput. Graph. Interact. Tech. **1**(2), 1–16 (2018)

21. Shi, L., Hassanieh, H., Davis, A., Katabi, D., Durand, F.: Light field reconstruction using sparsity in the continuous Fourier domain. ACM Trans. Graph. **34**(1), 1–13 (2014)

22. Wang, Z., Bovik, A.C., Sheikh, H.R., Simoncelli, E.P.: Image quality assessment: from error visibility to structural similarity. IEEE Trans. Image Process. **13**(4), 600–612 (2004)

23. Wu, G., Zhao, M., Wang, L., Dai, Q., Chai, T., Liu, Y.: Light field reconstruction using deep convolutional network on EPI. In: Proceedings of IEEE Conference on Computer Vision and Pattern Recognition (2017)

24. Xie, F., Mishchuk, P., Hunt, W.: Real time cluster path tracing. In: SIGGRAPH Asia 2021 Technical Communications (2021)

25. Xu, Z., Bi, S., Sunkavalli, K., Hadap, S., Su, H., Ramamoorthi, R.: Deep view synthesis from sparse photometric images. ACM Trans. Graph. **38**(4), 1–13 (2019)

Crowd Simulation with Detailed Body Motion and Interaction

Xinran Yao[1], Shuning Wang[1], Wenxin Sun[1], He Wang[2], Yangjun Wang[3], and Xiaogang Jin[1(✉)]

[1] State Key Lab of CAD&CG, Zhejiang University, Hangzhou 310058, People's Republic of China
jin@cad.zju.edu.cn
[2] University of Leeds, Leeds, UK
[3] CROS of Tencent Games, Shenzhen, People's Republic of China

Abstract. Crowd simulation methods generally focus on high fidelity 2D trajectories but ignore detailed 3D body animation which is normally added in a post-processing step. We argue that this is an intrinsic flaw as detailed body motions affect the 2D trajectories, especially when interactions are present between characters, and characters and the environment. In practice, this requires labor-intensive post-processing, fitting individual character animations onto simulated trajectories where anybody interactions need to be manually specified. In this paper, we propose a new framework to integrate the modeling of crowd motions with character motions, to enable their mutual influence, so that crowd simulation also incorporates agent-agent and agent-environment interactions. The whole framework is based on a three-level hierarchical control structure to effectively control the scene at different scales efficiently and consistently. To facilitate control, each character is modeled as an agent governed by four modules: visual system, blackboard system, decision system, and animation system. The animation system of the agent model consists of two modes: a traditional Finite State Machine (FSM) animation mode, and a motion matching mode. So an agent not only retains the flexibility of FSMs, but also has the advantage of motion matching which adapts detailed body movements for interactions with other agents and the environment. Our method is universal and applicable to most interaction scenarios in various environments in crowd animation, which cannot be achieved by prior work. We validate the fluency and realism of the proposed method by extensive experiments and user studies.

Keywords: Crowd simulation · Agent-based · Terrain-adaptive

1 Introduction

High-fidelity crowd animation has been a central topic in various graphics applications and can be used in many applications such as computer games, industry films, and virtual reality. From a macroscopic perspective, the fidelity of crowd motion is determined by the group behavior, such as the authenticity of trajectories and the rationality of crowd movement [9]. From a microscopic point of

N. Magnenat-Thalmann et al. (Eds.): CGI 2022, LNCS 13443, pp. 227–238, 2022.
https://doi.org/10.1007/978-3-031-23473-6_18

view, detailed individual motions also greatly affect the realism of crowd animation. While much effort has been spent on the former, the effort spent on the latter has mainly focused on single character animation. There has been little effort in systematic in-depth integration of both.

To address the aforementioned problems, we co-model crowd motions and individual motions, and propose a crowd behavior and animation control framework using a three-level hierarchy. The top level is the global control of crowd motions. The middle level targets the behavioral motions of different groups within the crowds. The low level governs the individual motions and agent interactions with other agents and the environment. We exhaustively evaluate our systems at different levels with both quantitative and qualitative metrics. The results show that our system can efficiently generate physically plausible and visually pleasing crowd motions with detailed individual motions and interactions. Formally, we propose a new three-level control framework for realistic crowd simulation with detailed individual motions. Also, we propose a new agent model for intelligent agent behaviors with awareness of the surroundings.

2   Related Work

Crowd simulation raises numerous challenges e.g. modeling, authoring, rendering, animation, navigation, behavior, and perception [28,29,33].

2.1   Crowd Simulation

The classic method of crowd simulation is based on a force model [9]. In order to simulate a more real trajectory in crowds, a new mechanical model [2] is proposed to simulate the following movement. On the other side, the force-based model produces problems such as oscillation and bottleneck congestion [10]. So the agent-based crowd model comes into being. The crystal model [19] takes the influences of multiple factors into account and integrates the theories of sociology and anthropology into crowd simulation. Shao et al. [25] propose a more flexible model named automatic pedestrian model to simulate crowd. In terms of performance, the hierarchy structure for scene management can greatly improve the search, and it is widely used in games [21] and swarm simulation [22]. Similarly, Low et al. [18] also propose an agent-based crowd simulation framework dividing the perception model into high level and low level.

To further improve the decision-making ability of individual agents, Markov decision process is introduced into crowd simulation [24]. Besides, many new methods are proposed to improve the decision-making ability of agents with the rise of deep learning and reinforcement learning. Dünmez et al. [3] use the reinforcement learning method to improve the ability of individual obstacle avoidance. To achieve crowd simulation of intelligence, only four agents can be trained as leaders [27], followed by the Boids model [23]. Individual obstacle avoidance can also be improved with reinforcement learning [3].

Our research is categorically different from the above methods in that we focus on the integration of crowd simulation with detailed individual motions. Rather than employing character animation techniques as a separate step, we deeply root individual motions into crowd simulation.

Besides simulation, different metrics have been proposed to validate simulation fidelity, where comparing simulations with real data becomes popular [7,8,30–32]. However, these methods are designed to compare two sets of 2D trajectories. Given our aim is to generate detailed individual motions among crowds, they cannot be employed to evaluate our framework. We, therefore, propose our own quantitative and qualitative metrics in terms of physical plausibility and visual realism.

2.2 Motion Matching

Hoyet et al. [13] confirm that enhancing the animation adaptiveness to the environment can improve the authenticity of the simulation results by adding shoulder movement in crowd simulation. Considering the authenticity of leg movements, Narang et al. [20] propose a motion simulation method based on gait constraints. However, the above methods only simulate the scenes on flat ground. Recently, deep learning has been used in various games [16]. The PFNN model [12] can enable individuals to complete a series of complex actions, which can well adapt to terrain changes.

In addition to terrain adaptiveness, interaction with other objects is also within the scope of motion matching. Agrawal et al. [1] propose an action template that could realize a variety of footstep animations for specific tasks, such as sidestep. However, the matching of the above interactive actions depends on a large amount of data and can only be used on specific tasks. A collaborative animation/simulation model [5] is developed by embedding multiple character animation methods in the form of components within the same framework.

Our research is also orthogonal to motion matching. It depends on motion matching on the low-level motion generation, but focuses on how agents are influenced by high level information such as crowd or local group behaviors.

3   Overview

The whole simulation scene is under the control of a hierarchical structure called "Global-Group-Individual". At the individual level, an agent model is built to achieve auto-perception, auto-decision, and cooperation with other group members. The animation system, as a co-simulation system, is constructed by a motion matching mode implemented by a phase-functioned neural network (PFNN) model [12] and a traditional animation mode implemented by finite state machine (FSM) [6]. An overview of our method is shown in Fig. 1.

4   Hierarchical Control

In our system, the structure has three levels: global, group, and individual.

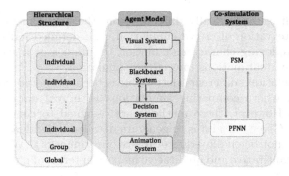

Fig. 1. The overview of our approach. The whole framework consists of three parts: hierarchy structure, agent model, and co-simulation system.

Global. This level acts as a global control to manage the information that needs to be broadcast. For environmental information management, the global level abstracts the scene into a waypoint map [4] and a grid map as shown in Fig. 2. Waypoint maps describe the feasible areas and the location of obstacles in the scene. The grid map G is defined as $G = (C_x, C_y, w, h, d)$, in which C_x and C_y is the position of the lower left corner of the map on the horizontal axis and the vertical axis, w is the width of the map, h is the height of the map, and d is the size of grids. Every grid $g(i, j)$ stores the pointer to the head of a doubly linked list. The position of each individual is stored in a linked-list node and linked to an appropriate list head. The relation between individual position (p_x, p_y) and grid $g(i, j)$ can be expressed as $i = \lfloor \frac{p_x - C_x}{d} \rfloor, j = \lfloor \frac{p_y - C_y}{d} \rfloor$.

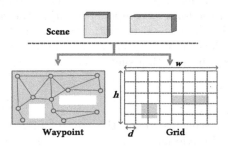

Fig. 2. The schematic diagram of the abstract structure of global level. Waypoint map and grid map are used to represent the entire scene. In the grid map, w and h are the width and the height of the map, respectively.

Group. This level acts as the role of a leader, responsible for controlling the individuals in a group, updating their information and coordinate motions, such as moving to a specific target.

Individual. This layer has two motion components: individual and group members. The former deals with the plausibility of individual motions, and the latter ensures that the individual motions are also consistent with group behaviors.

5   Agent Model

Figure 4 illustrates the agent model which consists of four modules: visual system, blackboard system, decision system, and animation system. The four models correspondingly simulate four functions of human beings: perception, memory, decision-making, and behavior.

5.1   Visual System

The scope of human observation is assumed to be a fan-shaped area centered on the agent location. Based on this assumption, the visual system is divided into three layers: short-distance perception, mid-distance perception, and long-distance perception. Figure 3 depicts the structure of the visual system.

Fig. 3. The structure of visual system. The visual system is divided into three layers. Different layers correspond to different viewing distance and viewing angle.

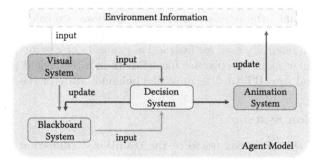

Fig. 4. The framework of the agent model. Based on the external environment information, the visual system passes the information to the blackboard system and the decision system. According to the information from pre-order systems, the decision system sends the decision results to the animation system. Then the animation system controls the agent to move or interact with other agents.

The grid map is used to get the information of the short-distance and mid-distance perception layers. We inspect the nodes in the covered grids after selecting a rough rectangular range based on the double length of the visual distance. For the mid-distance perception layer or other layers whose visual angle less is than 180°, the coverage area can be narrowed by a straight line passing through the center and perpendicular to the forward direction of the agent. The ray method is used in the long-distance layer. The position of the agent and the emission angles are sampled within the visual angle range.

5.2   Blackboard System

The blackboard system is organized as a dictionary data structure with the item name as keywords and item information as contents. A blackboard is separated into two parts to store individual attributes and memorize knowledge respectively. The individual attributes, defining the characteristics of agents. Memory knowledge has three blocks of content: public, friend, and private. Only the owner of the blackboard has the authority to modify the contents while other individuals have the authority to notify the modification.

5.3   Decision System

The decision system is composed of motion decision and behavioral decision. Motion decision, which determines the movement speed of the agent in the next frame, is influenced by the target position and the surrounding environment. It is divided into two parts: pathfinding implemented by waypoint maps and collision avoidance based on a social force method. The pathfinding part determines the general direction of individual movement while the collision avoidance part adjusts the local movement speed taking the surrounding environment into consideration. The attractive force is calculated according to the moving speed determined by pathfinding. Based on the visual system's perception of the surrounding individuals, the repulsive forces and frictions are calculated according to the distance to the surrounding individuals perceived by the visual system. Behavior Tree is generally used for fast-action games to create interactive characters with a similar social intelligence like soldiers in a battlefield [14,17]. Therefore, our method uses BT to determine the behavior state of the next frame.

5.4   Animation System

The animation system is composed of the traditional animation state machine [6] and the PFNN model [12]. Animation state machine is responsible for controlling actions that interact with other objects. The PFNN model replaces the animation related to the interaction of the terrain in the traditional animation state machine, so as to ensure the adaptability of the agent to the terrain in the process of movement.

6   Co-simulation System

6.1   Mode Switch

The switching process is shown in Fig. 6. We propose a method based on the interpolation of intermediate transition animations to realize the fluent switch between the PFNN model and the animation state machine, in which a transition clip is inserted between the traditional animation state machine and the PFNN model.

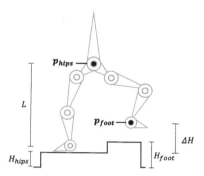

Fig. 5. The diagram of foot position in IK. This figure shows how the foot movement adapts to height on uneven ground. Here p_{hips} represents the position of the agent's center and p_{foot} represents the position of the agent's foot.

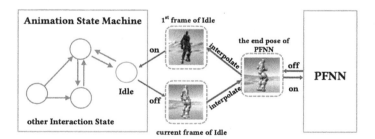

Fig. 6. The process of mode switches between the animation state machine and the PFNN model. We interpolate a transition animation between the traditional animation state machine and the PFNN model.

6.2   Inverse Kinematic

In the PFNN mode, IK is realized by the geometrical analysis method, which is offered by the IK components of Unity [15]. With the IK result, we update the position of each joint. In the animation state machine mode, we only need to set an appropriate foot position as the endpoint for IK, and the height of position can be sampled from height maps. However, the feet will slide on the ground if the foot height of each frame is directly set as the height of the ground. The relationship between foot positions and terrain height is shown in Fig. 5 and the calculation process is described as follows:

1. Get the current center position p_{hips} and foot position p_{foot} for every frame;
2. According to the projection position of p_{hips} and p_{foot} on the ground, the height under them, h_{hips} and h_{foot}, are sampled directly;
3. Calculate the target height difference between the foot and the ground $\Delta H = L - (L + h_{hips} - p_{foot}.y) = p_{foot}.y - h_{hips}$, where L is the height difference between the hips and the ground;
4. Calculate the actual height difference $p_{foot}.y = H_{foot} + \Delta H * \max(\frac{L + h_{hips} - h_{foot}}{L}, 0)$, where $\max(\frac{L + h_{hips} - h_{foot}}{L}, 0)$ is the regulator of height difference. When the sampled height of the foot is larger than that of the hips, the affection of ΔH decreases, and the regulator is smaller therefore. The more similar the sampled heights are, the closer the actual height of the foot to ΔH.

7 Results

All simulation results in this paper are achieved through the game engine Unity, 2017.1.5F1 version, and the program runs in the environment with Intel Core i7-8700 CPU and NVIDIA GeForce RTX 2070 GPU.

Fig. 7. Crowd behaviors simulated by our method. The whole team moves toward the same goal (left) and each individual tends to avoid collision with others (right).

Fig. 8. Results of terrain adaptiveness for training data. Movements can well adapt to different kinds of terrains. Even on an unusual terrain (the left figure), the joint angle can be adjusted to adapt to the terrain.

7.1 Behaviour Simulation

For all the presented results in the scenario, the red and blue teams are against each other, and the goal of a group always finds the enemy members. Figure 7(left) shows that both teams have a tendency to move towards the nearest enemy member no matter whether the group members are gathered or dispersed at present, and the movement is influenced by the group's overall goal. In Fig. 7(right), the individual movement trajectory clearly shows the collision avoidance with obstacles and other individuals.

7.2 Animation Simulation

This section focuses on the animation adaptiveness to terrain and shows the results from multiple perspectives. Figure 8 shows the results of terrain adaptiveness for training data, and Fig. 9 shows the animation result of the character moving on a very steep cliff. As can be seen from the figure, the new environment also gives rise to new motions, such as climbing a cliff, jumping, and maintaining body balance while sliding down a cliff with the help of arms. In addition, in order to verify the necessity of adding IK, in the process of experiment, we also compared the situation of with and without IK. We define a slipping error to represent the degree of foot slipping. For each foot landing, the position where the toe joint first contacts the ground is taken as the landing point, and the horizontal distance between the toe joint and the landing point in subsequent frames is calculated.

Fig. 9. Results of terrain adaptiveness for testing data. Our method can also produce acceptable results on special terrains such as a cliff.

Table 1. Average penetration error about movement

Terrain type	Our method with IK(cm)	Our method without IK (cm)	FSM (cm)
Flat	**0.000470**	0.001627	1.232807
Uneven	**1.136922**	3.756697	2.595681

Table 2 shows the average slipping errors on the flat and uneven ground caused by different methods. The results of the table show that the foot slipping produced by our method is much more slighter than that of the animation state machine, and the phenomenon is further weakened with the assistance of IK.

Another experiment mainly studies the clipping in the crowd animation. Table 1 shows the average penetration errors calculated from each method on different terrains when characters are moving. The results show that our method with IK produces the least penetration error and can effectively weaken the penetration phenomenon.

Table 2. Average slipping error

Terrain type	Our method with IK(cm)	Our method without IK(cm)	FSM(cm)
Flat	10^{-6}	0.115825	22.974229
Uneven	**2.603551**	3.05557	15.985041

7.3 User Study

To evaluate the smoothness of mode switching in the animation system, we conduct a user study with two clips of the comparison videos, one is a single confrontation while another is a group confrontation. Each video contains two segments, one is simulated by our method and the other only by the animation state machine [6]. Participants were asked to rate the videos on two dimensions, fluency and reality. The score is on a scale of 1 to 9, with a lower score indicating better performance in the first segment on that dimension, and vice versa. Results show that the average score of the single confrontation is 3.10 on fluency and 3.71 on reality, respectively. It is clear that our method outperforms the traditional method in terms of both fluency and reality. In terms of group confrontation, the fluency score and the reality score are 5.14 and 5.10 respectively, which is still better than the traditional animation state machine method [6].

8 Conclusion and Future Work

We have presented a novel hierarchical crowd behavior and animation control framework with detailed body locomotion and interaction, which can control at various levels consistently and support the interaction of multiple agents/groups in complex terrain scenes. Under control of the hierarchy structure, the information is propagated from level to level, which simplifies the complexity of scene management and improves the efficiency of information transfer. The four modules in the agent model are complementary to each other, which together make the agent motion realistic, intelligent, and flexible. At the same time, in order to perform terrain adaptiveness, the PFNN model is employed into the animation state machine. This co-simulation can simulate a variety of interactive tasks on different kinds of terrains.

Our method has some limitations. The motion matching method in our implementation can only control characters with a fixed skeleton structure. In addition, our simulation results of motion matching are highly dependent on the quality of the dataset. In the future, we would like to improve the ability of decision-making by the state-of-art technology, such as reinforcement learning to further strengthen the intelligence of agents. Generating crowd animation through the learned motion matching model [11] or the neural state machine [26] is also an interesting direction to explore.

Acknowledgement. Xiaogang Jin was supported by the National Natural Science Foundation of China (Grant No. 62036010) and the Key Research and Development Program of Zhejiang Province (Grant No. 2020C03096).

References

1. Agrawal, S., van de Panne, M.: Task-based locomotion. ACM Trans. Graph. (TOG) **35**(4), 82:1–82:11 (2016)
2. Chraibi, M., Tordeux, A., Schadschneider, A.: A force-based model to reproduce stop-and-go waves in pedestrian dynamics. In: Knoop, V.L., Daamen, W. (eds.) Traffic and Granular Flow '15, pp. 169–175. Springer, Cham (2016). https://doi.org/10.1007/978-3-319-33482-0_22
3. Dönmez, H.A.: Collision avoidance for virtual crowds using reinforcement learning. Master's thesis (2017)
4. Felder, A., Van Buskirk, D., Bobda, C.: Automatic generation of waypoint graphs from distributed ceiling-mounted smart cameras for decentralized multi-robot indoor navigation. In: Proceedings of the 13th International Conference on Distributed Smart Cameras, pp. 1–7 (2019)
5. Gaisbauer, F., Lehwald, J., Agethen, P., Sues, J., Rukzio, E.: Proposing a co-simulation model for coupling heterogeneous character animation systems. In: Proceedings of the 14th International Joint Conference on Computer Vision, Imaging and Computer Graphics Theory and Applications, VISIGRAPP, pp. 65–76 (2019)
6. Gillies, M.: Learning finite-state machine controllers from motion capture data. IEEE Trans. Comput. Intell. AI Games **1**(1), 63–72 (2009)
7. Guy, S.J., van den Berg, J., Liu, W., Lau, R., Lin, M.C., Manocha, D.: A statistical similarity measure for aggregate crowd dynamics. ACM Trans. Graph. (TOG) **31**(6), 1–11 (2012)
8. He, F., Xiang, Y., Zhao, X., Wang, H.: Informative scene decomposition for crowd analysis, comparison and simulation guidance. ACM Trans. Graph. (TOG) **4**(39), 50 (2020)
9. Helbing, D., Farkas, I., Vicsek, T.: Simulating dynamical features of escape panic. Nature **407**(6803), 487–490 (2000)
10. Helbing, D., Johansson, A.: Pedestrian, crowd, and evacuation dynamics. In: Encyclopedia of Complexity and System Science, pp. 6476–6495 (2009)
11. Holden, D., Kanoun, O., Perepichka, M., Popa, T.: Learned motion matching. ACM Trans. Graph. (TOG) **39**(4), 53 (2020)
12. Holden, D., Komura, T., Saito, J.: Phase-functioned neural networks for character control. ACM Trans. Graph. (TOG) **36**(4), 42:1–42:13 (2017)
13. Hoyet, L., Olivier, A.H., Kulpa, R., Pettré, J.: Perceptual effect of shoulder motions on crowd animations. ACM Trans. Graph. (TOG) **35**(4), 53:1–53:10 (2016)

14. Johansson, A., Dell'Acqua, P.: Emotional behavior trees. In: 2012 IEEE Conference on Computational Intelligence and Games (CIG), pp. 355–362 (2012)

15. Juliani, A., et al.: Unity: a general platform for intelligent agents. arXiv preprint arXiv:1809.02627 (2018)

16. Justesen, N., Bontrager, P., Togelius, J., Risi, S.: Deep learning for video game playing. IEEE Trans. Games 12(1), 1–20 (2020)

17. Llobera, J., Boulic, R.: A tool to design interactive characters based on embodied cognition. IEEE Trans. Games 11(4), 311–319 (2019)

18. Low, M., Cai, W., Zhou, S.: A federated agent-based crowd simulation architecture. In: The 2007 European Conference on Modelling and Simulation, Prague, Czech Republic, pp. 188–194. Citeseer (2007)

19. Manenti, L., Manzoni, S.: Crystals of crowd: modelling pedestrian groups using mas-based approach. In: Proceedings of the 12th Workshop on Objects and Agents, Rende (CS), Italy, 4–6 July 2011, CEUR Workshop Proceedings, vol. 741, pp. 51–57 (2011)

20. Narang, S., Best, A., Manocha, D.: Simulating movement interactions between avatars & agents in virtual worlds using human motion constraints. In: 2018 IEEE Conference on Virtual Reality and 3D User Interfaces (VR), pp. 9–16 (2018)

21. Nystrom, R.: Game programming patterns (2014)

22. Ren, J., Sun, W., Manocha, D., Li, A., Jin, X.: Stable information transfer network facilitates the emergence of collective behavior of bird flocks. Phys. Rev. E 98(5), 052309 (2018)

23. Reynolds, C.W.: Flocks, herds and schools: a distributed behavioral model. In: Proceedings of the 14th Annual Conference on Computer Graphics and Interactive Techniques, pp. 25–34 (1987)

24. Ruiz, S., Hernandez, B.: Real time Markov decision processes for crowd simulation. GPU Zen, pp. 323–341 (2017)

25. Shao, W., Terzopoulos, D.: Autonomous pedestrians. Graph. Models 69(5–6), 246–274 (2007)

26. Starke, S., Zhang, H., Komura, T., Saito, J.: Neural state machine for character-scene interactions. ACM Trans. Graph. (TOG) 38(6), 209:1–209:14 (2019)

27. Sun, L., Zhai, J., Qin, W.: Crowd navigation in an unknown and dynamic environment based on deep reinforcement learning. IEEE Access 7, 109544–109554 (2019)

28. Thalmann, D.: Crowd simulation. Wiley encyclopedia of computer science and engineering (2007)

29. van Toll, W., Pettré, J.: Algorithms for microscopic crowd simulation: advancements in the 2010s. Comput. Graph. Forum 40(2), 731–754 (2021)

30. Wang, H., Ondřej, J., O'Sullivan, C.: Path patterns: analyzing and comparing real and simulated crowds. In: ACM SIGGRAPH Symposium on Interactive 3D Graphics and Games 2016, pp. 49–57 (2016)

31. Wang, H., Ondrej, J., O'Sullivan, C.: Trending paths: a new semantic-level metric for comparing simulated and real crowd data. IEEE Trans. Visual Comput. Graphics 23(5), 1454–1464 (2017)

32. Wang, H., O'Sullivan, C.: Globally continuous and non-Markovian crowd activity analysis from videos. In: Leibe, B., Matas, J., Sebe, N., Welling, M. (eds.) ECCV 2016. LNCS, vol. 9909, pp. 527–544. Springer, Cham (2016). https://doi.org/10.1007/978-3-319-46454-1_32

33. Zhou, S., et al.: Crowd modeling and simulation technologies. ACM Trans. Model. Comput. Simul. (TOMACS) 20(4), 1–35 (2010)

Towards Rendering the Style of 20th Century Cartoon Line Art in 3D Real-Time

Peisen Xu[✉] and Davide Benvenuti

Nanyang Technological University, 50 Nanyang Avenue, Singapore 639798, Singapore
{peisen001,dbenvenuti}@ntu.edu.sg

Abstract. Al Hirschfeld (1903–2003) is one of the foremost representatives of a great generation of cartoon line artists. He extensively drew the American popular culture of the whole 20th century at its peak of liveliness and pushed beyond the conventional and commercial cartoon art with his exclusive focus on the minimalistic and expressive usage of pen-and-ink lines. However, the expressiveness of his line style has not been fully exploited in 3D real-time. We observe a lack of workflow and graphical tools to create his style. Thus, this essay proposes Hirschfeld's artworks as style guides to design and develop 3D line art characters in real-time animation. An innovative workflow focusing on the artistic directed control of the selection and the thickness of lines is explored and examined to assist the creation of 3D real-time line art and animation.

Keywords: Real-time rendering · Computer animation · Stylised rendering · Cartoon line art

1 Introduction

Before the popularity of computer-generated imagery (CGI) productions, cartoon line art was dominant in the animation art of the 20th century. Traditional 2D animation relied heavily on the expressiveness of the lines. Many of these animation styles were inspired by the cartoonists and caricaturists of the same era. Al Hirschfeld is known as one of the line artists that has heavily influenced the 2D animation style. His art style can be generally described as elegant, minimalistic, and accurate. Eric Goldberg, a renowned animator at Disney, incentivised the efforts in making Hirschfeld's style appear in major 2D animation productions. He brought Hirschfeld's style into the 1992 animated feature film Aladdin, as the character Genie, and in the 1999 animated short Rhapsody in Blue. However, it is not common to observe the direct adaption of his style in 3D animation, and there has been no scholarly discussion on how to recreate his style in 3D real-time.

The production of 3D animation has been traditionally focusing on photorealistic rendering methods. At the same time, there has been a persistent interest in exploiting the artistic potential and the variety of the rendered imageries in both industry and academia. Combining the 3D geometries with 2D stylised strokes is one of the main concerns in computer animation. Most previous research generally focuses on predicting the important strokes from a 3D model to be rendered and stylised in real-time. On the other hand, the last century has seen many video games utilising the real-time line rendering method to achieve a different look, notably the Borderlands series (2009–2019), Okami (2006), and Guilty Gear Xrd (2014). Nonetheless, few of them have conducted qualitative analysis on the unique style of certain influential cartoon line artists and addressed the difficulties of problem-solving in transforming their artistic language to 3D real-time. Besides, there is a lack of developed tools that enable artists to create expressive 3D line art in real-time.

In this case, Hirschfeld has developed his distinctive style with the exaggerated shape of the characters, unique selection of lines, and the precise control of the line texture and thickness, which is often hard to recreate in 3D computer graphics without paying special attention on the underlying geometry and the style and selection of rendered strokes. Thus, this research effort is motivated by the strong interest in experimenting with the certain line drawing style represented by Hirschfeld, which, to our knowledge, has not been found in the imagery results of any previous efforts in real-time line rendering.

With this goal in mind, we experimented with recreating some of his drawings in 3D and rendering them with stylised lines. In this process, we discovered that controlling the line visibility and line thickness in 3D is essential for creating the Hirschfeld-inspired minimalistic and smooth contours, and tools for edge marking and line weight control are helpful for these purposes. However, these tools are not available in the current real-time game engines. Thus, we developed a workflow that allows users to design and create real-time 3D line art and animation inspired by Hirschfeld's artworks.

This research makes the following contributions:

1. A workflow in the real-time game engine with tools that enable artists to manually mark edges for rendering, control line thickness at each individual vertex with a line weight map and real-time fine-toning.
2. An animation tool that interpolates the line thickness between keyframes, achieving smooth line transformation.
3. As part of the ongoing exploration of the usage of non-photorealistic rendering in computer animation, this research will imply the combination of line rendering techniques and the visual analysis of line art as a possible future direction to expand the aesthetic style in real-time line rendering.

2 Related Works

2.1 Contour Extraction

Image-space algorithm is most popular in real-time applications because of the simplicity in usage and advantages in performance [2]. Saito and Takahashi [19] proposed an "enhanced technique" to draw "comprehensible lines" over 3D objects in the image space using "Geometric Buffer", the screen-space information of the 3D scene stored in the memory. In practice, depth buffer (z-buffer) is often used in combination with normal buffer to extract the lines from the 3D geometry [11]. Colour buffer is also used for silhouette detection [10]. An edge detector such as the Sobel operator is often applied to the buffer.

Another method that is commonly used is the two-pass hardware rendering technique [2], which is also known as the "inverted hull" technique. Generally, the geometry is rendered normally in the first pass, and then the mesh is enlarged and rendered again with only back faces enabled. In this way, the outer silhouette of the geometry can emerge behind the normal mesh. This method can be found in several early research [7,18] and more recent research effort utilises programmable vertex shader to achieve this effect with one pass [4], but the performance is similar. Besides, this method is widely applied in Blender or Sketchfab to quickly add outlines to a stylised character mesh. The extracted contours can be complemented by other types of contours based on surface features, such as the creases, suggestive contours, ridges and valleys and apparent ridges [6]. Nonetheless, the style of these rendered lines is often too generic to depict the expressiveness of Hirschfeld's line art.

With the advent of GPU programming, more implementations utilise different shader programs in GPU [8,9], such as the geometry shader program, taking advantage of its accessibility to the adjacency information and its ability to generate extra geometry for line stylisation. The performance is also significantly improved [20]. However, most game engines such as Unity and Unreal Engine do not provide native support for adjacency information considering the optimisation of their rendering pipeline. This can only be circumvented by pre-calculating the adjacency information and attaching it as an additional buffer to the shader program.

Most recent efforts concerning contour extraction and stylised caricature generation involve the usage of machine learning methodologies [12,13,15,21]. These methods usually use 2D images as input and generate the stylised output automatically without or with limited interactivity. This research focuses more on enabling user interaction in a 3D real-time environment with a traditional graphical pipeline. Similar real-time tools have been developed for rendering 3D objects in a wide range of watercolour styles [16].

2.2   Line Stylisation

Previous research efforts on real-time stylised line rendering normally separate the pipeline into stroke extraction, chaining, smoothing and stroke rendering [2]. The visibility of the contour lines is computed either in object space with quantitative invisibility [1], with hybrid methods such as the item buffer [3], or with a new type of data structure named the segment atlas [5]. These methods are complex in both implementation and usage, and the frame rate of the real-time application is often limited by screen resolution.

Some other research extends the two-pass hardware rendering method by adding variable thickness to the outlines [4,14]. These methods base the line thickness on the principles detected from the topology of the mesh, such as the surface curvature, mesh density and lighting conditions etc. Although they produce lines with variable thickness, users cannot manually control the line thickness in specific regions. Moreover, Xu et al. [22] have developed a framework for stylised line animation that consists of three modules: 3D line extraction, curve rendering, and stroke tools. The first module computes the vectorised 2D lines from 3D objects based on occlusion. The second converts the lines to Disk B-spline curve format for stylisation. The third captures the user's input for further manipulation of the strokes. On the other hand, the developers of Guilty Gear have shared their workflow of using the vertex colour to store the thickness information of the outlines and surface textures with rectangular black bars for inner contour lines [17]. This workflow allows the artist to make manual adjustments to the thickness of the outline by changing vertex colour and the inner lines by changing UV.

2.3   Offline Rendering

More sophisticated line rendering and stylisation can be achieved by offline rendering such as Blender's Freestyle renderer. They assume that line drawing is a process that can be decomposed into four stages: line selection, chaining, splitting, and ordering. To test the functionality of Freestyle, we closely examined one of Hirschfeld's caricatures of Louis 'Satchmo' Armstrong, and reproduced it in 3D (Fig. 1).

Fig. 1. Louis 'Satchmo' Armstrong by Al Hirschfeld

Figure 2 is rendered using Freestyle line renderer. The silhouette (the boundary between the visible and the hidden faces) and the creases (the edges between two faces with an angle smaller than the threshold, which is 134°) are rendered. To achieve the minimalistic effect, the original artwork uses only the essential lines. One continuous line spans different body parts. This visual nuance can be reflected in 3D with Freestyle's line omission and line chaining functions. In addition, the surface lines on the face and the body of the character which cannot be represented by contours, silhouette or creases are painted as textures onto the object. Furthermore, Freestyle's edge mark function allows some edges (such as the edges on the collars) to be manually marked and rendered.

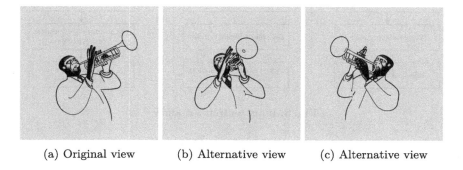

| (a) Original view | (b) Alternative view | (c) Alternative view |

Fig. 2. Offline rendering of the character in Blender Freestyle

The style of each stroke can also be adjusted in the Freestyle line renderer. The outer silhouette of the character is generated with thicker lines, line chaining and variation of thickness along the stroke. The lines are made smoother by applying the Bezier curve to the line geometry. On the other hand, the detailed lines, such as lines on the trumpet, are made thinner.

3 Approaches

From our observation of Hirschfeld's line arts, to achieve the minimalistic effect, the choice of which lines to draw and which to ignore is important. Thus, in this aspect, we found the edge mark function in Blender's Freestyle helpful. However, there is no counterpart to this function in current real-time rendering engines. Furthermore, another important characteristic of Hirschfeld's style is the stroke with varied thickness, often with thin ends. We aim to achieve this visual nuance with our line weight map approach as the initial rough input, and real-time line editing tools for fine-tuning. The 3D models are created in Blender and rendered in Unity. An overall input-output workflow is shown in Fig. 3.

3.1 Edge Marking

The process of manually marking the edges for real-time line rendering is done inside Blender. This is inspired by Blender's Freestyles edge mark function. Edge marks can be helpful for rendering the additional edges which can not be covered by contours or surface textures. To bring a similar function to real-time, additional edge marking information needs to be attached to the mesh on export. Thus, we developed a tool for automatically generating an additional UV map for recording the information of the marked edges. The users are able to manually select edges for marking, then the processing script will iterate through

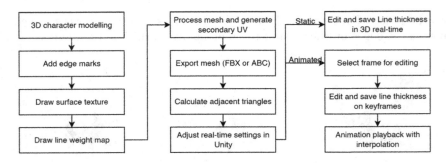

Fig. 3. Input/output workflow

all of the edges on the mesh and create a struct for each edge containing the indices of the two end vertices and a binary value, 0 for the normal edge and 1 for the marked edge. Besides, the script also checks if the edge is loose, and then marks the loose edge and creates a zero-area triangle on those edges. This is to prevent loose edges from being discarded in Unity. As a final step, the processing script iterates through each triangle. For each edge in the triangle, the edge type (either 0 or 1) is recorded in the V value of the UV coordinate of the first vertex in the edge. This process is shown in Algorithm 1.

Algorithm 1. Edge mark processing algorithm

$normalEdge \leftarrow 0$
$markedEdge \leftarrow 1$
for $edges$ in mesh.edges **do**
    if $edge$ is marked **then**
        $edge \leftarrow markedEdge$
    else
        $edge \leftarrow normalEdge$
    end if
end for
for $face$ in mesh.faces **do**
    $uv.v0 \leftarrow edge0.type$
    $uv.v1 \leftarrow edge1.type$
    $uv.v2 \leftarrow edge2.type$
end for

3.2   Geometry Shader Line Rendering

The silhouette edges and the marked edges of the objects are extracted in the geometry shader program. We circumvented the limitation of the geometry shader program in the game engine by utilising additional buffers to store the pre-computed adjacency information. The interface for this pre-processing step and the generated custom file is shown in Fig. 4. After that, in the application run-time, the geometry shader program iterates through each triangle in the mesh, and determines whether it is front-facing by comparing it with the view direction. If so, a similar operation is performed on each of its adjacent triangles to check whether any of them is back-facing. If a back-facing adjacent triangle is found, the edge between these two triangles is identified as a silhouette edge. Besides, we also check the vertex coordinate on the additional UV. If it is marked as 1, then the edge which contains this vertex as the first vertex is marked for rendering.

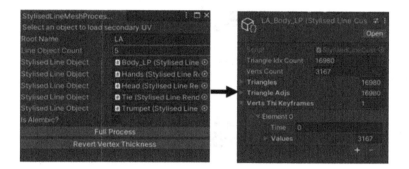

Fig. 4. Pre-processing UI and generated custom data

3.3 Line Weight Map

To enable the adjustment of the line thickness, the shader program reads from a grey-scale image map, named line weight map. This map contains the information on the weight for line thickness on each vertex. In the geometry shader program, the amount of offset on each vertex is controlled by multiplying the general line thickness and the corresponding line weight on the vertex. The line weight map is set as the initial condition for the variable line thickness in the stylised line object, while we also added support for more dynamic control of line thickness.

3.4 Editing the Line Thickness in Real-Time

To modify and fine-tune the line thickness, the user normally needs to update the line weight map in an external image editing software. We aim to improve the efficiency of this process by adding control to the line thickness in the real-time engine.

The process of editing the 3D line thickness is separated into four steps: centre vertex selection, control for the radius of influence, editing the line thickness and saving the modified thickness in offline storage. Additionally, we added the tool of "fill" and "erase" for more convenience in editing. A typical user interface is shown in Fig. 5.

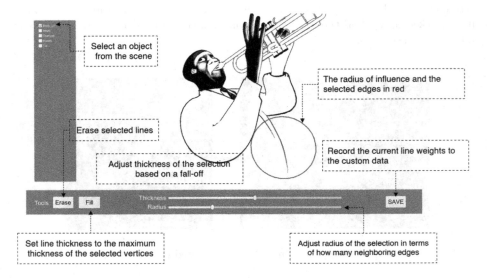

Fig. 5. Line thickness editing interface

The information of the modified line weight is recorded in the alpha channel of the vertex colour property of the mesh. To improve visual clarity, the selected edges and the radius of influence are coloured in red when editing. For better performance, the process of detecting the line selection and modifying the line thickness is mostly operated on GPU. Figure 6 shows our rendering pipeline for real-time line editing.

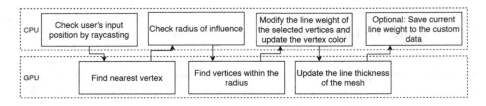

Fig. 6. Line editing pipeline

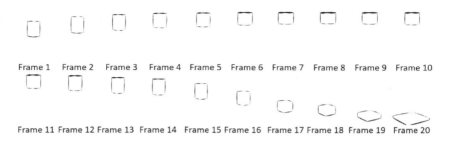

Fig. 7. Stylised line animation

3.5 Recording Line Thickness in Real-Time Animation

Our workflow can also be applied to real-time animation. We currently support the alembic format. For animated mesh, we added additional control to pause, preview and adjust the frames of the animation. The modified line thickness can be recorded on the selected frames and interpolated between each keyframe. An example is shown in Fig. 7. This is specifically applicable in cartoonish rigging and animation to enable smooth blending of line thickness when the mesh is squashed and stretched.

4 Results

We tested the workflow on AMD Ryzen 7 3700X 8-Core Processor 3.59 GHz, Nvidia GeForce RTX 2070 SUPER and 16 GB RAM with three characters: the trumpeter model, the pianist model and the "Apple of My Eye" model.

With the combination of the edge mark function and the line weight map, we can achieve the result close to the offline rendering in Blender and recreate Hirschfeld's line art in 3D real-time. The same trumpeter model is rendered in real-time (Fig. 8) with the line weight map (Fig. 8d). We also tested the workflow with the pianist character mesh inspired by Hirschfeld's drawing of George

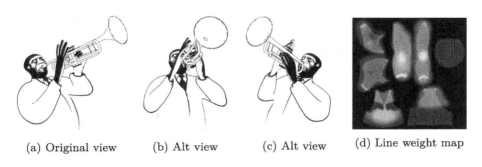

(a) Original view   (b) Alt view   (c) Alt view   (d) Line weight map

Fig. 8. Real-time rendering of the character in Unity

Gershwin. Figure 9 shows the comparison between the real-time line rendering and the original drawing.

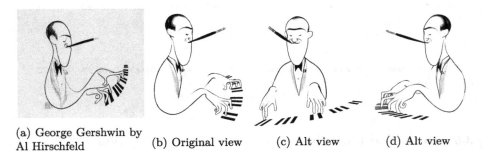

(a) George Gershwin by Al Hirschfeld   (b) Original view   (c) Alt view   (d) Alt view

Fig. 9. Real-time rendering of the pianist character in Unity

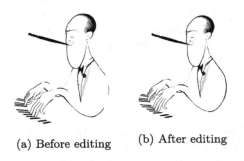

(a) Before editing   (b) After editing

Fig. 10. Fixing the breaking lines

From a certain camera angle, the line is breaking up, causing unwanted extra line segments to emerge on the mesh. In this case, our fill and erase functions can be useful to help remove these extra segments or connect the breaking lines from multiple perspectives. An example is shown in Fig. 10.

Finally, this workflow is applied to an animated character mesh called "Apple of My Eye", created by Davide Benvenuti, to exemplify the generalisability of the approach. Figure 11 shows several frames of the result. Table 1 is a detailed comparison of the performance.

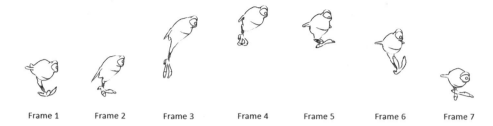

| Frame 1 | Frame 2 | Frame 3 | Frame 4 | Frame 5 | Frame 6 | Frame 7 |

Fig. 11. Real-time animation of the low-poly "Apple of My Eye" model

Table 1. Details on the performance

Name	Vert count	Animated?	Frame rate
Trumpeter	73627	No	127
Pianist	18534	No	375
Pianist (Animated)	21156	Yes	47
Apple of my Eye	10428	Yes	108

5 Conclusion and Future Works

This research addressed the lack of efforts in adapting the influential art style of cartoon line art in the 20th century in 3D real-time by experimenting with adapting selected artworks by Hirschfeld in the real-time engine. We developed a set of tools each solves a specific problem in this adaptation process. The edge mark tool is developed for the artistic directed selection of specific edges for real-time rendering. The line weight map is implemented to achieve the minimalistic effect, as well as control the varied thickness of lines. And real-time line thickness editing tool is designed and developed for fine-tuning the results from different perspectives.

With the tools above, a workflow for adapting Hirschfeld's style as static line art in 3D real-time is suggested. Besides, this research also explored creating real-time 3D character animation with an extension of the tools above. This workflow utilises the alembic format to store the information of the cartoonish animation. Using the real-time line editing tool, the custom rendering pipeline not only lets users modify line thickness at certain keyframes but also automatically interpolates the thickness between two consecutive recorded keyframes.

One of the major issues with producing 3D line character animation with this workflow is line flickering when the frame rate is around 40–50 frames per second. This issue can be circumvented by creating the mesh with a low poly count or disabling line editing when not used. However, a more desirable solution is to implement the temporal anti-aliasing technique in the current pipeline. This will also enable support for more objects in the same scene, which is often useful in real-time video games.

Finally, this workflow can be expanded in the future to incorporate more styles from other 20th century cartoon line artists, such as the style of Ronald Searle (1920–2011) and Gerald Scarfe (1936-).

References

1. Appel, A.: The notion of quantitative invisibility and the machine rendering of solids. In: Proceedings of the 1967 22nd National Conference, pp. 387–393 (1967)
2. Bénard, P., Hertzmann, A.: Line drawings from 3D models. arXiv preprint arXiv:1810.01175 (2018)
3. Brown, I., Arandjelović, O.: Making Japenese ukiyo-e art 3D in real-time. Sci **2**(2), 32 (2020)
4. Chen, D., Zhang, Y., Liu, H., Xu, P.: Real-time artistic silhouettes rendering for 3D models. In: 2015 8th International Symposium on Computational Intelligence and Design (ISCID), vol. 1, pp. 494–498. IEEE (2015)
5. Cole, F., Finkelstein, A.: Two fast methods for high-quality line visibility. IEEE Trans. Visual Comput. Graphics **16**(5), 707–717 (2009)
6. DeCarlo, D., Finkelstein, A., Rusinkiewicz, S., Santella, A.: Suggestive contours for conveying shape. In: ACM SIGGRAPH 2003 Papers, pp. 848–855 (2003)
7. Gooch, B., Sloan, P.P.J., Gooch, A., Shirley, P., Riesenfeld, R.: Interactive technical illustration. In: Proceedings of the 1999 Symposium on Interactive 3D Graphics, pp. 31–38 (1999)
8. Hermosilla, P., Vázquez, P.P.: NPR effects using the geometry shader. In: GPU Pro 360, pp. 33–49. AK Peters/CRC Press (2018)
9. Hermosilla, P., Vázquez Alcocer, P.P., et al.: Single pass GPU stylized edges (2009)
10. Herring, D.G., McGraw, T.: Inter-color NPR lines: a comparison of rendering techniques. Comput. Games J. **5**(1), 39–53 (2016)
11. Hertzmann, A.: Non-photorealistic rendering and the science of art. In: Proceedings of the 8th International Symposium on Non-Photorealistic Animation and Rendering, pp. 147–157 (2010)
12. Jang, W., Ju, G., Jung, Y., Yang, J., Tong, X., Lee, S.: StyleCariGAN: caricature generation via StyleGAN feature map modulation. ACM Trans. Graph. **40**(4), 1–16 (2021). https://doi.org/10.1145/3450626.3459860
13. Li, H., Sheng, B., Li, P., Ali, R., Chen, C.P.: Globally and locally semantic colorization via exemplar-based broad-GAN. IEEE Trans. Image Process. **30**, 8526–8539 (2021)
14. Matsuo, T., Mikami, K., Watanabe, T., Kondo, K.: Shape oriented line drawing in real-time 3DCG. In: SIGGRAPH Asia 2011 Posters, p. 1 (2011)
15. Mitchell, J.L., Brennan, C., Card, D.: Real-time image-space outlining for non-photorealistic rendering. In: ACM SIGGRAPH 2002 Conference Abstracts and Applications, SIGGRAPH 2002, p. 239. Association for Computing Machinery, New York (2002). https://doi.org/10.1145/1242073.1242252
16. Montesdeoca, S.E.: Real-time watercolor rendering of 3d objects and animation with enhanced control. Ph.D. thesis, Nanyang Technological University (2018)
17. Motomura, J.C.: GuiltyGearXrd's art style: the X factor between 2D and 3D (2015). https://www.youtube.com/watch?v=yhGjCzxJV3E
18. Raskar, R., Cohen, M.: Image precision silhouette edges. In: Proceedings of the 1999 Symposium on Interactive 3D Graphics, pp. 135–140 (1999)

19. Saito, T., Takahashi, T.: Comprehensible rendering of 3-D shapes. In: Proceedings of the 17th Annual Conference on Computer Graphics and Interactive Techniques, pp. 197–206 (1990)
20. Sander, P.V., Nehab, D., Chlamtac, E., Hoppe, H.: Efficient traversal of mesh edges using adjacency primitives. ACM Trans. Graph. (TOG) **27**(5), 1–9 (2008)
21. Xie, M., Xia, M., Li, C., Liu, X., Wong, T.T.: Seamless manga inpainting with semantics awareness. ACM Trans. Graph. (SIGGRAPH 2021 Issue) **40**(4), 96:1–96:11 (2021)
22. Xu, X., Seah, H.S., Qian, K., Benvenuti, D.: A framework for stylized animation from 3D line extraction. In: International Workshop on Advanced Imaging Technology (2017)

Detection and Recognition

Face Detection Algorithm in Classroom Scene Based on Deep Learning

Yi Zhang and Chongwen Wang[✉]

Beijing Institute of Technology, No. 5 Yard, Zhong Guan Cun South Street, Beijing , China
wcwzzw@bit.edu.cn

Abstract. With informatisation progresses in education, the application of artificial intelligence technology in education is increasing day by day. Although some breakthroughs have been made, the application in specific scenes (such as classroom scenes) faces many difficulties, such as small target detection, severe occlusion, etc. We propose a target detection algorithm based on video data for the classroom scene, which combines the optical flow information to improve the accuracy and alleviate the impact of occlusion. We also put forward the counting method suitable for classroom scenes, which can be used as the evaluation standard of attendance rate, head-up rate, and other indicators in classroom quality evaluation.

Keywords: Target detection · Optical flow method · Video analysis · Face detection

1 Introduction

With the development of educational informatisation, deep learning and other technologies in education are also gradually increasing. For example, the target detection algorithm can evaluate the probabilities of attendance, coming late, early leaving, and other indicators in teaching quality evaluation. However, the mainstream object detection algorithms such as YOLO, SSD, and faster RCNN have poor performance in college classroom scenes. We hope to propose a face detection algorithm suitable for classroom scenes and video data, especially for small targets and severe occlusion.

Target detection algorithms have made significant progress in accuracy and realtime performance. However, the image target detection network is usually detected after extracting keyframes when processing video data. The subsequent tasks such as tracking and motion prediction are also based on the bounding boxes. This method has good realtime performance, but some semantic information hidden between frames is ignored. In addition, it is difficult to deal with the occlusion problem, which is mainly limited by datasets and the setting of parameters. People usually adjust the threshold of the NMS [1] algorithm to balance the undetected error and residual error or use specific algorithms such as GAN [2] and composite network to alleviate the occlusion problem.

Although the deep learning method has been widely used in target detection, we still need to study many problems in video target detection. For example, this paper aims at the

© The Author(s), under exclusive license to Springer Nature Switzerland AG 2022
N. Magnenat-Thalmann et al. (Eds.): CGI 2022, LNCS 13443, pp. 255–265, 2022.
https://doi.org/10.1007/978-3-031-23473-6_20

large classroom in colleges and universities, with many people and small targets. There is a problem of severe occlusion and small target detection in this scene. Therefore, we combine optical flow information, design a video target detection algorithm, and apply it to practical problems. We prove the algorithm can accurately detect students in classroom scenes.

2   Related Works

2.1   Overview of Target Detection

With the development of deep learning, there has been a lot of progress and many algorithms with good performance in target detection. We will introduce target detection in detail from two aspects of image target detection and video target detection.

Image Target Detection
Image target detection algorithms are mainly divided into region proposal and end-to-end algorithms.

The algorithm based on region proposal, also known as the two-stage algorithm, needs to select the candidate region before extracting the feature and judging the category. The standard algorithms are fast RCNN and faster RCNN [3]. D2det [4] introduces dense regression to solve precise positioning and classification and predict multiple thick frame offsets of object proposals.

End-to-end target detection algorithms mainly include YOLO [5], SSD, etc., also known as single-stage target detection algorithms. Instead of region nomination, they regard target detection as a complete algorithm and directly regress the image features extracted by a convolution neural network to obtain the position and category of target objects. Yolof [6] only uses the one-level feature layer for detection and introduces two key components: expansion encoder and uniform matching, which improves performance.

Remarkably, several models with promising results have emerged in face detection recently. Tinaface [7] adopts the scale-invariant method to process the image pyramid to capture large-scale changes to achieve good detection results. Retinaface [8] adds the face key point branch and context modelling module and introduces the multi-loss function and self-monitoring method. It's detection speed is not limited by the number of faces.

Video Target Detection
Video target detection is mainly divided into deep-learning-based methods and detection and tracking-based methods.

Video detection algorithms based on deep learning, such as DFF [9], scholars hope to use the motion information of the target in the video for detection, so they propose the concept of keyframe and carry out end-to-end training, which ensures the accuracy of detection and improves the defect of approximate but inaccurate features. Ba Griffin [10] et al. proposed uncalibrated motion and detection-based depth estimation, derived analysis models and corresponding solutions, and developed a recursive neural network

(RNN) to predict depth according to motion and boundary box to improve the general applicability in different fields.

The representative work of the video detection algorithm based on detection and tracking is TCNN [11], which can solve the problem of temporal and spatial consistency of targets in the video. TCNN links the detection frames extracted from each frame together in chronological order and then uses a neural network to classify and score, and finally completes the tracking. MW Ashraf [12] and others use the region nomination method and optical flow information to detect small video targets using the attention mechanism at the pixel level. Roam [13] uses LSTM to solve the problem of target tracking, which is composed of a tracking module and model assistance update module, which can update the tracking model online.

2.2 Optical Flow Method

Hron Schunck proposed the gradient-based optical flow algorithm. This algorithm designs a total error parameter. When this parameter reaches the minimum value, it is considered that the calculated optical flow field is optimal, and the iterative formula of the optical flow field is obtained. Hron Schunck's algorithm can measure the roughness of the optical flow field. Jiang [14] et al. learned optical flow motion from sparse correspondence, significantly reducing video memory use and maintaining high accuracy.

With the development of deep learning technology, many methods of predicting optical flow using neural networks have appeared in recent years. These methods usually use multiplicative interaction to simulate the relationship between images. Differences and optical flow can then be inferred from potential variables. Flownet [15] inputs two frames of adjacent images, first extracts the respective characteristic pictures of the two images and obtains the final optical flow prediction through a series of convolution layers and inverse convolution layers. Mask flownet [16] is a relatively new improvement, and its effect on the Kitti data set is also excellent. It is mainly aimed at the problem of some occluded areas in the background after the foreground moves. Yang G [17] et al. learned optical flow from unlabeled image sequences under enhanced self-supervised.

3 Proposed Method

3.1 Model Overview

Aiming at the problem of face detection in the classroom environment, we propose a one-stage detection network combined with optical flow named FFnet (Flow Face network), as shown in Fig. 1. The ideas to improve the detection accuracy of small targets in video data are as follows: (1) based on YOLOX processing image RGB three-channel information, add two-dimensional optical flow information to enrich inter-frame semantics. (2) Refer to the soft NMS [18] algorithm and improve the Seq NMS [19] algorithm to make it suitable for complex scenes with high target overlap in the classroom. (3) Sort [20] algorithm is used to track to judge whether new students appear and leave the classroom.

Firstly, we extract the optical flow information by flownet and save it in a two-dimensional matrix with the same shape as the picture. The optical flow information matrix of the previous frame and the RGB image information of the current frame are spliced according to the channel dimension. The optical flow information matrix of the first frame is 0.

3.2 Network Design

The architecture of FFnet refers to YOLOX, as shown in Fig. 1. It can be divided into three parts: CSPDarknet, FPN, and Yolo head. The feature of input pictures will first be extracted in CSPDarknet. In the backbone part, three feature layers will be obtained for the following network construction step. Through the FPN network, three enhanced features can be obtained. We use YOLO head to obtain the prediction results finally.

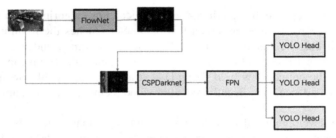

Fig. 1. The architecture of the FFnet.

Feature Extraction

Because we use additional two-dimensional optical flow information, the input layer dimension of the feature extraction network is set to 5 * w * h.

The backbone feature extraction network used by FFnet is CSPDarknet, with four essential characteristics.

1. The residual network is used. The whole CSPdarknet part is composed of residual convolution. The residual network is easy to optimise and can improve the accuracy by increasing the depth. Its internal residual block uses a jump connection, which alleviates the problem of gradient disappearance caused by increasing the depth in-depth neural network.
2. The focus network structure is used to take a value for every other pixel of the input data; that is, each feature layer will extract four independent feature layers and stack the four independent feature layers. The width and height information is concentrated in the channel information, and the input channel is expanded by four times. The architecture of focus is shown in Fig. 2.
3. SiLU activation function (Eq. 1) is used. SiLU is an improved version of sigmoid and ReLU. SiLU has the characteristics of no upper bound and lowers bound, smooth and non-monotonic. The effect of SiLU on the deep model is better than that of ReLU.

4. The SPP structure is used to extract features through the maximum pool of different pool core sizes to improve the receptive field of the network. In yolov4, spp is used in FPN. In FFnet, the spp module is used in the backbone feature extraction network.

$$f(x) = x \cdot sigmoid(x) \tag{1}$$

We add the attention module based on cspdarknet and use the CBAM attention mechanism for the three feature graphs output by the backbone network. In addition, we use EIOU loss as the loss function to focus the regression process on the high-quality anchor box to achieve higher convergence speed and accuracy.

Feature Fusion
In the feature fusion stage, we select three feature layers for fusion. These three feature layers come from different positions of CSPDarknet, which are located in the middle layer, the lower layer, and the bottom layer, respectively. When the input is (640,640,5), the shapes of the three feature layers are feat1 = (80,80,256), feat2 = (40,40,512), feat3 = (20,20,1024). We refer to the way of PAnet for feature fusion.

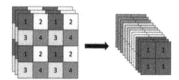

Fig. 2. The architecture of the focus

Obtain Prediction Results
Through the FPN feature fusion layer, we obtain three enhanced feature layers P3_out, P4_out, and P5_Out, the shapes of these three enhanced features are (20,20,1024), (40,40,512), (80,80,256) respectively, and then we use the feature layers of these three shapes to pass them into YOLO head to obtain the prediction results. The structure of the YOLO head is shown in the Fig. 3.

The YOLO head is designed to be decoupled, which divides classification and regression into two parts, which are combined at the time of final prediction. Three prediction results can be obtained for each feature layer: reg: the regression parameters used to judge each feature point. After the regression parameters are adjusted, the prediction box can be obtained; obj: used to judge whether each feature point contains an object; cls: used to judge the type of object contained in each feature point. Stack the three prediction results, and the result obtained by each feature layer is, out (h, w, 4 + 1 + num_classes).

3.3 Improved Seq NMS

Seq NMS is proposed for the video target detection task. Firstly, sequence selection is carried out, all detection frames with scores greater than the threshold are selected, the

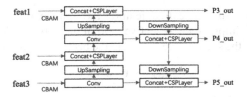

Fig. 3. The architecture of the feature fusion part of FFnet

detection frames at the corresponding positions in the front and rear frames are matched, and the average value or maximum value is selected for rescoring, and then NMS is used for suppression. Hard NMS is used in Seq NMS as a way of inhibition.

To make the algorithm more suitable for classroom scenes, we do not use the average and maximum rescoring methods of traditional Seq NMS. Still, it carries out weighted rescoring based on frame spacing. At the same time, this paper combines soft NMS and Seq NMS to improve traditional Seq NMS suppression steps. The improvement methods are introduced in detail below.

In this paper, the traditional Seq NMS rescoring algorithm is improved. The confidence U_n of the detection frame in the current frame is rescored as $0.8U_n + 0.1U_{n-1} + 0.1U_{n+1}$, which alleviates the false detection and missing detection caused by simply taking the average value, the erroneous detection caused by taking the maximum value, and the missing detection caused by taking the minimum value. Still, it will be more dependent on the detection performance of the network.

3.4 Face Count

In this paper, the sort algorithm is used to track the detection box to judge whether there are new students and students are leaving the classroom. With the help of the front and rear frame matching of the detection box, the counting function is realized, and the number of detection boxes judges the existing number in the classroom.

Counting Algorithm Based on Classroom Scene
Based on the sort algorithm, when the IOU between a target detected and the bounding box with all existing target prediction results in the selected frame is less than the specified threshold, it is considered that there is a new target to be detected.

The time interval of frame selection is enlarged to reduce the influence of occlusion in the classroom and adapt to the problem that the target in the classroom environment is relatively static. Select one frame every two seconds. When a target loses the matching frame in five adjacent frames, it is considered that the target disappears, and the face count decreases by one. On the contrary, when a target appears in five adja-cent frames, it is assumed that a new target appears, and the face count increases by one.

4   Experience

4.1   Dataset

We use the dataset collected in the Beijing Institute of Technology classroom to train the model. The dataset is divided into three types by classroom size: large, medium, and tiny. We sample the same number of frames in each class-room size to ensure good data distribution.

There are ten videos in the classroom face dataset, including two videos in large classrooms, five in medium-sized classrooms, and three in small classrooms. Each video is about 45 min. We extract one frame of the video every two seconds for annotation. In addition, we also randomly labeled some data for image face detection, which is divided into the training set and test set. The training set contains 477 pieces, of which 80 pieces are from large classrooms, 124 pieces are from small class-rooms and 273 pieces are from medium-sized classrooms. There are 171 pictures in the test set, including 32 from large classrooms, 95 from medium-sized classrooms, and 44 from small classrooms. The training set contains 11207 face areas and the test set contains 3972 face areas.

Due to the face dataset of the classroom being small, it is easy to be over-fitting when training large networks. This paper uses the widerface dataset for pre-training.

To enable the algorithm to deal with both picture target detection and video target detection simultaneously, we use the image and video datasets to train the model. When using an image dataset, to fit the model's input shape, the image's optical flow information is set to 0 (Fig. 4).

Fig. 4. Some pictures of the classroom face dataset

4.2 Pretreatment

The dataset is expanded by image inversion, image rotation, and scaling before train-ing to alleviate the lack of classroom face data and enhance the model's generalization. The first method is image flipping. Vertical flipping has no significance for the detection of classroom scenes, so we only flip the image horizontally. The second method is image rotation. We only rotated the image at a small angle. The specific rotation angle value is set to $\{-20, -10, 10, 20\}$. The third method is to zoom the im-age. While keeping the image size unchanged, zoom in, that is, cut the corresponding size at the center of the image, and fill the corresponding position of the image with a 0-pixel value when zooming out. The zoom ratio is $\{0.9, 1.1\}$.

4.3 Parameter Setting

Our experiment uses the PyTorch framework. The GPU is GTX 3090, 24GB. This experiment involves two parts: first, the training of the optical flow prediction network, and then the training of the target detection network.

Firstly, this paper trains the optical flow prediction network. The results of extracting optical flow information are shown in Fig. 5.

In this paper, the specific network super parameter details in the target detection network training process are as follows. When initializing the backbone network, select to import part of network model parameters pre-trained by the voc2007 dataset to accelerate the convergence speed. For the input layer, assign the pre-training values of the three channels of the pre-training model to the first three channels. The initial values of the last two channels are generated based on Gaussian distribution. The SPP kernel sizes are set to (5, 9, 13). Firstly, the widerface data set is used to sup-plement 0 matrices for optical flow information for 20000 iterations of training. Then the classroom face data set and video optical flow information are used for 20000 iterations of training. To balance the effect of image target detection and video target detection, 100 iterations of widerface without optical flow information and 100 itera-tions of classroom face data set with optical flow information are cycled, and the training is repeated and alternately trained ten times.

Fig. 5. The results of extracting optical flow information

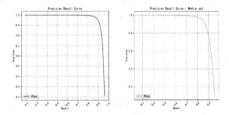

Fig. 6. The PR curve of FFnet. Left: he PR curve of FFnet on the classroom face dataset. Right: The PR curve of FFnet on the widerface dataset.

4.4 Result

We use optical flow information to assist target detection to realize the function of face detection and counting in the classroom scene. The detection results and counting results are shown below. We compare the performance of different networks on the widerface dataset and classroom face dataset, show the performance of FFnet on the classroom face dataset after combining optical flow information and compare the accuracy of FFnet using different NMS algorithms.

Table 1. AP of several neural networks on widerface.

Network	AP
Faster RCNN(resnet)	0.604
Faster RCNN(RPN)	0.731
Retinaface	0.914
TinaFace	0.924
FFnet	0.916

Table 2. Performance of several networks on single frame classroom face dataset.

	AP	FPS
FFnet	0.926	22.4
Faster RCNN(FPN)	0.901	10.2
Faster RCNN(ResNet)	0.794	15.3
Retinaface	0.922	24.3
TinaFace	0.911	26.2

Table 3. Performance of FFnet on single frame classroom face dataset.

Soft-nms	Seq-nms	Our nms	AP
√			0.913
	√		0.908
		√	0.932

To evaluate the effect of the network model, we evaluate the network model from the aspects of accuracy, speed, and model size. It can be seen from Table 1 that in this paper, on the classroom face dataset, the single-frame accuracy mAp reaches 0.926. Combined with the video optical flow information, the map reaches 0.932. The mAp on the widerface dataset reaches 0.916, which is a little higher than Retinaface, and a little lower than TinaFace. It can be considered that the network structure proposed in this paper has better detection performance for small faces and can extract more effec-tive features for small targets.

It can be seen from Table 2 that FFnet is superior to the two-stage detection network in terms of detection rate. Because the model proposed in this paper needs to use the optical flow network to extract the optical flow information, which combines the target detection network and the optical flow extraction network, the detection with optical flow depends on the generation of optical flow data, in the absence of optical flow information, the detection speed is limited by the reasoning speed of optical flow network. In the presence of optical flow information, the detection speed of FFnet can reach 22.4 (FPS). Without considering the optical flow prediction network, the model size of FFnet is 99.1(M), which is close to TinaFace.

It can be seen from Table 3 that the improved Seq NMS proposed by us can significantly improve the accuracy. FFnet using the improved Seq NMS algorithm finally achieved an accuracy of 0.932 on the classroom face dataset.

Figure 6 shows the PR curve of the classroom face dataset and the widerface(medium) dataset after training. On the classroom face dataset, when the recall rate reaches 0.9, the precision rate begins to decline significantly. On the widreface dataset, when the recall rate reaches 0.8, the precision rate begins to decline significantly.

5   Conclusion

Based on processing RGB three-channel information of the image, we add two-dimensional optical flow information to enrich semantic knowledge between frames and relieve the detection problem caused by occlusion. By extracting optical flow information, the existing classroom face datasets are enriched. Referring to the soft NMS algorithm, we improve the Seq NMS algorithm to make it suitable for complex scenes with high target overlap in the classroom. We propose FFnet, which uses optical flow information to assist target detection. It achieves an accuracy of 0.912 on the classroom face dataset and can effectively detect faces in the classroom scene. Using a sort algorithm for tracking, a student counting algorithm suitable for the classroom scene is proposed to judge whether new students and students are leaving the classroom.

In the follow-up work, we will focus on further improving the detection accuracy, optimizing the algorithm model structure to make the algorithm more suitable for the classroom scene, and putting forward a new optimization scheme for the complex problem of dense optical flow calculation. In the next step, we plan to put forward a more efficient method for the target with severe occlusion to improve the detection performance of FFnet in practical application as much as possible.

References

1. Neubeck, A., Van Gool, L.: Efficient non-maximum suppression. In: 18th International Conference on Pattern Recognition (ICPR 2006), pp. 850–855 (2006)
2. Goodfellow, I.J., Pouget Abadie, J., Mirza, M., et al: Generative adversarial networks. In: Advances in Neural Information Processing Systems, pp. 2672–2680 (2014)
3. Ren, S., He, K., Girshick, R., et al.: Faster RCNN: towards real-time object detection with region proposal networks. Adv. Neural. Inf. Process. Syst. **28**, 91–99 (2015)

4. Cao, J., Cholakkal, H., Anwer, R.M., et al.: D2det: towards high quality object detection and instance segmentation. In: Proceedings of the IEEE/CVF Conference on Computer Vision and Pattern Recognition, pp. 11485–11494 (2020)
5. Bochkovskiy, A., Wang, C.Y., Liao, H.Y.M.: Yolov4: optimal speed and accuracy of object detection. arXiv preprint arXiv:10934 (2020)
6. Chen, Q., Wang, Y., Yang, T., et al.: You only look one-level feature. In: Proceedings of the IEEE/CVF Conference on Computer Vision and Pattern Recognition, pp. 13039–13048 (2021)
7. Zhu, Y., Cai, H., Zhang, S., et al.: TinaFace: strong but simple baseline for face detection. arXiv preprint arXiv:2011.13183(2020)
8. Deng, J., et al.: Retinaface: single-shot multi-level face localisation in the wild. In: Proceedings of the IEEE/CVF Conference on Computer Vision and Pattern Recognition, pp. 5203–5212 (2020)
9. Zhu, X., Xiong, Y., Dai, J., et al.: Deep feature flow for video recognition. In: Proceedings of the IEEE Conference on Computer Vision and Pattern Recognition, pp. 2349–2358 (2017)
10. Griffin, B.A., Corso, J.J.: Depth from camera motion and object detection. In: Proceedings of the IEEE/CVF Conference on Computer Vision and Pattern Recognition, pp. 1397–1406 (2021)
11. Nam, H., Baek, M., Han, B.: Modeling and propagating CNNs in a tree structure for visual tracking. arXiv preprint arXiv:1608.07242 (2016)
12. Ashraf, M.W., Sultani, W., Shah, M.: Dogfight: detecting drones from drones videos. In: Proceedings of the IEEE/CVF Conference on Computer Vision and Pattern Recognition, pp. 7067–7076 (2021)
13. Yang, T., Xu, P., Hu, R., et al: ROAM: recurrently optimizing tracking model. In: Proceedings of the IEEE/CVF Conference on Computer Vision and Pattern Recognition, pp. 6718–6727 (2020)
14. Jiang, S., Lu, Y., Li, H., et al.: Learning optical flow from a few matches. In: Proceedings of the IEEE/CVF Conference on Computer Vision and Pattern Recognition, pp. 16592–16600 (2021)
15. Fischer, P., Dosovitskiy, A., Ilg, E., et al.: FlowNet: learning optical flow with convolutional networks. arXiv preprint arXiv:1504.06852 (2015)
16. Zhao, S., Sheng, Y., Dong, Y., et al: MaskFlownet: asymmetric feature matching with learnable occlusion mask. In: Proceedings of the IEEE/CVF Conference on Computer Vision and Pattern Recognition, pp. 6278–6287 (2020)
17. Yang, G., Ramanan, D.: Upgrading optical flow to 3D scene flow-through optical expansion. In: Proceedings of the IEEE/CVF Conference on Computer Vision and Pattern Recognition, pp. 1334–1343 (2020)
18. Bodla, N., Singh, B., Chellappa, R., et al.: Soft-NMS--improving object detection with one line of code. In: Proceedings of the IEEE International Conference on Computer Vision, pp. 5561–5569 (2017)
19. Han, W., Khorrami, P., Paine, T.L., et al.: Seq-NMS for video object detection. arXiv preprint arXiv:1602.08465 (2016)
20. Bewley, A., Ge, Z., Ott, L., et al.: Simple online and realtime tracking. In: 2016 IEEE International Conference on Image Processing (ICIP). IEEE, pp. 3464–3468 (2016)

GRVT: Toward Effective Grocery Recognition via Vision Transformer

Shu Liu[1,3], Xiaoyu Wang[1,3], Chengzhang Zhu[2,3(✉)], and Beiji Zou[1,3]

[1] School of Computer Science and Engineering, Central South University,
Changsha 410083, China
[2] School of Literature and Journalism, Central South University,
Changsha 410083, China
anandawork@126.com
[3] Hunan Engineering Research Center of Machine Vision and Intelligent Medicine,
Changsha 410083, China

Abstract. Grocery recognition aims to classify items by visual features of the image. The intention is to improve retailing experience, manage inventory and help visually impaired people. It is an important task in computer vision. Most previous works utilize global image features with a unique decision rule to recognize groceries and products via convolutional neural network (CNN) models. Such methods work on different CNN architectures to explore more accurate and representative features. However, fine-grained characteristics are not considered in feature extraction. Recently, vision transformer (ViT) models achieve success in multiple computer vision tasks. And fine-grained visual categorization is leveraging self-attention mechanism of ViT to learn discriminative regions and features. In this paper, we propose a novel ViT based framework named grocery recognition vision transformer (GRVT). It integrates multiple granularity scales of patches by multi-scale patch embedding to introduce robust image representation without incurring excessive computation cost. The mixed attention selection module guides the network to choose these discriminative patches and crucial regions for fine-grained feature extraction. Our GRVT achieves the state-of-the-art performance on Freiburg Groceries Dataset and Grocery Store Dataset.

Keywords: Grocery recognition · Fine-grained visual categorization · Vision transformer · Multi-scale patch embedding · Mixed attention selection

1 Introduction

Grocery recognition is a novel and practical research topic in computer vision and deep learning area. It plays a vital role in many applications in retail. Automatic grocery recognition is beneficial for retail and on-shelf product management. On the one hand, grocery recognition based on deep learning can be used for an automatic checkout system and improves customers' shopping experience by reducing waiting time [1]. On the other hand, it is able to develop better replenishment and planogram by monitors and to improve turnover and profits. For customers who are visually impaired, grocery recognition on mobile devices can assist them to distinguish products and accomplish shopping independently in their daily life [2].

Generally, grocery recognition is a classification task of computer vision. Its target is to distinguish different images into corresponding labels correctly. A classification system includes image capturing, image preprocessing, feature extraction, feature classification and the output of recognition [3]. Traditional feature extraction needs hand-crafted features which are not suitable for products that are changing day by day and also suffer from low accuracy. With the development of deep learning, the convolutional neural network (CNN) based image classification method obtains great success in recent years [4]. And promoted the development of related research fields such as object detection [5] and segmentation [6]. Recently, vision transformer (ViT) [7] shows better performance in image classification. ViT and its variants also achieve great success in popular tasks and further exceeds CNNs in particular aspects [8–10]. That shows the potential of transformer in capturing global and local information.

However, there is still a blank for transformer in grocery recognition. In this paper, we explore the capabilities of ViT in such task. An effective grocery recognition framework based on ViT, named GRVT, is presented. To be specific, to enhance generalizability on the patches of ViT, we propose a multi-scale patch embedding (MSPE) module to enable the network to integrate multiple scales of input. Moreover, mixed attention selection (MAS) module calculates attention scores across different sets of patch embeddings to choose discriminative and crucial regions. We evaluate our model on popular datasets including Freiburg Groceries Dataset [11] and Grocery Store Dataset [12], and our GRVT outperforms existing methods on these benchmarks. The main contributions are summarized as follows:

- To the best of our knowledge, we are the first to implement ViT model on grocery recognition task and explore its transfer learning performance. And ViT produces competitive results with CNN models.
- We introduce GRVT, a novel and compact architecture for grocery recognition that fuses multi-scale patch embeddings and computes mixed attention to choose crucial local regions.
- We verify the effectiveness of our framework on grocery datasets, and the experiment results show our GRVT achieves better performance than existing public works.

2   Related Work

Fine-grained visual categorization (FGVC) is a challenging task because of high intra-class variances and low inter-class variances. Datasets are mainly weakly-supervised with only class labels. Methods on FGVC are focusing on local regions to capture discriminative features as a categorization basis. Hu et al. [13] proposed weakly supervised data augmentation network (WS-DAN) to generate attention maps with discriminative parts, and then utilized data augmentations to reinforce the learning procedure. Chen et al. [14] proposed a destruction and construction learning (DCL) by region confusion mechanism and injected more discriminative local details into the classification network. Muktabb et al. [15] integrated a local concepts accumulation layer emphasize local features and showed effect gains. Ji et al. [16] proposed an attention convolutional binary neural tree which characterizes the coarse-to-fine hierarchical feature learning process, and used the attention transformer module to enforce the network to capture discriminative features. He et al. [17] firstly introduced ViT to fine-grained recognition, transformer architecture for fine-grained recognition (TransFG) selects discriminative image patches and adopts contrastive loss to enlarge the distance between sub-classes.

Grocery recognition aims at classifying objects in supermarket scenarios, like fruits, milk, and snacks. It could be considered a FGVC task. There is low inter-class variance, for example, apples come in a great many varieties, and their color and shape are familiar even if customers can not distinguish them easily. Furthermore, there is also high intra-class variance, a Golden-Delicious apple in different angles or lighting conditions can vary much in vision. Besides, it has some other characteristics which make the task more challenging. In grocery shops, products can be put on the shelf or piled up in a container. The object scale is not definite, the background could be other products and environment conditions are unconstrained. In recent studies, grocery recognition methods exploit deep neural networks (DNN) models as a feature extractor. The unique decision rule is adopted to classify low-dimensional vectors such as support vector machines (SVM) to identify retail goods [12]. Ciocca et al. [18] proposed a multi-task learning network to leverage hierarchical annotations based on the CNN feature extractor. Noy et al. [19] and Nayman et al. [20] adopted neural architecture search (NAS) on grocery product recognition by introducing expert advice and architecture pruning. Wei et al. [1] proposed a retail product checkout (RPC) dataset and an automatic checkout (ACO) task. Wang et al. [21] proposed self attention based DCL to learn crucial region information to classify retail product images in the laboratory environment. Leo et al. [22] systematically study DNNs and ensemble DNNs on grocery recognition and found that model ensemble shows significant improvement.

3   Method

Here we explore the model performance in the application of grocery recognition. To better elaborate our framework, we first reviewed the ViT model design, and the overall GRVT architecture and its two modules are then introduced.

3.1   Vision Transformer

Transformer [23] has achieved outstanding performance in natural language processing due to its capacity and superiority in multi-head attention mechanism.

Due to the potential of transformer-based vision models, the number of ViT variants is increasing, such as data-efficient image transformer (DeiT) [24], pyramid vision transformer (PVT) [25], Swin Transformer [26].

Vision transformer applies a standard transformer [23] directly into images with least modifications [7]. For an image of $X \in \mathbb{R}^{H*W*C}$, where H, W are the original resolution of image and C is the number of channels, flatten it into patches $X_p \in \mathbb{R}^{N*C}$, where P denotes the size of each patch and $N = HW/P^2$. The patches as a sequence are linearly projected E into a D-dimention latent embedding space. The linear projection can be written as

$$T = [X_p^1 E, X_p^2 E, \cdots, X_p^N E] \tag{1}$$

In bidirectional encoder representations from transformers (BERT) [27] model, the first token is $[cls]$, it is a randomly initialized vector and represents classification result of the whole sequence after the encoder layer. Similar to BERT's class token, a learnable embedding vector X_{cls} and position embedding E_{pos} are extended. In Eq. 2, the final sequence Z_0 serves as the input of the transformer encoder.

$$Z_0 = [X_{cls}, T] + E_{pos} \tag{2}$$

The transformer encoder consists of a series of multi-head self-attention (MSA) and multi-layer perceptron (MLP) blocks. Before every block, layer normalization (LN) is applied. MSA consists of several attention layers in parallel to learn from different spaces, and the number of layers in MSA is K. The encoding procedure can be described as Eq. 3 and Eq. 4, where Z_l denotes the encoded image representation. After multi layers' encoding, X_{cls} is the global feature representation for final classification.

$$Z_l^{'} = MSA(LN(Z_{l-1})) + Z_{l-1}, l = 1, \cdots, L \tag{3}$$

$$Z_l = MLP(LN(Z_l^{'})) + Z_l^{'}, l = 1, \cdots, L \tag{4}$$

3.2 GRVT Architecture

The pretrained ViT model on high resolution and large datasets could facilitate to better transfer learning results on middle and small benchmarks [7]. In this sense, ViT could achieve promising performance in grocery recognition. However, the granularity of the patch scale is single, and it is unable to adapt the requirements for scenarios of stores where objects can vary a lot in images. To this end, we propose a simple but effective GRVT architecture that utilizes multi-scale patch embedding and mixed attention selection module to filter out high-confidence patches for final encoding. The overview of our framework is illustrated in Fig. 1.

3.3 Multi-scale Patch Embedding

Multi-scale feature representation can help networks better detect and recognize objects [8,25]. Chen et al. [28] proposed a dual-branch transformer called

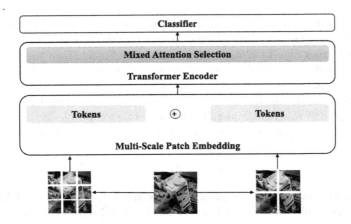

Fig. 1. The architecture of GRVT framework. Images are firstly split into a different scale of patches which are projected with their position embeddings and class embeddings. Image tokens are concatenated subsequently and input to the transformer encoder. Crucial and discriminative regions used for final classification are filtered by calculated attention weights from transformer encoder layers.

CrossViT that integrates different sizes of patches. Because the patch sizes are different in resolution, image patches are processed by separate encoder branches. Our MSPE module aims to integrate different granularity scales of patches as the input of the transformer encoder, with the same backbone architecture and very low computational cost. As shown in Fig. 2, let an image firstly be resized to $H_S \times W_S$ and $H_L \times W_L$. Patch number in each branch is $N_S = H_S W_S / P^2$, $N_L = H_L W_L / P^2$. For each patch embedding, we extend linear projection with their corresponding X_{cls} and E_{pos} following Eq. 1 and Eq. 2. Then we concatenate Z_0^S and Z_0^L as the final embedding of the encoder as Eq. 5. Dual granularities of token representations are complemented with each other.

$$Z_0 = [Z_0^S, Z_0^L] \tag{5}$$

3.4   Mixed Attention Selection

ViT feeds forward all patches across transformer encoder layer. Patch usually plays a different role in an image, it could be a part of the object, or invalid background. Noises can be harmful to the result if background patches are not filtered. The discriminative and crucial parts can guide the model to achieve better performance [17]. Here we propose a mixed attention selection module that fuses dual tokens' information and utilizes attention results across layers to filter out important parts. Figure 3 illustrates the design of MAS. The input of the encoder layers remains unchanged except for the last one. Multi-head self-attentions are calculated layer by layer, and N means the number of patches and

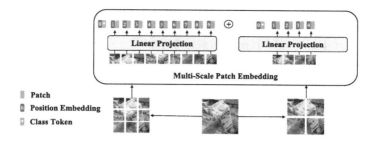

Fig. 2. Illustration of MSPE module. Images are divided into different scales of patches which are projected with position embedding and class embedding subsequently. Embeddings are concatenated into a sequence of tokens for the input of transformer encoder.

class tokens in Eq. 6. The attention weights $\boldsymbol{a}$ in every layer are accumulated by K attention heads in Eq. 7 and Eq. 8.

$$N = 1 + N_S + 1 + N_L \tag{6}$$

$$a_l^i = [a_l^{i_1}, a_l^{i_2}, \cdots, a_l^{i_N}], i \in 0, 1, \cdots, K \tag{7}$$

$$\boldsymbol{a}_l = [a_l^0, a_l^1, \cdots, a_l^K], l \in 1, 2, \cdots, L-1 \tag{8}$$

Different tokens get mixed step by step across layers of the encoder, and the class token can guide the model to capture global representation. We follow TransFG [17] to obtain unified weights $\boldsymbol{a}_{final}$ by recursively multiplying raw attention matrix. The calculation can be written as

$$\boldsymbol{a}_{final} = \prod_{l=0}^{L-1} \boldsymbol{a}_l \tag{9}$$

The part selection of TransFG [17] selects index of maximum value in $\boldsymbol{a}_{final}$ for each attention heads, which does not adapt for the characteristics of multi-scale patch embedding. The MSPE introduces two sets of patch tokens. N_S and N_L are not quantitatively equal and single attention selection is not robust. To solve these problems, we develop the MAS module to handle mixed attention and conduct a balanced selecting strategy to choose crucial patches. As Eq. 10, I denotes the balanced sampled top M indexes of K attention heads in different sets of patches respectively.

$$I = A_1^1, A_2^1...A_M^1, \cdots, A_1^K, A_2^K...A_M^K \tag{10}$$

Then we concatenate corresponding patches in Z_{L-1} as the final tokens in Eq. 11. GRVT focuses on the principle part to discover subtle differences with selected tokens. After the final layer, we integrate X_{cls}^S and X_{cls}^L as the final class token.

$$Z_{mix} = [X_{cls}^S, X_{cls}^L | Z_{L-1}^i], i \in I \tag{11}$$

$$Z_{cls} = mean(X_{cls}^S, X_{cls}^L) \tag{12}$$

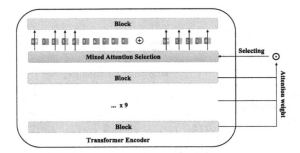

Fig. 3. Illustration of MAS module. Attention weights are gathered together and are calculated to filter out discriminative patches with a higher overall score.

4   Experiments

4.1   Datasets and Implementation Details

Freiburg Groceries Dataset (FGD) [11] is a challenging dataset due to the variety of objects and consists of 25 classes of groceries. The dataset mainly considers real-life scenes which include multi viewpoints of individual objects and packed shelves. Photos are taken in sophisticated lighting conditions with reflections and shadows at different stores. Grocery Store Dataset (GSD) [12] contains natural grocery items and refrigerated product images. The labels include coarse-grained and fine-grained classes with a hierarchical structure. It mainly includes vegetables, fruits, and packages. The coarse-grained class number is 43 and the fine-grained class number is 81. Furthermore, there are product descriptions with nutrition values to help visually impaired users in shops.

GRVT models are trained on 224×224 resolution images for fair comparison. Firstly, images are resized to 300×300 and then cropped to 224×224 for model inputs. For the MSPE module, images are resized 112×112 for another scale. The patch size $P = 16$ as the standard ViT-B-16 model. The learning rate is set to 0.03 with cosine annealing and the optimizer is stochastic gradient descent with a momentum of 0.9 and 0.0001 weight decay. The attention dropout rate is 0.1 and attention head number $K = 12$. The loss function is cross entropy loss and training iterations are 15,000. All experiments are performed with two Nvidia RTX 3090 GPUs, using Pytorch 1.9.0 with CUDA 11.1 and APEX with FP16 training.

4.2   Comparison with the State of the Art

We compare our GRVT against recent works, which are mostly based on CNN models that are trained end-to-end to classify images, or used as feature extractors for the subsequent decision rule. Table 1 shows the comparison results on FGD. ViT [7] performs better than public works' best result [20], and is closed to that of fine-grained approaches [14,17]. GRVT improves 0.63% accuracy than the standard ViT and exceeds the fine-grained approaches, which indicates the

Table 1. Comparison of different methods on FGD.

Method	Backbone	Acc
Baseline [11]	AlexNet	78.9
ASAP [19]	NAS	89.3
XNAS [20]	NAS	93.7
ResNet50 [4]	ResNet	91.94
ResNet101 [4]	ResNet	92.04
WS-DAN [13]	Inception	91.26
DCL [14]	ResNet	94.70
ViT [7]	ViT	94.53
Swin-B [26]	ViT	**95.25**
PVT-M [25]	ViT	93.02
TransFG [17]	ViT	94.92
GRVT	ViT	<u>95.16</u>

effectiveness of our method. As for comparison on GSD in Table 2, ViT outperforms the ensemble CNN models [22] and CNN based fine-grained methods [13, 14] in both label structures. Nevertheless, our GRVT further achieves 0.66% and 0.4% improvement. Compared to TansFG [17], ours also shows the superiority. GRVT brings multi-scale patch representation and makes the model learn more diverse, robust patches from the different granularity of tokens. Besides, the MAS module makes regions with discriminative information can be focused on the last transformer encoder layer. Although Swin Transformer [26] performs best on FGD, but falls behind our GRVT on GSD, mainly because the GSD category is more closed to a FGVC task. PVT [25] needs fewer parameters and computation but suffers from accuracy results.

Table 2. Comparison of different methods on GSD.

Method	Backbone	Acc/Fine	Acc/Coarse
DenseNet169 [12]	DenseNet	85.0	85.2
DN+MTL [18]	DenseNet	89.13	94.33
ResNet50 [22]	ResNet	90.58	93.61
ResNet101 [22]	ResNet	92.55	94.87
Ensemble [22]	CNNs	93.48	95.84
WS-DAN [13]	Inception	87.67	91.43
DCL [14]	ResNet	93.36	95.25
ViT [7]	ViT	94.59	<u>96.70</u>
Swin-B [26]	ViT	93.12	95.58
PVT-M [25]	ViT	91.50	94.19
TransFG [17]	ViT	<u>94.85</u>	95.78
GRVT	ViT	**95.25**	**97.10**

Table 3 tabulates the model efficiency, measured by the number of parameters (#Params) and computational costs (FLOPs). Generally, the ViT-based models have more parameters, with better performance than ResNet models. TransFG [17] introduces an overlapping patch sampling method to avoid information loss around patch edges, however, the total number of the patch is increased a lot. Compared to ViT [7], for the same image resolution 224×224, TransFG brings 65% more patches to calculate, while GRVT needs 25% more computational cost.

Table 3. Comparison of computational efficiency.

Method	#Params	FLOPs
ResNet50 [4]	26M	4.1G
ResNet101 [4]	45M	7.9G
ViT [7]	87M	17.6G
Swin-B [26]	88M	15.1G
PVT-M [25]	44M	6.7G
TransFG [17]	87M	27.8G
GRVT	87M	21.0G

4.3   Ablation Study

In order to investigate the effectiveness of MSPE and MAS modules, as well as the impact of parameter M in MAS, we conduct ablation studies in the following.

Effect of MSPE. MSPE introduces dual granularities of image patches. As shown in Table 4, it improves 0.31% and 0.42% evaluation result on FGD and GSD, respectively. The diversity of image patches improves the model's robustness and generalization capability.

Effect of MAS. MAS calculates attentions in encoder layers and samples those with high attention scores in a balanced way. Without considering noisy backgrounds, GRVT can focus on informative regions and capture important local features. Table 4 shows that MAS further achieves 0.32% and 0.24% improvement on two datasets.

Impact of Parameter M. MAS selects Top M patch indexes according to the result of a_{final}, where M refers the number of patches to be chosen in each attention head. As shown in Table 5, the best accuracy is achieved when $M = 3$. If M is too small, only a few patches can be selected for final encoding and predicting, which are not robust enough. If M is too big, each attention head produces too many indexes which would be redundant and the result becomes inconspicuous.

Table 4. Ablation studies of MSPE and MAS.

ViT	MSPE	MAS	FGD	GSD
✓			94.53	94.59
✓	✓		94.84	95.01
✓	✓	✓	**95.16**	**95.25**

Table 5. Quantitative results of parameter M in MAS module.

Method	FGD	GSD
GRVT ($M = 1$)	94.68	95.17
GRVT ($M = 3$)	**95.16**	**95.25**
GRVT ($M = 5$)	94.91	95.21

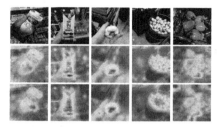

(a) Attention visualization on FGD   (b) Attention visualization on GSD

Fig. 4. Examples of visualization results on (a) Freiburg Grocery Dataset and (b) Grocery Store Dataset. The first row is the original image, the second row is the single branch attention map, and the third row is the attention map fused from two branches. Attention maps are overlaid on raw images for better visualization. (Color figure online)

4.4 Visualization

Figure 4 shows our visualization results on randomly selected images from both datasets. Attention maps from backbone encoder are transformed into the input space for better visualization. It can be observed that GRVT successfully captures discriminative regions such as product packages, edges, logos, and patterns, and also recognizes fruits and vegetables' shape, corners, and color. The background and shelf are purple and blue, while the important parts of products get more attention. For comparison of single branch and fused multi-scale attention maps, the latter shows more red and yellow regions on body of products, indicating the effectiveness of our GRVT.

5   Conclusion

In this work, we investigate the effectiveness of ViT on grocery recognition task, and demonstrate it can get better performance than CNN models. Furthermore, we propose a novel fine-grained grocery recognition framework named GRVT without introducing much computational cost, which outperforms recent works on grocery datasets. As GRVT achieves encouraging results, we believe that the transformer-based models have great potential for computer vision tasks, especially on grocery recognition. However, ViT models require more memory and computational resources, which may not suitable for lightweight needs and reality applications. In the future, we will further study transformer-based lightweight and efficient models that are possible for deployment on mobile devices.

Acknowledgements. This work was supported in part by the National Natural Science Foundation of China under Grant 61902435, in part by the International Science and Technology Innovation Joint Base of Machine Vision and Medical Image Processing in Hunan Province under Grant 2021CB1013, and in part by the Fundamental Research Funds for the Central Universities of Central South University. We are grateful for resources from the High Performance Computing Center of Central South University.

References

1. Wei, X.S., Cui, Q., Yang, L., Wang, P., Liu, L.: RPC: a large-scale retail product checkout dataset. arXiv preprint arXiv:1901.07249 (2019)
2. Leo, M., Furnari, A., Medioni, G.G., Trivedi, M., Farinella, G.M.: Deep learning for assistive computer vision. In: Leal-Taixé, L., Roth, S. (eds.) ECCV 2018. LNCS, vol. 11134, pp. 3–14. Springer, Cham (2019). https://doi.org/10.1007/978-3-030-11024-6_1
3. Wei, Y., Tran, S., Xu, S., Kang, B., Springer, M.: Deep learning for retail product recognition: challenges and techniques. Comput. Intell. Neurosci. **2020**, 23 (2020). https://doi.org/10.1155/2020/8875910. Article ID: 8875910
4. He, K., Zhang, X., Ren, S., Sun, J.: Deep residual learning for image recognition. In: 2016 IEEE Conference on Computer Vision and Pattern Recognition, pp. 770–778 (2016)
5. Ren, S., He, K., Girshick, R., Sun, J.: Faster R-CNN: towards real-time object detection with region proposal networks. In: Cortes, C., Lawrence, N., Lee, D., Sugiyama, M., Garnett, R. (eds.) Advances in Neural Information Processing Systems, vol. 28. Curran Associates, Inc. (2015)
6. He, K., Gkioxari, G., Dollár, P., Girshick, R.: Mask R-CNN. In: 2017 IEEE International Conference on Computer Vision, pp. 2980–2988 (2017)
7. Dosovitskiy, A., et al.: An image is worth 16 × 16 words: transformers for image recognition at scale. In: International Conference on Learning Representations (2021)
8. Zhu, X., Su, W., Lu, L., Li, B., Wang, X., Dai, J.: Deformable DETR: deformable transformers for end-to-end object detection. In: International Conference on Learning Representations (2021)
9. Zheng, S., et al.: Rethinking semantic segmentation from a sequence-to-sequence perspective with transformers. In: Proceedings of the IEEE/CVF Conference on Computer Vision and Pattern Recognition, pp. 6881–6890 (2021)
10. Esser, P., Rombach, R., Ommer, B.: Taming transformers for high-resolution image synthesis. In: Proceedings of the IEEE/CVF Conference on Computer Vision and Pattern Recognition, pp. 12873–12883 (2021)
11. Jund, P., Abdo, N., Eitel, A., Burgard, W.: The freiburg groceries dataset. arXiv preprint arXiv:1611.05799 (2016)
12. Klasson, M., Zhang, C., Kjellström, H.: A hierarchical grocery store image dataset with visual and semantic labels. In: 2019 IEEE Winter Conference on Applications of Computer Vision, pp. 491–500. IEEE (2019)

13. Hu, T., Qi, H., Huang, Q., Lu, Y.: See better before looking closer: weakly supervised data augmentation network for fine-grained visual classification. arXiv preprint arXiv:1901.09891 (2019)
14. Chen, Y., Bai, Y., Zhang, W., Mei, T.: Destruction and construction learning for fine-grained image recognition. In: 2019 IEEE/CVF Conference on Computer Vision and Pattern Recognition, pp. 5157–5166 (2019)
15. Srivastava, M.M.: Bag of tricks for retail product image classification. In: Campilho, A., Karray, F., Wang, Z. (eds.) ICIAR 2020. LNCS, vol. 12131, pp. 71–82. Springer, Cham (2020). https://doi.org/10.1007/978-3-030-50347-5_8
16. Ji, R., et al.: Attention convolutional binary neural tree for fine-grained visual categorization. In: 2020 IEEE/CVF Conference on Computer Vision and Pattern Recognition, pp. 10468–10477 (2020)
17. He, J., et al.: TransFG: a transformer architecture for fine-grained recognition. arXiv preprint arXiv:2103.07976 (2021)
18. Ciocca, G., Napoletano, P., Locatelli, S.G.: Multi-task learning for supervised and unsupervised classification of grocery images. In: Del Bimbo, A., et al. (eds.) ICPR 2021. LNCS, vol. 12662, pp. 325–338. Springer, Cham (2021). https://doi.org/10.1007/978-3-030-68790-8_26
19. Noy, A., et al.: ASAP: architecture search, anneal and prune. In: International Conference on Artificial Intelligence and Statistics, pp. 493–503. PMLR (2020)
20. Nayman, N., Noy, A., Ridnik, T., Friedman, I., Jin, R., Zelnik, L.: XNAS: neural architecture search with expert advice. In: Advances in Neural Information Processing Systems, vol. 32 (2019)
21. Wang, W., Cui, Y., Li, G., Jiang, C., Deng, S.: A self-attention-based destruction and construction learning fine-grained image classification method for retail product recognition. Neural Comput. Appl. **32**(18), 14613–14622 (2020). https://doi.org/10.1007/s00521-020-05148-3
22. Leo, M., Carcagnì, P., Distante, C.: A systematic investigation on end-to-end deep recognition of grocery products in the wild. In: 2020 25th International Conference on Pattern Recognition, pp. 7234–7241. IEEE (2021)
23. Vaswani, A., et al.: Attention is all you need. In: Guyon, I., et al. (eds.) Advances in Neural Information Processing Systems, vol. 30. Curran Associates, Inc. (2017)
24. Touvron, H., Cord, M., Douze, M., Massa, F., Sablayrolles, A., Jégou, H.: Training data-efficient image transformers & distillation through attention. In: International Conference on Machine Learning, pp. 10347–10357. PMLR (2021)
25. Wang, W., et al.: Pyramid vision transformer: a versatile backbone for dense prediction without convolutions. In: Proceedings of the IEEE/CVF International Conference on Computer Vision, pp. 568–578 (2021)
26. Liu, Z., et al.: Swin transformer: hierarchical vision transformer using shifted windows. In: Proceedings of the IEEE/CVF International Conference on Computer Vision, pp. 10012–10022 (2021)
27. Devlin, J., Chang, M.W., Lee, K., Toutanova, K.: BERT: pre-training of deep bidirectional transformers for language understanding. arXiv preprint arXiv:1810.04805 (2018)
28. Chen, C.F.R., Fan, Q., Panda, R.: CrossViT: cross-attention multi-scale vision transformer for image classification. In: Proceedings of the IEEE/CVF International Conference on Computer Vision, pp. 357–366 (2021)

A Transformer-Based Cloth-Irrelevant Patches Feature Extracting Method for Long-Term Cloth-Changing Person Re-identification

Zepeng Wang, Xinghao Jiang, Ke Xu$^{(\boxtimes)}$, and Tanfeng Sun

School of Cyber Science and Engineering, Shanghai Jiao Tong University,
Shanghai, China
{wzp.ck,xhjiang,113025816,tfsun}@sjtu.edu.cn

Abstract. Long-term person re-identification is a more practical research task in person retrieval fields because the object retrieved may appear for a more extended period in the actual situation. To overcome the disturbances caused by different clothes of the same person or similar clothes between other people, this paper proposes a Transformer-based Cloth-irrelevant Patches (TCiP) feature extracting method, which combines local features robust to clothes changing. It contains three main modules: (1) A transformer network is used as the backbone to extract patch features for its high performance in many vision tasks. The vital feature extractability of the transformer in cloth-changing Re-ID is proved in this paper. (2) Patch selector is a novel patches sequence recombine module guided by a human parsing model. (3) Considering that there are also additional identity-related features in the clothing areas, an Inverse Cloth-Id (ICI) loss is proposed for innovatively extracting cloth-irrelevant but identity-related features. The experimental results in this paper validate the validity of our method on cloth-changing person Re-ID. Moreover, it also proved the generality of general Re-ID benchmarks. Code is available at https://github.com/oliverck/TCiP.

Keywords: Person re-identification · Long-term cloth-changing Re-ID · Computer vision · Transformer

1 Introduction

Person re-identification (Re-ID) is a practical application study used for suspect tracking, loss person tracking, smart city construction, etc. The target of Re-ID is to match images of the same person captured from non-overlapping cameras with different views [18,21]. Common difficulties in person Re-ID include diverse backgrounds, illumination, and so on due to changing the capture device, location, and sunlight intensity. The primary research focuses on extracting discriminated features, reducing different cameras' differentiation, and eliminating incorrect label noise. These methods archive great performance in common Re-ID datasets, such as Market-1501 [20], MSMT17 [15].

N. Magnenat-Thalmann et al. (Eds.): CGI 2022, LNCS 13443, pp. 278–289, 2022.
https://doi.org/10.1007/978-3-031-23473-6_22

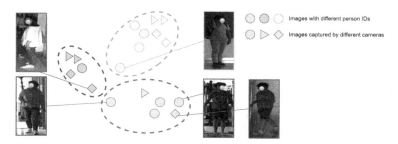

Fig. 1. The distribution of images features on cloth-changing Re-ID. Different color means images with different identities. Different shapes represent images captured by different cameras. The images are sampled from LTCC [13], and the feature distribution is generated by ResNet-50 [4] and calculated by the euclidean metric. (Color figure online)

But benchmarks above focus on retrieving a person within a short period called the Short-Term Cloth-Consistent (STCC) Re-ID. And methods designed for STCC can not be applied appropriately in the Long-Term Cloth-Changing (LTCC) Re-ID task. The STCC Re-ID methods consider the whole feature of the human body, such as the clothes' appearance. But LTCC Re-ID captures people over more extended periods. Their clothing and other variable appearances may change. Moreover, in STCC Re-ID, there are also hard cases where the judgment is wrong because different pedestrians may have similar clothes. As illustrated in Fig. 1, we get the red identity as the top-1 result wrongly when we calculate the feature distance to the blue identity wearing yellow. In the blue identity samples, the discrepancy between features caused by different clothes is much more significant than that brought by different capture devices. Therefore, previous methods focusing on global features perform poorly on cloth-changing Re-ID.

To deal with the clothes variance problem, we proposed a method to extract the local features invariant to a long-time spane. First, we apply a transformer network as the backbone to extract the local feature of each patch in the picture. Second, we use a human parsing method to localize the position of the biometric area, clothes area, and background area as patch-level. Moreover, we combine the biometric-related (bio-rel) patches sequence, and clothes-related (cloth-rel) patches sequence separately. As there are also high-relevant features to identity hidden in the cloth-rel area, such as body shape, it is not wise to discard these areas' information. So we propose an Inverse Cloth-Id (ICI) loss to extract cloth-irrelevant features from cloth-related patches. The contributions of our work are summarized as follows:

1. A novel Transformer-based Cloth-irrelevant Patches (TCiP) feature extracting method is proposed in our paper, aiming to localize the key and stable patches for long-term person re-identification.
2. We creatively propose an Inverse Cloth-Id (ICI) loss to extract the biometric feature hidden in clothes appearance.

3. Our method is validated on the popular clothes-changing Re-ID dataset, LTCC. We also prove the applicability of the proposed method on traditional Re-ID datasets like Market-1501 and MSMT17.

2 Related Work

2.1 Cloth-Changing Person Re-identification

Cloth-changing person re-identification methods proposed recently focus on how to extract local features preciously. As STCC methods using appearance information (including clothes appearance) perform poorly in LTCC Re-ID, several methods using additional information to localize key features have been proposed. CESD [13] is proposed to utilize body shape embedding to distill the identity-relevant feature and disentangle the identity-irrelevant feature. Biometric-Clothes Network (BC-Net) [19] compares the feature distance between the query samples and gallery samples by replacing the clothes area in the query with all clothes templates in the template pool. However, this method causes a lot more computational cost. FSAM [6] aims to extract body shape with a more accurate and fine-grained method. Additional contour sketch information [8,17] was proposed to be used for gait recognition, which can guide the retrieval result of person Re-ID.

Unlike the methods above, our model not only focuses on extracting cloth-irrelevant biometric features but also utilizes the potential long-term characteristics hidden in clothes regions.

2.2 Vision Transformer

Transformer has achieved great improvement not only in the field of natural language processing, but also in most computer vision fields, such as image classification [2,11], action recognition [10,12]. ViT was proposed to process images as sequences similar to patches in NLP. In the Re-ID field, TransReID [5] appends side information like camera ids in patch embedding processing and generates overlapping patches to preserve the patches neighboring local structures.

Different from the transformer network above, we propose to extract different local features by combining different sequences of patches. A patch select module is proposed to categorize patches into different categories to generate sequences guided by a human parsing module.

2.3 Human Parsing

Human parsing is a fine-grained semantic segmentation that aims to assign image pixels from the human body to semantic categories, e.g., arm, leg, glove, dress. Since human parsing has a good performance in separating the clothes region, biometric region, and background region from an image, we use a noise-tolerant human parsing method SCHP [9] to guide our network extracting biometric feature, cloth-unrelated feature.

3   Methodology

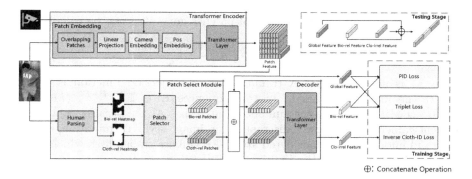

Fig. 2. The framework of the proposed TCiP. Patch Embedding module transfers the original image matrix to vector-like patches sequence as input of transformer encoder layer. Patch Select Module (PSM) calculates the Bio-rel Heatmap (BrH) and Cloth-rel Heatmap (CrH) for combining different patches into a new sequence. The sequence containing partial patches is processed to extract local features in the decoder layer. Moreover, the Inverse Cloth-Id (ICI) loss is used to mine long-term stable features hidden in clothes regions.

Due to the clothes appearance feature can not be used to identify a person in cloth-changing person Re-ID and clothes feature may disturb the retrieval result, we propose a cloth-irrelevant but identity-relevant local feature extracting method, a Transformer-based Cloth-irrelevant Patches (TCiP) feature extracting network. We adopt the transformer as a backbone to extract partial features, including clothes, biometrics, and background features. Then we use a human parsing module to localize patches containing clothes-related (cloth-rel) and biometric-related (bio-rel) features separately. We can combine the bio-rel patches sequence and the cloth-rel patches sequence. To extract long-term features related to person identity from cloth-rel patches, we propose an Inverse Cloth-Id (ICI) loss. The framework of our proposed network is shown in Fig. 2, we will introduce modules in our network in the following sections.

3.1   Transformer Encoder

It is proved that the transformer can achieve comparable results to CNN-based frameworks on Re-ID benchmarks [5]. Moreover, inspired by the structure that the transformer can decompose the image into multiple patches to extract local features, we use transformer layers as a local feature extracting backbone. Moreover, following TransReID, we better apply some modifications for applying transformer on the Re-ID task. The patch embedding module converts the given person image $x \in \mathbb{R}^{H \times W \times C}$ to patches sequence $e \in \mathbb{R}^{P \times D}$, where W, H, C denotes the height, width, and channel dimension of the input image sample. Furthermore, the expected P patches feature dimension is D. The traditional

ViT splits the images into N non-overlapping patches, neglecting the neighboring local structures around the patches. So we use a sliding window to generate overlapping patches. The step stride of the window is denoted as S, the image patch size as $H_p \times W_p$. The number of patches generated can be calculated as follow:

$$N = \lfloor \frac{H + S - H_p}{S} \rfloor \times \lfloor \frac{W + S - W_p}{S} \rfloor \tag{1}$$

where $\lfloor \cdot \rfloor$ is floor function. A trainable linear projection function is used to convert the images patches to vector sequences $E \in \mathbb{R}^{N \times P \times D}$, (i.e., $E = [e_1, e_2, ..., e_N]$), where N is the number of batch size. As the pictures captured by different cameras may cause a discrepancy in image style, illumination, etc., the camera id information is considered appended camera embedding, which follows the method Side Information Embedding (SIE) [5].

3.2   Patch Select Module (PSM)

In cloth-changing person Re-ID, clothing features cannot be used as unique features to distinguish identity and may even cause negative distractions. So we proposed a patch select module. We use SCHP [9] to label pixel-level masks of a person image, which contains biometrics, clothes, and background area. The patches sequence can be split into bio-rel patches sequence and cloth-rel patches sequence. Then the local features can be extracted from these sequences by the transformer layer.

Human Parsing. To separate the clothes area from the person image, we use extra information from human parsing to guide the patch selector. In this paper, we adopt the SCHP [9] network trained on LIP, which contains 20 labels (including 'Background', 'Hair', 'Upper-clothes', 'Face', 'Left-arm', and etc.). We grouped these 20 categories into 'Bio', 'Cloth', and 'Background'. 'Bio' contains human parsing labels related to the human body, like 'Face', 'Hair', and 'Left-arm'. And 'Cloth' includes the changeable clothing label, such as 'Upper-clothes', 'Hat' and 'Sunglasses'. Then we can get the pixel-level human parsing mask $H_{pixel} \in \mathbb{R}^{H \times W \times 3}$ with 3 channels, 'Bio', 'Cloth' and 'Background', where H_{pixel} is an $(0,1)$-matrix. As each patch contains $H_p \times W_p$ pixels, we convert the pixel-level mask to a patch-level heatmap the same size as the patch number calculated by Eq. (1). So the bio-rel heatmap and cloth-rel heatmap can be calculated as follows:

$$H_{Br} = \text{Pool}(H_{pixel}[0]) \tag{2}$$

$$H_{Cr} = \text{Pool}(H_{pixel}[1]) \tag{3}$$

where H_{Br} represents bio-rel heatmap, $\text{Pool}(\cdot)$ is a 2D average pooling function with kernel size $\{H_p, W_p\}$ and split window stride S and $H_{pixel}[0]$ represents the bio-rel pixel-level heatmap. As defined in Eq. (3), cloth-rel heatmap H_{Cr} can be calculated in the same way, just replace $H_{pixel}[0]$ with $H_{pixel}[1]$. As illustrated in Fig. 2, the bio-rel heatmap highlights the key biometric area in a person image but has a small region. It means the local feature extracted from there is high reliability but less information. Since the cloth region occupies a more significant proportion, the information about identity becomes less once we just abundant the cloth-rel region. So the critical problem is extracting long-term biometric information from cloth-rel patches.

Patch Selector. With the two heatmap matrices extracted above, we can combine the bio-rel patch sequence P_{Br} and cloth-rel patch sequence P_{Cr} by selecting from all patches generated by the transformer encoder. Nevertheless, generating patch sequences with different lengths for each sample in GPU parallel computing is not wise. To combine the patch sequence efficiently in parallel batch processing, we generate the cloth-irrelevant patch sequence as follows:

$$P_{Br} = P \odot H_{Br} + M \tag{4}$$

where $M \in \mathbb{R}^{P \times D}$ is a masking vector for padding. In order to alleviate the gradient explosion or gradient disappearance problem caused by the all-zero patch vector generated by $P \odot H_{CiP}$, we use a learnable mask token vector T_M to replace the all-zero patch following SimMIM [16]. M can be represented in the form of $\{M_1, M_2, ..., M_j, ..., M_P\}$, and the definition of M_j can be formulated as:

$$M_j = \begin{cases} T_M, & \text{if } H_{Br}[j] == 0 \\ 0, & \text{else.} \end{cases} \tag{5}$$

The M_j in Eq. (5) denotes the j-th patch mask. When the j-th patch is cloth-relevant, we replace it with T_M. And P_{Cr} can be calculated in the same way with H_{Cr}.

Then we use a transformer layer as a decoder to process the bio-rel patch sequence and cloth-rel patch sequence with latent features to local features separately.

3.3   Inverse Cloth-Id Loss

As mentioned above, there are also long-term bio-rel features hidden in the cloth-rel region. In order to make full use of these features, instead of discarding much information in vain, we propose an Inverse Cloth-Id (ICI) loss. As we want to extract local features unrelated to clothes Id, we train the network with ICI loss such that local feature F_{Ci} is as uncorrelated as possible from clothes Id. The ICI loss L_{ICI} can be formulated as:

$$L_{ICI} = e^{-L_{CloId}(F_{Ci})} \tag{6}$$

where L_{CloId} is the cross-entropy loss using clothes Id as the ground truth label. In the LTCC dataset, there are only labels to distinguish different clothes from the same person. We get the unique clothes label by combining the person label and clothes label of each person, which means that the clothes label between different people can not be the same even if they wear similar clothes. For global feature F_{glo} and biometric local feature F_{Br}, we use traditional cross-entropy loss L_{PId} with person id as ground truth label and triplet loss [1] L_{tri} to backward.

3.4 Training and Testing

With the processing of TCiP, we can get three different features, the global feature F_{glo}, the bio-rel feature F_{Br}, and the cloth-irrel feature F_{Ci}. The training loss of our network can be formulated as follows:

$$
\begin{aligned}
L_{total} = & \alpha \times (L_{PId}(F_{glo}) + L_{PId}(F_{Br})) \\
& + \beta \times (L_{tri}(F_{glo}) + L_{tri}(F_{Br})) \\
& + \gamma \times L_{ICI}
\end{aligned}
\tag{7}
$$

where α, β, γ is hyper-parameters, and we set $\alpha = \beta = 1$ and $\gamma = 1000$ in our experiment.

In the testing stage, we concatenate the three features above to generate the whole feature as follows:

$$
F_{whole} = \{\lambda_1 F_{glo}, \ \lambda_2 F_{Br}, \ \lambda_3 F_{Ci}\}
\tag{8}
$$

where $\lambda_1, \lambda_2, \lambda_3$ are hyper-parameters to weight the global feature and local features. $\lambda_1, \lambda_2, \lambda_3$ are all set to 1.0 in the experiment.

4 Experiment

4.1 Datasets and Evaluation Protocals

Datasets. To evaluate the effectiveness of solving the cloth-changing problem of our proposed method, we valid TCiP on a widely-used cloth-changing person Re-ID dataset, LTCC [13]. LTCC contains 17238 sample images of 152 person identities. 91 identities appear with different clothes and 61 identities without clothes changing. Furthermore, there are 12 cameras to capture different views in LTCC. To demonstrate the generality of our method on the Re-ID tasks, we evaluate our method on Market-1501 [20] and MSMT17 [15] to validate the applicability of our model on benchmark datasets for standard Re-ID without clothes changing.

Evaluation Protocols. To evaluate our method, we adopt the rank-k accuracy and mean Average Precision (mAP) to compare the performance of different methods. Following LTCC setting [13], two kinds of test settings are defined as follows:

1. **Standard Setting (SS).** The images in the gallery with the same identity and the same camera view with query images are discarded when calculating scores.
2. **Cloth-changing Setting (CS).** Based on SS, samples with the same clothing id are also removed. This evaluation setting can more intuitively show the performance of the Re-ID method for the cloth-changing situation.

We test on Market-1501 and MSMT17 with SS as default.

4.2   Implementation Details

We adopted ViT-BoT [5] pretrained by ImageNet as our backbone. The input size of the person image is resized to 256×128. And data augmentation methods in the training stage contain random horizontal flipping, padding, random cropping, and random erasing. The batch size is 64, with 8 images per person id and 2 images per clothes id. SGD optimizer is employed with the weight decay of $1e - 4$. The learning rate is initialized as $5e - 5$ with cosine learning rate decay. All experiments are trained for 120 epochs with one Nvidia Geforce 3090 GPU.

Table 1. Comparison with state-of-the-art methods on the cloth-changing datasets, LTCC. "General" means the method is designed for standard Re-ID task and "Cloth-Changing" means for the cloth-changing task. "CS" and "SS" denote "Cloth-changing Setting" and "Standard Setting" evaluation protocols. "R-k" denotes the rank-k accuracy (%), and "mAP" denotes the mean Average Precision (%). The best score is **bolded** and the second is underlined.

Methods	Type	LTCC			
		CS		SS	
		mAP	R-1	mAP	R-1
ResNet-50 [4]	General	9.02	20.08	25.98	58.82
PCB [14]		10.03	23.52	27.52	61.86
ISP [22]		11.9	27.8	29.6	66.3
CESD [13]	Cloth-Changing	12.40	26.15	34.31	71.39
GI-ReID [8]		13.17	28.11	36.07	73.59
FSAM [6]		16.2	38.5	35.4	73.2
CAL [3]		<u>18.0</u>	**40.1**	<u>40.8</u>	<u>74.2</u>
TCiP (ours)		**19.31**	<u>38.78</u>	**41.9**	**74.24**

4.3   Comparison on the Cloth-Changing Dataset

The experiment of our method on LTCC [13] is shown in Table 1. It is shown that the proposed TCiP method outperforms all compared methods in mean average precision (mAP) on LTCC. Our method has a 3.11% and 6.5% improvement in the mAP metric compared to FSAM. However, the Rank-1 metric only increased by 0.28% and 1.04%. We analyze why our method significantly improved mAP without the same scale increase in Rank1 value compared to FSAM and CAL. Our method focuses on the critical partial feature apart from the clothes-changing feature. However, even in long-term person Re-ID, clothing may not change significantly even with different clothes labels. As illustrated in Fig. 3, the same person may appear at different times, wearing slightly different but generally similar clothing. This also fits the cloth-changing setting as long as the labels of clothes are different. In this situation, methods that also use information about clothes can better retrieve the same person with similar outfits. At the same time, it has also led to increased misjudgments among people with similar clothes. This is why our method performs better than other methods in mAP. The above data and analysis prove that the proposed TCiP can solve the problem of changing clothes in person re-identification better than the previous methods. By splitting the clothes and biometric areas, our method can eliminate clothing distractions as much as possible, whether it is cunningly positive. So our approach can solve the cloth-changing situation well, which is proved by mAP growth.

Table 2. Experiment on standard datasets, Market-1501, MSMT17.

Methods	Market-1501		MSMT17	
	mAP	R-1	mAP	R-1
PCB [14]	81.6	93.8	40.4	68.2
IANet [7]	83.1	94.4	46.8	75.7
FSAM [6]	85.6	94.6	–	–
CAL [3]	**87.5**	**94.7**	<u>57.3</u>	<u>79.7</u>
TCiP (ours)	<u>86.65</u>	93.71	**66.01**	**83.68**

Fig. 3. The hard samples for training in LTCC. Pictures of each column have the same person id and different clothes ids.

Table 3. Ablation experiment on LTCC dataset. "F_{Br}" denotes using the biometric-related local feature, which extracts guided by human parsing. "Mask" denotes using mask token as illustrated in Eq. 5. "F_{Ci}" denotes cloth-irrelevant local features extracted with the guidance of ICI loss.

Backbone	F_{Br}	Mask	F_{Ci}	CS		SS	
				mAP	R-1	mAP	R-1
ResNet-50 [4]	–	–	–	9.02	20.08	25.98	58.82
TransReID [5]	–	–	–	15.69	28.06	33.06	64.5
ViT-BoT	–	–	–	16.52	30.87	34.81	67.34
	✓	–	–	18.36	35.46	40.17	72.21
	✓	✓	–	**19.62**	<u>37.24</u>	<u>41.18</u>	<u>72.62</u>
	✓	✓	✓	<u>19.31</u>	**38.78**	**41.9**	**74.24**

4.4   Experiment on Standard Re-ID

To verify the generality of our method, we train and test TCiP on two standard Re-ID datasets, Market-1501 and MSMT17. We use identity as clothes Id in the training stage. The performance on standard person Re-ID datasets without clothes changes is shown in Table 2. TCiP performs on par with other comparison methods on the Market-1501 and is better than all compared methods on the MSMT17. So TCiP proposed for changing clothes can also be applied appropriately to the standard Re-ID datasets without cloth-changing challenges.

4.5   Ablation Study

We validate the effectiveness of the proposed modules in TCiP in Table 3. The first ViT-BoT row shows that the transformer-based backbone performs much better than ResNet-50 in clothes-changing Re-ID, which is the same as its superiority in other CV fields. By comparing the first three rows where ViT-BoT is, locating biometric features through human parsing can bring significant improvements. Moreover, the learnable mask token vector proposed in Eq. 4 and Eq. 5 can get a significant increase. As shown in the last row of Table 3, the appending of ICI loss to extract cloth-irrelevant local feature is crucial as this feature significantly improves the Rank-1 metric in both CS and SS settings. Although the value of mAP in the CS setting remains at the level where the cloth-irrelevant local feature is not used, the improvement of other indicators due to the introduction of clothing information is considerable. The Rank-1 value gets a 1%–2% increase by the confidential information in the clothes region. It is consistent with our expected assumption that the clothing region features contain helpful information for person identity comparison. Moreover, it also shows that our proposed cloth-irrelevant local feature has improved in applying clothes-changing methods on standard Re-ID. So ICI loss digs out more key information hidden in the clothing area, bringing more key information.

4.6   Limitations

Although the proposed method performs well in cloth-changing Re-ID, it relies on human parsing performance and will bring additional computational costs. As illustrated in Fig. 3, people who change clothes may not significantly differ in appearance because they may not change the main clothing or retain a similar style. So the key to the research is how to consider clothing features adaptively.

5   Conclusion

In this paper, we propose that there is a lot of redundancy or even hostile interference areas in person images. The key to extracting robust identify-relevant features is to combine partial features reasonably. So we propose a novel Transformer-based Cloth-irrelevant Patches (TCiP) feature extracting method, which separates all patches into biometric-related patches, clothes-related patches, and background with the guidance of a human parsing module. And an Inverse Clothes Id (ICI) loss function is proposed to extract long-term local features from the clothes-related patches without the clothes-changing situation's disturbances. These experiments prove the effectiveness of our proposed method that TCiP archives the state-of-the-art performance on cloth-changing person Re-ID and standard person Re-ID benchmarks.

Acknowledgements. This work was funded by the Nature Natural Science Foundation of China (62002220).

References

1. Cheng, D., Gong, Y., Zhou, S., Wang, J., Zheng, N.: Person re-identification by multi-channel parts-based CNN with improved triplet loss function. In: Proceedings of the IEEE Conference on Computer Vision and Pattern Recognition, pp. 1335–1344 (2016)
2. Dosovitskiy, A., et al.: An image is worth 16×16 words: transformers for image recognition at scale. arXiv preprint arXiv:2010.11929 (2020)
3. Gu, X., Chang, H., Ma, B., Bai, S., Shan, S., Chen, X.: Clothes-changing person re-identification with RGB modality only. In: CVPR (2022)
4. He, K., Zhang, X., Ren, S., Sun, J.: Deep residual learning for image recognition. In: Proceedings of the IEEE Conference on Computer Vision and Pattern Recognition, pp. 770–778 (2016)
5. He, S., Luo, H., Wang, P., Wang, F., Li, H., Jiang, W.: TransReID: transformer-based object re-identification. In: Proceedings of the IEEE/CVF International Conference on Computer Vision, pp. 15013–15022 (2021)
6. Hong, P., Wu, T., Wu, A., Han, X., Zheng, W.S.: Fine-grained shape-appearance mutual learning for cloth-changing person re-identification. In: Proceedings of the IEEE/CVF Conference on Computer Vision and Pattern Recognition, pp. 10513–10522 (2021)
7. Hou, R., Ma, B., Chang, H., Gu, X., Shan, S., Chen, X.: Interaction-and-aggregation network for person re-identification. In: Proceedings of the IEEE/CVF Conference on Computer Vision and Pattern Recognition, pp. 9317–9326 (2019)
8. Jin, X., et al.: Cloth-changing person re-identification from a single image with gait prediction and regularization. arXiv preprint arXiv:2103.15537 (2021)
9. Li, P., Xu, Y., Wei, Y., Yang, Y.: Self-correction for human parsing. IEEE Trans. Pattern Anal. Mach. Intell. **44**(6), 3260–3271 (2022)
10. Li, X., Hou, Y., Wang, P., Gao, Z., Xu, M., Li, W.: Trear: transformer-based RGB-D egocentric action recognition. IEEE Trans. Cogn. Dev. Syst. **14**(1), 246–252 (2022)
11. Liu, Z., et al.: Swin transformer: hierarchical vision transformer using shifted windows. In: Proceedings of the IEEE/CVF International Conference on Computer Vision, pp. 10012–10022 (2021)
12. Plizzari, C., Cannici, M., Matteucci, M.: Spatial temporal transformer network for skeleton-based action recognition. In: Del Bimbo, A., et al. (eds.) ICPR 2021. LNCS, vol. 12663, pp. 694–701. Springer, Cham (2021). https://doi.org/10.1007/978-3-030-68796-0_50
13. Qian, X., et al.: Long-term cloth-changing person re-identification. In: Proceedings of the Asian Conference on Computer Vision (2020)
14. Sun, Y., Zheng, L., Yang, Y., Tian, Q., Wang, S.: Beyond part models: person retrieval with refined part pooling (and a strong convolutional baseline). In: Ferrari, V., Hebert, M., Sminchisescu, C., Weiss, Y. (eds.) ECCV 2018. LNCS, vol. 11208, pp. 501–518. Springer, Cham (2018). https://doi.org/10.1007/978-3-030-01225-0_30
15. Wei, L., Zhang, S., Gao, W., Tian, Q.: Person transfer GAN to bridge domain gap for person re-identification. In: Proceedings of the IEEE Conference on Computer Vision and Pattern Recognition, pp. 79–88 (2018)
16. Xie, Z., et al.: SimMIM: a simple framework for masked image modeling. In: International Conference on Computer Vision and Pattern Recognition (CVPR) (2022)

17. Yang, Q., Wu, A., Zheng, W.S.: Person re-identification by contour sketch under moderate clothing change. IEEE Trans. Pattern Anal. Mach. Intell. **43**(6), 2029–2046 (2021)

18. Ye, M., Shen, J., Lin, G., Xiang, T., Shao, L., Hoi, S.C.: Deep learning for person re-identification: a survey and outlook. IEEE Trans. Pattern Anal. Mach. Intell. **44**(6), 2872–2893 (2021)

19. Yu, S., Li, S., Chen, D., Zhao, R., Yan, J., Qiao, Y.: COCAS: a large-scale clothes changing person dataset for re-identification. In: Proceedings of the IEEE/CVF Conference on Computer Vision and Pattern Recognition, pp. 3400–3409 (2020)

20. Zheng, L., Shen, L., Tian, L., Wang, S., Wang, J., Tian, Q.: Scalable person re-identification: a benchmark. In: Proceedings of the IEEE International Conference on Computer Vision, pp. 1116–1124 (2015)

21. Zheng, L., Yang, Y., Hauptmann, A.G.: Person re-identification: past, present and future. arXiv preprint arXiv:1610.02984 (2016)

22. Zhu, K., Guo, H., Liu, Z., Tang, M., Wang, J.: Identity-guided human semantic parsing for person re-identification. In: Vedaldi, A., Bischof, H., Brox, T., Frahm, J.-M. (eds.) ECCV 2020. LNCS, vol. 12348, pp. 346–363. Springer, Cham (2020). https://doi.org/10.1007/978-3-030-58580-8_21

Learning Unified Binary Feature Codes for Cross-Illumination Palmprint Recognition

Jianxiong Wei[1], Lunke Fei[1(✉)], Shuping Zhao[1], Shuyi Li[2], Jie Wen[3], and Jinrong Cui[4]

[1] The School of Computer Science and Technology,
Guangdong University of Technology, Guangzhou, China
`flksxm@126.com`
[2] Department of Computer and Information Science, University of Macau,
Taipa, Macau, China
[3] The Bio-Computing Research Center, Harbin Institute of Technology,
Shenzhen, China
[4] The College of Mathematics and Informatics, South China Agricultural University,
Guangzhou, China

Abstract. Palmprint recognition has recently attracted broad attention due to its rich discriminative features, contactless collection manner and less invasive. However, most existing methods focus on within-illumination palmprint recognition, which requires the similar illumination of query samples acquisition as the gallery samples, significantly limiting its practical applications in the open environment. In this paper, we propose a cross-illumination palmprint recognition method by jointly learning the unified binary feature descriptors of multiple illumination palmprint images. Given two different illuminations of palmprint images, we first calculate the direction-based ordinal measure vectors (DOMVs) to sample the important palmprint direction features. Then, we jointly learn a unified feature mapping that project the two-illumination DOMVs into binary feature codes. To better exploit the palm-invariant features of multi-illumination samples, we make the binary feature codes as similar as possible by minimizing the feature distance between the two illumination samples of the same palm. Moreover, we maximize the variances of all binary feature codes among the training samples for each illumination, such that the discriminative power can be enhanced in an unsupervised manner. Finally, we convert the binary feature codes of a palmprint image into a block-wise histogram feature descriptor for cross-illumination palmprint recognition. Experimental results on three cross-illumination palmprint datasets show that our proposed method achieves competitive cross-illumination palmprint recognition performance in comparison with the state-of-the-art palmprint feature descriptors.

Keywords: Biometric · Palmprint recognition · Cross-illumination palmprint recognition · Binary feature code learning

N. Magnenat-Thalmann et al. (Eds.): CGI 2022, LNCS 13443, pp. 290–301, 2022.
https://doi.org/10.1007/978-3-031-23473-6_23

1   Introduction

Biometrics recognition refers to automatically recognizing people based on one's inherent physiological or behavioral characteristics, which has become one of the most popular personal authentication technologies because of its security and convenience [1]. So far there have been various biometric traits such as face [2], fingerprint [3] and gait [4] that have been successfully developed for biometrics recognition. Even so, different biometrics technologies usually have different advantages and disadvantages, and no biometrics can meet all requirements of practical applications. For example, as one of the most popular biometrics, face recognition has achieved great success in many real-world applications such as security checks, mobile phone unlocking and electronic payment. However, during the period of COVID-19, people usually wear masks making most existing face recognition systems less effective. In addition, fingerprint usually needs to be captured in a contact-based manner, making it easily leak onto the fingerprint recognition systems. In recent years, palmprint recognition has attracted increasing attention due to its several advantages such as rich characteristics, contactless acquisition manner and less invasive properties [5]. Therefore, palmprint recognition has great potential for practical application, and the past decade has witnessed remarkable progress in palmprint recognition [6,7].

In general, palmprint recognition mainly consists of four stages: image acquisition, image pre-processing, feature extraction and feature matching. Image acquisition aims to sample palmprint data via an imaging acquisition device such as a camera. Image pre-processing is to detect and crop the regions of interest (ROIs) of palmprint images for feature extraction. The objective of feature extraction is to extract the discriminative features to make palmprint images of different palms separable. Finally, the goal of feature matching is to classify different palmprint features from different palms. Compared with other three stages, how to extract the discriminative palmprint features play a key role in palmprint recognition because it significantly affects the final recognition performance. In recent years, there have been many feature extraction methods proposed for palmprint representation and recognition, such as the coding-based methods, structure-based methods, statistic methods, subspace methods, and deep learning-based methods. For example, Xu et al. [8] proposed a discriminative and robust competitive code method based on principal directions of palmprint images. Li et al. [9] proposed a new iterative closest point (ICP) method to accurately correct the translational and rotational variations between palmprint images. Jing et al. [10] proposed a supervised group-sparse coding (DLEM-SGSC) method based on a dual Laplace mixture error model for robust palmprint recognition against various contaminants. Fei et al. [11] proposed a multi-feature learning method to represent the multiple type features of palmprint images. Shao et al. [12] designed a new meta-Siamese network (MSN) to utilize shot less learning for small sample palmprint recognition. It is noted that most existing palmprint literature only studies the within illumination palmprint recognition. In other words, most existing palmprint recognition methods require the illuminations of the query and gallery palmprint images are the same.

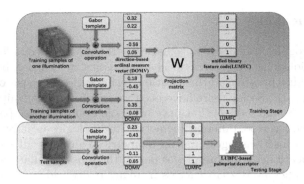

Fig. 1. The flowchart of the proposed LUBFC method. Given two illuminations of training samples, we first extract their direction-based ordinal measure vectors to sample the important direction features of palmprint images, and then jointly learn the feature mapping functions that convert double-illumination DOMVs into unified binary feature codes. For each test image, the DOMVs are first formed and then encoded into binary feature codes using the learned feature mapping. Finally, these binary feature codes are grouped into block-wise histogram feature vectors (LUMFC-based palmprint descriptor) for cross-illumination palmprint recognition.

However, in real applications, query samples are possibly captured under a very different illumination environment from the gallery samples, making most existing feature extraction methods less effective. How to extract the robust palmprint features to illumination changes remains an interesting and challenging problem.

In this paper, we propose an illumination-invariant palmprint feature learning method for cross-illumination for palmprint recognition, where the query palmprint images are captured from different illuminations from the gallery samples. Figure 1 shows the basic idea of the proposed method. Unlike most existing methods that learn features from raw pixels, our proposed method first extracts the direction-based ordinal measure vectors (DOMVs) from different illuminations of palmprint images. Then, a unified feature map function is jointly learned to project multi-illumination DOMVs into binary feature vectors, which have the minimized feature distance for the intra-palm samples, such that the multi-illumination of the intra-class palmprint images can achieve the common feature representation. Moreover, the variance of the learned binary features among all training samples is maximized, such that the discriminative ability of the learned features can be improved. Lastly, the learned binary feature codes are clustered into histogram descriptors for cross-illumination palmprint recognition. Experimental results on the widely used PolyU multi-illumination palmprint database show that the proposed method outperforms the state-of-the-art palmprint methods.

The main contributions of this paper can be summarized as follows:

- We propose a joint feature learning method to learn the illumination-invariant palmprint feature descriptors for cross-illumination palmprint recognition, where the query palmprint images are captured under different illuminations from the gallery samples. To the best of our knowledge, this is the first work with an attempt to study cross-illumination palmprint recognition.

- We formulate a simple yet effective optimization objective function for the proposed method, which can obtain a closed-form solution for the learned feature map function. Moreover, the proposed method can be easily learned with limited training samples such as one training image per palm for each illumination. Therefore, our proposed method has a fast-learning speed.
- We conduct extensive experiments on three two-illumination palmprint image datasets for both cross-illumination identification and verification, and the experimental results clearly show the effectiveness of the proposed method.

The rest of this paper is organized as follows. Section 2 elaborates our proposed cross-illumination palmprint recognition method. Section 3 analyzes the experimental results. Finally, Sect. 4 offers the conclusion of this paper.

2   Learning Robust Representation of Cross-Illumination Palmprint Images

In this section, we first elaborate the LUBFC learning method, and then show how to use LUBFC for cross-illumination palmprint recognition.

2.1   Multi-illumination Palmprint Recognition

The direction information is one of the most important features of palmprint images, which has shown strong discriminability for palmprint recognition. Inspired by this, in this work, we aim to learn an illumination-invariant direction feature descriptor for cross-illumination recognition. Specifically, we used the direction-based ordinal measure vectors (DOMV) [13] to capture the informative direction information of multiple illumination palmprint images, and then jointly learn the unified binary feature codes of the multiple illumination images.

For forming the DOMV of a palmprint image, twelve directions of Gabor filters are first used to convolve the palmprint image to obtain the directional responses on twelve directions. For each pixel of the palmprint image, the directional response differences between each pair of neighboring directions are subsequently concatenated to form the DOMV of the pixel. Let $X^1 = [x_1^1, x_2^1, \cdots, x_N^1]$ and $X^1 = [x_1^2, x_2^2, \cdots, x_N^2]$ be the DOM-Vs of the pixels of all training palmprint images captured under two different illuminations, where N is the total number of the training DOMVs. x_i^1 and x_i^2 represent the i-th DOMVs extracted from two different illuminations of palmprint images of the same palm. Our proposed LUBFC method aims to learn a unified feature projection that maps the DOMVs of two different illuminations into binary codes as:

$$b_i^1 = 0.5 \times (sgn(W^T x_i^1) + 1), \tag{1}$$

and

$$b_i^2 = 0.5 \times (sgn(W^T x_i^2) + 1), \tag{2}$$

where $W = [w_1, w^2, \cdots, w^k] \in R^{d \times K}$ represents the unified feature projection functions. d is the size of the DOMV and K is the feature projection function number. b_i^1 and b_i^2 are the binary feature codes learned from the DOMVs of two different illuminations of palmprint images, respectively. $sgn(u)$ equals to 1 when $u > 0$ and -1 otherwise.

To better learn the illumination invariant features of multiple illumination palmprint images, we have the main aim that the intra-palm binary feature codes learned from two different illuminations of samples are as similar as possible. Moreover, the inter-palm binary features codes should be as different as possible to enhance the discriminative power of the learned binary features. To achieve these objectives, we formulate the following objective function for the multi-illumination palmprint feature learning:

$$\max J(W) = J_1 + J_2 + \lambda J_3$$
$$= \sum_{i=1}^{N} (||b_i^1 - \bar{b}^1||_F^2 + ||b_i^2 - \bar{b}^2||_F^2 - \lambda||b_i^1 - b_i^2||_F^2), \tag{3}$$

where $\bar{b}^1$ and $\bar{b}^2$ are the mean of the learned binary features, i.e., $\bar{b}^1 = \frac{1}{N} \sum_{i=1}^{N} b_i^1$ and $\bar{b}^2 = \frac{1}{N} \sum_{i=1}^{N} b_i^2$. $||.||_F$ is the matrix Frobenius norm. The objective function consists of three constraint terms. The third item aims to make the features learned from two illuminations of palmprint images similar. The first and second constraint items ensure that the features are variant so as to enhance their discriminative power. λ is a weight parameter to balance the importance of the third constraint. By relaxing the sign function to its magnitude [14], we rewrite the objective function to the following form:

$$J = \sum_{i=1}^{N} (||W^T x_i^1 - W^T \bar{x}^1||_F^2 + ||W^T x_i^2 - W^T \bar{x}^2||_F^2 - \lambda||W^T x_i^1 - W^T x_i^2||_F^2)$$
$$= ||W^T X^1 - W^T \bar{X}^1||_F^2 + ||W^T X^2 - W^T \bar{X}^2||_F^2 - \lambda||W^T X^1 - W^T X^2||_F^2)$$
$$= tr(W^T X^1 (X^1)^T W - 2W^T X^1 (\bar{X}^1)^T W + W^T \bar{X}^1 (\bar{X}^1)^T W)$$
$$+ tr(W^T X^2 (X^2)^T W - 2W^T X^2 (\bar{X}^2)^T W + +W^T \bar{X}^2 (\bar{X}^2)^T W)$$
$$- \lambda tr(W^T X^1 (X^1)^T W - 2W^T X^1 (X^2)^T W + W^T X^2 (X^2)^T W)$$
$$= tr(W^T Y W), \tag{4}$$
$$s.t. \, W^T W = I,$$

where $Y = X^1(X^1)^T - 2X^1(\bar{X}^1)^T + \bar{X}^1(\bar{X}^1)^T + X^2(X^2)^T - 2X^2(\bar{X}^2)^T + \bar{X}^2(\bar{X}^2)^T - \lambda X^1(X^1)^T + 2\lambda X^1(X^2)^T - \lambda X^2(X^2)^T$, $\bar{X}^1 = [\bar{x}^1, \bar{x}^1, \cdots, \bar{x}^1]$,

---

Algorithm 1. LUBFC

Input: The DOMVs $X^1 = [x_1^1, x_2^1, \cdots, x_N^1]$ and $X^1 = [x_1^2, x_2^2, \cdots, x_N^2]$, of training sample set, parameter λ

Initialization: $\lambda = 100$.

   while W is unknown **do**

   1.Forming Y based on Eq. (4);

   2.Calculating the eigen-vectors of Y;

   3.Forming mapping matrix W by concatenating the eigen-vectors of Y;

   4.return W.

   end while

Output: Feature mapping matrix W.

$\bar{x}^1 = \frac{1}{N} \sum_{i=1}^{N} x_i^1$, $\bar{X}^2 = [\bar{x}^2, \bar{x}^2, \cdots, \bar{x}^2]$, $\bar{x}^2 = \frac{1}{N} \sum_{i=1}^{N} x_i^2$. The orthogonal constraint $W^T W = I$ makes the basis feature projection function independent, where I is an identity matrix. Therefore, the feature projection function can be optimized by calculating the eigen-function of Y. Algorithm 1 summarizes the optimization of the LUBFC method.

2.2 Feature Representation and Matching

Having obtained the feature mapping function, i.e., W, a new pawprint image can be easily converted into its binary feature code vectors. It is noted that different regions of a palmprint image usually have obvious different characteristics. To better represent the position-specific features of a palmprint, we calculate the block-wise histograms of the binary feature codes as the final feature representation. Specifically, we first convert the binary feature code vectors into an integer value for each pixel of the palmprint image. Then, we divide the decimal feature map into a group of non-overlapping blocks, the sizes of which are empirically set to 16 × 16 pixels in this paper. Third, we calculate the histogram for each block and concatenate the histogram of all blocks into a vector-based feature descriptor as the final representation. In the matching stage, we use the simple yet effective Chi-square distance [15] to measure the similarity of the histogram-based feature descriptors of palmprint images. Figure 2 illustrates the pipeline of the LUBFC-based representation and matching.

3 Experiments

In this section, we conduct cross-illumination palmprint recognition experiments to evaluate the proposed method on the widely used PolyU multi-spectral palmprint image database [16].

3.1 PolyU Multi-spectral Palmprint Image Database

The PolyU multi-spectral palmprint image database consists of 24,000 samples, which were captured from both palms of 250 volunteers (195 males and 55

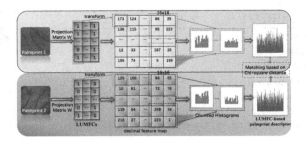

Fig. 2. Forming block-wise histogram feature descriptors.

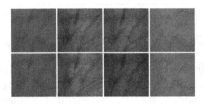

Fig. 3. Some typical palmprint images of the multi-spectral palmprint databases. The samples from the first and second were captured in the first and second sessions, respectively. The samples of the first to fourth columns were captured under the red, blue, green, and NIR illuminations, respectively. (Color figure online)

females) under four different illuminations, including the red, blue, green and near-infrared (NIR) illumination. Specifically, all the multi-illumination palmprint samples were collected in two independent sessions with an average time interval of approximately 9 days. In each session, each individual was asked to provide six images for each palm under each illumination. As a result, each palm contributed 24 samples under the four illuminations. Therefore, the multi-illumination database contains four independent datasets, each of which consists of 6,000 images from 500 different palms for each illumination. Figure 3 shows some typical examples of the multi-illumination palmprint samples. It can be seen that there are obvious differences among different illuminations of the palmprint images. It is noted that the samples captured under the invisible NIR illumination actually capture the palm vein information, which shows very different characteristics from the visible illumination, as shown in Fig. 3. For this reason, in our experiments, we use the palmprint images captured under Red, Blue and Green illuminations to conduct cross-illumination recognition experiments. In addition, all palmprint images were cropped into regions of interest with the sizes of 64×64 pixels.

Table 1. The identification results (average accuracy ± standard error) of different methods on the PolyU multi-spectral palmprint database.

Methods	Blue− >Green	Blue− >Red	Green− >Red	Green− >Blue	Red− >Blue	Red− >Green
CompCode	96.25 ± 0.19	90.88 ± 0.34	92.41 ± 1.26	96.16 ± 0.37	89.07 ± 0.94	92.54 ± 0.07
HOL	96.73 ± 0.46	76.19 ± 1.16	83.55 ± 0.74	96.77 ± 0.27	72.66 ± 0.81	81.27 ± 0.72
ALDC	98.42 ± 0.14	88.41 ± 1.41	93.22 ± 1.32	98.54 ± 0.22	78.14 ± 0.55	89.21 ± 0.77
NDI	98.79 ± 0.21	91.35 ± 0.71	94.77 ± 1.00	98.59 ± 0.18	83.66 ± 0.96	91.93 ± 0.54
LLDP	98.93 ± 0.20	88.31 ± 0.86	93.11 ± 0.36	98.72 ± 0.34	82.59 ± 0.20	90.44 ± 0.39
DoN	93.31 ± 0.45	82.52 ± 0.81	92.80 ± 0.71	92.48 ± 0.94	80.94 ± 0.78	86.37 ± 0.80
SDDLM	91.09 ± 0.43	88.37 ± 0.81	88.61 ± 0.72	90.56 ± 0.54	88.46 ± 0.41	88.90 ± 0.67
LUBFC	**99.52 ± 0.08**	**95.77 ± 0.19**	**97.13 ± 0.29**	**99.36 ± 0.14**	**92.24 ± 0.41**	**96.82 ± 0.21**

3.2 Cross-Illumination Palmprint Identification

In general, palmprint identification aims to identify the personal ID of a query sample based on a group of labeled galley samples. In this experiment, we form three two-illumination palmprint datasets to conduct cross-illumination identification, including Red+Blue, Red+Green and Blue+Green (referred to "A+B"). For each "A+B" dataset, we randomly select a palmprint image from "A" and a palmprint image from "B" to form a training sample set, such that the training set contains two samples for each palm with two different illuminations, which are used to learn the unified feature projection, i.e., W. Having obtained the feature projection, we can calculate the block-wise histogram feature descriptors for all the samples of the "A+B" dataset. Then, we randomly select one sample from "A" as the labeled gallery samples and use all samples from "B" as the query samples to calculate the rank-one identification accuracy of the query samples.

To better evaluate our proposed method, we also implemented several state-of-the-art methods, including Competitive code (CompCode) [17], HOL [18], ALDC [19], NDI [20], LLDP [21], DoN [22] and SDDLM [23] and compared them with the proposed method. For a fair comparison, all methods were repeated 10 times and the average identification accuracies are reported. Table 1 tabulates the average rank-one identification accuracies of different methods, where "A− >B" represent the gallery samples are from "A" and the query samples are from "B". It can be seen that the proposed method consistently outperforms the seven compared methods by significantly improving the identification accuracy over the other methods. This is because our proposed method can accurately extract the illumination-invariant palm orientation features and greatly preserve the original orientation features of the palmprint. In addition, our proposed LUBFC can extract the unified feature representation of multiple illumination palmprint images by projecting the multi-illumination palmprint images into a common binary feature space. Therefore, the gap between the two different illuminations of samples can be well reduced, such that a higher cross-illumination identification accuracy can be obtained.

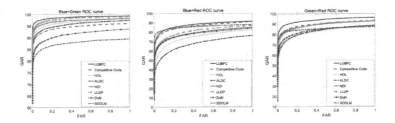

Fig. 4. The ROCs of different methods on the Blue+Green, Blue+Red, and Green+Red datasets, respectively. (Color figure online)

3.3   Cross-Illumination Palmprint Verification

Palmprint verification is to answer the question that a query palmprint image is from the same palm of a gallery sample or not. Compared with palmprint identification, palmprint verification is a one-by-one matching procedure whether they belong to the same palm. A match is considered as a genuine match if the two compared palmprint images are from the same palm, or otherwise an impostor match. In this experiment, we compare each palmprint image from one illumination with each palmprint image from another illumination. There are 6000 palmprint images for each of the Red, Green and Blue illuminations in the PolyU. Therefore, for each "A+B" dataset, the total number of verification matches 6000 × 6000 = 36,000,000, which contains 12 * 12 * 500 = 72,000 genuine matches and 35,928,000 impostor matches.

For our proposed method, we first calculate the matching scores for each pair of two compared palmprint images based on Chi-square distance, and then compute the false acceptance rate (FAR) and the true acceptance rate (GAR) based on the adaptive matching threshold. Moreover, we compare the FAR and GAR with the state-of-the-art palmprint descriptors such as the SDDLM methods. Figure 4 shows the ROCs (FAR versus GAR) of the proposed method in comparison with the seven baseline methods. It can be seen that the proposed method can obtain a higher GAR than the compared methods against the same FAR. The possible reason is that our method can efficiently learn the illumination-invariant features from multiple illumination palmprint images, such that the genuine matches between two illuminations of intra-class samples can be well detected.

3.4   Parameter Analysis

In this subsection, we analyze the sensitivity of the balance parameter λ of the proposed LUBFC. To the best of our knowledge, there is no effective way to obtain the optimal value of the balance parameter. In this work, we set λ to the values of different orders of magnitude, including 0.0001, 0.001, 0.01, 0.1, 1, 10, 100, and 1000, and then calculate the average rank-one identification accuracy of the proposed method on the "blue+green" dataset. Figure 5 shows the average

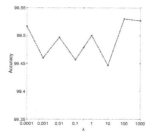

Fig. 5. The average rank-one identification accuracies for the proposed method versus different values of λ on the "blue+green" dataset. (Color figure online)

accuracy of the proposed method versus different values of λ. It can be seen that the proposed method achieves the best identification accuracy when λ is set to the values ranging from 100 to 1000. The possible reason is that a larger value of the balance parameter can highlight the similarity of the cross-illumination palmprint features, such that more unified representation can be obtained of the cross-illumination palmprint images. In addition, the identification result of our proposed method is slightly fluctuate with the values of the λ, demonstrating the less sensitivity of the proposed method to the balance parameter.

3.5   Computational Complexity Analysis

In this subsection, the computational complexity of the proposed method is analyzed. It is worth noting that the proposed LUBFC method can achieve the closed-form solution of feature projection, such that the proposed method can be efficiently trained. For example, the time cost time of training feature projection is about 15 s on the Red+Blue dataset. Moreover, we further test the time cost of the proposed method on feature extraction and matching. Table 2 tabulates the average time taken for feature extraction and matching of the proposed method in comparison with the representative palmprint descriptors. It is seen that the proposed method takes approximately 0.01 to 0.02 s more time than the other compared methods for feature extraction. The possible reason is that our proposed method needs to first extract DOMV from palmprint images and then extract the illumination-invariant features, while the traditional methods usually directly extract features from raw pixels of palmprint images. In addition, our proposed method has a faster feature matching speed than most compared methods due to its simple yet effective matching scheme. Therefore, considering the promising cross-illumination recognition accuracy, our proposed method has a good trade-off when both recognition performance and efficiency are concerned.

Table 2. The average time (s) taken for feature extraction and matching of different methods.

Methods	Feature extraction (s)	Matching (s)
CompCode	0.0326	0.0039
HOL	0.0369	0.0048
ALDC	0.0394	0.0050
NDI	0.0379	0.0154
LLDP	0.0370	0.0058
DoN	0.0269	0.0141
SDDLM	0.0231	0.0053
LUBFC	0.0488	0.0046

4   Conclusion

In this paper, we propose an illumination-invariant palmprint feature descriptor learning method for cross-illumination palmprint recognition. To reduce the gap between two different illuminations of palmprint images, we make the learned feature codes as similar as possible for the intra-palm samples with different illuminations. Further, we maximize the feature variances for all training samples of each illumination to make the learned feature discriminative. Experimental results on the PolyU multi-illumination palmprint database show that the proposed method achieves better or very competitive cross-illumination palmprint recognition performance when compared with the state-of-the-art methods. How to extend the proposed method for cross one to multiple illumination palmprint recognition seems to be an interesting further work.

Acknowledgement. This work was supported in part by the National Natural Science Foundation of China under Grants 62176066 and 62106052, in part by the Natural Science Foundation of Guangdong Province under Grant 2019A1515011811, and in part by the Guangzhou Science and technology plan project under Grant 202002030110.

References

1. Anil, K.J., Arun, R., Salil, P.: An introduction to biometric recognition. IEEE Trans. Circ. Syst. Video Technol. **14**(1), 4–20 (2004)
2. Bin, S., Ping, L., Chenhao, G., Kwan-liu, M.: Deep neural representation guided face sketch synthesis. IEEE Trans. Vis. Comput. Graph. **25**(12), 3216–3230 (2019)
3. Sidra, A., Po, Y., Saleha, M., Ping, L., Bin, S.: An accurate multi-modal biometric identification system for person identification via fusion of face and finger print. World Wide Web **23**(2), 1299–1317 (2020). https://doi.org/10.1007/s11280-019-00698-6
4. Marín-Jiménez, M.J., Castro, F.M., Delgado-Escaño, R., Kalogeiton, V., Guil, N.: UGaitNet: multimodal gait recognition with missing input modalities. IEEE Trans. Inf. Forensics Secur. **16**, 5452–5462 (2021)

5. Lin, Z., Lida, L., Anqi, Y., Ying, S., Meng, Y.: Towards contactless palmprint recognition: a novel device, a new benchmark, and a collaborative representation based identification approach. Pattern Recogn. **69**, 199–212 (2017)
6. Shuping, Z., Bob, Z.: Joint constrained least-square regression with deep convolutional feature for palmprint recognition. IEEE Trans. Syst. Man Cybern. Syst. **52**(1), 511–522 (2022)
7. Lunke, F., Shuping, Z., Wei, J., Bob, Z., Jie, W., Yong X.: Toward efficient palmprint feature extraction by learning a single-layer convolution network. IEEE Trans. Neural Netw. Learn. Syst. 1–12 (2022)
8. Yong, X., Lunke, F., Jie, W., David, Z.: Discriminative and robust competitive code for palmprint recognition. IEEE Trans. Syst. Man Cybern. Syst. **48**(2), 232–241 (2018)
9. Li, W., Bob, Z., Lei, Z., Jingqi, Y.: Principal line-based alignment refinement for palmprint recognition. IEEE Trans. Syst. Man Cybern. Part C **42**(6), 1491–1499 (2012)
10. Kunlei, J., Xinman, Z., Xuebin, X.: Double-Laplacian mixture-error model-based supervised group-sparse coding for robust palmprint recognition. IEEE Trans. Circ. Syst. Video Technol. **32**(5), 3125–3140 (2022)
11. Lunke, F., Bob, Z., Lin, Z., Wei, J., Jie, W., Jigang, W.: Learning compact multifeature codes for palmprint recognition from a single training image per palm. IEEE Trans. Multim. **23**, 2930–2942 (2021)
12. Huikai, S., Dexing, Z., Xuefeng, D., Shaoyi, D., Raymond, N.J.V.: Few-shot learning for palmprint recognition via meta-Siamese network. IEEE Trans. Instrum. Meas. **70**, 1–12 (2021)
13. Lunke, F., Bob, Z., Yong, X., Zhenhua, G., Jie, W., Wei, J.: Learning discriminant direction binary palmprint descriptor. IEEE Trans. Image Process. **28**(8), 3808–3820 (2019)
14. Jun, W., Ondrej, K., Shih-Fu, C.: Semi-supervised hashing for scalable image retrieval. In: CVPR, pp. 3424–3431 (2010)
15. Albert, S., Peter, M.B.: A scaled difference chi-square test statistic for moment structure analysis. Psychometrika **66**(4), 507–514 (2001). https://doi.org/10.1007/BF02296192
16. PolyU multispectral palmprint database. http://www.comp.polyu.edu.hk/biometrics/MultispectralPalmprint/MSP.htm
17. Wenming, Y., Xiaola, H., Fei, Z., Qingmin, L.: Comparative competitive coding for personal identification by using finger vein and finger dorsal texture fusion. Inf. Sci. **268**, 20–32 (2014)
18. Wei, J., Rongxiang, H., Yingkei, L., Yang, Z., Jie, G.: Histogram of oriented lines for palmprint recognition. IEEE Trans. Syst. Man Cybern. Syst. **44**(3), 385–395 (2014)
19. Lunke, F., Bob, Z., Wei, Z., Shaohua, T.: Local apparent and latent direction extraction for palmprint recognition. Inf. Sci. **473**, 59–72 (2019)
20. Lunke, F., Bob, Z., Yong, X., Liping, Y.: Palmprint recognition using neighboring direction indicator. IEEE Trans. Hum. Mach. Syst. **46**(6), 787–798 (2016)
21. Yuetong, L., et al.: Local line directional pattern for palmprint recognition. Pattern Recogn. **50**, 26–44 (2016)
22. Qian, Z., Ajay, K., Gang, P.: A 3D feature descriptor recovered from a single 2D palmprint image. IEEE Trans. Pattern Anal. Mach. Intell. **38**(6), 1272–1279 (2016)
23. Shuping, Z., Bob, Z.: Learning salient and discriminative descriptor for palmprint feature extraction and identification. IEEE Trans. Neural Netw. Learn. Syst. **31**(12), 5219–5230 (2020)

Colors, Paintings and Layout

SemiPainter: Learning to Draw Semi-realistic Paintings from the Manga Line Drawings and Flat Shadow

Keyue Fan, Shiguang Liu$^{(\boxtimes)}$, and Wenhuan Lu$^{(\boxtimes)}$

College of Intelligence and Computing, Tianjin University, Tianjin 300350, China
{lsg,wenhua}@tju.edu.cn

Abstract. Semi-realistic paintings are widely used in game concept art, film posters and animation, etc. However, none of existing work can reproduce this type of art. We propose the SemiPainter to generate semi-realistic paintings from line drawings based on a deep learning network. We divide the complex work into two parts, generating the shadow from a line drawing and a simple flat shadow image at first, then generating flat color from line drawings. We merge these two paintings and get the final result. We use two networks with U-Net structure to realize these two stages of work. In order to ensure the global consistency of picture illumination, we add the lighting direction to the shadow network. The color of each part of the painting is uncertain, so color hints from users is provided when coloring, so that the network can realize controllable colorization. To the best of our knowledge, this is the first framework for reproducing semi-realistic paintings.

Keywords: Colorization · Line drawings · Semi-realistic paintings

1 Introduction

In animation, video games and films, the creation of 2D paintings such as illustration and game concept art is a very important work. Semi-realistic paintings (Fig. 1(a)) is a style between flat color paintings and realistic paintings. In recent years, the semi-realistic painting is a very popular 2D painting style, which is difficult to simulate by current methods.

Compared with the flat color paintings (Fig. 1(b)), which only relies on lines and flat colors with a few light and shade, semi-realistic paintings need a large number of shadows to express the structure and content. It is difficult to generate semi-realistic paintings directly by existing image generation methods because our goal is to generate animation characters with different appearances. Meanwhile, different artists have different styles, so it is non-trivial to build a large enough database with consistent style.

This work was partly supported by the Natural Science Foundation of China under grant no. 62072328.

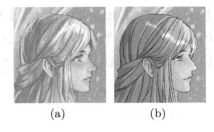

(a)   (b)

Fig. 1. Compared to flat color paintings, semi-realistic paintings rely on rich and continuous shadow to express the structure and content.

Because manual creation is complex, it is impossible to let models perform as a human and learn to work with the existing technology. Our purpose is not to teach the model to create, but to better assist artists and art lovers in painting. Some work has been proposed to colorize the line art, but no work focuses on generating semi-realistic paintings. In this paper, we propose SemiPainter, a framework based on neural networks that can generate semi-realistic paintings.

Some painters draw a black-and-white painting with shadow structure first, and then use the single channel adjustment in Photoshop to colorize the shadows in different layers. Inspired by this method, we also divide our generation work into two stages: semi-realistic shadow drawing and coloring. We designed ShadowNet and ColorNet to realize these two parts of work, respectively.

Because the line art can only provide limited structural information, it is difficult to generate shadows from it, too. Existed work such as ShadeSketch [42] and SmartShadow [38] have proposed some methods to generate shadows from the line arts, but only flat and discontinuous shadows are generated. Some work [5,14] attempts to generate continuous shadows, but the structure of these shadows is not clear. These methods cannot generate acceptable shadows for hair and pleats, which are common in a large number of animation paintings.

Since the animation paintings are various, artists often use their imagination to draw some colors that rarely appear in the real pictures, such as pink or blue hair. At the same time, the colors of objects on the picture are also rich and diverse. In the view of the model, generating purple skirts or pink skirts is all acceptable. Zhang et al. [39] indicated that users can provide color hints to guide colorization. We learn from their ideas. While providing line arts, we also add user color hints to realize user controllable colorization. But so far, there is no work to discuss the generation of semi-realistic paintings, and existing methods cannot complete this work.

In order to generate semi-realistic shadows, we use a global illumination vector and a flat shadow. The global light can ensure the rationality and correctness of the overall illumination. Because local shadows are complex, if we only rely on the information provided by the global lighting, we cannot generate the complex shadows for pleats, hair and other items in the paintings. In order to generate a better shadow structure, we provide a hint shadow for the network. This shadow is very simple, without any light and shade changes, and only provides some local shadow information. We can see from the experiment in Sect. 4 that, providing this information greatly improves the quality of the generated semi-realistic shadows. Then we draw flat colors for lines under the guidance of user color hints, and compose the resulting shadows and colors to produce the final result.

Artists and amateurs can use SemiPainter to quickly generate semi-realistic paintings. Because the shadows and colors were divided into two layers before composition, they can further refine it to produce high-quality paintings in a shorter time, which makes the method more practical.

We summarize our contributions as follows:

- We propose SemiPainter based on deep learning techniques. To the best of our knowledge, this is the first framework to generating semi-realistic paintings.
- We divide the complex generation work into two parts: shadow generation and flat color drawing, which improves the result quality of each part. Meanwhile, this method can produce shadow and color images respectively, and support the refinement of the two images.
- We use a flat shadow to guide shadow generation, which produces a better semi-realistic shadow.
- We draw a flat color image from the line art and then compose it with the shadow image to avoid the color confusion caused by directly coloring the shadow image.

2   Related Work

2.1   Deep Learning Based Art Paintings Generation

Generating semi-realistic paintings is a branch of art painting reproduction. There have been many works focusing on art painting generation based on deep learning. Some style transfer methods [9,12,18,19,27,30] can convert an art painting from one style to another, but these methods do not support the restoration of texture and shadow information from highly simplified line art. Image to image translation methods [3,15,22,43] have also realized the transformation of the original picture into art paintings, but the generation results are uncontrollable. Lin et al. [23] and Xue [35] convert the line arts into Chinese traditional paintings based on the deep neural network. Some works [16,32] simulate pencil drawings based on deep learning. Some painting generation works [13,28,44] can generate paintings by learning the artist's painting strokes. These are the generation methods for specific painting styles and cannot be used for the generation of semi-realistic paintings.

2.2   Deep Learning Based Shadow Generation

Some shadow generation methods [8,14] use deep learning framework to predict normal map from the line drawings, then the final result is generated by

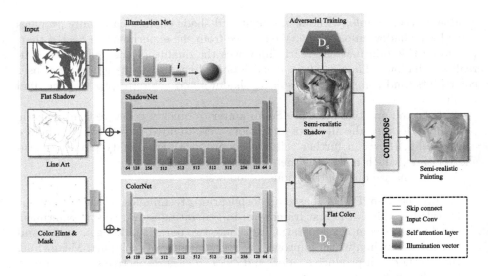

Fig. 2. Our method consists of three branches. Each convolution block contains a 4 × 4 convolution layer and a ReLU layer. In addition to the decoder of the colorNet, other blocks also include a normalization layer. Shadows and lines are single-channel grayscale images, and color hints are 4-channel images including a mask. (Color figure online)

positive lamination after rendering, Su et al. [33] proposed a semi-automatic normal map generation method. However, there are disadvantages in the shadows generated by this method. Compared with the 3D structure, the result is more like relief. Shadowsketch [42] can automatically generate flat shadows from line arts. It can generate different shadows according to different lighting directions. SmartShadow [38] is a user interactive flat shadow generation framework. However, these methods focus on generating flat shadows and their results usually lack details.

2.3 Line Art Colorization

Sangkloy et al. [31] used cGAN to generate a real image from the line draft. Autopainter [29] first used cGAN network for automatic cartoon image colorization. Style2paints [39] proposed a deep learning colorization model guide by user color hints. The two-stage design effectively divides the complex coloring task into two simpler and more targeted subtasks, which can generate high-quality flat color paintings. Ye et al. [36] used the U-Net structure and applied the residual block to the deep network model to make the color of the image more stable. In order to colorize the whole page of the cartoon instead of a single storyboard, Hensman et al. [11] proposed a colorization method based on cGAN. Furusawa et al. [7] proposed an interactive coloring model to provide different hair and clothing color for different characters. Chen et al. [2] colored cartoon line arts by providing coherent colors for regions that have similar semantics to those in the reference image. Li et al. [21] realized the process of directly generating colored cartoon image from a few sketches, through the generated results were questionable. These works generate flat color paintings, which cannot generate semi-realistic images.

2.4   Photo Colorization

Many researchers consider the coloring of black-and-white natural pictures, including automatic method [4,5,17,25,26,40] and semi-automatic method. We refer the reader to a recent review [24]. Among the semi-automatic colorization methods, the reference color is provided by user color hints [41], reference image [6,10], or palettes [1,34]. Instead of coloring paintings, these methods all focus on photos. Our result generated in the first stage is not a real natural image, if coloring with these method, we will get chaotic results.

3   Methods

Our method is divided into two parts: shadow generation and line art coloring. In Sect. 3.1, we will introduce the method of generating semi-realistic shadow according to line arts and simple flat shadows. Then, in Sect. 3.2, we discuss coloring line arts with flat color according to user color hints and masks. In Sect. 3.3, we describe our image composition methods for fusing semi-realistic shadows and flat colors to acquire semi-realistic paintings.

3.1   Shadow Generation

In the generation process, the global illumination information is important. In order to generate coordinated shadow, we use an illumination vector i to encoding global light direction. Because the line arts provides too little information while the details of shadows are complex, if we only rely on the information provided by the global illumination, we cannot obtain appropriate shadows for pleats, hair, etc. Therefore, we provide a simple flat shadow to guide the generation of semi-realistic shadows.

The shadow generation network is named shadowNet with a GAN structure. We use an U-Net network as the generator and a patch discriminator [20]. The input of shadowNet is a line art and a reference shadow. Both of the two pictures are single channel black-and-white images. The illumination vector i is extended and input into the decoder together with the image features.

We do not need the user to give the illumination direction, but use a global illumination prediction network G_i to predict the illumination vector of reference shadow provided by the user. The structure of G_i is shown in the orange part of Fig. 2, which can produce the 3×1 vector i. We find that the local information may affect the global shadow generation, so we add a self attention module to the network, so that the model can pay attention to the global information and focus on the important part of the picture.

The structure of shadowNet is shown in the blue part of Fig. 2. Each blue convolution block in the shadow generator G_s consists of a 4×4 conv layer, a Relu layer and an instance norm layer. We add a self attention layer after the last down sampling block. For each line art x_l, hint shadow x_s, and global illumination vector i, we get the $\hat{y}_s$ generated by $G_s(x_l, x_s, i)$, and get ground truth as y_s. Discriminator D_s produce adversarial loss by $\hat{y}_s$ and y_s The loss function can be expressed as:

$$
\begin{aligned}
L(G_s, D_s) = \ & \mathbb{E}_{x_l, x_s, y_s}[\alpha_1 \|y_s - \hat{y}_s\|_1 + \alpha_2 L_{percp}(y_s, \hat{y}_s) \\
& - \lambda_1 log(D_s(y_s)) - \lambda_1 log(1 - D_s(\hat{y}_s)))]
\end{aligned}
\tag{1}
$$

where L_{percp} is the perceptual loss. We add this loss to improve the quality of generated pictures. We set α_1 and α_2 to 10 and λ_1 to 5, respectively.

3.2 Line Art Colorization

Coloring the shadow directly will magnify the artifacts of shadow images generated by the first stage and lead to chaotic colors. Therefore, we choose to generate a flat color from the line art directly, and then mix the flat color with the shadow generated by previous stage. We use a color image generator G_c and a paired discriminator D_c to realize it. Our network recognizes different picture structures, such as hair, face, etc. The network paints the flat color on the same part of the picture based on the user hints.

The structure of the coloring network is shown in the green part of Fig. 2. The color points are input into a 7×7 conv layer. After extracting the shallow color features, they are added with the line art vector and down sampling by 4×4 conv layers. In order to improve the color saturation and richness of the generated results, we do not use the normalization layer in the process of up sampling. As the painting requires harmony in hue and contents, global information also needs to be considered. The color of the current position may be affected by the hue of the whole image, so we introduce the attention module, which can make the generated results more coordinated. In order to further improve the color saturation, we add the SSIM loss L_{SSIM} to the loss function.

For each line art x_l and color hints h, we record the results generated by $G_c(x_l, h)$ as $\hat{y}_c$ and ground truth as y_c. We train the network by optimizing the following loss function:

$$
\begin{aligned}
L(G_c, D_c) = \ & \mathbb{E}_{x_l, h, y_c}[\beta_1 \|y_c - \hat{y}_c\|_1 + \beta_2 L_{SSIM}(y_c, \hat{y}_c) \\
& - \lambda_2 log(D_c(y_c)) - \lambda_2 log(1 - D_c(\hat{y}_c))) - \gamma R(y_c)]
\end{aligned}
\tag{2}
$$

$$
R(y_c) = \frac{1}{n} \sum_{c=1}^{3} \sum_{i=1}^{n} (y_c - \overline{y}_c)
\tag{3}
$$

where n is the number of pixels in the y_c, c is the numbers of image channels. In the first training stage, in order to enrich the colors, we added a regular term $R(\cdot)$, which will make our network tend to generate rich colors faster.

We set the γ to 5 in the first training stage. In the second training stage, in order to stabilize the generation results and avoid generating too many artifacts, we set the γ as 0 to remove this loss. We set β_1 and β_2 to 10, λ_2 to 5 in all training stage.

3.3 Composing Shadow and Color

After observing the semi-realistic works, we found that the shadow giving the image a 3D structure is mainly realized by deepening the current color and increasing the saturation. Therefore, we use the shadow image to increase the saturation and brightness of the color image in the HSV space proportionately. The composition function is written as:

$$S_{comp} = min[1, (1 + S_{sd}) \cdot S] \tag{4}$$

$$V_{comp} = \frac{\eta(1 + S_{sd})}{2} \cdot V + (1 - \eta) \tag{5}$$

where S and V are the S and V channels of flat color picture respectively, S_{comp} and V_{comp} are the S and V channels of final semi-realistic painting, S_{sd} is semi-realistic shadow. We set the η to 2/3.

Line art   Flat shadow   ShadeSketch   ShadeSketch   DeepNormal   Ours
                                        w/o adj

Fig. 3. Comparison among the results of our shadowNet, ShadeSketch [42], and the DeepNormal [14] methods. The final result of ShadeSketch has been adjusted in lightness, and we also compare with their results that without adjustment.

(a)   (b)   (c)   (d)   (e)

Fig. 4. Pix2pix (b) [15], PaintsChainer (c) [37] and Style2paint (d) [39] are compared with our method (e) using the same input (a). Our method can generate results with shadow structure, while other methods fail to yield usable results or can only generate flat color paintings.

4   Experiments

In this section, we show the results of our framework. We compare our method with existing shadow generation methods and other line art coloring methods. The results show that only our method can generate semi-realistic paintings. We also showed some ablation experiments.

4.1   Qualitative Results

ShadowNet. In Fig. 3, we compare our shadow results with ShadeSketch [42] and DeepNormal [14]. ShadeSketch generated only flat shadow. Meanwhile, the shadows in their results are incoherent and questionable, especially the shadows on the face. The results provided by Deepnormal have poor stereoscopic shadows and look more like indentations on paper. The results show that our method can generate semi-realistic shadow, and these results are more significant on face images.

ColorNet. In order to test our method, we invited artists to draw 23 line arts and flat shadows, we then provided different color hints for them to produce some results. We compared the final results with the latest cartoon line arts colorization method PaintsChainer [37] and Style2paints [39], and also with the image to image method Pixel2Pixel [15]. Figure 4 shows the comparison results. It can be seen that only our method can generate semi-realistic painting. Image to image method cannot output usable results. PaintsChainer cannot draw accurately color and can only produce flat color. Although high-quality results are generated by Style2paints, they can only obtain flat color paintings.

4.2   Numerical Results

We also perform some numerical comparisons. We compare the quality of results generated by our method and Style2paints. The results are shown in Table 1.

The first three items VIF, SSIM and PSNR measure the similarities between the simulation results and the groundtruth. These three groups of results are

| (a) | (b) | (c) | (d) | (e) |

Fig. 5. Image (a) is the line art, image (b) is the semi-realistic shadow and image (e) is our final result. Directly generating a flat color image (c) cannot generate the result with shadow structure. Directly coloring the shadow (d) will cause chaotic results.

obtained on the 78 images manually selected from danboo-img. From the numerical results, we can see that, compared with Style2paints, our results are more similar to groundtruth, which further shows that our method can generate semi-realistic paintings. The last item is the entropy of images, which represents the amount of information contained in the picture. The higher the EN value, the more likely the image is to be of high quality. This group of results was obtained on the test set of 23 hand drawn line arts. Our results also obtained higher scores in this item.

Table 1. A comparison between the results of style2paints and ours.

	VIF ↑	SSIM ↑	PSNR ↑	EN ↑
Style2paints	0.0884	0.3812	11.3978	6.3601
Ours	0.1127	0.4669	13.9610	6.8665

4.3   User Study

In order to further evaluate our method, we did a user study. We use our method, PaintsChainer and Style2paints to convert the line arts drew by artists into colored pictures, and the generated results of each line art are put into a group. For each user, we randomly select three groups of images from the generated results, and ask users to select the image that is visually closest to the semi-realistic style as shown in Fig. 1(a).

We received 53 questionnaires from users, of which 14 were artists or professional students. The results are shown in Table 2.

Table 2. In the table, we use "Prof" to represent artists and professional students, "NorProf" to represent non professional users.

	PaintsChainer	Style2paints	Ours
Prof	7.14%	4.76%	88.10%
NonProf	6.84%	23.08%	70.09%

The 88.10% of the semi-realistic paintings selected by professionals come from our results, which demonstrates that compared with other methods, professionals believe that our framework generate qualified semi-realistic paintings. Even among the users who do not know much about art painting and various painting methods, most users still think our method produces better results.

4.4 Ablative Study

Figure 5 shows the result of ablative study. In Fig. 5(c), we show the flat colors results without the addition of shading, and in Fig. 5(d) we show the results of directly coloring the shadows, which creates a color confusion and generates high contrast paintings.

If the flat color results have too high saturation, it will lead to the high saturation in the final results. Therefore, when inputting color hints to training the colorNet, we increase the saturation of the color hints, making the model more inclined to generate the result of low saturation.

5   Conclusion and Future Work

We proposed a semi-automatic method, using flat shadows and color hints to generate semi-realistic paintings, which cannot be achieved by other methods. We also show the acceptable final results in the experiments. But there are still limitations in our work. The maximum size we can generate is 512×512, when a high-resolution image is input, the effect of the shadowNet will decline. Specifically, the model only blurs the reference shadow but cannot complete the shadow for the whole image. Meanwhile, there are still large gaps between our results and real semi-realistic paintings drawn by real artists.

In the future work, we will try to use the high resolution image generation models to achieve higher quality results. We will also consider the automatic refinement of semi-automatic paintings.

References

1. Bahng, H., et al.: Coloring with words: guiding image colorization through text-based palette generation. In: Ferrari, V., Hebert, M., Sminchisescu, C., Weiss, Y. (eds.) ECCV 2018. LNCS, vol. 11216, pp. 443–459. Springer, Cham (2018). https://doi.org/10.1007/978-3-030-01258-8_27
2. Chen, S.Y., et al.: Active colorization for cartoon line drawings. IEEE Trans. Vis. Comput. Graph. **28**(2), 1198–1208 (2022)
3. Chen, Y., Lai, Y.K., Liu, Y.J.: CartoonGAN: generative adversarial networks for photo cartoonization. In: 2018 IEEE/CVF Conference on Computer Vision and Pattern Recognition, pp. 9465–9474 (2018)
4. Cheng, Z., Yang, Q., Sheng, B.: Deep colorization. In: IEEE International Conference on Computer Vision (ICCV), pp. 415–423 (2015)

5. Deshpande, A., Lu, J., Yeh, M.C., Chong, M.J., Forsyth, D.: Learning diverse image colorization. In: 2017 IEEE Conference on Computer Vision and Pattern Recognition (CVPR), pp. 2877–2885 (2017)
6. Fang, F., Wang, T., Zeng, T., Zhang, G.: A superpixel-based variational model for image colorization. IEEE Trans. Vis. Comput. Graph. **26**(10), 2931–2943 (2020)
7. Furusawa, C., Hiroshiba, K., Ogaki, K., Odagiri, Y.: Comicolorization: semi-automatic manga colorization. In: SIGGRAPH Asia Technical Briefs, pp. 1–4 (2017)
8. Gao, Z., onetsuji, T.Y., Takamura, T., Matsuoka, T., Naradowsky, J.: Automatic illumination effects for 2D characters. In: NIPS Workshop on Machine Learning for Creativity and Design (2018)
9. Gatys, L.A., Ecker, A.S., Bethge, M.: Image style transfer using convolutional neural networks. In: 2016 IEEE Conference on Computer Vision and Pattern Recognition (CVPR), pp. 2414–2423 (2016)
10. He, M., Chen, D., Liao, J., Sander, P.V., Yuan, L.: Deep exemplar-based colorization. ACM Trans. Graph. **37**(4), 1–16 (2018)
11. Hensman, P., Aizawa, K.: cGAN-based manga colorization using a single training image. In: 2017 14th IAPR International Conference on Document Analysis and Recognition (ICDAR), vol. 03, pp. 72–77 (2017)
12. Huang, X., Belongie, S.: Arbitrary style transfer in real-time with adaptive instance normalization. In: 2017 IEEE International Conference on Computer Vision (ICCV), pp. 1510–1519 (2017)
13. Huang, Z., Zhou, S., Heng, W.: Learning to paint with model-based deep reinforcement learning. In: 2019 IEEE/CVF International Conference on Computer Vision (ICCV), pp. 8708–8717 (2019)
14. Hudon, M., Grogan, M., Pagés, R., Smolić, A.: Deep normal estimation for automatic shading of hand-drawn characters. In: Leal-Taixé, L., Roth, S. (eds.) ECCV 2018. LNCS, vol. 11131, pp. 246–262. Springer, Cham (2019). https://doi.org/10.1007/978-3-030-11015-4_20
15. Isola, P., Zhu, J.Y., Zhou, T., Efros, A.A.: Image-to-image translation with conditional adversarial networks. In: 2017 IEEE Conference on Computer Vision and Pattern Recognition (CVPR), pp. 5967–5976 (2017)
16. Jin, Y., Li, P., Sheng, B., Nie, Y., Kim, J., Wu, E.: SRNPD: spatial rendering network for pencil drawing stylization. Comput. Animation Virtual Worlds **30**(3–4), e1890 (2019)
17. Jin, Y., Sheng, B., Li, P., Chen, C.L.P.: Broad colorization. IEEE Trans. Neural Netw. Learn. Syst. **32**(6), 2330–2343 (2021)
18. Johnson, J., Alahi, A., Fei-Fei, L.: Perceptual losses for real-time style transfer and super-resolution. In: Leibe, B., Matas, J., Sebe, N., Welling, M. (eds.) ECCV 2016. LNCS, vol. 9906, pp. 694–711. Springer, Cham (2016). https://doi.org/10.1007/978-3-319-46475-6_43
19. Kolkin, N., Salavon, J., Shakhnarovich, G.: Style transfer by relaxed optimal transport and self-similarity. In: 2019 IEEE/CVF Conference on Computer Vision and Pattern Recognition (CVPR), pp. 10043–10052 (2019)
20. Li, C., Wand, M.: Precomputed real-time texture synthesis with Markovian generative adversarial networks. In: Leibe, B., Matas, J., Sebe, N., Welling, M. (eds.) ECCV 2016. LNCS, vol. 9907, pp. 702–716. Springer, Cham (2016). https://doi.org/10.1007/978-3-319-46487-9_43
21. Li, J., Gao, N., Shen, T., Zhang, W., Mei, T., Ren, H.: SketchMan: learning to create professional sketches, pp. 3237–3245. Association for Computing Machinery, New York (2020)

22. Liao, J., Yao, Y., Yuan, L., Hua, G., Kang, S.B.: Visual attribute transfer through deep image analogy. ACM Trans. Graph. **36**(4), 1–15 (2017)
23. Lin, D., Wang, Y., Xu, G., Li, J., Fu, K.: Transform a simple sketch to a Chinese painting by a multiscale deep neural network. Algorithms **11**(1), 1–18 (2018)
24. Liu, S.: Two decades of colorization and decolorization for images and videos. arXiv: 2204.13322 (2022)
25. Liu, S., Zhang, X.: Automatic grayscale image colorization using histogram regression. Pattern Recogn. Lett. **33**(13), 1673–1681 (2012)
26. Liu, S., Zhang, X.: Image colorization based on texture map. J. Electron. Imaging **22**(1), 1–9 (2013)
27. Liu, S., Zhu, T.: Structure-guided arbitrary style transfer for artistic image and video. IEEE Trans. Multimed. **24**, 1299–1312 (2022)
28. Liu, S., et al.: Paint transformer: feed forward neural painting with stroke prediction. In: 2021 IEEE/CVF International Conference on Computer Vision (ICCV), pp. 6578–6587 (2021)
29. Liu, Y., Qin, Z., Wan, T., Luo, Z.: Auto-painter: cartoon image generation from sketch by using conditional Wasserstein generative adversarial networks. Neurocomputing **311**, 78–87 (2018)
30. Park, D.Y., Lee, K.H.: Arbitrary style transfer with style-attentional networks. In: 2019 IEEE/CVF Conference on Computer Vision and Pattern Recognition (CVPR), pp. 5873–5881 (2019)
31. Sangkloy, P., Lu, J., Fang, C., Yu, F., Hays, J.: Scribbler: controlling deep image synthesis with sketch and color. In: 2017 IEEE Conference on Computer Vision and Pattern Recognition (CVPR), pp. 6836–6845 (2017)
32. Sheng, B., Li, P., Gao, C., Ma, K.L.: Deep neural representation guided face sketch synthesis. IEEE Trans. Vis. Comput. Graph. **25**(12), 3216–3230 (2019)
33. Su, W., Du, D., Yang, X., Zhou, S., Fu, H.: Interactive sketch-based normal map generation with deep neural networks. Proc. ACM Comput. Graph. Interact. Tech. **1**(1), 1–17 (2018)
34. Xiao, C., et al.: Example-based colourization via dense encoding pyramids. Comput. Graph. Forum **39**(1), 20–33 (2020)
35. Xue, A.: End-to-end Chinese landscape painting creation using generative adversarial networks. arXiv: 2011.05552 (2020)
36. Ye, R.T., Wang, W.L., Chen, J.C., Lin, K.W.: Interactive anime sketch colorization with style consistency via a deep residual neural network. In: 2019 International Conference on Technologies and Applications of Artificial Intelligence (TAAI), pp. 1–5 (2019)
37. Zan, T.: Paintschainer (2017). https://petalica-paint.pixiv.dev/index_zh
38. Zhang, L., Jiang, J., Ji, Y., Liu, C.: SmartShadow: artistic shadow drawing tool for line drawings. In: 2021 IEEE/CVF International Conference on Computer Vision (ICCV), pp. 5371–5380 (2021)
39. Zhang, L., Li, C., Wong, T.T., Ji, Y., Liu, C.: Two-stage sketch colorization. ACM Trans. Graph. **37**(6), 1–14 (2018)
40. Zhang, R., Isola, P., Efros, A.A.: Colorful image colorization. In: Leibe, B., Matas, J., Sebe, N., Welling, M. (eds.) ECCV 2016. LNCS, vol. 9907, pp. 649–666. Springer, Cham (2016). https://doi.org/10.1007/978-3-319-46487-9_40
41. Zhang, R., et al.: Real-time user-guided image colorization with learned deep priors. ACM Trans. Graph. **36**(4), 1–11 (2017)
42. Zheng, Q., Li, Z., Bargteil, A.: Learning to shadow hand-drawn sketches. In: 2020 IEEE/CVF Conference on Computer Vision and Pattern Recognition (CVPR), pp. 7434–7443 (2020)

43. Zhu, J.Y., Park, T., Isola, P., Efros, A.A.: Unpaired image-to-image translation using cycle-consistent adversarial networks. In: 2017 IEEE International Conference on Computer Vision (ICCV), pp. 2242–2251 (2017)
44. Zou, Z., Shi, T., Qiu, S., Yuan, Y., Shi, Z.: Stylized neural painting. In: 2021 IEEE/CVF Conference on Computer Vision and Pattern Recognition (CVPR), pp. 15684–15693 (2021)

Hierarchical Bayesian Network Modeling and Layout of Huizhou Traditional Villages in Geographic Environment

Zude Zheng, Lin Li[✉], Xiang Wang, and Xiaoping Liu

School of Computer Science and Information Engineering,
Hefei University of Technology, Hefei, China
lilin_julia@hfut.edu.cn

Abstract. The causes of Huizhou traditional villages are complex. This paper gives a parameter description covering the whole village and generates a hierarchical Bayesian network. By learning the parameters, this network extracts the layout pattern of the villages. Sampling results from hierarchical Bayesian networks guide road generation, house generation and placement. It can generate specific layout results according to different geographical environments, and the validity of the layout results is proved by experiments.

Keywords: Village layout · Bayesian network · Scene design

1 Introduction

Scene generation has been one of the research hotspots in computer graphics. It's generally divided into two application categories: architectural modeling and layout modeling. In particular, the architectural modeling represent shapes and facades of buildings by synthesizes geometries and textures; the layout modeling establishes the placement of objects of the scene by studding the relationship model between different object elements to meet the design requirements. The formation of traditional villages is influenced by history and geographical environment, so there are few studies on the layout of traditional villages. Previous research has focused on the local patterns of village, and do not explore the macroscopic rules of village layout.

The aim at this paper is to provide a complete, macroscopic village layout model for messy village data. This model permits the automatic generation of traditional villages using hierarchical Bayesian network trained in real-villages data. Take the Huizhou traditional village as an example, the first stage of the model is to infer the structure of the hierarchical Bayesian network based on the interdependence or causality data parameters. These parameters can reflect the characteristics of Huizhou traditional villages. Using geographic Environment information as a priori, the model uses a hierarchical Bayesian network to sample out road information, house information and housing adjacencies. The model

N. Magnenat-Thalmann et al. (Eds.): CGI 2022, LNCS 13443, pp. 318–329, 2022.
https://doi.org/10.1007/978-3-031-23473-6_25

uses L-system to guide road generation by combining the research theory of alleys in Huizhou traditional villages and road sampling results to realize the dynamic evolution process of roads. Upon the completion of the village's skeleton, the road networks to divide the area into blocks, which are the smallest zones surrounded by road. The model then used Markov chain Monte Carlo (MCMC) methods of the layout of houses. The main contributions of our work are in particular:

- A structured quantitative representation of Huizhou traditional villages layout is proposed by combining the qualitative research results.
- A hierarchical Bayesian network adapted to the representation of traditional village layout is proposed, and a reliable model is obtained by structural learning.
- The model is the first to comprehensively complete the layout of the entire village.

2   Related Work

This paper focuses on the study of the layout of outdoor architectural scenes, which can be divided into layout of modern city and layout of historic city and village. Therefore, the following is introduced based on both aspects.

2.1   Layout of Modern City

Most of the researches on urban layout focus on the geometric properties of cities, and there can be classified into generation of parcels and road network growth. The earliest research of generation of parcels by Greuter et al. [8] divided the region into square cells and generating building layouts using a pseudo-random method. Vanegas et al. [25, 26] devised an interactive system which uses geometrical and behavioral modelling for designing region. Streamline-based segmentation methods [28] and differential evolutionary algorithms [9] are also used for land segmentation. Peng [21] proposed a tiling-based approach to solve the problem of generating layouts of deformable templates. By formulating the tiling problem as a global optimization problem solved by a specialized solver. The algorithm also works well for city layout. Hua [12]'s approach translates functional goals and aesthetic principles into linear representations and quickly generates a logical layout of the city. Pueyo [22] is able to scale down the real-world city layout and retain the same layout.

  The other option is road network growth and realize the layout of the region formed by the road network as the boundary. The road network can be considered as a growing structure and can be simulated by L-system. Parish and Müller [20] extended Open L-system to grow a road network. Chen [4] used tensor fields to guide the road network generator. With the development of deep learning, the data-driven approach has also been adopted to learn to understand the intrinsic relationships between road networks. Kempinska [14] proposed a convolutional neural network auto encoder to train road network images, capture patterns of urban road networks using low-dimensional vectors, and generate new road networks. Generative adversarial networks (StreetGAN [11], SGAN [13]) are also used to generate road networks that maintain the consistency of the training dataset. RoadNetGAN [19] is the first application of NetGAN [3] to urban road network road generation.

The local layout of a city revolves around the generation and layout of a group of buildings in a region. It is essentially an optimization problem. Markov chain Monte Carlo [24], simulated annealing algorithms [1] and polygon domain relocation algorithms [10] are commonly used for local layout.

2.2 Layout of Historic City and Village

Most layout of historic city and village researches are done to preserve cultural heritage or to generate 3D feature scenes. For the aerial map of South African villages, Glass [7] used Voronoi diagrams to delineate the region. Li [15] proposed a Markov Monte Carlo-based stochastic optimization method for the construction and layout of Huizhou residential clusters. Ren et al. [23] used interactive evolutionary computation to address the layout problem of outdoor scenes. Emilien [6] proposed a local-to-global approach that generates village and road networks. Mizdal [18] proposed a solution that analyzes the terrain, defines the appropriate regions for the villages and generates the roads that connect the villages. There are many researchers [2,5,17,27] who chose a timeline based approach to village layout.

It can be seen that the layout of historic city and village is still mainly based on rules and optimization methods, lacking relevant data support, and less integrated with professional fields.

3 Description and Definition of Data

The dataset used in this paper has a total of 10 villages, containing 459 blocks and 6741 houses. And the data can be divided into four categories according to types: village data, road data, block data and house data. Table 1 shows the full parameter content. The following will detail the definition range of some parameters:

Mountain and River Alignment: This paper defines the geographical environment in which Huizhou traditional villages are located. Their alignments are divided into four types: east-west alignment, north-south alignment, northeast-southwest alignment, and southeast-northwest alignment.

Primary Road Alignment and Position: The alignment of the primary road is consistent with the range of geographic alignments defined above. The position of the primary road refers to its relative position in the village and is divided into nine types (eight basic directions and center).

Village Type: According to the characteristics of the geographical environment in which the Huizhou traditional villages are located, Liu [16] divided them into mountain pass type, mountain depression type and waterfront type.

Table 1. Description of the data of the Huizhou traditional villages

Data type	Parameters
Village data	*mountain existence, river existence, mountain alignment, river alignment, village type*
Road data	*angle, length, primary road positon, primary road alignment*
Block data	*block Hu Moments, block long side, block short side, block area, distance from the village center*
House data	*number of houses, number of materials, number of floors, material, floor, house area, convexity, adjacency, house short side, house long side*

Block Hu Moments: Hu Moments are used for the block shape identification and matching, which have been proved to be invariant to translation, scale, rotation and reflection.

Convexity: The house shapes are classify into two types, convex polygons house and concave polygons house. For the interior angle corresponding to each vertex α if $0° < \alpha < 180°$, the house is a convex polygon.

4 Hierarchical Bayesian Network Modeling

The causes of Huizhou traditional villages are complex, and there are sequential relationships among various kinds of data. This paper proposes a hierarchical Bayesian network to model the data, and the output of its upper layer is used as the input of the lower layer to achieve the layout of Huizhou traditional villages.

4.1 Hierarchical Bayesian Network Structure Learning

Given the variables and training data, a Bayesian network needs to be constructed for these variables such that the posterior probability of the structure of the network and the data structure given by the parameters is maximized. Structure learning is an NP-hard problem, and this paper uses the maximum-minimum hill climbing algorithm (MMHC) for structure learning of Bayesian networks.

In the actual village development process, alignment of mountains and rivers will influence the primary road, so the hierarchical Bayesian networks first use geographic environmental information as a priori conditions to study its influence on road generation.

The primary road and the alleyways form the road network, and the closed area of the road forms a block, so the geographic environment information, road information and block information become the priori conditions for the formation of houses. The number of various house materials and the number

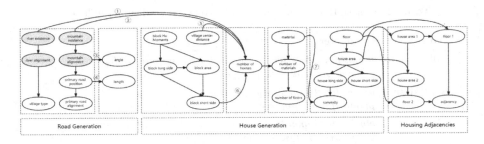

Fig. 1. Hierarchical Bayesian network modeling result

of various house floors in a single block are counted in the village data. The relationship between these quantitative parameters and the shape and size of houses is also important to consider.

In Huizhou traditional villages, there may be tandem or parallel combinations between residential houses. There are also some accessory spaces such as kitchens and utility rooms next to the residential houses, and they may be quite different from the main building in both shape and size. The adjacency between residential houses should also be considered in the village layout. After the houses are generated, various information of the houses will be used as a priori conditions to establish the adjacency of the houses.

4.2   Hierarchical Bayesian Network Parameter Learning

The Fig. 1 shows the structure learning results of the hierarchical Bayesian network. The hierarchical Bayesian network can be divided into three major parts: road generation, house generation and housing adjacency. The first layer is the primary road generation, the alignment and position of the primary road can be obtained by sampling the Bayesian network with the geographic environment information (yellow nodes) as input. We define $\mathbf{Q}$ as the variable to be sampled and $\mathbf{E}$ as the evidence node:

$$\mathbf{Q_1} = \{Q_{village\ type}, Q_{primary\ road\ position}, Q_{primary\ road\ alignment}\} \quad (1)$$

$$\mathbf{E_1} = \{E_{mountain\ existence}, E_{mountain\ alignment}, \\ E_{river\ existence}, E_{river\ alignment}\} \quad (2)$$

$\mathbf{Q_1}$ is the set of nodes sampled in the first round. After generating the primary road using the P mode of L-system, the angle and length of the road are continued to be sampled for the road part in order to generate the alleyways. Meanwhile, $\mathbf{Q}$ and $\mathbf{E}$ are updated as follows:

$$\mathbf{Q_2} = \{Q_{length}, Q_{angle}\} \quad (3)$$

$$\mathbf{E_2} = \{E_{primary\ road\ alignment}, E_{primary\ road\ position}, \mathbf{E_1}\} \quad (4)$$

$\mathbf{E_2}$ adds the position and alignment results of the primary road sampled in the first round to the original evidence nodes. From the Fig. 1, we can find that the *angle* and *length* attributes of the roads are mainly influenced by the alignment of the mountain and the position of primary road.

House generation starts on the third layer. The values of five nodes in the third layer can be filled according to the generated results of the road generation part of the previous layer. The village road skeleton forms blocks, for each block, the four nodes *block Hu Moments, block long side, block short side* and *block area* describe the information of the shape and size of the block itself. Node *center distance* describes the distance from the block to the village center.

In the previous structure learning, we found that the node *mountain existence* and the node *river existence* in the first layer also affects node *number of houses*, and the number of houses determines the number of houses with different types of materials. In the fourth layer we sample the number of houses in the block separately:

$$\mathbf{Q}_4 = \{Q_{number\ of\ houses}\} \tag{5}$$

$$\mathbf{E}_4 = \{E_{mountain\ existence}, E_{river\ existence}, E_{village\ center\ distance}, \mathbf{E}_3\} \tag{6}$$

$\mathbf{E}_3$ denotes the four evidence nodes describing the block information in the third layer. In the fifth layer, the sampling is repeated for different material nodes until the sum of their numbers and the sum of floors numbers are greater than the result of $Q_{number\ of\ houses}$:

$$\mathbf{Q}_5 = \{Q_{number\ of\ materials}, Q_{number\ of\ floors}, Q_{material}\} \tag{7}$$

$$\mathbf{E}_5 = \{E_{number\ of\ houses}\} \tag{8}$$

The sixth layer is a sampling of the remaining information of the house, but the sixth layer is also not independent. From the data we found that the node *material* is one of the factors affecting the concavity of the house, so the material information of the house becomes the a priori condition of the sixth layer:

$$\mathbf{Q}_6 = \{Q_{house\ short\ side}, Q_{house\ long\ side}, Q_{floor}, Q_{house\ area}, Q_{convexity}\} \tag{9}$$

$$\mathbf{E}_6 = \{E_{material}\} \tag{10}$$

The last layer is special, and the connection between the nodes of the last layer and the nodes of the sixth layer (blue arrows in the Fig. 1) does not indicate causality. $\mathbf{Q}$ and $\mathbf{E}$ of the seventh layer are updated as:

$$\mathbf{Q}_7 = \{Q_{adjacency}\} \tag{11}$$

$$\mathbf{E}_7 = \{E_{house\ area\ 1}, E_{house\ area\ 2}, E_{floor\ 1}, E_{floor\ 2}\} \tag{12}$$

After inferring the structure of the Bayesian network, the probability distribution of the parameters of the Bayesian network needs to be learned using the given sample data to update the original prior distribution of the variables.

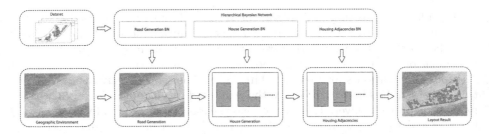

Fig. 2. Huizhou traditional village layout process

The maximum likelihood estimation in parameter learning requires high sample requirements, especially when the data are not uniformly distributed, and over-fitting can easily occur. In this paper, Bayesian estimation is used for parameter learning of Bayesian networks.

5   Huizhou Ancient Village Generation

In order to generate diverse and reasonable Huizhou traditional villages, we design a hierarchical Bayesian network layout framework. The complete layout framework is shown in the Fig. 2. Taking the geographic environment as input, we perform road generation process based on the sampling results of the road part of the hierarchical Bayesian network, combined with the L-system, After the sampling of the house generation part and housing adjences part is finished, the houses are placed in block using Markov chain Monte Carlo method to get the layout result of the whole village.

5.1   Road Skeleton Generation

According to Liu [16]'s theory, the village was initially composed of several settlements living near water, and generally developed and grew according to a most suitable river course, which is called the growth spine. The growth spine determines the main direction of the spatial form of Huizhou traditional villages. The secondary axes often depend on the growth of the main axes, and together with the main axes, they form the growth skeleton of the villages.

Based on the theory of village layout mentioned above, this paper uses L-system to simulate the growth process of roads. The L-system defines four modes of road growth, P mode for generating the primary road (main axis of growth); N mode for generating the alleyways (secondary axis of growth); B mode for encircling the alleyways and generating the block and E mode for extending the alleyways. As shown in the Fig. 3. After generating the primary road, the B and E modes are used alternately until the stopping condition is reached.

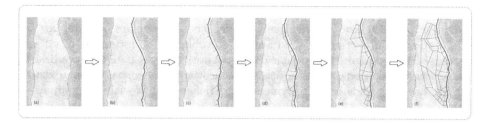

Fig. 3. A typical progression of our L-system. On an empty map (a). green is the mountain. P mode for primary road growth (b). N mode for generating the alleyways (c). B mode for encircling the alleyways and generating the blocks (d). Alternating B mode and E mode for road growth (e). Road skeleton growth completed (f) (Color figure online)

5.2   House Placement

We use the Metropolis-Hastings (MH) algorithm for house placement, which is a representative algorithm for Markov chain Monte Carlo. In this paper, we define $q(x, x')$ as $N(0, 5)$. $C(x)$ is the cost function of the placement of the house here, consisting of the cost of exceeding the boundary $C_b(x)$, the cost of overlapping with other houses $C_o(x)$, and the cost of maintaining a relative relationship with other houses $C_m(x)$. Specifically defined as:

$$C(\mathrm{x}) = \beta_1 C_b(x) + \beta_2 C_o(x) + \beta_3 C_m(x) \tag{13}$$

β is the weight of the cost. The algorithm starts by picking a random location inside the block as the initial state s_0 for the house placement. Sampling is performed according to the proposed distribution $q(x, x')$. The house is moved according to the sampling result and get the candidate state s'. We calculate the acceptance probability $\alpha(x, x')$ and compare it with u, which is sampled the uniform distribution in the interval $(0, 1)$, to determine whether to accept s'.

6   Experiment

6.1   Comparison with Other Methods

The layout of historic city and village is a problem faced to a special field with large differences, and there is no unified method to measure the result of layout. Most researchs on layout of historic city and village have been carried out in five parts: data support, geographical environment, road generation, house placement and house diversity, as shown in Table 2.

Most of the methods carry out the process of layout lacking data support, and the rules for generating data such as houses and roads are defined by the authors. Most of the methods achieve the road generation of villages, but in the part of house placement afterwards, the houses are simply placed at reasonable locations on both sides of the road. Blocks are not formed between the roads, and also the types of houses are relatively single. These papers are suitable for the formation of small settlement, and are not suitable for the formation of villages with high housing density and dense road network, such as Huizhou traditional villages. Our proposed layout model is the most comprehensive among existing works, and also yields more convincing and richer results with the support of data.

Table 2. Research content of historical layout of the city and the village paper, T indicates that the method was studied in this part, F indicates that it was not studied in this part

METHOD	Data support	Geographical environment	Road generation	House placement	House diversity
Glass [7]	T	F	T	F	F
Emilien [6]	F	T	T	T	F
Williams [27]	F	F	T	T	F
Li [15]	F	F	F	T	T
Ren [23]	T	F	F	T	T
Mizdal [18]	F	T	T	T	F
Berwaldt [2]	F	T	T	T	F
Mas [17]	F	T	T	T	T
Clappers [5]	F	T	F	T	T
Ours	T	T	T	T	T

6.2   Bayesian Network Accuracy Verification

In order to verify whether the nodes in the upper layer of the hierarchical Bayesian network are a priori conditions for the lower layer Bayesian network, we designed Leave-one-out experiments aiming to calculate the scores of the original Bayesian network and the Bayesian network after removing the edges that link the upper layer nodes to the lower layer nodes. The experiments use three scoring functions: K2, BDeu and BDs. The higher one has the higher probability of the occurrence of this structure under the dataset.

Bayesian network structure scores were calculated on road generation BN and house generation BN, respectively, as shown in Table 3 and 4. The results show that the original model is the best fit to the sample data under all three scoring functions. The experiments demonstrate that the dependencies between layers in our designed Bayesian network structure are realistic.

Table 3. Road Generation BN Leave-one-out experiments result.

Model	BDeu	K2	BDs
Road Generation BN	−30868.4	−31146.1	−31008.3
Model without edge 3	−31083.4	−31378.0	−31230.8
Model without edge 4	−31255.6	−31537.3	−31400.4

Table 4. House generation BN Leave-one-out experiments result.

Model	BDeu	K2	BDs
House generation BN	−104567.9	−107980.4	−106366.1
Model without edge 1	−105907.8	−108834.2	−107607.2
Model without edge 2	−105998.7	−108813.5	−107697.7
Model without edge 5	−109680.5	−111380.5	−111413.8
Model without edge 6	−109896.4	−111438.0	−111586.6
Model without edge 7	−104694.0	−108120.8	−106489.3

Fig. 4. Generated (right) and Real (left) Villages

6.3 Example Comparison

We simulated the generation of three different types of villages (mountain pass type, mountain depression type and waterfront type) under different geographical environments respectively. And we compare them with the real existing Huizhou traditional villages (Baichuan village, Honghu village and Xiangfeng village). As shown in Fig. 4. Our results prove that by learning from existing villages, the layout framework of Huizhou villages we design can adapt to different geographical environments, generate reasonable road network, building modeling and architectural layout.

7   Conclusion

We propose a method for generating the layout of Huizhou traditional villages based on hierarchical Bayesian network structure, and design Leave-one-out experiments to verify the effectiveness of hierarchical Bayesian network by three scoring functions, and our method can conform to the layout characteristics and patterns of Huizhou traditional villages to a certain extent. However, our method also has some shortcomings: There is no research on the buildings with special functions in Huizhou traditional villages. These special buildings may be the influencing factors of the layout of Huizhou ancient villages. The amount of data in Huizhou traditional villages is not large enough, which makes the accuracy and diversity of inference results of Bayesian network need to be improved.

References

1. Bao, F., Yan, D.M., Mitra, N.J., Wonka, P.: Generating and exploring good building layouts. ACM Trans. Graph. **32**(4), 1–10 (2013)
2. Berwaldt, N.L.P., Bettker, R.V., Pozzer, C.T.: Procedural generation of favela layouts on arbitrary terrains. In: 2020 19th Brazilian Symposium on Computer Games and Digital Entertainment (SBGames), pp. 136–144 (2020)
3. Bojchevski, A., Shchur, O., Zügner, D., Günnemann, S.: NetGAN: generating graphs via random walks. In: International Conference on Machine Learning, pp. 610–619 (2018)
4. Chen, G., Esch, G., Wonka, P., Müller, P., Zhang, E.: Interactive procedural street modeling. In: SIGGRAPH 2008: Proceedings of the 35th Annual Conference on Computer Graphics and Interactive Techniques 27, pp. 1–10 (2008)
5. Clappers, L.: Simulation-based believable procedurally generated video-game villages. Thesis (2021)
6. Emilien, A., Bernhardt, A., Peytavie, A., Cani, M.P., Galin, E.: Procedural generation of villages on arbitrary terrains. Visual Comput. **28**(6), 809–818 (2012)
7. Glass, K.R., Morkel, C., Bangay, S.D.: Duplicating road patterns in South African informal settlements using procedural techniques. In: Proceedings of the 4th International Conference on Computer graphics, Virtual Reality, Visualisation and Interaction in Africa, pp. 161–169 (2006)
8. Greuter, S., Parker, J., Stewart, N., Leach, G.: Real-time procedural generation ofpseudo infinite'cities. In: Proceedings of the 1st International Conference on Computer Graphics and Interactive Techniques in Australasia and South East Asia, pp. 87-ff (2003)
9. Hakli, H.: A performance evaluation and two new implementations of evolutionary algorithms for land partitioning problem. Arab. J. Sci. Eng. **45**(4), 2545–2558 (2020)
10. Hartmann, S., Krüger, B., Klein, R.: Content-aware re-targeting of discrete element layouts. Proc. Int. Conf. Comput. Graph. Vis. Comput. Vis. **23**, 173–182 (2015)
11. Hartmann, S., Weinmann, M., Wessel, R., Klein, R.: StreetGAN: towards road network synthesis with generative adversarial networks. In: 25th International Conference on Central Europe on Computer Graphics, Visualization and Computer Vision (WSCG), pp. 133–142 (2017)
12. Hua, H., Hovestadt, L., Tang, P., Li, B.: Integer programming for urban design. Eur. J. Oper. Res. **274**(3), 1125–1137 (2019)

13. Jetchev, N., Bergmann, U., Vollgraf, R.: Texture synthesis with spatial generative adversarial networks. arXiv preprint arXiv:08207 (2016)
14. Kempinska, K., Murcio, R.: Modelling urban networks using variational autoencoders. Appl. Netw. Sci. **4**(1), 1–11 (2019)
15. Li, S.L., Li, L., Ming-Wei, C., Cao, L., Jia, W., Liu, X.P.: Rapid modeling of Chinese Huizhou traditional vernacular houses. IEEE Access **5**, 20668–20683 (2017)
16. Liu, R., Jin, N.: Illustrations of Huizhou Traditional Architectures. China Architecture & Building Press, Beijing (2015)
17. Mas, A., Martin, I., Patow, G.: Simulating the evolution of ancient fortified cities. Comput. Graph. Forum **39**(1), 650–671 (2020)
18. Mizdal, T.B., Pozzer, C.T.: Procedural content generation of villages and road system on arbitrary terrains. In: 2018 17th Brazilian Symposium on Computer Games and Digital Entertainment (SBGames), pp. 205–2056 (2018)
19. Owaki, T., Machida, T.: RoadNetGAN: generating road networks in planar graph representation. In: Yang, H., Pasupa, K., Leung, A.C.-S., Kwok, J.T., Chan, J.H., King, I. (eds.) ICONIP 2020. CCIS, vol. 1332, pp. 535–543. Springer, Cham (2020). https://doi.org/10.1007/978-3-030-63820-7_61
20. Parish, Y.I., Müller, P.: Procedural modeling of cities. In: Proceedings of the 28th Annual Conference on Computer Graphics and Interactive Techniques, pp. 301–308 (2001)
21. Peng, C.H., Yang, Y.L., Wonka, P.: Computing layouts with deformable templates. ACM Trans. Graph. **33**(4), 1–11 (2014)
22. Pueyo, O., Sabriá, A., Pueyo, X., Patow, G., Wimmer, M.: Shrinking city layouts. Comput. Graph. **86**, 15–26 (2020)
23. Ren, P., Fan, Y., Zhou, M., Wang, Z., Du, G., Qian, L.: Graphics: rapid three-dimensional scene modeling by sketch retrieval and auto-arrangement. Computers **64**, 26–36 (2017)
24. Talton, J.O., Lou, Y., Lesser, S., Duke, J., Měch, R., Koltun, V.: Metropolis procedural modeling. ACM Trans. Graph. **30**(2), 1–14 (2011)
25. Vanegas, C.A., Aliaga, D.G., Benes, B., Waddell, P.A.: Interactive design of urban spaces using geometrical and behavioral modeling. ACM Trans. Graph. **28**(5), 1–10 (2009)
26. Vanegas, C.A., Kelly, T., Weber, B., Halatsch, J., Aliaga, D.G., Müller, P.: Procedural generation of parcels in urban modeling. Comput. Graph. Forum **31**(2pt3), 681–690 (2012)
27. Williams, B., Headland, C.J.: A time-line approach for the generation of simulated settlements. In: 2017 International Conference on Cyberworlds (CW), pp. 134–141 (2017)
28. Yang, Y.L., Wang, J., Vouga, E., Wonka, P.: Urban pattern: layout design by hierarchical domain splitting. ACM Trans. Graph. **32**(6), 1–12 (2013)

AE-GAN: Attention Embedded GAN for Irregular and Large-Area Mask Face Image Inpainting

Yongtang Bao[1], Xinfei Xiao[1], and Yue Qi[2,3,4(✉)]

[1] College of Computer Science and Engineering, Shandong University of Science and Technology, Qingdao 266590, China
{baozi0221,xinfeixiao}@sdust.edu.cn
[2] State Key Laboratory of Virtual Reality Technology and Systems, Beihang University, Beijing 100191, China
qy@buaa.edu.cn
[3] Virtual Reality Research Institute, Beihang University of Qingdao Research Institute, Qingdao 266100, China
[4] Peng Cheng Laboratory, Shenzhen 518055, China

Abstract. Existing image inpainting methods have shown promising results for regular and small-area breaks. However, restoration of irregular and large-area damage is still tricky and achieves mediocre results due to the lack of restrictions on the center of the hole. In contrast, face inpainting is also problematic due to facial structure and texture complexity, which always results in structural confusion and texture blurring. We propose an attention embedded adversarial generative network (AE-GAN) in the paper to solve this problem. Overall our framework is a U-shape GAN model. To enable the network to capture the practical features faster to reconstruct the content of the masked region in the face image, we also embed the attention mechanism that simplifies the Squeeze-and-Excitation channel attention mechanism and then set it reasonably in our generator. Our generator is chosen the U-net structure as a backbone. Because the structure can encode information from low-level pixels context features to high-level semantic features. And it can decode the features back into an image. Experiments on CelebA-HQ datasets demonstrate that our proposed method generates higher quality inpainting, results in consistent and harmonious facial structures and appearance than existing methods, and achieves state-of-the-art performance.

Keywords: Face inpainting · Attention mechanism · Adversarial generative network model

1 Introduction

Face images are the most popular types of images in daily life. In contrast, face images are degraded and destroyed Fig. 1(b), resulting in face pieces of information in the images being unrecognizable. They degraded due to noise,

N. Magnenat-Thalmann et al. (Eds.): CGI 2022, LNCS 13443, pp. 330–341, 2022.
https://doi.org/10.1007/978-3-031-23473-6_26

(a) Original   (b) Input   (c) Ours

Fig. 1. Example results generated by the proposed network on CelebA-HQ.[Best viewed with zoom-in].

blur, low resolution, compression, mosaic, scratch, or a combination of them. Face image inpainting Fig. 1 has attracted significant attention, aiming to obtain a clear and fidelity area of the face in the image. Face inpainting methods fill missing or masked regions with synthesized face contents. It is useful for face recognition [1], face detection, segmentation, 3D face reconstruction, face super-resolution [12], and other fields.

Among various approaches, deep-learning-based image inpainting methods have attracted a lot of attention [14]. The first deep-learning-based image inpainting method is Context Encoders (CE) proposed by Deepak Pathak et al. [19]. It generates the missing region content directly by encoding, inferring, and decoding the semantic features of the damaged image. Yu et al. [26] proposed generative image inpainting with contextual attention (CA). It updates the unknown region by roughly repairing the missing region using the coarse-to-fine method and then finding comparable blocks in the known region by the overall image content. Jingyuan Li et al. [11] used a one-shot fill approach to repair the image, but a circular inference approach, starting from the edge of the mask toward the hole center by inferring the appropriate pixels to fill, and achieved better results on the larger mask problem (Fig. 4(c)). Jialun Peng et al. [20] considered that the images might not have unique results in the inference process and proposed the VQ-VAE model of Generating Diverse Structure(Fig. 4(d)). Zhihua Chen et al. [3] combine color feature and space distance between two patches to search for the optimized patch to avoid texture inconsistency These methods have achieved some degree of success in completing the missing regions of a generic image. When used for face image restoration, they may produce problems such as missing texture, structural discordance, and facial artifacts. The main reason for such results is that these generic image drawing methods do not consider the human face's special characteristics (e.g., symmetry relations, harmony relations) in their approach.

Alternatively, these methods are more challenging to repair the problem of large masks. However, in practical scenarios, more than half of the face may be obscured, such as smearing [22], damage, and other problems, resulting in missing face information and making it challenging to generate full faces.

Our methodological innovations are summarized below:

1. We propose an AE-GAN model, a GAN [5] network model with U-net as the skeleton, embedded with our designed attention mechanism. The model is better at extracting and reconstructing features.

2. We design a PSE Attention mechanism to be embedded in our proposed to get AE-GAN to recover a more reasonable face region texture and structure with more weights.

3. Our experiment on benchmark datasets, including CelebA-HQ, demonstrates the superiority of our proposed method in quality.

2   Related Work

2.1   Face Inpainting

Compared to general images, most of the existing image restoration methods, due to their characteristics, such as symmetry and visually reasonable face structure, as well as gender, age, and other identifying information need to be considered, make most of the existing image restoration methods, perform poorly on face image restoration tasks. However, there are methods proposed specifically for face images, such as Li et al. [13] used face parsing to propose the loss of semantic parsing. Song et al. [23] trained an additional network to recover face landmarks and face parsing and then trained faces with masked images to complete the network. However, using prior knowledge consumes a lot of computational resources, and these methods do not direct the network to focus on the texture of the facial components. Tong Zhou et al. [28] proposed a face seven-component discriminator, using facial landmarks to locate four key facial components: i.e., both eyes, the nose, and the mouth, to solve the problem.

2.2   Generative Adversarial Network

Generative adversarial network (GAN) has been successful in the areas of image editing [25], image generation [2], style transfer [4], and others. Many recently proposed image inpainting methods are based on GAN [5]. When applied to face inpainting, these deep-learning methods synthesize plausible contents for missing facial key parts from random noise. A typical example is that Chen et al. [7] proposed Globally and Locally Consistent Image Completion (GLCIC). They combine a global discriminator with a missing region to ensure that the missing area is consistent with the whole image. They use dilated convolution to increase the receptive field. While these methods can generate visually plausible image structures and textures, they usually create distorted structures or blurry textures inconsistent with surrounding areas.

2.3   Attention Mechanism

Yu et al. [26] propose a fine-grained network containing contextual attention modules that learn the correlation between missing and unhidden patches to maintain contextual consistency. Subsequently, some methods directly use coarse-to-fine networks with contextual attention; for example, GConv converts the binary mask proposed by PConv [15] into a learnable value as a gating mechanism, while Xiong et al. [15] use object contours as prior knowledge to aid recovery. On the other hand, other methods choose to use contextual attention differently. For example, Saigon et al. [21] designed a parallel decoding network to replace the coarse-to-fine structure, thereby reducing the number of parameters. However, Zeng et al. [27] proposed an attention-shifting network that utilizes attention learned from higher-level features to reconstruct low-level features. In addition, the CSA layer [16] learned the correlation between plaques within the masking area.

In summary, previous attention-based approaches learned long-term correlations to search for similar feature-level patches as a filling reference. However, due to the lack of direct supervision of the parameters of the attention module, the learned attention is not reliable enough.

3   Method

3.1   Motivation and Framework

Face images are the most widely used among many images in daily life, so face image processing has been paid attention to by many researchers. In recent years, the GAN model has been widely used because of its excellent performance in the field of re-image generation. But because the GAN [16] is essentially a fixed probability after training to obtain the target probability distribution. It is generally a generative network and a discriminant network to play a game to get the target probability distribution. However, there is often an overfitting phenomenon, resulting in image details being smoothed and missing. When the face details are missing, face images will often be fidelity, especially when the damaged part of the face image is too large. To generate more realistic results, we propose that the first stage is a network designed based on the GAN model to generate a cursory result. Then we used the generated result for the second stage, which refines the input. So our network is a GAN network, consisting of a U-shape type generative network and a multi-scale discriminator. Since U-Net has excellent feature fusion, it will pass the shallow feature information through skip-connection to the deep information in the encoder for deep fusion. The method can solve the problem of many missing images during reconstruction. The overall framework of our inpainting network is shown in Fig. 2. In Fig. 2, on the left is our U-shape module and a VGG19 pre-trained model to compute perceptual and stylistic loss, and on the right is a demonstration of a multi-scale discriminator. We designed a AE Basic Block module to embed our PSE attention mechanism.

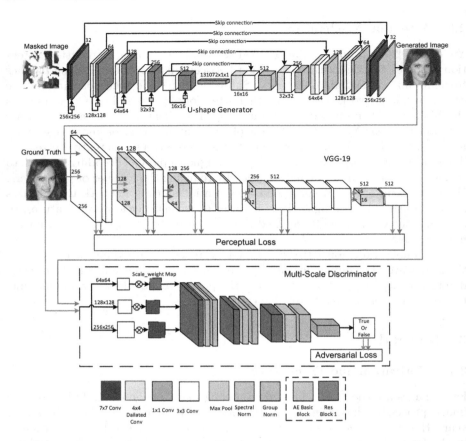

Fig. 2. Overview of our network architecture. It consists of three main modules: attention embedded U-Net structure generator in the Sect. 3.2, Multi-scale discriminator in the Sect. 3.3, attention embedded basic block (AE Basic Block) in the Sect. 3.4 and the attention is entitled PSE attention in the Fig. 3. [Best viewed with zoom-in].

3.2 U-shape Generator

It is well known that most deep models consist of an encoder, a decoder, and a discriminator. The encoder is used to learn the contextual features of the damaged image, the decoder is used to decode the features to generate the missing image content, and the discriminator is used to determine whether the restored content is accurate. In order to reconstruct structurally sound and texture realistic face images from the damaged face images, our architecture is designed as follows.

The generator is under the U-shape framework and is used to extract content features from the original image. In our encoder, the first convolution layer is set to a 7 × 7 convolution kernel with Padding set to 3, retaining as much information as possible about the original image. The subsequent four layers are

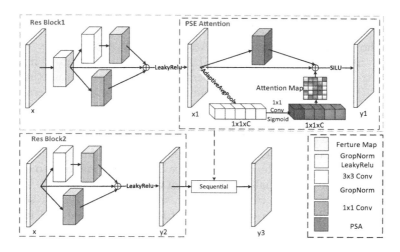

Fig. 3. Attention embedded basic block in the Sect. 3.4(AE Basic Block)

commonly used to get 3×3 convolution layers. After passing through the 3×3 convolutional layers, the feature maps are processed by a Group Normalization layer and a LeakyRelu activation function, finally sent to the Res Block1 module shown in Fig. 3. The Res Block1 module we designed is a feature map x. Firstly x is subjected to Group Normalization operation and LeakyReLu activation operation to obtain f(x). Then f(x) is subjected to 3×3 Conv and Group Normalization operation to get z_1 and convolved with 1×1 to obtain z_2. Finally, integrate the three parts to a Res Block and add one 1×1 convolution to preserve as complete information as possible and transmit it to the PSE Attention Module. In our upsampling section, we use a 4×4 Dailated convolution to increase the perceptual field and recover more information. Deeper integration of the shallow information of skip connection. Each group is followed by a Seq Block, a combination of Res Block1 and Res Block2 in Fig. 3

3.3 Multi-scale Discrimnator

Most of the previous discriminators are single discriminators or different discriminators at different scales, and our discriminator is a discriminator whose inputs are generative graphs downsampled by 1, 1/2, 1/4 respectively and then given different Scale_weight inputs to our designed discriminator. In our discriminator, we use spectral normalization [18] because GAN networks can be unstable during adversarial training and the resultant edges are too smooth. In contrast, spectral normalization gives the discriminator Lipschitz continuity, which makes the discriminator satisfy Lipschitz continuity and limits the drastic function changes, thus making the model more stable.

3.4   Embedded PSE Attention Block

Figure 3 shows that our partial SE Attention(PSE Attention) is embedded behind an inception module. Our PSEAttention is the original image first subjected to the AdaptiveAvgPool operation, which transforms the original H × W × C (H: Hight, W: weight, C: channel) sized feature map is transformed into a 1 × 1 × C sized feature map. As a result, the sensory field becomes larger to obtain the global field of view. Therefore, better can get the global information and retain the texture features. Then, the 1 × 1 × C feature map is fully connected, the importance of each channel is predicted by the fully connected layer, and the feature maps reweight the importance of different channels to obtain the Attention map of H × W. Finally, the fusion of Gan operation and PSA results is performed to retain the face region as a high-weight feature, remove some noise interference from the background, improve the network speed and reduce the parameter calculation.

4   Loss Function

Adversarial Loss. The generated image I_{out} is continuously brought close to the original image I_{gt} by adversarial training to generate images that are more realistic in structure and texture, and we use adversarial loss:

$$L_{adv} = \min_G \max_D \mathbb{E}_{I_{gt},E_{gt}}\Big[logD(I_{gt},E_{gt})\Big] + \mathbb{E}_{I_{gt},E_{gt}}\Big[logD(1-I_{out},E_{out})\Big] \quad (1)$$

Perceptual Loss. To constrain the original maps I_{gt} and generated maps I_{out} in the depth feature map, we use the perceptual loss [8] L_{perc}. It measures the L_1 distance between the depth feature map by the pertrained VGG-19 network on ImageNet:

$$L_{perc} = \mathbb{E}\Big[\sum_i \lambda_i \parallel \Phi_i(I_{out}) - \Phi_i(I_{gt}) \parallel_1 \Big] \quad (2)$$

where λ_i are the balancing weights. Φ_i are the is the activation of i-th layer of the VGG-19 model which corresponds to the activation maps from layers relu1_1, relu2_1, relu3_1, relu4_1 and relu5_1.

Pixel Loss. The Pixel Loss calculates the pixel-to-pixel loss of the predicted I_{out} and target images I_{gt}:

$$L_{pix} = \sum_i \Big[\parallel \Phi_i(I_{out}) - \Phi_i(I_{gt}) \parallel_1 \Big] \quad (3)$$

Identity Loss. In order not to lose identity information during network training, the Identity loss was introduced, mainly by obtaining from the pre-trained model Res50 the original maps I_{gt} and generated maps I_{out} in the depth feature map, to ensure that the generated face image structure identity is reasonable:

$$L_{id} = \mathbb{E}\Big[\sum_i \lambda_i \parallel \Phi_i(I_{out}) - \Phi_i(I_{gt}) \parallel_1 \Big] + \mathbb{E}\Big[\sum_j \lambda_j \parallel \Phi_j(I_{out}) - \Phi_j(I_{gt}) \parallel_1 \Big] \quad (4)$$

In summary, the joint loss is written as:

$$L_{joint} = \lambda_{adv}L_{adv} + \lambda_{perc}L_{perc} + \lambda_{pix}L_{pix} + \lambda_{id}L_{id} \tag{5}$$

where λ_{adv}, λ_{perc}, λ_{pix} and λ_{id} are the tradeoff parameters, and we empirically set $\lambda_{adv} = 0.1$, $\lambda_{perc} = 10$, $\lambda_{pix} = 5$ and $\lambda_{id} = 1$.

5   Experiment

5.1   Datesets and Evaluation Metric

Dataset. We evaluate our method on datasets of CelebA-HQ [9]. CelebA-HQ dataset: It is a high-quality version of the human face dataset CelebA [17] with 30,000 aligned face images. We follow the split in CelebA-HQ that produces 28,000 training images and 2,000 validation images.

Compared Methods. Compared Methods. We compare our method with a number of state-of-the art methods as listed: CA [27]: It is a generative model with different receptive fields in different branches. RFR [11]: It is a way of Recurrent Feature Reasoning. VQ-VAE [20]: It is a way of VAE.

Evaluation Metric. We perform evaluations by using four widely adopted evaluation metrics: 1) Frechet Inception Score (FID) [6] that evaluates the perceptual quality by measuring the distribution distance between the synthesized images and real images; 2) peak signal-to-noise ratio (PSNR); and 3) structural similarity index (SSIM) [24].

5.2   Implementation Details

We train our models on the training set and evaluate our model on the testing set. In training, we use images of resolution 256×256 with irregular masks [15]. All results given in this paper are not post-processed. Our implementation is with Pytorch v1.8.0, CUDNN v8.0.5, and CUDA v111.1. The hardware is an Intel CPU i7 (2.20 GHz) and GeForce RTX 3060 Laptop GPU. Our model costs 49.37 ms and 146.11 ms per image on GPU for testing images with sizes 256×256. We use Adam optimizer and leave other parameters as Keras default. Our model uses a batch size of 4 and 100 epochs of training and sets.

5.3   Qualitative Comparison

Figure 4 shows a comparison of our method with the three state-of-the-art methods CA [26], RFR [11] and VQ-VAE [20] on the dataset CelebA-HQ. The second column Fig. 4(b), method CA, shows that the overall image lacks light texture from the restoration results, as the method extracts similar areas from other regions of the image to fill in, and the method does not fit when the broken area is too large. The third column Fig. 4(c) is method RFR, and from the results, we see that the mask area appears indistinctly removed. Hence, the method infers that it will leave an underground situation in the same mask case. The fourth

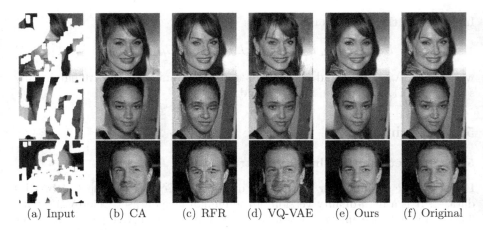

(a) Input   (b) CA   (c) RFR   (d) VQ-VAE   (e) Ours   (f) Original

Fig. 4. Qualitative comparison on CelebA-HQ: (a) input corrupted images, (b) CA, (c) RFR, (d)VQ-VAE, (e) ours, (f) ground-truth images [Best viewed with zoom-in].

Table 1. The table shows performance metrics for the training of different inpainting methods with either narrow or wide masks.

Method	PSNR ↑	SSIM ↑	FID ↓
CA	17.5403	0.6082	109.415
RFR	21.0492	0.6506	73.752
VQ-VAE	20.2262	0.6723	78.968
Existing attention	17.7604	0.7362	62.114
OURS	22.5838	0.7730	48.982

column Fig. 4(d) shows the method VQ-VAE, and from the results, we see that the image appears to have misaligned artifacts due to an incomplete restoration. So the results of our restoration method are significantly better than the other methods. With a large mask (40%–50%) coverage, we generate an image structure that is more consistent in structure and semantics.

5.4 Quantitative Comparison

We also performed a quantitative analysis, mainly by comparing the peak signal-to-noise ratio (PSNR), in terms of structural similarity index (SSIM), and mean L_1 loss, and the results are in Table 1, are in is in the data set CelebA-HQ dataset on irregular masks generating graphs are calculated with the original graph and compared with CA, RFR, VQ-VAE. Our method has significantly higher results on PSNR, SSIM and lower results on mean L_1 loss.

5.5 Ablation Studies

In this section, we would like to verify the effect of our contributions separately. Here we mainly illustrate the effectiveness of the PSE Attention module. As described in Sect. 3.2, the attention mechanism has a role in improving the image quality, mainly by adding different weights to different pixels to improve the restoration quality. As shown in Fig. 5(b), the result of removing our designed PSE Attention with Fig. 5(c) is the result of restoring the input Image, showing that our result is more realistic and no white artifacts appear. We removed the PSE Attention mechanism in our module, the calculation of the generator images for SSIM, PSNR, and FID, and the rendering attention line in Table 1 showed the exiting attention module. These results are the same as the previous setup for our experiment configuration.

(a) Input   (b) Existing Attention   (c) PSE Attention

Fig. 5. Comparison results for different attention manners. From the left to the right are: (a) Input, (b) Existing attention, (c) PSE attention.

6 Conclusion

This paper proposes a two-stage model that embeds attention mechanisms to repair. The first stage is the rough extraction feature stage; in this stage, we chose a pre-training model. The second stage is the U-shaped network used to refine the texture of the face image generated in the first stage. This method prevents the generation of chaotic structure and lack of detail problems. Experimental results demonstrate that our method performs better than the existing state-of-the-art face-inpainting methods. Moreover, our approach facilitates Face Recognization, Fake Face Detection, and Face Super-Resolution. However, our practice has drawbacks, such as limited application scenarios and poor effect on large angled faces in an image. We will address these drawbacks in future work.

Acknowledgments. We would like to thank the anonymous reviewers for their valuable suggestions. This paper is supported by the Shandong Provincial Natural Science Foundation (ZR2020MF132), the National Natural Science Foundation of China (No. 62072020), the Leading Talents in Innovation and Entrepreneurship of Qingdao (19-3-2-21-zhc), and the Key-Area Research and Development Program of Guangdong Province (No. 209B010150001).

References

1. Aleem, S., Yang, P., Masood, S., Li, P., Sheng, B.: An accurate multi-modal biometric identification system for person identification via fusion of face and finger print. World Wide Web **23**(2), 1299–1317 (2019). https://doi.org/10.1007/s11280-019-00698-6
2. Badatia, P., Tasgaonkar, P.P.: Crowd counting and density estimation using multicolumn discriminator in GAN. In: 2018 International Conference on Advances in Computing, Communications and Informatics (ICACCI), pp. 1179–1183 (2018). https://doi.org/10.1109/ICACCI.2018.8554372
3. Chen, Z., et al.: Structure-aware image inpainting using patch scale optimization. J. Vis. Commun. Image Represent. **40**, 312–323 (2016). https://doi.org/10.1016/j.jvcir.2016.06.029, https://www.sciencedirect.com/science/article/pii/S1047320316301262
4. Gatys, L.A., Ecker, A.S., Bethge, M.: Image style transfer using convolutional neural networks. In: 2016 IEEE Conference on Computer Vision and Pattern Recognition (CVPR), pp. 2414–2423 (2016). https://doi.org/10.1109/CVPR.2016.265
5. Goodfellow, I., et al.: Generative adversarial networks. Commun. ACM **63**(11), 139–144 (2020). https://doi.org/10.1145/3422622, https://doi.org/10.1145/3422622
6. Heusel, M., Ramsauer, H., Unterthiner, T., Nessler, B., Hochreiter, S.: GANS trained by a two time-scale update rule converge to a local nash equilibrium. In: 30th Proceedings Conference on Advances in Neural Information Processing System (2017)
7. Iizuka, S., Simo-Serra, E., Ishikawa, H.: Globally and locally consistent image completion. ACM Trans. Graph. **36**(4) (2017). https://doi.org/10.1145/3072959.3073659, https://doi.org/10.1145/3072959.3073659
8. Johnson, J., Alahi, A., Fei-Fei, L.: Perceptual losses for real-time style transfer and super-resolution. In: Leibe, B., Matas, J., Sebe, N., Welling, M. (eds.) ECCV 2016. LNCS, vol. 9906, pp. 694–711. Springer, Cham (2016). https://doi.org/10.1007/978-3-319-46475-6_43
9. Karras, T., Laine, S., Aittala, M., Hellsten, J., Lehtinen, J., Aila, T.: Analyzing and improving the image quality of stylegan. In: 2020 IEEE/CVF Conference on Computer Vision and Pattern Recognition (CVPR), pp. 8107–8116 (2020). https://doi.org/10.1109/CVPR42600.2020.00813
10. Ke, Q., Ming, L.D., Daxing, Z.: Image steganalysis via multi-column convolutional neural network. In: 2018 14th IEEE International Conference on Signal Processing (ICSP), pp. 550–553 (2018). https://doi.org/10.1109/ICSP.2018.8652324
11. Li, J., Wang, N., Zhang, L., Du, B., Tao, D.: Recurrent feature reasoning for image inpainting. In: 2020 IEEE/CVF Conference on Computer Vision and Pattern Recognition (CVPR), pp. 7757–7765 (2020). https://doi.org/10.1109/CVPR42600.2020.00778
12. Li, L., Tang, J., Ye, Z., Sheng, B., Mao, L., Ma, L.: Unsupervised face super-resolution via gradient enhancement and semantic guidance. The Vis. Comput. **37**(9), 2855–2867 (2021). https://doi.org/10.1007/s00371-021-02236-w
13. Li, Y., Liu, S., Yang, J., Yang, M.H.: Generative face completion. In: 2017 IEEE Conference on Computer Vision and Pattern Recognition (CVPR), pp. 5892–5900 (2017). https://doi.org/10.1109/CVPR.2017.624
14. Liu, B., Li, P., Sheng, B., Nie, Y., Wu, E.: Structure-preserving image completion with multi-level dynamic patches. The Vis. Comput. **35**(1), 85–98 (2019). https://doi.org/10.1007/s00371-017-1454-x

15. Liu, G., Reda, F.A., Shih, K.J., Wang, T.-C., Tao, A., Catanzaro, B.: Image inpainting for irregular holes using partial convolutions. In: Ferrari, V., Hebert, M., Sminchisescu, C., Weiss, Y. (eds.) ECCV 2018. LNCS, vol. 11215, pp. 89–105. Springer, Cham (2018). https://doi.org/10.1007/978-3-030-01252-6_6

16. Liu, H., Jiang, B., Xiao, Y., Yang, C.: Coherent semantic attention for image inpainting. In: 2019 IEEE/CVF International Conference on Computer Vision (ICCV), pp. 4169–4178 (2019). https://doi.org/10.1109/ICCV.2019.00427

17. Liu, Z., Luo, P., Wang, X., Tang, X.: Deep learning face attributes in the wild. In: 2015 IEEE International Conference on Computer Vision (ICCV), pp. 3730–3738 (2015). https://doi.org/10.1109/ICCV.2015.425

18. Miyato, T., Kataoka, T., Koyama, M., Yoshida, Y.: Spectral normalization for generative adversarial networks. arXiv preprint arXiv:1802.05957 (2018)

19. Pathak, D., Krähenbühl, P., Donahue, J., Darrell, T., Efros, A.A.: Context encoders: Feature learning by inpainting. In: 2016 IEEE Conference on Computer Vision and Pattern Recognition (CVPR), pp. 2536–2544 (2016). https://doi.org/10.1109/CVPR.2016.278

20. Peng, J., Liu, D., Xu, S., Li, H.: Generating diverse structure for image inpainting with hierarchical vq-vae. In: 2021 IEEE/CVF Conference on Computer Vision and Pattern Recognition (CVPR), pp. 10770–10779 (2021). https://doi.org/10.1109/CVPR46437.2021.01063

21. Sagong, M.c., Shin, Y.g., Kim, S.w., Park, S., Ko, S.j.: Pepsi : fast image inpainting with parallel decoding network. In: 2019 IEEE/CVF Conference on Computer Vision and Pattern Recognition (CVPR), pp. 11352–11360 (2019). https://doi.org/10.1109/CVPR.2019.01162

22. Sheng, B., Li, P., Gao, C., Ma, K.L.: Deep neural representation guided face sketch synthesis. IEEE Trans. Visual Comput. Graphics **25**(12), 3216–3230 (2019). https://doi.org/10.1109/TVCG.2018.2866090

23. Song, L., Cao, J., Song, L., Hu, Y., He, R.: Geometry-aware face completion and editing. In: Proceedings of the AAAI Conference on Artificial Intelligence, vol. 33, pp. 2506–2513 (2019). https://doi.org/10.1609/aaai.v33i01.33012506

24. Wang, Z., Bovik, A., Sheikh, H., Simoncelli, E.: Image quality assessment: from error visibility to structural similarity. IEEE Trans. Image Process. **13**(4), 600–612 (2004). https://doi.org/10.1109/TIP.2003.819861

25. Wu, X., Xu, K., Hall, P.: A survey of image synthesis and editing with generative adversarial networks. Tsinghua Sci. Technol. **22**(6), 660–674 (2017). https://doi.org/10.23919/TST.2017.8195348

26. Yu, J., Lin, Z., Yang, J., Shen, X., Lu, X., Huang, T.S.: Generative image inpainting with contextual attention. In: 2018 IEEE/CVF Conference on Computer Vision and Pattern Recognition, pp. 5505–5514 (2018). https://doi.org/10.1109/CVPR.2018.00577

27. Zeng, Y., Fu, J., Chao, H., Guo, B.: Learning pyramid-context encoder network for high-quality image inpainting. In: 2019 IEEE/CVF Conference on Computer Vision and Pattern Recognition (CVPR), pp. 1486–1494 (2019). https://doi.org/10.1109/CVPR.2019.00158

28. Zhou, T., Ding, C., Lin, S., Wang, X., Tao, D.: Learning oracle attention for high-fidelity face completion. In: 2020 IEEE/CVF Conference on Computer Vision and Pattern Recognition (CVPR), pp. 7677–7686 (2020). https://doi.org/10.1109/CVPR42600.2020.00770

Synthesis and Generation

Procedural Generation of Landscapes with Water Bodies Using Artificial Drainage Basins

Roland Fischer[(✉)], Judith Boeckers, and Gabriel Zachmann

University of Bremen, Bremen, Germany
{r.fischer,zach}@uni-bremen.de
https://cgvr.informatik.uni-bremen.de/

Abstract. We propose a method for procedural terrain generation that focuses on creating huge landscapes with realistically-looking river networks and lakes. A natural-looking integration into the landscape is achieved by an approach inverse to the usual way: After authoring the initial landmass, we first generate rivers and lakes and then create the actual terrain by "growing" it, starting at the water bodies. The river networks are formed based on computed artificial drainage basins. Our pipeline approach not only enables quick iterations and direct visualization of intermediate results but also balances user control and automation. The first stages provide great control over the layout of the landscape while the later stages take care of the details with a high degree of automation. Our evaluation shows that vast landscapes can be created in under half a minute and that it is quite easy to create landscapes closely resembling real-world examples. Moreover, our implementation is easy to extend and can be integrated smoothly into existing workflows.

Keywords: Procedural generation · Water bodies · Procedural rivers · Terrain generation · Drainage basins

1 Introduction

Procedural generation of 3D landscapes is a research topic of great relevance for many fields and industries. An old but still relevant challenge, however, is to produce realistic and detailed terrains while keeping the workload in check. Naturally, there has always to be a trade-off between control and automation. Numerous works with widely different focuses and approaches have been presented. Some put the focus on highly realistic terrains and take a computationally expensive simulation-based approach, others employ simpler and faster methods such as noise to generate still plausible and more varied results.

A sub-topic that got little attention despite being highly relevant for large landscapes is the procedural generation and plausible integration of water bodies. Mostly, these water bodies are simply added to the already computed terrain which tends to not look realistic. Rivers, their natural processes, and interaction

N. Magnenat-Thalmann et al. (Eds.): CGI 2022, LNCS 13443, pp. 345–356, 2022.
https://doi.org/10.1007/978-3-031-23473-6_27

with the terrain have been extensively studied in related fields such as geology, ecology, and hydrology [3,4,21]. However, relatively few works focused on procedural generation of 3D representations of them in near real-time speed. Existing scientific models and simulations, one popular model being optimal channel networks (OCNs) [1,20], usually employ only 2D representations, are more focused on analyzing existing landscapes than creating novel ones, or are very time-consuming to perform. For a more detailed overview of digital rivers creation throughout the various related research fields, we refer to Brown et al. [2].

We propose a method and pipeline for quick and easy procedural generation of large, plausible-looking landscapes with a special focus on believable water bodies. Our main contribution is an approach that mimics the mutual influence between terrain and water bodies by first generating the rivers and lakes based on artificial drainage basins, and then computing the final terrain. Our method carefully balances control and automation, and features distinct river deltas. To demonstrate our approach, we have developed a prototype application using a pipeline approach that makes it easy to evaluate intermediate results and emphasizes an agile workflow. Finally, we have conducted an extensive evaluation.

2   Related Work

One approach for procedural terrain generation is to use subdivision techniques and noise functions, as they are able to produce fractal-like structures, which are also often found in nature. Moreover, such techniques are, generally, relatively easy to use, highly scalable, and computed quickly. A comprehensive overview of various noise functions is given by Lagae et al. [17]. The drawbacks of those techniques are the intrinsic lack of control over global features, and the un-intuitive parameters, which make it hard to create geologically plausible landscapes.

A popular approach to providing intuitive control to the user is to add an authoring phase at the beginning, most often in form of a user sketch that acts as a high-level constraint for the subsequent terrain generation [11,23].

An approach to create more realistic terrains is to mimic or simulate natural processes such as plate tectonics [7,19], precipitation and other climate-related factors [6,10], and thermal or hydraulic erosion [5,18,22]. However, despite efforts to speed up the computations, most simulation-based approaches are very time-consuming, especially if applied on large-scale terrain. Another disadvantage is the lack of intuitive control over the generated terrains.

Realistic-looking large-scale terrains also can be created using example-based procedural generation techniques such as texture synthesis. These methods typically rely on user sketches and digital elevation models (DEMs) [12,14,26]. Naturally, example-based methods are limited by the available example data and can only replicate terrain features and landforms that are represented in the input DEM. Also, high-level geological constraints and the correct relations between large-scale features such as drainage basins are usually not taken into account.

Relatively few works explicitly focus on procedural rivers and water bodies as initial terrain-defining elements. Kelly et al. [16] first proposed the idea of procedurally generating terrain based on river networks and corresponding drainage basins. Here, the river networks were generated based on constrained midpoint displacement, and then the terrain was computed accordingly. Derzapf et al. [8] employed a similar approach but applied it on a planetary scale. In the work by Teoh [24], the terrain generation starts, too, by first procedurally creating river networks. In this case, rivers are grown from randomly placed outlets around the land region. In contrast to these works, Genevaux et al. [15] explicitly take hydrological knowledge into account. Additionally, initial user sketches provide more control. Based on the sketch, a river-network graph is created, river segments get classified into different types of watercourses, and the surrounding terrain gets computed using a hierarchical terrain construction tree. Zhang et al. [25] present a similar approach but generate the rivers based on Tokunaga river networks and calculate the surrounding terrain using a diffusion process.

For a more comprehensive overview and discussion of procedural terrain generation techniques, we refer to the recently presented work by Galin et al. [13].

3   Overview of Our Approach

As we prioritize a quick and easy generation over absolute realism, we have decided against simulation-based approaches. Also, we found the approach of first generating the terrain and then adding rivers to it using pathfinding algorithms not convincing, as this does not respect geomorphological constraints. We instead propose to follow the more natural "rivers first" approach, specifically, first generating river networks based on artificial drainage basins and then modeling the final terrain after them.

To provide a quick workflow, we employ a pipeline approach in which each step should be computed in a matter of seconds, be repeatable if modifications are desired, and the results directly be applied on a proxy mesh for inspection. We have used heightmaps as data structures, as they have a smaller memory footprint and provide much greater compatibility with external applications than voxels. Figure 1 depicts a high-level overview of our approach. We start with the general landscape layout by letting the user author the landmasses using marker-based curves. Then, different regions can be marked (e.g. flatland, or

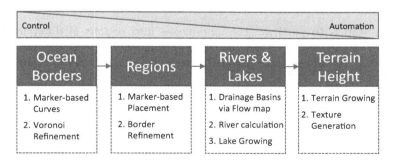

Fig. 1. Overview of our procedural generation pipeline. The first stages feature more user control, the latter ones provide more automation.

mountains). Following this, the river networks, including lakes, are computed based on artificial drainage basins. Finally, the terrain height gets computed based on the previous steps. In the earlier stages, we emphasize providing the user with more control over the algorithm, while the later stages have a higher degree of automation. The reasoning for this is that the user should have a great influence over the general layout of the landscape, which are defined in the earlier stages of the pipeline, but not be overwhelmed with a host of detail decisions.

4   Our Terrain Generation Pipeline in Detail

Due to space constraints, we still had to omit a number of technical details, but the interested reader can find them in our technical report [9].

4.1   Ocean Borders

To define the overall shape of a landmass, the user can place marker objects throughout the scene, from which we compute a closed curve by interpreting the markers as control points of a cubic spline, see Fig. 2 (1). Multiple landmasses can be built by repeating the process. The markers contain location information, a rotation, and a strength parameter (curvature of the tangent). To get a more natural look, we have developed a border refinement method for constrained randomization based on Voronoi diagrams. Each Voronoi region gets classified to represent landmass or ocean, depending on if the corresponding Voronoi site is inside or outside the spline, see Fig. 2 (2). The black ellipse depicts the initial spline, and the white outline the ocean border. To efficiently produce finer, more detailed borders (yellow outline), a second iteration can be applied in which additional Voronoi sites are placed around the previously computed border. The second iteration can also be applied using a noise-based priority queue. Although computationally more expensive, it produces more varied results through more inhomogeneous region growth and can lead to the formation of small islands. Figure 2 shows an island after the first iteration of border refinement (3), and two iterations with noise-based sampling (4).

4.2   Regions

The next step is to partition the landmasses into regions of different terrain types such as flatland, mountain, or desert. We again focused on giving the user great control by allowing the manual distribution of regions over the terrain. A region is defined similarly to the coastlines in the previous step by placing region markers. This time they contain parameters regarding the terrain type, the extent, and its border, which is randomized using noise.

4.3   River Networks and Lakes

When analyzing naturally generated terrain, the landscape can be divided into drainage basins – areas where water is collected by surface runoff. They are often

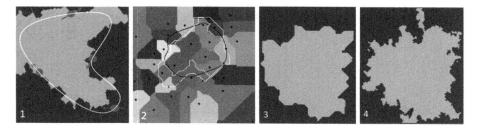

Fig. 2. (1): Authoring of the general shape of the landmass using marker objects (spline control points). (2): Border refinement based on Voronoi diagrams. The black ellipse depicts the initial spline, the white outline the ocean border after the first iteration, and the yellow one the after two iterations. (3): A terrain after one border-refinement iteration. (4): A terrain after two border-iterations with noise-based sampling. (Color figure online)

separated by mountains or hills. This means that by artificially generating those drainage basins, we know afterward where we can place hills and mountains. To generate the drainage basins, we have developed a method inspired by optimal channel networks [1,20]. Similarly to them, we define a finite graph $G(V, E)$ over a regular grid spanning the landscape. The nodes $v \in V$ correspond to the cells of the grid, and the edges $e \in E$ link neighboring nodes and enable the flow of water between them. We then construct a spanning forest F over G that acts as a flow graph/flow network, i.e., G gets partitioned into a number of spanning trees T – acyclic, directed, rooted sub-graphs. Each outlet acts as a root of one of these trees, which each represent one river network or its drainage basin.

Our procedure is shown in Fig. 3 and starts by placing down several potential outlets around the coasts (left image) and mountain regions. The separation between those outlets happens so that the rivers can be generated differently based on terrain type. Then, we compute the drainage basins by construction of the spanning forest that indicates the flow directions. This is done by calculating random flow directions for all cells in the uniform grid and storing them in a flow map (middle image) that procedurally connects all cells from mountain and flatland regions. This process starts at the river outlets by adding all outlet cells into a fringe set. Then, consecutively, random cells from this set get selected and their unsearched, valid neighbor cells get processed by assigning the flow direction (pointing to the current cell) and, in turn, adding them to the fringe set. By using a random selection order, we guarantee a homogeneous growth of the spanning trees and, thus, the drainage basins. The number of outlets influences the shape of the river networks. The fewer outlets are generated compared to the number of river sources, the higher the branching factor in the final river networks will be.

Then, we proceed to generate the actual rivers. A possible approach for this would be to distribute water over the grid, calculate the amount that would flow through each cell, and place rivers where a specified threshold is exceeded. However, this would lead to a relatively even distribution of river sources. Instead,

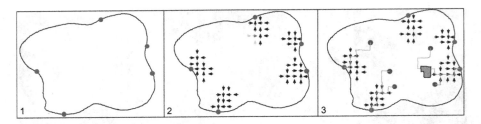

Fig. 3. River computation: First (1), random outlets are selected at the ocean borders (red dots). Then (2), we compute the flow directions across the land (arrows), starting at the outlets and then consecutively and randomly selecting previously evaluated cells (green arrow) to process their unprocessed neighbors (grey arrows). Eventually (3), we randomly place river sources (blue dots) and create the actual rivers by following the flow map (blue lines). Lakes are grown from random points on the river. (Color figure online)

we place the river sources randomly and then follow the flow directions until the ocean is reached (right image of Fig. 3). The amount of river sources placed is again controlled by the user and can be set separately for mountain and flatland regions. Users also can set the chance for a river to be a dried-out riverbed. In our implementation, each river adds a certain amount of strength to a cell when flowing through it, thus, when two rivers join, their respective strength is combined from thereon. Based on this strength, we calculate the width of the river and accordingly assign more cells to it. Figure 4 (top left) depicts a color-coded example of various rivers and their respective strength.

For each cell a river travels through, there is a chance to generate a lake. The size of the lake depends on the strength of the river. In addition, the size is limited by user-set maxima and minima. To produce lakes that vary in shape, a user-controlled noise function is applied to the lake borders. The lake generation is also limited to one lake per river source and a user-controlled region-based limit. After generating a lake, the river generation continues. Figure 4 (right) shows an example terrain with lakes and river networks.

With our approach, we are also able to generate distinct river deltas by performing a second, locally-bound iteration of generating drainage basins and then rivers. However, here we reverse the process: we select a river cell instead of a coastline cell as the starting point from which we compute the flow map; in this case only a regional one. Then, we select multiple coastline cells to be outlets from where the distributaries of the delta are created by following the computed regional flow directions back to the original river cell. We allow this process to randomly occur in the general vicinity of the ocean, see Fig. 4 (bottom left).

4.4   Terrain

After generating the rivers and lakes, we "grow" the terrain starting at the water bodies. To do this, we employ a height-based priority queue. The initial height of

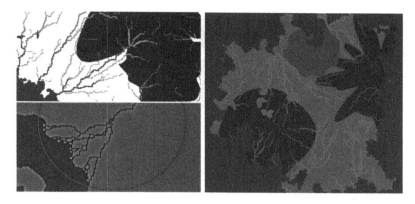

Fig. 4. Top left: A map highlighting the river strength with different colors (green indicating weak rivers and red strong ones). Bottom left: An example of a river delta, the red dot depicts the position from which the river delta computation was started, the circle shows the radius of the local flow map, and the yellow dots mark the stream outlets. Right: A terrain with rivers of varying width, lakes, and color-coded regions. (Color figure online)

water cells increases from the outlet onward based on a region-based steepness, although a distance-based curve is possible too. When a cell is removed from the queue, all the neighbors that have not been traversed yet will receive a new height by the addition of a growth value. The growth value is calculated by taking into account the terrain growth factor of the cell's region, neighboring regions, and a random value obtained from noise functions that also depend on the region. The exact height calculation for a cell x' which is the neighbor of an already computed cell x is described by the following equation:

$$h(x') = h_x + s_t \cdot b_d + s_r \cdot (1 - b_d) + |n_t \cdot a_t| \tag{1}$$

In this, h_x is the height of cell x, s_t is the region-dependent growth factor which itself is computed using a distance-based interpolation between all regions in the area, b_d is a distance-based blending factor, s_r a growth factor for rivers, n_t the noise output whose frequency is again terrain-dependent, and a_t is a terrain-dependent amplitude. The latter is calculated as $a_t = s_t \cdot k_t$ in which k_t is a terrain-dependent noise strength. Figure 5 (left) shows an example terrain with computed height.

4.5 Visualization

To visualize the generated terrain, we generate a textured mesh based on the heightmap. The user can choose from multiple rendering modes using different textures, which are illustrated in Fig. 5: the region mode visualizes each region with a separate color, the normal-texture mode displays a color gradient that is dependent on the height, and the height mode displays a black and white

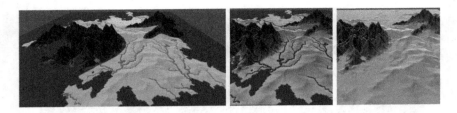

Fig. 5. An example of a final terrain with computed height using different rendering modes. From left to right: region mode, normal-texture mode, and height mode.

normalized heightmap as texture. Additionally, the mesh can be flattened to a plane for easier evaluation of earlier stages.

5   Evaluation

We start the evaluation with a brief complexity analysis: The run-time complexity of our pipeline is $O(n_c \cdot n_s \cdot n_l)$ with n_c being the number of grid cells, n_s being the number of river sources, and n_l being the number of lakes. This means that we have a linear time complexity. Similarly, the space complexity is $O(n_c)$.

5.1   Performance Evaluation

All measurements were done using an Intel i7 7800x processor, 16 GB of main memory, and an Nvidia GeForce 2070 graphics card. As the performance is mainly dependent on the number of grid cells n_c, we conducted all measurements with sizes of $n_c = 512^2, 1024^2, 2048^2$ and took the median of 20 runs.

In Fig. 6 we illustrate the computational time of the whole pipeline over the different grid sizes, whereby the timings of the individual pipeline steps are stacked on top of each other. As we can see, the computation is very fast: depending on the grid size, the whole process is done in a couple of seconds (25 s for the biggest tested grid size). Various single steps are being computed

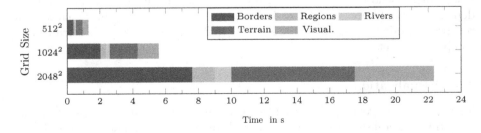

Fig. 6. The calculation times for the complete pipeline over multiple grid sizes. Even with a grid size of 2048^2 the whole pipeline gets computed in under 25 s.

nearly in an instant. Looking at the timings for the individual pipeline steps, the calculation of the regions and rivers is the fastest and, compared to the other steps, negligible throughout all resolutions. At lower resolutions of 512^2, the calculation of the terrain's height and the visualization take the most time with 0.39 and 0.38 s, respectively. At higher resolutions of 2048^2, however, the border computation takes the longest with 7.6 s, followed by the terrain with 7.5 s. The reason for this is that the computational time of most pipeline steps growths with factors closely around the expected one of 4 that corresponds to the linear growth regarding the number of grid cells (quadratic regarding grid side-length) which we established in the theoretical complexity analysis. The time for the border calculation, in practice, growth with factors around 5, though.

Investigating deeper what exactly causes the computational time in the individual steps, we find that in the river step the calculation of the drainage basins via the flow map takes up $> 88\%$ of the time while the following computation of rivers and lakes takes nearly no time, see Table 1. Accordingly, the number of rivers and lakes does not have a significant effect. The main factor regarding the performance is therefore the overall grid resolution. Some other parameters, however, also have a notable influence

Table 1. Detailed timings of some pipeline steps (resolution: 2048^2).

Step	Substep	Time in ms
Borders	Refine. (1i)	851
	Refine. (2i)	1601
	Refine. (2i+N)	7600
Rivers	Drainage B	796
	Rivers+Lakes	100
Visual.	Mesh	800
	Textures	3426

on the needed time for computation. For instance, in the first pipeline step, the second iteration of border refinement takes considerably longer than the first one, as a higher number of Voronoi points is used. Also, if the second refinement iteration is applied with additional noise (default setting), it takes even more time to compute, as in this case, we use a priority queue. This is also the reason for the higher practical growth factor of this step. Regarding the visualization step, the computation of the textures takes roughly four-fifths of the time of the step while the mesh generation itself only takes one-fifth.

5.2   Qualitative Evaluation

To our knowledge, there are no metrics to quantify the quality and realism of procedural terrains and water bodies. Thus, in order to evaluate the terrain generated with the proposed system and to showcase its versatility, we did a qualitative evaluation. For this, we have created several landscapes with different settings, which can be seen in Fig. 7, and reviewed the production process as well as the results regarding usability, flexibility, and plausibility. With our system, it is possible to produce a vast variety of shapes for the coastline. Single continents, as well as island groups, can be created by varying the number and position of land markers. Generally, we found the process very efficient and flexible; simpler shapes can be realized very quickly with just a few markers, but by using a greater number, the user also can create more complex worlds. Similarly, the whole process to create a terrain is very easy and straightforward,

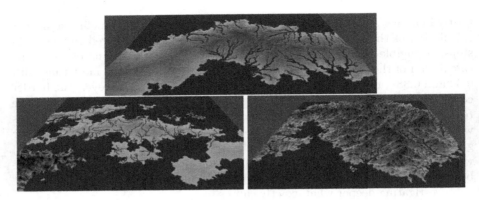

Fig. 7. Example landscapes generated with our system. Note the high variability and plausibility.

as our pipeline design allows for quick iterations and the saving of intermediate results. Also, although we provide many parameters to fine-tune each step, in most cases the majority of them don't necessarily have to be changed and our pre-configured default settings will suffice. Thanks to our focus on water bodies and the approach to create river networks before the final terrain, the procedural landscapes produced with our system are quite natural looking and feature plausibly embedded river networks that recreate the typical dendric structures from the real ones. In general, we found that the generated results look very plausible and, presumably, the majority of different demands on the produced landscapes can be satisfied.

To further evaluate the plausibility of the generated terrains, we have compared them with real-world terrain based on publicly available height data. For this comparison, we took DEMs, constructed 3D meshes of them, and attempted to replicate the real terrain as closely as possible with our system while only investing a reasonable amount of time (a couple of minutes). As an example, we randomly took a section of the Severo-Evensky District in Magadan Oblast in Russia (61.21703, 160.21836) as a real-world reference. Figure 8 shows the comparison between the mesh representations of both landscapes, the left image shows the real terrain, and the right one our systems replication of it. As can be seen, it is possible to recreate a similar general shape of the coastline. Also, the mountain ranges are distributed with a good approximation of reality. It is not possible to perfectly match the terrain near the world border, as the real map is a part of a larger landscape but our algorithm does not have information beyond the borders. However, the inland parts of the river networks were generated in a believable way. Even though the pathways of the riverbeds differ from the original directions, the individual parts of river networks have similar overall shapes.

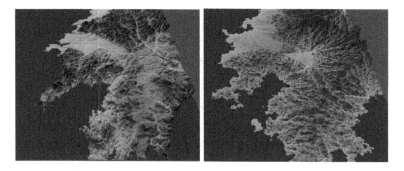

Fig. 8. Comparison of a real world's terrain (left) and our recreation (right), both visualized with meshes. Note that our recreation is quite similar.

6 Conclusion

We have presented a system for the procedural generation of vast landscapes with a focus on the natural and realistically-looking integration of water bodies. We achieved this by first generating river networks and lakes based on drainage basins and then the actual terrain. A quick and agile workflow is facilitated thanks to our pipeline design in which each stage is computed and visualized in a matter of seconds. According to our performance measurements, a high-fidelity landscape can be computed in under 25 s. In order to balance the amount of control, usability, and efficiency, we have designed the first pipeline stages to allow the authoring of the general landscape and its layout, while the later stages are more automation-heavy on the terrain details. Of course, our methods in the various stages of our pipeline are easily modifiable to much more or even less control, so it can be easily adapted to different needs in different workflows. Our qualitative evaluation demonstrated the great variability of our approach and a dedicated comparison with real-world terrain based on DEM data illustrated the capability to quickly create terrains strongly resembling the real ones.

References

1. Balister, P., et al.: River landscapes and optimal channel networks. Proc. Natl. Acad. Sci. **115**(26), 6548–6553 (2018)
2. Brown, R., Pasternack, G.: How to build a digital river. Earth-Sci. Rev. **194**, 283–305 (2019)
3. Carrara, F., Altermatt, F., Rodriguez-Iturbe, I., Rinaldo, A.: Dendritic connectivity controls biodiversity patterns in experimental metacommunities. Proc. Natl. Acad. Sci. USA **109**, 5761–5766 (2012)
4. Carraro, L., et al.: Generation and application of river network analogues for use in ecology and evolution. Ecol. Evol. **10** (2020)
5. Cordonnier, G., et al.: Large scale terrain generation from tectonic uplift and fluvial erosion. Comput. Graph. Forum **35** (2016)

6. Cordonnier, G., Ecormier, P., Galin, E., Gain, J., Benes, B., Cani, M.P.: Interactive generation of time-evolving, snow-covered landscapes with avalanches. Comput. Graph. Forum **37** (2018)
7. Cortial, Y., Peytavie, A., Galin, E., Guérin, E.: Procedural tectonic planets. Comput. Graph. Forum **38**, 1–11 (2019)
8. Derzapf, E., Ganster, B., Guthe, M., Klein, R.: River networks for instant procedural planets. Comput. Graphi. Forum **30**, 2031–2040 (2011)
9. Fischer, R., Boeckers, J., Zachmann, G.: Procedural generation of landscapes with water bodies using artificial drainage basins. Tech. rep., University of Bremen (2022). https://cgvr.informatik.uni-bremen.de/papers/cgi22/TR.pdf
10. Fischer, R., Dittmann, P., Weller, R., Zachmann, G.: Autobiomes: procedural generation of multi-biome landscapes. Vis. Comput. **36**, 1–10 (2020)
11. Gain, J., Marais, P., Straßer, W.: Terrain sketching. In: I3D 2009, pp. 31–38 (2009)
12. Gain, J., Merry, B., Marais, P.: Parallel, realistic and controllable terrain synthesis. Comput. Graph. Forum **34** (2015)
13. Galin, E., et al.: A review of digital terrain modeling. Comput. Graph. Forum **38** (2019)
14. Guérin, E., et al.: Interactive example-based terrain authoring with conditional generative adversarial networks. ACM Trans. Graph. **36** (2017)
15. Génevaux, J.D., Galin, E., Guérin, E., Peytavie, A., Benes, B.: Terrain generation using procedural models based on hydrology. ACM Trans. Graph. **32**, 13 (2013)
16. Kelley, A., Malin, M., Nielson, G.: Terrain simulation using a model of stream erosion. In: ACM SIGGRAPH Comput. Graph. **22**, pp. 263–268 (1988)
17. Lagae, A., et al.: A survey of procedural noise functions. Comput. Graph. Forum **29** (2010)
18. Lim, F., Wei, T.Y., Bhojan, A.: Visually improved erosion algorithm for the procedural generation of tile-based terrain. In: VISIGRAPP (2022)
19. Michel, É., Emilien, A., Cani, M.P.: Generation of folded terrains from simple vector maps. In: Eurographics (2015)
20. Rigon, R., Rinaldo, A., Rodriguez-Iturbe, I., Bras, R., Ijjasz-Vasquez, E.: Optimal channel networks - a framework for the study of river basin morphology. Water Resour. Res. **29**, 1635–1646 (1993)
21. Rosgen, D.L.: A classification of natural rivers. CATENA **22**, 169–199 (1994)
22. Stava, O., Benes, B., Brisbin, M., Krivanek, J.: Interactive terrain modeling using hydraulic erosion. In: Symposium on Computer Animation, pp. 201–210 (2008)
23. Talgorn, F.X., Belhadj, F.: Real-time sketch-based terrain generation. In: Computer Graphics International, pp. 13–18 (2018)
24. Teoh, S.T.: RiverLand: an efficient procedural modeling system for creating realistic-looking terrains. In: Bebis, G., et al. (eds.) ISVC 2009. LNCS, vol. 5875, pp. 468–479. Springer, Heidelberg (2009). https://doi.org/10.1007/978-3-642-10331-5_44
25. Zhang, H., Qu, D., Hou, Y., Gao, F., Huang, F.: Synthetic modeling method for large scale terrain based on hydrology. IEEE Access **4**, 6238–6249 (2016)
26. Zhou, H., Sun, J., Turk, G., Rehg, J.: Terrain synthesis from digital elevation models. IEEE Tran. Visual. Comput. Graph. **13**, 834–48 (2007)

High-Fidelity Dynamic Human Synthesis via UV-Guided NeRF with Sparse Views

Zhifeng Xie[1(✉)], Zhaosheng Wang[1], Sen Wang[1], Yuzhou Sun[1], and Lizhuang Ma[2]

[1] Shanghai University, Shanghai, China
{zhifeng_xie,auggstwang,wangsen,sunyuzhou}@shu.edu.cn
[2] Shanghai Jiao Tong University, Shanghai, China
ma-lz@cs.sjtu.edu.cn

Abstract. In the field of dynamic human synthesis, some recent works try to decompose a non-rigidly deforming scene into a canonical neural radiance field and use a set of deformation fields for mapping observation-space points to the canonical space, thereby enabling them to learn the dynamic scene from images. Due to the highly under-constrained optimization cased by deformation field without prior and the insufficient of surface appearance information cased by sparse views, the rendering result exists obvious appearance artifacts. In this paper, to address the problem of artifacts, we present a novel method called UV-guided Neural Radiance Fields (UVNeRF), consisting of three modules: Canonical Space Mapping Module (CSMM), Texture Space Mapping Module (TSMM), UV-guided Neural Rendering Module (UVNRM). CSMM map observation-space points to the canonical space based 3D human skeletons which can regularize learning of the deformation field. TSMM map canonical-space points to the texture space for obtaining a rough human surface representation on the UV space as the extra information. UVNRM render the image result using the outputs of CSMM and TSMM. The experimental studies on Human3.6M and ZJU-MoCap dataset show that our approach gains noteworthy enhancements comparing recent dynamic human synthesis methods.

Keywords: Human synthesis · Neural radiance field · Canonical space

1 Introduction

Dynamic human synthesis amis to produce high-fidelity human rendering from arbitrary viewpoints and poses. It has been an important task in the field of computer vision and computer graphics, which has a variety of applications such as free-viewpoint videos, telepresence, video games and movies. Traditional methods mainly rely on a dense array of cameras [28] and the fitting of template mesh [25]. Those methods need complex hardware and only apply in constrained environments.

N. Magnenat-Thalmann et al. (Eds.): CGI 2022, LNCS 13443, pp. 357–368, 2022.
https://doi.org/10.1007/978-3-031-23473-6_28

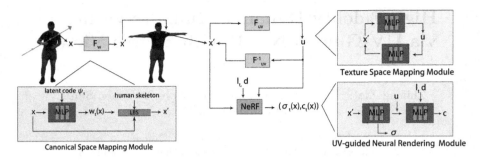

Fig. 1. Overview of our method. Our method consists of three modules: canonical space mapping module (Sect. 3.1), texture space mapping module (Sect. 3.2) and UV-guided neural rendering module (Sect. 3.3).

Recently, to solve the problem of applicable range, some people try to use neural radiance field (NeRF) [14] for syntheizing dynamic human with sparse multi-view video. Their methods [10,15,16,18,27] decompose a video into a canonical NeRF and a set of deformation fields that map observation-space points to the canonical space. Although those methods achieve task of dynamic human synthesis, their results still exist obvious appearance artifacts due to two reasons. On the one hand, deformation field without prior is extremely under-constrained. On the other hand, the sparsity of input views make learned surface appearance information less than the dense views.

To overcome these problems, we propose a novel method for dynamic human synthesis, named UV-guided Neural Radiance Fields (UVNeRF). As shown in Fig. 1, our method includes three modules:Canonical Space Mapping Module (CSMM), Texture Space Mapping Module(TSMM), UV-guided Neural Rendering Module (UVNRM). CSMM can introduce blend weight field [8] to decoupule human pose in the observation space and convert it into canonical space. TSMM can train uv mapping MLP to regress a 2D UV coordinate at each point from canonical space to texture space, and another inverse MLP to map the 2D UV coordinate in the texture space back to canonical space. UVNRM integrates the uv code into with richer appearance information into canonical NeRF to guide and render high-fidelity dynamic human synthesis. Moreover, we evaluate our method on the H36M [6] and ZJU-MoCAP [16] datasets that capture dynamic humans in complex motions with synchronized cameras. Our method exhibits noteworthy performances on novel view and novel pose synthesis.

In summary, this work has the following contributions:

– We propose a novel method called UV-guided Neural Radiance Fields to achieve high-fidelity dynamic human synthesis from a sparse multi-view video.
– We construct a cycle mapping structure between canonical space and texture space to efficiently regress 2D uv coordinates and yield a coarse human representation.
– We propose UV-guided neural rendering to integrate the uv code including richer appearance information into the pipeline of dynamic human synthesis.

2   Related Work

2.1   Dynamic Human Synthesis

Given multi-view video, some methods [2,22] adopted the traditional modeling and rendering pipeline to synthesize dynamic human. Although their results were impressive, they relied on a dense array of cameras to achieve high-fidelity synthesis. To reduce the amount of input views, some people tried to use NeRF for the task of dynamic human synthesis from a sparse multi-view video. Neural Body [16] implicitly represented human body at different video frames from the same set of latent codes, which were anchored to the vertices of a deformable mesh. Animatable NeRF [15] and HumanNeRF [27] decomposed multi-view inputs into deformatable field decoupling human pose and a canonical NeRF rendering novel view. However, these methods still exist appearance artifacts due to under-constrained deformation field and the inadequate surface information from the sparsity of input. Comparably, our method introduces blend weight field with priors to solve under-constrained problem and learn a coarse human representation in the texture space for gaining rich surface information under the sparse inputs, which eliminates appearance artifacts.

2.2   Neural Rendering

A lot of works has shown significant progress on 3D scene modeling and novel view synthesis using differentiable neural rendering manner based explicit representations, such as point clouds [12], voxels [1] or meshes [9,11]. Although those methods were easy to edit and render, their results were constrained in resolution. Recently, some methods [14] have implicitly represent 3D scene, which achieved impressive results for synthesizing novel views. However, these methods were only applicable to rigid deformation fields. Some researchers [18] tried to extend implicit representation to non-rigid deforming, such as dynamic human synthesis. But their methods could not decouple and drive human pose. In contrast, we combine implicit functions with deformable field for representing the dynamic human, achieving high-fidelity rendering results.

2.3   Image-Based Rendering

IBR aim to synthesize novel views from image space without recovering detailed 3D geometry. Previous work [3] used light field interpolation to produce novel views. But the range of novel viewpoints were limited. To synthesize more novel views, some work [17,26] tried to estimate depth maps from input views as proxy geometries, warping observed images into the novel view. Though these methods extended the renderable range, the unstable proxy geometries often failed to produce the high-quality rendering results. Comparably, we propose texture space mapping to obtain the uv code, which can guide the rendering of high-quality appearance and geometry in novel views.

3 Method

As shown in Fig. 1, our method consists of three modules: Canonical Space Mapping Module, Texture Space Mapping Module and UV-guided Neural Rendering Module.

3.1 Canonical Space Mapping Module

In this module, we leverage human priors [13] to learn deformation field for decouping human poses, which can help us solve the under-constrained problem. Our deformation field is based on skeleton-driven deformation framework [8] which defines K skeletons and produce K transformation matrices $G_k \in SE(3)$ where SE(3) is a set of matrices of rigid transformation. The deformation field can be divided into two parts: blend weight field and canonical space mapping. Blend weight field use a MLP to estimate weights of human skeletons. And then we utilize the linear blend skinning algorithm [8] with blend weights to map a canonical space point $x^{'}$ to the observation space x:

$$x = (\sum_{k=1}^{K} \omega(x)_k G_k)x^{'}, \tag{1}$$

where $\omega(x)_k$ is the blend weight of k-th part. Similarly, if we know the blend weights of an observation-space point x, we can transform that point to the canonical space using the following:

$$x^{'} = (\sum_{k=1}^{K} \omega^{'}(x)_k G_k)^{-1}x, \tag{2}$$

where $\omega^{'}(x)_k$ is the blend weight function defined in the observation space. As shown in Fig. 1, given K synchronized videos of a performer captured at sparse viewpoints with T frames, we leverage SMPL model as our 3D statical body S to regularize the learned blend weights. For any given points sampled from frame $t \in \{1, ..., T\}$, we first find the closest surface point on the SMPL mesh. Then, the init blend weight is computed by performing barycentric interpolation of the blend weights of three vertices on the corresponding mesh fact. A MLP network F_w is used to learn a residual vector conditioned on the latent code ψ_t. The neural blend weight field w_t at frame t is defined as:

$$w_t(x) = norm(F_w(x, \psi_t) + w_0(x, S_t)), \tag{3}$$

where w_0 is the initial blend weights computed based on statical body model S_t; $norm(w) = w/\sum \omega_i$. For observation-space point x, we use the Eq. 2 with the blend weight $\omega^{'}(x)_k \in w_t(x)$ and G_k defined in S_t to compute the corresponding texture coordinate $x^{'}$ in the canonical space.

3.2   Texture Space Mapping Module

Comparing with the dense views, we observe that inputs whose views are sparse easily render results containing appearance artifacts. The reason is that sparse views include less appearance information than the dense. To solve this problem, a natural idea is seeking for more appearance information for rendering high-fidelity images.

Inspired by AtlasNet [21], we model an coarse object human 2D surface as an unwrapped atlas in the texture space and let it as extra appearance information for guiding rendering. As shown in Fig. 1, for the canonical space point x', we use a MLP network F_{uv} to map it into texture space:

$$F_{uv} : x' \rightarrow \boldsymbol{u}. \tag{4}$$

where $\boldsymbol{u} = (u, v)$ is a 2D UV coordinate for parameterizing texture space. The output of network is represented by a 2D unit sphere where $\boldsymbol{u}$ is interpreted as a point, which is best for objects with genus 0(such as SMPL model).

Because directly mapping a 3D point to the texture space often leads to the learned human surface which is a highly distorted and a degenerate result that some varying points are mapped to the same point in the texture space. The ideal result is instead to uniformly map the 2D surface onto the texture space and occupy the entire texture space. In order to achieve the goal, we utilize another MLP network F'_{uv} to project the 2D texture space into 3D canioncal space:

$$F'_{uv} : \boldsymbol{u} \rightarrow x'. \tag{5}$$

It can help us to reason about a coarse 2D surface of the object human body in the texture space and avoid to generate distorted and degenerate results.

3.3   UV-Guided Neural Rendering Module

Our rendering module is similar to canonical NeRF [6], including density field and radiance field. First, we utilize a MLP network F_σ to regress density. As shown in Fig. 1, for the frame t, the volume density σ_t is predicted as a function of the canonical space coordinate x' and the latent code l_t, which is defined as:

$$\sigma_t(x') = M_\sigma(\gamma(x'), \gamma(l_t)). \tag{6}$$

where M_σ represents an MLP network with four layers and γ represent positional encoding. Then, our radiance field F_c is different from the canonical NeRF. The one we use combined with uv code encoding from texture space coordinates u and view direction code from a 2D vector (θ, ϕ). The uv code including more appearance information can effectively guide the estimation of radiance and the view direction code which have the information of camera view can be used for synthesizing novel views. As shown in Fig. 1, for the frame t, the radiance c_t is predicted as a function of the canonical space coordinate x' and the latent code l_t, the viewing direction d and the uv coordinate $\boldsymbol{u}$, which is defined as:

$$c_t(x') = M_c(\gamma(x'), \gamma(l_t), \gamma_d(d), \gamma_u(\boldsymbol{u})). \tag{7}$$

where M_c represents an MLP network with four layers, and γ_d and γ_u are positional encoding functions for viewing direction and uv coordinate, respectively. Finally, given volume density and radiance, we utilize the classical volume rendering techniques to render the dynamic human body into a 2D image. For the frame t and camera ray r, the rendered color $\tilde{C}_t(r)$ of the corresponding pixel can be computed by the following equation:

$$\tilde{C}_t(r) = \sum_{n=1}^{N} T_n(1 - exp(-\sigma_t(x_n^{'})\delta_n))c_t(x_n^{'}), \tag{8}$$

$$T_n = exp(-\sum_{m=1}^{n-1} \sigma_t(x_m \delta_m)). \tag{9}$$

where $\delta_n = ||x_{n+1}^{'} - x_n^{'}||_2$ is the distance between adjacent sampled points and N is the count of sampling points along camera ray r.

3.4 Loss

Given a multi-view input, we learn the UV-guided neural radiance fields by optimizing the following objective function:

$$\mathcal{L} = \mathcal{L}_c + \mathcal{L}_{bw}. \tag{10}$$

where $\mathcal{L}_c$ and $\mathcal{L}_{bw}$ are color loss and blend weights loss, respectively.

Color Loss. This loss minimizes the error between the rendered images and the corresponding observed frames, which is defined as the following:

$$\mathcal{L}_c = \sum_{r \in \mathcal{R}} ||\tilde{C}_t(r) - C_t(r)||_2 \tag{11}$$

where $\mathcal{R}$ is the set of rays passing through image pixels; $\tilde{C}_t(r), C_t(r)$ represent the predicted color and the ground truth color of the pixel, respectively.

Blend Weights Loss. We utilize a consistency loss between blend weight fields. According to Eq. (1) and Eq. (2) in Sect. 3.1, two corresponding points at canonical and observation spaces should have the same blend weights. Given an observation-space point x at frame t, we map it to the canonical space point using $T_t(x)$. The consistency loss between blend weight fields is defined as:

$$\mathcal{L}_{bw} = \sum_{x \in \mathcal{X}_t} ||w_t(x) - w^{can}(T_t(x))||_1. \tag{12}$$

where $\mathcal{X}_t$ is the set of 3D points sampled within the 3D human bounding box at frame t; w_t and w^{can} are blend weights in the observation-space and canonical space, respectively.

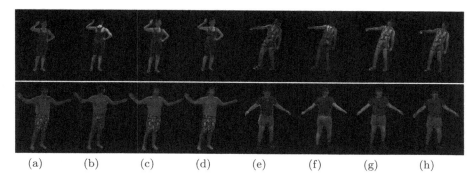

(a)   (b)   (c)   (d)   (e)   (f)   (g)   (h)

Fig. 2. Qualitative results of novle view on the H36M dataset. (a) and (e) are the ground truth. (b) and (f) are the NHR [23] which has difficulty in controlling the viewpoint. (c) and (g) are the A-NeRF [15] which exists obvious appearance artifacts. Compared with them, our method(d) and (h) achieve high-quality rendering of the target view.

4 Experiments

4.1 Dataset

H36M [7] is a multi-view dynamic human video dataset recording human poses using the marker-based motion capture system and 4 cameras. It includes 11 subjects. For evaluating our network, we select 8 subjects: S1, S5, S6, S7, S8, S9 and S11. The training process uses three cameras and the test process uses one. The SMPL parameters from the 3D human poses can be estimated using [7] and the foreground humans can be segmented using [4].

ZJU-MoCap [16] is a multi-view dynamic human video dataset recording human poses using the marker-based motion capture system and 21 cameras. We use four subjects, "Twirl", "Taichi", "Waarmup" and "Punch1", to evaluate our network. The setting is as same as the Neural Body for comparing it.

4.2 Training

We train the parameters of $F_w, F_{uv}, F_{uv}^{-1}, F_\sigma, F_c, \{\psi_t\}$ and $\{l_t\}$ jointly based on the input video. We set the learning rate as $5e^{-4}$ and decay exponentially to $5e^{-5}$ along the optimization where our training adopts Adam optimizers as same as [15]. Our network trained on a Titan XP. For a three-view video, we choose 260 frames for training and 130 frames for eval. One training take around 200k iterations (about 24 h).

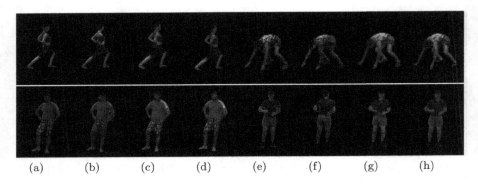

(a)   (b)   (c)   (d)   (e)   (f)   (g)   (h)

Fig. 3. Qualitative results of novle pose on the H36M dataset. (a) and (e) are the ground truth. (b) and (f) are the NHR [23] which has difficulty in controlling the viewpoint. (c) and (g) are the A-NeRF [15] which exists obvious appearance artifacts. Compared with them, our method(d) and (h) achieve high-quality rendering of the target view.

Table 1. Results of novel view and novel pose synthesis on H36M dataset in terms of PSNR and SSIM(higher is better).

	PSNR				SSIM			
	NT	NHR	A-NeRF	Ours	NT	NHR	A-NeRF	Ours
Novel view	20.42	20.93	23.00	**24.28**	0.850	0.866	0.891	**0.905**
Novel pose	19.88	20.35	21.58	**21.83**	0.842	0.858	0.860	**0.868**

4.3   Comparisons

Baselines. We evaluate our method on image synthesis using two metrics: peak signal-to-noise ratio (PSNR) and structural similarity index (SSIM). We compare our method with state-of-the-art image synthesis methods [15,16] that also utilize SMPL priors. 1) Animatable NeRF [15] use a deformation field based on the skeleton-driven deformation framework based on SMPL model mapping observation-space points to the canonical space, and then send the mapped points into NeRF to get synthesis results, which is the state of art method on H36M datasets. 2) Neural Body [16] condition on a set of structed latent codes anchored on SMPL model, which encodes local geometry and appearance with a SparseConvNet to represent a dynamic human, which is the state of art method on ZJU-MoCap datasets. Besides those, we also compare some other methods: Neural Textures [20] and NHR [23].

Results of Novel View Synthesis and Novel Pose Synthesis. We synthesize novel views and novel poses of training video frames in order to comparison. Table 1 show the quantitative comparison of our method with NT [20], NHR [23] and A-NeRF [15] on the H36M dataset. Our method integrating uv code into

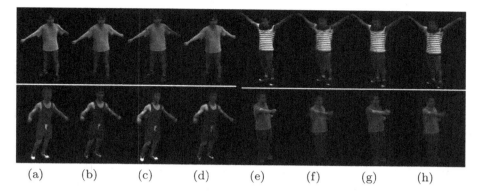

(a) (b) (c) (d) (e) (f) (g) (h)

Fig. 4. Qualitative results of novel pose synthesis on the ZJU-MoCap dataset. (a) and (e) are the ground truth. (b) and (f) are the A-NeRF [15]. (c) and (g) are the NB [16]. A-NeRF and NB tend to generate rendering results with appearance artifacts. Compared with them, our method (d) and (h) achieve high-quality rendering of the target view.

Table 2. Results of novel view and novel pose synthesis on ZJU-MoCap dataset in terms of PSNR and SSIM (higher is better).

	PSNR				SSIM			
	NHR	A-NeRF	NB	Ours	NHR	A-NeRF	NB	Ours
Novel view	23.25	27.10	**28.90**	27.36	0.905	0.949	**0.967**	0.951
Novel pose	21.88	23.16	23.06	**23.86**	0.863	0.893	0.879	**0.897**

the pipeline of dynamic human synthesis achieves the best performance across all metrics. As we can see the qualitative comparison in the Fig. 2, NHR is difficulty to control the synthesis of novel view and the previous state-of-art method A-NeRF still exist obvious appearance artifacts due to inadequate information from the sparsity of input views. We learn a coarse human representation to rich appearance information to effectively reduce the appearance artifacts of rendering results. Table 2 shows the quantitative comparison on the ZJU-MoCap dataset with NT, NHR, A-NeRF and NB [16]. Our method is higher than the NT, NHR and A-NeRF across all metrics. Although NB gives best performance in the quantitative comparison of the novel view synthesis due to local latent struct code, which also weaken the performance of novel pose synthesis, our method achieves the best performance across all metrics on the novel pose synthesis. As shown in the Figs. 3 and 4, our rendering results have least appearance artifacts in the qualitative comparison of novel pose synthesis.

4.4 Ablation Study

We conduct ablation studies on one subject (S11) of the H36M dataset in terms of the novel view synthesis performance. First, we analyze the effects of uv coding.

Then we explore the performances of our models trained without blend weights loss.

Impact of Uv Coding. For comparison, we train a model without uv coding that are proposed in Sect. 3.2. As shown in Table 3, all metrics are lower than the complete model. As we can see the qualitative comparison in Fig. 5, the rendering result without uv coding is high-distorted and the complete model renders high-quality result.

Impact of Blend Weights Loss. We compare our model with the one which have no blend weights loss. Table 3 shows that blend weights loss improves the performance on novel view and novel pose synthesis. The qualitative comparison is presented in Fig. 5. The rendering without blend weights loss is obviously blurry. In compared, the image synthesized by our complete model is high-fidelity.

Table 3. Comparison of models trained without uv coding(w/o_uv) or blend weights loss(w/o_bwl) on the subject "S11" terms of PSNR and SSIM(higher is better).

	PSNR			SSIM		
	w/o_uv	w/o_bwl	full	w/o_uv	w/o_bwl	full
Novel view	24.55	26.20	**26.48**	0.902	0.920	**0.925**
Novel pose	22.76	21.88	**22.93**	0.853	0.863	**0.877**

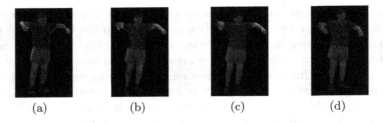

(a)   (b)   (c)   (d)

Fig. 5. Comparison of models trained with different settings on the subject "S11". (a) (b) and (c) are the ground truth, result of the model without uv code and without bwloss, respectively. (d) is the rengdering of complete model.

5   Conclusion

We propose a method for high-fidelity dynamic human synthesis using a sparse set of cameras, called UV-guided Neural Radiance Fields(UVNeRF). Experiments on the H36M dataset and ZJU-MoCap dataset demonstrated that the propose model achieves significant performances on images synthesis under novel views and novel human poses. Because our deformation field is based on SMPL model which cannot represent the complex non-rigid deformations of garments, such as loose clothes. In the future, we hope to construct a new human model and introduce feature interaction [5,19,24] that can represent local garment deformations for handling the problem of complex garments.

Acknowledgements. This work was supported by the Shanghai Natural Science Foundation of China under Grant No. 19ZR1419100.

References

1. Aliev, K.-A., Sevastopolsky, A., Kolos, M., Ulyanov, D., Lempitsky, V.: Neural point-based graphics. In: Vedaldi, A., Bischof, H., Brox, T., Frahm, J.-M. (eds.) ECCV 2020. LNCS, vol. 12367, pp. 696–712. Springer, Cham (2020). https://doi.org/10.1007/978-3-030-58542-6_42
2. Alldieck, T., Magnor, M., Bhatnagar, B.L., Theobalt, C., Pons-Moll, G.: Learning to reconstruct people in clothing from a single RGB camera. In: Proceedings of the IEEE/CVF Conference on Computer Vision and Pattern Recognition, pp. 1175–1186 (2019)
3. Davis, A., Levoy, M., Durand, F.: Unstructured light fields. Comput. Graph. Forum. **31**, 305–314. Wiley Online Library (2012)
4. Gong, K., et al.: Instance-Level human parsing via part grouping network. In: Ferrari, V., Hebert, M., Sminchisescu, C., Weiss, Y. (eds.) ECCV 2018. LNCS, vol. 11208, pp. 805–822. Springer, Cham (2018). https://doi.org/10.1007/978-3-030-01225-0_47
5. Guo, H., Sheng, B., Li, P., Chen, C.P.: Multiview high dynamic range image synthesis using fuzzy broad learning system. IEEE Trans. Cybernet. **51**(5), 2735–2747 (2019)
6. Huang, Z., Xu, Y., Lassner, C., Li, H., Tung, T.: Arch: animatable reconstruction of clothed humans. In: Proceedings of the IEEE/CVF Conference on Computer Vision and Pattern Recognition, pp. 3093–3102 (2020)
7. Ionescu, C., Papava, D., Olaru, V., Sminchisescu, C.: Human3. 6m: large scale datasets and predictive methods for 3D human sensing in natural environments. IEEE Trans. Pattern Anal. Mach. Intell. **36**(7), 1325–1339 (2013)
8. Lewis, J.P., Cordner, M., Fong, N.: Pose space deformation: a unified approach to shape interpolation and skeleton-driven deformation. In: Proceedings of the 27th Annual Conference on Computer Graphics and Interactive Techniques, pp. 165–172 (2000)
9. Liao, Y., Schwarz, K., Mescheder, L., Geiger, A.: Towards unsupervised learning of generative models for 3D controllable image synthesis. In: Proceedings of the IEEE/CVF Conference on Computer Vision and Pattern Recognition, pp. 5871–5880 (2020)
10. Liu, L., Habermann, M., Rudnev, V., Sarkar, K., Gu, J., Theobalt, C.: Neural actor: neural free-view synthesis of human actors with pose control. ACM Trans. Graphics **40**(6), 1–16 (2021)
11. Liu, L., et al.: Neural rendering and reenactment of human actor videos. ACM Trans. Graphics **38**(5), 1–14 (2019)
12. Lombardi, S., Simon, T., Saragih, J., Schwartz, G., Lehrmann, A., Sheikh, Y.: Neural volumes: learning dynamic renderable volumes from images. arXiv preprint arXiv:1906.07751 (2019)

13. Loper, M., Mahmood, N., Romero, J., Pons-Moll, G., Black, M.J.: SMPL: a skinned multi-person linear model. ACM Trans. Graph. **34**(6), 1–16 (2015)

14. Mildenhall, B., Srinivasan, P.P., Tancik, M., Barron, J.T., Ramamoorthi, R., Ng, R.: NeRF: representing scenes as neural radiance fields for view synthesis. In: Vedaldi, A., Bischof, H., Brox, T., Frahm, J.-M. (eds.) ECCV 2020. LNCS, vol. 12346, pp. 405–421. Springer, Cham (2020). https://doi.org/10.1007/978-3-030-58452-8_24

15. Peng, S., et al.: Animatable neural radiance fields for modeling dynamic human bodies. In: Proceedings of the IEEE/CVF International Conference on Computer Vision, pp. 14314–14323 (2021)

16. Peng, S., Neural body: Implicit neural representations with structured latent codes for novel view synthesis of dynamic humans. In: Proceedings of the IEEE/CVF Conference on Computer Vision and Pattern Recognition, pp. 9054–9063 (2021)

17. Penner, E., Zhang, L.: Soft 3D reconstruction for view synthesis. ACM Trans. Graphics **36**(6), 1–11 (2017)

18. Pumarola, A., Corona, E., Pons-Moll, G., Moreno-Noguer, F.: D-NeRF: neural radiance fields for dynamic scenes. In: Proceedings of the IEEE/CVF Conference on Computer Vision and Pattern Recognition, pp. 10318–10327 (2021)

19. Sheng, B., Li, P., Gao, C., Ma, K.L.: Deep neural representation guided face sketch synthesis. IEEE Trans. Visual Comput. Graphics **25**(12), 3216–3230 (2018)

20. Thies, J., Zollhöfer, M., Nießner, M.: Deferred neural rendering: image synthesis using neural textures. ACM Trans. Graphics (TOG) **38**(4), 1–12 (2019)

21. Vakalopoulou, M., et al.: AtlasNet: multi-atlas non-linear deep networks for medical image segmentation. In: Frangi, A.F., Schnabel, J.A., Davatzikos, C., Alberola-López, C., Fichtinger, G. (eds.) MICCAI 2018. LNCS, vol. 11073, pp. 658–666. Springer, Cham (2018). https://doi.org/10.1007/978-3-030-00937-3_75

22. Weng, C.Y., Curless, B., Kemelmacher-Shlizerman, I.: Photo wake-up: 3D character animation from a single photo. In: Proceedings of the IEEE/CVF Conference on Computer Vision and Pattern Recognition, pp. 5908–5917 (2019)

23. Wu, M., Wang, Y., Hu, Q., Yu, J.: Multi-view neural human rendering. In: Proceedings of the IEEE/CVF Conference on Computer Vision and Pattern Recognition, pp. 1682–1691 (2020)

24. Xie, Z., Zhang, W., Sheng, B., Li, P., Chen, C.P.: BaGFN: broad attentive graph fusion network for high-order feature interactions. IEEE Trans. Neural Netw. Learn. Syst. Early Access (2021)

25. Xu, L., Xu, W., Golyanik, V., Habermann, M., Fang, L., Theobalt, C.: Event-Cap: monocular 3d capture of high-speed human motions using an event camera. In: Proceedings of the IEEE/CVF Conference on Computer Vision and Pattern Recognition, pp. 4968–4978 (2020)

26. Zhang, B., Sheng, B., Li, P., Lee, T.Y.: Depth of field rendering using multilayer-neighborhood optimization. IEEE Trans. Visual Comput. Graphics **26**(8), 2546–2559 (2019)

27. Zhao, F., Yang, W., Zhang, J., Lin, P., Zhang, Y., Yu, J., Xu, L.: Human-NeRF: generalizable neural human radiance field from sparse inputs. arXiv preprint arXiv:2112.02789 (2021)

28. Zhou, T., Tucker, R., Flynn, J., Fyffe, G., Snavely, N.: Stereo magnification: learning view synthesis using multiplane images. arXiv preprint arXiv:1805.09817 (2018)

Rec2Real: Semantics-Guided Photo-Realistic Image Synthesis Using Rough Urban Reconstruction Models

Hui Miao[1], Feixiang Lu[2], Tiancheng Xu[1], Liangjun Zhang[2],
and Bin Zhou[1,3(✉)]

[1] State Key Laboratory of Virtual Reality Technology and Systems,
Beihang University, Beijing, China
`zhoubin@buaa.edu.cn`
[2] Robotics and Autonomous Driving Laboratory, Baidu Research, Nashville, USA
[3] Peng Cheng Laboratory, Shenzhen, China

Abstract. We present a novel and effective photo-realistic image generation pipeline using the rough 3D reconstruction models from the Google Earth 3D map. Our goal is to transfer the images (rendered from the 3D models) from the reconstruction style (rec-style) to the photo-realistic style (real-style). To achieve this, we propose a bidirectional transferring approach that takes semantics as guidance. Specifically, we first design an unpaired patch-to-patch image translation method to transfer the images from real-style to rec-style, which can generate paired training data and introduce supervised information. Then, we fine-tune an auto-encoder network to transfer the images from rec-style to real-style. Our approach can generate arbitrary camera-view images with ground-truth annotations automatically, which can be used in AD perception tasks such as 2D detection and instance segmentation. Experiments show the effectiveness of our approach, which can generate diverse and photo-realistic images.

Keywords: Semantics-guided image synthesis · Reconstruction models · Image style transfer

1 Introduction

With the development of artificial intelligence technology, autonomous driving (AD) has made dramatic progress in recent years. Only with the accurate vehicle perception results can autonomous vehicles plan safe paths and be further controlled [27]. Therefore, the perception module plays an essential role in AD. Many AD datasets (*e.g.*, KITTI [7], NuScene [1]) have been widely used in various perception tasks. However, collecting and annotating these real captured data is time-consuming. In addition, these datasets are captured from the fixed camera views, which are limited to acquiring novel view data from the arbitrary camera views. Therefore, some researchers use the model-rendering data, which is obtained from the simulated environments [15,22,31]. In this way, diverse traffic scenarios and weather conditions can be simulated. On the other hand, most

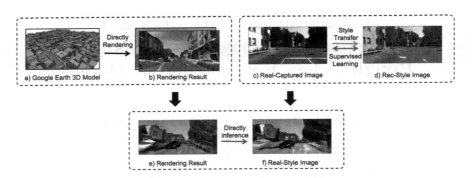

Fig. 1. Three stages of our data generation pipeline.

of these simulators are based on gaming engines (*e.g.*, Unity [22], Unreal [5]) and heavily rely on a large scale of handcrafted 3D assets. Besides, it is not easy to build detailed 3D models and adjust lighting that is consistent with the real world. Thus, many sensor data generation methods (*e.g.*, [3,8,16,28,29]) begin to take advantages of the real-world data. However, these methods also need to collect a large amount of data such as camera images and LiDAR points in advance. In addition, the generated images are limited to the camera views, which are often similar to the initial training images. Our goal is to generate diverse and photo-realistic images with corresponding ground-truth annotations under arbitrary camera views at a low cost. Instead of building a 3D virtual city by artists, it is natural to use the existing urban reconstruction results, such as the Google Earth 3D map.

In photogrammetry, the urban reconstruction can provide both geometric and texture information. The reconstruction results of cities [18] that present the real-world scenes to the greatest extent can be used as 3D model assets in simulators. However, the reconstruction results often have some defects resulting in image warping. Thus, we propose an image quality improvement method to refine coarse images that are rendered from reconstruction models.

In order to make our rendering results based on reconstruction models more realistic, we combine vehicle mesh models with 3D reconstruction urban models to construct traffic scenes as real as possible. Besides, the texture of our vehicle models is reconstructed from the real world, which reduces the domain gap between the rendering data and real-world data. Furthermore, the semantic labels of scenes and the instance labels for vehicles can be generated automatically, which are useful for AD perception tasks such as 2D detection and instance-level segmentation.

In this paper, we propose a novel data generation pipeline that combines the urban and vehicle reconstruction models with deep learning-based image style transfer. As shown in Fig. 1, we design a bidirectional transfer approach. Firstly, we render images from the reconstruction models (*e.g.*, Google Earth 3D map). The style of the initial rendering results can be defined as *rec-style*. Then we transfer real-captured images (*e.g.*, KITTI) to *rec-style*. Similarly, the style of real-captured images can be defined as *real-style*. We can get paired training data for *rec-to-real* training with this *real-to-rec* process, which is guided by the scene semantics. Finally, our *rec-to-real* neural network, which can be seen as an image improvement method, can refine the quality of initial rendering results.

In summary, our contributions are as follows:

1) We present a novel image generation pipeline, which benefits from urban and vehicle reconstruction models. With this method, we can generate photo-realistic images in arbitrary camera views.
2) We design a semantics-guided image quality improvement method, which can refine the initial rendering results and reduce the domain gap between rendering data and real-captured data.
3) Our method simulates the real AD scenarios and can automatically generate multi-view data with corresponding ground-truth annotations. Our results can be used as training data for specific AD perception tasks such as 2D detection and instance-level segmentation. Besides, we compare with other style transfer methods and highlight the fidelity of our results.

2 Related Work

2.1 Data Collection Methods

It is well known that labeled data and neural networks are two critical components of deep learning. To some extent, data plays a fundamental role. To solve the problem of data scarcity, many real-captured datasets (*e.g.*, NuScene [1], and KITTI-360 [12]) have been built and released. However, the process of data collection and annotation is labor-intensive and costly. Therefore, how to generate and synthesize training data with corresponding annotations has been an important topic.

Many approaches [5,22] focus on collecting training data from simulators recently. However, most of these data are based on a rendering engine (*e.g.*, Unreal, Unity), introducing the domain gap between rendering data and real-captured data. Besides, simulators need a lot of handcrafted 3D assets, which are also expensive and time-consuming.

To reduce the domain gap between rendering data and real-captured data, many researchers begin to synthesize data based on real-captured 2D and 3D data. [3,28] collect multi-sensor data in advance, but the preprocessing of these data is time-consuming and labor-intensive. [13,17] use 3D information to edit existing datasets, which limits the diversity of data.

2.2 Urban Scene Reconstruction

With the development of 3D reconstruction and photogrammetry, urban scene reconstruction has gradually received wide attention in the literature. There are two types of techniques that can be used to accomplish this task: 1) Simultaneous Localization and Mapping (SLAM) [4] (*e.g.*, LILO [30], Orb-slam2 [19]);

2) Structure from Motion (SfM) [26] combined with Multi-View Stereo recon-struction (MVS) [9] (*e.g.*, MVE [6], COLMAP [23,24]). The SLAM-based meth-ods generally focus on real-time reconstruction, while the SfM-based techniques reconstruct the urban scene offline. Although the reconstruction results con-tain real-world spatial structure and texture information, the models have some defects (*e.g.*, distortion, incompletion), which limit the use of the reconstruction models.

2.3   Image Style Transfer

The style transfer methods can be categorized into one-to-one image transla-tion [2,10,21] and many-to-many image translation [20,32] according to the input images. Swapping autoencoder [21] encodes an image into a structure code and a texture code and swaps these two components to produce a realistic image, which inspires our image quality improvement method. CycleGAN [32], which translates images from a source domain X to a target domain Y, learns two mapping functions $G: X \rightarrow Y$ and $F: Y \rightarrow X$ combined with two dis-criminators D_X and D_Y. Although these methods can produce high-quality and photo-realistic images, the many-to-many translation techniques cannot capture fine-grained semantic and structure information, and the one-to-one translation methods cannot deal with dataset-to-dataset translation.

3   Method

We argue that high-quality simulation data can be obtained under the con-straints of reconstruction information. However, it is difficult to use the recon-struction models directly, which always exist some defects (*e.g.*, distortion, incompletion). Thus, we present a novel and effective data generation pipeline for producing high-quality data using the reconstruction models. As shown in Fig. 1, our approach can be divided into three stages. Firstly, we obtain the rendering images based on the dynamic vehicle objects and Google Earth 3D Models, which can be seen as the reconstruction results (Sect. 3.1). Then we transfer the style of the existing dataset (*e.g.*, KITTI) to rec-style due to the lack of supervised information for rec-to-real translation (Sect. 3.2). After that, we fine-tune an auto-encoder neural network to transfer the style of images from rec-style to real-style based on the swapping auto-encoder [21] pre-trained model. Finally, we use the trained model to directly infer the rec-style images, which are obtained from the rendering engine (Sect. 3.3).

3.1   Rec-Style Image and Annotation Generation

Our goal is to produce high-quality simulation data based on the reconstruction models, including the dynamic elements and the static urban scene environments. Towards this goal, we need first to build a simulated environment, which can render rec-style images and corresponding annotations automatically.

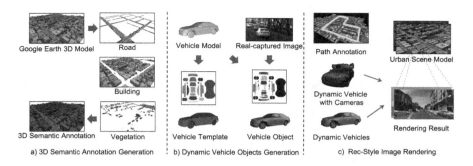

a) 3D Semantic Annotation Generation | b) Dynamic Vehicle Objects Generation | c) Rec-Style Image Rendering

Fig. 2. Our rec-style image synthesis includes three steps: 1) 3D semantic annotation generation; 2) dynamic vehicle elements with reconstruction texture generation; 3) rec-style images with corresponding annotations rendering.

In order to generate accurate semantic annotations, which can be used to guide image refinement, we manually label semantic annotations on the 3D model (Fig. 2(a)). To simulate realistic scenes and generate training data for AD, the dynamic vehicle objects should be added (Fig. 2(b)). Similar to static scene models, we use vehicle models reconstructed from real-captured images as dynamic objects. Specifically, we use the part-based texture inpainting neural network [17] to reconstruct the texture of the vehicles in ApolloCar3D dataset [25]. Then these textures can be mapped to vehicle templates (*e.g.*, [14]), which can synthesize diverse vehicle 3D models.

Based on the reconstructed urban scenes and vehicle models, we simulate dynamic urban scenes from the view of autonomous vehicles (Fig. 2(c)). We manually label paths on the reconstruction models before adding dynamic vehicles into reconstructed urban scenes. After that, vehicles with realistic textures can go along a path randomly. In this process, we simulate four cameras that are virtually mounted on a self-driving vehicle in the 3D scenes. Thus, we can obtain the multi-view image data during the driving. Besides, to maintain the texture color, which is captured from the real world, we don't introduce additional lighting during rendering. Since each vehicle is an independent model, the corresponding mask can be rendered as an instance segmentation annotation, which can be used to calculate the 2D bounding box. In a word, we can get multi-view AD simulation data with corresponding annotations, including semantic segmentation, vehicle instance segmentation, and vehicle 2D bounding boxes.

3.2   Real-to-Rec Style Transfer

While the rec-style rendering results based on the reconstruction models can present real-world scenes to the greatest extent, these images still exist a domain gap due to the defects (*e.g.*, distortion, incompletion) of the reconstructed scenes. Section 3.2 and Sect. 3.3 mainly focus on this problem. Obviously, it is necessary

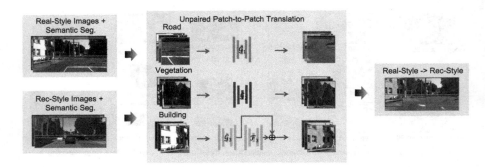

Fig. 3. The patch-to-patch translation neural network for different semantic classes.

to introduce real-style data as references, so we use KITTI [7], which is similar to our rec-style data in the style of scenes. However, it is difficult to only use the KITTI dataset and our rec-style data to improve realism due to a lack of effective supervised information. Thus, we first transfer the KITTI dataset to rec-style, which introduces reconstruction defects. After that, we obtain the paired images that can be used as supervised information to train a neural network to repair defects of images (Sect. 3.3).

Specifically, we train an unpaired patch-to-patch translation neural network based on CycleGAN [32] for each semantic class. As shown in Fig. 3, we consider three semantic classes, including road, vegetation, and building. According to the semantic segmentation map $\mathcal{I}_{seg}$, the pixel-connected regions $Mask_c$ and 2D bounding boxes $Boxes_c$ of the specific class c can be calculated. Based on the original images $\mathcal{I}_{ori}$ and $Boxes_c$, the RGB patches P_c^* of class c can be cropped. P_c^* is image patches for real-style data or rec-style data of class c, and can be further expressed as P_c^{real} and P_c^{rec}. Besides, we define the real-style domain of class c as X_c and the rec-style domain as Y_c.

The patch-to-patch category-specific neural network (Fig. 3) based on Cycle-GAN mainly includes two mapping functions: $\mathcal{G}_c : X_c \rightarrow Y_c$ and $\mathcal{F}_c : Y_c \rightarrow X_c$. It is worth noting that compared to the building, the style of road and vegetation are uniform within each dataset, so the output of $\mathcal{G}_c$ is the result of style transfer for these two classes. On the contrary, each building has its own style, and our goal is to transfer to rec-style while maintaining the original color and basic structure, so we use the combination of the output of $\mathcal{G}_c$ and $\mathcal{F}_c$ as the result of building. This process can be formulated as

$$P_c^{rec'} = \begin{cases} \mathcal{G}_c(P_c^{real}) & c=1,2 \\ \alpha\mathcal{G}_c(P_c^{real}) + (1-\alpha)\mathcal{F}_c(\mathcal{G}_c(P_c^{real})) & c=3 \end{cases}, \quad (1)$$

where α is a weight for the output of $\mathcal{G}_c$ and $\mathcal{F}_c$, and $P_c^{rec'}$ is the image patch with rec-style. After this operation, the patch $P_c^{rec'}$ can be put back into the original image $\mathcal{I}_{ori}$ according to $Mask_c$ and $Boxes_c$, which can be formulated as

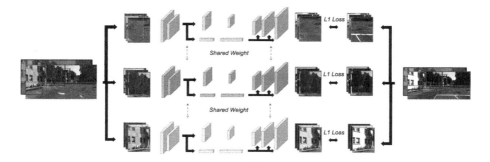

Fig. 4. Rec-to-Real image refinement neural network architecture.

$$\mathcal{I}_{res}^{rec'} = \mathbb{C}_{c=0}^{n}(\mathcal{R}(P_c^{rec'}, \mathcal{I}_{ori}, Mask_c, Boxes_c)), \tag{2}$$

where $\mathcal{R}$ is an operation that puts $P_c^{rec'}$ back to the original image, n is the number of categories (*e.g.*, 3), $\mathbb{C}$ is an operation that combines the result for each category, and $\mathcal{I}_{res}^{rec'}$ is the rec-style image, which is transferred from real-style by semantic category.

3.3   Rec-to-Real Image Refinement

Our approach exploits paired images generated in Sect. 3.2 to train a semantic-based rec-to-real image refinement neural network. Figure 4 shows our network architecture, which is based on the pre-trained swapping autoencoder [21]. Here, we still only consider three categories, including road, vegetation, and building. Similar to the patch extraction in Sect. 3.2, we compute the patch $P_c^{rec'}$ and P_c^{real} of class c from paired images generated in Sect. 3.2. For each semantic class, the rec-style image patches are first encoded as a structure code and a texture code. At the stage of the decoder, the texture code is injected, which is consistent with StyleGAN2 [11]. Based on the output of decoder $P_c^{real'}$, the loss function can be defined as:

$$L = \Sigma_{c=1}^{n} L1(P_c^{real'}, P_c^{real}), \tag{3}$$

where n is the number of classes. After training, we use the trained model to directly improve our rec-style images generated in Sect. 3.1. For the sky part and vehicle part, we use original rendering results, which have fewer defects. Similar to the training process, the rendering images are cropped as patches at the inference stage, which introduces the distortion caused by patch boundaries. Thus, we calculate the mean value on both sides of the patch boundaries to further refine images. Figures 5, 7, and 8 show our final results.

4   Experiments and Discussion

Our approach can be used to generate high-quality data with corresponding annotations based on reconstruction models. The quality of reconstruction models is essential for our data generation, so we first discuss the impact of reconstruction models. Then we compare our method with CycleGAN [32] and evaluate the fidelity of the generated data. Finally, the importance of semantic patches in the generation process is analyzed.

4.1   The Impact of Reconstructed Scenes

Reconstruction models play an important role in our data generation pipeline. As shown in Fig. 5, we compare the initial rendering results and improved results based on models with different qualities. Obviously, the higher quality model produces better rendering results and improved results (green boxes), and the lower quality model produces poorer results (yellow boxes).

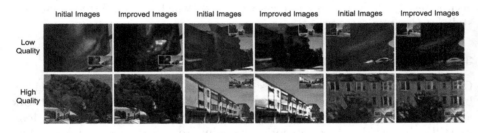

Fig. 5. Initial rendering results and improved results based on models with different quality. The higher quality model produces better results (green boxes), and the lower quality model produces poorer results (yellow boxes). (Color figure online)

4.2   Comparison with Style Transfer Methods

To justify the diversity and fidelity of our generated data, we compare our method with CycleGAN [32], which includes rendering-to-ApolloScapes translation and rendering-to-KITTI translation. Figure 7 shows that the results based on CycleGAN are uncontrollable and overfitted to the reference dataset, i.e. ApolloScapes (the second row) and KITTI (the third row). Moreover, the results in the last three rows are all transferred from the initial rendering results (the first row). The results of the CycleGAN-based method change the semantic structure of the source data (i.e. the initial rendering results). In contrast, our generated data are from the real scenes in the Google Earth 3D map, so the initial rendering data is full of diversity. The most direct way to maintain data diversity is to decrease structure bias towards the initial rendering results.

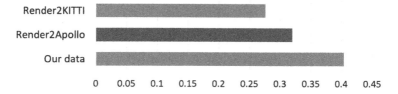

Fig. 6. Results of our human perceptual study where we ask participants to choose which image is more realistic.

As shown in Fig. 6, we conduct a human perceptual study to demonstrate the realism of the improved results, which are compared with CycleGAN results (Fig. 7). We show the same 50 sets of images to 5 participants. Participants are asked to choose the most realistic one in each set of images. Figure 6 shows that our results are more realistic in 40% of the images.

Fig. 7. The first row is the initial rendering results. We compare our method (the last row) with CycleGAN [32], which includes rendering-to-ApolloScapes translation (the second row) and rendering-to-KITTI translation (the third row).

4.3 The Validity of Our Method

In order to verify the validity of our data, we train a *Mask-RCNN* model on the KITTI dataset and evaluate it on different synthetic data, including initial rendering results, handcrafted-model-based rendering data, and our generated data. Table 1 demonstrate that our data has higher fidelity than others.

Table 1. The 2D detection and instance segmentation performance on different synthetic data.

Methods	2D Det. (mAP) ↑	Ins. Seg. (mAP) ↑
Rec-Style data	0.256	0.238
Handcrafted-model-based data	0.307	0.249
Our data	**0.320**	**0.284**

4.4 The Impact of Semantic Patches

As a highlight in Sect. 3.3, we propose a semantics-guided patch-based image improvement method. To demonstrate the effectiveness of semantic patches, we train a network that encodes and decodes the images directly. Figure 8 shows that our patch-based method can learn more details.

Fig. 8. To demonstrate the effectiveness of semantic patches, we train a network that encodes and decodes the images directly (the first row). And the results of our patch-based method are in the second row.

5   Conclusions and Limitations

In this paper, we present a novel and effective photo-realistic image generation pipeline with 3D reconstruction models. Based on the dynamic and static reconstruction results, we can obtain the rendering results with some defects. After unpaired patch-to-patch translation, the paired training data can be generated. Then, we propose an image improvement method to refine the rendering results to produce high-quality images with the paired training data. Although our method can reduce some defects, generating photo-realistic images remains challenging when reconstructed models are heavily distorted, which will be our future work.

Acknowledgement. We thank reviewers for their comments to improve the paper. And we thank Yuexin Ma for her suggestions for this paper. This work was supported in part by National Key Research and Development Program of China (2019YFF0302902), and National Natural Science Foundation of China (61932003).

References

1. Caesar, H., et al.: nuScenes: a multimodal dataset for autonomous driving. arXiv preprint arXiv:1903.11027 (2019)
2. Chen, D., Yuan, L., Liao, J., Yu, N., Hua, G.: StyleBank: an explicit representation for neural image style transfer. In: Proceedings of the IEEE Conference on Computer Vision and Pattern Recognition, pp. 1897–1906 (2017)
3. Chen, Y., et al.: GeoSim: realistic video simulation via geometry-aware composition for self-driving. In: CVPR, pp. 7230–7240 (2021)
4. Davison, A.J.: Real-time simultaneous localisation and mapping with a single camera. In: IEEE International Conference on Computer Vision, vol. 3, pp. 1403–1403. IEEE Computer Society (2003)
5. Dosovitskiy, A., Ros, G., Codevilla, F., Lopez, A., Koltun, V.: CARLA: an open urban driving simulator. In: Conference on Robot Learning, pp. 1–16. PMLR (2017)
6. Fuhrmann, S., Langguth, F., Moehrle, N., Waechter, M., Goesele, M.: MVE-an image-based reconstruction environment. Comput. Graph **53**, 44–53 (2015)
7. Geiger, A., Lenz, P., Stiller, C., Urtasun, R.: Vision meets robotics: the KITTI dataset. Int. J. Robot. Res. **32**(11), 1231–1237 (2013)
8. Guo, H., Sheng, B., Li, P., Chen, C.P.: Multiview high dynamic range image synthesis using fuzzy broad learning system. IEEE Trans. Cybernet. **51**(5), 2735–2747 (2019)
9. Hartley, R., Zisserman, A.: Multiple View Geometry in Computer Vision. Cambridge University Press (2003)
10. Johnson, J., Alahi, A., Fei-Fei, L.: Perceptual losses for real-time style transfer and super-resolution. In: Leibe, B., Matas, J., Sebe, N., Welling, M. (eds.) ECCV 2016. LNCS, vol. 9906, pp. 694–711. Springer, Cham (2016). https://doi.org/10.1007/978-3-319-46475-6_43
11. Karras, T., Laine, S., Aittala, M., Hellsten, J., Lehtinen, J., Aila, T.: Analyzing and improving the image quality of stylegan. In: Proceedings of the IEEE/CVF Conference on Computer Vision and Pattern Recognition, pp. 8110–8119 (2020)
12. Liao, Y., Xie, J., Geiger, A.: Kitti-360: a novel dataset and benchmarks for urban scene understanding in 2D and 3D. arXiv preprint arXiv:2109.13410 (2021)
13. Liu, Z., et al.: 3D part guided image editing for fine-grained object understanding. In: Proceedings of the IEEE/CVF Conference on Computer Vision and Pattern Recognition, pp. 11336–11345 (2020)
14. Lu, F., et al.: PerMO: perceiving more at once from a single image for autonomous driving. arXiv preprint arXiv:2007.08116 (2020)
15. Lu, P., Zhu, F., Li, P., Kim, J., Sheng, B., Mao, L.: Hierarchical rendering system based on viewpoint prediction in virtual reality. In: Magnenat-Thalmann, N., et al. (eds.) CGI 2020. LNCS, vol. 12221, pp. 24–32. Springer, Cham (2020). https://doi.org/10.1007/978-3-030-61864-3_3
16. Manivasagam, S., et al.: LiDARsim: realistic lidar simulation by leveraging the real world. In: CVPR, pp. 11167–11176 (2020)
17. Miao, H., Lu, F., Liu, Z., Zhang, L., Manocha, D., Zhou, B.: Robust 2D/3D vehicle parsing in arbitrary camera views for CVIS. In: Proceedings of the IEEE/CVF International Conference on Computer Vision, pp. 15631–15640 (2021)
18. Moulon, P., Monasse, P., Marlet, R.: Global fusion of relative motions for robust, accurate and scalable structure from motion. In: ICCV, pp. 3248–3255 (2013)

19. Mur-Artal, R., Tardós, J.D.: ORB-SLAM2,: an open-source slam system for monocular, stereo, and RGB-D cameras. IEEE Trans. Rob. **33**(5), 1255–1262 (2017)
20. Park, T., Efros, A.A., Zhang, R., Zhu, J.-Y.: Contrastive learning for unpaired image-to-image translation. In: Vedaldi, A., Bischof, H., Brox, T., Frahm, J.-M. (eds.) ECCV 2020. LNCS, vol. 12354, pp. 319–345. Springer, Cham (2020). https://doi.org/10.1007/978-3-030-58545-7_19
21. Park, T., Zhu, J.Y., Wang, O., Lu, J., Shechtman, E., Efros, A., Zhang, R.: Swapping autoencoder for deep image manipulation. Adv. Neural. Inf. Process. Syst. **33**, 7198–7211 (2020)
22. Rong, G., et al.: LGSVL simulator: a high fidelity simulator for autonomous driving. arXiv preprint arXiv:2005.03778 (2020)
23. Schönberger, J.L., Frahm, J.M.: Structure-from-motion revisited. In: Conference on Computer Vision and Pattern Recognition (CVPR) (2016)
24. Schönberger, J.L., Zheng, E., Frahm, J.-M., Pollefeys, M.: Pixelwise view selection for unstructured multi-view stereo. In: Leibe, B., Matas, J., Sebe, N., Welling, M. (eds.) ECCV 2016. LNCS, vol. 9907, pp. 501–518. Springer, Cham (2016). https://doi.org/10.1007/978-3-319-46487-9_31
25. Song, X. ,et al.: Apollocar3d: a large 3D car instance understanding benchmark for autonomous driving. In: Proceedings of the IEEE Conference on Computer Vision and Pattern Recognition, pp. 5452–5462 (2019)
26. Ullman, S.: The interpretation of structure from motion. Proc. R. Soc. Lond. Ser. B Biol. Sci. **203**(1153), 405–426 (1979)
27. Van, N.D., Sualeh, M., Kim, D., Kim, G.W.: A hierarchical control system for autonomous driving towards urban challenges. Appl. Sci. **10**(10) (2020)
28. Yang, Z., et al.: SurfelGan: synthesizing realistic sensor data for autonomous driving. In: CVPR, pp. 11118–11127 (2020)
29. Zhang, B., Sheng, B., Li, P., Lee, T.Y.: Depth of field rendering using multilayer-neighborhood optimization. IEEE Trans. Visual Comput. Graphics **26**(8), 2546–2559 (2019)
30. Zhang, Y.: LILO: a novel lidar-IMU SLAM system with loop optimization. IEEE Trans. Aerosp. Electr. Syst. **58** (2021)
31. Zhu, F., Lu, P., Li, P., Sheng, B., Mao, L.: Gaze-contingent rendering in virtual reality. In: 37th Computer Graphics International Conference on Advances in Computer Graphics CGI 2020, pp. 16–23 (2020)
32. Zhu, J.Y., Park, T., Isola, P., Efros, A.A.: Unpaired image-to-image translation using cycle-consistent adversarial networks. In: Proceedings of the IEEE International Conference on Computer Vision, pp. 2223–2232 (2017)

3D Digital City Structure Model Based on Image Modeling Technology

Zhen Wang[1,2]($\boxtimes$), Xiaoxuan Li[3], and Hengshuo Xu[4]

[1] Shenyang Ligong University, Shenyang, Liaoning, China
1803562307@pku.edu.cn
[2] Beijing Virtual Simulation and Visualization Engineering Technology Research Center, Beijing, China
[3] Department of Geography and Geoinformation Science, George Mason University, Fairfax, VA, USA
[4] Nankai University, Tianjin, China

Abstract. Considering that the traditional three-dimensional (3D) digital city structure model has a poor reconstruction effect in terms of reconstruction time and optical flow direction, this study proposed a 3D digital city structure model based on image modeling technology. By assessing the error between digital city image points and 3D structure points, 3D structure feature points of the digital city were obtained. Combining with image modeling technology, the matching feature points of 3D structures in the digital city were collected, and the initial matching point pairs of 3D digital city structures were selected. The spatial coordinate system of the digital city was calculated by parametrizing the camera model, and the dynamic texture matching points of the digital city 3D structure were extracted using image modeling technology to determine 3D spatial orientation. Finally, the 3D digital city structure model was constructed by converting the camera coordinate system and urban actual coordinate system. Experimental results suggested that the 3D digital city structure model based on image modeling technology can shorten the reconstruction time of digital city 3D structures and improve the accuracy of the direction angle of optical flow.

Keywords: Image modeling technology · Digital city · 3D structure · Camera

1 Introduction

A Digital city refers to the space virtual information platform constructed by computer technology, multimedia technology, and database technology. By utilizing the remote sensing positioning system and geographic information system to virtually build the natural resources, social resources, and other related information through the network, the 3D description of urban data can be realized to provide essential services for urban development and management [1]. The digital city supports the planning, construction, and development of urban areas through advanced information technology, which can effectively improve comprehensive management efficiency and promote sustainable urban development [2]. Therefore, developing a 3D digital city structure model has become a

N. Magnenat-Thalmann et al. (Eds.): CGI 2022, LNCS 13443, pp. 381–392, 2022.
https://doi.org/10.1007/978-3-031-23473-6_30

priority in relevant fields. Currently, the 3D digital city structure model is still based on the traditional measurement and modeling methods, mainly based on expensive drone images with significant errors and high work intensity. The resulting digital city model is not satisfying for multiple reasons [3]. Therefore, based on image modeling technology, this paper introduces the 3D digital city structure model, which brings new impetus to the development of the digital city.

Pan [4] proposed a 3D digital city structure modeling method based on shape retrieval, which was used to solve the problem of excessive energy consumption when developing 3D structure models. Firstly, the collected urban resource information is calibrated by pixels, and the local feature scene of the digital city is constructed using the image points of a single-scene structure model. The shape feature of the 3D digital city structure model is calculated by averaging the feature values. Then a cluster analysis was applied to determine the local component of the digital city to obtain the distance between the local shapes of the digital city. The simulation of real-world scenarios can be conducted using shape retrieval functions, and finally, 3D digital city structure modeling is completed.

The experimental results show that the 3D digital city structure model based on shape retrieval can effectively reduce the uncertainty in the modeling process and save energy. Zhu [5] uses a UAV to reconstruct the 3D structure model of a building to investigate the performance of the 3D digital city structure model. First, Zhu used aviation equipment to shoot buildings from multiple angles. The sampling analysis was conducted to process collected images and generate a pixel database using similar images. The scanner was used to scan various landmarks of the building, which was then compared to the information in the pixel database. Finally, the image modeling technology is used to reconstruct the 3D digital city structure model on the matching results.

2   Design of 3D Digital City Structure Model

2.1   Development of a Parametric Camera Model

In the process of developing the 3D digital city structure model, the initial values of the camera parameters of the aerial camera and the original coordinate points are determined. These configurations are then compared with the corresponding points in the collected images in 3D space [6] and used to develop a new 3D digital city model using camera-based parameters. The steps for 3D modeling are illustrated as follows:

$K_i = diag(f_i, f_i, 1)$ represents the intrinsic parametric camera model, where f_i is the camera's extrinsic parameters, and K_i is a sequence matrix to map out 3D coordinate points. The parametric camera model Θ_{it} can be expressed using the Eq. (1) below:

$$\Theta_{it} = (\theta_{i1}, \theta_{i2}, \theta_{i3}, t_{i1}, t_{i2}, t_{i3}, f) \tag{1}$$

where θ_{i1}, θ_{i2}, and θ_{i3} are the rotation coefficients in the parametric camera model. t_{i1}, t_{i2}, and t_{i3} are the translation coefficients in the parametric camera model, and f is the camera focus factor. A 3D point in the digital city X can be transformed into a location X' in parametric camera model using the equation of pixel transformation [7] shown below:

$$X' = \frac{(R_i)[X_j - c_i]}{p(\Theta_i, X)} \tag{2}$$

where $p(\Theta, X)$ is the image function, Θ_i is the camera parameter, R_i represents the pixel location of the 3D digital city structure images. X_j is the intersection between the surface and optical axis, and c_i represents any 3D digital city point.

The 3D coordinate point X' was transformed to x' in camera parameter model coordinates using the Eq. (3) below:

$$x' = \begin{bmatrix} fX'_x/X'_z \\ fX'_y/X'_z \end{bmatrix} \tag{3}$$

where fX'_x and fX'_y are the pixel size and value of the 2D coordinate system of the parametric camera model, respectively.

The camera parameter can be calculated using Eq. (4) as follows:

$$\Theta_i = \frac{[x \leftrightarrow x']e}{p(\Theta_i, X)} \times u_{ij}(x)r_{ij} \tag{4}$$

where $x \leftrightarrow x'$ is the corresponding pixel set on the digital city image, r_{ij} is the error between the pixel points of the parametric camera model and the actual 3D model of the digital city, e is the position error distance between the 3D model of the digital model and the real measured point. e and r_{ij} are therefore expressed as follows:

$$e = \sum_{i \in I} \sum_{j \in \chi(i)} f(r_{ij})\Theta_i \tag{5}$$

$$r_{ij} = \frac{m_{ij} - u_{ij}}{\Theta_i \times e} \tag{6}$$

where I represents the 3D digital city pixel set. $\chi(i)$ is the ith point of the camera pixel in digital city.

The three-dimensional coordinates were transformed into camera parameters, and the conversion from three-dimensional coordinates to two-dimensional coordinates was completed. The investigation of the camera parameter model is finished.

2.2 Extraction of Dynamic Texture Matching Points of 3D Digital City Structure Model

Before constructing the 3D digital city structure model based on image modeling technology, the dynamic texture matching points of the 3D digital city structure model are extracted according to the parametric camera model [8], which is illustrated in the steps shown below:

$$N = \sum_{i=0}^{L-1} n_i \tag{7}$$

n_i represents the total number of pixels in the parametric camera model; N is the pixel set acquired by the camera, and L is the dynamic texture value in the camera model. And the percentage of total dynamic texture point values by camera pixel set (p_i) can be calculated by the Eq. (8):

$$p_i = n_i/N \qquad (8)$$

p_A and p_B represent the probability values of the matched points of dynamic texture, which can be calculated as follows:

$$p_A = \sum_{\tau=0}^{\tau} p_i \qquad (9)$$

$$p_B = \sum_{i=\tau+1}^{L-1} p_i \qquad (10)$$

where τ was set to the dynamic texture threshold [9], pixels of the camera image limited by dynamic texture points can be classified into two categories: A and B. A represents the background of the 3D digital city structure model, ranging from 0 to τ. B is the dynamic texture of the digital city, ranging from $\tau + 1 \sim L - 1$ [10].

μ_0, the average dynamic texture value of the camera images, which can be calculated using the Eq. (11):

$$\mu_0 = p_A \mu_A + p_B \mu_B = \sum_{i=0}^{L-1} i p_i \qquad (11)$$

where μ_A and μ_B denote the average dynamic texture A and B in the 3D digital city structure model.

The dynamic texture variance σ^2 of the 3D digital city structure model of categories A and B, therefore, can be calculated using Eq. (12):

$$\sigma^2 = p_A(\mu_A - \mu_0)^2 + p_B(\mu_B - \mu_0)^2 \qquad (12)$$

Assuming that the optimal dynamic texture threshold is τ^* and any point $p(x, y)$ is located in the 3D structure image coordinates of the digital city $I(x, y)$. When the optimal threshold of dynamic texture is $\tau^* < f_{qpt}(x, y)$, the coordinate $p(x, y)$ is located in the dynamic texture area. However, when the threshold is $\tau^* > f_{qpt}(x, y)$, the coordinate $p(x, y)$ is not located in the dynamic texture area. Here the $p(x, y)$ can be expressed as follows:

$$p(x, y) = \begin{cases} 1, f_{qpt}(x, y) > \tau^* \\ 0, f_{qpt}(x, y) \leq \tau^* \end{cases} \qquad (13)$$

A method for building a 3D digital city structure model based on image modeling technology was proposed. The parametric camera model is used to calculate the dynamic texture point positions of the 3D digital city structure model. Then the corresponding points in the digital city model are extracted [11]. θ is the dynamic texture orientation angle of the 3D structure model and can be calculated using the Eq. (14):

$$\theta = \tan(v/\mu) \qquad (14)$$

where v represents the vertical coefficients for dynamic textures of 3D structures and μ is the horizontal coefficient of the dynamic texture of 3D structures.

The dynamic texture matching point $p^*(x, y)$ of the 3D digital city structure model can be obtained using Eq. (15):

$$p^*(x, y) = \begin{cases} 1, fangle(x, y) > \theta \\ 0, fangle(x, y) \leq \theta \end{cases} \tag{15}$$

where $fangle(x, y)$ is the direction threshold of the dynamic texture, and θ is the direction angle [12].

The dynamic texture point position of the 3D digital city structure model was calculated based on the parametric camera model, and then the adaptive texture point threshold $fangle(x, y)$ is determined using a dynamic texture recognition algorithm, and the dynamic texture matching points $p^*(x, y)$ in the 3D structure are extracted based on the pixel points of the parametric camera model.

2.3 Selecting Initial Matching Point Pairs for the 3D Structure of Digital Cities

When searching for initial matching point pairs for the 3D digital city structures, the feature point $\omega'(x, y)$ can be obtained using the Eq. (16) [13]:

$$\omega'(x, y) = \frac{\theta(x, y) \otimes [e, r_{ij}]}{(x, y)} \tag{16}$$

where (x, y) represents the feature point of digital city images, $\theta(x, y)$ is the gratitude of feature point, r_{ij} is the error between digital city image and 3D structure point, and e represents the geolocation error between digital city image and 3D structure point.

The Euclidean distance from the to-be-matched point to the nearby point is calculated using Eq. 17:

$$d(\Phi) = \frac{\sqrt{\{s_{k1}, s_{k2}, s_{k3}\} \times [I_k \cdot I_m]}}{(\lambda) * (\lambda)^n} \tag{17}$$

where $\{s_{k1}, s_{k2}, s_{k3}\}$ is defined as the 3D feature set of digital city image I_k. I_m is the corresponding image of the digital city image I_k. (λ) denotes the mapping relation between the match point and the 2D structure of the digital city. $(\lambda)^n$ denotes the mapping relation between the match point and the 3D structure of the digital city.

The shortest distance between the point v_{ki} and its matching point on I_m can be expressed using the Eq. (18):

$$\Gamma\left(I_m = \frac{I_m}{v_{ki}\{v_{mi}\}} \times \frac{d(\Phi)}{\{s_{k1}, s_{k2}, s_{k3}\}}\right) \tag{18}$$

where $\{v_{mi}\}$ is the point set that will be matched to v_{ki}.

Therefore, 3D digital city structure feature points are derived based on the difference between digital city image points and 3D structure points. By applying the image modeling technology, the 3D digital city structure matching feature points can be obtained, and its initial matching points can also be identified.

2.4 Building 3D Digital City Structure Model

The steps of building a 3D digital city structure model are illustrated as follows: (i) calculating the spatial coordinate system from the parametric camera model; (ii) extracting the matching points of dynamic textures of the 3D digital city structure model using image model building technology and determining 3D spatial orientation [14]; and (iii) constructing the 3D digital city structure model by transforming camera coordinate system and city coordinate system.

Supposing the pixel coordinates of the parametric camera model is $Q_\varepsilon - Y_\varepsilon A_\varepsilon C_\varepsilon$ where C_ε is the horizontal position, A_ε is the vertical position, Y_ε is the width dimension position, $Q_j - YA$ is the digital city coordinate system, $Q_k - VX$ is the camera configuration coordinate system, and H_ω is the city image in the camera [15]. Point H_ω can be calculated from the coordinate system visual variance H_1, H_2:

$$\begin{cases} C_\varepsilon = \frac{xk}{1000q} \\ q_\omega = \chi_1 - \chi_2 \end{cases} \tag{19}$$

where C_ε is the coordinates of H_ω in parametric camera model coordinate system, x is the distance between the horizontal arises, k is the actual focal length of the camera, q_ω is the visual difference of the parametric camera model, and χ_1 and χ_2 are the actual horizontal and vertical coordinates of the actual pixels, respectively.

By expressing the 3D city structure image as the parametric camera model pixel coordinate system, the horizontal and vertical coordinate positions in the 3D digital city structure will not change. After relocating the initial position [16], the digital city 3D structure's transformation can be achieved using Eq. (20):

$$\begin{bmatrix} i \\ j \\ 1 \end{bmatrix} = \begin{bmatrix} \vartheta_i & 0 & -V_0\vartheta_i \\ 0 & \vartheta_j & -v_0\vartheta_j \\ 0 & 0 & 1 \end{bmatrix} \cdot \begin{bmatrix} V \\ v \\ 1 \end{bmatrix} = N_2 \begin{bmatrix} V \\ v \\ 1 \end{bmatrix} \tag{20}$$

where N_2 is the transformation matrix of the 3D digital city structure model, (v, v) is the horizontal and vertical coordinates on the parametric camera model H_ω, (v_0, v_0) represents the horizontal and vertical coordinates on the original 3D digital city structure coordinate system, ϑ_i means the width of the pixel of the 3D digital city structure image [17, 18], and ϑ_j denotes the height of the pixel of the 3D digital city structure image. Based on the pinhole imaging principle, the pixel width and height coordinates of the point H_ω is:

$$\begin{cases} Y_e = C_\omega \frac{i_1}{k} \\ A_e = C_\omega \frac{j_1}{k} \end{cases} \tag{21}$$

where (i_1, j_2) are the coordinates of the digital city image captured by the camera. Let $Q_\omega - Y_\omega A_\omega C_\omega$ to be the actual city coordinate system, C_ω represents the height position of the building of the city, A_ω represents the front position of the corresponding digital city 3D structure, Y_ω represents the horizontal position of the digital city 3D structure. Then the transformation of the parametric camera model to the 3D digital city structure model can be achieved via the following equation:

$$
\begin{bmatrix} Y_{\overline{\omega}} \\ A_{\overline{\omega}} \\ C_{\overline{\omega}} \\ 1 \end{bmatrix} = \begin{bmatrix} 1 & 0 & 0 & 0 \\ 0 & \cos(\alpha) & -\sin(\alpha) & 0 \\ 0 & \sin(\alpha) & \cos(\alpha) & 0 \\ 0 & z & 0 & 1 \end{bmatrix} \cdot \begin{bmatrix} Y_{\varepsilon} \\ A_{\varepsilon} \\ C_{\varepsilon} \\ 1 \end{bmatrix} = \begin{bmatrix} Y_{\varepsilon} \\ A_{e} \\ C_{e} \\ 1 \end{bmatrix} \tag{22}
$$

According to Eq. (22), the 3D digital city structure model can be constructed by transforming the camera coordinate system and the actual city coordinate system [19, 20]:

$$
\begin{bmatrix} Y_{\overline{\omega}} \\ A_{\overline{\omega}} \\ C_{\overline{\omega}} \\ 1 \end{bmatrix} = N \begin{bmatrix} i_1 \\ j_2 \\ 1 \end{bmatrix} \tag{23}
$$

In summary, the principles of developing the 3D digital city structure model were sufficiently explained, which can be further implemented to construct 3D digital city structures.

3 Comparative Experiment Analysis

3.1 Simulation Experiment Platform Setup

TO verify the effectiveness of applying the image modeling technology in developing the 3D digital city structure model, 3D structure images were selected from the 3D digital city structure database which is a computer system operated in Widows 7 with 4.2 GHz and 4 GB memory. The system was coded using C++ programming language and Matlab. The simulation interface is shown in Fig. 1.

Fig. 1. Simulation interface

3.2 Experiment Result Analysis

Based on the method proposed in this paper, a 3D digital city structure model was constructed, and a visualization process was applied to the study areas, as shown in Fig. 2.

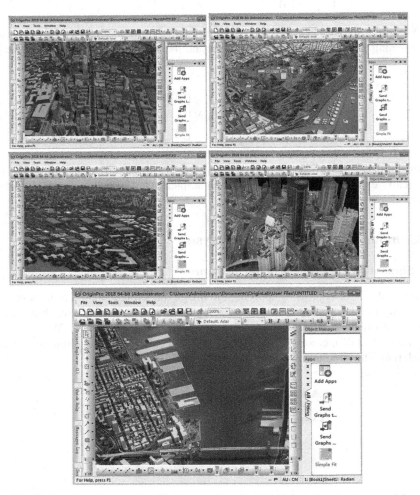

Fig. 2. Preview of some visualization results using 3D digital city structure model.

Based on the results shown in Fig. 2, the 3D digital city structure model developed in this paper has several distinct advantages (Fig. 2): (1) detailed textures, (2) boundaries are not blurred, (3) details of cities are accurately presented and reconstructed, (4) better visualization effects.

On the platform shown in Fig. 1, digital city structure models from [4] and [5] were used to compare with the 3D digital city structure model proposed in this paper. The experimental factors include the model building time and optical flow direction angle. Here are the results of the model building time as shown in Fig. 3, a–c for study area 1.

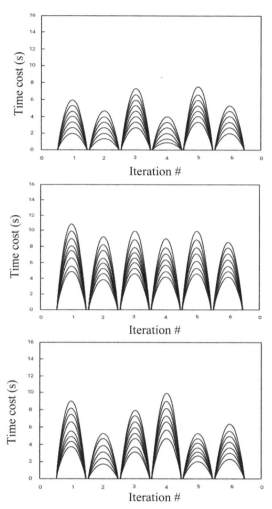

Fig. 3. Test results of 3D digital city structure model: (a) image-based 3D digital city structure model (upper panel), (b) 3D digital city structure model from [4] (middle panel), (c) 3D digital city structure model from [5] (lower panel)

It took less than 8 s for the proposed 3D digital city structure model to accomplish the modeling tasks. In comparison, it took 8 to 11 s for the 3D digital city structure model from [4] and 5 to 10 s for the 3D digital city structure model from [5] to finish the process. Considering the time cost of three 3D digital city structure models, the 3D digital city structure model from the literature [4] took the longest time in the multiple experiments. The image modeling technology for the 3D digital city structure model took the shortest time during the construction process. The evident results suggested that constructing a parametric camera model can (i) obtain the camera's position and states, (ii) provide reliable data support for the digital city structure model rebuilding, and (iii) substantially reduce the time cost during the reconstruction process. Furthermore, the comparison results of three different 3D digital city structure models are shown in Table 1.

Table 1. The time cost of constructing 3D structures using different models

Study area #	Time cost of model reconstruction/s		
	3D digital city structure model based on image modeling technology	3D digital city structure model [4]	3D digital city structure model [5]
2	23.6	56.9	96.4
3	25.8	68.4	98.7
4	27.9	69.3	95.6
5	25.4	78.9	87.1
Average	25.7	68.4	94.5

It can be found that the maximum, average, and minimum time costs of the 3D digital city structure model based on image modeling technology are 27.9 s, 25.7 s, and 23.6 s. These numbers are all much less than those using other modeling technology [4, 5], indicating that the proposed method has the highest efficiency performance and can be widely used and promoted. The relatively low cost is mainly due to the camera parameter settings used in the proposed model, such that the status and location of the camera were set to support the information data construction in the 3D digital city structure model. It is therefore verified that the imaged-based modeling building technology for the 3D digital city structure model has high efficiency for model reconstruction.

In terms of the optical flow direction angle (θ), the more accurate the optical flow direction angle calculation, the higher the accuracy of the digital 3D image matching point and the higher the accuracy of the digital city 3D model. The optical flow direction angles from the three 3D digital city structure models are shown in Table 2.

Table 2. Results of optical flow direction angle using 3D digital city structure models

Test #	Optical flow direction angle			
	3D digital city structure model based on image modeling technology	3D digital city structure model from [4]	3D digital city structure model from [5]	Actual optical flow direction angle
1	30	32	30	30
2	35	34	30	35
3	20	20	35	20
4	65	65	50	65
5	40	42	35	40

Table 2 showed that after five iterations, the optical flow direction angle calculated from the proposed 3D digital city structure model perfectly matched the actual optical flow direction angle, demonstrating that the accuracy of the developed 3D digital city structure model reached 100%. The 3D digital city structure model from the literature [4], however, can only achieve 40% and 20% accuracy, respectively. By comparing the calculation results from the three 3D digital city structure models, it can be concluded that the 3D digital city structure model based on the imaged modeling technology in this paper can accurately calculate the optical flow direction angle and has higher accuracy.

4 Conclusion

This paper proposed an imaged modeling technology for the 3D digital city structure model research, which was used to develop a novel 3D digital city structure model by (i) parametrizing the camera model, (ii) extracting dynamic texture matching points of the 3D digital city structure model, and (iii) determining the digital city 3D structure's initial matching point pairs. The experiment results show that the model proposed has better rebuild effects in terms of clear feature boundaries, detailed city textures, and relatively low time costs.

References

1. 江明明. 基于倾斜摄影测量技术的三维数字城市建模. 测绘与空间地理信息000(003), 189–190 (2017)
2. 朱庆, 李世明, 胡翰,等. 面向三维城市建模的多点云数据融合方法综述. 武汉大学学报(信息科学版)43(12), 209–218 (2018)
3. 余忠迪, 李辉, 巴芳,等. 基于消费者级无人机的城市三维建模.国土资源遥感30(117(02)), 70–75 (2018)
4. 潘美莲. 单幅结构场景图像的三维建模与仿真技术. 计算机仿真036(002), 166–170 (2019)

5. 朱剑伟. 一种基于无人机影像的建筑物三维模型重建方法. 测绘通报**2018**(S1), 129–133 (2018)
6. 田婧. 基于立体成像技术的三维环境设计建模方法研究. 现代电子技术**43**(575(24)), 80–82+86 (2020)
7. 余忠迪, 李辉, 巴芳,等. 基于消费者级无人机的城市三维建模. 国土资源遥感**030**(002), 67–72 (2018)
8. 葛余超, 李锋, 詹勇. 一种基于三维模型的数据降维方法. 测绘通报**2019**(S2), 89–91+100 (2019)
9. 刘志, 潘晓彬. 基于渲染图像角度结构特征的三维模型检索方法. 计算机科学**045**(0z2), 251–255 (2018)
10. 徐金财、李朝奎、陈建辉. 一种基于3ds Max与Smart 3D的三维模型构建方法. 测绘通报**524**(11), 64–68 (2020)
11. 任帅, 王震, 苏东旭,等. 基于三维模型贴图与结构数据的信息隐藏算法. 通信学报**40**(05), 215–226 (2019)
12. 张宝平, 黄庆丰. 关于三维城市景观实体准确测量优化建模仿真. 计算机仿真**35**(05), 235–238 (2018)
13. 杜金莲, 徐硕, 赵枫朝. 基于二维数字地图的三维城市建模方法研究. 系统仿真学报**30**(10), 119–125 (2018)
14. 王装, 魏冬梅. 城市居住空间形态特征数字化建模仿真研究. 计算机仿真**036**(007), 219–222 (2019)
15. 陈苹. 多平台摄影结合在同项目多区域多精度快速实景三维建模中的应用. 测绘通报**2019**(S2), 144–146 (2019)
16. Santhanavanich, T., Coors, V.: CityThings: an integration of the dynamic sensor data to the 3D city model. Environ. Plan. B **48**(3), 417–432 (2021)
17. Zheng, L., An, H., Zhang, Y.: Research on 3D data modeling of virtual city environment based on GIS. Microprocess. Microsyst. **12**(1), 103392–103399 (2020)
18. Naoki, K., Tomohiro, F., Nobuyoshi, Y.: Future landscape visualization using a city digital twin: integration of augmented reality and drones with implementation of 3D model-based occlusion handling. J. Comput. Des. Eng. **15**(2), 2–16 (2022)
19. Youssef, A., Prisyazhnuk, S., Petrov, A., et al.: Using free lidar data with aerial photogrammery images for construction of 3D building models for openstreetmap. IOP Conf. Ser.: Mater. Sci. Eng. **753**(1), 032081–032092 (2020)
20. Feng, Z., Li, H., Zeng, W., et al.: Topology density map for urban data visualization and analysis. IEEE Trans. Visual Comput. Graph. **27**(2), 828–838 (2021)

AR and User Interfaces

Augmented Reality-Based Home Interaction Layout and Evaluation

Ningxin Chen, Zheng Lu, Xinhui Yu, Liuming Yang, Pengfei Xu[✉], and Yachun Fan

Beijing Normal University, Beijing 100875, China
xupf@bnu.edu.cn

Abstract. This paper proposes an indoor scene layout interactive assessment method based on augmented reality (AR) to solve the problems of lacking an intuitive and systematic assessment of indoor scene layout and inefficient human moving for layout readjustment. This paper evaluates the indoor layout from accessibility, ventilation, and illumination and proposes the home interactive evaluation system AR-IHES (Augmented Reality Based Interactive Home Evaluation System) to give evaluation opinions and layout adjustment methods. The accessibility is assessed by using an avatar free-roaming in the scene, ventilation by simulating the natural wind field with a particle system, and illumination by calculating the cumulative influence of each light source at each point of the room. Then, we project the layout into AR, and users wearing AR devices obtain rich evaluation opinions, and freely adjust the design through gestures. The experimental results show that the assessment method can provide real-time feedback of objective and scientific evaluation results and provide users with corresponding modification opinions, which solve both the problems of tricky indoor scene layout evaluation and inefficient adjustment.

Keywords: Indoor scene evaluation · Avatar · Interactive layout

1 Introduction

Indoor scene layout implicitly affects people's living experience, daily mood, and efficiency [1, 2]. The scientific and in line with a personal assessment of indoor layout has important practical significance. A comprehensive indoor layout assessment method should consider both the subjective feelings of people and the scientific nature of the layout itself, which is a complicated problem. Firstly, in assessing personal feelings, it is often necessary to walk into the actual scene. When the indoor layout does not meet expectations, it is required to readjust the indoor layout manually; such assessment methods are time-consuming and laborious. Secondly, there are limited methods to evaluate the scientific nature of the indoor layout, mainly using specific indicators in engineering simulation, in which the range of evaluation objects is narrow, and its arithmetic power requirements are high [3–5].

This paper proposes an indoor scene layout interactive system based on AR (AR-IHES). Our main contributions are as follows: (1) We propose a scientific, objective,

N. Magnenat-Thalmann et al. (Eds.): CGI 2022, LNCS 13443, pp. 395–406, 2022.
https://doi.org/10.1007/978-3-031-23473-6_31

and effective assessment method, which combines three key factors: accessibility, ventilation, and illumination. These three factors can greatly influence people's feelings in an indoor scene. (2) We use an avatar as an important agent in the whole assessment process which means we can simulate people with different heights, weights, and other features to get an overall perspective. Avatar will be roaming the indoor scene to get the assessment. This paper proposes a virtual human expansion indoor roaming algorithm based on the traditional algorithm to improve the long-distance roaming ability to the marginal scenes by reasonably expanding the room area. (3) We add an interactive feature to the assessment which enables people to wear AR headsets, freely walk, feel and adjust indoor scene layout. Users can integrate their own preferences with scientific suggestions to get the final satisfactory layout.

2   Related Work

2.1   Indoor Scene Layout Assessment

Indoor layout assessment needs to be based on a priori knowledge of ergonomics. In the illumination assessment, the Kruithof curve defines the relationship between different color temperatures, illumination levels, and human comfort [6], and Kakitsuba et al. did a further study on it [7]. In the ventilation assessment, Wargocki confirmed it significantly impacts human comfort and health [8]. Huang, Hygge, et al. established the relationship between indoor ventilation and many humane factors. [9, 10]. Ching found that windows and doors always play a significant role in the ventilation process [11].

Existing Indoor layout assessments are mainly used to solve the problems that arise in the automatic synthesis of indoor scenes. Issues related to scene synthesis results are monotonous and cannot match real-time reality. Yu et al. propose a method to automatically add details at the location pointed by the user [12]. Savva et al. use the relationship between indoor objects to generate suggested indoor objects [13]. Merrell et al. use priories to synthesize the design, but they do not consider people's subjective preferences, and the final layout has convergence [14]. To functionally assess indoor suitability in a specific location, Zhang et al. extract objects from 2D floor plans and established relationships between objects and objects [15]. In addition, Zhao et al. divide the evaluation levels of the artistic furniture layout rationality index and finally realized the standard evaluation of creative furniture layout rationality [16], but the application to real life is not wide enough. Fu et al. propose the human-centered metrics HCMs, which integrate the human-object and human-environment relationships [17] but fail to combine the natural human feelings, lacking the participation of real people.

2.2   Avatar-Based Indoor Scene Layout

In the individual reconstruction to simulate the natural person, it is used to relate the floor area of the avatar with height and weight [18] and Liu substitutes the Kuehnapfel formula [19] to calculate the human surface area BSA (m^2). A common approach for avatar is to make it move iteratively and accomplish tasks such as planning the fastest escape path through real-time statistics [20–22]. There are two main types of roaming algorithms for indoor pathfinding [23]. One is to compute the indoor scene directly and plan the complete path, such as the improved fast extended random tree algorithm (M-RRT) [24] with the improved sparse A* search (SAS) algorithm [25]. The other is by directly moving objects [26]. However, these algorithms face problems such as the long-running time, and unreachable marginal space, while the avatar expansion indoor roaming algorithm proposed in this paper can solve these problems.

2.3 Interactive Indoor Scene Layout

AR "seamlessly" integrates real-world information with virtual and allows people to interact. Liebmann et al. respond to 3D objects by matching markers to user input tracks and using tags such as the corresponding one-to-one with interactive events [27]. Vuletic's system integrates virtual reality and human/finger pose tracking in real-time [28]. Yoon proposes the ease of technical implementation is a higher priority in practice [29]. Regarding specific interaction tools, Riedlinger compares HoloLens and Tango and gives more detailed advice on task scheduling [30]. In conclusion, this paper is the first work to combine augmented reality with indoor interaction layout evaluation, making the indoor layout more convenient and evaluation results more intuitive.

3 Overview

This section outlines the augmented reality-based indoor scene interaction evaluation system AR-IHES, summarized in Fig. 1. This paper first applies augmented reality to indoor interaction layouts to solve the problem of users who cannot quickly move and add new furniture. Users wearing HoloLens2 augmented reality devices, using gestures, can achieve a variety of functions such as adding, deleting, zooming in and out of furniture, and personalizing their rooms. In addition to the interactive layout, augmented reality will enable users to fully feel the details of ventilation and illumination. Every layout is not perfect. Next, there may be many practical problems, such as narrow aisles, the overall room utilization is not extensive, etc. Therefore, this paper proposes an assessment method based on avatar assessing accessibility, ventilation, and illumination, which will be elaborated on Sects. 4–5. Finally, the method makes specific suggestions for the placement and size of doors, windows, and lamps.

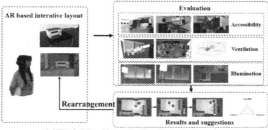

Fig. 1. Overview of the AR-IHE. Use AR to design personalized scenes. The system evaluates accessibility, ventilation, and illumination, gives suggestions, and the user makes a re-layout.

4 Accessibility Assessment Based on Avatar Roaming

We propose to use avatars to imitate humans and perform interactive operations such as purposeful walking, and viewing to determine the accessibility of indoor objects, the range of vision, etc. The assessment results align with interior design knowledge.

4.1 Avatar-Based Indoor Scene Layout

The traditional avatar random roaming always lacks roaming the edges and it's unacceptable in the indoor scene layout. We propose an indoor scene expansion roaming algorithm to solve this by reasonably expanding the room area, repeatedly detecting the furniture position in the time frame sequence, and changing the roaming trajectory of the virtual human in real-time. The algorithm steps are as follows:

- *Input*: Avatar roaming range
- *Output*: Avatar roaming result.
- *Step1*: Open a new clock cycle and the guide block appears randomly in the roaming range acting as the endpoint of the avatar's pathfinding.
- *Step2*: The avatar pursues the guide block with the shortest path.
- *Step3*: judge whether the position relationship between the avatar and the guide block satisfies inequality (2); if it does, repeat Step1; otherwise, continue.
- *Step4*: Determine whether the avatar chases the guide block for more than one clock cycle; if it is satisfied, repeat Step1; otherwise, continue Step2.
- *Step5*: If the user ends the roaming, it ends.

The roaming room is considered a rectangle. The absolute position of the avatar in the room is R, $R = [P_{x1}, P_{x2}, P_{y1}, P_{y2}]$, where P_{x1}, P_{x2} is the distance from the left to right sides, P_{y1}, P_{y2}, the top to bottom. The actual roaming position range quadratic is R', whose area is larger and $P'_{x1}, P'_{x2}, P'_{y1}, P'_{y2}$ are the corresponding values. Let k be the expansion factor Δt, and the R, R' should satisfy the following equation.

$$\min\{P_{x1} - P_{x2}, P_{y1} - P_{y2}\} \leq k|P'_i - P_i| \leq \max\{P_{x1} - P_{x2}, P_{y1} - P_{y2}\} \quad (1)$$

Denote $|P'_i - P_i|$ an expansion factor, and it is determined as a hyperparameter 10. For non-rectangular rooms, the algorithm is still applicable by splitting the non-rectangular room into rectangles, as shown in Fig. 2.

When the guide block location P_L is determined, the avatar calls the pathfinding algorithm to pursue it, following the shortest path principle. When the following decision formula calculating the angle between P_a and P_L is satisfied:

$$\frac{P_a \cdot P_L}{|P_a||P_L|} \leq \Delta c \quad (2)$$

, guide block changes its position randomly. Usually, P_a and P_L satisfy (2) and go to the next cycle. However, the obstacle will lead to a stationary blocking stat. The system

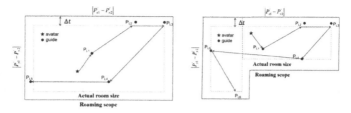

Fig. 2. Avatar roaming schematic, first is a rectangle, and second is a non-rectangular room

introduces a clock mechanism, when the virtual human moves more than one clock T, it will forcibly changes the L position and enters the next cycle,

$$T = \frac{d}{v * k} \tag{3}$$

, where d is the length of the sloping side of the room, v is the virtual human moving speed, and k is the jitter coefficient to cover the large area or long distance scenario.

4.2 Accessibility Assessment

The simulation process should be "natural and objective" [27]. The system simulates humans with different heights, weights, and ages and translates them to the avatar's height H, floor space S, and daily walking speed V. The system first calculates the floor surface S as BSA (m^2) by substituting the Kuehnapfel formula [26],

$$BSA = 0.0151 \times W^{0.4259} \times H^{0.5751} \tag{4}$$

To evaluate the home accessibility, the system represents the ground in a matrix, and the number of units of avatar N are based on the Chinese rule of Nine,

$$N = \lceil 52 \times BSA \rceil \tag{5}$$

The system is designed with five types of avatars representing different persons, ID1~5 for adult females, adult males, elderly, children, and the obese. The movement information is represented by the roaming matrix M_r, which is initialized to 0. In each frame, the points of the avatar passing through increment by 1. The currently available area ratio is obtained by calculating the ratio of non-zero values within one clock cycle, which is E_a. Search M_r, the maximum dwell time point reflects the location of the layout that may be modified. With sufficient time, Table 1 shows the same avatar within different layouts, and Fig. 3 shows the different views with different avatars.

Table 1. Roaming in different Tests using ID1 adult female adult

No.	Schematic	Available	Suggestion
a		66.13%	The layout is more reasonable.
b		47.03%	Modify the location of the yellow cabinet in the lower right corner of Figure 5b
c		26.90%	Modify the black table at the bottom of Figure 5c.

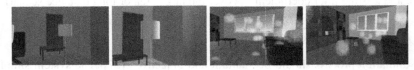

Fig. 3. Comparative display chart of virtual human view, from the left to right, top to down, the figure is 20 cm view, 100 cm view, 150 cm view, small animal view

5 Ventilation and Illumination Assessment

Factors such as ventilation and lighting are fully considered for a well-designed indoor scene. This system combines numerical evaluation with AR feeling while giving corresponding suggestions. Firstly, ventilation assessment uses a particle system to simulate the flow of wind. In the illumination section, the cumulative illumination impact of each light source is calculated to evaluate the indoor lighting situation.

5.1 Indoor Ventilation Assessment

Several studies have found windows and doors always matter and air often flows from the window to the door [11]. Therefore, we bind the wind field with them [17] as in Fig. 4-a, and the remaining vents such as exhaust fans will be given other fields. Firstly, users can feel the wind in AR since the particles are visible, as in Fig. 4 b–c.

Next, the room ventilation performance will be assessed in terms of the extent and distribution of particle dispersion, following the ideal fluid motion differential equations - Euler's set of equations.

$$\begin{cases} \frac{du}{dt} = \frac{\partial u}{\partial t} + u\frac{\partial u}{\partial x} + v\frac{\partial u}{\partial y} + w\frac{\partial u}{\partial z} = f_x - \frac{1}{\rho}\frac{\partial p}{\partial x} \\ \frac{dv}{dt} = \frac{\partial v}{\partial t} + u\frac{\partial v}{\partial x} + v\frac{\partial v}{\partial y} + w\frac{\partial v}{\partial z} = f_y - \frac{1}{\rho}\frac{\partial p}{\partial y} \\ \frac{dw}{dt} = \frac{\partial w}{\partial t} + u\frac{\partial w}{\partial x} + v\frac{\partial w}{\partial y} + w\frac{\partial w}{\partial z} = f_z - \frac{1}{\rho}\frac{\partial p}{\partial z} \end{cases} \quad (6)$$

Fig. 4. a: Indoor layout wind field schematic; b–c: virtual human in different parts of the room

, where $u, v, and w$ are the velocity components of the mass respectively, and the initial velocity is $0; f_x, f_y$ and f_z are the forces per unit mass acting on the mass, specifically the combined force of the wind field; and p is the mass velocity.

The room is divided evenly into s cells, preset to 10^3 as a hyperparameter. The room is represented by a space matrix V_r, indicating the number of particles per unit space, initialized to 0. The assessment starts at t_{stable} seconds after particle distribution reaches a steady state, at which time the set of particle coordinates P is obtained, then traverse P to update V_r,

$$V_r[a][b][c] += 1, if Pi.location in cell(a, b, c) \tag{7}$$

After updating the matrix, the sum of non-zero points in the matrix can be calculated as S, which represents the area reached by the particles. In addition, the number of air changes is also a critical reference indicator [32] and we will compute it as T. The evaluation of the ventilation E_v is obtained by combining above two:

$$E_v = \sigma_1(1 - \frac{T - 0.45}{0.25}) + \sigma_2(\frac{S}{1000}) \tag{8}$$

, where σ_1, σ_2 are the evaluation weights, $\sigma_1, \sigma_2 \in [0, 1], \sigma_1 + \sigma_2 = 1$.

5.2 Illumination Assessment

Indoor light assessment is similar to ventilation. Firstly, users can directly feel the light intensity in AR, as in Fig. 5. Secondly, the room is divided into 10^3 cells for a 3D matrix $I_r, I_r(x, y, z)$ indicating the influence of each light source on (x, y, z) unit,

$$I_r(x, y, z) = \sum_i w_i \times \alpha_i \tag{9}$$

w_i is i-th light intensity, when it is parallel light, $\alpha_i = 1$; when a point light,

$$\alpha_i = \frac{1}{(x - x_i)^2 + (y - y_i)^2 + (z - z_i)^2} \tag{10}$$

Unlike ventilation, light does not need to be simulated in the whole room while only focus on the cells related to people standing and sitting.

The illumination assessment is mainly based on the Building Lighting Design Standard to determine the average illuminance (Eav),

$$Eav = \phi \times N \times CU \times K \div S \tag{11}$$

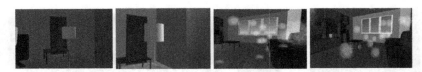

Fig. 5. In the left 2 figures, when the user approaches the lamp, it automatically lights up; away, turns off. In the right 2 figures, the user can feel the natural light within a day.

, where Φ is the total luminous flux value, N is the number of lamps; CU is the space utilization coefficient; K = 0.8; S is the floor area.

After calculation, we will compare it with the standard value and make suggestions. Assume the sum of all light sources is L_{sum}, and the final illumination evaluation E_l can be obtained by combining the illumination distribution with Eav,

$$E_l = \beta_1 \times \sum_{x,y,z}^{10} \frac{I_r(x, y, z)}{0.5 \times L_{SUM}} + \beta_2 \times Eav \tag{12}$$

6 Experiment

In this section, we first show representative evaluation results in terms of accessibility, ventilation, and lighting in different indoor layouts, then we do a user study to validate the effectiveness. Experiments are tested on Intel Core i7-12700 4.70 GHz 16 GB RAM PC, 2019.4.27f1c1 unity, HoloLens2.0. We used a dataset of Alibaba 3D Future Model, containing all common indoor objects.

6.1 Evaluation Results Under Different Layouts

Table 2 shows the comparison of the results of the evaluation methods under three different layouts in the same bedroom scene which clearly reflect the assessment result. Table 3 gives the above results in a typical non-rectangular scene.

Table 2. Assessment of accessibility, light, and ventilation under different layouts. At the accessibility row, the darker color means obstruction; ventilation, more wind flowing through the place; illumination, strong light at that place.

	Layout 1	Layout 2	Layout 3
Accessibility			
Ventilation			
Illumination			

Table 3. Evaluation of accessibility, ventilation, and light in non-rectangular rooms

	Accessibility	Ventilation	Illumination
Heat Map			

6.2 User Study

A total of eight users were invited to conduct the experiment. The overall user experiment was divided into three parts: (1) Users were introduced to how to use the system. (2) Two scenes were randomly assigned to each user, and the users performed two rounds of interaction layouts with system suggestions (3) Each user fill in a questionnaire and we ask more persons to calculate the scenes.

Table 4 shows the evaluation results of four types of scenes, three different layouts and one after another. It is clear that grades generally increase in the two turns.

Furthermore, we design a questionnaire: Q1: "Accessibility assessment is valid." Q2: "Ventilation assessment is valid." Q3: "Lighting assessment is valid." Q4: "AR interaction helps you" Q5: "System is easy" Q6: "You'd like to recommend this system to others." The options are 0–4 from totally disagree to strongly agree. Results show users are generally satisfied with at least 2.625 on average and we do not encounter extremely bad answers. Among them, a 25-year-old computer practitioner who will start a family said that he would be willing to use this system for his new house decoration. We also asked 30 users to score all layouts from 0 (bad) to 1 (good) in Fig. 6. The overall

Table 4. Four groups of 3D scenes with different layouts, and the corresponding evaluation scores. Take the children's room as an example. Scene 1 is the original layout in which the carpet cushions and cabinets are so close. The user gets the advice and adjusts them and moves the window from personal preferences. Then system assesses again that the wind field distribution range is small after window adjustment. The user adjusts it back and subsequently.

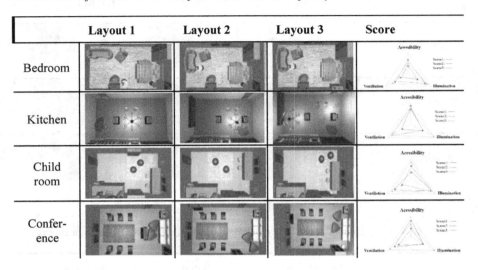

	Layout 1	Layout 2	Layout 3	Score
Bedroom				
Kitchen				
Child room				
Conference				

assessment is good. Considering subjective user preferences, it is acceptable that layout 2 has a lower score in the bedroom and children's room.

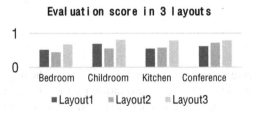

Evaluation score in 3 layouts

Bedroom   Childroom   Kitchen   Conference

■ Layout1   ■ Layout2   ■ Layout3

Fig. 6. Three layouts generated by the interaction evaluation in four different sets of scenarios, scored by 30 users respectively

The current approach has several limitations. First, our approach focuses on large home objects, for which small objects lack corresponding evaluation. Second, the assessment algorithms cannot characterize richer scene semantics.

7 Conclusion

This paper proposes an AR-IHES interactive evaluation system to assess the interior scene layout and assist users in optimizing it in AR. The assessment is in three parts: accessibility, ventilation, and illumination based on the avatar and interactive indoor scene layout. The results show it can provide real-time feedback and scientific suggestions which solves inefficient indoor layout adjustment and difficult assessment.

Acknowledgements. This research was partially supported by the National Key R&D Program of China (No. 2020YFC1523302), National Nature Science Foundation of China (No. 61972041, No. 62072045), and Innovation & Transfer Fund of Peking University Third Hospital (No. BYSYZHKC2021110).

References

1. Kim, J., Hong, T., Jeong, J., et al.: An integrated psychological response score of the occupants based on their activities and the indoor environmental quality condition changes. Build. Environ. **123**, 66–77 (2017)
2. Kim, J., Dear, R.D.: Workspace satisfaction: the privacy-communication trade-off in open-plan offices. J. Environ. Psychol. **36**, 18–26 (2013)
3. Chiang, C.M., Lai, C.M., Chou, P.C., et al.: the study on the comprehensive indicators of indoor environment assessment for occupants health in Taiwan. Build. Environ. **37**(4), 387–392 (2017)
4. Feng, Z., Yu, C.W., Cao, S.J.: Fast prediction for indoor environment: models assessment. Indoor Built Environ. **28**(6), 1–5 (2019)
5. Zhao, K., Jiang, Z., Li, D., et al.: Outdoor environment assessment tool for existing neighbourhoods based on the multi-criteria decision-making method. Build. Environ. **209**, 108687 (2021)
6. Ashdown, I., Eng, P.: The Kruithof curve: a pleasing solution (2015)
7. Kakitsuba, N.: Comfortable indoor lighting conditions for LEDlights evaluated from psychological and physiological responses. Appl. Ergon. **82**, 102941 (2019)
8. Wargocki, P., Sundell, J., Bischof, W., et al.: Ventilation and health in non-industrial indoor environments: report from a European multidisciplinary scientific consensus meeting (EUROVEN). Indoor Air **12**(2), 113–128 (2010)
9. Li, H., Zhu, Y., Qin, O., et al.: A study on the effects of thermal, luminous, and acoustic environments on indoor environmental comfort in offices. Build. Environ. **49**, 304–309 (2012)
10. Hygge, S., Knez, I.: Effects of noise, heat and indoor lighting on cognitive performance and self-reported affect. J. Environ. Psychol. **21**(3), 291–299 (2001)
11. Ching, F.D., Binggeli, C.: Interior Design Illustrated. Wiley, USA (2012)
12. Yu, L.F., Yeung, S.K., et al.: The Clutterpalette: an interactive tool for detailing indoor scenes. IEEE Trans. Vis. Comput. Graph. **22**, 1138–1148 (2016)
13. Savva, M., Chang, AX., Agrawala, M.: SceneSuggest: context-driven 3D scene design (2017)
14. Merrell, P., Eric, S., Zeyang, L., et al.: Interactive furniture layout using interior design guidelines. ACM Trans. Graph. **30**(4), 1–10 (2011)
15. Zhang, S., Zhang, Y., Ma, Q., et al.: PLACE: proximity learning of articulation and contact in 3D environments (2020)
16. Zhao, W.: Rationality evaluation of art furniture layout based on scene simulation. In: International Conference on Virtual Reality and Intelligent Systems (2019)
17. Fu, Q., Fu, H., Yan, H., et al.: Human-centric metrics for indoor scene assessment and synthesis. Graph. Models **110**, 101073 (2020)
18. Gao, Y., Ma, Y., Zhao, Z., et al.: Statistical analysis of the correlation between the contact area of human barefoot morphological characteristics and height and body mass. Chin. Tissue Eng. Res. **25**(32), 6 (2021)

19. Liu, G.H., Sheng, D.: Comparison of formulas for calculating human surface area based on three-dimensional measurements. J. Anat. **5**, 6 (2019)
20. Rahman, A., Mahmood, A.K.: Agent-based simulation using prometheus methodology in evacuation planning. In: International Symposium on Information Technology, vol. 3, pp. 1–8. IEEE (2008)
21. Gwynne, S., Galea, E.R., Owen, M.: A review of the methodologies used in the computer simulation of evacuation from the built environment. Build. Environ. **34**(6), 741–749 (1999)
22. Pan, X., Han, C.S., Dauber, K., et al.: A multi-agent based framework for the simulation of human and social behaviors during emergency evacuations. Ai Soc. **22**(2), 113–132 (2007)
23. Zhang, K., Ji, Y., Bo, J., et al.: Deep learning-based algorithm for indoor simple environment pathfinding. Internet Things Technol. **10**(4), 5 (2020)
24. Hoyet, L., Spies, C., Plantard, P., et al.: Influence of motion speed on the perception of latency in avatar control. In: 2019 IEEE International Conference on Artificial Intelligence and Virtual Reality (2019)
25. Zhang, S., Lv, M., Yang, C.: Real-time 3D route planning based on modified rapidly exploring random-tree algorithm. In: 2019 IEEE 2nd International Conference on Electronic Information and Communication Technology (ICEICT) (2019)
26. Fu, Z., Ding, M., Yu, X.: A study of pathfinding algorithms in game programming. J. Hunan Univ. Technol. **21**(4), 4 (2007)
27. Liebmann, F., et al.: Pedicle screw navigation using surface digitization on the Microsoft HoloLens. Int. J. Comput. Assist. Radiol. Surg. **14**(7), 1157–1165 (2019). https://doi.org/10.1007/s11548-019-01973-7
28. Vuletic, T.: Systematic literature review of hand gestures used in human computer interaction interfaces. Int. J. Hum. Comput Stud. **129**, 74–94 (2019)
29. Yoon, L., Yang, D., Kim, J., et al.: Placement retargeting of virtual avatars to dissimilar indoor environments. IEEE Trans. Vis. Comput. Graph. **28**, 1619–1633 (2020)
30. Riedlinger, U., Oppermann, L., et al.: Tango vs. HoloLens: a comparison of collaborative indoor AR visualisations using hand-held and hands-free devices. Multimodal Technol. Interact. **3**(2), 23 (2019)

LiteAR: A Framework to Estimate Lighting for Mixed Reality Sessions for Enhanced Realism

Chinmay Raut[1], Anamitra Mani[2(✉)], Lakshmi Priya Muraleedharan[2], and Raghavan Velappan[2]

[1] Indian Institute of Technology Madras, Chennai 600036, Tamil Nadu, India
[2] Samsung Research Institute India Bangalore, Bagmane Constellation Business Park, Bengaluru 560037, Karnataka, India
{anam.mani,lakshmi.m,raghavan.v}@samsung.com

Abstract. We propose an end-to-end learning based method to estimate irradiance in real-time given a single input limited field of view image from a mobile phone camera. We further develop a technique inspired by physically based rendering to take advantage of spatially varying environment to illuminate virtual objects in augmented reality sessions to make them look more realistic. We integrate the Inertial Measurement Unit sensor to dynamically estimate illumination, making the mixed reality experience interactive. Our solution runs in real-time on mobile phones, with significantly lower computational requirements and enhanced realism in comparison to state-of-the-art methods.

Keywords: Illumination estimation · Augmented reality · Mobile mixed reality

1   Introduction

One of the main challenges in making augmented reality accessible is to make it seem as realistic as possible. Virtual objects should be indistinguishable from the real world in AR sessions. Lighting plays a major role in rendering objects realistically. While direct light is important in rendering shadows, indirect light is essential for realistic renders. The environment surrounding an object acts as an indirect light source and hence contributes to the illumination of the object. It is extremely important to estimate this diffuse lighting accurately for realistic rendering to enhance augmented reality experiences. Image-based lighting is a physically-based rendering method to illuminate objects using an environment map.

In the context of AR, a panorama surrounding the AR object can be used as an environment map. However, on a mobile phone, the camera captures only a small fraction of the panorama. Therefore, it is very difficult to predict the complete environment map from camera images. Recent works propose a learning based method to predict illumination using a single input image from the rear camera. However, most of these methods assume that the mobile phone is at the

N. Magnenat-Thalmann et al. (Eds.): CGI 2022, LNCS 13443, pp. 407–423, 2022.
https://doi.org/10.1007/978-3-031-23473-6_32

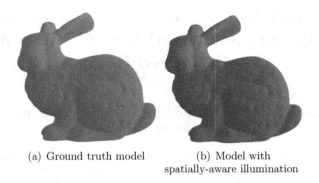

(a) Ground truth model   (b) Model with
                            spatially-aware illumination

Fig. 1. The environmentally-aware illumination of the object enhances its realism in an AR scene.

centre of the environment and thus predict an environment map surrounding the phone. While this may work for most cases, it is not necessarily true as often the virtual object to be placed in an AR session is placed away from the mobile phone camera. Sometimes the real-world objects surrounding the virtual object may alter the environment map. Thus, for realistic rendering it is essential to take into account the immediate environment surrounding the virtual object. Figure 1(b) shows how the environmentally aware illumination enhances the realism of a virtual object in Fig. 1(a).

Our contribution includes,

1. A framework to estimate illumination in real-time for augmented reality experiences on mobile phones by representing the dynamically changing irradiance map as a set of spherical harmonics and training a light-weight neural network on the same.
2. Utilizing scene geometry estimation to update the object's local environment and using this information to enhance object illumination for realism.
3. Use of the Inertial Measurement Unit (IMU) sensor present in the phone to update lighting instead of relying on calling the neural network per frame, which in turn reduces computational cost while achieving realistic illumination.

2   Related Work

After demonstrating a way to capture illumination using a mirrored sphere, earlier works in illumination estimation use a light probe to predict scene lighting. Debevec [5] presented a way to construct an omnidirectional HDR using multiple photographs of a mirrored sphere taken under varying exposures. This HDR can in turn be used to render additional objects in the scene. Prakash et al. [17] use a specular sphere to sample radiance for mobile augmented reality. Debevec presented a way to capture illumination using hybrid 3D spheres [6]. Beyond mirrored balls, known 3D objects have also been used to estimate illumination. Mandl [15] used a combination of pose estimation and illumination estimation neural networks to accurately estimate lighting using a light probe. Calian et al. [2] made use of human faces to predict illumination. However, for mobile AR experiences, the necessity of having a known light probe in the environment ruins the user experience. Thus, we need a probeless illumination estimation method.

Apart from using single object probes, scene properties have also been used to explore illumination estimation. The scene appearance is determined by a variety of factors like the scene geometry, material properties, lighting, etc. One way to estimate scene illumination is to optimize these properties to find the best representation of the scene. However, with limited inputs, the problem becomes an under-constrained optimization problem, and thus the probability of the error multiplying is high. Thus, when using an optimization method, the work either makes certain assumptions about the scene or expects the user to manually provide ground truth. Karsch et al. [11] expect user annotations to estimate initial geometry and lighting. Zhang et al. [22] require depth information and expect users to manually provide ground truth for lightsource locations. One more method matches the image to the most similar cropped image from a database of panoramas, assuming that similar images share illumination estimates. Although probe based techniques produce good results, they are not practical for commercial mobile augmented reality since they require the presence of a light probe in the scene. Recent work has explored end-to-end neural network based solutions to estimate illumination based on input images and additional information.

Most recently, learning based methods have been found to produce seamless augmented reality experiences. Gardner et al. [7] proposed a learning-based method that predicts indoor illumination based on a single image. Their network contained global and local branches and was trained on LDR panoramas of indoor scenes. They further used 2100 HDR panoramas to fine tune the model. They do not take into consideration depth data, and therefore they fail to capture spatially varying lighting information. However, their method is considered state-of-the-art for indoor illumination estimation. Cheng et al. [4] utilize views from both the front and rear cameras of mobile devices to train a neural network with two different branches concatenating to produce spherical harmonics. However, the model is not optimized and is not suitable to run in real-time. Legendre et al. [12] create their own dataset by capturing illumination information through a mirrored ball along with the image from the rear camera. They formulate the problem so as to output the HDR image containing lighting information using the cropped input image from the rear camera. They use L2 loss and discriminatory loss to fine tune the network. Deeplight et al. [12] capture illumination using a mirrored sphere placed 60 cm in front of the camera. However, the placement of the virtual objects rarely coincides with that. Often, they are placed on surfaces visible in the scene and are closely surrounded by other real objects. They do not take into consideration spatially varying lighting and therefore fail to capture true illumination at the local position.

Song et al. [19] proposed a fully differential modular network consisting of 4 components, namely: geometry estimation, scene completion, and LDR-to-HDR estimation. By splitting the network into four components, it becomes easier to optimize the modules individually and, consequently, the whole network. However, the complete model becomes bulky and it is difficult to run in real-time on a mobile phone. Zhao et al. [23] calculate spherical harmonics directly from point cloud data [14] inspired from Monte Carlo integration [18]. They expect rgb-d data as input and warp the point cloud data to a global panorama. Although predicting SH directly from point cloud data reduces the complexity of the model, the model requires RGB-D input, which in itself is sparse in nature.

Other recent works for immersion during interaction in VR include tracking and rendering of contacts with tangible objects in VR [20], Recently mixture graphs [1] have been designed to compute correctly pre-filtered volume lighting. An efficient approach for high quality GPU-based rendering of line data with ambient occlusion and transparency effects has been discussed in [9].

Considering the existing methods for estimating illumination, they are still far from solving the illumination estimation problem for augmented reality scenes for mobile environment. The probe base method ruins the user experience for mobile AR users and hence is impractical. The scene-property based illumination estimation methods expect user intervention in terms of initial geometry and light source estimations. Some of the learning based methods do produce seamless augmented reality experiences. However, the majority of them are not suitable for real-time operation or are not practical for mobile augmented reality experiences. Learning based methods rely on neural networks to dynamically update lighting. However, depending on the complexity of the model, using a neural network might not be suitable to run per frame because of the required computational power. When considering mixed reality applications for mobile, we can also make use of other sensors present in the device to make the process computationally lighter. We propose a learning based method that integrates depth sensors and IMU sensors for dynamic lighting.

3   Illumination Estimation

Figure 2 illustrates the complete proposed pipeline for illumination estimation for mobile augmented reality. The input module has three streams, one each for camera input, which is passed through a neural network to produce global spherical harmonics; depth input, which is used to update lighting based on the local environment of the virtual object; and the angle of rotation of the phone about the vertical axis whenever the user rotates the phone. The input data from the camera is processed to estimate global spherical harmonics by passing it through the neural network model trained using the Matterport 3D dataset [3]. A depth image is used to obtain point cloud data, which is further used to update global spherical harmonics based on the immediate local environment surrounding the virtual object. We also keep track of the rotation of the mobile phone to update spherical harmonics using fast spherical harmonics rotation.

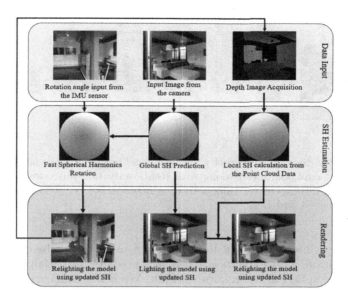

Fig. 2. Complete data pipeline showcasing all the modules and the flow of the proposed process

Table 1. Standard variables

Symbol	Variable
SH_{lm}	Spherical harmonics coefficient l of band l
L	Radiance at the point
R	Radius of the sphere we query points from
r	Distance of a point from the center of the sphere
$sign(d)$	$sign(d)$ function outputs -1 or 1 depending on which side of the center the point lies along axis d
SH_g	Global Spherical harmonics coefficients
SH_l	Local Spherical harmonics coefficients
D	Maximum distance between any two points in the point cloud dataset
y	SH band 2 with 5 componentes that we want to rotate
P	A function which projects a normal vector into the second band of spherical harmonics. It takes a normalized three dimensional vector as input and outputs a 5 dimensional SH vector
M	3×3 rotation matrix. It's the rotation that we want to somehow apply to our SH vector
U	The 5×5 (unknown) rotation matrix that want to apply to y
N	Set of five three-dimensional normalized vectors

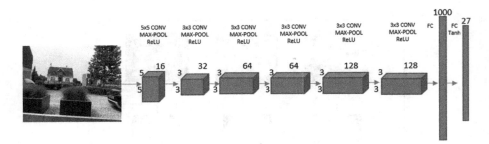

Fig. 3. Network diagram to predict global spherical harmonics. We use blocks of convolutional and max-pool layers along with ReLU activation function followed by two fully connected layers. We use Tanh activation function before the last layer to restrict output between −1 and 1.

We explain each step in detail in this section using four subsections, namely: data preparation, global spherical harmonics prediction, spatially varying environment, and spherical harmonics rotation. We define standard variables and their symbols in Table 1.

3.1   Data Preparation

We use publicly available Matterport 3D dataset [3] consisting of panoramas of indoor scenes and viewpoint images (rear camera images) for the same. One set of observations consists of a rear camera image and a panorama. There are a total of 10,800 panoramic scenes in the dataset. Each panorama contains 18 viewpoint images taken from multiple angles. For training purposes we choose 6 viewpoints separated by 60° each with vertical camera alignment.

Fig. 4. Input from rear camera and corresponding panorama

Figure 4 depicts one instance of the dataset containing the rear camera input image used as training data and the corresponding panorama from which we calculate spherical harmonics. We split the data into training and validation sets with a ratio of 3:1. To enhance the dataset, we add color tints so that there is enough variance in the dataset.

3.2 Global Spherical Harmonics Prediction

We use an image captured using the rear camera as the input and produce nine spherical harmonics for each channel. We formulate this as a regression problem and utilize convolutional neural network followed by fully connected layers. We begin by resizing the image to 480∗320 pixels. We design a block of convolutional layer followed by a max-pool layer with ReLU activation function. We increase the depth of each layer to extract more features in subsequent layers. Then, afterward, to reduce the output to 27 components, we use fully connected layers. Finally, we pass the output through the Tanh function to restrict predicted coefficients between −1 and 1. Figure 3 demonstrates the model architecture.

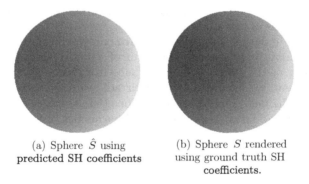

(a) Sphere $\hat{S}$ using
predicted SH coefficients

(b) Sphere S rendered
using ground truth SH
coefficients.

Fig. 5. We calculate l2 loss between these images and aim to minimize it along with minimizing the l2 loss between SH coefficients themselves.

We use mean squared error on predicted SH coefficients as our loss function and ADAM as our optimizer. A small difference in SH coefficients can lead to a significant change in illumination. Using only 27 coefficients might be an under-constrained problem that can lead to errors in illumination estimation. As shown in Fig. 5, we introduce render loss as an additional loss function in which we render a sphere $hatS$ using predicted SH coefficients and calculate l2 loss with respect to the sphere S rendered using ground truth SH coefficients.

3.3   Spatially Varying Environment

We must take into account the spatially varying environment, especially around the virtual object, to make the augmented reality experience more realistic. Another popular problem in mixed reality is geometric estimation of the scene. A lot of newer mobile devices have an integrated Lidar sensor to capture depth images. For devices without a depth sensor, several approaches like estimating structure from motion with the help of camera images from multiple angles and sensor data [21], estimating depth from a single image [10,13] have filled in the role of depth estimation. Since most mixed reality sessions devote certain computational power to geometry estimation, we can leverage the same for realistic relighting of the virtual objects placed in the scene.

The inspiration for relighting the object from local point cloud data comes from Monte Carlo integration, wherein we treat every point queried from a sphere of certain radius surrounding the virtual object as a point light source. However, since the distance between these points and the virtual object is less, we approximate integration to summation. We first downsample the data uniformly. We arranged the point cloud data in a K-Dimensional tree (KDTree) data structure [8]. The time complexity for querying neighbours is reduced from N to $log N$. We query all the points lying in a sphere of a certain radius. We experiment with different values of this radius.

We focus on updating the spherical harmonic coefficients of the first two bands. We calculate irradiance in the form of spherical harmonic coefficients using the colour of the point and its distance from the object. To obtain the local SH coefficient, we integrate weighted irradiance based on distance over all of the points in the ball point query. Equations 1–3 use queried points and their radiance values to update the local spherical harmonics of band 1.

$$SH_{10} = \sum (L * (R - r)/R) * sign(x) \tag{1}$$

$$SH_{11} = \sum (L * (R - r)/R) * sign(y) \tag{2}$$

$$SH_{12} = \sum (L * (R - r)/R) * sign(z) \tag{3}$$

where R is the radius of the sphere we query points from. r is the distance of a point from the centre of the sphere. These local coefficients are used to update global SH coefficients based on a distance measure, as shown in Eq. 5. We use alpha as the measure of distance, which is calculated using Eq. 4.

$$Alpha = R/D \tag{4}$$

$$SH_g = alpha * SH_g + (1 - alpha) * SH_l \tag{5}$$

3.4   Spherical Harmonics Rotation

Panoramic images capture more details in the horizontal direction since the distribution of radiance varies more in the horizontal direction. In a mobile mixed reality session, the user places a virtual object in the scene captured by the camera. After placing the object, the user might move around the object, but the surrounding environment would remain the same. Thus, the only way object illumination would change is if the object is moved and placed somewhere else or if there is some change in the environment. To keep track of the scene, we use sparse optical flow. Even if the scene itself does not change, if the user moves around the object, the illumination would change because of the rotation.

Table 2. LiteAR renders of various models (a) bunny, (b) dragon, (c) teapot, and (d) Lucy in various environments. The model takes the image as an input and produces 27 spherical harmonics coefficients as irradiance.

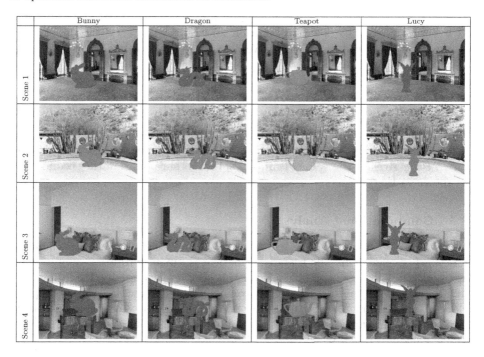

We track the rotation around the vertical axis and update spherical harmonics accordingly. We utilize the IMU sensor present in mobile phones to track rotation. Thus, instead of calling the neural network every frame, we rotate the environment map whenever the user rotates the phone about the vertical axis triggered by the IMU sensor. We implement zonal harmonics for fast spherical harmonics rotation calculation [16]. Using zonal harmonics, the total number of multiplication operations required for spherical harmonics rotation per channel is 118, which is significantly less than the 120 million multiplication operations required in a neural network. Furthermore, since we do not care about zonal harmonics themselves and only care about spherical harmonics rotation, we can make use of sparse data and formulate the rotation problem as finding the rotation matrices for each spherical harmonics band.

1. The first band does not change with rotation as its value remains constant.
2. The second band can be treated as a vector, which can be rotated by pre-multiplying by a rotation matrix corresponding to the angle of rotation.
3. The third band has five components. To find a rotation matrix for this band, we make use of the fact that rotation followed by projection is the same as projection followed by rotation. We demonstrate this using Eq. 6.

$$U * P(N) = P(M * N) \tag{6}$$

$$U * y = [P(M * N)] * P(N)^{-1} * y \tag{7}$$

We have to solve for U. We can choose N to be a set of five unit vectors as long as the projections of those vectors are linearly independent in order to solve for U. $U * y$ gives us the value of rotated spherical harmonics in the second band as shown in Eq. 7.

3.5 Computational Analysis

The model is designed to have less than 120M multiplication and accumulation functions to make it mobile friendly. Spherical Harmonics rotation only requires 118 multiplication operation thus is very cheap computationally. Updating local lighting based on the immediate environment depends on the density of point cloud data. We first down sample the point cloud data since reducing density eliminates redundancy with negligible change in the results. Our neural network model runs at 30 FPS using Intel(R) Core(TM) i7-6700HQ CPU.

Table 3. Comparison of global illumination estimation by different models with the ground truth. We use various learning based methods to render the Stanford bunny and demonstrate the same to compare realism.

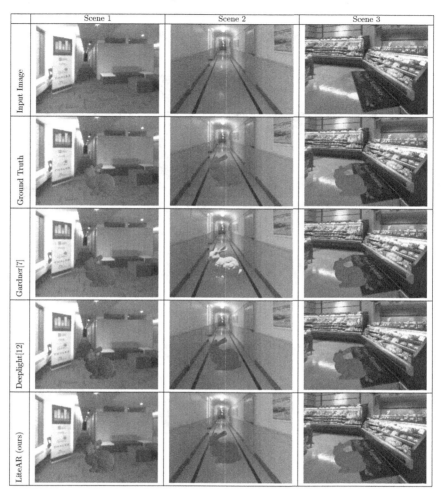

4 Results and Discussion

With 10,800 panoramic scenes and 6 viewpoints for each scene, we have 64,000 distinct observations in our dataset. To improve the illumination variance, we add color tints to produce two more sets of observations for every one set of observations. We split the dataset into training and testing data respectively, with a 75%–25% split. We train our model LiteAR on this data and evaluate the results. Table 2 shows renders of different models rendered using spherical harmonics produced by our model. We compare the results to recent state-of-the-

418   C. Raut et al.

Table 4. Comparison of rendering based on global illumination and spatially aware illumination. We use depth image to obtain point cloud data which is further used to update global spherical harmonics.

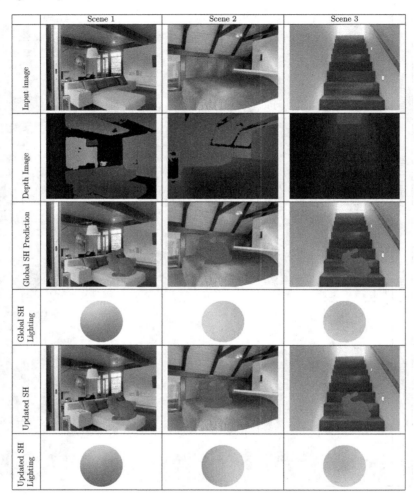

Table 5. L2 loss on global spherical harmonics for different models

Model	l2 loss
Gardner [7]	0.18
Deeplight [12]	0.28
PointAR [23]	0.21
LiteAR (ours)	0.24

Table 6. Computational complexity in terms of the number of parameters and multiply accumulates (MACs) where M stands for million

	Number of parameters (M)	MACs (M)
Gardner [7]	20	3800
Deeplight [12]	3.5	300
PointAR [23]	1.4	790
LiteAR (ours)	2.2	120

(a) Global SH Render   (b) Spatially Aware SH Render

Fig. 6. (a) depicts rendering of Stanford bunny using spherical harmonics predicted by the neural network and (b) depicts the same using updated spherical harmonics after taking into consideration the immediate local environment

art lighting estimation research in Table 3. It is important to note that we target mobile AR applications and, thus, model complexity is as important a metric as accuracy. Furthermore, the objective is to improve realism. Thus, making the model look more realistic is essential as opposed to only improving the model to minimize errors on global lighting information.

Table 3 compares bunny renderings using different models. Each model only uses a single input image to predict illumination. Deeplight and LiteAR produce similar results when getting the ambient lighting right. Gardner's [7] method fails to estimate indirect lighting correctly when there is a light source present in the image, as can be seen in the second example. For evaluation, we use $l2$ loss to compare model accuracy for global lighting information. We calculate $l2$ loss by computing the average $l2$ distance between spherical harmonics coefficients produced by our model (SH_g) and ground truth spherical harmonics coefficients (SH_{gt}).

Our neural network model for global spherical harmonics prediction produces better results, i.e., less l2 loss than deeplight [12] and comparable results to that of Gardner [7] as shown in Table 5 and PointAR [23] while being 40 times less computationally expensive than Gardner's [7] method and 6 times less computationally expensive than PointAR [23]. Table 6 compares the model complexities for our method against the state of the art. The model proposed by Gardner

Table 7. Comparison of illumination estimation predicted by the neural network to those estimated by rotating initially predicted spherical harmonics. We use spherical harmonics predicted using one frame and perform SH rotation on them. We then use rotated frames to predict spherical harmonics using the neural network. We compare renderings obtained by both the methods. We also demonstrate the visual difference in illumination and structural similarity index measure (SSIM)

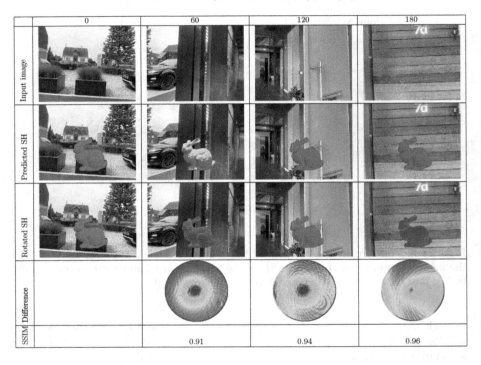

et al. [7] has more than 20M parameters, resulting in more than 3800M multiply accumulates (MACs). This makes it unsuitable for mobile augmented reality applications. LiteAR has 3 times and 6 times fewer MACs compared to Deeplight and PointAR [23] respectively, therefore making it suitable to run in real time even on mobile phones. Table 5 demonstrates the l2 loss for each model. LiteAR produces better results than Deeplight for global illumination estimation and comparable results to PointAR. However, the l2 loss on global lighting estimation is not a direct metric of measuring realism as the local environment can greatly influence lighting. Spatially varying environmental lighting modules visibly improve the realism of the model. Thus, even with less accurate global lighting prediction compared to other models, LiteAR produces results that are more realistic.

Table 4 demonstrates lighting estimation after taking into account the spatially variable environment. In the first and second examples, point cloud data samples consists of the green-coloured sofa and purple-coloured bed, respectively. These points are located beneath the model, affecting primarily the SH_1 harmonic. Wherein, in the third example, the stairs and walls affect every spherical harmonic in the first band, more so SH_{10} because of the proximity of the stairs. The visual appearance of the model is enhanced greatly and thus helps make the mixed reality experience feel more realistic. Figure 6 demonstrates the improvement in lighting with a closer look at Scene 2 from Table 4. The purple color of the bedsheet affects the lighting of the bunny from below. The updated lighting demonstrates the purple shade on the chest and legs of the bunny, thus making it more realistic.

With a light neural network combined with spherical harmonics rotation based on the input from the IMU sensor, the whole pipeline is mobile-friendly being able to render models at high frame rates. Instead of calling a neural network every frame, in order to make the pipeline even lighter, we use spherical harmonics rotation based on IMU sensor input. Table 7 demonstrates bunny rendering with spherical harmonics predicted by a neural network for every image and compares it to bunny rendering with spherical harmonics predicted once and then rotated by a given angle. The comparison showed a high structural similarity index between lighting estimated using the neural network directly and using SH rotation after estimating once. The rotation operation only requires less than 120 multiply accumulates compared to millions for calling the neural network, therefore reducing the computational load.

5   Conclusion and Future Work

In conclusion, the LiteAR pipeline operates much faster than the state-of-the-art methods while slightly compromising the global illumination estimation accuracy. However, the dataset used to train the model did not have enough variance with respect to illumination. Therefore, the accuracy could be improved with a more varied dataset. Moreover, after updating lighting based on the local spatial environment, the renders look more realistic. Using integrated sensors like the IMU sensor makes the process much faster with minimal visual compromise in estimating illumination.

The dataset to train the model to predict global spherical harmonics consisted of indoor images taken from multiple angles. Most of the photographed rooms share similar lighting for multiple photos. Thus, there is little variation in labels in the form of spherical harmonics. This may lead to over-fitting, as the model would try to find an optimal solution. We solve this problem using data augmentation by introducing colour tints. However, the dataset could be naturally enriched by introducing pictures taken with different mobile phone cameras and of different places under varying lighting.

For considering the local environment to update lighting, experimenting with different values for the radius to sample points and alpha coefficient to update global spherical harmonics gives varying results. Thus, a method could be developed to dynamically select values for the radius and alpha coefficient.

A confidence score along with the spherical harmonics would be helpful to determine the best set of spherical harmonic coefficients predicted by the model. Thus, the most accurate SH prediction could be used along with the input from the IMU sensor instead of calling the neural network model every few frames.

References

1. Althelaya, K.A., Agus, M., Schneider, J.: The mixture graph-a data structure for compressing, rendering, and querying segmentation histograms. IEEE Trans. Vis. Comput. Graph. **27**, 645–655 (2021)
2. Calian, D.A., Lalonde, J.F., Gotardo, P., Simon, T., Matthews, I., Mitchell, K.: From faces to outdoor light probes. In: Computer Graphics Forum, vol. 37, pp. 51–61. Wiley Online Library (2018)
3. Chang, A., et al.: Matterport3D: learning from RGB-D data in indoor environments. arXiv preprint arXiv:1709.06158 (2017)
4. Cheng, D., Shi, J., Chen, Y., Deng, X., Zhang, X.: Learning scene illumination by pairwise photos from rear and front mobile cameras. In: Computer Graphics Forum, vol. 37, pp. 213–221. Wiley Online Library (2018)
5. Debevec, P.: Rendering synthetic objects into real scenes: bridging traditional and image-based graphics with global illumination and high dynamic range photography. In: ACM SIGGRAPH 2008 Classes, pp. 1–10 (2008)
6. Debevec, P., Graham, P., Busch, J., Bolas, M.: A single-shot light probe. In: ACM SIGGRAPH 2012 Talks, p. 1 (2012)
7. Gardner, M.A., et al.: Learning to predict indoor illumination from a single image. arXiv preprint arXiv:1704.00090 (2017)
8. Greenspan, M., Yurick, M.: Approximate KD tree search for efficient ICP. In: Fourth International Conference on 3-D Digital Imaging and Modeling 2003, 3DIM 2003. Proceedings, pp. 442–448. IEEE (2003)
9. Groß, D., Gumhold, S.: Advanced rendering of line data with ambient occlusion and transparency. IEEE Trans. Vis. Comput. Graph. **27**, 614–624 (2021)
10. Hambarde, P., Murala, S.: S2DNet: depth estimation from single image and sparse samples. IEEE Trans. Comput. Imaging **6**, 806–817 (2020)
11. Karsch, K., Hedau, V., Forsyth, D., Hoiem, D.: Rendering synthetic objects into legacy photographs. ACM Trans. Graph. (TOG) **30**(6), 1–12 (2011)
12. LeGendre, C., et al.: DeepLight: learning illumination for unconstrained mobile mixed reality. In: Proceedings of the IEEE/CVF Conference on Computer Vision and Pattern Recognition, pp. 5918–5928 (2019)
13. Liu, F., Shen, C., Lin, G.: Deep convolutional neural fields for depth estimation from a single image. In: Proceedings of the IEEE Conference on Computer Vision and Pattern Recognition, pp. 5162–5170 (2015)
14. Liu, W., Sun, J., Li, W., Hu, T., Wang, P.: Deep learning on point clouds and its application: a survey. Sensors **19**(19), 4188 (2019)
15. Mandl, D., et al.: Learning lightprobes for mixed reality illumination. In: 2017 IEEE International Symposium on Mixed and Augmented Reality (ISMAR), pp. 82–89. IEEE (2017)

16. Nowrouzezahrai, D., Simari, P., Fiume, E.: Sparse zonal harmonic factorization for efficient SH rotation. ACM Trans. Graph. (TOG) **31**(3), 1–9 (2012)
17. Prakash, S., Bahremand, A., Nguyen, L.D., LiKamWa, R.: GLEAM: an illumination estimation framework for real-time photorealistic augmented reality on mobile devices. In: Proceedings of the 17th Annual International Conference on Mobile Systems, Applications, and Services, pp. 142–154 (2019)
18. Robert, C.P., Casella, G.: Monte Carlo integration. In: Robert, C.P., Casella, G. (eds.) Monte Carlo Statistical Methods, pp. 71–138. Springer, New York (1999). https://doi.org/10.1007/978-1-4757-3071-5_3
19. Song, S., Funkhouser, T.: Neural illumination: lighting prediction for indoor environments. In: Proceedings of the IEEE/CVF Conference on Computer Vision and Pattern Recognition, pp. 6918–6926 (2019)
20. de Tinguy, X., Pacchierotti, C., Lécuyer, A., Marchal, M.: Capacitive sensing for improving contact rendering with tangible objects in VR. IEEE Trans. Vis. Comput. Graph. **27**, 2481–2487 (2021)
21. Zanfir, A., Marinoiu, E., Sminchisescu, C.: Monocular 3D pose and shape estimation of multiple people in natural scenes-the importance of multiple scene constraints. In: Proceedings of the IEEE Conference on Computer Vision and Pattern Recognition, pp. 2148–2157 (2018)
22. Zhang, E., Cohen, M.F., Curless, B.: Emptying, refurnishing, and relighting indoor spaces. ACM Trans. Graph. (TOG) **35**(6), 1–14 (2016)
23. Zhao, Y., Guo, T.: POINTAR: efficient lighting estimation for mobile augmented reality. In: Vedaldi, A., Bischof, H., Brox, T., Frahm, J.-M. (eds.) ECCV 2020. LNCS, vol. 12368, pp. 678–693. Springer, Cham (2020). https://doi.org/10.1007/978-3-030-58592-1_40

Personalized User Interface Elements Recommendation System

Hao Liu[1], Xiangxian Li[1], Wei Gai[1(✉)], Yu Huang[1], Jingbo Zhou[2],
and Chenglei Yang[1]

[1] Shandong University, Jinan, Shandong, China
gw@sdu.edu.cn
[2] Business Intelligence Lab, Baidu Research, Beijing, China

Abstract. This paper introduces a personalized user interface element recommendation system, in which the model can recommend personalized user interface elements by introducing user features and user evaluations in the offline training. Through experiments, we found that compared with common machine learning algorithms, the Field-aware Factorization Machine that introduced user feature intersections has achieved a better accuracy in the recommendation, which shows the advantages of introducing user features and feature intersections in the recommendation of interface elements.

Keywords: User interface · Field-aware factorization machine · Personalized recommendation

1 Introduction

Users interact with computer systems through the Graphical User Interface (GUI), from web pages and mobile applications to explanation equipment, self-service equipment in specific scenarios, as well as mixed reality (MR), virtual reality (VR), and other interactive environments [1, 7, 8]. Users are closely related to the GUI.

Usually, interface designers modify user interface (UI) elements (such as buttons, search boxes, etc.) according to the application theme and obtain user evaluations by A/B testing or user surveys before publishing. Considering the diversity of users, interface designers usually have to make trade-offs on existing designs. Therefore, when a user opens a web page or an application for the first time, the "average" interfaces are usually shown, i.e., pages that can be basically accepted by most users.

To solve the problem of how to provide a user-friendly and more suitable interface, many existing applications provide the option of manually setting interface parameters such as theme color and font size. However, the effect achieved by this method often has

Supported by the National Natural Science Foundation of China under Grant 62007021 and 61972233.
H. Liu and X. Li—Contributed equally to this work.

several limitations, including increasing the learning cost of user operations and making users spend more time in the adaptation of the interface.

Ideally, when a user opens applications or web pages, systems would automatically recommend personalized interfaces based on the "user profile" which outlines the target user and links user preferences to designs. In a general application or web page, the user needs to bind an account or provide personal information (usually gender and region) through input, and then the application or web page recommends content to users based on the behavioral data (such as hobbies, retrieving content, browsing records, etc.) [5, 9]. Some applications can use the extracted user information to push the designed user interface [7, 10]. However, the completeness and authenticity of the information provided by users are often limited, so the system may only provide the default interface or the specified interface with coarse-grained division.

For some widely used systems like campus systems, users' detailed personal information has been stored in the database. After the user logs in to the system, the corresponding personal comprehensive information can be obtained in the backend. In this situation, we propose an interface recommendation system that can be embedded in systems tied to user information. Unlike many existing recommendation works, our system is refined to the basic component of the user interface, such as buttons, search box, etc. The system we proposed relies on users' personal information in the database and the user's preference information on user interface elements and uses a model to fit the relationship between different types of user preference and user interface element solutions. In other words, this system aims to take user information into account, predict user preferences, and recommend personalized user interface elements.

Our main contributions are:

1. A user interface element personalized recommendation system is proposed, which learns user features and user evaluations offline through a machine learning model, and recommends detailed user interface elements for users online.
2. The performance of different models in the user interface element personalized recommendation system is explored through extensive experimental evaluation, and the significance of introducing user features and using feature intersection methods for user interface element recommendation is discussed.

This paper is organized as follows, in Sect. 2, we introduce the existing works on UI or UI element recommendation and the evaluation metrics commonly used in UI element recommendation. In Sect. 3, we introduce the structure of the recommender system for user interface element personalization and the selection of related models. Section 4 illustrates the process of data collection, discuss the feature intersection between user features and design element features, and analyze the effects of system recommendations. Section 5 is the summary and prospect of the work.

2   Related Works

2.1   Personalized User Interface

Recommendations about UI or UI elements are majorly based on users' usage records or historical information [3, 6, 18], and it is difficult to make personalized recommendations when the user opens it for the first time. So, we need to consider personalized recommendations based on user information.

In terms of recommending UI based on personalized information, Gossen et al. designed an adaptive Search UI for the Knowledge Journey Exhibit search system which divides users according to their ages (age 7–12 children group and adult group) [2]. In addition to the common design element variables (colors, patterns), adaptive objects are also considered, such as whether the menu list expands in a disc or drop-down style. Sarsam et al. classified users based on the five major personalities and separated two potential personality types (neuroticism and extra conscientiousness) after using the k-means cluster [16]. Reinecke et al. classified users based on cultural differences and defined the calculation of differences in cultures as the weighted sum of the user's living time in each country and evaluate by users' responses to preference questions [13]. Rim et al. used the Bayesian network and adapted the simulated annealing algorithm to learn the connection tree, and predict the probability distribution in the webpage content [15]. Users' age, major, gender, etc. are used as features to learn users' preferences of the color in the UI, as well as in contents, and files.

Methods of dividing groups by user characteristics and recommending the interface are usually to design an overall or partial user interface scheme by counting the overall characteristics of a certain group and estimating the effect according to user evaluations. These methods usually only focus on single characteristic and recommend the entire interface solution or the design element solution, which is coarse-grained in terms of user personalized recommendation and difficult to expand to more systems. The process of surveying and designing elements still has a significant time and manual investment for the designer. Therefore, there is a need for a personalized recommendation method involving a more detailed UI element.

Regarding more refined design element recommendation, the recent FEELER model learns user evaluations of design element solutions in a data-driven way [19], and the trained model predicts user evaluations based on design elements, thus realizing recommendations for designers to provide a reference. FEELER has a large number of user evaluations, and the obtained prediction model is a prediction for all users, but it is hard to collect massive data on ordinary systems. Therefore, instead of modeling the element solution and predicting the ideal one, a personalized recommendation model is established by introducing user characteristics in a small-scale data set.

2.2   Metrics

The evaluations of interface design are mainly divided into two types: evaluation of recommended solutions and user feedback. In the former type, Nawaz et al. used the time and number of clicks when entering the target page as the measurement [11]. Soh et al. used Mean Absolute Precession and Normalized Discounted Cumulative Gain of the predicted knot relative to the real situation as indicators [18]. Besides, Reinecke et al. used the absolute error to measure the gap between the predictions and the users' answers [13]. For the user feedback, there are three main methods:

Subjective measures. Subjective measures refer to the users' self-evaluation of the recommended results, such as users' self-evaluation of cognitive processes and mental efforts. Thereby directly estimate the task difficulty to evaluate the cognitive load. In addition, Questionnaires like SUS and UEQ are usually designed to measure user satisfaction UEQ [3]. Although subjective measures are easy to manage and analyze, they do not meet the runtime requirements of adaptive systems and may be less accurate when the user's cognitive state is very limited dual-tasks measures. The basis of dual-tasks measures is the resources required by humans to process a task are limited and sharable among concurrently executing tasks. With more resources allocated in the primary task and fewer resources in the secondary task, performance on the secondary task reflects the cognitive load.

Physiological measures. Objective ocular measures, such as the use of pupil dilation to assess cognitive load [6, 16], serve as physiological indicators of cognitive load such as muscle tone, pupil dilation, heart rate, blood pressure, and neuronal activity. Mydriasis is one of the most promising techniques, and researchers have used eye trackers to collect data on pupil diameter and correlate it with cognitive load.

Our work is a data-driven recommendation model, which mainly focuses on the evaluation indicators of the recommended solution. Since the data contains the subjective ratings of users, it reflects the fitting of user preferences to a certain extent. Therefore, the recommendation metrics are adopted in the experimental evaluation.

3   Recommendation System

3.1   Preliminaries

In the personalized user interface element recommendation system, the design element solution is defined as $\vec{s} = \{s_1, s_2, \ldots, s_n\}, \vec{s} \in S$, where s_j is the jth feature of the solution, such as color, length, radians, etc., and then denote the evaluations of solution $\vec{s}$ for user $\vec{u}$ of the as $y_{\vec{s}}^{\vec{u}}$.

For the personalized recommendation of design elements, facing a new user $\vec{u}_{new}$, if the evaluation $y_S^{\vec{u}_{new}}$ of the solution set S is ranked as $R_{groundtruth}$, we try to find the model $\varphi(\cdot, \cdot)$ to fit the evaluation and obtain the corresponding ranking $R_{predict}$, so that two rankings are as close as possible. This can be described as a recommending processing to optimize the target function $\mathrm{argmax}_{\varphi(\cdot,\cdot)} g\big(O_{groundtruth}, \varphi(u_{new}, S)\big)$, where $g(\cdot, \cdot)$ is a function used to determine the similarity between personalized recommendation and ground-truth. In our work, AP, NDCG and cosine similarity are used, which will be introduced in detail in the experiments below.

3.2   Processing

The recommendation system consists of the database (saving user information, design element solutions, and user evaluations of design element solutions) and the model, as shown in Fig. 1. The training stage is in the red dashed box. Participants with evaluations of the design element solutions are queried from the database, which include users' information feature U_{train}, design elements set S_{train}, and users' corresponding design element score set $y_{S_{train}}^{U_{train}}$. Splicing each user feature $\vec{u}$ in U_{train} with the design element $\vec{s}$ into a feature vector $\vec{x}$, the corresponding evaluation score $y_{\vec{s}}^{\vec{u}}$ is the label of the vector, all $\vec{x}$ and $y_{\vec{s}}^{\vec{u}}$ are combined as the training set D_{train} and trained by the model. The fitted model can predict user's score in the design element solution domain according to the input user characteristics.

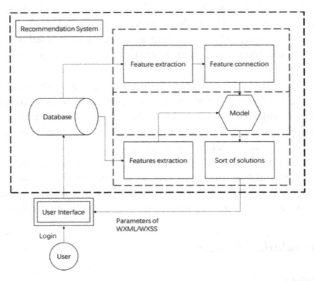

Fig. 1. The processing of user interface elements recommended personalization system.

For users who use the system, only need to provide personal information and the system converts information into user features and fits the scores. After sorting the scores, it can recommend personalized design element solutions for users.

3.3 Model

Since users' evaluations of design elements are the embodiment of user preference, the evaluation domain should reflect the degree of preference, the 5-point Likert scale is adapted in our work. Among the commonly used model in machine learning, Linear Regression (LR) is one of the most popularly used to fit data; and the Supporting Vector Regressor (SVR) model has better generalization ability in small-scale data; the Gradient Boosting Decision Tree (GBDT) is suitable for fitting continuous or non-continuous data. These models are used in many fields. However, for the personalized recommendation of design elements, there are still two main problems:

1) Features in the UI elements are mostly continuous (length, angle, etc.), which cause the problem of combinatorial explosion. In order to ensure the test quality, only a

small part of the entire design element domain is evaluated, so the obtained evaluation matrix will be sparse, which will make the model learning more difficult.

2) There may be interrelated features between user features and design element solution features, as well as between design element solution features, and how to effectively learn the information brought by feature intersection is also critical. The impact of feature intersection will be introduced in detail in Sect. 4.2.

To alleviate problems of sparsity and feature intersection, the Factorization Machine (FM) [8] is proposed to decompose sparse matrices and add feature intersection. For input feature x and predicted value $\hat{y}$, FM is defined as Eq. 1:

$$\hat{y} = w_0 + \sum_{i=1}^{n} w_i x_i + \sum_{i=1}^{n} \sum_{j=i+1}^{n} <v_i, v_j> x_i x_j \qquad (1)$$

where w_0 and w_i are the coefficients of the constant term and the first-order term. The first two terms of the polynomial are in the form of linear regression, and the third term is the quadratic term with the feature intersection. The coefficient of the quadratic term is obtained by matrix decomposition. The latent vector v corresponding to the feature is obtained by the dot product, which implements feature intersection, and the parameter estimation is more accurate in the case of sparseness.

FM proposes a solution to the sparse matrix and feature intersection, but each feature has only one latent vector, and the strength of intersection between different features is uncontrollable. For example, some features within user features are irrelevant.

To a lesser extent (such as age and gender, age and major), there is likely to be a strong correlation between user characteristics and design element solution characteristics, and within design element solution characteristics. Therefore, here we adopt the Field-aware Factorization Machine (FFM) [4] model that can describe the feature intersection in more detail, and the definition is shown in Eq. 2:

$$\hat{y} = w_0 + \sum_{i=1}^{n} w_i x_i + \sum_{i=1}^{n} \sum_{j=i+1}^{n} <v_{i,f_j}, v_{j,f_i}> x_i x_j \qquad (2)$$

Different from FM, FFM divides the features into different fields, and the hidden vector further becomes v_{i,f_i} corresponding to the field where the interactive object x_j is located, so as to provide features intersect. Different strength issues make the feature intersection more detailed. Some improvements after FFM, such as Field-weighted Factorization Machines [12], Bilinear-FM, etc., mainly solve the problem of FFM model in terms of computational performance, but are close to FFM in accuracy.

4 Experiments

4.1 Data Collection

The experimental data is collected through the WeChat applet, including two parts: user personal information and ratings of user interface elements. The tested need to fill in personal information (including gender, age, family location, ethnicity, major), and then complete the evaluation of the two user interface elements of the "find/reset" button and the search box. The evaluation interface is shown in Fig. 2 (a) and (b).

In terms of user information collection, because the proportion of ethnic groups other than Han in the collected data is too small ($\cong 5\%$), so that is not included. The final user features include gender, age, residence and major, namely, $\vec{u} \in U$, $\vec{u} = \{u_{\text{sex}}, u_{\text{age}}, u_{\text{location}}, u_{\text{major}}\}$, and the distribution of user features is shown in Table 1.

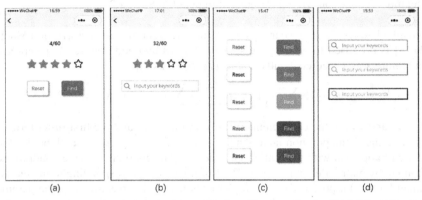

(a)   (b)   (c)   (d)

Fig. 2. The interface and solutions in data collection. The interface is divided into three parts, from top to bottom: evaluation progress, score, and plan. a) The interface of button scoring; b) the search box interface; (c) and (d) are the diagram of color in the User Interface Elements.

Table 1. Distribution of users' features.

Feature of users	Class	Font size and style
Sex	Male	65
	Female	96
Age	<20	18
	≥20 and <30	119
	≥30	24
Location	Shandong Provinces	103
	Yunnan Provinces	25
	Others	33
Major	Engineering	129
	Others	32

In terms of user evaluation, we adapted a 5-point Likert scale (1-dislike very much, 5-like very much). The button solution set S_{button} contains 120 types, of which the design solution $\vec{s} \in S_{button}$ contains feature vector $\vec{s} = \{s_{color}, s_{length}, s_{radius}\}$ (5 colors, 6 kinds of length, 4 kinds of lead angle radians), details are shown in Table 2, and color examples are shown in Fig. 2 (c). The set of solutions during user testing is 30% (36 types) randomly among all solutions. The set S_{search} of the search box contains 60 types, of which the design solution $\vec{s} \in S_{search}$ contains feature vector $\vec{s} = \{s_{color}, s_{length}, s_{radius}\}$ (3 colors, 5 thicknesses of lines, 4 min of lead angle radian). The is shown in Table 3, and color examples are shown in Fig. 2 (d). The set of solutions during testing is 30% random of all solutions (18 types).

In order to ensure the quality of the evaluation, we set up scoring screening rules (the tester does not know the specific rules) to filter out the users who give the same scores for all the button or search bar solutions; Same solutions will appear at random intervals in the evaluation, and we also filter out the users who have the same score for all the button or search box solutions. For users with a large gap in the evaluation of the same program, a total of 161 valid data were finally collected.

Table 2. Features in the button dataset.

Features of solutions	Categories	Notation
Color	#5AA2E0,#ffa032,#ff78a0, #7957dc, #c36e30	Hex-triplet code of color
Length	160, 180, 200, 220, 240, 260	Length of border, unit: rpx
Radius	0, 20, 40, 60	Radius of border, unit: rpx

Table 3. Features in the search bar dataset.

Features of solutions	Categories	Notation
Color	#d0d0d0, #808080, #000000	Hex-triplet code of color
Thick	1, 3, 5, 7, 9	Thick of border, unit: rpx
Radius	0, 20, 40, 60	Radius of border, unit: rpx

4.2 Feature Intersection

In order to further study the relationship between user characteristics and user preferences for design elements, we calculated the mutual information (MI) between all feature vector pairs (X_1, X_2) in the data and user evaluation Y. MI can measure the mutual relationship between the two variables. The degree of dependence, the eigenvector pair, and the MI formula for user evaluation are:

$$MI((X_1, X_2), Y) = \sum_{(i,j)\in(X_1,X_2)} \sum_{y\in Y} p((i,j), y)\log\frac{p((i,j),y)}{p(i,j)p(y)} \tag{3}$$

The heat map is drawn according to MI as shown in Fig. 3. The parts with high correlation in a) mainly focus on button color and user features, button color and button length, button color and button lead angle radian. In interface design, color is one of the most easily perceived variables by users. People of different ages and genders tend to have different preferences for colors, which is in line with practical considerations in design. b) The parts with a high correlation of search bar are mainly concentrated between age and the thickness of the search box line, and between the thickness of the search box line and the radian of the search box lead angle.

From the mutual information between features, we found there is a strong correlation between design element features, and some user features are also correlated with design element features. This correlation can theoretically provide information for a recommendation. To verify this, we take a comparative experiment in the following.

4.3 Metrics

The metrics for measuring the model are Mean Absolute Precession (MAP), Normalized Discounted Cumulative Gain (NDCG), and Cosine Similarity between the actual ranking and the predicted ranking. The MAP reflects the ranking performance. The higher the MAP, the higher the overlap between the recommended set and the actual set. It is defined as Eq. 4 and Eq. 5:

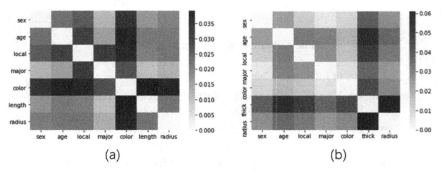

(a)   (b)

Fig. 3. Mutual information of user features and design element features, where a) is the mutual information of the button solution; b) is the mutual information of the search box solution.

$$AP_u = \frac{1}{m} \sum_{i=1}^{N} \left(\frac{s_i}{i} \left(\sum_{j=1}^{i} s_i \right) \right) \tag{4}$$

$$MAP = \frac{\sum_{u \in U} AP_u}{|U|} \tag{5}$$

where AP_u is the average precision of test user, N is the number of overlaps between the recommended ranking and the ground-truth, and m represents the top m solutions to be examined. The top m solutions in the ground-truth are marked as 1 and then is 0, corresponding score will be assigned for corresponding item in the recommended sorting. After AP_u calculated, MAP is the mean of the AP for all test users.

An index is evaluated by the NDCG ranking algorithm, which reflects the overall quality of ranking. The better the ranking, the greater the NDCG value, as shown in Eq. 6, 7, and 8. For N folds, each fold has M data. Mark all the data in the i-th fold as i, and find the corresponding data in the prediction data set as i. S_i represents the tokens in ground-truth, and s_i represents tokens in the predicted ranking.

$$DCG_{predict} = \sum_{i=1}^{N*M} \frac{2^{s_i} - 1}{log_2(i+1)} \tag{6}$$

$$DCG_{ground-truth} = \sum_{i=1}^{N*M} \frac{2^{S_i} - 1}{log_2(i+1)} \tag{7}$$

$$NDCG = \frac{DCG_{predict}}{DCG_{ground-truth}} \tag{8}$$

Cosine Similarity reflects the similarity between vectors. Since most of the vectors of the user interface element solution are continuous components, the greater the similarity between the recommended solution and the ground truth, it means the two are approximately similar, and can also be to a certain extent. It reflects the recommended performance. For vectors $\vec{s_k}$ and $\vec{s_l}$, the definition of Cosine Similarity and the average Cosine Similarity in vector sets S_1 and S_2 are as Eq. 9 and Eq. 10:

$$Cosine\ Similarity(\vec{s_k}, \vec{s_l}) = \frac{\vec{s_k} \cdot \vec{s_l}}{\| \vec{s_k} \| \| \vec{s_l} \|} \tag{9}$$

$$Average\ Cosine\ Similarity = \frac{\sum_{\vec{s_k} \in S_1} \sum_{\vec{s_l} \in S_2} Cosine\ Similarity(\vec{s_k}, \vec{s_l})}{\| S_1 \| \| S_2 \|} \tag{10}$$

4.4 Results

We divide the collected data into with and without user features groups: For with user features group, its feature vector $\vec{x} = \{x_0, x_1, \ldots, x_n\}$ is consisted by $\vec{u}$ and $\vec{s}$; for without user features group, the feature vectors only contain $\vec{s}$. Data set D = (X, Y) consists of feature vector set X and its corresponding score set Y. According to the design elements, it is divided into Button data set and Search bar data set.

We experimented with LR, SVR, GBDT, FM and FFM models, each of which fit two datasets with and without user features. In the testing phase, after the model predicts the

Table 4. Performance comparison of different machine learning methods.

Dataset	Button		Search bar	
Model	MAP	NDCG	MAP	NDCG
LR	0.2604	0.7327	0.3478	0.6920
LR (User)	0.2467	0.7315	0.3333	0.6891
SVR	0.2420	0.7328	0.3395	0.6922
SVR (User)	0.2591	0.7333	0.3280	0.6957
GBDT	0.2666	0.7315	0.3229	0.6906
GBDT (User)	0.2582	0.7331	0.3254	0.6934
FM	0.2119	0.7464	0.3279	0.6997
FM (User)	0.2296	**0.7477**	0.3363	0.7028
FFM	0.2726	0.7430	0.3568	0.7171
FFM (User)	**0.2969**	0.7459	**0.3578**	**0.7209**

user's rating on the design element solution domain, the predicted rating and the user rating are sorted to calculate indicators. Since there are 5 scores (1 to 5) in ground-truth, there are multiple possible rankings for design solutions. Note that different rankings will bring differences in evaluation, and some may even have large gaps. With this regard, we randomly sort the solutions with the same score for 50 times, calculate the result for each sorting, and the final result is the average of all sorting situations. In this way, the deviations between different situations are reduced to less than 0.008. Results of MAP and NDCG are shown in Table 4, where m of MAP is 3, and N of NDCG is 6, and k-folds cross validation (k = 5) is used. As shown in Table 4, in the Button and the Search bar dataset, the FFM model has achieved obvious performance gain on MAP, and FFM with user features is more accurate than that without user features. In terms of NDCG, FM and FFM are close and work better than other methods. For other machine learning methods, introducing user features does not improve the overall prediction, which shows the importance of feature intersection for getting a more accuracy recommendation solution.

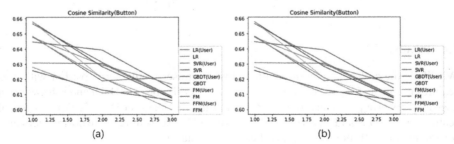

Fig. 4. Cosine similarity results. (a) Cosine similarity of models on the button dataset. (b) Cosine similarity of models on the search bar dataset.

Results of Cosine Similarity is shown in Fig. 4 (a) and (b), we calculated top 1, 2, 3 cases. In the Button dataset, the FFM model with user features has better performance in top-1 and top-2 accuracy, and on the Search bar dataset, the FFM with user features outperforms other models, which shows that while maintaining the recommendation accuracy, the FFM model with user features may have a high similarity to ground-truth in the case of indirect hits. And for other models, LR and GBDT are also recommended solutions that similar to ground-truth.

5 Conclusion and Feature Works

In this paper, we propose Personalized User Interface Elements Recommendation System based on user information. By introducing feature intersection by FFM, it provides more accurately recommend UI elements to new users. We found that users' evaluation of UI elements is related to the user's own characteristics, but also to the intersection of the characteristics of the user interface element solution itself.

For the future works, firstly, current work only recommends a single UI element, when multiple UI elements need to be recommended at the same time, the impact of their intersection on the overall interface need to be studied. Secondly, in addition to feature intersection, it will be interesting to improve existing models for the characteristics of user interface elements themselves. Going a step further, the impact of user preference on user interface elements on intersection efficiency, accuracy, and the trade-off between preference and efficiency are also worthy of in-depth discussion.

References

1. Ertugrul, E., Li, P., Sheng, B.: On attaining user-friendly hand gesture interfaces to control existing GUIs. Virtual Real. Intell. Hardw. **2**(2), 153–161 (2020)
2. Gossen, T., Nitsche, M., Vos, J., Nürnberger, A.: Adaptation of a search user interface towards user needs: a prototype study with children & adults. In: Proceedings of the Symposium on Human-Computer Interaction and Information Retrieval, pp. 1–10 (October 2013)
3. Hussain, J., et al.: Model-based adaptive user interface based on context and user experience evaluation. J. Multimodal User Interfaces **12**(1), 1–16 (2018). https://doi.org/10.1007/s12 193-018-0258-2
4. Juan, Y., Zhuang, Y., Chin, W.S., Lin, C.J.: Field-aware factorization machines for CTR prediction. In: Proceedings of the 10th ACM Conference on Recommender Systems, pp. 43–50 (September 2016)
5. Kolekar, S.V., Pai, R.M., MM, M.P.: Rule based adaptive user interface for adaptive E-learning system. Educ. Inf. Technol. **24**(1), 613–641 (2019)
6. Machado, E., et al.: A conceptual framework for adaptive user interfaces for older adults. In: 2018 IEEE International Conference on Pervasive Computing and Communications Workshops (PerCom Workshops), pp. 782–787. IEEE (March 2018)
7. Margaris, D., Spiliotopoulos, D., Vassilakis, C., Karagiorgos, G.: A user interface for personalized web service selection in business processes. In: Stephanidis, C., et al. (eds.) HCII 2020. LNCS, vol. 12427, pp. 560–573. Springer, Cham (2020). https://doi.org/10.1007/978-3-030-60152-2_41
8. Meng, X., et al.: A video information driven football recommendation system. Comput. Electr. Eng. **85**, 106699 (2020)

9. Moran, K., Bernal-Cárdenas, C., Curcio, M., Bonett, R., Poshyvanyk, D.: Machine learning-based prototyping of graphical user interfaces for mobile apps. IEEE Trans. Softw. Eng. **46**(2), 196–221 (2018)
10. Müller, F., Schmitz, M., Funk, M., Günther, S., Dezfuli, N., Mühlhäuser, M.: Personalized user-carried single button interfaces as shortcuts for interacting with smart devices. In: Extended Abstracts of the 2018 CHI Conference on Human Factors in Computing Systems, pp. 1–6 (April 2018)
11. Nawaz, M., Motiwalla, L., Deokar, A.V.: Adaptive user interface for a personalized mobile banking app. In: Adjunct Publication of the 26th Conference on User Modeling, Adaptation and Personalization, pp. 141–142 (July 2018)
12. Pan, J., et al.: Field-weighted factorization machines for click-through rate prediction in display advertising. In: Proceedings of the 2018 World Wide Web Conference, pp. 1349–1357 (April 2018)
13. Reinecke, K., Bernstein, A.: Predicting user interface preferences of culturally ambiguous users. In: CHI 2008 extended abstracts on Human Factors in Computing Systems, pp. 3261–3266 (2008)
14. Rendle, S.: Factorization machines. In: 2010 IEEE International Conference on Data Mining, pp. 995–1000. IEEE (December 2010)
15. Rim, R., Amin, M.M., Adel, M.: Bayesian networks for user modeling: Predicting the user's preferences. In: 13th International Conference on Hybrid Intelligent Systems (HIS 2013), pp. 144–148. IEEE (December 2013)
16. Sarsam, S.M., Al-Samarraie, H.: Towards incorporating personality into the design of an interface: a method for facilitating users' interaction with the display. User Model. User-Adap. Inter. **28**(1), 75–96 (2018). https://doi.org/10.1007/s11257-018-9201-1
17. Sheng, B., Li, P., Zhang, Y., Mao, L., Chen, C.P.: GreenSea: visual soccer analysis using broad learning system. IEEE Trans. Cybern. **51**(3), 1463–1477 (2020)
18. Soh, H., Sanner, S., White, M., Jamieson, G.: Deep sequential recommendation for personalized adaptive user interfaces. In: Proceedings of the 22nd International Conference on Intelligent User Interfaces, pp. 589–593 (March 2017)
19. Zhou, J., et al.: Intelligent exploration for user interface modules of mobile app with collective learning. In: Proceedings of the 26th ACM SIGKDD International Conference on Knowledge Discovery & Data Mining, pp. 3346–3355 (August 2020)

Medical Imaging

A Feature Point Extraction Method for Capsule Endoscope Localization

Jiaxing Ma[1]([✉]), Yinghui Wang[1]([✉]), Pengjiang Qian[1], and Gang Lin[2]

[1] School of Artificial Intelligence and Computer Science, Jiangnan University,
Wuxi 214122, China
6201924122@stu.jiangnan.edu.cn, wangyh@jiangnan.edu.cn
[2] Gastroenterology Department, Affiliated Hospital of Jiangnan University, Wuxi 214122, China

Abstract. Wireless capsule endoscopy (WCE) has emerged as a popular non-invasive imaging tool for inspection of human Gastrointestinal (GI) tract. If a displacement technique based entirely on visual features is used for WCE positioning, a suitable visual feature extraction technique is important. In this paper, an improved ORB algorithm is proposed to extract feature points from capsule endoscopy images. Because of the complexity of the scene in the digestive tract and the insignificant image variation, the adaptive threshold is proposed to be calculated using the coefficient of variation in the feature point extraction stage, which improves the ability of the algorithm to extract feature points in homogeneous area features. Then, the feature points are further filtered using the quadtree method to eliminate over-concentration and overlapping feature points. In the feature point description phase, BEBLID is used to enhance the saliency of the feature description. Finally, the Hamming distance is used to match points and RANSAC is used to avoid mismatches. The experimental results show that the improved algorithm has better stability and adaptability to capsule endoscopic images, and effectively improves the matching accuracy on the basis of satisfying the real-time performance.

Keywords: Wireless capsule endoscopy · Feature extraction · Adaptive thresholding · BEBLID

1 Introduction

In contrast to conventional wired endoscopes, wireless capsule endoscopy (WCE) works with a small, swallowable endoscope that is housed in a capsule and has come into common use as a non-invasive, painless, cross-contamination-free clinical imaging and diagnostic tool for the human digestive system. However, both acquisition path planning and lesion diagnosis [1] cannot be separated from the specific location of the WCE [2–4] within the cavity. Currently commercially available WCEs are mainly positioned using magnetic positioning techniques [5–7], which require expensive equipment and do not provide direct information about the distance the capsule is moving through the gastrointestinal tract, so a visual odometry method for capsule endoscopic positioning was developed. However, current SLAM (Simultaneous Localization and Mapping) [8, 9] methods that enable good camera localization and SFM (Structure from Motion) [10] methods for 3D structure recovery are almost ineffective for internal cavity video, mainly due to the inability to extract and track features caused by the high luminosity of the internal surface of the gastrointestinal cavity and the low frequency of the video frames.

For WCE localization needs more attention to the effective extraction of feature points, there are mainly SIFT (Scale Invariant Feature Transform) [11] method based on scale space, SURF (Speeded Up Robust Features) algorithm [12], FAST (Features from Accelerated Segment Test) algorithm [13] and ORB (Oriented FAST and Rotated BRIEF) [14], etc. To this end, an improved ORB method is proposed in this paper. For feature point detection, dynamic local thresholds are calculated for improvement based on neighborhood image blocks using coefficients of variation, and then feature points are managed and optimized using quadtrees. In the feature description stage, BEBLID (Boosted Efficient Binary Local Image Descriptor) [21] is then used to describe the feature points so that they can also be extracted on WCE images. Experiments show that the method is better adapted to the extraction of WCE video feature points, especially for less variable capsule endoscopic image regions with almost no loss of speed, and provides good support for WCE wireless capsule localization.

The structure of the remaining sections of this paper is shown below. The related work on feature point extraction is presented in Sect. 2. An overview of our approach is given in Sect. 3. The improved feature point detection method, feature point optimization method and feature point description technique proposed in this paper are described in detail in Sect. 4. Experimental metrics and results for real capsule endoscopy image datasets are discussed in Sect. 5. Section 6 contains the conclusions.

2 Related Work

Among the many classical methods for feature point extraction, SIFT is a scale space-based feature point detection method proposed by Lowe in 2004 [11]. The algorithm takes full account of changes in the illumination, scale and rotation of the image during the transformation process, but is computationally complex and cannot compute SIFT features and implement localization in real time on the CPU of an ordinary computer. Based on the SIFT algorithm, Bay proposed the SURF algorithm in 2006 [12], which uses Hessian matrices and reduced-dimensional feature descriptors to improve the execution efficiency of the SIFT algorithm to a certain extent and provides the possibility for the algorithm to run in real time on a computer. When processing WCE images, these algorithms are still too time consuming to meet the demands of real time. In addition, other features exist to improve computational speed by appropriately reducing accuracy and robustness, in particular the FAST algorithm proposed by Rosten et al. between 2006 and 2010 [13], which is known for its speed and uses the grey value of each pixel in a given field and the grey value of the centroid to determine whether the centroid is a corner point; as the algorithm only detects corner points, it is not scale invariant or directional; and the FSAT algorithm can only be used for the detection of feature points and cannot describe them in detail. To address these above shortcomings of the FSAT algorithm, Rublee et al. proposed a fast binary descriptor ORB [14] based on BRIEF

(Binary Robust Independent Elementary Features) [15] in 2011. The ORB offers a good compromise between accuracy and speed, maintaining rotation and scale invariance while achieving significant speed improvements. The BRIEF algorithm generates binary feature descriptions by randomly selecting pixels in the image window of feature points to compare grey values. However, in the process of comparing pixel grey values, only the relationship between pixel point grey values is used. Failure to make full use of the grey value information around a pixel point can result in a loss of image information. For this reason, this paper uses the BEBLID [18] descriptor to describe feature points, by which each descriptor obtains more spatially supported visual information, thus reducing the sensitivity of the feature description to noise.

In addition, Spyrou et al. [16] performed a comparative evaluation of each of these feature extraction methods on capsule endoscopic images. ORB feature points have a great advantage in terms of speed compared to other algorithms, but the number of ORB feature points that can be extracted when performing feature point detection is very sparse, with most feature points appearing in more textured image regions or even resulting in feature point redundancy, while regions with weak or lacking texture have almost no feature points. To address this problem, Mur-Arta uses double threshold and quadtree in ORB_SLAM3 [18] to optimize feature point extraction, but the algorithm still uses artificially set thresholds and does not consider pixel neighborhood correlation as a condition for truly adaptive extraction. Ma et al. [19] used dynamic local threshold instead of fixed threshold, and were able to extract more feature points by calculating local thresholds based on neighborhood image blocks. However, this method only simply considers the average grey value, which leads to much less effectiveness in this method on capsule endoscopic images. To this end, this paper uses the coefficient of variation [20] to calculate the difference in grayscale values between pixel points, which improves the feature point extraction capability of the original ORB algorithm in regions where the capsule endoscope image does not change significantly, based on the realization of automatic feature point extraction; subsequently, a quadtree is used to average and distribute the feature points to achieve a more uniform distribution of feature points over the whole image area. Experiments have verified the effectiveness and robustness of this method in this paper for WCE videos.

3 Method Overview

Overall, our approach first uses a feature point extraction method based on a local adaptive threshold calculated by the coefficient of variation, then averages and distributes the feature points using a quadtree, and uses the more accurate BEBLID descriptor to describe the feature points in the feature description stage. The method is shown in Fig. 1.

In the original FAST algorithm, the choice of threshold value determines the result of the extraction. According to the principle of the algorithm, the smaller the threshold, the more feature points are extracted and vice versa. Due to the complexity and variability of the intracavity scene captured by the capsule endoscope, the fixed threshold selection of FAST is not adapted to the feature extraction needs of the intracavity scene. To do this, we propose to divide the image by blocks, with each block counting as a separate region

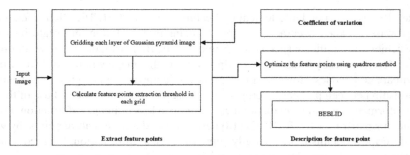

Fig. 1. Technology roadmap for the methodology in this paper

and the grey value of each pixel point counting as a sample value, and then calculate the coefficient of variation between the grey values of the pixel points as a threshold for the current block.

In addition, to solve the problem of concentrated or even redundant feature points, this paper uses quadtrees in [18] to filter and homogenize the extracted feature points. The process is to consider an image as a node, if the number of feature points in the node is greater than 1, then the node is divided into 4 nodes, if the number of feature points is 0, then the node is deleted; then, this operation is repeated until the number of nodes is greater than the number of feature points needed or it can no longer be divided.

Finally, further considering the requirement of real time, our method uses the BEBLID method for the description of the extracted feature points. The BEBLID descriptor presents features based on the comparison of pixel pairs, the key to its comparative speed is the limited number of comparisons, which is also essentially a compromise in the pursuit of speed at the expense of partial accuracy.

4 Method Detail Description

4.1 Adaptive Thresholds

The FAST algorithm [13] determines whether a candidate pixel point is a feature point by comparing the greyscale of the pixels around it. With the candidate pixel point p as the centre, the grey scale values of 16-pixel points of a circle of radius 3 are calculated and compared with point p. These points are numbered clockwise from 1 to 16. If the absolute value of the difference in grey level between N consecutive pixel points of these 16-pixel points and the central pixel point p is greater than or equal to t (t is a threshold), this detection point is judged to be a feature point. In practice, to speed up the determination process the difference in greyscale between point p and pixels 1, 5, 9 and 13 can be calculated and if there are three differences greater or less than t, further comparisons are made with other pixels. If the condition is not met, point p is simply excluded.

A fixed threshold approach would make the computation simple and reduce computation time, but such an approach used on high light and little variation capsule endoscopic images does not meet the requirements for feature point extraction, for this reason this paper proposes the use of a coefficient of variation to calculate the threshold t to improve this problem and achieve the need for adaptivity.

The coefficient of variation is a normalized measure of the degree of dispersion of a probability distribution and can be used to measure the degree of variation of individual pixel points. When the scale of measurement differs too much between data, the coefficient of variation can be used to remove the effect of the scale of measurement. The coefficient of variation is calculated as shown in Eq. (1).

$$c_v = \frac{\sigma}{\mu} \tag{1}$$

where c_v is the coefficient of variation, σ is the standard deviation of the sample and μ is the mean of the sample.

To calculate the adaptive threshold using the coefficient of variation, the entire image is first gridded according to a set grid size, with each grid acting as a separate image region. Calculate the threshold t in each grid by (2).

$$t = \frac{D_i}{M_i} * \alpha (i = 1, 2, \ldots) \tag{2}$$

where D_i denotes the standard deviation of the grayscale values of the pixel points in grid i, and M_i denotes the mean of the grayscale values of the pixel points in grid i. α can be calculated from (3).

$$\alpha = \frac{M_i}{M_i'} \tag{3}$$

$$M_i' = \frac{\sum_{j=1}^{n_i} f_i(x, y) - f_i(x, y)_{max} - f_i(x, y)_{min}}{n_i - 2} \tag{4}$$

where M_i' is the truncated mean of the grayscale values of the pixel points in grid i, n_i denotes the number of pixel points in grid i, $f_i(x, y)$ denotes the grayscale value at (x, y) in grid i, $f_i(x, y)_{max}$ denotes the maximum value of the grayscale value in grid i, and $f_i(x, y)_{min}$ denotes the minimum value of the grayscale value in grid i.

4.2   Feature Point Homogenization

The original ORB algorithm tends to concentrate on texture-rich regions when extracting feature points, and regions with less texture or lack of texture yield fewer feature points, which can result in feature point aggregation and feature point redundancy. In order to achieve a more uniform distribution of feature points in capsule endoscopy images, this paper adopts a homogenization strategy.

The extraction of feature points is first accomplished using the dynamic local threshold-based FAST algorithm proposed in Sect. 4.1. To further homogenize the feature points in the image, the two-dimensional space of the image is chunked using a quadtree, and then the feature points in each chunk are processed. The steps are as follows.

Step 1. Take the entire image is used as the initial node of the quadtree to obtain the initial quadtree structure.

Step 2. Judge all the nodes in the image. If the number of feature points in the node is 0, the node is deleted, if the number of feature points in the node is equal to 1, the node is no longer divided. If the number of feature points in the node is greater than 1, then the node continues to be split into four child nodes.

Step 3. Repeat the second step until the number of nodes reaches the set number of required feature points or no further splitting is possible, then the splitting of the quadtree ends.

Step 4. Select the feature points contained in each node. If the number of feature points is greater than 1, the feature point with the largest response value is selected to represent the node.

By the above method, feature points can be evenly distributed within the capsule endoscope image area.

4.3 BEBLID Descriptor

BEBLID [21] is a binary descriptor that uses a Boosting scheme to select the most discriminative pixels in a local image region. BEBLID is similar to BRIEF in that it is a binarization method, also based on differences in grey values, but BEBLID calculates the average difference in grey values within a region. A fixed number of square areas of different sizes are selected around the feature point and each pair of square areas is of the same size, which describes the feature point by calculating the difference in the average grey value of the pixel points in each pair of square blocks. The extraction function $f(x)$ for the BEBLID feature descriptor is defined as shown in Eq. (5).

$$f(x; p_1, p_2, s) = \frac{1}{s^2} \left(\sum_{q \in R(p_1, s)} I(q) - \sum_{r \in R(p_2, s)} I(r) \right) \tag{5}$$

where (q), $I(r)$ are the grey scale values of pixel points q and r, $R(p_1, s)$, $R(p_2, s)$ are square borders centred on p_1, p_2 and of size.

5 Experimental Results and Analysis

This section shows the setting of our experimental parameters, the selection of data sets, the selection of evaluation criteria, the experimental results, the experiments on parameter variation and the comparative analysis of the methods.

5.1 Selection of Datasets

The proposed method in this paper was evaluated on a dataset of 120 capsule endoscopy videos collected by PillCam at a resolution of 576×576 pixels, each of approximately 2.5 h duration, for a total of 45,000 frames, containing the complete video of the full procedure performed using the capsule endoscope. The videos were captured using PillCam capsules at the Gastroenterology Department of the Jiangnan University Hospital. The dataset includes a large number of videos from the stomach, colon and small intestine sites, and only video frames from the small intestine site are used for evaluation in this paper, excluding video clips from the stomach and colon sites from this study.

5.2 Evaluation Criteria

Four evaluation criteria were used in the experiments of this paper. The first criterion is the number of feature points, which is one of the most intuitive criteria for the effectiveness of feature point extraction.

The second criterion is the matching accuracy, which is calculated as shown in Eq. (6).

$$precision = \frac{m_c}{m} * 100\% \tag{6}$$

where m_c refers to the number of matches that were correctly matched and m refers to the number of matches that did not eliminate incorrect matches.

The third criterion is the image operation time. The third criterion is image manipulation time. In this paper, the operation time includes feature point extraction time, description time and matching time. Input processing time and metric calculation time are not considered.

The fourth criterion is the directional error, which means that the camera motion between frames is recovered by matching the correspondence between the feature points, but often there are deviations between the resulting camera motion and the true motion because of the presence of mismatching.

5.3 Experimental Results

In this section the feasibility of our method on capsule endoscopic images will be verified. Since does not exist any ground truth data set for the problems at hand, the only feasible way to evaluate the proposed approach was to use simulated scale and rotation transformations of sampled video frames.

We used the same evaluation method as in [17], specifically, in order to obtain a representative set of frames from the capsule endoscope video, selected video frames from the dataset were rotated transformed and/or scaled transformed at a frame rate of 5 fps. Then, we extracted feature points from both frames and, using RANSAC (Random Sample Consensus) [22], we determined the internal correspondences between the original video frames and the rotated video frames. Based upon these correspondences we estimated a transformation matrix, from which it was trivial to extract rotation and/or scale accordingly. Finally, we estimate rotation (orientation) and/or displacement (scaling) errors in comparison to the corresponding known artificial values.

For the determination of the set of the tentative correspondences, it must lead to more random experiments, so we set 30 experiments and take the average of 30 experiments as the average errors.

Figure 2(a) shows a real capsule endoscope image, the object to be matched is obtained by rotation and scaling on the basis of the real capsule endoscope image. In the experiments, the images to be matched were in two cases. In the first, only the rotation was performed without scaling, and a total of 8 different rotation angles were tested, from 5 to 45°, with a rotation step of 5°. In the second, the images were scaled by 0.9 on the basis of 8 different rotation angles.

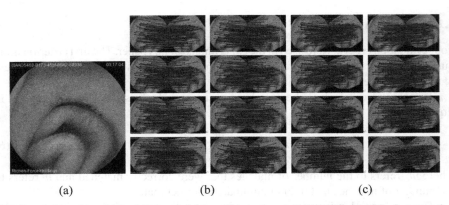

(a)   (b)   (c)

Fig. 2. (a) Capsule endoscopic image of the small bowel area. (b) Matching results for a rotation of 8 angles. (c) Matching results scaled to 0.9 and rotated by 8 angles. The green line indicates a correct match and the red line indicates an incorrect match. (Color figure online)

Table 1. Mean absolute orientation errors for each rotation angle at the original and 0.9 scales.

Angle (degrees)	No-scale (degrees)	Scale (degrees)
5	21.4035	13.3594
10	4.3211	0.2672
15	36.0287	6.7480
20	35.1488	2.0812
25	2.0323	0.6260
30	3.8051	0.3977
35	4.7720	5.5424
40	3.7651	4.5578

Figure 2(b) and 2(c) show the results for each of the two cases. The results are shown from left to right, with the angles increasing in order from top to bottom. Figure 2(b) and 2(c) show us the method in this paper is able to extract sufficient feature points and accomplish matching on both scaled and capsule endoscopic images that undergo different angular rotations. However, the matching results are relatively similar and it is difficult to visually distinguish the differences. In order to analyze the algorithm performance differences in more detail, the mean absolute orientation errors of the eight selected image sets were counted, as shown in Table 1. Where Angel true angle, No-scale indicates error without scaling and Scale indicates error with scaling. The error with scaling is smaller than the error without scaling. Without scaling the error is higher between 5 and 20°, while with scaling it is higher only at 5°.

5.4 Comparative Analysis of Methods

In this section we present a comparative analysis of the results of the proposed method and other similar methods on capsule endoscopic images in order to give a clearer indication of the advantages of our method. In the experiments, the feature extraction methods in ORB [14], the current best visual feature-based displacement technique ORB_SLAM3 [18], and our proposed improved method were used to obtain comparative results on the dataset in Sect. 5.3, respectively.

Table 2. Number of feature points extracted by the [14, 18] and our method.

Angle actual	[14] No-scale	[18] No-scale	Ours no-scale	[14] Scale	[18] Scale	Ours Scale
5	148	464	**507**	136	459	**507**
10	171	468	**507**	139	480	**505**
15	170	482	**507**	143	474	**505**
20	172	482	**507**	143	483	**506**
25	199	482	**507**	169	482	**506**
30	208	486	**507**	175	482	**507**
35	218	484	**507**	177	481	**503**
40	210	477	**504**	191	474	**503**

Table 3. Matching accuracy extracted by the [18] and our method.

Angle actual (degrees)	[18] No-scale (%)	Ours no-scale (%)	[18] Scale (%)	Ours scale (%)
5	62.5430	61.4458	52.8986	**54.2587**
10	50.1832	**52.7508**	45.3571	**45.5975**
15	48.9437	**52.4845**	54.0146	**55.1839**
20	51.2027	**55.3459**	58.5185	52.9032
25	49.1525	**57.4675**	54.6387	**55.1155**
30	54.5139	51.7886	53.9855	51.3245
35	49.3243	**53.3762**	56.8905	47.5570
40	47.8571	**53.5032**	53.0466	52.8846
Avg	51.71505	54.7703	53.6688	**51.8531**

The first evaluation criterion is quantity. We set the number of target feature points to 500. Table 2 shows the number of feature points extracted by the methods of the [14, 18] and our method. Where Avg is the average number for 8 sets of experiments. In both cases, the average number of feature points extracted by [14] is 187 and 159, and the average number of feature points extracted by [18] is 478 and 476, which are far from the extraction requirements. Our improved method achieves the target number we set for the extraction in different angle transformations and scenes with or without scaling. The resulting experiments show that our improved ORB algorithm outperforms both the ORB method and the method in ORB_SLAM3 for extraction on capsule endoscopy images.

The second evaluation criterion is the accuracy rate. Compared to the method in ORB_SLAM3 and our method, the ORB algorithm extracts a much smaller number of feature points on the capsule endoscopic image. Since we care about extracting enough feature points while ensuring the accuracy rate of matching, we exclude the ORB method. As shown in Table 3, in the case without scaling, the average accuracy of [18] is 51.7150% and that of our method is 54.7703%. In the case with scaling, the average accuracy of our method is 1.8157% lower than that of [18], but there are still four angles under which our method is superior.

The third criterion is time. The experimental results are shown in Fig. 3. The computation time of our improved ORB method and the method in ORB_SLAM3 are both higher than that of the ORB method. However, considering that the number of feature points extracted by ORB is much less, it can be excluded. Although the extraction speed of the optimized ORB algorithm is slower than before the optimization, it can maintain almost the same computation time as the method in ORB_SLAM3 when the results are better. The real-time requirements of the system can be met.

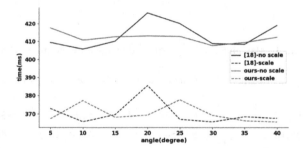

Fig. 3. Average extraction times for [18] and our method with and without scaling.

The fourth criterion is orientation error. Table 4 shows the orientation errors at eight angles for the methods of [14, 18] and our method with and without scaling. Where No-scale indicates no scaling, Scale indicates scaling and Avg indicates the average error over the 8 angles. As can be seen from Tables, in the absence of scaling, the mean error was 28.2001° for [14], 15.4883° for [18] and 13.9095° for our method. With scaling, the mean error for [14] is 14.5736 degrees and for [18] is 21.2225°, our method is only 4.1975°. The experimental results show that our method outperforms other methods and is robust on capsule endoscopic images.

Table 4. Orientation errors with and without scaling in the [14, 18] and our method.

Angle actual (degrees)	[14] No-scale (degrees)	[18] No-scale (degrees)	Ours no-scale (degrees)	[14] Scale (degrees)	[18] Scale (degrees)	Ours Scale (degrees)
5	26.6887	20.1484	21.4035	0.3835	37.5493	13.3594
10	34.4837	11.3446	**4.3211**	16.9175	11.0954	**0.2672**
15	80.6692	40.2004	**36.0287**	2.6067	17.0243	6.7480
20	6.6569	7.6963	35.1488	35.5334	23.4020	**2.0812**
25	24.9077	13.7508	**2.0323**	5.1912	45.4308	**0.6260**
30	23.3149	9.3273	**3.8051**	11.3170	2.8833	**0.3977**
35	28.7053	19.8742	**4.7720**	26.4908	31.7732	**5.5424**
40	0.1743	1.5647	3.7651	18.1486	0.6219	4.5578
Avg	28.2001	15.4883	**13.9095**	14.5736	21.2225	**4.1975**

6 Conclusions

This paper proposes an improved ORB algorithm based on local adaptive threshold, quadtree and BEBLID descriptors is proposed for the purpose of stable extraction of feature points on capsule endoscopic images. The method in this paper is based on the ORB algorithm, focusing on the feature point extraction phase and the feature point description phase for research and improvement. First, a feature point extraction method based on the calculation of local adaptive thresholds for the coefficient of variation is adopted, which allows for the uniform extraction of feature points on capsule endoscopy images. Then, feature points are managed and optimized using a quadtree approach to avoid excessive concentration and overlap of feature points. In the feature point description stage, the BEBLID descriptor is used for feature description. Through the validation of the capsule endoscopy image dataset, the improved ORB algorithm proposed in this paper has better performance in capsule endoscopy images, effectively improving the number of feature points extracted and the accuracy of feature matching, and the feature points can be evenly distributed within the image, which is a good adaptation to the weak texture region like capsule endoscopy images.

Acknowledgments. This work was supported by the National Natural Science Foundation of China [grant numbers 61872291, 62172190], and The Innovation & Entrepreneurship Plan of Jiangsu Province (JSSCRC2021532).

References

1. Charfi, S., El Ansari, M.: A locally based feature descriptor for abnormalities detection. Soft. Comput. **24**(6), 4469–4481 (2019). https://doi.org/10.1007/s00500-019-04208-8

2. Pahlavan, K., Bao, G., Ye, Y.: Rf localization for wireless video capsule endoscopy. Int. J. Wirel. Inf. Netw. **19**(4), 326–340 (2012)

3. Than, T.D., Alici, G., Zhou, H.: A review of localization systems for robotic endoscopic capsules. IEEE Trans. Biomed. Eng. **59**(9), 2387–2399 (2012)

4. Herp, J., Deding, U., Buijs, M.: Feature point tracking-based localization of colon capsule endoscope. Diagnostics. **11**(2), 193 (2021)

5. Bianchi, F.: Hybrid 6-DoF magnetic localization for robotic capsule endoscopes compatible with high-grade magnetic field navigation. IEEE Access. **10**, 4414–4430 (2022)

6. Liu, S., Kim, J., Hong, A.: Six-dimensional localization of a robotic capsule endoscope using magnetoquasistatic field. IEEE Access. **10**, 22865–22874 (2022)

7. Liu, S.: Three-dimensional localization of a robotic capsule endoscope using magnetoquasistatic field. IEEE Access. **8**, 141159–141169 (2020)

8. Mur-Artal, R., Montiel, J.M., Tardós, J.D.: ORB-SLAM: A versatile and accurate monocular SLAM system. IEEE Trans. Robot. **31**(5), 1147–1163 (2015)

9. Mur-Artal, R., Tardós, J.D.: ORB-SLAM2: An open-source SLAM system for monocular, stereo, and RGB-D Cameras. IEEE Trans. Robot. **33**(5), 1255–1262 (2017)

10. Schonberger, J.L., Frahm, J.M.: Structure-from-motion revisited. In: Proceedings of the IEEE Conference on Computer Vision and Pattern Recognition, CVPR 2016, pp. 4104–4113. IEEE, Las Vegas (2016)

11. Lowe, G.: Distinctive image features from scale-invariant keypoints. Int. J. Comput. Vis. **60**(2), 91–110 (2004)

12. Bay, H., Tuytelaars, T., Van Gool, L.: SURF: Speeded up robust features. In: Leonardis, A., Bischof, H., Pinz, A. (eds.) ECCV 2006. LNCS, vol. 3951, pp. 404–417. Springer, Heidelberg (2006). https://doi.org/10.1007/11744023_32

13. Rosten, E., Porter, R., Drummond, T.: Faster and better: a machine learning approach to corner detection. IEEE Trans. Pattern Anal. Mach. Intell. **32**(1), 105–119 (2010)

14. Rublee, E., Rabaud, V., Konolige, K.: ORB: an efficient alternative to SIFT or SURF. In: Proceedings of the IEEE International Conference on Computer Vision, ICCV 2011, pp. 2564–2571. IEEE, Barcelona (2011)

15. Calonder, M., Lepetit, V., Strecha, C., Fua, P.: BRIEF: binary robust independent elementary features. In: Daniilidis, K., Maragos, P., Paragios, N. (eds.) ECCV 2010. LNCS, vol. 6314, pp. 778–792. Springer, Heidelberg (2010). https://doi.org/10.1007/978-3-642-15561-1_56

16. Spyrou, E., Iakovidis, D.K., Niafas, S.: Comparative assessment of feature extraction methods for visual odometry in wireless capsule endoscopy. Comput. Biol. Med. **65**, 297–307 (2015)

17. Spyrou, E., Iakovidis, D.K.: Video-based measurements for wireless capsule endoscope tracking. Meas. Sci. Technol. **25**(1), 5002–5038 (2014)

18. Campos, C., Elvira, R., Rodríguez, J.J.G.: ORB-SLAM3: An accurate open-source library for visual, visual-inertial, and multimap SLAM. IEEE Trans. Robot. **37**(6), 1874–1890 (2021)

19. Ma, C., Hu, X., Xiao, J.: Homogenized ORB algorithm using dynamic threshold and improved Quadtree. Math. Probl. Eng. **2021**(1), 1–19 (2021)

20. Kesteven, G.L.: The coefficient of variation. Nature **158**(4015), 520–521 (1946)

21. Suarez, I., Sfeir, G., Buenaposada, J.M.: BEBLID: boosted efficient binary local image descriptor. Pattern Recognit Lett. **133**, 366–372 (2020)

22. Tran, Q.-H., Chin, T.-J., Carneiro, G., Brown, M.S., Suter, D.: In defence of RANSAC for outlier rejection in deformable registration. In: Fitzgibbon, A., Lazebnik, S., Perona, P., Sato, Y., Schmid, C. (eds.) ECCV 2012. LNCS, vol. 7575, pp. 274–287. Springer, Heidelberg (2012). https://doi.org/10.1007/978-3-642-33765-9_20

Automated Diagnosis of Retinal Neovascularization Pathologies from Color Retinal Fundus Images

Rahma Boukadida[1,2](✉) ⓘ, Yaroub Elloumi[1,3,4] ⓘ, Rostom Kachouri[3] ⓘ,
Asma Ben Abdallah[1], and Mohamed Hedi Bedoui[1] ⓘ

[1] Medical Technologie and Image Processing Laboratory, Faculty of Medicine,
University of Monastir, Monastir, Tunisia
rahmaboukadida@yahoo.com
[2] Faculty of Sciences of Monastir, University of Monastir, 1002 Monastir, Tunisia
[3] Gaspard- Monge Computer Science Laboratory, Université Gustave Eiffel CNRS, ESIEE,
Paris, France
[4] ISITCom Hammam -Sousse, University of Sousse, Sousse, Tunisia

Abstract. The retinal Neo-Vascularization (NV) is the abnormal growth of new blood vessels in the retina, which leads to a severe reduction on visual acuity and blindness. It is a main biomarker to screening several diseases, where the Proliferative Diabetic Retinopathy (PDR) and Wet Age-related Macular Degeneration (WAMD) are the most common ones. The NV severity requires a fast screening to avoid severe degradation. However, it is labor intensive and time-consuming for the ophthalmologists.

In this paper, we suggest an automated screening method that automatically detects NV from fundus photography and classify it as PDR, WAMD and Healthy. For this purpose, the image is preprocessed and then provided a transfer learned model of the VGG16 neural network. The method was evaluated using a dataset containing 395 fundus photographs of retinal images where an accuracy of 98.30%, a sensitivity of 98.66%, a specificity of 98.33% were achieved. In addition, the areas under curve in terms of classes were between 98% and 100%.

Keywords: Retinal neovascularization · Wet Age-Related Macular Degeneration · Proliferative Diabetic Retinopathy · Deep Learning · Transfer Learning

1 Introduction

Neo-Vascularization (NV) is an abnormal formation of new blood vessels, usually in or under the retina. It is caused by a severe lack of oxygen in the retinal capillaries. The new vessels are thin, tortuous and fragile. They may easily start leaking blood on surface of retina and cause severe vision loss, even blindness [1]. NV is associated with a range of ocular disorders, including Age-related Macular Degeneration (AMD), Diabetic Retinopathy (DR), retinopathy of prematurity, corneal neovascularization, retinal vessel occlusion, and neovascular glaucoma. Among these neovascularization-related diseases, AMD and DR are the leading causes of visual impairment in the world [2] which are targeted in this study.

AMD causes severe vision loss in developed countries, particularly in people aged 65 and older. It is considered as the third leading cause of irreversible vision loss worldwide. By 2040, AMD will affect 288 million people worldwide [2]. AMD can be classified into two types. The Dry AMD which is characterized by the appearance of drusens as shown in Fig. 1(b). The Wet AMD (WAMD) occurs due to a Choroidal Neovascularization (CNV) which is an abnormal blood vessel formation from choroid region of the retina, as shown in Fig. 1(c). The WAMD progresses faster and leads to an irreversible loss of sight.

DR is another common cause of human vision loss, which affects actually 463 million people worldwide and 700 million by 2045 [3,4]. DR has been categorized into two types, Non-proliferative Diabetic Retinopathy (NPDR) and Proliferative Diabetic Retinopathy (PDR). The latter is the most severe stage of DR, which corresponds to 9% of DR affected people [5]. PDR is characterized by neovascularization with or without pre-retinal or vitreal hemorrhages. The detection of PDR in early stage in order to stop or delay its progression leads to avoid vision loss and blindness [6].

The early detection of WAMD and PDR is essential to preserve the visual acuity. The NV, in particular caused by WAMD and PDR, have similar neovascular changes, related to the color and the shape whatever the retinal pathology is. Consequently, it is hard to distinguish between PDR and WAMD. However, misdiagnosis or failure to diagnose results in inadequate medical therapy which leads to severe aggravation of vision and blindness.

In this work, we aim to propose an automated method to differentiate between normal, WAMD and PDR cases through fundus images, in order to save patients from the risk of blindness. Also, it is inexpensive and non-invasive technique and thus, an ideal screening technology to be adopted for the detection of WAMD and PDR.

The paper is organized as follows. Section 2 discusses the related work. The suggested method for WAMD and PDR detection is presented in Sect. 3. The evaluation of the proposed method and performance parameters is done in Sect. 4, followed by conclusion in the last section.

2   Related Work

Recently, several deep learning systems have been developed for the classification of color fundus photographs into AMD severity scales [7, 8]. These severity scales have included both binary (e.g., Dry vs. WAMD) and multi-class (e.g., the 9-step AREDS Severity Scale and a 4-class AMD classification) systems. The work described by Peng et al. [9] uses a DL model called « DeepSeeNet», to classify fundus images automatically by the the Age Related Eye Disease Study (AREDS). Experiment results show that the proposed model achieves an accuracy of 0.671 and a kappa of 0.558. Grassmann et al. [10] proposed a deep learning based classification architecture to predict the severity of AMD. In this study, an ensemble of several convolutional neural networks was used to classify among 13 different classes of AMD. The experimentation is processed using the

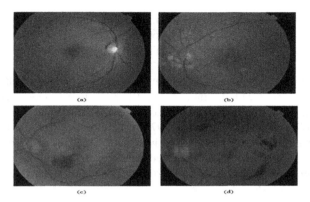

Fig. 1. Fundus images: (a) normal, (b) Dry AMD, (c) WAsMD, (d) PDR image.

AREDS dataset. The accuracy of classifying fundus photographs into 13 different AMD classes was only 63.3%. Keel et al. [11] proposed an algorithm for detecting WAMD based on fundus photography from a private dataset. The work described by Heo et al. [12] developed a DL-based diagnostic tool to detect and differentiate between Dry and WAMD using fundus photographs. The dataset was composed of 399 fundus images. The experimental results show that the proposed model achieves 90.86% accuracy with preprocessing for classification into three classes. Burlina et al. [13] proposed a method a DL algorithm to identify the class of AMD using color fundus photographs from the AREDS. The performances of two-four classes of AMD classification were 93.4%, 81.5%, and 79.4%, respectively.

It is noteworthy that ophthalmologists must distinguish between RDNP and PDR, as the diagnoses have different treatments and prognosis for blindness. There are several works for DR diagnosis at image level based on DL. Pratt et al. [14] proposed a CNN model to evaluate the severity of DR. The classification provides 5 grades such as No DR, Mild DR, Moderate DR, Severe DR and Proliferative DR. EyePACS database was used for training. The proposed model achieved a classification accuracy of 75%. Shanthi et al. [15] present a DL architecture to classify the input into 4 categories. Training and testing were performed, respectively, with 710 and 303 fundus images from the MESSIDOR database. The work described by Riaz et al. [16] presented a CNN for DR classification into 5 classes. The network was implemented on EyePACS/Kaggle and MESSIDOR databases. The performance was evaluated on 1747 images from the MESSIDOR database and 17,978 images from the EyePACS/Kaggle database. Wan et al. [17] evaluated 4 types of CNN architectures to classify DR into 5 categories (0–4). Liu et al. [18] described a challenge named "Diabetic Retinopathy (DR)-Grading and Image Quality Estimation Challenge" in conjunction with ISBI 2020 to hold three sub-challenges and develop deep learning models for DR image assessment and grading. The performance was evaluated using the DeepDRiD dataset containing 2,000 regular DR images and 256 ultra-widefield images. The weighted kappa for DR grading ranged from 0.93 to 0.82. Dai et al. [19] proposed a CNN model to evaluate the severity of DR. Images were obtained from the Shanghai Integrated Diabetes Prevention and Care System study.

The grading of diabetic retinopathy as mild, moderate, severe and proliferative achieves area under the curves of 0.943, 0.955, 0.960 and 0.972, respectively. All the networks were provided with transfer learning capability and hyperparameter tuning. Most of the training database is EyePACS/Kaggle.

Although several automated DL systems have been found to simultaneously detect DR and AMD using color fundus images. In [20], the authors propose a DL model called Retinet, that classifies the fundus image into normal, AMD and DR classes. The dataset integrates 62578 fundus images where 197 ones are on the Wet and Dry AMD stage which are selected from the UCH-AMD private database. They achieved prediction rate is about 88%. Gonzalo et al. [21] proposed an automated diagnosis of DR and AMD using a pre-trained DL system based in color fundus images. Then, validation was tested on Messidor and the AREDS dataset.

In order to develop and test the accuracy of their DLs, the majority of the research that detects AMD has used the AREDS database. On the other hand, the research that detects DR has used the EyePacs database. However, there is no method that proposes to differentiate only between the WAMD and PDR. In this regard, the contribution of this paper is to propose a method to differentiate between PDR and WAMD using small publicly available data sets.

3   Automated Diagnosis of WAMD and PDR

3.1   Proposed Method

Our objective is to propose an automated method for differentially between normal, WAMD, and PDR images. In this context, The VGG-16 neural network is applied to image classification and is frequently found in related works. This work focuses on evaluating the application of VGG-16 neural network with transfer learning to classify the input image into 3 categories (Healthy image, WAMD image, PDR image) as illustrated in the Fig. 2. Furthermore, this work highlights the necessary pre-processing step to ensure the quality of images used in the training.

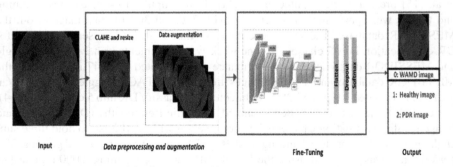

Fig. 2. Diagram of our proposed method.

3.2 Data Preprocessing and Augmentation

Preprocessing is necessary to make the new vessels visible in a fundus image. The green channel is extracted from the RGB fundus images. This channel is selected because the blood vessels, including those associated with neovascularization, appear clearer in this channel than in the other channels. Then, to improve the visibility of the blood vessels, Contrast Limited Adaptive Histogram Equalization (CLAHE) is used [22, 23]. CLAHE adjusts the contrast of the image in order to ensure that the blood vessels become brighter than the background. The preprocessed images are shown in Fig. 3 c1, c2, c3. The size of the input retinal images is 224 × 224 pixels.

To increase the diversity of the dataset and improve the robustness of the DL model, we applied data augmentation methods. For this purpose, all images are flipped and shifted horizontally and vertically and rotated with an angle of 5°, as presented in Fig. 4.

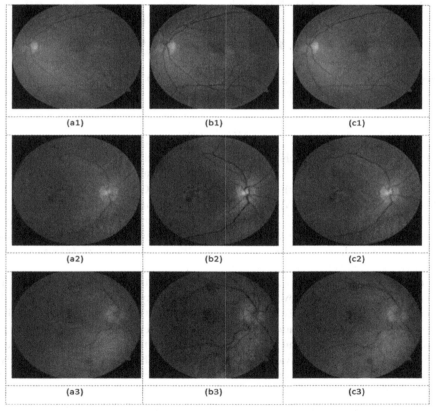

Fig. 3. Pre-processing: a1, a2 and a3, healthy, WAMD and PDR image; b1, b2 and b3, green channels of images; c1, c2 and c3, pre-processed images (Color figure online)

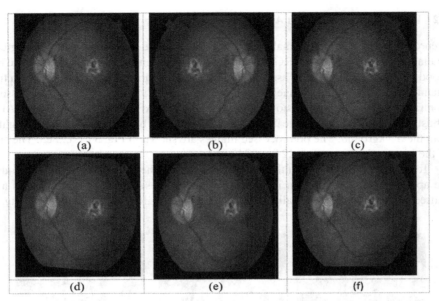

Fig. 4. Data augmentation (a) original input, (b) horizontal flip, (c) vertical flip, (e) rotation with 5° of the image, (f) width shift, (g) height shift

3.3 Transfer Learning of VGG16 Architecture

In this study, the VGG-16 architecture was applied to achieve transfer learning. VGG-16 is a convolutional neural network by VGGNet (Visual Geometry Group), which was developed by Oxford University Visual Geometry Group researchers to compete in the ImageNet Large-Scale Visual Recognition Challenge (ILSVR) in 2014 [22]. The architecture is composed of 13 convolutional layers, interspersed with 5 pooling layers and ending with 3 dense layers (see Fig. 2). The pre-trained CNN model was trained using ImageNet which is a large public dataset that contains 1,000,000 images to be classified into 1,000 classes.

The retinal fundus dataset was utilized to train the pre-trained network, after applying pre-processing on it. To achieve the transfer, the top 2 layers of the pre-trained model, which are employed to classify 1000 classes, were removed and replaced by an a three layers. The first layer is a flatten in order to align all features into a single row. The second layer applies a dropout function to prevent overfitting, with a threshold equal to 0.5. Then, a SoftMax activation function as a classifier with 3 nodes to supply 3 output classes. The new network was re-trained with retinal fundus images dataset with learning rate of 0.00001.The loss function was minimized using a stochastic gradient descent optimizer with momentum =0.9. While the number of epochs was 30 epochs. After repeated testing, the batch size was set as 4. The main hyper parameters used for training are summarized in Table 1.

Table 1. .

Hyperparameter	Value
Optimizing function	SGD—Stochastic Gradient Descent
Epochs	30
Batch size	4
Learning rate	0.00001
Dropout	0.2
Loss function	Categorical cross entropy

4 Experimental Results

4.1 Dataset

Based on the state of the art study, the databases do not contain enough PDR and WAMD fundus images. For this purpose, we construct a database of 395 images where fundus images are collected from different databases. The dataset contains 115 WAMD images, 114 PDR images and 166 healthy images. The image resources used are collected from four publically accessible databases: ODIR, RFMiD, REFUGE, Dataset from fundus images for the study of DR. The number of images is detailed in Table 2.

ODIR [24]: The Ocular disease intelligent recognition (ODIR) database comprises of pairs of fundus images of 5000 patients labeled for eight categories of ophthalmological diseases. RFMiD [25]: It consists of 3200 fundus images captured using three different fundus cameras with 46 conditions annotated through adjudicated consensus of two senior retinal experts. REFUGE [26]. The REFUGE dataset (Retinal-Fundus-Glaucoma-Challenge) contains 400 fundus images. With 89 AMD images. Dataset from fundus images for the study of DR [27]. This dataset consist of 757 color fundus images acquired at the Department of Ophthalmology of the Hospital de Clínicas, Facultad de Ciencias Médicas (FCM), Universidad Nacional de Asunción (UNA), Paraguay. The acquisition of the retinographies was made through the Visucam 500 camera of the Zeiss brand. Two expert ophthalmologists have classified the dataset.

4.2 Evaluation Metrics

In order to evaluate the performance of our method, we use four parameters, which are sensitivity (Sens), specificity (Spec), accuracy (ACC) and AUC, given in Eqs. (1)–(3), respectively.

$$\text{Sensitivity} \ = \ \text{TP} \ / \ (\ \text{TP} \ + \ \text{FN} \ ) \tag{1}$$

$$\text{Specificity} \ = \ \text{TN} \ / \ (\ \text{TN} \ + \ \text{FP} \ ) \tag{2}$$

$$\text{Accuracy} \ = \ (\ \text{TP} \ + \ \text{TN}) \ / \ (\ \text{TP} \ + \ \text{TN} \ + \ \text{FP} \ + \text{FN} \ ) \tag{3}$$

Table 2. Datasets description

Bases de données	Number of healthy images	Number of WAMD images	Number of PDR images
ODIR [17]	-	36	-
RFMiD [18]	0	38	0
REFUGE [19]	-	41	0
Dataset from fundus images for the study of DR [20]	166	0	114
Total	166	115	114

where TP, TN, FP and FN are respectively the true positive, the true negative, the false positive and the false negative detected images.

AUC is the area under the Receiver Operating Curve (ROC) and it provides the probability that the model ranks a positive example more highly than a negative example. ROC is a plot between two parameters: True Positive Rate (TPR) and False Positive Rate (FPR). The first in the Y-axis and the second is on the X-axis. TPR is equal to sensitivity, and FPR is the complement of Specificity. Equation (4) shows the parameter FPR.

$$FPR = FP / (FP + TN)   \tag{4}$$

4.3   Performance Evaluation of Proposed Method

The method was developed using the Python language. The pre-processing is executed using the OpenCV library. We trained our model using the "Keras" API. The training and testing steps are executed on the cloud service "google Colab".

The dataset in splitting where 70% of the data are used for training, 15% for validation and 15% for testing. The accuracy and loss curves on the training and validation set as depicted in Fig. 5. The X-axis represents the epoch count, the left Y-axis represents the loss value, and the right Y-axis represents the training accuracy.

In addition, the confusion matrix of the test set depicting the true versus the predicted class of 59 fundus images. Figure 6 shows the confusion matrix. Furthermore, our algorithm successfully identified all fundus images with WAMD and PDR. Thus, 25 images showing a healthy fundus were identified correctly as such, resulting a specificity of 98% and sensitivity of 96% for this class. Our results demonstrate that our method is able to differentiate between WAMD and PDR up to 98.30%. The sensitivity of the system is 98.66% and the specificity is 98.33%.

Figure 7 shows Receiver Operator Characteristic (ROC) curve of each class. The AUC of the model reached 100%, 98%, and 98.81% for detecting WAMD, Healthy images and PDR images.

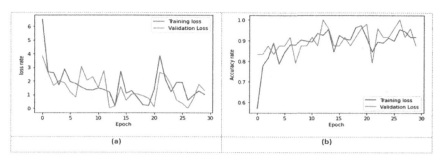

Fig. 5. Evaluation of training performance in terms of epochs: (a) Training and validation loss values; (b) Training and validation accuracy values

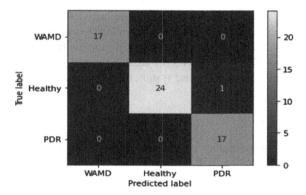

Fig. 6. Confusion matrix

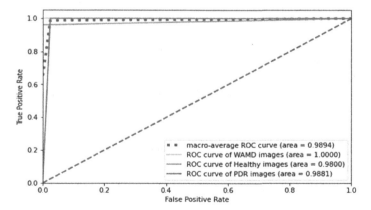

Fig. 7. Receiver operating characteristic curves for each class

5   Conclusion

PDR and WAMD are common retinal diseases. If not treated timely, they can cause irreversible central vision loss. In this paper, we proposed a diagnostic system for automatic and early identification of WAMD and PDR. For this purpose, we use a deep learning approach based transfer learning with the VGG16 neural network using fundus images. The images of the inputs are directly introduced into the network by processing them in advance. The images are preprocessed and resized. The data augmentation is used to increase the data set. The main features used to detect diseases are extracted automatically.

The experimental results demonstrate the reliability of the proposed method. Our proposed method has achieved an ACC of 98.30%, a sensitivity of 98.66%, a specificity of 98.33% and a AUC of 98.94%. Further, the results suggest that this method may provide an efficient, cost-effective and precise diagnosis of healthy, PDR and WAMD fundus images. Hence proper treatment can be provided to impede the progression of the diseases. Also, this method is the first attempt to differentiate fundus images into normal, dry AMD, and wet AMD classes. Furthermore, this suggested contribution is able to be implemented into a mobile End-To-End system for retinal pathology screening [28, 29].

References

1. Yu, S., Xiao, D., Kanagasingam, Y.: Machine learning based automatic neovascularization detection on optic disc region. IEEE J. Biomed. Health Inform. **22**(3), 886–894 (2018). https://doi.org/10.1109/JBHI.2017.2710201
2. Wong, W.L., et al.: Global prevalence of age-related macular degeneration and disease burden projection for 2020 and 2040: a systematic review and meta-analysis. Lancet Global Health **2**(2), e106–e116 (2014). https://doi.org/10.1016/S2214-109X(13)70145-1
3. International Diabetes Federation. International diabetes federation diabetes atlas.. https://www.diabetesatlas.org/en/
4. Elloumi, Y., Abroug, N., Bedoui, M.H.: End-to-end mobile system for diabetic retinopathy screening based on lightweight deep neural network. In: Bouadi, T., Fromont, E., Hüllermeier, E. (eds.) IDA 2022. LNCS, vol. 13205, pp. 66–77. Springer, Cham (2022). https://doi.org/10.1007/978-3-031-01333-1_6
5. Boukadida, R., Elloumi, Y., Akil, M., Bedoui, M.H.: Mobile-aided screening system for proliferative diabetic retinopathy. Int. J. Imaging Syst. Technol. **31**(3), 1638–1654 (2021). https://doi.org/10.1002/ima.22547
6. Elloumi, Y., Ben Mbarek, M., Boukadida, R., Akil, M., Bedoui, M.H.: Fast and accurate mobile-aided screening system of moderate diabetic retinopathy. In: Thirteenth International Conference on Machine Vision, Rome, Italy, p. 93. January 2021. https://doi.org/10.1117/12.2588505
7. Sayadia, S.B., Elloumi, Y., Kachouri, R., Akil, M., Abdallah, A.B., Bedoui, M.H.: Automated method for real-time AMD screening of fundus images dedicated for mobile devices. Med. Biol. Eng. Compu. **60**(5), 1449–1479 (2022). https://doi.org/10.1007/s11517-022-02546-8
8. Elloumi, Y., Akil, M., Boudegga, H.: Ocular diseases diagnosis in fundus images using a deep learning: approaches, tools and performance evaluation. In: Real-Time Image Processing and Deep Learning 2019, Baltimore, United States, p. 30, May 2019. https://doi.org/10.1117/12.2519098

9. Peng, Y., *et al.*: DeepSeeNet: a deep learning model for automated classification of patient-based age-related macular degeneration severity from color fundus photographs. Ophthalmology **126**(4), 565–575 (2019). https://doi.org/10.1016/j.ophtha.2018.11.015

10. Grassmann, F., *et al.*: A deep learning algorithm for prediction of age-related eye disease study severity scale for age-related macular degeneration from color fundus photography. Ophthalmology **125**(9), 1410–1420 (2018). https://doi.org/10.1016/j.ophtha.2018.02.037

11. Keel, S., *et al.*: Development and validation of a deep-learning algorithm for the detection of neovascular age-related macular degeneration from colour fundus photographs. Clin. Experiment. Ophthalmol. **47**(8), 1009–1018 (2019). https://doi.org/10.1111/ceo.13575

12. Heo, T.-Y., *et al.*: Development of a deep-learning-based artificial intelligence tool for differential diagnosis between dry and neovascular age-related macular degeneration. Diagnostics **10**(5), 261 (2020). https://doi.org/10.3390/diagnostics10050261

13. Burlina, P., Pacheco, K.D., Joshi, N., Freund, D.E., Bressler, N.M.: Comparing humans and deep learning performance for grading AMD: a study in using universal deep features and transfer learning for automated AMD analysis. Comput. Biol. Med. **82**, 80–86 (2017). https://doi.org/10.1016/j.compbiomed.2017.01.018

14. Pratt, H., Coenen, F., Broadbent, D.M., Harding, S.P., Zheng, Y.: Convolutional Neural networks for diabetic retinopathy. Procedia Comput. Sci. **90**, 200–205 (2016). https://doi.org/10.1016/j.procs.2016.07.014

15. Shanthi, T., Sabeenian, R.S.: Modified Alexnet architecture for classification of diabetic retinopathy images. Comput. Electr. Eng. **76,** 56–64 (2019). https://doi.org/10.1016/j.compeleceng.2019.03.004

16. Riaz, H., Park, J., Choi, H., Kim, H., Kim, J.: Deep and densely connected networks for classification of diabetic retinopathy. Diagnostics **10**(1), 24 (2020). https://doi.org/10.3390/diagnostics10010024

17. Wan, S., Liang, Y., Zhang, Y.: Deep convolutional neural networks for diabetic retinopathy detection by image classification. Comput. Electr. Eng. **72,** 274–282 (2018). https://doi.org/10.1016/j.compeleceng.2018.07.042

18. Liu, R., *et al.*: DeepDRiD: diabetic retinopathy—grading and image quality estimation challenge. Patterns **3**(6), 100512 (2022). https://doi.org/10.1016/j.patter.2022.100512

19. Dai, L., *et al.*: A deep learning system for detecting diabetic retinopathy across the disease spectrum. Nat. Commun. **12**(1), 3242 (2021). https://doi.org/10.1038/s41467-021-23458-5

20. Ghebrechristos, H., Alaghband, G., Hwang, R.Y.: RetiNet — feature extractor for learning patterns of diabetic retinopathy and age-related macular degeneration from publicly available datasets. In: 2017 International Conference on Computational Science and Computational Intelligence (CSCI), Las Vegas, NV, USA, pp. 1643–1648. December 2017. https://doi.org/10.1109/CSCI.2017.286

21. González-Gonzalo, C., *et al.*: Evaluation of a deep learning system for the joint automated detection of diabetic retinopathy and age-related macular degeneration », *Acta* Ophthalmology **98**(4), pp. 368-377 (2020. https://doi.org/10.1111/aos.14306

22. Simonyan, K., Zisserman, A.: Very Deep convolutional networks for large-scale image Recognition (2014). https://doi.org/10.48550/ARXIV.1409.1556

23. Boudegga, H., Elloumi, Y., Akil, M., Hedi Bedoui, M., Kachouri, R., Abdallah, A.B.: Fast and efficient retinal blood vessel segmentation method based on deep learning network. Comput. Med. Imag. Graph **90** 101902 (2021). https://doi.org/10.1016/j.compmedimag.2021.101902

24. OIA-ODIR: [En ligne]. Disponible sur: https://odir2019.grand-challenge.org

25. RFMid: https://riadd.grand-challenge.org/download-all-classes/

26. refuge-AMD. https://refuge.grand-challenge.org/iChallenge-AMD/

27. Castillo Benítez, V.E., *et al.*: Dataset from fundus images for the study of diabetic retinopathy. Data in Brief **36**, 107068 (2021). https://doi.org/10.1016/j.dib.2021.107068

28. Elloumi, Y.: Cataract grading method based on deep convolutional neural networks and stacking ensemble learning. Int. J. Imaging Syst. Tech. **32**(3), 798–814 (2022). https://doi.org/10.1002/ima.22722
29. Mrad, Y., Elloumi, Y., Akil, Y., Bedoui, M.H.: Fast and accurate method for glaucoma screening from smartphone-captured fundus images. IRBM **43**, 279–289 (2021). https://doi.org/10.1016/j.irbm.2021.06.004

Segmentation

DDCNet: A Lightweight Network with Variable Receptive Field for Real-Time Portrait Segmentation in Complex Environment

Dongjin Huang$^{(\boxtimes)}$, Di Wu, Jinhua Liu, and Yushan Lv

Shanghai University, Shanghai, China
`djhuang@shu.edu.cn`

Abstract. Due to the complex and diverse structure of the portrait boundary, it is a great challenge to segment the portrait from the natural background efficiently and accurately. We propose a new lightweight real-time semantic segmentation network-DDCNet, for portrait segmentation in complex background. Firstly, we propose a deformable depthwise separable convolution block, which combines deformable convolution with depthwise separable convolution, so that the network can fully obtain global and local information while reducing time consumption, and effectively reduce the complexity of the model. Secondly, we propose a detail selection block, which improves the segmentation accuracy of the network by selecting the information supplemented by skip connection. Finally, we propose a novel loss to improve the robustness of portrait segmentation in natural background. Our model has few parameters (0.122M) and FLOPs (0.092G). Experimental results show that our method could efficiently obtain the accurate segmentation image in real-time and achieve state-of-the-art comprehensive performance on the public datasets EG1800 and Conference Video Segmentation Dataset. User study shows that our method is favored by the most testers.

Keywords: Portrait segmentation · Lightweight · Deformable convolution · Deep learning

1 Introduction

Portrait segmentation is an important subset of semantic segmentation, which aims to divide images into portrait and background by classifying each pixel. Portrait segmentation is a preprocessing operation used to study and analyze human behavior, and it makes important contributions to subsequent studies such as 3D reconstruction and tracking recognition [1].

Traditional segmentation methods [2,3] are generally based on the color or natural structure of the image, rely on data-driven and prone to low-frequency "smearing" or high-frequency "chunky" artifacts [4]. In recent years, semantic segmentation network based on deep learning has developed rapidly, but it is still

N. Magnenat-Thalmann et al. (Eds.): CGI 2022, LNCS 13443, pp. 465–476, 2022.
https://doi.org/10.1007/978-3-031-23473-6_36

a huge challenge to create a network that balances real-time, lightweight, and accuracy [5]. Because the segmentation task needs to solve two contradictory problems at the same time, that is, to save low-level features while acquiring high-level semantic information [6]. In order to ensure the effect of high accuracy, researchers try to place multiple receptive fields on layers of the network to enhance global and local information, but the parallel operation brings time consumption. Another common method uses a two-branch network, such as [5,7,8]. The two branches are used to obtain low-level features and high-level semantics but increases the model's complexity.

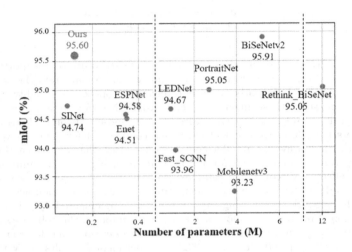

Fig. 1. Comparison of model complexity and accuracy on EG1800. The horizontal axis is parameters, and the vertical axis is the mIoU.

To solve these problems, we propose a DDCNet module with deformable depthwise separable convolution block (DDC) and detail selection block (DS). The DDC module proposed by us combines deformable convolution [9] with depthwise separable convolution [10], so that the module can automatically adjust the receptive field according to the characteristics of objects, so as to achieve the purpose of enhancing global and local information without time consumption. The parameters brought by deformable convolution and FLOPs are offset by the feature of depthwise convolution, thus reducing the complexity of the module. The DS module we proposed sets two thresholds to remove the noise in the high resolution feature map in the skip connection and retain the details that are discarded during the encoding process, so makes the supplementary detailed information effective and can bring better segmentation results to high-level semantics. In addition, we calculate the weighted loss for the part of the prediction error of each picture, so as to improve the robustness of the network for the classification of portraits.

Experiments show that, for public complex background datasets, compared with the existing efficient and the latest network, our model achieves a superior balance in complexity and accuracy, as shown in Fig. 1.

2 Related Work

Due to the limitations of the classification standards of traditional methods and the improvement of the computing performance of equipment in recent years, portrait segmentation based on deep learning has become the mainstream research methods.

Real-Time Network: ENet [11] proposed a deep and narrow shape network structure, which effectively improves the speed of the network, but loses a certain degree of accuracy. As an effective real-time segmentation model, BiSeNet [7] is not suitable for low-resolution images due to the limitations of its up-sampling module. BiSeNetV2 [8] uses two branches to calculate low-level features and high-level features, and there is an auxiliary segmentation head in the network structure to enhance training. The multi-path structure will cause time consumption to a certain extent. Rethinking BiSeNet [12] solves the time-consuming problem of multipath in [7] and proposes a new network block, which reduces the size of the filter in a geometric progression, and reduces the computational complexity, but the amount of parameters is still huge. LEDNet [13] uses channel split and channel shuffle operations to enhance the fusion of information. The core idea of MobileNet [14] is to replace standard convolution with depthwise convolution with filtering function and pointwise convolution with linear combination, which can basically not lose accuracy and reduce network complexity. MobileNetV2 [15] adds a novel residual connection to [14], which can use low dimensional input to achieve the same effect as [14]. MobileNetV3 [16] introduced the SE and proposed a novel architecture design based on complementary search technology.

Portrait Segmentation Network: Shen et al. [17] proposed a portrait segmentation network to classify portraits and backgrounds, and created the first dataset of human portraits-EG1800. Kuang et al. [18] proposed a stream-based network and established a video conference segmentation dataset that can be used for portrait segmentation. Zhang [19] proposed a portrait segmentation network-PortraitNet, which can run on mobile devices and has superior segmentation effects, and has extraordinary performance on the EG1800 dataset. Hyojin Park et al. [20] proposed an extremely lightweight model named ExtremeC3Net, which segmentation accuracy is only slightly lower than that of [19]. Hyojin Park [6] also proposed an extremely lightweight portrait segmentation network-SINet, which is based on [21] and achieved higher segmentation accuracy than [20].

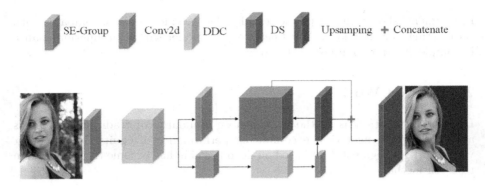

Fig. 2. Structure of DDCNet. To facilitate understanding, information sets A, B and C in the figure only represent conceptual information, not real information set images. SE-Group represents grouping convolution with SE structure.

3   Our Methods

In this section, we explained the network structure of DDCNet, as shown in Fig. 2. The DDC module we proposed has a deformable receptive field, and the structure of the receptive field can be changed through backpropagation to better extract the detailed information of the complex structure of the portrait boundary (see Sect. 3.1). The DS module we proposed optimizes the traditional skip connection. By setting a threshold for the confidence of high-level semantics to control the information supplement of low-level features, the noise caused by jump connections is effectively removed, and the detailed information that is discarded in the encoding process is fully retained (see Sect. 3.2). In addition, we calculated a weighted loss for the mispredicted part of each picture, and added the result to the total loss of the network, which improved the network's robustness for portrait classification (see Sect. 3.3).

3.1   Deformable Depth Separable Convolution Block (DDC)

Inspired by depthwise convolution [10] and deformable convolution [9], we proposed a DDC block with deformable receptive field. The DDC module can not only pay attention to the detailed features that are not covered by the traditional convolution, but also does not bring additional calculation burden. Compared with the traditional convolution, it even reduces the amount of parameters and FLOPs.

For a traditional convolution kernel (kernel size is 3), its receptive field D can be formally expressed as:

$$D = (-1, -1), (-1, 0) \ldots, (0, 1), (1, 1) \tag{1}$$

For each pixel of the output feature map:

$$y(p_0) = \sum_{p_n \in D} w(p_n) \cdot x(p_0 + p_n) \tag{2}$$

where p_n traverses every position in D. For the DDC block, it first obtains the 9 offsets of each pixel through depthwise separable convolution, and then uses bilinear interpolation to make each offset position fall on the pixel. Each pixel p_0 after deformable convolution calculation can be expressed as:

$$y(p_0) = \sum_{p_n \in D} w(p_n) \cdot x(p_0 + p_n + \Delta p_n) \tag{3}$$

where $p_n + \Delta p_n$ represents the effective pixel offset.

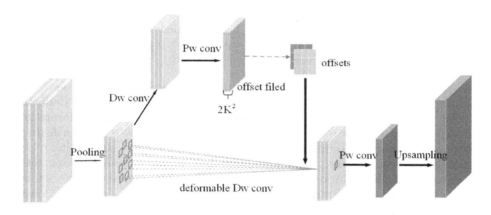

Fig. 3. The structure of DDC. Dw conv is depthwise convolution, Pw conv is pointwise convolution.

The DDC structure is shown in Fig. 3. We first perform a pooling operation on the feature map to further reduce the FLOPs and memory consumption. Then use the depth separable convolution to extract the offset, the resolution of the output feature map remains unchanged, and the depth becomes $2K^2$(K is kernel size). At this time, every $2K^2$ pixel at the same position corresponds to the offset of the corresponding pixel in the calculation process. Substitute the offset into the depthwise convolution to perform the operation of formula (3), and then perform the pointwise convolution operation to change the number of channels. Finally, a bilinear interpolation operation is performed to restore the resolution of the resulting feature map to the input size.

3.2   Detail Selection Block (DS)

Semantic segmentation models mostly use an encoder-decoder structure. The encoder down-samples the input image to extract detailed information, reducing the resolution of the feature map. The decoder up-samples the small-size

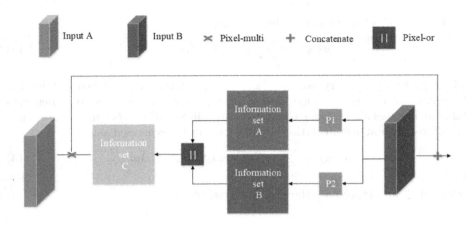

Fig. 4. Structure of DS block. Input a is a high-resolution feature map, input B is a low-resolution feature map, and P1 and P2 represent two confidence thresholds.

resolution feature map to restore its detailed information and resolution. The detailed information lost during down-sampling is difficult to recover perfectly during up-sampling. The network represented by [19] adds detailed information to high-level semantics by stitching high-resolution and low-resolution feature maps to obtain more accurate results. However, most studies, such as [5], when making jump connections, only simply splicing information, summing elements, or enhancing high-resolution feature maps with low-resolution attention vectors. This direct operation introduces detailed information that is ignored by down-sampling to the high-level semantics, and at the same time introduces noise information that is filtered out by downsampling. The final segmentation map is often not accurate enough. The structure of our proposed DS module is shown in Fig. 4. The DS block can calculate the confidence of the low-resolution feature map, and propose two confidence thresholds to control the position of the pixel of the supplementary high-resolution feature map, so as to block noise from interfering with the segmentation result. Specifically, the DS block uses the softmax function to calculate the probability value of each pixel for the two categories of the feature map with the number of input channels of 2 (two categories). And store the position of the pixel with the maximum probability value less than P1 as the information set A, and store the position of the pixel with the difference between the two probability values less than P2 as the information set B. Perform a 'union' operation on A and B to get the detailed information to select the set C. Multiplying C with the high resolution feature map for pixel correspondence, and the result is spliced with the low-resolution feature map, which introduces the details of low-level features to the high-level semantics, while avoiding the inflow of the information of the pixel where the noise is located. We set P1 to 0.9 and P2 to 0.3. At this time, the network can obtain the best segmentation results.

3.3 Loss Function

Models used for portrait segmentation often additionally calculate the loss of the boundary part of the portrait to accurately segment the results [19]. Calculating the boundary of the portrait requires preprocessing of GroundTruth, which is equivalent to providing trimap to the model. We found that the error prediction part of the model is mostly concentrated on the portrait boundary. Calculating the weighted loss for this part helps to improve the segmentation result without preprocessing GroundTruth. Our total loss TL is:

$$TL = L_{i \in P}(y_i, p_i) + \lambda L_{i \in F}(y_i, p_i) \tag{4}$$

$$L = -\sum_{i=1}^{n}(y_i \cdot \log(p_i) + (1 - y_i)\log(1 - p_i)) \tag{5}$$

$$F = G_{i \in P}(y_i, y_{p_i}) \tag{6}$$

where L is the cross entropy loss function, P is the collection of all pixels in the picture, F is the set of pixels with incorrect predictions, p_i is the predicted probability, y_i is the label. G is the 'XNOR' operation, and y_{pi} is the predicted label value derived from p_i. λ is a hyperparameter, we set it to 0.5.

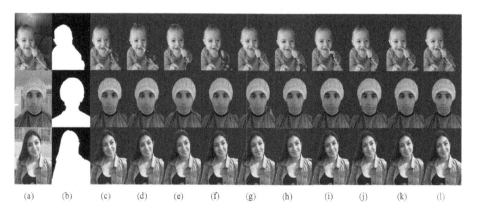

Fig. 5. Comparison of EG1800 segmentation results. (a) Image, (b) GroundTruth, Model: (c) ESPNet [21], (d) Fast_SCNN [5], (e) MobileNetV3 [16], (f) SINet [6], (g)BiSeNetV2 [8], (h) PortraitNet [19], (i)LEDNet [13], (j) Rethink_BiSeNet [12], (k)ENet [11], (l) DDCNet.

4   Experimental Results and Analysis

4.1   Visual Comparison and Index Analysis

We evaluated our network on the public portrait dataset EG1800 [17]. Due to the damage of some URLs, we did not get all the data of EG1800. We could only get 1579 pictures, including 1309 pictures in the training set and 270 pictures in the test set. We trained all methods using the incomplete dataset.

During training, we controlled the batch size to 8, and trained a total of 300 epochs. The learning rate for the first 150 epochs is 0.0005, then decay to 0.000125 by stepwise. All experiments are performed under the Pytorch framework, and the GPU is configured with NVIDIA GeForce GTX 1070 with cuda 10.2.

Figure 5 shows the visual segmentation results of DDCNet and other lightweight models. When the person in the image is occluded by the object, the segmentation accuracy of the ESPNet, Fast_SCNN and SINet model near the occluder is affected. MobileNetV3, Rethink_BiSeNet and PortraitNet have obvious phenomenon of incorrect classification of pixels in the foreground or background. DDCNet can better identify people and occlusions and perform segmentation without generating classification errors. BiSeNetV2 and ENet are inaccurate in the segmentation of character boundaries, and DDCNet classification is more detailed and correct. Experiments show that the segmentation quality of DDCNet is better than other models, and it has the best and stable overall performance.

Figure 6 shows the ROC curve and PR curve of DDCNet on the EG1800 dataset and the video conference segmentation data set. The AUC value on the EG1800 dataset is 0.9873, the average accuracy (AP) is 0.9904, and the AUC value on the video conference segmentation dataset is 0.9985, and the AP is 0.9956.

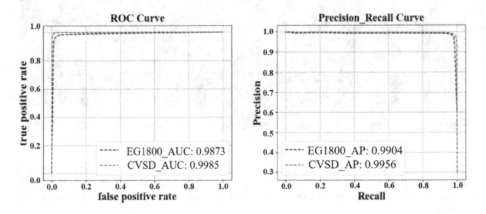

Fig. 6. ROC curve and PR curve of DDCNet on EG1800 and Conference Video Segmentation Dataset. The red line represents Conference Video Segmentation Dataset, the blue line represents EG1800. (Color figure online)

Table 1. Performance comparison of models on EG1800. We measure FPS on a NVIDIA GeForce GTX 1070 GPU environment with input size 224 × 224. The maximum scores are highlight in red, our results are hightlight in bold.

Methods	Paras(M)	FLOPs(G)	mIoU(%)	F1(%)	Acc(%)	Recall(%)	AUC	FPS
ENet [11]	0.349	0.346	94.51	74.46	96.52	97.13	0.982	52
PortraitNet [19]	2.698	0.334	95.05	89.31	96.41	98.15	0.985	99
MobileNetV3 [16]	3.910	0.252	93.23	65.28	95.71	96.64	0.980	71
ESPNet [21]	0.345	0.328	94.58	86.76	96.62	97.39	0.984	125
LEDNet [13]	0.919	1.076	94.67	73.17	96.64	97.09	0.984	62
Fast_SCNN [5]	1.136	0.159	93.96	71.76	96.26	96.67	0.983	196
Rethink_BiSeNet [12]	12.042	2.256	94.78	72.66	96.71	97.92	0.983	72
SINet [6]	0.087	0.064	94.74	88.35	96.80	96.92	0.984	100
BiSeNetV2 [8]	5.191	3.375	95.91	76.19	97.05	98.35	0.987	111
DDCNet (ours)	**0.122**	**0.092**	**95.60**	89.66	97.29	**97.48**	0.987	**47**

Table 2. Performance comparison of models on Conference Video Segmentation Dataset.

Methods	mIoU(%)	F1(%)	Acc(%)	Recall(%)	AUC
DDCNet(ours)	97.36	96.53	99.18	99.22	0.999

In order to qualitatively evaluate the experiment, we use the parameters (Paras), FLOPs, F1-score (F1), Accuracy (Acc), Recall, mIoU, AUC and FPS as performance evaluation indicators.

Table 1 shows the comparison results of our model with other models on the EG1800. Our model effectively controls the parameters and FLOPs while achieving superior results in real-time (47FPS). In all comparative experiments done on the EG1800, our model achieved the best F1, accuracy and AUC values. BiSeNetV2 has the highest mIoU (95.91%), but this model requires a large number of parameters and FLOPs, and requires relatively high experimental equipment. On the basis of maintained a comparable mIoU to BiSeNetV2, DDC-Net improves accuracy and F1, and reduces 97.8% of parameters and 97.3% of FLOPs. Compared with the extremely lightweight model SINet, DDCNet only increased the parameters of 35.84K and the FLOPs of 0.02G while achieving better results in five indicators: mIoU, F1, accuracy, recall and AUC.

We applied our model to the Conference Video Segmentation Dataset [18] and achieved excellent results. The results are shown in Table 2. Experiments prove that our model has good generalization ability for portrait datasets in different complex environments.

Table 3. Comparison of accuracy of convolution kernels of different sizes in DDC blocks (EG1800). The maximum score is highlight in bold.

Kernel_Size	3	5	3 and 5
mIoU(%)	94.92	94.98	**95.60**

Table 4. Comparison of accuracy of convolution kernels of different sizes in DDC blocks (EG1800). The maximum score is highlight in bold.

P1	mIoU(%)		
	P2		
	0.7	0.8	0.9
0.3	95.27	95.48	**95.60**
0.2	95.59	95.32	95.41
0.1	95.55	95.35	95.52

4.2 Ablation Study

In order to illustrate the effectiveness of each module, and to explore the optimal parameters of each module, we did an ablation experiment on EG1800. As shown in Table 3, we explored the impact of changes in the size of the convolution kernel in the DDC block on the segmentation performance. Experiments show that the combination of 3 and 5 for the kernel size can achieve the highest mIoU. As shown in Table 4, we explored the impact of the combination of different information confidence thresholds in the DS block on the segmentation performance. Experiments show that when the confidence level P1 of the information set A is set to 0.9 and the confidence level P2 of the information set B is set to 0.1, the model can reach the highest mIoU. We analyze that the combination of confidence in other information leads to the decrease in mIoU of the final segmentation result because: 1) The information confidence is too broadly, the DS module introduces noise in skip connection. 2) The confidence level is too strict, the model has an over-fitting phenomenon.

4.3 User Study

We randomly selected 6 images from the EG1800 and entered them into each model in Table 1, and obtained 60 segmented images, which were divided into 10 groups of data according to the number of models. Results are presented in random order to avoid subjective bias. We sent questionnaires to 20 users and asked them to select the model which have the best effect in overall, internal and edge. The votes for our method are 20, 18 and 17. Studies have shown that our method produces the most user-friendly results compared to existing portrait segmentation methods.

5   Conclusion

In this paper, we propose a lightweight portrait segmentation model-DDCNet. Deformable convolution is introduced and combined with depthwise separable convolution, which enables the network to fully extract feature information while reducing the parameters and FLOPs. In the skip connection, the thresholds are set for the confidence of high-level semantics to avoid the introduction of noise. In Conference Video Segmentation Dataset and EG1800, DDCNet achieves excellent segmentation results compared with the existing lightweight semantic segmentation models.

In the next step, we will continue to expand our work. We will pay more attention to the complex and diverse structure of the portrait boundary and the occluded objects in front of the portrait, and integrate the method into the reconstruction workflow.

Acknowledgements. This work was supported by the Shanghai Natural Science Foundation of China under Grant No.19ZR1419100 and the Shanghai talent development funding of China under Grant No. 2021016.

References

1. Miao, J., Sun, K., Liao, X., Leng, L., Chu, J.: Human segmentation based on compressed deep convolutional neural network. IEEE Access **8**, 167,585–167,595 (2020). http://doi.org/10.1109/ACCESS.2020.3023746
2. Chuang, Y.Y., Curless, B., Salesin, D.H., Szeliski, R.: A Bayesian approach to digital matting. In: Proceedings of the 2001 IEEE Computer Society Conference on Computer Vision and Pattern Recognition. CVPR 2001, vol. 2, pp. II-II (2001). http://doi.org/10.1109/CVPR.2001.990970
3. Pare, S., Kumar, A., Bajaj, V., Singh, G.K.: A multilevel color image segmentation technique based on cuckoo search algorithm and energy curve. Appl. Soft Comput. **47**, 76–102 (2016). https://doi.org/10.1016/j.asoc.2016.05.040
4. Xu, N., Price, B., Cohen, S., Huang, T.: Deep image matting. In: Proceedings of the IEEE Conference on Computer Vision and Pattern Recognition, pp. 2970–2979 (2017). http://doi.org/10.1109/CVPR.2017.41
5. Poudel, R.P., Liwicki, S., Cipolla, R.: Fast-SCNN: fast semantic segmentation network. arXiv preprint arXiv:1902.04502 (2019)
6. Park, H., Sjosund, L., Yoo, Y., Monet, N., Bang, J., Kwak, N.: SiNet: extreme lightweight portrait segmentation networks with spatial squeeze module and information blocking decoder. In: Proceedings of the IEEE/CVF Winter Conference on Applications of Computer Vision, pp. 2066–2074 (2020). http://doi.org/10.1109/WACV45572.2020.9093588
7. Yu, C., Wang, J., Peng, C., Gao, C., Yu, G., Sang, N.: BiSeNet: bilateral segmentation network for real-time semantic segmentation. In: Ferrari, V., Hebert, M., Sminchisescu, C., Weiss, Y. (eds.) ECCV 2018. LNCS, vol. 11217, pp. 334–349. Springer, Cham (2018). https://doi.org/10.1007/978-3-030-01261-8_20
8. Yu, C., Gao, C., Wang, J., Yu, G., Shen, C., Sang, N.: Bisenet v2: bilateral network with guided aggregation for real-time semantic segmentation. Int. J. Comput. Vis. **129**(11), 3051–3068 (2021). http://doi.org/10.1007/s11263-021-01515-2

9. Dai, J., et al.: Deformable convolutional networks. In: Proceedings of the IEEE International Conference on Computer Vision, pp. 764–773 (2017). http://doi.org/10.1109/ICCV.2017.89

10. Chollet, F.: Xception: Deep learning with depthwise separable convolutions. In: Proceedings of the IEEE Conference on Computer Vision and Pattern Recognition, pp. 1251–1258 (2017). http://doi.org/10.1109/CVPR.2017.195

11. Paszke, A., Chaurasia, A., Kim, S., Culurciello, E.: Enet: a deep neural network architecture for real-time semantic segmentation. arXiv preprint arXiv:1606.02147 (2016)

12. Fan, M., et al.: Rethinking BiseNet for real-time semantic segmentation. In: Proceedings of the IEEE/CVF Conference on Computer Vision and Pattern Recognition, pp. 9716–9725 (2021). http://doi.org/10.1109/CVPR46437.2021.00959

13. Wang, Y., et al.: LedNet: a lightweight encoder-decoder network for real-time semantic segmentation. In: 2019 IEEE International Conference on Image Processing (ICIP), pp. 1860–1864 (2019). http://doi.org/10.1109/ICIP.2019.8803154

14. Howard, A.G., et al.: Mobilenets: efficient convolutional neural networks for mobile vision applications. arXiv preprint arXiv:1704.04861 (2017)

15. Sandler, M., Howard, A., Zhu, M., Zhmoginov, A., Chen, L.C.: Mobilenetv 2: Inverted residuals and linear bottlenecks. In: Proceedings of the IEEE Conference on Computer Vision and Pattern Recognition, pp. 4510–4520 (2018). http://doi.org/10.1109/CVPR.2018.00474

16. Howard, A., et al.: Searching for mobilenetv3. In: Proceedings of the IEEE/CVF International Conference on Computer Vision, pp. 1314–1324 (2019). http://doi.org/10.1109/ICCV.2019.00140

17. Shen, X., et al.: Automatic portrait segmentation for image stylization. Comput. Graphics Forum 35, 93–102 (2016). http://doi.org/10.1111/cgf.12814

18. Kuang, Z., Tie, X.: Flow-based video segmentation for human head and shoulders. arXiv preprint arXiv:2104.09752 (2021)

19. Zhang, S.H., Dong, X., Li, H., Li, R., Yang, Y.L.: PortraitNet: real-time portrait segmentation network for mobile device. Comput. Graph. 80, 104–113 (2019). http://doi.org/10.1016/j.cag.2019.03.007

20. Park, H., Sjösund, L.L., Yoo, Y., Bang, J., Kwak, N.: Extremec3Net: extreme lightweight portrait segmentation networks using advanced c3-modules. arXiv preprint (2019). https://doi.org/10.48550/arXiv.1908.03093

21. Mehta, S., Rastegari, M., Caspi, A., Shapiro, L., Hajishirzi, H.: ESPNet: efficient spatial pyramid of dilated convolutions for semantic segmentation. In: Ferrari, V., Hebert, M., Sminchisescu, C., Weiss, Y. (eds.) ECCV 2018. LNCS, vol. 11214, pp. 561–580. Springer, Cham (2018). https://doi.org/10.1007/978-3-030-01249-6_34

A Chromosome Segmentation Method Based on Corner Detection and Watershed Algorithm

Zhifeng Zhang, Jinhui Kuang[✉], Xiao Cui, Xiaohui Ji, Junxia Ma, Jinghan Cai,
and Zhe Zhao

Zhengzhou University of Light Industry, Zhengzhou 450001, China
1129452025@qq.com

Abstract. Karyotype analysis is an effective tool for chromosome disease diagnosis, and the number and morphological characteristics of chromosomes can be medically analyzed and described by image processing technology. Chromosome image segmentation is the basis of karyotype analysis. Chromosome images have the characteristics of high adhesion, overlapping and nesting, which is a difficult problem in chromosome image segmentation at present. In order to effectively solve the problem of chromosome adhesion or overlap, this paper innovatively applies watershed algorithm based on gray difference transformation and corner detection to chromosome image segmentation. The algorithm uses gray difference transformation in preprocessing to reduce the phenomenon of image over-segmentation caused by watershed algorithm and separate lightly adhered chromosomes. For overlapping chromosomes, corner detection is used to find the best corner of chromosome segmentation, and then the overlapping chromosomes are separated. Through experiments on 100 chromosome images, the accuracy of chromosome segmentation is 96.2%.

Keywords: Karyotype analysis · Chromosome image segmentation · Watershed algorithm · Corner detection

1 Introduction

Chromosome is the carrier of human genetic information. Chromosome abnormalities will lead to human genetic diseases. Karyotype analysis is an important means to diagnose genetic diseases [1]. Karyotype analysis consists of four steps: Firstly, human cell samples were obtained, slides were made and karyotype images were collected; Secondly, the karyotype image is preprocessed, including noise reduction and enhancement; Then, the segmentation, counting and classification of chromosome karyotype images are completed; Finally, the karyotype image analysis report is generated [2]. The normal human chromosome image and karyotype are shown in Fig. 1.

 Chromosome image segmentation is the basis of chromosome karyotype analysis. In order to realize the subsequent steps such as counting and classification in karyotype analysis, each chromosome needs to be extracted from the image. Because the chromosomes are distributed in three-dimensional space in the production process, the

N. Magnenat-Thalmann et al. (Eds.): CGI 2022, LNCS 13443, pp. 477–488, 2022.
https://doi.org/10.1007/978-3-031-23473-6_37

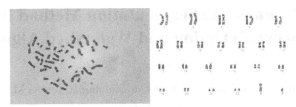

Fig. 1. Normal human chromosome image and karyotype

chromosomes often appear as adhesion, overlap, overlap and nesting in the image. The focus of this paper is to separate these adherent or overlapping chromosomes, and select G-banding chromosomes for experiments. The banding chromosome is different from the color banding chromosome in M-FISH database [3], and the G-banding chromosome has clear banding patterns, which is widely used in the study of chromosome diseases. At present, many scholars have made different contributions to the segmentation of adherent chromosomes or overlapping chromosome clusters [4].

In the traditional chromosome image processing methods, Grisan et al. [5] and Madian et al. [6] used the threshold segmentation method to process the chromosome image. The algorithm obtained the concave convex points by calculating and comparing the curvature of the edge points of the target object one by one, and then paired them into a cutting line, and compared the parallelism between the cutting lines with the width of a single chromosome, so as to correctly cut or adhere the overlapping chromosomes. However, when the chromosomes are bent and overlapped, The algorithm will misjudge the effectiveness of cutting points, resulting in the reduction of segmentation accuracy. Arora et al. [7, 8] proposed a chromosome segmentation method based on geometric calculation. The algorithm first tracks the contour line of overlapping chromosomes, then finds all cutting points of overlapping chromosomes, and then selects a specific number of cutting points to separate chromosomes based on computational geometry. The algorithm focuses on the separation of overlapping chromosomes, but it does not get high segmentation accuracy. Yilmaz et al. [9] cut the chromosome by extracting the chromosome skeleton and endpoint, and using the curvature to obtain the concave point. By comparing the end-to-end skeleton with the overlapping region, the best candidate chromosome is obtained. The algorithm has high segmentation accuracy, but the author did not explain the source of chromosome data set and the accuracy of overlapping chromosome segmentation. Manohar et al. [10] used the segmentation algorithm based on watershed to segment chromosomes in M-FISH data set. The proposed algorithm can achieve efficient segmentation of chromosomes in the data set, but the algorithm only has obvious segmentation effect on slightly adherent chromosomes, and it is difficult to separate overlapping chromosomes.

How to segment overlapping or adherent chromosomes is still a key problem to be solved in chromosome image segmentation, which is very important for the results of chromosome karyotype analysis. Therefore, this paper proposes a solution, that is, the gray difference transform is applied to the watershed algorithm and combined with corner detection to accurately segment the chromosome image. Firstly, the gray difference transform is applied to the preprocessing of chromosome image to preserve more edge regions of chromosome features, reduce the noise in the image and prevent over segmentation in the follow-up. Secondly, the hole filling algorithm is used for the threshold processed binary image to remove the holes in the chromosome. At the same time, the result of morphological boundary extraction is used as the input image in watershed transform for segmentation. For the impurities, single chromosome and chromosome cluster in the image, the rule-based target object classification decision-making process is used to distinguish chromosomes and impurities. Finally, according to the characteristics of the obtained overlapping chromosomes, the corner detection algorithm is adopted to find out the corner with large gray difference between the edge pixel and the center pixel in the region as the segmentation point, segment the overlapping chromosomes and output the processed image [11]. The algorithm flow of chromosome image segmentation is shown in Fig. 2.

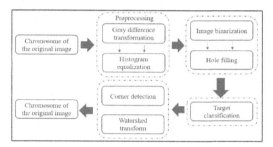

Fig. 2. Chromosome segmentation algorithm flow

2 Method

In human chromosome image analysis, the image quality can affect the accuracy of the final analysis effect. Preprocessing and counting of images are required [12]. Chromosome image preprocessing is to reduce irrelevant information in the image, retain useful information, enhance the detectability of chromosome feature edges, and then improve the reliability of chromosome image segmentation, counting and classification. Due to the low resolution of chromosome images, it is necessary to preprocess them before image segmentation to enhance the image quality.

2.1 Image Denoising

Image denoising is a method to enhance image quality [13]. The image after gradient transformation can reflect the boundary of the object. Because the noise may have the same gradient value as the image edge, it is easy to produce too many minimum points in the image, resulting in the phenomenon of over segmentation in the segmentation using watershed algorithm [14].

In order to solve the phenomenon of over segmentation, this paper replaces the gradient transformation algorithm based on the gray difference transformation of non-adjacent pixels in eight-neighborhood for the first time. The gray difference transformation of non-adjacent pixels in the eight-neighborhood needs to traverse different directions, calculate the difference, and determine the transformation direction according to the differences. As shown in Fig. 3, the whole image is traversed by sliding the window. When the window slides, the gray value of the corresponding point in the image is the value of each small grid in the window. The gray value of the pixel at the center of the window is obtained by the combination of the gray difference of two non-adjacent pixels in its eight-neighborhood. As shown in formula (1). The image obtained by this method is the gray difference image.

$$D_{iff}(i,j) = \sum_{m,n=1}^{8} |u_m - u_n|, u_m \text{ and } u_n \text{ not adjacent} \qquad (1)$$

Because the gray difference between the pixels in the eight-neighborhood at the noise is very small, the value of this point is also very small in the gray difference map; On the contrary, at the boundary point, the value of the point is very large. The gray difference transformation can effectively reduce the noise on the chromosome image, and the edge of each chromosome is very clear.

u_1	u_2	u_3
u_4	$u_{i,j}$	u_5
u_6	u_7	u_8

Fig. 3. 3×3 window

2.2 Histogram Equalization Enhancement

Image equalization is to convert the unbalanced histogram corresponding to the original image through some method, so that the histogram can be evenly distributed, and then the overall contrast effect of the image can be significantly improved [15]. The denoised chromosome image is used as the input of histogram equalization, and the pixel gray in the image is mapped and transformed to make the gray density of the transformed image evenly distributed. The image histogram equalization steps are as follows:

Step 1: set the total pixels of the original image as N and the number of gray levels as L;
Step 2: calculate the total number of pixels of each gray level of the image n_k. Calculate the normalized gray value r_k of the input image;
Step 3: calculate the probability of each gray level in the image as: $p_r(r_k) = n_k/N$, calculate the cumulative sum s'_k;
Step 4: calculate the corresponding gray level m of each gray level and obtain the mapping relationship of gray levels: $r_k \Rightarrow s_m$;
Step 5: get the number of pixels n'_k, solve the probability of each gray level pixel: $p_s(s_k) = n'_k/N$.

After image preprocessing, the effect diagram is shown in Fig. 4.

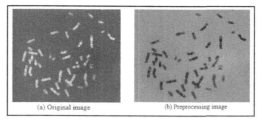

Fig. 4. Preprocessing result image: Fig. a is chromosome images to be processed; Fig. b is preprocessed chromosome images

2.3 Target Classification

After the above treatments, some irrelevant substances other than those outside the chromosomes will still be present in the chromosome image, such as impurities such as nuclei, cell debris. To achieve accuracy in subsequent operations, impurities need to be distinguished from chromosomes and impurities removed. Currently, impurity removal algorithms mostly remove irrelevant objects in their images depending on the size of the target, convex hull, etc. [16], however, relying solely on these characteristics does not effectively eliminate impurities and will even remove the research subjects together. To avoid chromosome missorting as well as to effectively remove impurities, five features including area, mean area, width, mean width, and chromosome backbone crossing points were selected.

1. Area (SA): area of a single chromosome;
2. Average area (AA): the sum of the total areas of all chromosomes divided by the number of chromosomes;
3. Width (SW): the area of a single chromosome divided by the corresponding backbone length of that chromosome;
4. Average width (AW): the sum of the total areas of all chromosomes divided by the sum of the backbone lengths of the chromosomes;
5. Number of intersections (NI): the number of intersections that adhere to or overlap the chromosome backbone.

Where, the width is obtained from its area divided by the skeleton length. Skeletonization [17] is to remove unwanted contour points and keep only the skeleton points, so the skeleton length can be regarded as the chromosome length, and the number of intersections of the skeleton can also be used as an important feature to judge chromosome clusters. With the above features set as rules and applied in a tandem fashion, the chromosome image impurity removal decision-making pipeline based on the tandem rule is illustrated in Fig. 5. The impurity removal effect is shown in Fig. 6.

2.4 Chromosome Segmentation

Combined with the principle of watershed algorithm [18, 19], this paper segments the chromosomes without adhesion or slight adhesion, and extracts the boundary of the

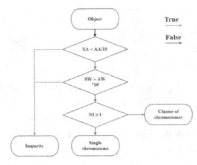

Fig. 5. Flowchart of target object classification: green line segments represent meeting judgment conditions; red line segments represent not meeting judgment conditions (Color figure online)

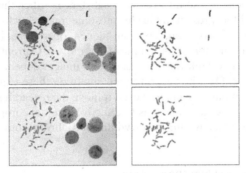

Fig. 6. Impurity removal result image: on the left is the image of the chromosome containing more impurities; on the right is the result diagram of the removal of impurities after passing through the process described above

processed chromosome image for watershed algorithm segmentation. Let the image processed by the filling algorithm be A, and B is a disc-shaped structuring element. Finally, the boundary of A is

$$\beta(A) = A - (A \ominus B) \tag{2}$$

Apply watershed transform to boundary $\beta(A)$, which is helpful to remove the impurities in the image background, and finally get the chromosome image segmentation results, as shown in Fig. 7.

The improved watershed algorithm proposed in this paper has a good effect on the segmentation of slightly adherent chromosomes, and can improve the recognition rate and accuracy of chromosome segmentation. Based on this, Shi-Tomasi corner detection algorithm is introduced to segment chromosomes by detecting their intersections [20, 21].

The idea of Shi-Tomasi corner detection algorithm is to use a fixed window to slide in any direction in the image, and determine whether there are corners in the window by comparing the gray level changes of pixels in the window before and after sliding. The schematic diagram of the window is shown in Fig. 8.

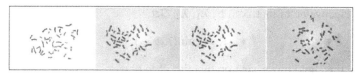

Fig. 7. Images after segmentation of lightly adherent chromosomes: each separated chromosome is distinguished by a different color in the figures (Color figure online)

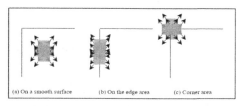

(a) On a smooth surface   (b) On the edge area   (c) Corner area

Fig. 8. Schematic diagram of window movement: Fig. a is on a smooth surface; Fig. b is on the edge area; Fig. c is on the corner area

In the image coordinate $x_0 = (x, y)$, translate the window by $[u, v]$, then the gray value of the image before and after the movement changes to:

$$E(u,v) = \sum_{x,\,y} w(x, y) \left[I(x + u, y + v) - I(x, y) \right]^2 \tag{3}$$

where $w(x, y)$ is the weighting function located at x_0; $I(x, y)$ is the gray value of pixel at x_0, and $I(x + u, y + v)$ is the gray value of pixel at coordinate $(x + u, y + v)$. From the total differential formula:

$$I(x + u, y + v) = I(x, y) + I_x u + I_y v + o(u_2 + v_2) \tag{4}$$

It can be obtained from formula (3)

$$E(u, v) = \sum_{x,\,y} w(x, y) \left(u^2 I_x^2 + 2uv I_x I_y + v^2 I_y^2 \right) \tag{5}$$

Continue to convert Eq. (10) above into matrix form:

$$E(u, v) = [u, v] \left(\sum_{x,\,y} w(x, y) \begin{bmatrix} I_x^2 & I_x I_y \\ I_x I_y & I_y^2 \end{bmatrix} \right) \begin{bmatrix} u \\ v \end{bmatrix} \tag{6}$$

Then:

$$M = \sum_{x,\,y} w(x, y) \begin{bmatrix} I_x^2 & I_x I_y \\ I_x I_y & I_y^2 \end{bmatrix} \tag{7}$$

M is a 2-dimensional matrix, the above Eq. (7) can be simplified to

$$E(u, v) = [u, v] M \begin{bmatrix} u \\ v \end{bmatrix} \tag{8}$$

Let the eigenvalue of matrix m be λ_1, λ_2. Set

$$R = \min(\lambda_1, \lambda_2) \tag{9}$$

Perform threshold processing on function R to obtain

$$R > \text{threshold} \tag{10}$$

The local maximum of R is calculated, and then the corner is detected by non-maximum suppression of R.

Most of the corners detected by this algorithm are not necessary to segment overlapping chromosomes, which will increase the detection time and reduce the segmentation accuracy.

In order to improve the accuracy of overlapping chromosome segmentation, the improved Shi-Tomasi corner detection algorithm needs to be used. Firstly, before solving the response function R, filter the pixels in the image to find the corner to be selected. Secondly, by comparing whether the gray difference between the central pixel and each edge pixel in the detection window is in a given interval, we can determine whether they are similar. Finally, the corner to be selected is determined by the value of the number n of similar points. The algorithm steps are:

Step 1: set the gray value of a point on the image as I, filter the pixel points by using the difference equation, and get I_x^2, I_y^2 and $I_x I_y$;
Step 2: I_x^2, I_y^2 and $I_x I_y$ do bilateral filtering, remove isolated points in the image, and take the solution result as the element in matrix M;
Step 3: compare the gray values of the central pixel and the edge pixel in the detection window, judge whether the difference is within a fixed threshold, and take the obtained similar pixel as the corner to be selected;
Step 4: solve the response function r of the pixel through formula (10), suppress the non-maximum value, and judge whether the corner to be selected is a segmentation point.

An improved corner detection algorithm removes a large number of irrelevant corners from chromosome images and only preserves junctions where the gray scale changes are more pronounced at chromosome intersections. The algorithm connects two points by calculating the nearest point between them and use it as a dividing line to cut adherent or overlapping chromosomes. The corner detection result image is shown in Fig. 9, and finally the segmentation result image is shown in Fig. 10.

3   Experimental Results and Analysis

To verify the effectiveness of the proposed segmentation method to resolve overlapping chromosome images, experiments were performed on 100 images of G-banded chromosomes provided by the Third Hospital of Peking University. There are 4591 chromosomes in the image, of which 523 are mutually adhered and 126 are mutually overlapped. The different methods segmentation results were analyzed in terms of the

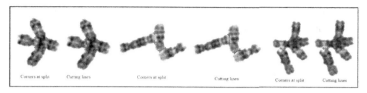

Fig. 9. Corner detection results: the images on the left are the marked optimal cutting corners; the images on the right are cut lines

Fig. 10. Results of correct segmentation of overlapping chromosomes: the overlapping chromosomes in the above picture can be correctly segmented

angle at which overlapping or adhered chromosomal regions were correctly segmented. If a chromosomal region was algorithmically processed to correctly extract the chromosomes in that region, then the adhered or overlapping regions were considered correctly segmented, and the chromosome segmentation accuracy was derived from Eq. (11).

$$accuracy = \frac{\text{no. of correctly segmented chromosomes}}{\text{total no. of chromosomes}} \tag{11}$$

Comparison of the experimental results with different algorithms is shown in the table below.

Table 1. Comparison with the previously proposed algorithms

Method	No. of chromosomes	Correct number	Accuracy
Grisan et al. [5]	6683	6282	94%
Manohar et al. [10]	920	864	94%
Yilmaz et al. [9]	6678	6531	97.8%
Proposed	4591	4416	96.2%

It can be seen from the comparative data in Table 1 that this method has ideal results for chromosome segmentation, and the segmentation accuracy is higher than that in literature [5] and literature [10]. Yilmaz's segmentation accuracy is very high, but the author did not give the segmentation accuracy of adherent or overlapping chromosomes. Literature [1] used Yilmaz's method to re-experiment and obtained 86.96% segmentation accuracy. In order to verify the segmentation accuracy of overlapping or adherent chromosomes in this paper, the experimental results of chromosome segmentation are

Table 2. The accuracy of different algorithms for the segmentation of adherent chromosomes, where 'T' means adherent chromosomes

Method	No. of adherent chromosomes ('T')	Accuracy
Grisan et al. [5]	819	90%
Arora et al. [8]	1178	96.7%
Proposed	523	96.9%

Table 3. The correct rate of segmentation of overlapping chromosomes by different algorithms, where 'X' means overlapping chromosomes

Method	No. of overlapping chromosomes ('X')	Accuracy
Grisan et al.[5]	201	90%
Arora et al. [8]	189	81%
Proposed	126	91.3%

presented in the form of Table 2 and Table 3. It can be concluded that this paper marks the corners at the segmentation of overlapping chromosomes through the corner detection algorithm to determine the optimal segmentation corners, which improves the accuracy of segmentation of adherent or overlapping chromosomes. The segmentation effect is shown in Fig. 11.

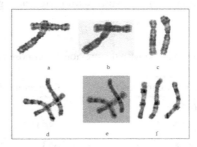

Fig. 11. Segmentation results of overlapping chromosomes: Fig. a and d are chromosomes to be segmented; Fig. b and e are the chromosomes after segmentation; Fig. c and f show the separated chromosomes

The segmentation accuracy of 100 images in this experiment is higher. However, the segmentation effect of the algorithm for complex chromosome clusters with overlapping heads and tails in chromosome images needs to be further improved. Because the wrong segmentation of chromosome will cause the destruction of chromosome structure, and it is difficult to repair the chromosome in the later stage, it will also bring unnecessary trouble to the subsequent karyotype analysis. Therefore, the head tail overlapping complex chromosome clusters can still meet the needs of normal chromosome karyotype analysis by relying on a small amount of subsequent manual intervention.

4 Conclusion

Chromosome image segmentation is the key step to complete chromosome karyotype analysis. The result of chromosome image segmentation can directly affect the accuracy and efficiency of analysis. In order to improve the accuracy of segmentation of adherent or overlapping chromosomes, this paper analyzes the characteristics of human chromosome image, and applies the watershed algorithm based on gray difference transformation combined with corner detection to segment human chromosome image. Firstly, the algorithm can identify a single chromosome and chromosome cluster. By introducing corner detection into chromosome image segmentation, the adherent or overlapping chromosomes are segmented and marked. Finally, the watershed algorithm based on gray difference transformation is used to segment the chromosomes in the image. The experimental results show that the process can correctly segment the overlapping or adherent chromosomes without damaging the chromosome characteristics. However, for complex chromosome clusters with overlapping heads and tails in chromosome images, the solution proposed in this paper can not segment effectively, which will be the focus of this paper in the future. At the same time, in order to realize the universality of this method, this paper will also try to promote this segmentation method, such as medical image segmentation of human brain or image segmentation in other fields.

Acknowledgements. The research was supported in part by the National Natural Science Foundation of China (Grant No. 61975187), the scientific and technological project of Henan Province (Grant No. 212102210382, No. 212102210410 and No. 222102210030), and the co-working space Project of Zhengzhou University of Light Industry (Grant No. 2020ZCKJ216).

References

1. Lin, C., et al.: Chromosome cluster identification framework based on geometric features and machine learning algorithms. In: 2020 IEEE International Conference on Bioinformatics and Biomedicine (BIBM), pp. 2357–2363 (2020)
2. Song, J., Yu, J., Tian J., et al.: Study on reducing birth defects by amniotic fluid karyotype analysis. J. Hebei Med. Univ. **43**(02), 173–176+217 (2022)
3. Karvelis, P.S., Tzallas, A.T., Fotiadis, D.I., Georgiou, I.: A multichannel watershed-based segmentation method for multispectral chromosome classification. IEEE Trans. Med. Imaging **27**(5), 697–708 (2008)
4. Munot, M.V.: Development of computerized systems for automated chromosome analysis: current status and future prospects. Int. J. Adv. Res. Comput. Sci. **9**(1), 782–791 (2018)
5. Grisan, E., Poletti, E., Ruggeri, A.: Automatic segmentation and disentangling of chromosomes in Q-band prometaphase images. IEEE Trans. Inf Technol. Biomed. **13**(4), 575–581 (2009)

6. Madian, N., Jayanthi, K.B.: Overlapped chromosome segmentation and separation of touching chromosome for automated chromosome classification. In: 2012 Annual International Conference of the IEEE Engineering in Medicine and Biology Society, pp. 5392–5395 (2012)
7. Pastore, R., Khan, I., Mufti, F.: Computational geometry-based overlapping chromosome images management. J. Multimed. Process. Technol. (JMPT) **5**(4), 129–133 (2014)
8. Arora, T., Dhir, R.: A novel approach for segmentation of human metaphase chromosome images using region based active contours. Int. Arab J. Inf. Technol. **16**(1), 132–137 (2019)
9. Yilmaz, I.C., Yang, J., Altinsoy, E., Zhou, L.: An improved segmentation for raw G-band chromosome images. In: 2018 5th International Conference on Systems and Informatics (ICSAI), pp. 944–950 (2018)
10. Manohar, R., Gawande, J.: Watershed and clustering based segmentation of chromosome images. In: 2017 IEEE 7th International Advance Computing Conference (IACC), pp. 697–700 (2017)
11. Hu, T., Mao, J.: PCB image mosaic based on downsampling and improved Shi-Tomasi corner detection algorithm. Electron. Meas. Technol. **44**(22), 134–140 (2021)
12. Wayalun, P., Kubola, K.: Adaptive image enhancement for automatic complicated G-band chromosome number determination. In: 2019 12th Biomedical Engineering International Conference (BMEiCON), pp. 1–5 (2019)
13. Li, M.: Research on wavelet image denoising algorithm based on new threshold function. Control. Eng. **8**(12), 2360–2365 (2021)
14. Rahali, R., Ben Salem, Y., Dridi, N., Dahman, H.: Drosophila image segmentation using marker controlled watershed. In: 2020 17th International Multi-Conference on Systems, Signals & Devices (SSD), pp. 191–195 (2020)
15. Yelmanov, S., Hranovska, O., Romanyshyn, Y.: A new approach to the implementation of histogram equalization in image processing. In: 2019 3rd International Conference on Advanced Information and Communications Technologies (AICT), pp. 288–293 (2019)
16. Altinsoy, E., Yang, J., Yilmaz, C.: Fully-automatic raw G-band chromosome image segmentation. IET Image Proc. **14**(9), 1920–1928 (2020)
17. Cai, X., Yang, Z., Cai, R., Yakun, G.E., Yang, B.: Image skeleton extraction method based on diffuse filling. J. Syst. Simul. **32**(08), 1455–1464 (2020)
18. Sang, Y., Li, X.L.: Colony image segmentation based on improved watershed algorithm. Electron. Meas. Technol. **42**(06), 87–93 (2019)
19. Xia, M., Zhou, J., Wang, J., Shi, D., Cao, Q.: Research on image processing algorithm based on watershed segmentation. Sci. Technol. Horiz. (17), 71–77 (2019)
20. Huang, Y., et al.: Image mosaic algorithm based on improved fast Shi Tomasi feature point detection algorithm. Mech. Des. Res. **34**(04), 70–77 (2018)
21. Mu, Z., Li, Z.: A novel Shi-Tomasi corner detection algorithm based on progressive probabilistic hough transform. In: 2018 Chinese Automation Congress (CAC), pp. 2918–2922 (2018)

Voxel-Based 3D Shape Segmentation Using Deep Volumetric Convolutional Neural Networks

Yuqi Liu[1], Wei Long[2], Zhenyu Shu[3(✉)], Shun Yi[4], and Shiqing Xin[5]

[1] College of Information Science and Electronic Engineering, Zhejiang University, Hangzhou, China
[2] Polytechnic Institute, Zhejiang University, Hangzhou, China
[3] School of Computer and Data Engineering, NingboTech University, Ningbo, China
shuzhenyu@nit.zju.edu.cn
[4] School of Mechanical Engineering, Zhejiang University, Hangzhou, China
[5] School of Computer Science and Technology, ShanDong University, Jinan, China

Abstract. 3D shape segmentation serves as the base of semantic shape analysis and becomes a hot research topic in recent years. Many segmentation methods are devised by feeding surface based geometric descriptors into a deep neural network. Most of the existing approaches assume that the surface variation information is rich enough to characterize a 3D shape, and thus perform all the constituent steps on the triangle mesh representation. However, triangle based learning networks suffer from how to define the convolutional operator, unlike the trivial situation of regular pixels or voxels. Observing that the volumetric representation is the dual of the surface representation, we design a volumetric encoder-decoder architecture, named V-SegNet, which works by lifting surface based geometric features to the enclosed voxels and then training a deep volumetric network. In the inference stage, we build the voxelization of a given 3D object, then predict the label for each voxel lying in the interior of the given shape, and finally generate the labeling information for each triangle face. The experimental results show that V-SegNet, working in a surface-volume-surface fashion, further improves the segmentation performance.

Keywords: 3D shape segmentation · Voxel · Deep learning · Shape analysis

1 Introduction

Segmentation of 3D shapes has become a fundamental task in shape analysis [1] due to the arises of a large amount of 3D shape data on the Internet in recent years. These 3D shapes are usually acquired by depth sensors using 3D geometric representations in the forms of polygon meshes and point clouds. And the purpose is to segment 3D shapes into labeled meaningful (semantic) parts.

Y. Liu and W. Long—Contribute equally to this work.

© The Author(s), under exclusive license to Springer Nature Switzerland AG 2022
N. Magnenat-Thalmann et al. (Eds.): CGI 2022, LNCS 13443, pp. 489–500, 2022.
https://doi.org/10.1007/978-3-031-23473-6_38

These labeled 3D objects have been proven essential to many computer graphics applications, such as skeleton extraction [2], objection detection [3], 3D object reconstruction [4] to name a few.

A common idea of segmentation is computing the geometric features on each faces directly using hand-crafted geometric descriptors and then clustering them into several groups in the feature space, at last, projecting the labels back on the 3D shape to obtain the final segmentation results. However, the 3D shape segmentation task is still challenging from many aspects, including the ambiguity between subtle creases and boundaries of parts, the variety of shape parts, and the integration of local and global features. To overcome these challenges and increase the segmentation performance, two trends of techniques are developed.

One trend is combining features of faces on the models using multiple geometric descriptors together. The motivation is that describing the shapes from different perspectives is better than from a single aspect for segmentation. The other trend is to use learning-based techniques and prior knowledge to improve the segmentation results. In the state-of-the-art methods, these techniques are used widely, such as formulating the objective function as a Conditional Random Fields (CRF) model [5], training convolutional neural networks (CNNs) to generate mesh representations from low-level features [6], and so on. However, the semantic information of each mesh also requires the connection and position information between the various components of the model. It is difficult to learn this information only by the feature descriptor of each mesh. Therefore, [7] encodes the mesh model into voxels and applies 3D CNN to learn position features. However, on one hand, voxels with a large resolution will bring high computational complexity, which might make segmentation methods unpractical to handle complex 3D shapes. On the other hand, voxels with a small resolution will lead to severe information loss, preventing segmentation methods from achieving satisfactory performance.

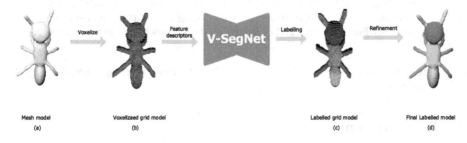

Fig. 1. The overview of our algorithm. (a) The mesh model to segment. (b) The voxelized model contains not only the geometric features on the surface but also the inner space information, which becomes the input of V-SegNet and is quite different from existing 3D shape segmentation methods. (c) The output of V-SegNet composes the labeled voxels. (d) The final labeled mesh model refined by the graph-cuts algorithm.

To address these problems, we propose a novel 3D mesh segmentation method based on the deep learning method, which combines voxels and feature descriptors. We propose to use voxel grids to divide the 3D shape mesh into voxels before segmentation and give each voxel a feature descriptor of the contained mesh, unlike former works directly segment on the mesh model. Benefiting from using the volumetric neural network that takes both the geometric features on shapes' surfaces and the 3D voxel data as input, our method considers the whole shape of 3D models, including the surface and the inner space, which can obtain more satisfactory segmentation results. The intermediate and final segmentation results of our approach and an overview of our algorithm are shown in Fig. 1. To summarize, our contributions in this work are listed as follows.

- We propose a novel method for 3D shape segmentation by taking into account both geometric features of each face and relative positions between various parts of shapes, which leads to more satisfactory segmentation results.
- Extensive experimental results illustrate that our method outperforms state-of-the-art 3D segmentation methods on several public benchmarks.

2   Related Work

Earlier work leverages a single 3D shape feature descriptor in mesh segmentation [8]. The representatives include Gaussian Curvature (GC) [9], Average Geodesic Distance (AGD) [10], Shape Diameter Function (SDF) [2], and so on. Previous work usually first extracts geometric feature vectors of each mesh, then applies clustering means to get the labeling result. However, one feature descriptor can only describe the geometric feature in one aspect and is insufficient to be employed to obtain satisfactory segmentation results for any 3D shape.

To deal with this problem, later studies rely more on multiple shape geometric descriptors. Kalogerakis et al. [11] employ a Conditional Random Field model to segment 3D meshes by combining multiple shape geometric descriptors. Guo et al. [6] fuse multiple shape geometric descriptors of each mesh into a 2D matrix, and then applied a deep convolution neural network to segment on this matrix. However, those methods only combine a variety of feature descriptors and do not extract the relative position relationship between meshes.

Over the last few years, benefiting from the advances in deep learning and the boost of 3D shape repositories, approaches using deep learning methods to solve 3D shape segmentation tasks are rapidly growing. Due to the directness and good representation of 3D shapes, many researchers use 3D voxels to segment 3D shapes. Maturana et al. [12] and Qi et al. [13] propose the voxel-based 3D CNN architectures to tackle shape classification tasks. Wang et al. [7] propose VoxSeg-Net based on attention feature aggregation to implement the segmentation task. To reduce the computation cost, Riegler et al. [14] show a novel representation of 3D shapes employing octree structure, making it appropriate for deep learning in high-resolution inputs. Wang et al. [15] propose an octree-based 3D CNN, which can dramatically reduce the computation cost.

Fig. 2. The comparison of the results among our method and Guo et al. [6], which show the key advantage of our method. The left segmentation result is the ground-truth. The middle segmentation result is obtained by using our method, while the right one is got by using the method proposed in Guo et al. [6].

There are also some methods which directly segment 3D shapes on their mesh models. Kalogerakis et al. [11] propose a segmentation method based on multi-view 2D projection. Yu et al. [16] propose a 3D shape segmentation method based on recursive neural networks. Hu et al. [17] define mesh-based convolution operators to aggregate local features of neighboring faces and implement pooling and upsampling of shape surfaces. MeshCNN [18] defines the convolution and pooling methods on edges of 3D meshes and successfully applies them to segmentation. MeshWalker [19] represents 3D meshes by multiple random walk sequences along the surfaces and employs a recurrent neural network for training.

3   V-SegNet Framework

Our framework aims to segment 3D shapes by estimating the labels of all faces on the 3D models. In the first stage of our pipeline, we compute each face's geometric features in the 3D mesh model and voxelize the 3D model. We take the mean of the feature vector on the face contained in each voxel as the feature vector of the voxel. The next stage is the proposed network named V-SegNet, which consists of a volumetric encoder-decoder architecture and volumetric residual blocks. The input of V-SegNet is the feature vector of each voxel, and the output is the probability distribution of each voxel assigned with each label. V-SegNet labels each voxel with its corresponding feature vector. Finally, we label each face on the mesh model according to the corresponding voxels' labels, and further improve the segmentation quality by applying the graph-cuts algorithm [20]. The details are described in the following.

The key advantage of our method lies in that our method can successfully capture the spatial information of the shapes, instead of considering the geometric features on the surfaces only. As shown in Fig. 2, the segmentation result at the right does not correctly label the middle of the glasses, as the middle and the adjacent lenses have similar geometric features. In contrast, the segmentation result at the middle shows that our voxel-based method is capable of learning the inner spatial information of shape to more accurately segment each component.

3.1   Generating the 3D Shape Feature Input

Past methods usually perform segmentation by clustering the features on the faces of 3D models, which neglects the inner information of the shapes. To consider both surface and the inner information of 3D shapes, we propose to voxelize the 3D mesh model and use the feature vector of voxels as the input of V-SegNet.

The proposed network segments 3D shapes based on features, which are firstly computed from the 3D mesh model. Instead of training a 3D CNN as the direct feature extractor, we choose three hand-crafted feature descriptors to obtain the geometric information contained in 3D shapes, including GC, AGD, and SDF. These feature descriptors provide good extraction of local and global features of 3D shapes and have shown excellent performance in previous studies. Compared with using one single descriptor, we characterize a shape from different perspectives by using various feature descriptors.

The voxelization process then projects and discretizes the feature vector of each face on 3D mesh models to the corresponding voxel based on the volumetric resolution. To be more specific, the mesh model is placed inside its bounding box, which is actually a voxel grid of size $M \times N \times K$. We select the voxel grid's resolution under the balance between the size of the network and performance. In this paper, the resolution is experimentally set to be $80 \times 80 \times 80$ and the corresponding ablation study can be found in Sect. 4.3. The resolution can already split all 3D mesh models in our experimental datasets, where most of them contain no more than 30K faces, into suitable size voxels which contain approximately one face. It is worth pointing out that we recommend using higher resolution when dealing with 3D mesh models with more faces. In practice, we can also simplify input 3D shapes with large number of faces into coarser ones before segmentation.

For those voxels penetrated by one or more faces, we assign the mean of the feature vector of the face to the voxels. Otherwise, the voxels have no faces passing through in the inner spaces of 3D shapes are set to zeros. In the 3D voxelized model, the voxels that are traversed by the surface occupy only a small part of the voxel space. Those voxels with no feature vectors inside are not engaged in the computation of loss function to reduce the computational cost. With the voxelization process, we have a three-channel voxel grid of size $3 \times 80 \times 80 \times 80$ as the input of our V-SegNet.

3.2 The Architecture of V-SegNet

We use volumetric blocks extended from 2D CNN to design the V-SegNet. It includes volumetric basic block, volumetric residual block, volumetric down-sampling block, and volumetric up-sampling block [21]. The volumetric basic blocks consist of the convolution layer, batch normalization layer, and ReLU as the activation function.

As shown in Fig. 3, V-SegNet composes of an encoder-decoder structure with feature extraction shortcuts using volumetric residual blocks extended from 2D residual block [22] for labeling 3D features of voxel cubes in a voxel-to-voxel manner. V2V-PoseNet [21] inspired us in architecture. The number of the features' channel is first increased from 3 to 16 using a volumetric basic block of size $3 \times 3 \times 3$ empirically and down-sampled next with max-pooling. The features are then processed by three sequentially volumetric residual blocks to double the

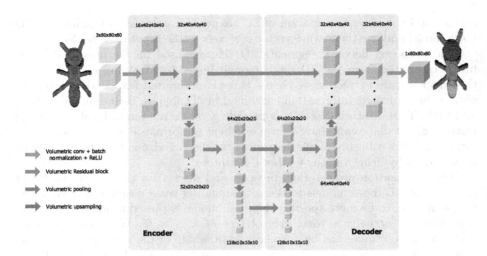

Fig. 3. The V-SegNet framework and its encoder-decoder architecture. The input is voxels with concatenated geometric features in a voxelized model. Volumetric residual block, volumetric down-sampling block, volumetric up-sampling block, and volumetric convolutional block are used to construct the networks. The output is a labeled voxel which is part of the target segmented model.

number of channels and extract the local information of the object. After that, the encoder uses volumetric basic blocks to obtain scale-invariant local features and deliver them to the next coarser level using max-pooling. Batch normalization and ReLU are employed after each volumetric convolution for accelerating the learning. In the bottleneck, we use one volumetric residual block to improve the labeling performance empirically. Next, the features of the coarser level are compressed and up-sampled with volumetric basic blocks. They are then concatenated with shortcuts from extracted finer level features using volumetric residual blocks for compensating the detail loss in max-pooling layers. In the

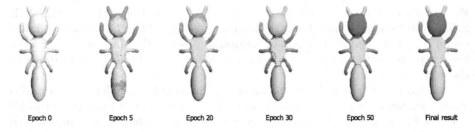

Fig. 4. Segmentation results of V-SegNet with different numbers of training epochs. As the number of training epochs grows, the segmentation result becomes more accurate.

end, the labeling values go through two consecutive volumetric residual blocks and two $1 \times 1 \times 1$ volumetric basic blocks to the final prediction.

The labeling results of V-SegNet on every voxel are then transformed back to each face of corresponding meshes. Note that a face may contain multiple labels if it intersects with several voxels. For this case, we determine the face's final label by a simple voting mechanism. Similar to other approaches, we also employ the graph-cuts algorithm to further refine the boundaries between segments.

We design the network in this way because of its efficiency on memory and computational time, as well as it combines multi-scale information as in U-net [23] and FCN [24]. V-SegNet has the capability to consider the geometric features on shapes' surfaces and their spatial information simultaneously to obtain more satisfactory segmentation results.

3.3   Network Training

Although geometric descriptors are invariant to rotate, V-SegNet has not been designed to automatically rotate the shapes to the same specific angle for both training and testing shapes. As a result, the deflective placements of shapes in different categories could cause accuracy to descend. Therefore, we manually rotate a shape along the x, y, z-axis $\pm 90°$ to expand it to several shapes of different placement if the original placement of this shape is skew. Theoretically, rotating the input 3D shapes smaller degrees can benefit data augmentation further, although it may increase the computational burden. We experimentally find that rotating $90°C$ is enough for getting satisfactory results.

The weights in V-SegNet are initialized using zero-mean Gaussian distribution with $\sigma = 0.001$. To train all the variants, we use ADAM with a fixed learning rate of 0.005 and betas of $(0.9, 0.99)$ using our PyTorch implementation of V-SegNet. We train the variants for 100 epochs because over-fitting occurs if more epochs are applied. The training set is shuffled before every epoch, and each mini-batch (4 shapes) is picked to ensure that each model is used only once in an epoch. To train V-SegNet, we use the cross-entropy loss over all the voxels that are not empty in a batch as the objective function. The loss L is defined as follows:

$$L = -\sum_{n=1}^{N} \sum_{i,j,k \in H} \log(\widetilde{y}_{y_n(i,j,k)}) \qquad (1)$$

where y_n is the ground-truth label and $\widetilde{y}$ is the predicted probability value on the true label in mini-batch n, and N denotes the mini-batch size. H represents the set of coordinates where the voxel model is not empty. As shown in Fig. 4, as the number of epochs grows, the segmentation results become more accurate.

4   Experimental Results

In this section, we evaluate the proposed approach and state-of-the-art methods on a large variety of shapes from selected datasets based on the accuracy of 3D shape segmentation results.

Table 1. The accuracy comparison of our method with other methods including Shape-Boost [5], Wang et al. [25], Guo et al. [6], ShapePFCN [11], MeshCNN [18] and Mesh-Walker [19], on the PSB dataset and the small COSEG dataset. "null" means that the results do not exist. "Our method" represents the segmentation results of our method refined by the graph-cuts algorithm.

Methods	ShapeBoost	Wang et al.	Guo et al.	ShapePFCN	MeshCNN	MeshWalker	Ours
Human	93.20%	55.60%	91.22%	**93.80%**	74.76%	87.02%	90.73%
Cup	99.60%	99.60%	**99.73%**	93.70%	95.86%	99.54%	99.60%
Glasses	97.20%	–	**97.60%**	96.30%	93.94%	96.11%	97.47%
Airplane	96.10%	–	96.67%	92.50%	84.36%	96.20%	**97.14%**
Ant	98.80%	–	98.80%	**98.90%**	91.83%	97.36%	98.26%
Chair	98.40%	**99.60%**	98.67%	98.10%	84.75%	97.61%	98.37%
Octopus	98.40%	–	**98.79%**	98.10%	98.21%	97.86%	98.11%
Table	99.30%	99.60%	99.55%	99.30%	96.78%	99.33%	**99.65%**
Teddy	98.10%	–	**98.24%**	96.50%	84.29%	95.57%	98.08%
Hand	88.70%	–	**88.71%**	88.70%	68.83%	83.31%	86.67%
Plier	96.20%	–	96.22%	95.70%	83.69%	92.24%	**96.43%**
Fish	95.60%	–	95.64%	95.90%	89.05%	94.58%	**96.44%**
Bird	87.90%	–	88.35%	86.30%	68.09%	92.76%	**92.84%**
Armadillo	90.10%	–	**92.27%**	93.30%	50.24%	89.12%	91.04%
Vase	85.80%	90.50%	89.11%	85.70%	68.94%	84.56%	**92.11%**
FourLeg	86.20%	54.30%	87.02%	89.50%	68.73%	80.93%	**91.04%**
Lamp	–	–	96.28%	87.70%	–	–	**97.25%**
Iron	–	–	97.37%	87.70%	–	–	**97.70%**
Guitar	–	–	97.15%	**97.90%**	–	–	96.93%
Candelabra	–	–	94.44%	**96.30%**	–	–	94.88%
Average	–	–	95.09%	93.76%	81.40%	92.76%	**95.54%**

4.1   Experimental Setting

Dataset. The benchmark datasets employed in our experiments are composed of two different datasets: the Princeton Segmentation Benchmark (PSB) [26] and the Shape COSEG Dataset [27], including the small COSEG dataset and the large COSEG dataset. Similar to [28], we also leave out three categories (Bearing, Mech, and Bust) in the PSB dataset because they lack the meaningful correspondences between segmentations.

We separate the PSB and the small COSEG datasets into two components. All categories take 12 shapes as the training set and the rest for testing. For

Table 2. The accuracy comparison of our method with three other methods, including MeshCNN [18], MeshWalker [19], and PDMeshNet [1], on the large COSEG dataset.

Methods	MeshCNN	MeshWalker	PDMeshNet	Ours
Tele-aliens	95.76%	**98.70%**	98.18%	98.07%
Chairs	94.54%	98.60%	97.23%	**98.89%**
Vases	93.49%	**99.00%**	95.36%	98.63%
Average	94.60%	**98.77%**	96.92%	98.53%

Table 3. Comparisons of using different geometric descriptors as the input of V-SegNet for 3D shape segmentation on 16 categories from the PSB dataset. "Pre-graphcuts" indicates the segmentation accuracy before the graph-cuts algorithm. "GC+AGD", "GC+SDF", and "AGD+SDF" means using the corresponding features as input and applying graph-cuts. "Ours" represents using "GC+AGD+SDF" as the input of our network and applying graph-cuts for post-processing.

Dataset	GC+AGD	GC+SDF	AGD+SDF	Pre-graphcuts	Ours
PSB	94.21%	94.44%	94.69%	93.18%	**95.25%**

the large COSEG dataset, we refer to [1,18,19] for division. Within each category, we repeatedly conduct the segmentation experiment with different random initialization three times to compute the average accuracy. The final accuracy of the proposed approach is compared with the state-of-the-art methods. It is noted that the compared methods are also refined by the graph-cuts algorithm.

Implementation Details. Our method is implemented in both PyTorch and Matlab. The whole network is trained on a single NVIDIA GeForce RTX 2080 Ti GPU, and our Matlab framework runs on Intel CoreTM i9 3.60 GHz CPU, 32 GB of RAM. Together with the consumption of shape preprocessing, it takes 6 min to train a shape containing 20K to 30K faces.

4.2   Comparison

We compare with the following seven traditional and state-of-the-art methods, including ShapeBoost [5], Wang et al. [25], ShapePFCN [11], MeshCNN [18], Guo et al. [6], MeshWalker [19], and PDMeshNet [1]. As in [5], the accuracy is computed as:

$$Accuracy = \sum_{t \in T} a_t \mathbf{g}_t (l_t) / \sum_{t \in T} a_t, \qquad (2)$$

where a_t is the area of the triangle t and l_t is the predicted segmentation label. $\mathbf{g}_t (l_t)$ is a function which equals to 1 if the prediction is correct and 0 otherwise.

Table 1 presents the statistical comparisons of the proposed approach and the above state-of-the-art methods on segmentation accuracy. It is obvious that categories with the least number of parts to label, such as *Cup, Octopus, Table* have the highest accuracy among all due to the clarity of the meaning on different parts. The lowest accuracy comes from the category of *Human* and *Hand*, which have the most ambiguity and more parts. It is harder to distinguish each finger than segment the palm and the fingers, and also difficult to tell the explicit boundary between the upper arm and lower arm. It can be observed that the accuracies of our proposed method are comparable to the state-of-the-art methods: ShapeBoost [5], Wang et al. [25], ShapePFCN [11], Guo et al. [6], MeshCNN [18], and MeshWalker [19]. Among the state-of-the-art methods, Guo et al. [6] have the best performance. Furthermore, our overall average segmentation accuracy outperforms all other competing methods. Table 2 shows the comparison between our method and three approaches on the large COSEG dataset.

4.3 Ablation Studies

Here, we demonstrate the effectiveness of using several geometric descriptors as feature extractors on meshes. The input of V-SegNet is composed of three heuristically designed geometric features, including GC, AGD, and SDF. Table 3 shows the average segmentation accuracy for 16 categories in the PSB dataset. The highest accuracy is obtained when all three descriptors are employed in generating the network's input, while the accuracy is lower when one of the descriptors is not used. Table 3 also shows the segmentation accuracy of our method before applying graph-cuts.

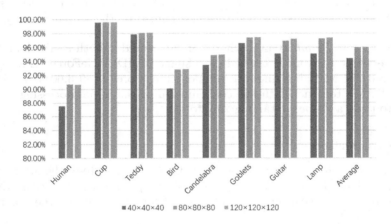

Fig. 5. Comparison of segmentation accuracy at different voxel resolutions.

To test the effect of voxel resolution on our method, we conduct experiments at different resolutions. Figure 5 shows the segmentation accuracies of our approach on eight classes of models at $40 \times 40 \times 40$, $80 \times 80 \times 80$, and $120 \times 120 \times 120$ resolutions, respectively. It can be seen that the resolution $80 \times 80 \times 80$ is sufficient to extract rich shape features on the datasets used in our experiments, while keeping the computation burden as low as possible.

5 Limitation and Future Work

First, it is non-trivial to design a deep neural structure capable of dealing with the placement differences between shapes in the training and testing sets. We need to integrate an automatic shape alignment algorithm into our framework in the future.

Second, it is assumed that the category of the model is known such that only shapes in the same category are taken as the testing set. We will connect a model classification network ahead of the V-SegNet to build a blind 3D shape segmentation framework.

6 Conclusion

In this paper, we propose a novel voxel-based method for segmenting 3D shapes using deep neural volumetric convolutional networks. With a voxelization process on the mesh models, our method can explore the cues from the surface and the inner space by employing both the part position information on the voxelized model and the feature descriptor information on the meshes. The experimental results illustrate that our method can achieve better performance than state-of-the-art methods.

Acknowledgments. This work is supported by the National Natural Science Foundation of China (61872321, 62172356, 61972350), Natural Science Foundation of Zhejiang Province (LY22F020026), and Ningbo Major Special Projects of the "Science and Technology Innovation 2025" (2020Z005, 2020Z007, 2021Z012).

References

1. Milano, F., Loquercio, A., Rosinol, A., Scaramuzza, D., Carlone, L.: Primal-dual mesh convolutional neural networks. In: Conference on Neural Information Processing Systems, pp. 952–963 (2020)
2. Shapira, L., Shamir, A., Cohen-Or, D.: Consistent mesh partitioning and skeletonisation using the shape diameter function. Vis. Comput. **24**(4), 249–259 (2008)
3. Lim, J.J., Khosla, A., Torralba, A.: FPM: fine pose parts-based model with 3D CAD models. In: Fleet, D., Pajdla, T., Schiele, B., Tuytelaars, T. (eds.) ECCV 2014. LNCS, vol. 8694, pp. 478–493. Springer, Cham (2014). https://doi.org/10.1007/978-3-319-10599-4_31
4. Huang, H., Kalogerakis, E., Yumer, E., Mech, R.: Shape synthesis from sketches via procedural models and convolutional networks. IEEE Trans. Vis. Comput. Graph. **23**(8), 2003–2013 (2016)
5. Kalogerakis, E., Hertzmann, A., Singh, K.: Learning 3D mesh segmentation and labeling. ACM Trans. Graph. **29**, 1–12 (2010)
6. Guo, K., Zou, D., Chen, X.: 3D mesh labeling via deep convolutional neural networks. ACM Trans. Graph. **35**(1), 1–12 (2015)
7. Wang, Z., Lu, F.: VoxSegNet: volumetric CNNs for semantic part segmentation of 3D shapes. IEEE Trans. Vis. Comput. Graph. **26**(9), 2919–2930 (2019)
8. Shu, Z., Qi, C., Xin, S., Hu, C., Wang, L., Zhang, Y., Liu, L.: Unsupervised 3D shape segmentation and co-segmentation via deep learning. Comput. Aid. Geom. Des. **43**, 39–52 (2016)
9. Gal, R., Cohen-Or, D.: Salient geometric features for partial shape matching and similarity. ACM Trans. Graph. **25**(1), 130–150 (2006)
10. Shapira, L., Shalom, S., Shamir, A., Cohen-Or, D., Zhang, H.: Contextual part analogies in 3D objects. Int. J. Comput. Vis. **89**(2–3), 309–326 (2010)

11. Kalogerakis, E., Averkiou, M., Maji, S., Chaudhuri, S.: 3D shape segmentation with projective convolutional networks. In: Proceedings of the IEEE Conference on Computer Vision and Pattern Recognition, pp. 3779–3788 (2017)
12. Maturana, D., Scherer, S.: VoxNet: a 3D convolutional neural network for real-time object recognition. In: IEEE/RSJ International Conference on Intelligent Robots and Systems (IROS), pp. 922–928. IEEE (2015)
13. Qi, C.R., Su, H., Nießner, M., Dai, A., Yan, M., Guibas, L.J.: Volumetric and multi-view CNNs for object classification on 3D data. In: Proceedings of the IEEE Conference on Computer Vision and Pattern Recognition, pp. 5648–5656 (2016)
14. Riegler, G., Osman Ulusoy, A., Geiger, A.: OctNet: learning deep 3D representations at high resolutions. In: Proceedings of the IEEE Conference on Computer Vision and Pattern Recognition, pp. 3577–3586 (2017)
15. Wang, P.S., Liu, Y., Guo, Y.X., Sun, C.Y., Tong, X.: O-CNN: octree-based convolutional neural networks for 3D shape analysis. ACM Trans. Graph. **36**(4), 1–11 (2017)
16. Yu, F., Liu, K., Zhang, Y., Zhu, C., Xu, K.: PartNet: a recursive part decomposition network for fine-grained and hierarchical shape segmentation. In: Proceedings of the IEEE/CVF Conference on Computer Vision and Pattern Recognition, pp. 9491–9500 (2019)
17. Hu, S.M., Liu, Z.N., Guo, M.H., Cai, J.X., Huang, J., Mu, T.J., Martin, R.R.: Subdivision-based mesh convolution networks. ACM Trans. Graph. **41**(3), 1–16 (2022)
18. Hanocka, R., Hertz, A., Fish, N., Giryes, R., Fleishman, S., Cohen-Or, D.: MeshCNN: a network with an edge. ACM Trans. Graph. **38**(4), 1–12 (2019)
19. Lahav, A., Tal, A.: MeshWalker: deep mesh understanding by random walks. ACM Trans. Graph. **39**(6), 1–13 (2020)
20. Boykov, Y., Veksler, O., Zabih, R.: Fast approximate energy minimization via graph cuts. IEEE Trans. Pattern Anal. Mach. Intell. **23**(11), 1222–1239 (2001)
21. Moon, G., Chang, J.Y., Lee, K.M.: V2V-PoseNet: voxel-to-voxel prediction network for accurate 3D hand and human pose estimation from a single depth map. In: Proceedings of the IEEE Conference on Computer Vision and Pattern Recognition, pp. 5079–5088 (2018)
22. He, K., Zhang, X., Ren, S., Sun, J.: Deep residual learning for image recognition. In: Proceedings of the IEEE Conference on Computer Vision and Pattern Recognition, pp. 770–778 (2016)
23. Ronneberger, O., Fischer, P., Brox, T.: U-net: convolutional networks for biomedical image segmentation. In: Navab, N., Hornegger, J., Wells, W.M., Frangi, A.F. (eds.) MICCAI 2015. LNCS, vol. 9351, pp. 234–241. Springer, Cham (2015). https://doi.org/10.1007/978-3-319-24574-4_28
24. Long, J., Shelhamer, E., Darrell, T.: Fully convolutional networks for semantic segmentation. In: Proceedings of the IEEE Conference on Computer Vision and Pattern Recognition, pp. 3431–3440 (2015)
25. Wang, Y., Gong, M., Wang, T., Cohen-Or, D., Zhang, H., Chen, B.: Projective analysis for 3D shape segmentation. ACM Trans. Graph. **32**(6), 1–12 (2013)
26. Chen, X., Golovinskiy, A., Funkhouser, T.: A benchmark for 3D mesh segmentation. ACM Trans. Graph. **28**(3), 1–12 (2009)
27. Wang, Y., Asafi, S., Van Kaick, O., Zhang, H., Cohen-Or, D., Chen, B.: Active co-analysis of a set of shapes. ACM Trans. Graph. **31**(6), 1–10 (2012)
28. Hu, R., Fan, L., Liu, L.: Co-segmentation of 3D shapes via subspace clustering. Comput. Graph. Forum **31**(5), 1703–1713 (2012)

Object Detection

Few-Shot Detection Based on an Enhanced Prototype for Outdoor Small Forbidden Objects

Jia Chen[1,2], Xinzhou Chen[1], Jin Huang[1,2(✉)], Xinrong Hu[1,2], and Tao Peng[1,2]

[1] Wuhan Textile University, Wuhan 430200, Hubei, China
derick0320@foxmail.com
[2] Engineering Research Center of Hubei Province for Clothing Information,
Wuhan 430200, Hubei, China

Abstract. In this paper, we propose an enhanced prototype based on a regional many-to-many attention mechanism for few-shot object detection of forbidden objects such as knives and sticks. Specifically, First, we use the original prototype to obtain the invariance of the image to better represent the invariant features of images. Then, we use the enhanced prototype to weight the support features of different query images of knives and sticks to avoid over-fitting. Finally, we use a joint regional consistency loss function to balance and maximize the consistency between the enhanced prototype and the original prototype, which facilitates online learning of invariant object features and improves the efficiency of object detection. The results of experiment show that the enhanced prototype can effectively detect knives and sticks, compared with state-of-art methods. Our method achieves significant improvements in both visual and quantitative evaluation metrics.

Keywords: Knife and stick detection · Few-shot object detection · Feature prototype · Regional attention mechanism

1 Introduction

Recently, security check has played an important part in public transport safety and prevention of terrorist attacks. Most of the existing indoor security checks are detected with the assistance of X-ray screening machines as well as computer vision technology. Existing indoor security check approaches [1–3] detect forbidden objects with X-ray technology. But there is few study of outdoor security check cause it is hard to detect the small objects such as knives and sticks in surveillance. To solve the problem, we propose an enhanced prototype few-shot object detection algorithm based on a regional many-to-many attention mechanism.we design augmented prototypes to learn invariant object features among different object categories, unlike the prototypes learned from each category individually [4–6], our enhanced feature prototypes are learned from all object categories, and the advantages are twofold; on the one hand, the extracted enhanced prototypes can characterize the rich contextual information of the image and invariants from all object categories. On the other hand, the region mixing consistency loss function makes the enhanced prototypes less affected by the data unbalance of different categories. Moreover, by fine-tuning, the enhanced prototype can be efficiently adapted to new categories with fewer data, especially new categories such as knives and sticks. We also propose a regional mixture consistency loss to maximize the consistency between the features of the augmented object and the original object. We produced a knife and stick dataset. In the training process, we train the model on a large number of rich base datasets and then fine-tune the model on a newly constructed training set that contains a small number of balanced training sets from the base dataset and the knives and sticks objects. Comparative experiments and rich visualizations on two benchmarks demonstrate the effectiveness of the proposed approach.

The contributions are summarized as follows:

- We propose an excellent enhanced prototype to obtain the invariant characteristics of knives and sticks.
- In order to implement few-shot object detection(FSOD) for knives and sticks, a new framework with enhanced prototype are designed.
- We design a new region blending consistent loss function that can make the object features after enhancement consistent with the original features.
- We collect a datasets for small forbidden objects such as knives, sticks.

2   Related Work

2.1   Few-Shot Learning

Few-shot learning is a technique that achieve accurate classification with a small amount of training data. Many new methods have emerged recently in few-shot learning, mainly in terms of models [7–9], algorithms [10–15], and other breakthroughs. Afrasiyabi, A. et al. [9] proposed Mixture-based Feature Space Learning(Mixt-FSL), method to model the base class with a mixture model by simultaneously training a feature extractor and learning the mixture model parameters online. This yields a richer and more discriminative feature space that can be used to classify new examples from few samples. Li, W.H. et al. [10] proposed Universal Representation Learning (URL), which learns a set of universal visual representations by extracting knowledge from multiple domain-specific networks after co-aligning their features with the help of adapters and central kernel alignment. Liang, H. et al. [11]proposed a novel noise-enhanced supervised autoencoder (NSAE) to capture a wider range of feature distribution variations. Guo, Y. et al. [12] proposed attentional weight generation by information maximization (AWGIM) for small number of shots learning, first, it maximizes the mutual information between the weights generated in the task and the data; this allows the generated weights to retain information about the task and the specific query samples. The second is the self-attentive and cross-attentive paths used to encode task contexts and individual queries. Zhu, Y. et al. [13] proposed a multi-attentive meta-learning (MattML) approach for shot less fine-grained image recognition. The proposed meta-learning method uses the attention mechanism of both the base learner and the task learner to capture the discriminative part of the image. The base learner is equipped with two convolutional block attention modules (CBAMs) and a classifier. These two CBAMs can learn diverse and information-rich parts. And the initial weights of the classifier are engaged by the task learner, which provides sensitive initialization of the classifier with respect to the task. To adapt the gradient-based meta-learning approach is used by updating the two CBAMs and the parameters of the participating classifiers, which helps the updated base learner to focus adaptively on the discriminative part. Baik, S et al. [14] introduced a new meta-learning framework with a loss function adapted to each task. The proposed framework is named Meta-Learning with Task-Adaptive Loss Function (MeTAL). According to so many previous studies, we believe that designing a robust prototype is the key technique to improve knife and stick detection in a real surveillance environment.

2.2 Attentional Mechanisms

Attention mechanisms were first developed for human vision and then applied to areas such as neural machine translation and image description generation since humans selectively focus on a portion of information that is useful to them and ignore information that is useless to them. Vaswani, A. et al. [16] proposed to learn self-attention in feature space. Memory-based VOS methods [17] use many-to-many attention to learn bootstrap information from memory features to query features, and graph attention methods [18–20] learn graph matching attention by modeling the input image as a bipartite graph. However, the direct use of these full-rank attentions in FSOD suffers from expensive computational costs, especially when the number of processed images increases. In this paper, we refer the attention mechanism to the process of generating enhanced prototypes to reduce the effect of data imbalance across different classes and enhance the generalization of invariant features over regions. It enables better detection of knives and sticks in real surveillance environments.

3   Methodology

In this section, we present our FSOD with Domain Agent Network Prototypes, as shown in Fig. 1.

3.1   Learning and Extraction of Common Generic Prototypes

The learning process of the common generic prototype in this paper. We first use the widely used Faster R-CNN as the base detection model, and given the input image, we first use feature extractors such as VGG-16, ResNet, etc. We cite the generality prototypes and descriptors of the paper by Aming Wu et al. [21] as in Eqs. 1, 2 and 3.

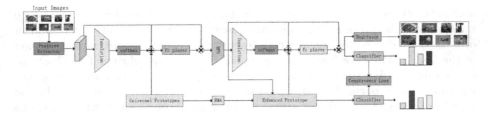

Fig. 1. few-shot detection architecture with enhanced prototype, involution and fc layer denote involution layer and fully connected layer respectively. $\oplus$ denote the residual operation, $\otimes$ denote the concatenation operation. We focus on improving the generalization ability of the detector by learning invariant object features. First, generic prototypes are learned from all object classes. Using the output of RPN (Region Proposal Network), we take the generic prototypes and obtain the augmented prototypes by many-to-many attention transformation. Next, enhanced object features are computed based on the enhanced prototypes. Finally, the region mixing consistency loss between the augmented features and the original features is computed

To extract the corresponding features $F \in \mathbb{R}^{w \times h \times m}$ where w, h and m denote width, height and number of channels, respectively. Then, the common generic prototype is defined as $C = C_i \in \mathbb{R}^m, i = 1, 2, ..., D$. Based on the defined prototype set C, this paper calculates the descriptors representing pixel-level information in the image.

$$\Gamma = W_g * F + b_g, \tag{1}$$

$$V_i = \sum_{j-1}^{wh} \frac{e^{\Gamma_{j,i}}}{\sum_{i-1}^{D} e^{\Gamma_{j,i}}} (F_j - c_i), \tag{2}$$

where $W_g \in \mathbb{R}^{3 \times 3 \times m \times D}$ and $b_g \in \mathbb{R}^D$ are convolutional parameters. $\Gamma_r \in \mathbb{R}^{D \times m}$ represents the output descriptors. $(F_j - c_i)$ indicates residual operation. In this paper, we use the residual operation to assign visual features to the corresponding prototypes, and finally we use the result of the connection of F and Γ as input to the RPN module.

$$P = RPN(\Psi([F, V_r W_p + b_p])), \tag{3}$$

where $V_r \in \mathbb{R}^{1 \times D \times m}$ is the result of V reconstruction, while $W_p \in \mathbb{R}^{D \times m \times m}$ and $b_p \in \mathbb{R}^m$ are fully connected layer parameters, By cascading operations, the feature symbol V can be fused into the original feature F, thus enhancing the representation of F. Ψ is composed of two convolutional layers with ReLU activation for transforming the result of cascading, and finally P is the output result of RPN and Roi Pooling, where n, s are the number of proposals and the proxy of proposals, and P is the feature dimension as F.

3.2   Regional Many-to-Many Attention Reinforcement Prototype Module

In this paper, we study the correlation between support and query images, and the construction of correlation is a many-to-many problem. To solve the appeal problem, in this paper, based on the previous [16,20,22,23], Leveraging the labeled support images and between each support query image pair to learn many-to-many attention, this paper uses the regional many-to-many attention mechanism of [24] to reduce the computational cost, we are given a query q and a pair of keys k-v, the new attention matrix of the decomposition is denoted as:

$$\hat{A} = A^{qt}A^{tk}, \tag{4}$$

where A^{qt} is the attention between query q and agent t and A^{tk} is the attention between agent t and key value k. which is defined as:

$$A^{qt} = \sigma(\frac{q(k)^T}{\sqrt{C_k}}), A^{tk} = \sigma(\frac{q^t(k)^T}{\sqrt{C_k}}), \tag{5}$$

In our setup, we set $C_q = C_k$. The category t sampled from the query image is called the domain proxy. Following Eq. 6 and Eq. 7, the attention matrix A^{Qt} and the attention matrix A^{tS} are calculated as follows:

$$A^{Qt} = \sigma(\frac{q^Q(k^t)^T}{\sqrt{C_k}}), A^{tS} = \sigma(\frac{q^t(k^S)^T}{\sqrt{C_k}}), \tag{6}$$

where q^t and k^t are the queries and keys of the agent features sampled from q^Q and k^Q. After that, we obtain the attention feature v^A, denoted as:

$$v^A = Av^S = A^{Qt}A^{tS}v^S, \tag{7}$$

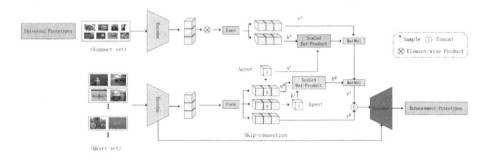

Fig. 2. Our enhanced prototype generated using ordinary generic prototypes and regional many-to-many attention, we decompose the full rank attention into the product of two smaller attentions, making our computational cost smaller.

As shown in Fig. 2, given the support set, the general prototype and the query set as inputs, two encoders sharing the same weights extract features for the support set and the query set, respectively. Then we compute two attention matrices: one is the correlation between the domain agent and the support set, and the other is the correlation between the domain agent and the query set. We derive the final attention features by weighting the support features using the above two attention matrices. After connecting the attention features with the feature values of the query set, we use the decoder to obtain the final enhanced prototype.

3.3 Two-Stage Fine-Tuning Method: Regionally Mixed Consistent Loss Function

First, our loss function is divided into four parts. The first part is from the RPN to distinguish foreground from background and refine bounding-box anchors. The second part is classified losses form the RMA incurs a classification loss for each point in the current query set and RPN. The third part is box regression loss. The last part is consistent loss. To better balance the gradient with the propagation loss, we choose the same KL-Divergence loss [21]. The overall joint loss function is as follows:

$$L = L_{rpn} + L_{cls} + L_{loc} + \eta L_{con}, \tag{8}$$

The most important part of the loss function is L_{cls}. It contains two classifications of losses form RMA module and RPN. This article discusses in detail the classification loss of RMA, The classification loss can be formulated as:

$$L_{clsrma} = -\frac{1}{|Q+1|} \sum_{(x,y) \in Q} log \frac{e^{T(F(x),v_y)}}{\sum_{k \in C_i} e^{T(F(x),v_k)}}, \tag{9}$$

We use the set of images of the query set as the set of query points $(x, y) \in Q$, where $T(F(x), v_k)$ denotes the similarity between sample x and the k-th class representation v_k predicted by the enhanced prototypes. η is a hyperparameter. During the training period, we used a two-stage fine-tuning approach to optimize our model. Specifically, in the base training phase, we use joint loss L to optimize the whole model based on the data-rich base class. After the base training phase, only the de-detection head of the last fully connected layer (for classification) is replaced. The new classification layer is randomly initialized. Furthermore, in several fine-tuning phases, we still employ loss L to fine-tune the whole model, based on a balanced training set consisting of a few base classes and new classes.

4 Experiment

4.1 Data Set Introduction

First is our own collected dataset of knives and sticks in the surveillance environment. We call the collected dataset the KS dataset. We follow the setup in [4, 32] to construct the few-shot detection dataset in order to evaluate it fairly, we set 5 new classes and 15 base classes for knives and sticks respectively. Each class has 20 images. Also, we use the same three class splits as in work [4], where each new class has only K object instances available and K is set to 1, 2, 3, 5, 10.

After that we used the same setup to do generalizability experiments with less sample dataset, for MS COCO [31], 20 categories overlapped with PASCAL VOC [29,30] as new categories with K = 10 and K = 30. The remaining 60 categories were used as base categories.

4.2   Ablation Studies in KS Dataset

In order to verify which module of the method in this paper is more relevant for tool and stick detection, we conduct ablation experiments for regional many-to-many attention, enhanced prototype, regional mixed consistent loss function, and with or without fine-tuning, respectively.

Table 1. AP (%) for 1, 2, 3, 5, 10 shot

Block	Dataset	Contain				1	2	3	5	10
Attention	KS	χ				37.5	41.7	46.4	53.9	58.3
Enhanced prototype	KS		χ			**36.6**	40.1	**40.3**	55.4	59.2
Loss	KS			χ		38.1	40.3	45.8	53.7	**50.1**
Finetune	KS				χ	37.2	**39.1**	46.6	**53.5**	58.8
All	KS					**44.1**	**48.3**	**51.4**	**56.1**	**62.0**

As shown in Table 1, χ indicates that this module is not included, keeping other conditions constant. The most significant effects on the experimental results are the enhanced prototype and the region loss consistency function. We can see that in the 1-shot case, several modules have little impact, and basically the detection efficiency is about the same; the most prominent is the 3-shot case, where the absence of the enhanced prototype leads to a significant decrease in the detection effect, with a drop of nearly 11.1%, indicating that the effect of the invariant features of the enhanced prototype to extract tools and sticks makes the detection effect also better; and then look at the 10-shot case. When the regional loss consistency function is removed, it will lead to the common generic prototype and enhanced prototype extracted at the beginning can not maximize consistency, making the learning of invariant object features poor, resulting in low detection efficiency.

After we studied each module, we found that the number of Enhanced Prototypes may affect the Enhanced Prototypes. To verify our conjecture, we continued the ablation study of the number of Enhanced Prototypes.

The number of enhanced prototypes is an important hyperparameter of the prototype formulation; if this number is too small, these prototypes may not adequately represent the features of the image, while on the other hand, if the number is too large it can lead to a large computational effort afterwards. Table 2 shows the impact of different number of enhanced prototypes on the performance. We can see that the best performance is achieved when 26 prototypes are used, and the performance decreases when the number is greater or less than 26, indicating that the number of enhanced prototypes affects the performance of the model.

Table 2. Ablation experiments with enhanced prototype numbers

Number/shot	1	2	3	5	10
10	38.1	44.9	46.8	53.3	57.6
12	38.7	45.0	47.3	53.9	58.0
14	38.9	45.4	48.0	54.0	58.8
16	39.3	45.9	47.9	54.2	58.9
18	39.6	46.2	48.6	54.6	59.4
20	42.0	46.8	48.8	54.9	59.7
22	42.5	47.0	49.1	55.0	60.1
24	42.6	47.3	49.5	55.5	59.8
26	**43.9**	**48.2**	**51.3**	55.7	**61.8**
28	42.1	47.8	49.6	**56.0**	58.3
30	40.8	47.3	49.2	55.4	59.6
32	40.7	47.0	48.9	55.1	59.4
34	40.2	46.6	48.7	54.8	60.0
36	39.9	46.2	47.9	54.7	58.9
38	39.4	45.7	47.5	54.3	58.7
40	38.8	45.1	46.6	53.9	58.3

4.3   Comparison Experiments in KS Dataset

In this section, the method of this paper is compared with detection performance and experimental visualization.

Table 3. AP (%) for 1, 2, 3, 5, 10 shot in KS dataset

Method/shot	1	2	3	5	10
Meta R-CNN	36.3	40.4	40.3	**56.2**	56.2
FSOD-VE	37.1	40.5	45.2	53.7	53.1
MPSR	37.3	41.2	42.4	54.5	56.2
Ours	**44.1**	**48.3**	**51.4**	56.1	**62.0**

Table 3 shows the performance of few-shot detections on the KS dataset. Compared with FSOD-VE, Meta R-CNN and MPSR, our method consistently outperforms them on 1-shot, 2-shot, 3-shot and 10-shot. It is only slightly smaller than Meta R-CNN by 0.1% on 5-shots, which further demonstrates the effectiveness of the proposed enhanced prototype for both knives and sticks.

Figure 3 shows the detection of our method and MSPR in a real environment with images from a new class of knives and sticks samples under the camera. The upper bar shows the MSPR detection effect, and the lower bar shows the detection effect of our method. It can be seen that in the first image, the prediction box of MSPR detection is larger than our method, in the second image, the detection of the tool is shifted and is not as accurate as ours, and in the third image, MSPR detects the shadow of the tool on the ground as the tool now, and there is a false detection situation.

Fig. 3. Detection visualization

4.4   Generalizability Experiments

Table 4. Few-shot detection performance on the PASCAL VOC dataset

Method/shot	Novel set 1					Novel set 1					Novel set 1				
	1	2	3	5	10	1	2	3	5	10	1	2	3	5	10
TFA	25.6	37.4	43.1	48.9	53.7	19.3	28.4	31.3	35.2	40.3	18.6	28.3	35.2	41.7	46.2
MPSR	41.5	42.3	49.7	54.5	61.0	25.2	30.1	40.3	40.7	48.1	32.7	34.1	42.4	47.9	50.2
Ours	**44.2**	**48.0**	**51.0**	**56.8**	**61.9**	**32.4**	**31.2**	**42.5**	**43.6**	**49.4**	**36.6**	**40.1**	**44.5**	**51.3**	**54.2**

Table 4 shows the results in PASCAL VOC. The performance decreases significantly as the number of new categories decreases. This indicates that solving the problem of fewer samples is crucial to improve the generalization of the detector. We can see that the proposed method consistently outperforms the two baseline methods. This indicates that the use of generic prototype augmentation helps to learn invariant object features, thus improving the performance. Also, it shows that focusing on invariance plays a key role in solving FSOD.

Table 5. Few-shot detection performance on the MS COCO dataset

Shot	Method	AP	AP_{75}	AP_S	AP_M	AP_L
10	Meta R-CNN	8.2	6.5	2.2	7.6	14.2
10	FSOD-VE	**12.6**	9.7	2.4	**13.9**	**19.9**
10	TFA	9.1	8.8	–	–	–
10	MPSR	9.4	9.4	3.1	8.1	16.0
10	Ours	11.6	**10.8**	**4.7**	12.2	18.1
30	Meta R-CNN	12.5	10.9	2.7	11.5	19.1
30	FSOD-VE	15.1	12.3	3.1	**16.0**	22.7
30	TFA	12.1	12.0	–	–	–
30	MPSR	13.7	13.5	4.1	12.8	22.9
30	Ours	**15.6**	**15.8**	**6.3**	15.2	**25.2**

Table 5 shows the performance of the few-sample detection on the MS COCO dataset. Although FSOD-VE performs better than our method in the 10-shot case, our method outperforms FSOD-VE on small objects. Also, the training of our method is much easier compared to FSOD-VE. Moreover, we do not use viewpoint information. These results further indicate that using the enhanced prototype helps to improve the generalization ability of the detector. The few-shot detection performance (%) on the MS COCO dataset.

5 Conclusion

To solve the problem of detecting knives and sticks in forbidden object detection, this paper proposes an enhanced prototype based on a regional many-to-many attention mechanism and develops a method for detecting few-shot targets using the enhanced prototype. The results of experiments under the knife and stick datasets collected by ourselves in the street environment show that the method applies well to the real environment, and the results on the public experimental dataset show the generalization of the method in this paper.

Acknowledgment. This work is supported by the Chen's research was sponsored by Natural Science Foundation of HuBei Province of China Award No.2020CFB801.

References

1. Akcay, S., Breckon, T.: Towards automatic threat detection: a survey of advances of deep learning within X-ray security imaging. Pattern Recogn. **122**, 108,245 (2022)

2. Mery, D., Kaminetzky, A., Golborne, L., Figueroa, S., Saavedra, D.: Target detection by target simulation in X-ray testing. J. Nondestruct. Eval. **41**(1), 1–12 (2022). https://doi.org/10.1007/s10921-022-00851-8

3. Hassan, T., Akcay, S., Bennamoun, M., Khan, S., Werghi, N.: Tensor pooling-driven instance segmentation framework for baggage threat recognition. Neural Comput. Appl. **34**(2), 1239–1250 (2022). https://doi.org/10.1007/s00521-021-06411-x

4. Liu, J., Song, L., Qin, Y.: Prototype rectification for few-shot learning. In: Vedaldi, A., Bischof, H., Brox, T., Frahm, J.-M. (eds.) ECCV 2020. LNCS, vol. 12346, pp. 741–756. Springer, Cham (2020). https://doi.org/10.1007/978-3-030-58452-8_43

5. Snell, J., Swersky, K., Zemel, R.: Prototypical networks for few-shot learning. In: Advances in Neural Information Processing Systems 30 (2017)

6. Wang, K., Liew, J.H., Zou, Y., Zhou, D., Feng, J.: PANet: few-shot image semantic segmentation with prototype alignment. In: Proceedings of the IEEE/CVF International Conference on Computer Vision, pp. 9197–9206 (2019)

7. Kang, B., Liu, Z., Wang, X., Yu, F., Feng, J., Darrell, T.: Few-shot object detection via feature reweighting. In: Proceedings of the IEEE/CVF International Conference on Computer Vision, pp. 8420–8429 (2019)

8. Wang, Y.X., Ramanan, D., Hebert, M.: Meta-learning to detect rare objects. In: Proceedings of the IEEE/CVF International Conference on Computer Vision, pp. 9925–9934 (2019)

9. Afrasiyabi, A., Lalonde, J.F., Gagné, C.: Mixture-based feature space learning for few-shot image classification. In: Proceedings of the IEEE/CVF International Conference on Computer Vision, pp. 9041–9051 (2021)

10. Li, W.H., Liu, X., Bilen, H.: Universal representation learning from multiple domains for few-shot classification. In: Proceedings of the IEEE/CVF International Conference on Computer Vision, pp. 9526–9535 (2021)

11. Liang, H., Zhang, Q., Dai, P., Lu, J.: Boosting the generalization capability in cross-domain few-shot learning via noise-enhanced supervised autoencoder. In: Proceedings of the IEEE/CVF International Conference on Computer Vision, pp. 9424–9434 (2021)

12. Guo, Y., Cheung, N.M.: Attentive weights generation for few shot learning via information maximization. In: Proceedings of the IEEE/CVF Conference on Computer Vision and Pattern Recognition, pp. 13499–13508 (2020)

13. Zhu, Y., Liu, C., Jiang, S.: Multi-attention meta learning for few-shot fine-grained image recognition. In: IJCAI, pp. 1090–1096 (2020)

14. Baik, S., Choi, J., Kim, H., Cho, D., Min, J., Lee, K.M.: Meta-learning with task-adaptive loss function for few-shot learning. In: Proceedings of the IEEE/CVF International Conference on Computer Vision, pp. 9465–9474 (2021)

15. Lin, C., Yuan, Z., Zhao, S., Sun, P., Wang, C., Cai, J.: Domain-invariant disentangled network for generalizable object detection. In: Proceedings of the IEEE/CVF International Conference on Computer Vision, pp. 8771–8780 (2021)

16. Vaswani, A., et al.: Attention is all you need. In: Advances in Neural Information Processing Systems 30 (2017)

17. Seo, S., Lee, J.-Y., Han, B.: URVOS: unified referring video object segmentation network with a large-scale benchmark. In: Vedaldi, A., Bischof, H., Brox, T., Frahm, J.-M. (eds.) ECCV 2020. LNCS, vol. 12360, pp. 208–223. Springer, Cham (2020). https://doi.org/10.1007/978-3-030-58555-6_13

18. Veličković, P., Cucurull, G., Casanova, A., Romero, A., Lio, P., Bengio, Y.: Graph attention networks. arXiv preprint arXiv:1710.10903 (2017)

19. Wang, H., Zhang, X., Hu, Y., Yang, Y., Cao, X., Zhen, X.: Few-shot semantic segmentation with democratic attention networks. In: Vedaldi, A., Bischof, H., Brox, T., Frahm, J.-M. (eds.) ECCV 2020. LNCS, vol. 12358, pp. 730–746. Springer, Cham (2020). https://doi.org/10.1007/978-3-030-58601-0_43

20. Zhang, C., Lin, G., Liu, F., Guo, J., Wu, Q., Yao, R.: Pyramid graph networks with connection attentions for region-based one-shot semantic segmentation. In: Proceedings of the IEEE/CVF International Conference on Computer Vision, pp. 9587–9595 (2019)

21. Wu, A., Han, Y., Zhu, L., Yang, Y.: Universal-prototype enhancing for few-shot object detection. In: Proceedings of the IEEE/CVF International Conference on Computer Vision, pp. 9567–9576 (2021)

22. Oh, S.W., Lee, J.Y., Xu, N., Kim, S.J.: Video object segmentation using space-time memory networks. In: Proceedings of the IEEE/CVF International Conference on Computer Vision, pp. 9226–9235 (2019)

23. Voigtlaender, P., Leibe, B.: Online adaptation of convolutional neural networks for video object segmentation. arXiv preprint arXiv:1706.09364 (2017)

24. Chen, H., Wu, H., Zhao, N., Ren, S., He, S.: Delving deep into many-to-many attention for few-shot video object segmentation. In: Proceedings of the IEEE/CVF Conference on Computer Vision and Pattern Recognition, pp. 14040–14049 (2021)

25. Zhang, C., Lin, G., Liu, F., Yao, R., Shen, C.: CANet: class-agnostic segmentation networks with iterative refinement and attentive few-shot learning. In: Proceedings of the IEEE/CVF Conference on Computer Vision and Pattern Recognition, pp. 5217–5226 (2019)

26. He, K., Zhang, X., Ren, S., Sun, J.: Deep residual learning for image recognition. In: Proceedings of the IEEE Conference on Computer Vision and Pattern Recognition, pp. 770–778 (2016)

27. Deng, J.: A large-scale hierarchical image database. In: Proceedings of IEEE Computer Vision and Pattern Recognition (2009)

28. Oh, S.W., Lee, J.Y., Sunkavalli, K., Kim, S.J.: Fast video object segmentation by reference-guided mask propagation. In: Proceedings of the IEEE Conference on Computer Vision and Pattern Recognition, pp. 7376–7385 (2018)

29. Everingham, M., Eslami, S., Van Gool, L., Williams, C.K., Winn, J., Zisserman, A.: The PASCAL visual object classes challenge: a retrospective. Int. J. Comput. Vis. 111(1), 98–136 (2015). https://doi.org/10.1007/s11263-014-0733-5

30. Everingham, M., Van Gool, L., Williams, C.K., Winn, J., Zisserman, A.: The PASCAL visual object classes (VOC) challenge. Int. J. Comput. Vis. 88(2), 303–338 (2010). https://doi.org/10.1007/s11263-009-0275-4

31. Lin, T.-Y., et al.: Microsoft COCO: common objects in context. In: Fleet, D., Pajdla, T., Schiele, B., Tuytelaars, T. (eds.) ECCV 2014. LNCS, vol. 8693, pp. 740–755. Springer, Cham (2014). https://doi.org/10.1007/978-3-319-10602-1_48

32. Yan, X., Chen, Z., Xu, A., Wang, X., Liang, X., Lin, L.: Meta R-CNN: towards general solver for instance-level low-shot learning. In: Proceedings of the IEEE/CVF International Conference on Computer Vision, pp. 9577–9586 (2019)

33. Wang, X., Huang, T.E., Darrell, T., Gonzalez, J.E., Yu, F.: Frustratingly simple few-shot object detection. arXiv preprint arXiv:2003.06957 (2020)

34. Wu, J., Liu, S., Huang, D., Wang, Y.: Multi-scale positive sample refinement for few-shot object detection. In: Vedaldi, A., Bischof, H., Brox, T., Frahm, J.-M. (eds.) ECCV 2020. LNCS, vol. 12361, pp. 456–472. Springer, Cham (2020). https://doi.org/10.1007/978-3-030-58517-4_27

Research on Real-Time Forestry Pest Detection Based on Improved YOLOv5

Jipeng Yu[1](✉), Taizhe Tan[1,2], and Yaoyu Deng[1]

[1] Guangdong University of Technology, Guangzhou, China
2112005210@mail2.gdut.edu.cn
[2] Heyuan Bay Area Digital Economy Technology Innovation Center, Heyuan, China

Abstract. Small object detection has always been a difficult point in the field of object detection. To achieve better detection performance of forestry pests, this paper proposes Mf-YOLOv5s. Based on YOLOv5s, we replace the PANet with M-BiFPN to explore the importance of different input features and add one more prediction head to enhance the detection of tiny pests. Then we insert the BoTR between backbone and neck to capture global contextual information by using self-attention mechanism. Furthermore, we use Copy-Pasting data augmentation strategy to expand the dataset, which can make the sample distribution evenly. We also add a D-CBAM to neck to explore the role of hybrid attention mechanism in small object detection. The experimental results show that the AP_{50} of Mf-YOLOv5s on the test set is 95.3%, which is 2.2% higher than YOLOv5s, the detection precision and recall are 2.9% and 3.1% higher, respectively.

Keywords: Pest detection · YOLOv5 · BiFPN · Transformer · D-CBAM

1 Introduction

The stability of forestry is crucial to the development of the world, and real-time pest detection technology is the key to the modernization of agriculture. Agriculture and forestry may suffer from pests and diseases at any time, which may lead to a reduction in food production and slow growth of forest trees, or cause extensive crop death and ecological degradation, and bring huge economic losses to agriculture and forestry [1]. Therefore, rapid detection and elimination of forestry pests prior to outbreaks is an important step in the task of pest control. Previously, forestry pest detection mainly used the light trapping method, capturing insects required manual identification and statistics, which was inefficient, labor-intensive, and poor in real-time, making it hard to meet the requirements of modern agricultural development [2].

In view of the challenge and particularity of pest identification in forestry, and the limitation that pest image classification effects are particularly dependent on pre-designed manual features, the object detection algorithm based on deep learning has also been applied by researchers to the field of pest image detection.

N. Magnenat-Thalmann et al. (Eds.): CGI 2022, LNCS 13443, pp. 515–526, 2022.
https://doi.org/10.1007/978-3-031-23473-6_40

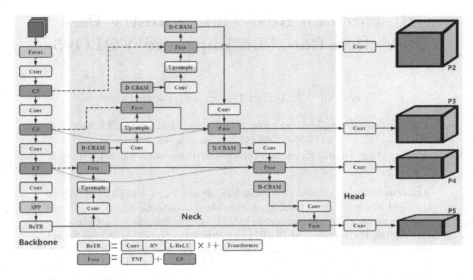

Fig. 1. The architecture of Mf-YOLOv5s. a) Adding a layer of transformer encoder block between backbone and Neck. b) The neck use the structure of M-BiFPN. c) Using D-CBAM can extract the attention area to help Mf-YOLOv5s focus on useful objects. d) Adding one more prediction head for tiny pests detection. In addition, the FNF module in the figure represents the fast normalized fusion approach in M-BiFPN.

Deven [3] et al. subjected three widely used object detection models to detect and identify insect datasets, Faster R-CNN [6] performed well with an accuracy of 95.33% in the same test environment. Lin [7] et al. designed an anchor-free object detection model, which achieved mean average precision(mAP) of 56.4% on the 24 small pest datasets. However, there are still limitations in pest detection methods. Specifically, small pest detection faces the following challenges: (1) In the existing object detection models, the shallow features of the backbone network are generally used to detect small objects, but the lack of semantic information in the shallow features makes the detection of small targets difficult; (2) Currently, the mainstream object detection algorithms widely use datasets (PASCAL VOC, COCO) with small training samples of small and medium targets, which makes the small targets not sufficiently learned during the model training process.

In this study, we propose Mf-YOLOv5s in response to the above problems. The framework of Mf-YOLOv5s is illustrated in Fig. 1. Based on the YOLOv5s, firstly, we use the Copy-Pasting data augmentation [9] strategy to amplify a small number of pest instances, so that the number of pest samples is more evenly distributed. Secondly, adding the Encoder module in the Transformer [10] structure to the end of the backbone, which helps to combine CNN's excellent local feature extraction capabilities with the Transformer's efficient ability to capture global information and context. Thirdly, considering the importance of different features during feature fusion process, the M-BiFPN module is used to replace the PANet [11]. Furthermore, we add one more prediction head to strengthen the detection ability of tiny insects. Finally, we also add hybrid attention mechanism D-CBAM to find the attention region of interest in images. On the test dataset, the AP value of Mf-YOLOv5s is 75.5%, which is better than YOLOv5s [22] by 2.2%.

2   Related Work

2.1   Data Augmentation

Data augmentation refers to increasing the number of training samples for neural network learning through resampling, rotation, translation and other methods. Whether in public datasets or datasets collected in the real world, the number of samples for small objects is generally small. Therefore, increasing the number of samples for small objects by means of data augmentation will help improve the detection performance of the model. Paper [9] proposed to copy-paste small samples in an image without overlapping with other targets, increasing the number of small targets in a single image. Common global pixel augmentation methods include random scaling, cropping, translation, rotation, etc. These methods can be used for training to expand the dataset and enhance the robustness of the model. Furthermore, Several researchers have also proposed methods for data augmentation for multiple image processing, such as MixUp [12] and Mosaic [13].

In this paper, the Copy-Pasting data augmentation strategy is used to expand the data set before training, so that the distribution is even among the samples. During training, we add global pixel augmentation methods such as random scaling, cropping, and translation. In addition, we also use two tricks MixUp [12] and Mosaic [13] to enhance the generalization ability of model and avoid overfitting.

2.2   Object Detection Models

CNN-based object detectors is mainly divided into two types: 1) one-stage detectors: YOLOv3 [8], YOLOv4 [13]. 2) two-stage detectors: Faster R-CNN [6], R-FCN [14]. With the rapid development of object detection, today's popular one-stage object detectors mainly have two kinds: anchor-based and anchor-free. The detectors of anchor-free are CenterNet [15], FCOS [16]. From the perspective of designing the network structure, a modern detectors is generally composed of two parts, an CNN-based backbone which is used for image feature extraction and a head, used to predict classes and bounding boxes for objects. In addition, Object detectors often insert some layers between the backbone and the head, researchers usually call it the neck of an object detector [24]. To sum up, a modern object detector is composed of the following parts.

Input. The input of an object detector is usually image, patches or image pyramid.

Backbone. Backbone which is usually pre-trained on ImageNet. For those detectors working on CPU, the backbone could be MobileNet [26,27] or ShuffleNet [25]. For those detectors running on GPU, the backbone could use VGG [4], ResNet [5]. These networks have strong feature extraction capabilities on task of image classification.

Neck. Usually, a neck is composed of several bottom-up paths and several top-down paths. It is designed to make full use of the features extracted by the backbone. Commonly used path-aggregation blocks in the neck have FPN [17], PANet [11], BiFPN [18].

Head. In image classification tasks, backbone cannot be used to predict the location information of objects. So head is used to predict the position coordinates and category of objects in the image. The head of object detectors mainly have two kinds: one-stage detector and two stage detector. Two-stage detector is relatively more accurate, especially in positioning. The one-stage detector is generally faster and easier to meet the real-time demand in practical application scenarios.

2.3   Overview of YOLOv5

YOLOv5 [22] is a one-stage object detection algorithm, which is similar to YOLOv4 [13], improved based on YOLOv3 [8]. With little reduction in mAP, the size of the weight file of YOLOv5 is small, which is nearly 90% smaller than YOLOv4, shorter training time and inference speed compare to YOLOv4. The network structure of YOLOv5 is divided into four parts: Input, Backbone, Neck and Head. Input includes data augmentation, adaptive image filling, and so on. The backbone mainly contains Focus module, CSPDarkNet53 and SPP layer. Neck uses the architecture of PANet [11]. Head is still using the detection head of YOLOv3 [8]. YOLOv5 contains four different network structures, including YOLOv5s, YOLOv5m, YOLOv5l and YOLOv5x. The depth, width, number of convolution kernels, and parameters of the four types of networks are increasing sequentially. Since the YOLOv5s model has good detection performance on a general dataset, we select it as our baseline.

3   Method

3.1   BoTR

In this paper, to explore Transformer [10] encoder block could capture global contextual information by using self-attention mechanism, and establish long-distance dependence on targets, we insert the encoder block of Transformer between the backbone and the neck. Because the resolution of the feature maps at the end of the backbone is relatively small. Applying Transformer encoder block on these feature maps will not introduce too much calculation and memory consumption. Combining the Transformer encoder block with the convolutional neural network, We can call it BoTR, which contains three convolution blocks and several Transformer encoders.

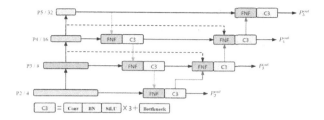

Fig. 2. The architecture of M-BiFPN. a) FNF represents fusing different features by using fast normalized fusion approach. b) C3 block contains two parts: three convolution blocks and several Bottlenecks. c) Adding one more prediction head to detect tiny objects. d) The green arrow and the red arrow denote the upsampling and downsampling operations, respectively. (Color figure online)

3.2   M-BiFPN

The feature fusion module used in YOLOv5 is PANet [11], which introduces global self-attention upsampling to restore pixel localization, it treats all input features equally. Since different input features usually contribute to the output feature unequally. Inspired by BiFPN [18], we consider using a new weighted fusion approach: fast normalized fusion [18]. By adding an additional weight for each input, the network could learn the importance of each input feature. In addition, YOLOv5 has three prediction heads to predict the category and location of objects. Since the pest dataset contains many extremely small pests, we specially add one prediction head to detect tiny objects. We replace PANet in the original version of YOLOv5 with improved BiFPN, and name the new feature network as M-BiFPN. Figure 2 shows the structure of M-BiFPN.

The formula of fast normalized fusion is as follows:

$$O = \sum_i^N \frac{w_i}{\epsilon + \sum_j w_j} \cdot I_i \tag{1}$$

where $w_i \geq 0$, and $\epsilon = 0.0001$ is a extremely small value to avoid numerical instability. Here we use a example to describe the two fused features processes at level 4 for M-BiFPN:

$$P_4^{td} = C3(\frac{w_1 \cdot P_4 + w_2 \cdot Up(P_5)}{w_1 + w_2 + \epsilon}) \tag{2}$$

$$P_4^{out} = C3(\frac{w_1' \cdot P_4 + w_2' \cdot P_4^{td} + w_3' \cdot Down(P_3^{out})}{w_1' + w_2' + w_3' + \epsilon}) \tag{3}$$

where P_4^{td} is the intermediate feature at level 4 on the top-down pathway, P_4^{out} represents the output feature map at level 4 on the bottom-up pathway. Up and Down represent upsampling and downsampling operations, respectively. To further improve detection accuracy, M-BiFPN uses the standard convolution with a convolution kernel of 1, and adds batch normalization and SiLU activation after convolution. But in [18], BiFPN use depthwise separable convolution for feature fusion to improve the efficiency. All other features are constructed in a similar way.

3.3   D-CBAM

CBAM [20] is a simple and effective convolutional neural network attention module. Furthermore, it is also an end-to-end general module that can be seamlessly integrated into any CNN architectures. In convolutional neural networks, the size of the receptive field determines the performance of spatial attention. A large receptive field can aggregate a wider range of contextual information, resulting in a stronger representation of spatial attention. In this paper, we insert attention mechanism in neck, and use dilated convolution to aggregate spatial features of two-dimensional spatial attention. The improved module is called D-CBAM.

4   Experiments

We evaluate Mf-YOLOv5s on the amplified pest test set. To measure the performance of the model, this paper uses AP (average of all 10 IoU thresholds, ranging from $[0.5: 0.95]$) and AP_{50} as evaluation indicators.

4.1   Copy-Pasting Strategy to Augment Dataset

The dataset used in this experiment comes from Baidu. It provides 2183 images, including 1693 images in the training set, 245 images in both validation set and test set.

Table 1. Comparison of the number of samples in the original and modified dataset.

Classes	Original			Modified		
	Training	Validation	Test	Training	Validation	Test
Boerner	1595	318	304	1994	636	608
Leconte	2216	594	596	2617	1188	1192
Linnaeus	818	292	284	1618	1074	1058
acuminatus	953	235	235	1753	960	960
armandi	1765	231	242	2167	462	484
coleoptera	2091	186	173	2489	372	346
linnaeus	909	0	0	2109	490	490

According to the statistical results in Table 1, the numbers of samples "Linneaus", "acuminatus" and "linneaus" in original dataset are insufficient. This will cause the model to be more inclined to learn features of other targets during the training process, while targets with a smaller number of samples will have poor generalization. Inspired by the copy-pasting data augmentation [9], we cut three kinds of insects with a small number, and then randomly folded and rotated the insects obtained after cutting, and pasted them on the image. Each paste operation should ensure that the pasted targets do not overlap with the existing targets on the image, which not only keeps the number of samples balanced, but also increases the diversity of small target locations. Due to lack of insect "linnaeus" in validation and test sets, three types of insects with fewer samples are randomly pasted onto each image in the validation and test sets. The training set use the same strategy for the first 400 images. The amplified dataset has 3073 insect images, including 2093 images in training set, 490 images in both validation and test sets.

4.2   Implementation Details

In the training phase, we use the same hyper-parameters as YOLOv5s. Specifically, our network is trained with Adam optimizer for 300 epochs, the initial learning rate being 0.0032 and the first 2 epochs are used for warm-up. The learning rate is reduced by using cosine decay rule. Weight decay and momentum are set as 0.00036 and 0.843, respectively. We initialize our network with the weights from YOLOv5s, because Mf-YOLOv5s and YOLOv5s share most part of backbone. By using part of pre-trained model from YOLOv5s, we can save lots of training time. The input images are set as 640, and a mini-batch of 32 images. In addition, we use MixUp and Mosaic data augmentation, and label smoothing regularization methods. Finally, using the SiLU activation function on backbone and neck.

The object size in the pest dataset accounts for less than 5% of the entire image, so the network needs to pay more attention to small-sized targets. The anchor boxes used by YOLOv5 model are counted on the COCO dataset, and some anchors are too large to be suitable for our pest detection task. The k-means algorithm is integrated in yolov5 during training, there is no need to additionally get the detection anchors adapted to the pest dataset. Therefore, the sizes of 12 anchors are $(21, 31)$, $(31, 21)$, $(43, 27)$, $(27, 45)$, $(35, 36)$, $(36, 46)$, $(46, 38)$, $(68, 38)$, $(39, 70)$, $(68, 53)$, $(54, 68)$, $(79, 77)$.

4.3   Performance Comparison

To compare the Mf-YOLOv5s with other classical object detection models in terms of performance, several models are trained and tested on the amplified dataset. Table 2 show the detection results of each model. Compared with YOLOv5s, our network adds a small amount of parameters and calculations, but it effectively improves the detection performance of tiny pests, AP and AP_{50} increased by 2.2% and 1.9%, respectively. Furthermore, YOLOv5m has more layers and larger width than YOLOv5s, it requires more parameters and computation, but Mf-YOLOv5s can greatly reduce the amount of parameters and calculations, the AP_{50} value is the same as YOLOv5m, the AP is 0.9% higher than YOLOv5m. YOLOv4-MF [28] is an excellent detector for pest detection, but our model has better performance in detecting pests. Compared with other excellent detection models, our model has a great Precision and Recall. The results also prove that the improved model in this paper has better performance in small object detection.

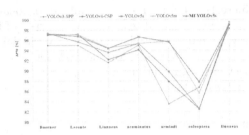

Fig. 3. AP values of different models on each object.

Figure 3 shows the detection performance of the test set for all insect classes on each model. The detection performance of Mf-YOLOv5s is higher than YOLOv3 and YOLOv5s, especially on "armindi". In addition, Mf-YOLOv5s has similar performance in detecting various categories compared with YOLOv5m, but YOLOv5m has a larger amount of parameters and calculations.

Table 2. Comparison of the comprehensive performance of each model. Params and GFLOPs denote the number of parameters and multiply-adds. YOLOv4-MF uses the same dataset as this paper, it only exposes AP values on the test set.

Indicators	YOLOv3	YOLOv4	YOLOv4-MF	YOLOv5s	YOLOv5m	Ours
AP^{test}	72.2%	73.3%	–	73.3%	74.6%	**75.5%**
AP_{50}^{test}	92.2%	92.9%	88.93%	93.4%	95.0%	**95.3%**
AP^{val}	72.5%	74.7%	–	72.8%	74.1%	**75.8%**
AP_{50}^{val}	92.6%	94.0%	–	92.9%	94.5%	**95.3%**
Precision	88.3%	61.0%	90.39%	87.4%	**91.4%**	91.3%
Recall	81.4%	**95.1%**	81.41%	85.7%	85.3%	86.3%
Params	9.6M	52.5M	38.10M	**7.1M**	21.1M	8.4M
GFLOPs	23.4	119.2	**4.05**	16.4	50.4	21.1
F1-score	0.847	0.743	0.84	0.86	0.882	**0.887**

Table 3. Abalation study on test set.

Methods	AP	AP_{50}	Parameter	GFLOPs
YOLOv5s	73.3%	93.4%	7.0M	16.4
+ M-BiFPN	74.6%	93.6%	8.33M	21.2
+ D-CBAM	74.8%	94.6%	8.37M	21.4
+ BoTR	75.5%	95.3%	8.37M	21.2

4.4 Training Results

The training loss and validation loss curves are shown together in Fig. 4, it can be seen from the figure that the loss value of Mf-YOLOv5s is lower than that of YOLOv5s on both the training set and the validation set. Furthermore, both models converged well and no overfitting occurred.

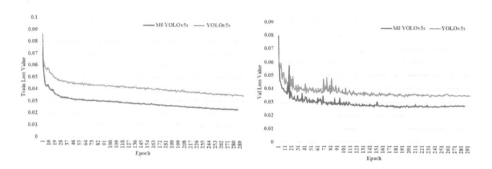

Fig. 4. Training loss and validation loss of the two models.

4.5 Ablation Studies

In order to verify that the improved part can indeed improve the detection performance, we design a series of experiments on the test set to test the effectiveness of the added modules. The impact of each component is listed in the Table 3.

Effect of M-BiFPN. From Table 3, replacing the PANet of YOLOv5s with M-BiFPN makes the number of parameters from 7.0M to 8.4M, and GFLOPs from 16.4 to 21.1. This increases the amount of paramaters and calculation, but AP value is improved.

Effect of BoTR. Adding the transformer encoder blocks to the end of the backbone, which not only allows the model to capture global features and rich contextual information, but also improves AP.

Effect of D-CBAM. Furthermore, to verify the improved attention mechanism D-CBAM has better performance than CBAM, no other modules are changed, we use two concatenate dilated convolution to replace the standard convolution of the spatial attention module in CBAM. The kernel size of dilated convolution is set to 3 or 7. We list out the results of CBAM and others on the test set, as shown in Table 4. In the process of convolutional aggregation of spatial information, the larger the receptive field, the richer the spatial context information that can be aggregated. When only adding a small number of parameters, cascading two dilated convolutions can explicitly adjust filter's receptive field and improve the AP.

Table 4. Performance of CBAM versus improved CBAM on the test set. CBAM-x means that the kernel size of dilated convolution is x. Params represents the parameter increment.

Model	AP	AP_{50}	Params
CBAM	74.8%	94.6%	21482
CBAM-3	75.3%	94.9%	21127
CBAM-7	**75.5%**	**95.3%**	21727

4.6   Visualization

We compare YOLOv5s with Mf-YOLOv5s in a visual experiment. Figure 5 shows the comparison of the detection results of the two algorithms. As can be seen from the figure, the use of YOLOv5s to detect the image have missed detection and false detection, while Mf-YOLOv5s does not exist.

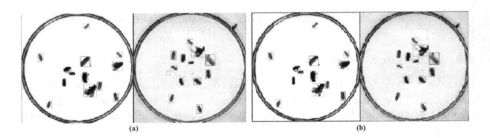

Fig. 5. Comparison of detection results of different detectors. (a) YOLOv5s; (b) Mf-YOLOv5s.

5   Conclusions

In this paper, we propose an improved YOLOv5s one-stage detector called Mf-YOLOv5s. Compared with other classic one-stage detectors, Mf-YOLOv5s is more efficient in detecting small targets, and the amount of model parameters and calculations are not significantly increased. In our network, we add some effective tricks to improve the detection effect of YOLOv5, such as M-BiFPN, BOTR, D-CBAM, and copy-paste data augmentation. Given its effectiveness and efficiency, we hope that Mf-YOLOV5s can serve as a strong detector to solve the problems of forest pest detection. We also believe that Mf-YOLOV5s can be extended to Solve many other industrial tasks. In addition, this work has only been done partly, and further improvements can be made in these areas: (1) collect images of real pest samples under natural background and manually label them, expand the dataset and sample categories. (2) Under the condition of satisfying speed and accuracy, further compress the model structure.

References

1. Ngugi, L.C., Abelwahab, M., Abo-Zahhad, M.: Recent advances in image processing techniques for automated leaf pest and disease recognition - a review. Inf. Process. Agric. **8**, 27–51 (2020)
2. Li, K., Zhu, J., Li, N.: Lightweight automatic identification and location detection model of farmland pests. Wirel. Commun. Mob. Comput. **2021**, 1–11 (2021)
3. Patel, D.J., Bhatt, N.: Insect identification among deep learning's meta-architectures using TensorFlow. Int. J. Eng. Adv. Technol. **9**(1), 1910–1914 (2019)
4. Simonyan, K., Zisserman, A.: Very deep convolutional networks for large-scale image recognition. arXiv preprint arXiv:1409.1556 (2014)
5. He, K., Zhang, X., Ren, S., Sun, J.: Deep residual learning for image recognition. In: Proceedings of the IEEE Conference on Computer Vision and Pattern Recognition, pp. 770–778 (2016)
6. Ren, S., He, K., Girshick, R., Sun, J.: Faster R-CNN: towards real-time object detection with region proposal networks. In: Advances in Neural Information Processing Systems 28, pp. 91–99 (2015)
7. Jiao, L., Dong, S., Zhang, S., Xie, C., Wang, H.: AF-RCNN: an anchor-free convolutional neural network for multi-categories agricultural pest detection. Comput. Electron. Agric. **174**, 105522 (2020)
8. Redmon, J., Farhadi, A.: YOLOv3: an incremental improvement. arXiv preprint arXiv:1804.02767 (2018)
9. Kisantal, M., Wojna, Z., Murawski, J., Naruniec, J., Cho, K.: Augmentation for small object detection. arXiv preprint arXiv:1902.07296 (2019)
10. Vaswani, A., et al.: Attention is all you need. In: Advances in Neural Information Processing Systems, pp. 5998–6008 (2017)
11. Liu, S., Qi, L., Qin, H., Shi, J., Jia, J.: Path aggregation network for instance segmentation. In: Proceedings of the IEEE Conference on Computer Vision and Pattern Recognition, pp. 8759–8768 (2018)
12. Zhang, H., Cisse, M., Dauphin, Y.N., Lopez-Paz, D.: mixup: beyond empirical risk minimization. arXiv preprint arXiv:1710.09412 (2017)
13. Bochkovskiy, A., Wang, C.Y., Liao, H.Y.M.: YOLOv4: optimal speed and accuracy of object detection. arXiv preprint arXiv:2004.10934 (2020)
14. Dai, J., Li, Y., He, K., Sun, J.: R-FCN: object detection via region-based fully convolutional networks. In: Advances in Neural Information Processing Systems, pp. 379–387 (2016)
15. Zhou, X., Wang, D., Krähenbühl, P.: Objects as points. arXiv preprint arXiv:1904.07850 (2019)

16. Tian, Z., Shen, C., Chen, H., He, T.: FCOS: fully convolutional one-stage object detection. In: Proceedings of the IEEE/CVF International Conference on Computer Vision, pp. 9627–9636 (2019)
17. Lin, T.Y., Dollár, P., Girshick, R., He, K., Hariharan, B., Belongie, S.: Feature pyramid networks for object detection. In: Proceedings of the IEEE Conference on Computer Vision and Pattern Recognition, pp. 2117–2125 (2017)
18. Tan, M., Pang, R., Le, Q.V.: EfficientDet: scalable and efficient object detection. In: Proceedings of the IEEE/CVF Conference on Computer Vision and Pattern Recognition, pp. 10781–10790 (2020)
19. Liu, S., Huang, D., Wang, Y.: Learning spatial fusion for single-shot object detection. arXiv preprint arXiv:1911.09516 (2019)
20. Woo, S., Park, J., Lee, J.-Y., Kweon, I.S.: CBAM: convolutional block attention module. In: Ferrari, V., Hebert, M., Sminchisescu, C., Weiss, Y. (eds.) ECCV 2018. LNCS, vol. 11211, pp. 3–19. Springer, Cham (2018). https://doi.org/10.1007/978-3-030-01234-2_1
21. Chen, L.C., Papandreou, G., Schroff, F., Adam, H.: Rethinking atrous convolution for semantic image segmentation. arXiv preprint arXiv:1706.05587 (2017)
22. glenn jocher et al: YOLOv5 (2021). https://github.com/ultralytics/yolov5
23. Howard, A.G., et al.: MobileNets: efficient convolutional neural networks for mobile vision applications. arXiv preprint arXiv:1704.04861 (2017)
24. Zhu, X., Lyu, S., Wang, X., Zhao, Q.: TPH-YOLOv5: improved YOLOv5 based on transformer prediction head for object detection on drone-captured scenarios. In: Proceedings of the IEEE/CVF International Conference on Computer Vision, pp. 2778–2788 (2021)
25. Ma, N., Zhang, X., Zheng, H.-T., Sun, J.: ShuffleNet V2: practical guidelines for efficient CNN architecture design. In: Ferrari, V., Hebert, M., Sminchisescu, C., Weiss, Y. (eds.) Computer Vision – ECCV 2018. LNCS, vol. 11218, pp. 122–138. Springer, Cham (2018). https://doi.org/10.1007/978-3-030-01264-9_8
26. Howard, A., et al.: Searching for MobileNetV3. In: Proceedings of the IEEE/CVF International Conference on Computer Vision, pp. 1314–1324 (2019)
27. Sandler, M., Howard, A., Zhu, M., Zhmoginov, A., Chen, L.C.: MobileNetV2: inverted residuals and linear bottlenecks. In: Proceedings of the IEEE Conference on Computer Vision and Pattern Recognition, pp. 4510–4520 (2018)
28. Zha, M., Qian, W., Yi, W., Hua, J.: A lightweight YOLOv4-based forestry pest detection method using coordinate attention and feature fusion. Entropy **23**(12), 1587 (2021)

Power Line Detection Based on Feature Fusion Deep Learning Network

Kuansheng Zou$^{(\boxtimes)}$, Zhenbang Jiang, and Shuaiqiang Zhao

School of Electrical Engineering and Automation, Jiangsu Normal University, Xuzhou, China
zoukuansheng@jsnu.edu.cn

Abstract. Nowadays, the network of transmission lines is gradually spreading all over the world. With the popularization of UAV and helicopter applications, it is of great significance for low-altitude safety aircraft to detect power lines in advance and implement obstacle avoidance. The Power Line Detection (PLD) in a complex background environment is particularly important. In order to solve the problem of false detection of power lines caused by complex background images, a PLD method based on feature fusion deep learning network is proposed in this paper. Firstly, in view of the problems of low accuracy and poor generalization by using the traditional PLD in complex background environments, a rough extraction module that makes full use of the fusion features is constructed, which is combined with the inherent features and auxiliary information of aerial power line images. Secondly, an output fusion module is constructed, the weights of which are actively learned in the network training session. Finally, the fusion module fuses the decisions of different depths for output. The experimental results show that the proposed method can effectively improve the accuracy of power line detection.

Keywords: Deep learning · Feature fusion · Power Line Detection · Auxiliary information

1 Introduction

With the advancement of the construction of the modern power grid system and the increasing demand for electricity, transmission lines have spread to all parts of the world in a complex network. It is also of great significance for safe low-altitude flight to detect power lines and implement obstacle avoidance. The Australian Transport Safety Report shows that between 1994 and 2004, there were 119 helicopter crashes into power lines, of which 45 were fatally injured and 22 were seriously injured [1]. Hitting power lines will cause serious damage to the helicopter. The U.S. military data report shows that 54 power line collisions occurred between 1997 and 2006, resulting in 13 deaths of military personnel and economic losses of up to 224 million US dollars [2]. Flight safety accidents threaten people's lives and cause huge economic losses.

Aircraft obstacle avoidance mainly depends on the pilot's reaction and experience. The aircraft in operation can avoid large obstacles, but small obstacles, especially for

N. Magnenat-Thalmann et al. (Eds.): CGI 2022, LNCS 13443, pp. 527–538, 2022.
https://doi.org/10.1007/978-3-031-23473-6_41

power lines, often fail to dodge, which in turn leads to disasters. The Power Line Detection (PLD) is mainly used for aircraft obstacle avoidance of power lines, which can identify the presence or absence of power lines within the visible range in advance, and use this as a judgment basis to remind the driver, and then take hovering measures if necessary to avoid disasters.

Mining the inherent features of power lines can help to improve the detection performance. The inherent features of power lines are listed as follows [3]. The brightness of multiple power lines is uniform and continuous, and the gray scale is similar. Looking down, the power line is brighter than the ground background, and the metal is bare brighter; The power line is close to a parallel line and runs through the whole image, and its width can be estimated to be 1~5 pixels; The ground background is complex. Ground objects such as road lane line, river, or other straight-line objects cause serious interference to the PLD.

Based on the inherent features of power lines and deep learning, a PLD method based on feature fusion deep learning network is proposed in this paper. The mainly contributions are summarized as follows. A rough feature extraction module is used at first, which is combined with the inherent features and auxiliary information of aerial power line images; a fusion output module with active weight learning is proposed.

2   Related Work

2.1   Related Deep Learning Models

In recent years, Convolutional Neural Networks (CNN) have been widely used in the field of image processing [4–7]. In 2012, Alex won the championship in the ImageNet LSVRC-2010 competition with the AlexNet [8] model, which brought a huge impact to academia and industry. Simonyan and Zisserman proposed the VGG model in [9], and won the second place in the ImageNet challenge classification task and the first place in the localization task. According to the size of the convolution kernel and the number of convolutional layers, the VGG model can be divided into 6 configurations, among which VGG19 has a better effect. In 2014, GoogleNet [10] won the first place in the ImageNet ILSVRC14 challenge, the network structure of which is constructed by using multi-scale processing. The inception module is proposed by them, which is a parallel multi-scale fusion module. The input feature matrix goes through four paths in parallel to get four outputs, height and width of the output four paths are the same, and based on this, the output fusion during the channel is performed.

The number of network layers of CNN gradually deepens, and the problem of accuracy decline occurs on the training set. In [11], ResNet is proposed, the network layers of which include convolutional layers and fully connected layers, excluding pooling layers and BN layers. To a certain extent, the ResNet network layers could be deepened while ensuring the accuracy of the training set.

The core idea of the ResNet is the residual module. In the residual structure, the gradient disappearance problem caused by the increase of depth is alleviated to a certain extent through skip connections. In the residual bottleneck structure, the 1×1 convolution at the head and the tail is used to adjust the dimension. The 1×1 convolution at the head can reduce the amount of computation by reducing the number of parameters, and the 1 × 1 convolution at the tail restores the image dimension.

2.2 Existing PLD Methods

Literature [12] is a classical method for PLD based on traditional image processing. RGB color space is converted into YCbCr color space at first, in order to reduce the interference of noise information through filtering and normalize the amplitude. Then, On the Y component, different types of image features are extracted through DCT, LBP and HOG respectively. The absolute value of the logarithm of the DCT domain discrete cosine coefficient is taken to emphasize the dynamic range. Finally, the extracted features are sent to Naive Bayes classifier, Random Forest classifier and SVM classifier respectively for recognition.

Although this kind of method is simple, it needs to manually set the feature extraction and feature matching methods. An end-to-end PLD system could be made based on deep learning methods. The PLD method based on deep learning does not require manual feature extraction of power lines, and the established CNN model can automatically extract effective features. Thus, some researchers have tried to apply CNNs to PLD.

Features are extracted through a CNN model before the enhanced display of power lines in literature [13], and then images are divided into two categories, with or without power lines. VGG19 model and the ResNet50 model are fine-tuned to adapt to the power line dataset in literature [14] and an end-to-end PLD method is proposed. The VGG19 model and the ResNet50 model are divided into five stages and the feature maps of these five stages are output. The feature maps of the five stages are input to the Naive Bayes classifier, the random forest classifier and the SVM classifier respectively for power scene discrimination. A fast PLD network for pixel-wise straight and curved PLD method is proposed in [15]. An edge attention fusion module and a high pass block are combined together by them, which extract semantic and spatial information to improve the PLD result along the boundary.

The Power Line Extraction (PLE) is the pixel-wise PLD method, which has been concerned and studied by more and more people. A PLE method based on weakly supervised learning, which solves the problem of labeling large-scale datasets is proposed in [16]. A PLE method based on pyramid patch classification, which uses a convolutional neural network-based classifier to help eliminate power line pseudo-targets is proposed in [17]. Generative adversarial network is combined with conic and hue perturbation to enhance datasets, and reduces model parameters and computational complexity through model pruning in [18]. Artificially synthesized power line images are used as training data, and a fast single-shot line segment detector is proposed in [19]. A real-time segmentation model for power lines is proposed in [20], in which the context branch utilizes the AFDB module to achieve efficient short-range feature extraction with a large receptive field, and the spatial branch helps to capture rich spatial information and utilizes classification with subnet-level skip connections. It recovers long-distance features and improves the performance of power line extraction. Liu draws on the Unet model for medical image segmentation, improves the Unet model and its variants to adapt to the power line dataset, and extracts the power lines from the image [21].

The above-mentioned methods mainly relies on inherent characteristics of deep learning network to improve detection performance. Better results may be obtained by establishing corresponding network modules based on mining the inherent features of power lines.

3   The Proposed Method

The residual bottleneck module proposed in the ResNet model can deepen the network while preventing over-fitting; the inception module proposed in the GoogleNet model can make full use of the information of different receptive fields for fusion; according to characteristics of power lines, the two above-mentioned modules are useful for PLD tasks. Based on the idea of residual bottleneck module and inception module, a PLD model is proposed based on feature fusion, combined with the unique characteristics of power lines in aerial power line images and the characteristics of auxiliary objects.

3.1   Overall Network Architecture Design

The CNN model is used as the backbone network in the proposed model, and the network architecture is shown in Fig. 1.

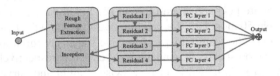

Fig. 1. The architecture diagram of PLD model

The power line image inputs to the network and enters the feature extraction module for rough feature extraction. The extracted rough features contain a lot of structural information. The features under different receptive field scales are synthesized, fused and output after the rough feature extraction module. Then the output feature maps enter the residual module again to further explore the feature information. Finally, the features extracted by residual module 1, residual module 2, residual module 3 and residual module 4 are used as the judgment basis, and four output results are obtained, and the four output results are fused and output by means of active weight learning.

3.2   Rough Feature Extraction Module Design

Rough feature extraction is the first step in the proposed PLD. Both the inherent features of power lines and the information of auxiliary objects are the key elements to identify power lines. The small receptive field pays more attention to the detailed information of the power line, while the large receptive field mainly focuses on the global information of auxiliary objects such as power poles and towers. Therefore, the feature information of different receptive fields is fully fused in the rough feature extraction stage. The structure of the rough feature extraction module is shown in Fig. 2. Different from the traditional feature extraction module, it can make full use of each convolutional layer to scale the receptive field, and then achieve the fusion effect of feature extraction under different receptive field scales.

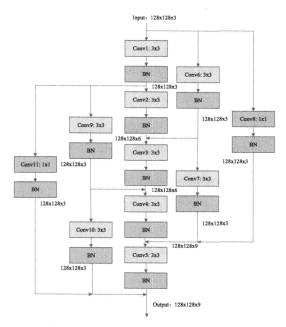

Fig. 2. Rough feature extraction module

The rough feature extraction module is mainly composed of 3 × 3 convolutional layers, 1 × 1 convolutional layers and BN layers. The main function of the BN layer is to speed up the training and convergence of the network, so the concatenation of the convolutional layer and the BN layer can be regarded as a convolutional layer. The main channel of the module consists of five 3 × 3 convolutional layers, the left and right branch 1 consists of two 3 × 3 convolutional layers respectively, and the left and right branch 2 consists of 1 × 1 convolutional layers. Literature [9] shows that the cascade of two 3 × 3 convolution kernels is equivalent to a 5 × 5 convolutional kernel, and the cascade of four 3 × 3 convolutional kernels is equivalent to a 9x9 convolutional kernel. Finally, the feature is roughly extracted. The convolutional layer 1 and the convolutional layer 2 are cascaded in parallel with the convolutional layer 6, which can be regarded as a 5 × 5 convolutional kernel and a 3 × 3 convolutional kernel for feature extraction and fusion output. Similarly, the combination of convolutional layer 3, 4 and 7, the combination of convolutional layer 2, 3 and 9, the combination of convolutional layer 4, 5 and 10, can be regarded as a 5 × 5 convolutional kernel and a 3 × 3 convolutional kernel for feature extraction and fusion output. The convolutional layer 6 and 7 are cascaded and connected in parallel with 8, which can be regarded as a 5 × 5 convolutional kernel and a 1 × 1 convolution kernel for feature extraction and fusion output. Similarly, the combination of convolutional layer 9, 10 and 11 can also be regarded as a 5 × 5 convolutional kernel and a 1 × 1 convolutional kernel after feature extraction and fusion output. Convolutional layer 1, 2, 3 and 4 are cascaded in parallel with convolutional layer 8, which can be regarded as a 9 × 9 convolutional kernel and a 1 × 1 convolutional kernel for feature extraction and fusion output. Similarly, the combination of convolutional layer 2, 3, 4, 5 and 11 can also be regarded as a 9 × 9 convolutional kernel and a 1 × 1 convolutional kernel after feature extraction and fusion output. Therefore, this model can use each convolutional layer to scale the receptive field without any difference, to achieve the fusion effect of feature extraction under different receptive field scales.

3.3 Residual Module

The residual module [11] can prevent overfitting while deepening the network. The residual module used in the model is shown in Fig. 3. The main path of the residual module has two 3 × 3 convolutional layers to extract features and two BNs. The layer speeds up the training and convergence of the network, and the identity-mapping branch is composed of a 1 × 1 convolutional layer and a BN layer to adjust the input and output channels of the module.

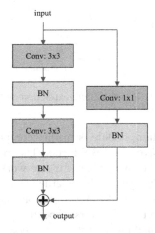

Fig. 3. Residual module used by the proposed model

3.4 Inception Module

The inception module [22] can perform feature fusion of different receptive fields on the features extracted by the residual module in the network. The inception module used in the model is shown in Fig. 4. It is divided into four path branches after image is input to the inception module. The first branch extracts features through the 1 × 1 convolutional layer and the BN layer. The second branch continuously passes through the combination of two 3 × 3 convolutional layers and BN layers after adjusting the channel dimensions of the 1 × 1 convolutional layer and the BN layer. The third branch performs feature extraction through a combination of 3 × 3 convolutional layers and BN layers after adjusting the channel dimensions of the 1 × 1 convolutional layer and BN layer. The fourth branch pools and sums image features. Finally, the features of the four branches are fused and output.

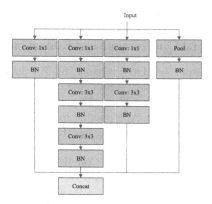

Fig. 4. Inception module used by the proposed model

3.5 Output Fusion Module Design

CNN is used for classification and recognition, and the abstract features finally extracted by the network are usually judged and output. The features extracted from the shallow layer of the CNN help to identify linear objects, and the auxiliary information such as power towers and other information extracted from the deep layer of the CNN can help to judge and distinguish between the power lines with other linear objects. In order to make full use of the power line's inherent features and auxiliary information in aerial images, the features extracted from different depths of the model are respectively judged, fused output. The structure of the fusion output module is shown in Fig. 5. The features extracted from each residual blocks are extracted to make judgments respectively, and finally the fusion output is performed by means of active weight learning, which can make comprehensive judgments by using the features of different stages.

The results of feature extraction through the residual block are expressed as $output_1$, $output_2$, $output_3$, $output_4$ respectively, and the 4-way output passes through the fusion module to obtain the final output result. The formula is as follows:

$$output = w1 \cdot output_1 + w2 \cdot output_2 + w3 \cdot output_3 + w4 \cdot output_4 \qquad (1)$$

The initial values of $w1$, $w2$, $w3$, $w4$ and are set to be 1/23, 2/23, 4/23, and 16/23, respectively, $w1 + w2 + w3 + w4 = 1$ as the conditional constraints of the formula; $w1$, $w2$, $w3$, $w4$ are used as the parameters of CNN through back-propagation, their weights are actively learned for iterative updates.

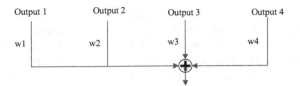

Fig. 5. The module of fusion output

4   Experimental Results and Analysis

4.1   Dataset, Experimental Configuration and Evaluation Metric

The public power line dataset is used in this paper [8]. The dataset contains two subsets, Infrared-IR and Visible Light-VL. Each subset contains two parts, Include and Exclude, and each part has 2000 images with 128 × 128 pixels. In this paper, the aerial image visible light dataset [8] is used for the experiments, and the dataset is divided into training set, cross-validation set and test set according to 3:1:1.

Experimental configuration is set as follows. The GPU model is NVIDIA GeForce RTX 2070 8G; the CPU model is Intel(R) Core(TM) i9-10900k CPU @ 3.70 GHz; the SSD is 512 GB and HDD is 1TB; the OS is 64-bit Windows 10; the programming language is Python 3.7; the running platform is Pycharm community; the loss function is CrossEntropyLoss; the optimization function is Adam [23]; the learning rate is 1e−3; the number of iterations are 200.

The accuracy rate is selected as the evaluation metric, and the formula is as follows:

$$Accuracy = \frac{Number\ of\ correct\ predictions}{Total\ number\ of\ predictions} \tag{2}$$

For the PLD task, it is a binary classification problem, and the above formula can be written as:

$$Accuracy = \frac{(TP + TN)}{(TP + FP + TN + FN)} \tag{3}$$

where TP indicates that the actual case is positive, and the prediction is positive; TN indicates that the actual case is negative, and the prediction is negative; FP indicates that the actual case is negative, and the prediction is positive; FN indicates that the actual case is positive, and the prediction is negative.

4.2   Experimental Comparison Results and Analysis

The proposed model is compared with the traditional image processing based methods at first [1]. Experimental results are shown in Fig. 6. SVM is used to classify LBP features in Exp. 1. NAIVEBAYES is used to classify LBP features in Exp. 2. RANDOMFOREST is used to classify LBP features in Exp. 3. SVM is used to classify HOG features in Exp. 4. NAIVEBAYES is used to classify HOG features in Exp. 5. RANDOMFOREST is used to classify HOG features in Exp. 6. SVM is used to classify CS_DCT features in Exp.7.

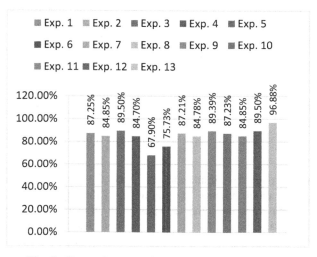

Fig. 6. Comparison experiment I of the proposed PLD

NAIVEBAYES is used to classify CS_DCT features in Exp. 8. RANDOMFOREST is used to classify CS_DCT features in Exp. 9. SVM is used to classify RS_DCT features in Exp. 10. NAIVEBAYES is used to classify RS_DCT features in Exp. 11. RANDOM-FOREST is used to classify RS_DCT features in Exp. 12. The proposed model is used to classify test set images in Exp. 13. In this set of experiments, the proposed model achieved the highest accuracy of 96.88%, which was 7.38% higher than the second place. It can be seen that on the visible light dataset, the proposed model has significant advantages over traditional image processing methods.

The proposed model is also compared with the commonly used deep learning methods, and the experimental results are shown in Fig. 7. The six models are tested respectively. The 'Pamodel' uses a layer of convolution to replace the rough feature extraction module of the proposed method. Due to the complex background in the dataset, some power lines are invisible due to factors such as temperature, weather, and illumination. Power lines have unique characteristics and auxiliary information, which are different from other types of objects. Thus, the accuracy of classical deep learning models is not good enough. Comparing the experimental results of the proposed 'Mymodel' with 'Pamodel', it can be seen that the effectiveness of the rough feature extraction module. In this set of experiments, the proposed model achieves the highest accuracy of 96.88%, which is 4.5% higher than the second place. It can be seen that on the visible light dataset, the proposed PLD model based on feature fusion has certain advantages over the classical deep learning model.

4.3 Robustness and Generalization Tests

In order to test the possibility of the proposed method in practical application, the digital image processing technology is used to process the power line data set. The foggy, strong light, snowfall and motion blur scenes are simulated that may exist in the actual

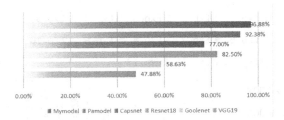

Fig. 7. Comparison experiment II of PLD

environment, and through the simulation case, tests the performance of the proposed PLD method in these environments. In order to verify the applicability of the proposed method in the new environment, other 200 power line images without the data sets are used to test the generalization of the proposed method. The performance metrics of the proposed method in above four scenes and generalization scene are shown in Table 1.

Table 1. The metrics of in the five scenes.

Scenes	Accuracy
Foggy	88.9%
Strong light	95.9%
Snow fall	89.5%
Motion blur	71.9%
Generalization scene	83.3%

Compared with the normal scene, the bias of accuracy in above-mentioned scenes is $-8.24\%, -1.01\%, -7.62\%, -25.78\%$, and -14.02% respectively. In total, the proposed method has a good robustness and generalization with these five scenes, except that motion blur will have a certain impact on the robustness of the performance.

5   Conclusion

The main work of this paper is summarized as follows. The important role of PLD in practical applications is mentioned at first. Then, classical image classification models are introduced for further used in PLD. Based on the advantages of classic models and the characteristics of power line images, a PLD method based on feature fusion is constructed in this paper. Finally, experiments are carried out with the visible light image dataset. Diverse experimental results show that the proposed method is effective, and have a good performance robustness and generalization.

For the issue of not so perfect performance robustness in a snowfall and foggy environment, the fusion of infrared images and visible light images can be introduced in the future. Since in the snowfall and foggy environment, although the power lines are indistinguishable from the background, the high-temperature power lines can be distinguished from the low-temperature background environment. For the issue of not so good performance robustness in a motion blur environment, In the future, more stable and active disturbance rejection UAV trajectory-tracking methods can be studied for get better image capture effect, and reduce motion blur in aerial images.

References

1. ASTB: Wire-Strike Accidents in General Aviation: Data Analysis 1994 to 2004. ATSB Transport Safety Investigation Report, Australian Govern (2006)
2. Song, B., Li, X.: Power line detection from optical images. Neurocomputing **129**, 350–361 (2014)
3. Zou, K., Jiang, Z., Zhang, Q.: Research progresses and trends of power line extraction based on machine learning. In: Proceedings of the 2nd International Symposium on Computer Engineering and Intelligent Communications, pp. 211–215. IEEE, Nanjing (2021)
4. Zhang, H., et al.: Attention-guided multitask convolutional neural network for power line parts detection. IEEE Trans. Instrum. Meas. **71**, 1–13 (2022)
5. Chen, Z., Qiu, J., Sheng, B., Li, P., Wu, E.: GPSD: generative parking spot detection using multi-clue recovery model. Vis. Comput. **37**(9–11), 2657–2669 (2021). https://doi.org/10.1007/s00371-021-02199-y
6. Masood, A., et al.: Automated decision support system for lung cancer detection and classification via enhanced RFCN with multilayer fusion RPN. IEEE Trans. Ind. Inform. **16**, 7791–7801 (2020)
7. Sheng, B., et al.: Retinal vessel segmentation using minimum spanning superpixel tree detector. IEEE Trans. Cybern. **49**, 2707–2719 (2019)
8. Krizhevsky, A., Sutskever, I., Hinton, G.E.: Imagenet classification with deep convolutional neural networks. In: Advances in Neural Information Processing Systems, pp. 1097–1105 (2012)
9. Simonyan, K., Zisserman, A.: Very deep convolutional networks for large-scale image recognition. arXiv 1409.1556 (2014)
10. Szegedy, C., et al..: Going deeper with convolutions. In: Proceedings of the IEEE Conference on Computer Vision and Pattern Recognition (CVPR), pp. 1–9. IEEE, Boston (2015)
11. He, K., Zhang, X., Ren, S., Sun, J.: Deep residual learning for image recognition. In: Proceedings of the IEEE conference on Computer Vision and Pattern Recognition (CVPR), pp.770–778. IEEE, Las Vegas (2016)
12. Yetgin, Ö., Gerek, Ö.: Automatic recognition of scenes with power line wires in real life aerial images using DCT-based features. Digit. Signal Process. **77**, 102–119 (2018)
13. Gerek, Ö., Benligiray, B.: Visualization of power lines recognized in aerial images using deep learning. In: Proceedings of the 26th IEEE Signal Processing and Communications Applications Conference, pp. 1–4. IEEE, Izmir (2018)
14. Yetgin, Ö., Benligiray, B., Gerek, O.: Power line recognition from aerial images with deep learning. IEEE Trans. Aerosp. Electron. Syst. **55**, 2241–2252 (2019)
15. Zhu, K., Xu, C., Wei, Y., Cai, G.: Fast-PLDN: fast power line detection network. J. Real-Time Image Process. **19**, 3–13 (2021). https://doi.org/10.1007/s11554-021-01154-3
16. Choi, H., Koo, G., Kim, B.J., et al.: Weakly supervised power line detection algorithm using a recursive noisy label update with refined broken line segments. Expert Syst. Appl. **165**, 113895.1–113895.9 (2021)
17. Li, Y., Pan, C., Cao, X., Wu, D.: Power line detection by pyramidal patch classification. IEEE Trans. Emerg. Top. Comput. Intell. **3**(6), 416–426 (2018)

18. Xu, G., Li, G.: Research on lightweight neural network of aerial power line image segmentation. J. Image Graph. **26**(11), 2605–2618 (2021)

19. Nguyen, V., Jenssen, R., Roverso, D.: LS-Net: fast single-shot line-segment detector. Mach. Vis. Appl. **32**(1), 1–16 (2020). https://doi.org/10.1007/s00138-020-01138-6

20. Gao, Z., Yang, G., Li, E., Liang, Z., Guo, R.: Efficient parallel branch network with multi-scale feature fusion for real-time overhead power line segmentation. IEEE Sens. J. **21**(10), 12220–12227 (2021)

21. Liu, J., Li, Y., Gong, Z., Liu, X., Zhou, Y.: Power line recognition method via fully convolutional network. J. Image Graph. **25**(5), 956–966 (2020)

22. Szegedy, C., Vanhoucke, V., Ioffe, S., Shlens, J., Wojna, Z.: Rethinking the inception architecture for computer vision. In: Proceedings of the 2016 IEEE Conference on Computer Vision and Pattern Recognition (CVPR), pp. 2818–2826. IEEE, Las Vegas (2016)

23. Ironside, N., et al.: Fully automated segmentation method for hematoma volumetric analysis in spontaneous intracerebral hemorrhage. Stroke **50**, 3416–3423 (2019)

Image Attention and Perception

Wider and Higher: Intensive Integration and Global Foreground Perception for Image Matting

Yu Qiao[1], Ziqi Wei[2], Yuhao Liu[1], Yuxin Wang[1(✉)], Dongsheng Zhou[3], Qiang Zhang[1], and Xin Yang[1]

[1] Computer Science and Technology, Dalian University of Technology, Dalian, China
wyx@dlut.edu.cn
[2] CAS Key Laboratory of Molecular Imaging, Institute of Automation, Beijing, China
[3] Dalian University, Dalian, China

Abstract. This paper reviews recent deep-learning-based matting research and conceives our wider and higher motivation for image matting. Many approaches achieve alpha mattes with complex encoders to extract robust semantics, then resort to the U-net-like decoder to concatenate or fuse encoder features. However, image matting is essentially a pixel-wise regression, and the ideal situation is to perceive the maximum opacity correspondence from the input image. In this paper, we argue that the high-resolution feature representation, perception and communication are more crucial for matting accuracy. Therefore, we propose an Intensive Integration and Global Foreground Perception network (I2GFP) to integrate wider and higher feature streams. Wider means we combine intensive features in each decoder stage, while higher suggests we retain high-resolution intermediate features and perceive large-scale foreground appearance. Our motivation sacrifices model depth for a significant performance promotion. We perform extensive experiments to prove the proposed I2GFP model, and state-of-the-art results can be achieved on different public datasets.

Keywords: Image matting · Integration · Global foreground perception

1 Introduction

Image matting has a wide application in film productions, image editing, live video, etc. Since the first success to explore image matting with convolutional neural networks [2], deep learning has contributed significantly to the performance improvement of alpha mattes. Xu *et al.* [17] combined RGB images with trimaps as conjoint input and proposed an encoder-decoder model to predict

---

Y. Qiao and Z. Wei—contribute equally to this work.

N. Magnenat-Thalmann et al. (Eds.): CGI 2022, LNCS 13443, pp. 541–553, 2022.
https://doi.org/10.1007/978-3-031-23473-6_42

Fig. 1. The alpha mattes produced by our I2GFP on the natural images.

alpha mattes, providing primary heuristics for most later researches. Many elaborated models [1,15] are proposed with potential modifications like skip connections, refinement modules, and additional branches to improve the visual and quantitative quality of alpha mattes. These models share an analogous pipeline and a complicated encoder architecture (Fig. 2(a)), the Resnet50 backbone in [15], the Xception-65 encoder in [5], the MobinleNetV2 model in [9] etc. Some trimap-free methods [11,22] also exploit deep models to generate alpha mattes. Complex encoders can extract advanced semantics and contribute to the shape completion of foreground objects. However, in this paper, we throw such a doubt: advanced semantics is the decisive element in image matting?

The essence of image matting is a pixel-wise estimation, which is a common understanding from the image synthesis equation [17]. The anticipated alpha matte should bridge an end-to-end correspondence between the input image and the foreground opacity. This assumption can authorize a great degree of arbitrariness on semantic information (Fig. 1): a half-length portrait or a head can suggest a human, several leaves or petals can represent a flower. Based on this observation, we can conclude that advanced semantics may not be the consequential factor for image matting. Instead of deep semantics, wider and higher feature representation, perception and communication are more crucial for high-quality alpha mattes.

In this paper, we abandon extremely advanced semantics in favor of intensive integration between various encoder features, and complement the global foreground perception branch to provide a highly expressive appearance. The schematic comparison between our motivation and general existing matting models is illuminated in Fig. 2. Specifically, we adopt a 4-stride output VGG-16 encoder to retain more input information and bridge intensive connections (IC) to the decoder stage. Each decoder block can catch all low-order layers to integrate wider representation, and the consistent resolution ($output\_stride = 4$) can enable such an incremental feature fusion. Simultaneously, we import a global foreground perception (GFP) branch to capture large-field appearance details. Generally speaking, high-resolution feature representation and extensive fore-

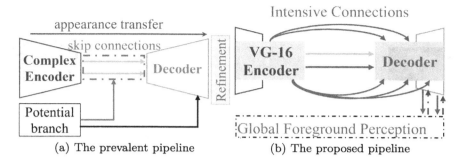

Fig. 2. The motivation of wider and higher compared to the prevalent pipeline of most existing matting researches [5,7,9,15]. We sacrifice model depth for a sustained intermediate resolution (output stride = 4) and bridge intensive connections to the decoder. Global foreground perception can contribute to more details.

ground appearance can maintain more details and textures, and their accumulation can provide wider attribute integration. Therefore, the proposed Intensive Integration and Global Foreground Perception network (I2GFP) can achieve a wider and higher alpha matte estimation. We conduct extensive experiments on public matting datasets, and the state-of-the-art performance can also verify the rationality of our motivation.

Our main contributions are summarized as follows:

- We propose the Intensive Integration and Global Foreground Perception network (I2GFP), providing a wider and higher feature representation with the sacrifice of model depth. Extensive experiments on public datasets can prove our motivation and the proposed model.
- We bridge Interleaved Connections (IC) between the encoder and decoder stage, enabling a wider feature communication.
- We present a Global Foreground Perception branch to capture and convert primitive appearance, which can complement rich foreground details.

2   Related Work

Here we briefly review traditional matting approaches, then enumerate recent deep-learning-based architectures and analyze their functions and universality.

Traditional Matting. Traditional approaches resort to color or texture distribution to estimate alpha mattes. They can be divided into two categories according to different ways of uncertainty expansion: sampling-based and affinity-based methods. Sampling-based solutions [4] connect the pixel-wise uncertainty in foreground and background to infer the labels of transition regions. As for affinity-based methods [6], they calculate the correlations between certain and transition regions, then propagate the labels to the whole image. Potential certainty is provided by trimap or scribbles priors, and both involve user interactions to indicate

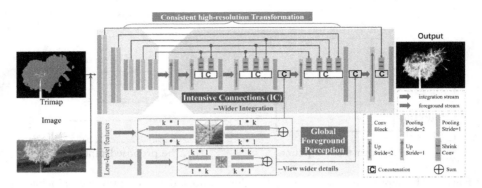

Fig. 3. The overall architecture of the proposed Intensive Integration and Global Foreground Perception network (I2GFP). We employ simple backbone to extract necessary semantics and utilize intensive connections to integrate different-level features. The global foreground perception can capture rich appearances to complement details.

some label attributes. Each pixel in trimap shares an explicit label correspondence, white-foreground, black-background and gray-transition. While scribbles have limited prior annotations suggested by several scribbles to represent foreground and background. Due to the restricted expressive ability of hand-crafted features, traditional matting approaches usually generate ambiguous alpha mattes when the input images have complex colors or textures.

Deep-Learning-Based Matting. Recent deep learning models can achieve comparable results benefiting from the structure representation of powerful convolution neural networks. Generally speaking, existing matting architectures have two solutions, with trimaps as confine and end-to-end automatic models. Xu *et al.* [17] employ concatenated RGB images and trimaps as input, regressing alpha mattes with an encoder-decoder model. Most later methods [1,5,15] follow this to design their models, using a complex encoder to extract advanced semantics and achieve original resolution with a U-Net like decoder. Hao *et al.* [9] and Dai [3] unify upsampling operators with the index functions to improve encoder-decoder network. Li *et al.* [7] utilize a guided contextual attention to improve the transmission of the opacity. Though the trimap expansions in SIM [14] can extend the range of transition capture, they require alpha categories.

Several researches [11,12,20,22] achieve trimap-free architectures, but they have limited generalization in natural images and also rely on complex encoders to extract extremely advanced semantics. There are also some methods relying on multiple stages or feedback to perform model optimization. [2] fuses trimap labeling and image matting as a two-phase framework. Interactions-based methods [16,18] resort to user feedback to refine alpha mattes. Some approaches [19] and [8] can produce results with additional guidance like masks, backgrounds.

3   Methodology

Our motivation is to provide wider and higher feature fields for alpha estimation. Although model depth can contribute to advanced semantics with an accumulated receptive field, we argue that extreme semantics are not consequential. On the one hand, the foreground classes enjoy a high granularity of freedom in natural matting images and bring huge ambiguity for vanilla semantics. It could be anything sharing a transparent uncertain region; even part of them can also be the target. On the other hand, image matting requires pixel-wise opacity and all alpha values expect a wider feature range and higher field to receive more opacity perception. The wider range can combine different-level feature representation, while the higher field can retain extensive appearances and details to enrich fine-grained prediction. Based on the above observations, we propose the Intensive Integration and Global Foreground Perception network (I2GFP), with intensive connections (IC) and global foreground perception (GFP), to achieve wider and higher feature representation. In this section, we first introduce the whole architecture Sect. 3.1, then the IC module Sect. 3.2 and GFP branch Sect. 3.3.

3.1   Network Architecture

The architecture of the Intensive Integration and Global Foreground Perception network (I2GFP) is illuminated in Fig. 3. We take an RGB image and trimap as concatenated input ($\mathbb{R}^{4 \times H \times W}$). Trimap is imported to suggest transition regions. To fully demonstrate the validity of I2 and GFP in capturing matting features, we harness original VGG-16 to capture necessary semantics and record the features from different blocks as $\mathcal{F}_E^i \in \mathbb{R}^{c \times h \times w}$, where i, c, h, and w denote the block index, channels, height, and width of features. We only reserve the stride=2 pooling operation in the first two blocks, thus can generate a high-resolution intermediate feature $\mathcal{F}_E^i \in \mathbb{R}^{c \times H/4 \times W/4}$, $i \in \{3, 4, 5\}$. This $output\_stride = 4$ design can extract sufficient semantics and preserve more initial attributes.

For the decoder stage, we adopt Intensive Connections (IC) to obtain a wider feature representation. We also propose a Global Foreground Perception (GFP) branch to provide necessary appearances. For a better training procedure, we incrementally add the IC and GFP module to achieve optimal convergence.

3.2   Intensive Connections

Although common skip connections can bridge the feature transport, each decoder layer can only observe the corresponding encoded features, resulting in direct calculation between skip connections and upsampled features: $\mathcal{F}_D^i = \Phi(\theta) \sim \mathcal{C}at\{\mathcal{F}_E^i, \mathcal{F}_U^{i-1}\}$, where $\mathcal{F}_D^i \in \mathbb{R}^{c \times h \times w}$ and $\mathcal{F}_U^i \in \mathbb{R}^{c \times h \times w}$ represent the i-layer encoder feature and i-layer unsampling feature. Such connection ignores the context relevance desired by image matting. Considering the example in Fig. 3, the stems, branches, and catkins of the dandelion correspond to a potentially different range of receptive fields, but the correlations and opacity between them are mutually enforced by each other. Therefore, we employ intensive connections (IC) to improve this correlation among different-level features.

Formally speaking, we define the calculation of step-wise convolution in decoder stage as follows:

$$\mathcal{F}_D^i = \Phi(\theta) \sim Cat\{\mathcal{F}_E^5, \mathcal{F}_E^4...\mathcal{F}_E^i, \mathcal{F}_U^i\}, \tag{1}$$

except for the output convolution, each decoder layer takes the last upsampling feature and all low-order encoder features as input to obtain wider feature representation. For example, the fourth decoder layer has a concatenated input of $\mathcal{F}_E^5$, $\mathcal{F}_E^4$ and $\mathcal{F}_U^4$, and output $\mathcal{F}_D^4$. IC can promote the communication between different receptive fields. We use shrink convolution to transport the encoder features with a channels of 16. The final output layer only takes $\mathcal{F}_U^1$ and $\mathcal{F}_E^1$ as input to preserve more primitive foreground appearance.

Compared to previous dense connections [21,23], IC has two novel parts for image matting. The first starts with the third encoding layer and ends with the third decoding layer, sharing consistent resolution, and we integrate them by shrinking convolution and the concatenation operation. The second part is the combination between the decoder features and the low-level information from GFP. The consistent high-resolution integration can promote context-related foreground communication, and the combination with primitive textures can provide more foreground details for alpha mattes.

3.3   Global Foreground Perception

Many matting works [3,17] combine the initial encoded features in the back-end layers of the decoder to supplement the foreground details. The deep network can extract abstract semantics, while the low-level features contain more primitive textures (appearances and details). Inspired by the large kernels in [10], we propose our global foreground perception (GFP) branch to capture low-level details. Given the RGB input, we first perform two downsampling convolutions to reduce calculation space. Then two global convolutional layers can perceive large-field foreground appearances with a large kernel size k. Specially, we employ a combination of $1 \times k + k \times 1$ and $k \times 1 + 1 \times k$ convolutions like [10], enabling more feature perception and integration in a large $k \times k$ region. k equals space size is the ideal receptive field for capturing the full foreground, but we use half the spatial size comprising the execution cost. GFP can perceive sufficient foreground appearances and details, and the large-kernel global convolutions can retain the contextual opacity variations within the RGB input.

Compared to Gloabl Convolutional Network [10], there are two main innovations of GFP. 1) We only use large kernels on the initial image features to extract foreground details and bridge the direct transformation between initial image features and alpha mattes. 2) Compared to the semantic problems, image matting requires much more foreground textures and boundaries from the input image. The large kernels in the two global convolutional layers of GFP are 255 and 127. Both are the largest size considering the GPU capacity. Small kernels like 3, 5 ... 15 can also extract image features, but they are separated from the requirements of alpha mattes for as many foreground details.

3.4   Loss Functions and Implementation Details

Loss functions. We use $\mathcal{L}_1$ loss, composition loss ($\mathcal{L}_{comp}$) and Laplacian loss ($\mathcal{L}_{lap}$) to ensure the pixel-wise accuracy, and $\mathcal{L}_{grad}$ loss to balance the gradient.

$$\mathcal{L}_1 = \sum_j |\alpha_p^j - \alpha_g^j|, \tag{2}$$

$$\mathcal{L}_{comp} = \sum_j |C_g^j - \alpha_p^j F_g^j - (1 - \alpha_p^j)B_g^j|, \tag{3}$$

$$\mathcal{L}_{grad} = \sum_j |\bigtriangledown \alpha_p^j - \bigtriangledown \alpha_g^j|, \tag{4}$$

$$\mathcal{L}_{lap} = \sum_{s=1}^{5} 2^{s-1}|L_{py}^s \alpha_p - L_{py}^2 \alpha_g|, \tag{5}$$

$$\mathcal{L}_{total} = \mathcal{L}_1 + \mathcal{L}_{comp} + \mathcal{L}_{grad} + \mathcal{L}_{lap}. \tag{6}$$

where α_p^j and α_g^j correspond to the alpha values at pixel j inside unknown regions, p and g denote the predicted and ground truth alpha mattes, $\alpha_p^j, \alpha_g^j \in [0, 1]$. L_{py}^s represents the Laplacian functions. And the final loss function is the direct linear combination of $\mathcal{L}_1$, $\mathcal{L}_{comp}$, $\mathcal{L}_{grad}$, and $\mathcal{L}_{lap}$.

Implementation Details. We employ the PyTorch deep learning framework to implement I2GFP, and the training environment is 4 Tesla V100 graphics cards. We first train the encoder-decoder integration model for $200,000$ iterations with a batch size of 10 and an initial learning rate of $4e^{-4}$. The VGG-16 backbone is loaded from the pre-trained model, and other parameters are randomly initialized from a Gaussian distribution. All training images are randomly cropped to 512×512, 640×640 or 800×800, then resized 512×512, thus the large kernels in the two global convolutional layers of GFP are 255 and 127, respectively. We also employ horizontal random flipping, jitter and affine translation to make data augmentation. We use the Adam optimizer to optimize the network and adopt the Cosine Annealing strategy to schedule the learning rate. We then add the GFP branch to train the whole model with the same hyperparameters. The first training stage takes three days, and the full I2GFP takes additional two days to achieve the best results.

4   Experiments

In this section, we evaluate the proposed I2GFP on the public matting datasets and natural images. The comparisons involve visual and quantitative demonstrations with the SOTA approaches and ablation study. The four evaluation metrics include the summation of absolute differences (SAD), mean square error (MSE), the gradient (Grad), and connectivity (Conn) proposed by [13]. Considering the fairness, most SOTA methods in our experiments are trimap-based. Unless otherwise noted, all metrics are calculated inside the transition regions–the lower the values of all evaluation metrics, the better the predicted alpha mattes.

4.1   Results on Adobe Composition-1k

The Adobe Composition-1k dataset is constructed by [17], which contains 431 different foreground images and corresponding alpha mattes for training while 50 for testing. We refer to the composition rules in [17] to generate a large-scale dataset with 43100 training images and 1000 testing examples. Here we compare I2GFP with CF [6] and deep learning models, including DCNN [2], DIM [17], Sample [15], CA [5], Index [9], AdaM [1], GCA [7], A^2U [3], Late Fusion [22], and HAttMatt [11].

The quantitative summary is reported in Table 1, and the best results are shown in bold. We can observe that I2GFP has clear advantages on the MSE and Gradient metrics compared to existing methods, corresponding to 3.66% and

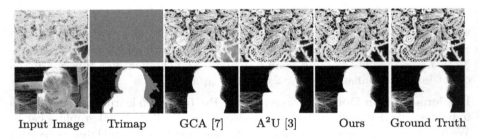

Input Image   Trimap   GCA [7] A^2U [3]   Ours   Ground Truth

Fig. 4. The visual comparisons with GCA [7] and A^2U [3] on the Adobe Composition-1K dataset [17]. The regions marked by the red rectangles are zoomed in at the corner.

Table 1. The quantitative results on the Adobe Composition-1K testing dataset [17]. "Base"-baseline model, "Base+IC"-add the IC module on the baseline. The combination of IC and GFP on the baseline is the full I2GFP model.

Methods	CF [6]	DCNN [2]	DIM [17]	Sample [15]	CA [5]	Index [9]	AdaM [1]
SAD↓	121.18	122.40	50.4	40.35	35.8	45.8	41.7
MSE↓	0.076	0.079	0.014	0.0099	0.0082	0.013	0.010
Grad↓	130.63	129.57	31.0	–	17.3	25.9	16.8
Conn↓	120.16	121.80	50.8	–	33.2	43.7	–
	GCA [7]	A^2U [3]	LF [22]	HAtt [11]	Base	Base+IC	I2GFP
SAD↓	35.28	**32.15**	49.02	45.04	41.82	35.46	32.20
MSE↓	0.0091	0.0082	0.020	0.015	0.0106	0.0084	**0.0079**
Grad↓	16.92	16.39	34.33	21.70	20.76	17.65	**15.64**
Conn↓	32.53	**29.25**	50.60	44.28	36.71	34.78	30.41

4.58% performance promotion, respectively. These improvements are benefiting from IC module and GFP branch. IC can consolidate the opacity consistency between different foreground parts via multi-scale feature communication. GFP can provide rich appearances to complement details and texture to further visual quality. By contrast, on the SAD and Conn metrics, I2GFP is slightly inferior to A^{2}U matting [3]. The potential analysis is that the affinity-aware functions in [7] can retain many sampling details. It is noted that most deep learning models [1,5,7,9,11,15,22] employ sophisticated backbones to extract more advanced semantics, and the performance of I2GFP indicates that wider and higher feature representation contributes better to alpha perception.

As shown in Fig. 4, we make the visual comparisons with GCA [7] and A^{2}U [3] matting. The I2GFP demonstrates more details and textures for common transition regions, like hairs and nets. The better visual presentation is mainly due to the GFP branch, which can supply more exquisite appearances. The high-resolution encoder-decoder motivation can also retain more primitive image features. Our VGG-16 backbone has limited ability to capture semantics as verified by many classification tasks and the improvement is basically from IC and GFP. Thus we can conclude that advanced semantics may not be the consequential factor for image matting.

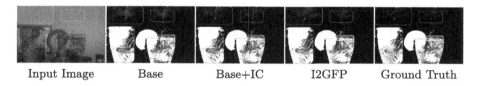

Input Image   Base   Base+IC   I2GFP   Ground Truth

Fig. 5. Ablation study: the suspended water droplets and the lines on the glass gradually clarify with the model components incremented (zoomed regions on the left).

Table 2. The quantitative results on the Distinctions-646 dataset [11]. The metrics about HAtt [11] are summarized on the full images. "I2GFP-f" represents our results on the full images. The other metrics are calculated inside the transition regions.

Methods	CF [6]	DIM [17]	Index [9]	GCA [7]	HAtt [11]	Base	Base+IC	I2GFP	I2GFP-f
SAD↓	146.66	44.15	34.47	26.59	48.98	31.12	28.99	**26.48**	30.57
MSE↓	0.141	0.031	0.019	0.015	0.009	0.015	0.013	**0.012**	0.005
Grad↓	356.50	39.08	28.31	19.50	41.57	18.86	15.40	**15.19**	21.45
Conn↓	143.12	44.65	33.37	**25.23**	49.93	31.62	28.52	26.39	30.91

4.2   Ablation Study

Here we perform an ablation study to verify different components. All models here are trained and evaluated on the Adobe dataset [17]. The *output_stride* = 4 encoder is cascaded with a U-Net like decoder to form the baseline model. As reported in Table 1, the baseline model can achieve better results than DIM [17] and Index [9], proving the validity of the higher motivation (*output_stride* = 4 can retain more primitive attributes). Then we add IC on the decoder stage to promote communications between different-level encoder features. IC can provide wider feature fields for each layer, and there is a noticeable improvement in all metrics after adding IC. The I2GFP is the full model with IC and GFP, which achieves the best results in Table 1.

The visual comparison from the Adobe Composition-1k testing set is shown in Fig. 5. Both IC and GFP can supply more details and texture, and we can observe that the suspended water droplets and the lines on the glass gradually become clear after adding different components.

4.3   Results on Distinctions-646

The Distinctions-646 dataset [11] consists of 596 distinct training alpha mattes and 50 testing ones. We compare I2GFP with some available methods, CF [6], DIM [17], Index [9], GCA [7], and HAtt [11]. The quantitative and qualitative results are shown in Table 2 and Fig. 6.

Compared to GCA, I2GFP improves 20% on MSE, 22.1% on Gradient, and is slightly worse than GCA on Connectivity. We can conclude that the wider and higher feature representation is robust and generalized for different datasets. The visual demonstration in Fig. 6 can clearly indicate the deficiency of Index and GCA. They both show poor performance on the net-like foreground, as shown in the first row of Fig. 6. Many holes in the net are fuzzed together, making it difficult to distinguish them directly even are zoomed in. With the detailed appearances provided by GFP, our model can handle such a situation impressively, and the textures of the nets are visible (Fig. 7).

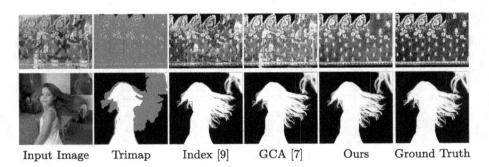

Input Image   Trimap   Index [9]   GCA [7]   Ours   Ground Truth

Fig. 6. The visual comparisons with IndexNet [9] and GCA [7] on the Distinctions-646 dataset [11]. The regions marked by the red rectangles are zoomed in at the corner of the alpha mattes to show more details.

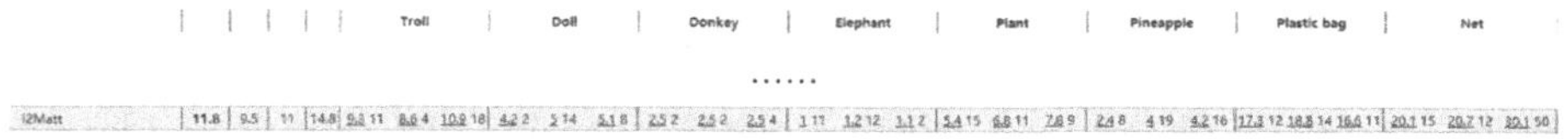

| | | | | | Troll | | Doll | | Donkey | | Elephant | | Plant | | Pineapple | | Plastic bag | | Net |

......

| I2Matt | | 11.8 | 9.5 | 11 | 14.8 | 9.1 11 | 8.0 4 10.9 10 | 4.2 2 | 5 14 | 5.1 8 | 2.5 2 | 2.6 2 | 2.5 4 | 3 11 | 1.2 12 | 1.1 7 | 5.4 15 | 6.8 11 | 7.6 9 | 2.6 8 | 4 19 | 4.2 16 | 17.3 12 18.5 14 16.6 11 | 20.1 15 | 20.7 12 | 20.1 50 |

Fig. 7. A screenshot from the benchmark website [13]. I2GFP gets an overall score of 11.8 and rank seventh among all published papers. Only our method employs a simple backbone and produces better results through wider and higher features.

4.4   Results on the Alpha Matting Benchmark

The visual results of the benchmark dataset are shown in Fig. 8. Without tricks, we can achieve the overall rank of 11.8 on this list, which ranks seventh among all published papers. Only our model employs a simple backbone to extract features, and the performance promotion is primarily from the well-designed intensive connections and global foreground perception. The alpha features from different levels share profound communications, and necessary foreground details are supplied to refine the boundaries and textures.

4.5   Results on Natural Images

Here we display additional results on natural images (Fig. 9). I2GFP can predict high-quality alpha mattes with complex backgrounds (the color disturbance and blur). The transition regions have a clear distinction to separate the foreground objects, which is mostly benefited from our wider and higher feature representation. Notably, the global foreground perception branch can provide essential appearances even affected by illumination (second example in Fig. 9). The trimaps are generated by off-the-shelf segmentation models, and the dependence on high-quality trimap is a problem existing in most current matting methods. However, trimaps can define the user interests, which restricts the valid applications for some trimap-free methods [11, 22].

Fig. 8. The alpha mattes of I2GFP on the benchmark images [13].

Fig. 9. The alpha mattes generated by I2GFP on the real-world images.

5   Conclusions and Future Works

In this paper, we review most existing matting architectures and introduce our motivation for wider and higher feature representation. We propose the Intensive Integration and Global Foreground Perception network (I2GFP) to achieve extensive feature representation, perception, and communication for alpha mattes. IC can promote feature communication between upsampling layers and different-level encoder attributes, while GFP branch can capture rich appearances with large kernels. We perform extensive experiments on public datasets and natural images. The results show that I2GFP can achieve state-of-the-art performance, proving the effectiveness of IC, GFP, and the wider and higher feature fields motivation. Besides, we will explore more flexible semantic modules to replace the existing pre-trained backbone in the future, which we believe can achieve a better performance/capacity trade-off.

References

1. Cai, S., et al.: Disentangled image matting. In: Proceedings of the IEEE/CVF International Conference on Computer Vision, pp. 8819–8828 (2019)
2. Cho, D., Tai, Y.-W., Kweon, I.: Natural image matting using deep convolutional neural networks. In: Leibe, B., Matas, J., Sebe, N., Welling, M. (eds.) ECCV 2016. LNCS, vol. 9906, pp. 626–643. Springer, Cham (2016). https://doi.org/10.1007/978-3-319-46475-6_39
3. Dai, Y., Lu, H., Shen, C.: Learning affinity-aware upsampling for deep image matting. In: Proceedings of the IEEE/CVF Conference on Computer Vision and Pattern Recognition, pp. 6841–6850 (2021)
4. Gastal, E.S.L., et al.: Shared sampling for real-time alpha matting. Comput. Graph. Forum 29, 575–584 (2010). https://doi.org/10.1111/j.1467-8659.2009.01627.x
5. Hou, Q., Liu, F.: Context-aware image matting for simultaneous foreground and alpha estimation. In: Proceedings of the IEEE/CVF International Conference on Computer Vision, pp. 4130–4139 (2019)
6. Levin, A., Lischinski, D., Weiss, Y.: A closed-form solution to natural image matting. IEEE Trans. Pattern Anal. Mach. Intell. 30(2), 228–242 (2008). https://doi.org/10.1109/TPAMI.2007.1177
7. Li, Y., Lu, H.: Natural image matting via guided contextual attention. In: Proceedings of the AAAI Conference on Artificial Intelligence, vol. 34, pp. 11450–11457 (2020)
8. Lin, S., Ryabtsev, A., Sengupta, S., Curless, B.L., et al.: Real-time high-resolution background matting. In: Proceedings of the IEEE/CVF Conference on Computer Vision and Pattern Recognition, pp. 8762–8771 (2021)
9. Lu, H., Dai, Y., Shen, C., Xu, S.: Indices matter: learning to index for deep image matting. In: Proceedings of the IEEE/CVF International Conference on Computer Vision, pp. 3266–3275 (2019)
10. Peng, C., Zhang, X., Yu, G., et al.: Large kernel matters-improve semantic segmentation by global convolutional network. In: Proceedings of the IEEE/CVF Conference on Computer Vision and Pattern Recognition, pp. 4353–4361 (2017)
11. Qiao, Y., Liu, Y., Yang, X., Zhou, D., et al.: Attention-guided hierarchical structure aggregation for image matting. In: Proceedings of the IEEE/CVF Conference on Computer Vision and Pattern Recognition, pp. 13676–13685 (2020)

12. Qiao, Y., et al.: Multi-scale information assembly for image matting. Comput. Graph. Forum **39**, 565–574 (2020). https://doi.org/10.1111/cgf.14168
13. Rhemann, C., Rother, C., Wang, J., Gelautz, M., Kohli, P., Rott, P.: A perceptually motivated online benchmark for image matting. In: Proceedings of the IEEE/CVF Conference on Computer Vision and Pattern Recognition, pp. 1826–1833 (2009)
14. Sun, Y., et al.: Semantic image matting. In: Proceedings of the IEEE/CVF Conference on Computer Vision and Pattern Recognition, pp. 11120–11129 (2021)
15. Tang, J., Aksoy, Y., Oztireli, C., Gross, M., Aydin, T.O.: Learning-based sampling for natural image matting. In: Proceedings of the IEEE/CVF Conference on Computer Vision and Pattern Recognition, pp. 3055–3063 (2019)
16. Wei, T., Chen, D., Zhou, W., et al.: Improved image matting via real-time user clicks and uncertainty estimation. In: Proceedings of the IEEE/CVF Conference on Computer Vision and Pattern Recognition, pp. 15374–15383 (2021)
17. Xu, N., Price, B., et al.: Deep image matting. In: Proceedings of the IEEE/CVF Conference on Computer Vision and Pattern Recognition, pp. 2970–2979 (2017)
18. Yang, X., Xu, K., Chen, S., et al.: Active matting. In: Proceedings of the Advances in Neural Information Processing Systems, pp. 4595–4605 (2018)
19. Yu, Q., Zhang, J., Zhang, H., et al.: Mask guided matting via progressive refinement network. In: Proceedings of the IEEE/CVF Conference on Computer Vision and Pattern Recognition, pp. 1154–1163 (2021)
20. Yu, Z., Li, X., Huang, H., Zheng, W., Chen, L.: Cascade image matting with deformable graph refinement. In: Proceedings of the IEEE/CVF International Conference on Computer Vision, pp. 7167–7176 (2021)
21. Zhang, Q., Cong, R., Li, C., et al.: Dense attention fluid network for salient object detection in optical remote sensing images. IEEE Trans. Image Process. **30**, 1305–1317 (2021). https://doi.org/10.1109/TIP.2020.3042084
22. Zhang, Y., et al.: A late fusion CNN for digital matting. In: Proceedings of the IEEE/CVF Conference on Computer Vision and Pattern Recognition, pp. 7469–7478 (2019)
23. Zhang, Z., Ma, J., Xu, P., Wang, W.: Dense attention-guided network for boundary-aware salient object detection. In: Lokoč, J., et al. (eds.) MMM 2021. LNCS, vol. 12572, pp. 148–161. Springer, Cham (2021). https://doi.org/10.1007/978-3-030-67832-6_13

Authenticity Identification of Qi Baishi's Shrimp Painting with Dynamic Token Enhanced Visual Transformer

Wenjie Chen, Xiaoting Huang, Xueting Liu, Huisi Wu, and Fu Qi[✉]

Shenzhen University, Shenzhen, China
qfu@szu.edu.cn

Abstract. Automatic recognition of Chinese ink paintings' authenticity is still a challenging task due to the high similarity between genuine and fake paintings, and the sparse discriminative information in Chinese ink paintings. To handle this challenging task, we propose the Dynamic Token Enhancement Transformer (DETE) to improve the model's ability to identify the authenticity of Qi Baishi's shrimp paintings. The proposed DETE method consists of two key components: dynamic patch creation (DPC) strategy and dynamic token enhancement (DTE) module. The DPC strategy creates patches with different sizes according to their contributions, forcing the network to focus on the important regions instead of meaningless ones. The DTE module gradually enhances the association between the class token and most impact tokens to improves the performance eventually. We collected a dataset of authenticity identification of Qi Baishi's shrimp paintings and validated our method on this dataset. The results showed that our method outperformed the state-of-the-art methods. In addition, we further validated our method on two public available painting classification datasets WikiArt and ArtDL.

Keywords: Fined-grained classification · Visual transformer · Qi Baishi's paintings

1 Introduction

There are many fake paintings in the painting market, which often cause huge economic losses to collectors and investors. Unfortunately, identifying the authenticity of a painting requires high professionalism, making the identification of paintings expensive. Therefore, it is essential to design a method to identify the authenticity of paintings. Most of the current methods for automatic classification of paintings are designed for western oil paintings [1–8], lacking methods for classifying Chinese ink paintings. Since Chinese ink paintings contain more blank regions than Western oil paintings and nature images, causing the imbalanced distribution of discriminative information in Chinese ink paintings. In this regard, the methods that are effective for classifying natural images [9–11] and western oil paintings do not perform well in Chinese ink paintings.

N. Magnenat-Thalmann et al. (Eds.): CGI 2022, LNCS 13443, pp. 554–565, 2022.
https://doi.org/10.1007/978-3-031-23473-6_43

Chinese ink paintings contain a lot of blank regions, which makes the discriminative feature sparse and scattered. If the visual transformer [10] uses a finer-grained patch creation strategy to capture small discriminative information in the image would undoubtedly increase the model's ability to distinguish fine-grained nuance. However, if the fine-grained patch creation strategy is also used for the image's blank regions, it will increase the model's unnecessary demand for computational resources. It can be observed that each region in the image contributes differently to the classification. Thus, we can use different grain patch creation strategies for an image. Therefore, we propose a fine-grained patch creation strategy for the regions that contribute significantly to the classification. In contrast, a coarser-grained patch creation strategy will be applied to the regions that contribute slightly to the classification. In this way, we can balance the model's computation resource requirement and fine-grained information handling ability.

In addition, each token in the token sequence inside the visual transformer contributes differently to the classification. To allocate the computing resource more properly and improve the model's performance, we identify the contribution of each token and improve the model's performance by dynamically enhancing the association between the class token and the most impact tokens. The key is to calculate the contribution of each token to the classification. In this paper, we proposed an attention weight aggregation method, which can accurately calculate the similarity between each token. With the help of aggregated attention weight, we can calculate the contribution of each token to the classification.

Overall, in this paper, we design the Dynamic Token Enhance Transformer (DTET) for identifying the authenticity of Qi Baishi's shrimp paintings, a typical type of Chinese ink painting. First, to improve the model's ability to recognize subtle differences, we design a dynamic patch creation strategy (DPC) to create patches with different sizes for different regions according to their contributions. In addition, we proposed a dynamic token enhancement (DTE) module to gradually enhance the association between the class token with the tokens that contribute significantly to the classification. Finally, we calibrate the model's predicted confidence by label smoothing, which improves the model's reliability.

2 Method

2.1 Network Framework

The architecture of our network is demonstrated in Fig. 1. Firstly, we generate a Class Activation Map (CAM) [12] by a pre-trained CNN model, which identify the contribution of each pixels to the classification. Then, we dynamically create the patches with different granularities regarding the mean contributions of that region. Thus, the model can better balance the computation resource requirement and the model's performance. In addition, we aggregate the attention weights of each transformer layer and identify the contribution of tokens inside the transformer to the classification. With the identified contribution of

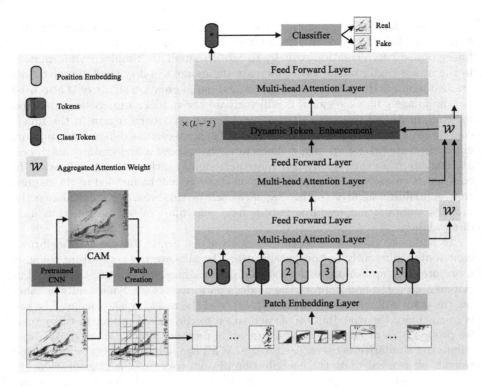

Fig. 1. Framework of our model. The model dynamically creates and embeds patches based on the CAM generated by the pre-trained CNN model. We further aggregate each transformer layer's attention weights to identify each token's contribution to the classification and enhance the classification performance with toke subsequences that most contribute to the classification.

the tokens, we can dynamically enhance the relationship between the class token and the most impact tokens, which helps to improve the model's performance.

2.2   Dynamic Patch Creation and Embedding Strategy

Since the information distributed in the spatial space in Qi Baishi's shrimp paintings is highly imbalanced, we create the patch with a different granularity for different regions in an image according to its contribution. Figure 2(a) is the CAM [12] generated by the pre-trained CNN model for an image, the red colour in the CAM identifies the contribution of the region to the classification. We use a finer granularity patch creation strategy for the image regions that contribute significantly to the classification. On the contrary, a coarser granularity patch creation strategy for the image regions where contributes slightly to the classification.

We create the patches with two different granularities according to the CAM in this paper. Let PS denote the coarse-grained patch size, and $\frac{PS}{2}$ stand for

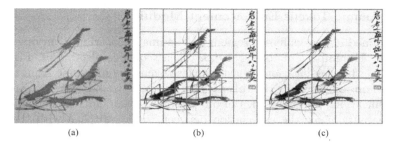

(a)   (b)   (c)

Fig. 2. Comparison of patches creation strategies. (a) CAM generated by the pre-trained CNN model; (b) the dynamic patches creation strategy in this paper; (c) the traditional patches creation strategy.

the fine-grained patch size. The input image is represented by $X = R^{C \times H \times W}$, where C, H and W are the numbers of channels, height and width of the image, respectively. $N_{sg} = \frac{H \times W}{PS}$ is the number of patches that will be created by coarse-grained patch creation strategy, and $N_{fg} = 4\frac{H \times W}{PS}$ is the number of patches will be created by fine-grained patch creation strategy.

First, we use a fine-grained patch creation strategy for the $p \times 100\%$ region of the image that contributes most to the classification and a coarse-grained patch creation strategy for the rest. Let P_{sg} and P_{fg} denote the image regions where the patch is created with coarse and fine granularity, respectively. P_{sg} and P_{fg} can be calculated by

$$P_{sg} = argtop(-cam, p \times N_{sg}), \tag{1}$$

$$P_{fg} = argtop(cam, (1 - p) \times N_{sg}), \tag{2}$$

where cam denotes CAM of the image. The $argtop(x, n)$ function is used to gather the position of the largest n values in x.

Then, we create and embed the coarse-grained and fine-grained patch according to P_{sg} and P_{fg}. We denotes them with X_{sg} and X_{fg}, respectively. The methods formulation is defined as follows

$$X_{sg} = F_{sg}(X, P_{sg}), \tag{3}$$

$$X_{fg} = F_{fg}(X, P_{fg}), \tag{4}$$

where $F_{sg}(\cdot)$ and $F_{fg}(\cdot)$ are the coarse-grained and fine-grained patch creation and embedding functions. we implement $F_{sg}(\cdot)$ and $F_{fg}(\cdot)$ with a convolutional layer. The convolution kernel size for $F_{sg}(\cdot)$ and $F_{fg}(\cdot)$ functions are PS and $\frac{PS}{2}$, respectively. The stride for convolution is equal to the kernel size.

Finally, by concatenating the coarse-grained, fine-grained, and the classification token X_{cls} together, we form the token sequence that will be fed into the transformer. The equation is given as follows

$$Y = cat(X_{cls}, X_{sg}, X_{fg}), \tag{5}$$

where Y is the token sequence that will be fed into the transformer model, whose length is $N = N_{sg} \times (1 - p) + N_{fg} \times p + 1$. $cat(\cdot, \cdot, \cdot)$ is a concatenate function.

2.3 Dynamic Tokens Enhancement Module

As mentioned above, different regions in the image contribute varying to classification. The impact of tokens in the token sequence also varies. Figure 3(c) shows that the classification's most impact tokens mainly come from the foreground of an image, while the tokens from the background contribute minor to the classification. The main idea of our dynamic token enhancement module is to gradually enhance the association between the class token with the tokens that contribute significantly to the classification.

The dynamic token enhancement module first requires accurately identifying each token's contribution to the classification. Serrano et al. [13] aggregate the attention weights in each transformer layer to improve accuracy in identifying the tokes' relationship, which we refer to as aggregated attention weights in this paper. However, as shown in Fig. 3(a), we find that the aggregated attention weight may not be accurate enough to calculate the tokens' contribution to classification. To obtain the tokens' contribution accurately, we calculate the contribution of each token to classification by two steps: the attention weights aggregation step and the token's contribution computing step.

In the attention weight aggregation step, we multiply the attention weights from each transformer layer to reduce the noise of the attention weights. We further normalize the aggregate attention weight with the $softmax$ function. We define the formulation as follows

$$Att_{agg}^i = \begin{cases} softmax(log(a^i \times (Att_{agg}^{i-1})^\top)), & i > 1 \\ softmax(log(a^i)), & i = 1 \end{cases} \tag{6}$$

where $Att_{agg}^i \in R^{(N+1) \times (N+1)}$, is the aggregated attention weight of the ith layer, and a^i denotes the attention weight of the ith transformer layer. Here we use the logarithmic to improve the numerical sensitivity while computing the aggregated attention weights by the $softmax$.

The aggregated attention weight identifies the relationship between each token in the token sequence, with similar tokens having higher attention weights and, conversely, lower similarity having lower aggregated attention weights.

In the token's contribution computing step, we calculate the contribution of each token to classification by calculating the similarity between each token to the class token X_{cls}, according to the aggregated attention weights. The method is given as follows,

$$Contri_k^i = softmax(log(a_{(1,\cdot)}^i \times Att_{agg}^{i-1})), \tag{7}$$

where $Contri_k^i$ denotes the contribution of the kth token, $k \in [2, N+1]$, to the classification in the ith layer. $a_{(1,\cdot)}^i$ stand for the first row of matrix a^i.

Then, we gather $N \times pe$ most significant contributed tokens by $Contri^i$. We first find out the tokens' position by

$$P_e = argtop(Contri^i, pe \times N). \tag{8}$$

Based on P_e, we can gather the most significant contributed tokens by

$$Y_e = gather(Y, P_e), \tag{9}$$

where $gather(Y, P_e)$ is a function to gather the tokens in the token sequence in Y by the tokens' position P_e. Y_e is the subset of Y, which contain the most significant contributed tokens in Y.

After that, to enhance the relationship between the classification token Y_{cls} with the most impact tokens, we concatenate the subsequence of tokens Y_e with the original token sequence Y_r, which can be defined as:

$$Y = cat(Y_r, Y_e), \tag{10}$$

where Y_r is a slice of Y, which is the first N token of Y, the length of the new token sequence Y becomes $(1 + pe) \times N$. By making full use of the most impact subsequence of tokens, the transformer model can improve the classification performance while slightly increasing computational resources requirement.

Like the classic visual transformer model [10] for image classification, we calculate the model's logistic prediction of image classification by a linear layer, formulated as

$$logits = FC(LN(Y_{cls})), \tag{11}$$

where FC is a linear layer. LN represents the layer normalization. Y_{cls} denotes the class token of the last transformer layer.

2.4 Loss Function

We take advantage of label smoothing, criticize and calibrate the model with label smoothing to improve the model's reliability, which is formulated as:

$$\mathcal{L}_{cls} = \sum_{i=1} -y_i^{LS} log(p_i), \tag{12}$$

where $y_i^{LS} = y_i(1 - \beta) + \frac{\beta}{K}$, is the smoothed y_i label. $\beta \in (0, 1)$ is the smoothing strength of the label. K is the number of class. p_i is the classification logistic predicted by the model for the ith sample.

3 Experiments

3.1 Experiments Settings and Evaluation Metrics

All models used for the experiments in this paper were implemented by PyTorch and experimented on NVIDIA RTX 3090. We optimize the model by Stochastic Gradient Descent (SGD) optimizer with an initial learning rate of 0.001, a momentum of 0.9, and a weight decay of 1.0×10^{-3}. During the model's training, we use a cosine schedule to adjust the learning rate of the optimizer. The model reaches convergence by 60 epochs in training, and the batch size is 64.

The model in this paper is fine-tuned on the ImageNet-1K pre-trained backbone. We employ ResNet-18 [9] as the helper model to generate the CAM.

In this paper, the classification performance is measured by accuracy, recall, and Expected Calibration Error (ECE) [14]. The ECE metric is used to measure the deviation of the predicted confidence from the true likelihood. When $ECE \rightarrow 0$ means the model's predicted confidence is closer to the true likelihood.

3.2 Validation Datasets and Data Preprocessing

In this paper, with the help of experts in Chinese ink painting study, we collected and created a dataset for identifying the authenticity of Qi Baishi's shrimp paintings. This dataset is to identify the authenticity of Qi Baishi's shrimp paintings. The dataset contains 256 genuine paintings by Qi Baishi and 173 fake paintings collected from the internet, similar to the genuines. The aspect ratios of the image in the dataset range from 1 : 1 to 1 : 3.8. In addition, We further validate the generalization of our model on two publicly painting classification datasets, WiKiArt [15] and ArtDL [16].

We pad zero to the image first, make sure the aspect ratio is 1 : 1, then resize the images to 224×224 and normalize each channel of the images with its mean and standard deviation. For data augmentation, we randomly select three different image transformation methods to transform the image. The image transformation methods including random resize, random cropping, random rotation, random flipping, random gaussian blur, random brightness transformation, random contrast transformation, random gamma transformation, random median filtering transformation, random noise injection, and random sharpening. We validate the methods with 5-fold cross-validation. The statistical results reported in the following are the mean of the 5-fold validations.

Table 1. Hyper-parameter selection in identifying the authenticity of Qi Baishi's shrimp paintings dataset. ↑: the larger the value, the better result, ↓: the smaller the value, the better the result.

p	Acc (%) ↑	Recall (%) ↑	ECE (%) ↓	pe	Acc (%) ↑	Recall (%) ↑	ECE (%) ↓
0.1	93.384	96.717	4.719	0.1	94.384	96.667	5.465
0.2	94.388	97.662	4.564	0.2	94.832	96.882	5.295
0.3	95.462	98.264	3.594	0.3	95.426	97.217	4.530
0.4	95.531	98.385	3.477	0.4	95.872	97.342	4.154
0.5	95.542	98.429	3.325	0.5	95.462	98.264	3.594
0.6	**95.720**	**98.562**	**3.236**	0.6	**95.467**	**98.562**	**3.236**

(a) Hyper-parameter selection for p .   (b) Hyper-parameter selection for pe.

3.3 Hyper-parameters Selection

The two modules involved in our model are the DPC and DTE module. In the DPC module, the hyper-parameter $p \in [0, 1]$ determines the number of patches created with fined-grained. As shown in Table 1(a), the model's performance is obviously affected by p when p is less than 0.3. When the value of p is over 0.3, the performance is less affected by p. Thus, we finally choose $p = 0.3$ as the hyper-parameter of DPC module to balance the performance and the computation resource requirements. For the DTE module, the hyper-parameter pe determines the length of the subsequence of tokens to enhance the performance. As shown in Table 1(b), the model's performance is obviously affected by pe when pe is less than 0.5, while pe is greater than 0.5, the performance is much insensitive to pe. Thus, we finally choose $pe = 0.5$ as the hyper-parameter of pe.

Table 2. Ablation studies in identifying the authenticity of Qi Baishi's shrimp paintings dataset.

Methods	Acc (%) ↑	Recall (%) ↑	ECE (%) ↓
Baseline	93.720	96.427	4.036
Baseline + DPC	95.244	96.887	3.864
Baseline + DTE	94.761	97.342	3.839
DETE	**95.462**	**98.264**	**3.594**

3.4 Ablation Studies

Table 2 shows the statistical results of the ablation studies. In the ablation studies, we use the ViT [10] as the baseline. The experimental results show that the DPC module effectively improve the model's ability to discriminate differences in images. By creating patches with different granularity according to the contribution of regions, the Baseline + DPC method significantly improved 1.504% in ACC metrics. In addition, by utilizing the most impact tokens to enhance the association between the class token and other tokens, the Baseline + DTE method achieves 1.041% and 0.915% improvements in ACC and Recall metrics, respectively. Finally, by simultaneously equipping both DPC and DTE in the Baseline, our DETE method can effectively achieved the classification performance in our ablation studies, as shown in Table 2.

3.5 Comparison with State-of-the-Art Methods

To further demonstrate the advantages of our method identifying the authenticity of Qi Baishi's shrimp paintings dataset, we also compared our proposed method with six state-of-the-art methods, including four CNN-based methods (i.e., ResNet-50 [9], CAL [17], SEF [18], and WS-DAN [19]) and two transformer-based methods (i.e., ViT [10], ViTPS [20]. Among them, CAL, SEF and ViTPS are state-of-the-art fined-grained methods.

Table 3 shows the statistical results of the comparison experiments on identifying the authenticity of Qi Baishi's shrimp paintings dataset. ResNet-50 [9] and Visual Transformer [10] are classical image classification methods not proposed

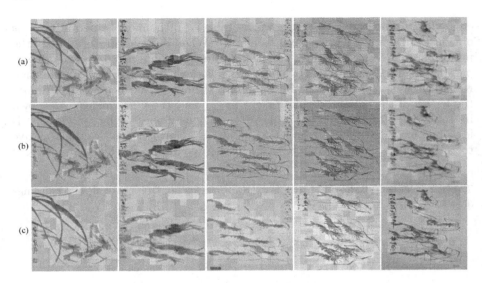

Fig. 3. Comparison of the contributions of tokens to the classification by different methods. The red pixels indicate the contribution of each token corresponding to the region of the image to the classification. (a): TransFG, (b): Single transformer layer's attention weights, (c): Ours. (Color figure online)

for fine-grained image classification. Therefore, the classification performance of Qi Baishi's shrimp painting classification is poor. CAL [17] improves the fine-grained classification performance by significant attentional features, while the limited training data constrain CAL. SEF [18] makes several sub-feature groups by rearranging and grouping features. By enhancing the semantics of the sub-feature of a global feature, SEF outperformed previous comparison methods. However, which is limited in helping the model recognizes the image's subtle differences. WS-DAN [19] identifies and erases the discriminative pixels in the image to force the model to learn more sophisticated features. However, the performance of WS-DAN is inferior when the training data is limited. ViTPS [20] progressively samples the critical regions in the image to keep the object structure in the image not being destroyed. However, ViTPS's sampling strategy is inefficient when the training data is limited.

With the help of the DPC and DTE module, our method improves the model's classification performance, even when the training data is limited. Since our method calibrates the predicted confidence in training, its ECE is the best compared with other methods. To verify the effectiveness of the proposed aggregated attention weight, we visualized the contribution of different tokens to classification. From Fig 3, we can observe that our method identifies the token's contribution to classification more accurately than comparison methods.

We further validated our model on two public available painting classification datasets. The experiments result in Table 3 shows that our method outperformance the state-of-the-art methods in WikiArt [15] and ArtDL [16] datasets.

Table 3. Statistic result for comparison with state-of-the art methods.

Methods	Years	Acc (%) ↑	Recall (%) ↑	ECE (%) ↓
Qi Baishi's shrimp paintings dataset				
ResNet-50 [9]	2015	84.273	82.968	16.698
WS-DAN [19]	2019	86.447	87.478	11.450
SEF [18]	2020	90.625	91.667	10.345
ViT [10]	2021	86.107	85.949	13.984
CAL [17]	2021	85.836	84.971	16.002
ViTPS [20]	2021	87.826	86.889	15.216
DETE (ours)	2022	**95.462**	**98.264**	**3.594**
ArtDL dataset				
ResNet-50 [9]	2015	72.624	72.346	16.354
ViT [10]	2021	73.352	73.989	13.257
WS-DAN [19]	2019	76.495	76.694	11.554
SEF [18]	2020	75.746	75.568	10.362
CAL [17]	2021	75.345	75.494	13.024
ViTPS [20]	2021	75.248	75.784	14.277
DETE (ours)	2022	**76.788**	**77.501**	**7.812**
WikiArt dataset				
ResNet-50 [9]	2015	74.374	74.867	14.698
ViT [10]	2021	75.791	75.724	12.448
WS-DAN [19]	2019	77.483	77.427	9.150
SEF [18]	2020	76.952	76.882	8.145
CAL [17]	2021	77.624	77.428	8.017
ViTPS [20]	2021	77.933	77.756	8.612
DETE (ours)	2022	**78.482**	**78.325**	**5.758**

3.6 Discussions and Limitations

As shown in Fig. 3(c), the proposed aggregated attention weight calculation method identifies the contributions of each token more efficiently than other existing methods. Based on this identified contribution, other transformer-based methods can also improve the computational efficiency by rearranging the tokens with the help of the proposed aggregated attention weights. On the other hand, similar to other methods, the proposed aggregated attention weight calculation method still may incorrectly mark the background regions of images as regions that contribute to the classification. As shown in Fig. 4, the algorithm for calculating the aggregated attention weights of images in this paper still has shortcomings in that the aggregated attention incorrectly marks the background regions of images as regions that contribute to the classification.

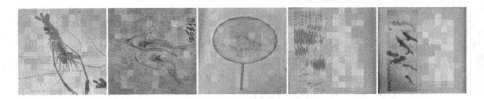

Fig. 4. Failure cases of the identified contribution of tokens to the classification by the aggregated attention weights of this paper.

4   Conclusion

The Qi Baishi's shrimp paintings contain many blank regions and the discriminative information of the painting are dispersed, leading the contribution of different region in the image to the classification is unbalanced. To handle the above problems, we first design the DPC module dynamically create the patch according to the contribution of the regions in the image. The DTE module enhances the relationship between the class token and the selected most impact tokens to improve classification performance. We collected the authenticity of Qi Baishi's shrimp paintings identification dataset and validated our method on this dataset. The results showed that our method outperformed the state-of-the-art methods. In addition, to verify the generalization ability of our method, we further validated our method on the publicly available painting classification datasets WikiArt [15] and ArtDL [16].

Acknowledgments. This work was supported in part by grants from the National Natural Science Foundation of China (Nos. 61973221 and 62002232), the Natural Science Foundation of Guangdong Province of China (No. 2019A1515011165), and the Shenzhen Research Foundation for Basic Research, China (No. 20200824213635001).

References

1. Mohammadi, M.R., Rustaee, F.: Hierarchical classification of fine-art paintings using deep neural networks. Iran J. Comput. Sci. **4**, 59–66 (2021)
2. Zhao, W., Zhou, D., Qiu, X., Jiang, W.: Compare the performance of the models in art classification. PLOS One 1–16 (2021)
3. Cetinic, E., Lipic, T., Grgic, S.: Fine-tuning convolutional neural networks for fine art classification. Expert Syst. Appl. **114**, 107–118 (2018)
4. Tan, W.R., Chan, C.S., Aguirre, H.E., Tanaka, K.: Ceci N'EST Pas Une pipe: a deep convolutional network for fine-art paintings classification. In: IEEE International Conference on Image Processing (ICIP), pp. 3703–3707 (2016)
5. Cömert, C., Özbayoğlu, M., Kasnakoğlu, C.: Painter prediction from artworks with transfer learning. In: International Conference on Mechatronics and Robotics Engineering (ICMRE), pp. 204–208 (2021)
6. Dobbs, Todd, Ras, Zbigniew: On art authentication and the Rijksmuseum challenge: a residual neural network approach. Expert Syst. Appl. **200**(C), 116933 (2022)

7. Cetinic, E., She, J.: Understanding and creating art with AI: review and outlook. ACM Trans. Multimed. Comput. Commun. Appl. (TOMM) **18**, 1–22 (2022)
8. Elgammal, A., Kang, Y., Leeuw, M.D.: Picasso, matisse, or a fake? automated analysis of drawings at the stroke level for attribution and authentication. In: Proceedings of the AAAI Conference on Artificial Intelligence, vol. 32 (2018)
9. He, K., Zhang, X., Ren, S., Sun, J.: Deep residual learning for image recognition. In: IEEE Conference on Computer Vision and Pattern Recognition (CVPR), pp. 770–778 (2016)
10. Dosovitskiy, A., et al.: An image is worth 16 × 16 words: transformers for image recognition at scale. In: International Conference on Learning Representations (ICLR) (2021)
11. Brock, A., De, S., Smith, S.L.: Characterizing signal propagation to close the performance gap in unnormalized resnets. In: International Conference on Learning Representations (ICLR) (2021)
12. Zhou, B., Khosla, A., Lapedriza, À., Oliva, A., Torralba, A.: Learning deep features for discriminative localization. In: IEEE Conference on Computer Vision and Pattern Recognition (CVPR), pp. 2921–2929 (2016)
13. Serrano, S., Smith, N.A.: Is attention interpretable? In: Proceedings of the 57th Conference of the Association for Computational Linguistics (ACL), pp. 2931–2951 (2019)
14. Guo, C., Pleiss, G., Sun, Y., Weinberger, K.Q.: On calibration of modern neural networks. In: International Conference on Machine Learning (ICML), vol. 70, pp. 1321–1330 (2017)
15. Saleh, B., Elgammal, A.: Large-scale classification of fine-art paintings: learning the right metric on the right feature. Int. J. Digit. Art Hist. (2) (2016)
16. Milani, F., Fraternali, P.: A dataset and a convolutional model for iconography classification in paintings. J. Comput. Cult. Heritage (JOCCH) **14**, 1–18 (2021)
17. Rao, Y., Chen, G., Lu, J., Zhou, J.: Counterfactual attention learning for fine-grained visual categorization and re-identification. In: Proceedings of the IEEE/CVF International Conference on Computer Vision (ICCV), pp. 1025–1034 (2021)
18. Luo, W., Zhang, H., Li, J., Wei, X.-S.: Learning semantically enhanced feature for fine-grained image classification. IEEE Signal Process. Lett. **27**, 1545–1549 (2020)
19. Hu, T., Qi, H.: See better before looking closer: weakly supervised data augmentation network for fine-grained visual classification. CoRR, abs/1901.09891 (2019)
20. Yue, X., et al.: Vision transformer with progressive sampling. In: Proceedings of the IEEE/CVF International Conference on Computer Vision (ICCV), pp. 387–396 (2021)

Modeling and Simulation

An Optimized Material Point Method for Soil-Water Coupled Simulation

Zhaoyu Xiong, Hao Zhang, Haipeng Li, and Dan Xu[✉]

Yunnan University, Kunming, China
lihaipeng@mail.ynu.edu.cn, danxu@ynu.edu.cn

Abstract. The interactions between soil and water are ubiquitous in reality, and the infiltration or flush by water often leads to soil's deformation and failure, which are very common in film scenes. In recent years, the material point method (MPM) has been applied to animate different materials with convincing effects, but soils, as a kind of widely spread natural material too, are relatively less considered yet. In this paper, we propose an optimized MLS-MPM to model soil-water mechanics. In our method, soil stress is updated with the increments of strain and vorticity, and a Drucker-Prager model with tension cut-off is employed to model the linear isotropic poroelasticity of soils. The plasticity model is implemented with a return mapping algorithm, being $O(n^3)$ faster than the traditional way. The soil-water coupling scheme is achieved by momenta exchange between them following Darcy's law. The method shows a great boost by reducing the number of matrix multiplication operations when computing stress and updating deformation gradient. The efficacy of our method is validated by a set of test scenes and benchmarks.

Keywords: Material point method · Physics-based modeling · Return mapping algorithm · Soil-water coupling · Drucker-Prager model

1 Introduction

Large scenes involving dynamic objects are often a necessary part that contributes to the visual experience of films. In the modern film industry, a great proportion of scenes are generated by digital animation and VFX compositing, as they are efficient to create dynamic objects, and physics-based simulation is a powerful tool for animating realistic and dynamic environments with systematic behaviors. Compared with the other popular numerical methods, the material point method (MPM) exhibits its adaptability with varying continuus materials and numerical stability, and its optimized variant, the moving least square MPM (MLS-MPM), shows 2× faster by reusing affine velocity to evaluate velocity gradient.

Through the aforementioned works, soils are still rarely considered yet and they attract our interest. Deformation and failure of soils are induced by shear force and tensile force, between which the former is primarily considered as the evaluation of soil strength in engineering. However, tensile strength also contributes to the shape

© The Author(s), under exclusive license to Springer Nature Switzerland AG 2022
N. Magnenat-Thalmann et al. (Eds.): CGI 2022, LNCS 13443, pp. 569–581, 2022.
https://doi.org/10.1007/978-3-031-23473-6_44

evolution of soil during deformation and failure [26] such as cracking. Inspired by geotechnical practices, we use a linear isotropic poroelasticity model to describe the constitutive behavior of soils. Among the common natural substances and phenomena, water is a ubiquitous one that frequently comes with soils and influences their shapes, for instance, infiltration and flushing. Therefore we extend the soil model to a two-way coupled one to capture their motion.

In this paper, we propose an optimized soil-water coupled MLS-MPM, which uses a Drucker-Prager poroelasticity model to animate soil and water. At the particle-to-grid stage, trial soil stress is updated with the increments of strain and vorticity that are derived from the affine velocity in APIC [15]. After that, the Drucker-Prager model predicts the state of trial stress by the shear failure criterion and the tensile failure criterion, and projects it back to the yield by the return mapping algorithm. Both two steps reduce the total number of matrix multiplications needed to achieve a significant boost. The soil-water coupling is implemented by the momentum exchange between phases following Darcy's law. Our method is naturally adaptive to varying types of soils described in a set of physical parameters.

The main contributions of this paper can be summarized as:

- An optimized MLS-MPM implementation for soil and soil-water coupled simulation, using two material point layers to represent different phases and exchange momenta.
- A linear isotropic Drucker-Prager poroelasticity model with tension cut-off for soils, where pore flow follows Darcy's law.
- The return mapping algorithm for soil's plasticity to reach an $O(n^3)$ boost, compared with the general way that updates deformation gradient using SVD.

2   Related Works

2.1   Computational Geomechanics

The effective stress theory gives the strain or strength behavior of porous granular media under pore pressure, and several well-known forms are often adopted in practice [11]. The formulations of multiphase governing equations include three major variants: $u - p$, $u - U$ and $u - v - p$, where u is soil displacement, p is pore pressure, U is water displacement and v is water velocity.

The widely used numerical methods include SPH, FEM, FDM and MPM [20]. FEM and FDM are error-prone in large deformations due to their complex remeshing and remapping scheme. SPH gets unstable when neighboring particles are insufficient, its boundary treatment is complicated as well. Compared with them, MPM has shown to be successful in problems involving large deformations in history-dependent materials, and has been applied to different geotechnical problems. The MPM representation of soil-water system can be categorized into two groups, using single or dual particle layers for two phases. While the latter guarantees the mess conservation in both phases, the former may cause loss of water mass, or neglect the relative velocity between soil skeleton and water [6]. So far the two-layer method has been used to model saturated [1] and unsaturated soils [6] with the $u - p$ and $u - U$ formulations.

Among the most used soil constitutive models in practice, the first generation, for instance, the Mohr-Coulomb criterion and the Drucker-Prager model, are still popular for their simplicity and computational efficiency [7]. While the Mohr-Coulomb model has a hexagon cone-shaped yield surface, the Drucker-Prager model is the smoothed variant, which is more convenient and efficient to implement.

2.2   Material Point Method

Compared with the previous Lagrangian-Eulerian hybrid solvers such as PIC and FLIP, MPM [23] gains its advantages over them from no advection term or mesh distortion. It is first introduced into computer graphics to simulate snow [21], and yet has been applied on a wide variety of materials and phenomena with good results, which include melting and solidification [22]; foams [4,19,28]; sands and debris [2,9]; cloth, knit and hair [14]; sauces [18]; baking and cooking materials [3]; rubbers [4]; magnetized materials [24]; etc.

A series of works put efforts into improving the computing efficiency or the numerical precision of MPM. The mapping schemes from APIC [15] and PolyPIC [8] improve the conservation of energy and angular momentum in particle-grid transfer. [10] uses the generalized interpolation material point (GIMP) method as well as the dynamic grid solution to improve the accuracy. The moving least square MPM (MLS-MPM) [12] eliminates the direct evaluation of the gradient of the shape function by reusing the affine velocity in APIC to achieve 2× faster speed. Moreover, in the Hierarchical Optimization Time (HOT) method [27], an efficient implicit time integration is proposed, which is irrespective of simulated materials and conditions.

2.3   CG Simulation of Porous Flow

Some works aim to reproduce granule-fluid mixture animation. [16] introduces a two-way coupling SPH to simulate porous flow. [2] proposes a semi-implicit MPM for the non-smooth rheology, treating granular matter as the compressible viscoplastic fluid with the D-P yield criterion, as well as a unilateral compressibility constraint. [25] suggests a two-grid MPM for sand-water mixtures. A similar approach is proposed to animate particle-laden flows with optimized time integration and discretization [9]. [5] also shows great results in the coupling of granular materials and fluids.

3   Physical Model

Our physical model is based on the mixture theory and the effective stress theory to model the coupled soil-water system, where the pore air is not considered. As explained by the effective stress theory, only the part of the total stress exerted on soil skeleton contributes to the soil strength, Terzaghi's principle describes the effective stress in soil-water mixture system:

$$\sigma'_{ij} = \sigma_{ij} - \delta_{ij}p^w, \tag{1}$$

where σ'_{ij} is the effective stress, σ_{ij} is the total stress, p^w is the pore pressure and δ_{ij} is the Kronecker delta function. The sign of pore pressure is defined as positive in compression.

For readability, our naming convention specifies normal symbols (e.g. ρ) for scalars, lower-cased bold symbols for vectors (e.g. $\boldsymbol{g}$) and upper-cased bold symbols (e.g. $\boldsymbol{F}$) for matrices. The superscript α of a quantity denotes the phase it refers to, which is either s for soil or w for water.

3.1   Governing Equations

The governing equations of the soil-water mixture system include the conservation of mass and momentum. With the material derivation of physical quantity ϕ with respect to phase α denoted as $\frac{D^\alpha \phi}{Dt} = \frac{\partial \phi}{\partial t} + \boldsymbol{v}^\alpha \cdot \phi$, they are respectively written as

$$\frac{D\rho}{Dt} + \rho \nabla \cdot \boldsymbol{v} = 0, \quad \rho \frac{D\boldsymbol{v}}{Dt} = \nabla \cdot \boldsymbol{\sigma} + \rho \boldsymbol{g}, \tag{2}$$

where ρ is the mixture density, $\boldsymbol{v}$ is the velocity, $\boldsymbol{\sigma}$ is the stress, and $\boldsymbol{g}$ is the gravitational acceleration. Given the soil density ρ^s, the water density ρ^w and the soil porosity θ, their densities in the soil-water mixture are $\overline{\rho}^s = (1-\theta)\rho^s$ and $\overline{\rho}^w = \theta \rho^w$, and $\rho = \overline{\rho}^s + \overline{\rho}^w$.

The momentum balance equations of the two phases are

$$\begin{aligned}
\overline{\rho}^s \frac{D^s \boldsymbol{v}}{Dt} &= \nabla \cdot (\boldsymbol{\sigma}^s - (1-\theta)\boldsymbol{\sigma}^w) + \overline{\rho}^s \boldsymbol{g} - \theta \boldsymbol{R}, \\
\overline{\rho}^w \frac{D^w \boldsymbol{v}}{Dt} &= -\nabla \cdot (\theta \boldsymbol{\sigma}_w) + \overline{\rho}^w + \theta \boldsymbol{R},
\end{aligned} \tag{3}$$

where $\boldsymbol{R}$ is the Darcy's drag force (see Sect. 3.3). The mass balance equations are

$$(1-\theta)\frac{D^s \rho}{Dt} + \overline{\rho}^s \nabla \cdot \boldsymbol{v}^s = 0, \quad \theta \frac{D^w \rho}{Dt} + \overline{\rho}^w \nabla \cdot \boldsymbol{v}^w = 0. \tag{4}$$

3.2   Soil Constitutive Model

Elasticity. Assume soils are linear isotropic elastic, we use Hooke's law to derive the trial stress after elastic deformation. The trial stress σ_{ij}^{*n+1} can be broken down into two parts, the rotational stress $\sigma_{ij}^{R^n}$ and the pure deformative stress $C_{ijkl}\Delta \varepsilon_{kl}$ (C is the stiffness tensor):

$$\sigma_{ij}^{*n+1} = \left(\sigma_{ij}^n + \sigma_{ik}^n \Delta \omega_{jk} + \sigma_{jk}^n \Delta \omega_{ik}\right) + C_{ijkl}\Delta \varepsilon_{kl}. \tag{5}$$

The strain $\Delta \varepsilon$ and the vorticity increment $\Delta \omega$ are both derived from the velocity gradient:

$$\Delta \varepsilon = \frac{\Delta t}{2}\left[\frac{\partial \boldsymbol{v}}{\partial \boldsymbol{x}} + \left(\frac{\partial \boldsymbol{v}}{\partial \boldsymbol{x}}\right)^T\right], \quad \Delta \omega = \frac{\Delta t}{2}\left[\frac{\partial \boldsymbol{v}}{\partial \boldsymbol{x}} - \left(\frac{\partial \boldsymbol{v}}{\partial \boldsymbol{x}}\right)^T\right]. \tag{6}$$

Plasticity. We take the Drucker-Prager model with tension cut-off [13] to apply soil plasticity, which consists of the shear failure criterion f_s and the tensile failure criterion f_t, both are functions of the effective shear stress τ and the spherical stress σ_m:

$$f_s = \tau + q_\varphi \sigma_m - k_\varphi, \quad f_t = \sigma_m - \sigma_t, \tag{7}$$

where $\sigma_m = \sum_i^d \sigma_i/3$, $\tau = \sqrt{\sum_{i,j}^d (\sigma_{ij} - \sigma_m \delta_{ij})^2/2}$, and the tensile strength $\sigma_t = k_\varphi/q_\varphi$ is defined as the maximum value of the spherical stress of the material. k_φ and q_φ are parameters of the D-P model determined by the cohesion c and the angle of internal friction φ of soil, the used inner adjustment is:

$$q_\varphi = \frac{6c \cos \varphi}{\sqrt{3}\,(3 + \sin \varphi)}, \quad k_\varphi = \frac{6c \sin \varphi}{\sqrt{3}\,(3 + \sin \varphi)}, \quad q_\psi = \frac{6 \sin \psi}{\sqrt{3}\,(3 + \sin \psi)}. \tag{8}$$

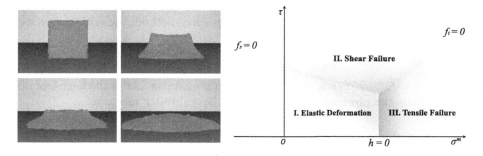

Fig. 1. Left: The shape evolution of a soil cube in different degrees of failure. Right: The yield surface of the D-P model on the $\sigma^m - \tau$ plane.

At first, the soil is assumed as perfectly elastic to derive the trial stress which is later evaluated by the criteria in Eq. 7. On the σ_m-τ plane, the trial stress point may fall on one of three subzones divided by $f_s = 0$, $f_t = 0$ and the bisector of their angle $h = \tau - \tau^p - \alpha^p(\sigma_m - \sigma_t)$, with the constants $\tau^p = k_\varphi - q_\varphi \sigma_t$ and $\alpha^p = \sqrt{1 + q_\varphi^2} - q_\varphi$. The state of the trial stress is predicted by the subzone it is on:

1. If $f_s \leq 0$ and $f_t \leq 0$ (subzone I in Fig. 1), the trial stress needs no plasticity correction.
2. If $f_s > 0$ and $h > 0$ (subzone II in Fig. 1), the shear failure occurs, and the stress point should be re-projected to $f_s = 0$ to regain stability.
3. If $f_t > 0$ and $h < 0$ (subzone III in Fig. 1), the tensile failure is declared, and the stress point should be projected to $f_t = 0$.

The detailed procedure of the above is described in Sect. 4.2.

3.3 Water Consititutive Model

In the free water condition, the Cauchy stress of water is

$$\boldsymbol{\sigma}^w = -p^w \boldsymbol{I}, \tag{9}$$

where $p^w = -\frac{\partial \Psi^w}{\partial J}$ is the water pressure, $\Psi^w = K^w(J-1)^2/2$ is the energy function, and K^w is the bulk modulus of water. Viscosity term and surface tension are not considered due to their little contribution. The momentum exchange term, Darcy's force, is the relative velocity between soil skeleton and water:

$$\boldsymbol{R} = -\frac{\gamma^w n}{k} \left(\boldsymbol{v}^w - \boldsymbol{v}^s \right), \tag{10}$$

where $\gamma^w = \rho^w g$ is the unit weight of water, k is the soil permeability. Darcy's force increases with higher permeability or porosity. When the soil is fully compact ($\theta = 0$), it falls back to the free water condition.

4 Implementation

Our method takes a semi-implicit time integration method, the critical timestep size Δt_{crit} follows the CFL condition:

$$\Delta t \le \Delta t_{crit} = \Delta x / c, \quad c = \sqrt{(K^u + 4G/3)/\rho}, \tag{11}$$

where $K^u = K^s + K^w/\theta$ is the undrained bulk modulus, Δx is the length of one grid cell, c is the pressure wave velocity in the soil-water mixture.

4.1 Particle-Grid Mapping Scheme

At P2G, nodal mass and velocity are collected by:

$$m_i^{\alpha,\,n} = \sum_p N_i\left(\boldsymbol{x}_p^{\alpha,\,n}\right) m_p^{\alpha,\,n}, \tag{12}$$

$$v_i^{\alpha,\,n} = \sum_p N_i\left(\boldsymbol{x}_p^{\alpha,\,n}\right) \left[v_p^{\alpha,\,n} + C_p^{\alpha,\,n}\left(\boldsymbol{x}_i - \boldsymbol{x}_p^{\alpha,\,n}\right)\right]. \tag{13}$$

The nodal soil porosity is calculated by:

$$\theta_i^n = 1 - \sum_p N_i\left(\boldsymbol{x}_p^{s,\,n}\right)\left(1 - \theta_p^n\right) m_p^{s,\,n}/m_i^{s,\,n}, \tag{14}$$

where the current porosity p is $\theta_p^{s,\,n} = 1 - (1 - \theta_p^0)/det(F_p^n)$, to guarantee that the porosity of cells where no soil particles are scattered is 1 other than 0.

At G2P, the new velocities and affine matrices are mapped back to particles by:

$$\widehat{v}_p^{\alpha,\,n+1} = \sum_i N_i\left(\boldsymbol{x}_i\right) v_i^{\alpha,\,n+1}, \tag{15}$$

$$\widehat{C}_p^{\alpha,\,n+1} = \sum_i N_i\left(\boldsymbol{x}_i\right) v_i^{\alpha,\,n+1}\left(\boldsymbol{x}_i - \boldsymbol{x}_p^{\alpha,\,n}\right)^T. \tag{16}$$

4.2 Update Stress

The soil trial stress is updated according to Sect. 3.2, where by utilizing $C = \frac{\partial v}{\partial x}$ in MLS-MPM, the direct evaluation of velocity gradient is eliminated. The plasticity correction may meet one of the 3 conditions:

1. $f_s \leq 0$ and $f_t \leq 0$. The trial stress is directly returned: $\sigma = \sigma^*$.
2. $f_s > 0$ and $h > 0$. A shear failure occurs. The corrected stress should be

$$\sigma_{ij} = \sigma_{ij}^R + C_{ijkl}\left(\Delta\varepsilon_{kl} - \Delta\varepsilon_{kl}^p\right), \tag{17}$$

and the condition $f_s(\sigma_{ij}^*) - \frac{\partial f_s}{\partial \sigma_{ij}}C_{ijkl}\Delta\varepsilon_{kl}^p = 0$ is implied by Taylor's first-order expansion. With the non-associative flow rule, the shear potential is $g_s = \tau + q_\psi \sigma_m$, then the plastic strain increment is

$$\Delta\varepsilon_{ij}^p = \mathrm{d}\lambda_s \frac{\partial g_s}{\partial \sigma_{ij}}, \quad \mathrm{d}\lambda_s = \frac{f_s\left(\sigma_{ij}^*\right)}{\frac{\partial f_s}{\partial \sigma_{ij}}C_{ijkl}\frac{\partial g_s}{\partial \sigma_{kl}}}. \tag{18}$$

The stress is corrected as

$$\sigma = \frac{\tau}{\tau^*}\left(\sigma^* - \sigma_m^* I\right) + \sigma_m I, \tag{19}$$

where $\sigma_m = \sigma_m^* - Kq_\psi\,\mathrm{d}\lambda_s$ and $\tau = k_\varphi - q_\varphi\sigma_m$.
3. $f_t > 0$ and $h < 0$. Tensile failure happens. The stress should be corrected following

$$\sigma_m = \sigma_m^* - K\Delta\varepsilon_m^p = \sigma_t, \tag{20}$$

where the increment of the plastic volumetric strain $\Delta\varepsilon_m^p = \Delta\varepsilon_{ij}^p\delta_{ij} = \mathrm{d}\lambda_t$ is derived from its Taylor's expansion $\mathrm{d}\lambda_t = \left(\sigma_m^* - \sigma_t\right)/K$. Therefore, the corrected stress is

$$\sigma = \sigma^* + \sigma_m\left(\sigma_t - \sigma_m^*\right)I. \tag{21}$$

4.3 Update Nodal Velocity

Recalling that $\sigma = \frac{1}{J}\frac{\partial \Psi}{\partial F}F^T$, the grid force discretization in MLS-MPM style is rewritten as:

$$f_i^n = -\sum_p N_i\left(x_p^n\right)V_p^n\sigma_p^{n+1}M^{-1}\left(x_i - x_p^n\right), \tag{22}$$

where $V_p^n = V_p^0 det\left(F_p^n\right)$ is the current volume of particle p, $M = \Delta x^2/4$ for quadratic $N_i(x)$. The momentum at grid node i of phase α is then

$$(m\widehat{v})_i^{\alpha,\ n+1} = (mv)_i^{\alpha,\ n} + (m_i^{\alpha,\ n}g + f_i^{\alpha,\ n} + d_i^{\alpha,\ n})\Delta t, \tag{23}$$

where the Darcy's drag force (see also Eq. 10) $d_i^{\alpha,\ n} = (-1)^{\delta_{\alpha w}}\theta_i m_i^s m_i^w R$. Therefore, the updated node velocity is $\widehat{v}_i^{n+1} = (m\widehat{v})_i^{n+1}/m_i^n$.

4.4   Boundary Conditions

The boundary conditions are applied on grids. Assume that the simulation space is an orthodox box, and no relative velocity between the boundary and particles, the free-slip condition is applied on the entire boundary $\partial\Omega$ for the water phase:

$$BC\left(v_i^w\right) = v_i^w - (n \cdot v_i^w)\,n, \quad x_i^w \in \partial\Omega^w, \tag{24}$$

to set the corresponding velocity component to zero.

For soil phase, the boundary is divided into the vertical boundary Ω_V^s and the horizontal boundary Ω_H^s, where $\partial\Omega_V^s \cup \partial\Omega_H^s = \partial\Omega^s$ and $\partial\Omega_V^s \cap \partial\Omega_H^s = \emptyset$. We enforce the Dirichlet boundary condition at the vertical boundary:

$$BC\left(v_i^s\right) = 0, \quad x_i^s \in \Omega_V^s, \tag{25}$$

to set the nodal velocity at the vertical boundary to zero. At the horizontal boundary, the Neumann boundary condition is applied:

$$BC\left(v_i^s\right) = \max\left(0,\ 1 - \mu_{fric}\frac{|n \cdot v_i^s|}{|v_i'^s|}\right)v_i'^s, \quad x_i^s \in \Omega_H^s, \tag{26}$$

by which the vertical component of velocity is enforced to be zero, and the horizontal component decrease in proportion to the original magnitude of the vertical velocity component as well as the dynamic friction factor μ_{fric}.

5   Results

To validate our method, we designed several experiments. All works are performed on a PC with Intel Core i7-10875H, NVIDIA GeForce RTX 2080 Super with Max-Q Design, 32 GB RAM, implemented on Houdini 19.0.

5.1   Performance

In usual MPMs, material plasticity is applied via the deformation gradient, where the trial deformation gradient F^* is decomposed into $F^* = U\Sigma V^T$ by SVD. The singular value matrix Σ indicates the stretch rate of the material at the spatial components. Given the stretch limit θ_s and the compression limit θ_c, the singular values are restricted within $[1 - \theta_c,\ 1 + \theta_s]$ to correct Σ as $\Sigma^\star$. The corrected deformation gradient is $F = U\Sigma^\star V^T$.

However, the time complexity of this procedure is $O(n^3)$ for n-order square matrices. Meanwhile, the return mapping algorithm only modifies the diagonal elements of σ in place, reducing the time complexity to $O(n)$. We compare them on the benchmark with different numbers of randomly generated particles. The benchmark is written in C++ with Eigen and compiled with -O3 level optimization. The result is given in Table 1. Despite the fluctuations, the average boost rate matches our analysis.

Table 1. Performance comparison on different numbers of particles

Particle #	100K	500K	1M	5M
Traditional (ms)	2366	12246	24029	115947
Ours (ms)	94	454	854	4212
Boost rate (%)	2417	2597	2714	2653

The traditional stress computation using polar decomposition $\boldsymbol{F} = \boldsymbol{RU}$ is also replaced by the elasticity model in Sect. 3.2. Although some fast polar decomposition methods for 2×2 and 3×3 matrices also reduce the number of matrix multiplication, our model does not involve an additional need to solve square root.

5.2   Soil Elastoplasticity

As introduced before, the return and mapping algorithm applies plasticity by projecting the trial stress point back to the yield surface. The left side of Fig. 1 shows the shape evolution of a soil cube with different degrees of failure, which gradually turns into a cone, consistent with the shape of the yield surface. We also demonstrate the effect of main soil parameters on the strength in Fig. 2, where from left to right, the soil spheres turn from sandy ($E = 10^6$ Pa, $c = 10$ Pa) to clayey ($E = 10^7$ Pa, $c = 10^4$ Pa).

Fig. 2. Shape evolution of three soil spheres of different strengths falling to the ground.

5.3   Soil-Water Coupling

The compressibility of pores allows variable porous flow velocity with respect to the water saturation. As the soil takes higher water pressure with a higher water content, the volume of pores is compressed as well, leading to a lower porosity. As per Darcy's law Eq. 10, the pore flow velocity is slower as the result. Figure 3 shows the infiltration process of a water cuboid on the top of a soil cube, and Fig. 4 gives two shots of the water-induced soil deformations, to validate the porous medium model.

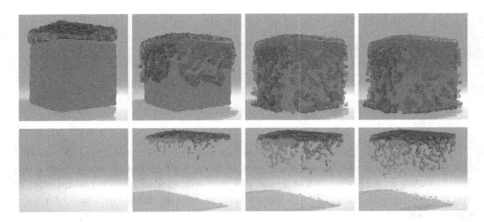

Fig. 3. Simulation of a water cuboid on the top of a soil cube. The bottom row shows the volume of water that flows into the soil pores.

Fig. 4. Examples of water-induced soil deformation.

6   Discussion

Performance. Our method benefits from the MLS-MPM and achieves a significant boost on the plasticity calculation by replacing SVD with a set of linear operations to update the deformation gradient of soil. Theoretically, this method can be extended to other kinds of materials of linear isotropic elastoplasticity to reduce the computation cost.

Limitations. Although our method introduces a performance improvement, the implementation of it appears more trivial than the general way, thus unreasonable parameters are more error-prone. Another noticeable problem is that when the soil has a low permeability, the stability may fluctuate and a smaller timestep may be required, the CFL condition gets insufficient to ensure the simulation stability under this circumstance. Meanwhile, [17] suggests an additional critical timestep depending on permeability.

Future Works. This paper just covers a small proportion of the diverse geomechanical behaviors. Meanwhile, the return mapping algorithm has a great potential to be extended to other isotropic and anisotropic plasticity models. We are also interested in a parallelized version to improve computing efficiency. Moreover, the conservation of vorticity may be a consideration [29].

Acknowledgment. This work was partially supported by the National Natural Science Foundation of China (Grant No. 62162068, 61540062), the Yunnan Ten Thousand Talents Program and Yunling Scholars Special Project (Grant No. YNWR-YLXZ-2018-022), the Yunnan Provincial Science and Technology Department-Yunnan University "Double First Class" Construction Joint Fund Project (Grant No. 2019FY003012), and the Graduate Research and Innovation Fund Project of Yunnan University (Grant No. 2021Y277).

References

1. Bandara, S., Soga, K.: Coupling of soil deformation and pore fluid flow using material point method. Comput. Geotech. **63**, 199–214 (2015). https://doi.org/10.1016/j.compgeo.2014.09.009
2. Daviet, G., Bertails-Descoubes, F.: A semi-implicit material point method for the continuum simulation of granular materials. ACM Trans. Graph. **35**(4), 1–13 (2016). https://doi.org/10.1145/2897824.2925877
3. Ding, M., Han, X., Wang, S., Gast, T.F., Teran, J.M.: A thermomechanical material point method for baking and cooking. ACM Trans. Graph. **38**(6), 1–14 (2019). https://doi.org/10.1145/3355089.3356537
4. Fang, Y., Li, M., Gao, M., Jiang, C.: Silly rubber: an implicit material point method for simulating non-equilibrated viscoelastic and elastoplastic solids. ACM Trans. Graph. **38**(4), 1–13 (2019). https://doi.org/10.1145/3306346.3322968
5. Fang, Y., et al.: IQ-MPM: an interface quadrature material point method for non-sticky strongly two-way coupled nonlinear solids and fluids. ACM Trans. Graph. **39**(4), 51:1–51:16 (2020). https://doi.org/10.1145/3386569.3392438
6. Feng, K., Huang, D., Wang, G.: Two-layer material point method for modeling soil–water interaction in unsaturated soils and rainfall-induced slope failure. Acta Geotech. **16**(8), 2529–2551 (2021). https://doi.org/10.1007/s11440-021-01222-9
7. Fern, E., Rohe, A., Soga, K., Alonso, E.: The Material Point Method for Geotechnical Engineering: A Practical Guide (2019). https://doi.org/10.1201/9780429028090
8. Fu, C., Guo, Q., Gast, T., Jiang, C., Teran, J.: A polynomial particle-in-cell method. ACM Trans. Graph. **36**(6), 1–12 (2017). https://doi.org/10.1145/3130800.3130878
9. Gao, M., et al.: Animating fluid sediment mixture in particle-laden flows. ACM Trans. Graph. **37**(4), 1–11 (2018). https://doi.org/10.1145/3197517.3201309
10. Gao, M., Tampubolon, A.P., Jiang, C., Sifakis, E.: An adaptive generalized interpolation material point method for simulating elastoplastic materials. ACM Trans. Graph. **36**(6), 1–12 (2017). https://doi.org/10.1145/3130800.3130879
11. Guerriero, V., Mazzoli, S.: Theory of effective stress in soil and rock and implications for fracturing processes: a review. Geosciences **11**(3), 119 (2021). https://doi.org/10.3390/geosciences11030119

12. Hu, Y., et al.: A moving least squares material point method with displacement discontinuity and two-way rigid body coupling. ACM Trans. Graph. **37**(4), 1–14 (2018). https://doi.org/10.1145/3197517.3201293
13. Huang, P., Li, S., Guo, H., Hao, Z.: Large deformation failure analysis of the soil slope based on the material point method. Comput. Geosci. **19**(4), 951–963 (2015). https://doi.org/10.1007/s10596-015-9512-9
14. Jiang, C., Gast, T., Teran, J.: Anisotropic elastoplasticity for cloth, knit and hair frictional contact. ACM Trans. Graph. **36**(4), 1–14 (2017). https://doi.org/10.1145/3072959.3073623
15. Jiang, C., Schroeder, C., Selle, A., Teran, J., Stomakhin, A.: The affine particle-in-cell method. ACM Trans. Graph. **34**(4), 1–10 (2015). https://doi.org/10.1145/2766996
16. Lenaerts, T., Adams, B., Dutré, P.: Porous flow in particle-based fluid simulations. ACM Trans. Graph. **27**(3), 1–8 (2008). https://doi.org/10.1145/1360612.1360648
17. Mieremet, M., Stolle, D., Ceccato, F., Vuik, C.: Numerical stability for modelling of dynamic two-phase interaction. Int. J. Numer. Anal. Meth. Geomech. **40**(9), 1284–1294 (2016). https://doi.org/10.1002/nag.2483
18. Nagasawa, K., Suzuki, T., Seto, R., Okada, M., Yue, Y.: Mixing sauces: a viscosity blending model for shear thinning fluids. ACM Trans. Graph. **38**(4), 95 (2019). https://doi.org/10.1145/3306346.3322947
19. Ram, D., et al.: A material point method for viscoelastic fluids, foams and sponges. In: Proceedings of the 14th ACM SIGGRAPH/Eurographics Symposium on Computer Animation, SCA 2015, pp. 157–163. Association for Computing Machinery, New York (2015). https://doi.org/10.1145/2786784.2786798
20. Soga, K., Alonso, E., Yerro, A., Kumar, K., Bandara, S.: Trends in large-deformation analysis of landslide mass movements with particular emphasis on the material point method. Géotechnique **66**(3), 248–273 (2016). https://doi.org/10.1680/jgeot.15.lm.005
21. Stomakhin, A., Schroeder, C., Chai, L., Teran, J., Selle, A.: A material point method for snow simulation. ACM Trans. Graph. **32**(4), 1–10 (2013). https://doi.org/10.1145/2461912.2461948
22. Stomakhin, A., Schroeder, C., Jiang, C., Chai, L., Teran, J., Selle, A.: Augmented MPM for phase-change and varied materials. ACM Trans. Graph. **33**(4), 1–11 (2014). https://doi.org/10.1145/2601097.2601176
23. Sulsky, D., Chen, Z., Schreyer, H.: A particle method for history-dependent materials. Comput. Methods Appl. Mech. Eng. **118**(1), 179–196 (1994). https://doi.org/10.1016/0045-7825(94)90112-0
24. Sun, Y., Ni, X., Zhu, B., Wang, B., Chen, B.: A material point method for nonlinearly magnetized materials. ACM Trans. Graph. **40**(6), 1–13 (2021). https://doi.org/10.1145/3478513.3480541
25. Tampubolon, A.P., et al.: Multi-species simulation of porous sand and water mixtures. ACM Trans. Graph. **36**(4), 1–11 (2017). https://doi.org/10.1145/3072959.3073651
26. Tang, L., Sang, H., Luo, Z., Sun, Y.: Advances in research on the mechanical behavior of the tensile strength of soils. Adv. Earth Sci. **30**(3), 297 (2015). https://doi.org/10.11867/j.issn.1001-8166.2015.03.0297
27. Wang, X., et al.: Hierarchical optimization time integration for CFL-rate MPM stepping. ACM Trans. Graph. **39**(3), 1–16 (2020). https://doi.org/10.1145/3386760

28. Yue, Y., Smith, B., Batty, C., Zheng, C., Grinspun, E.: Continuum foam: a material point method for shear-dependent flows. ACM Trans. Graph. **34**(5), 1–20 (2015). https://doi.org/10.1145/2751541
29. Zhu, J., et al.: Compensating the vorticity loss during advection with an adaptive vorticity confinement force. Comput. Animat. Virtual Worlds **32**(1), e1973 (2021). https://doi.org/10.1002/cav.1973

SlimFliud-Net: Fast Fluid Simulation Using Admm Pruning

Hao Xiang[1], Songyang Yu[2], Ping Li[3,4], Weiguang Li[2], Enhua Wu[5,6], and Bin Sheng[1(✉)]

[1] Department of Computer Science and Engineering, Shanghai Jiao Tong University, Shanghai, China
shengbin@sjtu.edu.cn
[2] China Ship Development and Design Center, Wuhan, China
[3] Department of Computing, The Hong Kong Polytechnic University, Hung Hom, Hong Kong
[4] School of Design, The Hong Kong Polytechnic University, Hung Hom, Hong Kong
[5] State Key Laboratory of Computer Science, Institute of Software, Chinese Academy of Sciences, Beijing, China
[6] Faculty of Science and Technology, University of Macau, Macau, China

Abstract. While data-driven fluid simulation methods greatly replace the physics-based fluid solver and achieve high quality results, it is a challenge to get enough realistic effect with less time. The Huge neural network models brought by the complexity of fluid data need to calculate a large number of parameters from the convolutional and full-connected layers in the forward propagation process, which lead to very long inference time and cannot meet the real-time requirements. Our method is based on a structural pruning method to reduce the number of parameters of a general fluid neural network model that imposes the admm constraints on original loss on training process and removes the convlutional filters at a certain rate according to their importance. We show the high quality results for velocity field reconstruction and advancing time from reduced parameters using our pruned fluid model, which has only 30%–50% parameters of the original model and greatly improves the inference speed of the model. It is a big step towards high-accuracy real-time fluid simulation.

Keywords: Fluid simulation · Neural network · Filter pruning

1 Introduction

Fluid reconstruction and evolution is an important work in the field of fluid simulation. Traditionally, fluids are reconstructed by Finite Element Method (FEM), Finite Difference Method (FDM), and Smoothed Particle Hydrodynamics (SPH) and its extended methods, resulting in a large linear system to be solved using numerical solvers. The huge problems in computation amount and time severely

---

H. Xiang and S. Yu—contribute equally to this work.

© The Author(s), under exclusive license to Springer Nature Switzerland AG 2022
N. Magnenat-Thalmann et al. (Eds.): CGI 2022, LNCS 13443, pp. 582–593, 2022.
https://doi.org/10.1007/978-3-031-23473-6_45

hinder their real-time performance, although they are getting better in terms of authenticity.

With the evolution of time, techniques combining neural networks and modern GPUs are flourishing in many fields. Autoencoders [1], long short-term memory (LSTM) [2], generative adversarial networks(GANs) [3], and continuous convolution [4] are new tools for studies associated with solver acceleration and detail enhancement. The combination of neural network and fluid simulation accelerates the inference speed of fluid simulation, making it possible to simulate real-time fluid in complex situations. DeepFluid [5] presents a novel generative model to simulate fluid behaviors from a set of reduced parameters. A convolutional neural network is trained on a collection of discrete, parameterizable fluid simulation velocity fields. Although this method simulates various fluid behaviors ranging from turbulent smoke to viscous liquids, however, the large network model caused by complexity of fluid data structure leads to amounts of computation in the process of fluid reconstruction and time advancing, resulting low inference speed. Besides, M Chu et al. [6] also presents a similar network like above model for generating corresponding velocity field frame from a density field frame. The large time consuming also emerge in this model. Furthermore, almost all fluid neural network models have the problem that the inference time is too long for many network parameters. At present, related work has improved its inference speed by pruning the neural network model. Therefore, in order to solve this problem, we use structural filter pruning combined with ADMM (Alternating Direction Method of Multipliers) to prune the fluid neural networks, which greatly reduces model parameters while maintaining the inference accuracy. After pruning, in the process of fluid reconstruction and time advancement, the network model will greatly reduce the inference time due to the reduction of the calculation amount, thereby enhancing the real-time performance of fluid simulation.

In this paper, we apply ADMM pruning method [7] to the field of fluid neural network, and perform pruning experiments on several fluid neural network models. The results show that the model obtained by pruning can be reduced in size by 30–50% while maintaining a similar visual effect. The results verify the feasibility of ADMM structured pruning algorithm in this field, and obtain a fluid neural network model with smaller scale and faster inference speed.

To summarize, the contribution of our work includes:

- The first work to perform structured pruning for fluid deep networks that considers the parameter redundancy of the neural network, which provides a new idea for accelerating fluid simulation
- A non end-to-end pruning strategy that integrates the advantages of both velocity reconstruction and advancing time, which ensuring high performance as well as high resolution
- A detailed analysis of the pruning feasibility in deep fluid networks from pruning performance and renderings.

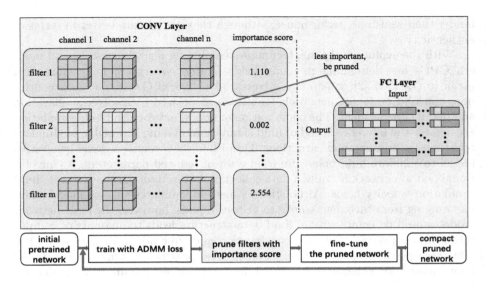

Fig. 1. The pruning framework of our proposed method. (Left) Filter pruning for convolutional layers. (Right) Row pruning for full-connected layers.For each convolution kernel of the convolution layer, we calculate their norm-2 value as the importance of each convolution kernel. According to the given pruning ratio of each layer and the number of filters of this layer N, through ADMM pruning algorithm (combined with filter pruning), the importance of N*ratio convolution kernels will tend to 0 after the model is trained. This means that these filters have less influence on the output result, so we can remove this part of filter. For the full-connected layer, we directly calculate the value of norm-2 for each neuron and then do the same with the above method. Pruning process is mainly divided into two stages. In the first stage, the model will be trained under the constraint of ADMM Loss until ADMM Loss converges to sparse weight. In the second stage, the model was pruned according to the sparsed weight, and then the precision of the pruned model through fine-tune will be improved.

2   Related Work

2.1   Fluid Simulation

Fluid Simulation refers computer graphics techniques for generating realistic animation of fluids such as water and smoke [8]. Approximating the solution to Navier-Stokes equation that govern real fluid physics is the mainstream idea in computer graphics. Eulerian method, Lagrangian method and hybrid method, are three typical viewpoints by discretizing the continuous field from different perspectives. Foster [9] and Stam [10] introduced Eulerian method and semi-Lagrangian advection step by discretizing a fluid on static unified grid. The physical properties are stored on the grid nodes and grid faces [11]. To capture more small scale details, a set of adaptive strategies, such as tall cells [12], far-field grids [13], and adaptive staggered-tiled grids [14] was proposed. Position-based-dynamics (PBD) [15] which relies on the Smoothed particle hydrodynamics(SPH) [16] kernel, simulates a position-based fluid in Lagranian way. Differentiation is performed on neighboring particles using a smooth kernel. Cornelis [17] and Bender [18] further solved the instability problem and achieved incompressibility. Zhu [19] combining particle-in-cell (PIC) method [20] and fluid-implicit-particle (FLIP) method [21] with a blending factor to animate sand as a continuous fluid. Jiang [22] employed a locally affine velocity descriptor to achieve a grid-particle interpolation step, whereas Fu [23] further improved energy and vorticity conservation by augmenting each particle with a polynomial descriptor.

2.2   Data-Driven Fluid Simulation

Data driven methods build a mathematical model using a large amount of historical data, and generates predictions based on the knowledge learned automatically [24]. Chu [25] trained a patch-based convolutional descriptor to locally synthesize high-resolution details from space-time flow repositories on regular grid. [26] formulates physics-based fluid simulation as a regression problem, estimating the acceleration of every particle for each frame. An LSTM based method for predicting changes of the pressure field for multiple subsequent time steps has been presented by [2]. [3] proposed a temporally coherent generative model addressing the super-resolution problem for fluid flows, generating consistent and detailed results by using a novel temporal discriminator, in addition to the commonly used spatial one. Stanton [27] proposed a state graph for simulation to describe unstructured Lagrangian particles. [28] and [29] employed graph convolution to extract topological features after dynamically building edges in the graph between neighboring particles. Ummenhofer [4] applied a spatial convolution operator as main differentiable operation on both fluid and boundary particles under the SPH framework. SPNets [30] achieved particle-particle pairwise interactions and particle-static object interactions by ConvSP and ConvSDF layers.

2.3   Fluid Acceleration

Some data-driven solvers [31,32] replaced the time-consuming procedure for solving Poission equation with neural networks, hence accelerating the simulation in Eulerian method. LSTM [2] and generative adversarial networks [3] are also served as acceleration approaches. Chu [33] presented an algorithm, efficient and parallelized domain decomposition based approach, to solving Poisson's equation on irregular domains. Gao [34] performed a memory-friendly GPU optimization for accelerating MPM simulation. Yang [1] used a neural projection operator composed of a lightweight network with an embedded recursive architecture to predict the behaviors of physical systems by learning constraints. GPU's parallel computing has been used in parallel training [35] and extended to support physical calculations for acceleration [36–39]. Hu [40,41] developed a differentiable programming language for simulation to optimize the calculation at the operating system level. Another different perspective of fluid acceleration is model reduction/compression, which simplifies the model for low computational complexity while preserving the features as much as possible. Treuille [42] first introduced model reduction for feature extraction to fluid simulation. Weight pruning methods, which have been applied to image classification task in computer vision (CV), aim to remove redundant or less importance weights. In [43], for each filter of the convolutional layer, the sum of the absolute value of its weight (l1-norm) is calculated as its importance score, and then the less important ones are pruned according to the importance score of each filter. In SFP [44], the l2-regularization of the filter weight is used to measure the importance, and soft filter pruning is performed accelerating deep convolutional networks. Although no previous study in data-driven fluid simulation methods has ever done so, the idea of network pruning is promising to be directly used to balance the contradiction between efficiency and performance in fluid simulation.

3 Method

3.1 ADMM Pruning Method

The classic ADMM algorithm is generally used for solving following two-block convex optimization problem:

$$\min_{x} \quad f(x) + g(y)$$
$$\text{s.t.} \quad Ax + By = c \tag{1}$$

where $x \in \mathbf{R^n}$ is the optimization variable of the objective function $f(x)$, $y \in \mathbf{R^m}$ is the optimization variable of the objective function $g(y)$, $A \in \mathbf{R^{p \times n}}, B \in \mathbf{R^{p \times m}}, c \in \mathbf{R^p}$. The function $f(x) \to \mathbf{R}$, $g(y) \to \mathbf{R}$ are both convex functions.

According to the Systematic DNN Weight Pruning framework by Zhang [7], the first pruning framework using ADMM, for weight parameters W_i, b_i of a certain layer i, weight pruning optimization problem can be expressed as similar form:

$$\min_{\{W_i\},\{b_i\}} \quad f(W_i, b_i) + \sum_{i=1}^{N} g_i(Z_i)$$
$$\text{s.t.} \quad W_i = Z_i, i = 1, 2, ...N. \tag{2}$$

$$g_i(W_i) = \begin{cases} 0, & if \quad card(W_i) \le l_i, \\ +\infty, & otherwise. \end{cases} \tag{3}$$

where $f(\{W_i\}, \{b_i\})$ expressed the total loss of the network, and $g_i(\Delta)$ is the indicator function of $S_i = \{W_i | card(W_i) \le l_i\}, i = 1, 2, ..., N$. $card(\Delta)$ returns the number of non-zero elements of its matrix argument and l_i is the desired number of weights in the i-th layer of the network.

It can be seen that the weight pruning problem is transformed into a convex optimization problem that can be solved by ADMM. According to ADMM solution, the optimization problem becomes one of finding the optimal solution to minimize the following objective function.

$$L_\rho(\{W_i\}\{b_i\}\{Z_i\}\{\Lambda_i\}) = f(\{W_i\}, \{b_i\}) + \sum_{i=1}^{N} g_i(Z_i)$$
$$+ \sum_{i=1}^{N} \|W_i - Z_i + U_i\|_F^2 + \sum_{i=1}^{N} \frac{\rho_i}{2} \|U_i\|_F^2 \tag{4}$$

Furthermore, the optimal solution can be solved iteratively by repeating the following steps until convergence. Please refer to [7] for soulution details.

$$
\begin{cases}
W_i^{k+1}, b_i^{k+1} = \underset{W_i, b_i}{\arg\min} L_\rho(W_i, b_i, Z_i^{k+1}, U_i^{k+1}) \\
Z_i^{k+1} = \underset{Z_i}{\arg\min} L_\rho(W_i^{k+1}, b_i^{k+1}, Z_i, U_i^k) \\
U_i^{k+1} = U_i^k + W_i^{k+1} - Z_i^{k+1}
\end{cases}
\tag{5}
$$

3.2 Original Model

For the selected model, we mainly adopted the network architecture from [5], used for velocity field reconstruction and advancing time from reduced representations, as illustrated in Fig. 2. This model is mainly composed of four parts: Encoder $\mathbf{G}^\dagger$, Decoder/Generator $\mathbf{G}$, Latent Space Network $\mathbf{T}$ and Discriminator $\mathbf{D}$. Take the example of the smoke, $\mathbf{c}$ is generally the combination of x-position and width of the smoke source, the current time or more extended parameters.

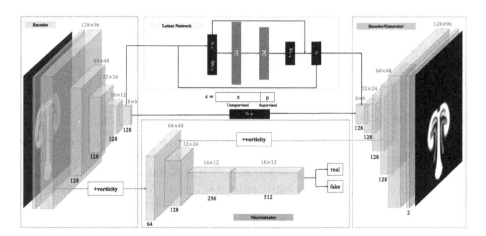

Fig. 2. A ResNet-based encoder-decoder generator, with latent network encoding corresponding parameters like x-position and width of smoke source. The generator compresses a velocity field u into a latent space representation c, which includes a supervised and unsupervised part (p and z). The latent space integration network finds mappings from subsequent latent code representations c_t and c_{t+1}. The discriminator shares a similar architecture with Encoder (velocity/vorticity as input and authenticity as output). Yellow, blue and balck boxes stand for the convolutional layers, full-connected layers and reduced representation of velocity frame. (Color figure online)

The Decoder/Generator $\mathbf{G}$ converts the reduced one-dimension representation $\mathbf{c}$ to a velocity field frame by series of convolutional layers with residual connections and full-connected layers. The Encoder $\mathbf{G}^\dagger$ structure which maps the velocity field frame into a parameterization $\mathbf{c}$ is approximately symmetric to the Decoder structure **G**. The Latent Space Integration Network **T** is actually a MLP (multi-perceptron) composed of multiple fully connected layers for advancing time from reduced representation. The reduced representation c_t will be updated to c_{t+1} by the latent network integration T.

The loss function for both Generator **G** and Encoder **G**† is:

$$L_G(\mathbf{c}) = \lambda_{\mathbf{u}}\|\mathbf{u_c} - \hat{\mathbf{u}}_{\mathbf{c}}\|_1 + \lambda_{\nabla\mathbf{u}}\|\nabla\mathbf{u_c} - \nabla\hat{\mathbf{u}}_{\mathbf{c}}\|_1 + \lambda_{\mathbf{p}}\|\mathbf{p} - \hat{\mathbf{p}}_{\mathbf{c}}\|_2^2 \tag{6}$$

where $\hat{\mathbf{p}}$ is the part of the latent space vector constrained to represent control parameters **p**, and $\lambda_{\mathbf{p}}$ is a weight to emphasize the learning of supervised parameters.

where $\hat{\mathbf{u}}_{\mathbf{c}} = \nabla \times G(\mathbf{c})$ for incompressible flows, $\hat{\mathbf{u}}_{\mathbf{c}} = G(\mathbf{c})$ for compressible flows and $\hat{\mathbf{p}}$ is the part of the latent space vector constrained to represent control parameters **p**. $\lambda_{\mathbf{u}}$, $\lambda_{\nabla\mathbf{u}}$ and $\lambda_{\mathbf{p}}$ are used to emphasize the reconstruction of either the velocities or their derivatives and learning of supervised parameters. The loss of the latent space integration network is designed to minimize errors accumulated in repeated latent space updates:

$$L_T(\mathbf{x}_t, \mathbf{x}_{t+w+1}) = \frac{1}{w} \sum_{i=t}^{t+w-1} \|\Delta\mathbf{z}_i - T_i\|_2^2 \tag{7}$$

where $\mathbf{x}_t = [\mathbf{c}_t; \Delta\mathbf{p}_t]$ is input vector with latent code $\mathbf{c}_t$ and position parameters' difference $\Delta\mathbf{p}_t$, T_i is recursively computed from t to i by window w, and $\Delta\mathbf{z}_t$ is the residual between two consecutive velocity field states.

3.3   Implementation

We perform structured pruning operations on a large number of convolutional and fully connected layers included in encoder, decoder, and latent integral network. The principle of pruning is shown in Fig. 1 Notably, we did not perform structured pruning on all convolutional layers. Due to AutoEncoders(Generator and Encoder) and Latent Network are trained separately rather than end-to-end models and structured pruning will reduce the number of output channels, we apply admm constraints to AutoEncoder and Latent Network respectively while maintaining latent variable **c**'s dimension consistent to ensure that the input and output of two module can be well coupled. Pruning criteria: In the process of pruning, for the convolutional layer, we pass the 2-norm of each convolution kernel of each layer, and decide to prune the smaller convolution kernel of 1-norm by size sorting. For full connection layer, we adopt row pruning and each node's is calculated and sorted by 2-norm.

According to equation (4) (6) (7), loss function of AutoEncoder **G**† + **G** and Latent Network **T** after applying admm constraints can be expressed as:

$$L_G(\mathbf{c}) = \lambda_{\mathbf{u}}\|\mathbf{u_c} - \hat{\mathbf{u}}_{\mathbf{c}}\|_1 + \lambda_{\nabla\mathbf{u}}\|\nabla\mathbf{u_c} - \nabla\hat{\mathbf{u}}_{\mathbf{c}}\|_1 + \lambda_{\mathbf{p}}\|\mathbf{p} - \hat{\mathbf{p}}_{\mathbf{c}}\|_2^2$$
$$+ \sum_{i=1}^{N} g_i(Z_i) + \sum_{i=1}^{N} \rho_i/2\|W_i - Z_i + U_i\|_F^2 - \sum_{i=1}^{N} \rho_i/2\|U_i\|_F^2 \tag{8}$$

$$L_T(\mathbf{x}_t, \mathbf{x}_{t+w+1}) = \frac{1}{w} \sum_{i=t}^{t+w-1} \|\Delta\mathbf{z}_i - T_i\|_2^2 + \sum_{i=1}^{N} g_i(Z_i)$$
$$+ \sum_{i=1}^{N} \rho_i/2 \|W_i - Z_i + U_i\|_F^2 - \sum_{i=1}^{N} \rho_i/2 \|U_i\|_F^2 \tag{9}$$

The constraint term makes part of weights of pretrained network to be zero or close to 0 after training and we set all the weights with a value 0 or close to 0. Finally, by retraining for restoring performance through the Fine-tune stage, slim models can be obtained. The results of pruned model are comparable to original model in visual effects. Please refer to Sect. 4.2 for more detailed results.

4   Experiments

4.1   Datasets

Kim et al. [5] proposed a velocity field image benchmark datasets. The dataset contains 2D smoke plume example and 3D smoke plume example. The training set for 2D smoke plume example consists of the combination of 5 samples with varying source widths w and 21 samples with varying x positions p_x. Each simulation is computed for 200 frames, using a grid resolution of 96 × 128 and a domain size of (1, 1:33). The network is trained with a total of 21000 unique velocity field samples.

The 3D smoke data samples in the original text are four types: Smoke&Sphere Obstacle, Smoke Inflow and Buoyancy, Rotating Smoke, Moving Smoke.

Smoke & Sphere Obstacle: 3-D example of a smoke plume interacting with a sphere computed on a grid of size 64 × 96 × 64. The training data consists of ten simulations with varying sphere positions, with the spaces between spheres centroid samples consisting of 0.06 in the interval [0:2; 0:8].

Smoke Inflow and Buoyancy: A collection of simulations for 5 inflow velocities (in the range [1:0; 5:0]) along with 3 different buoyancy values(from 6× $10e^{-4}$ to 1 × $10e^{-3}$) are generated.

Rotating Smoke: The model are trained for a smoke simulation sample with a periodically rotating source using 500 frames as training data.

Moving Smoke: A smoke source is moved in the XZ-plane along a path randomly generated using Perlin noise including 200 simulations on a grid of size 48 × 72 × 48 for 400 frames.

4.2   Quantitative Result

In the following, our results demonstrate that our slim models have better performance in terms of inference time, FLOPs and compressing ratio.

We compare original model and pruned model in terms of inference time, model size, Compressing ratio et al. Table 1 shows the inference performance for

Table 1. Inference performance for Original Model and Slim Model

Scene	Smoke Plume	Smoke Obstacle	Smoke Inflow	Moving Smoke
Grid resolution	96 * 128	64 * 96 * 64	112 * 64 * 32	48 * 72 * 48
Frames	21000	6600	3750	80000
Simulation time (s)	0.033	0.491	0.128	0.08
Eval. time (ms) [Batch]	0.052 [100]	0.999 [5]	0.958 [5]	0.52 [10]
Eval. time (ms) [Batch] - Slim	0.023[100]	0.455 [5]	0.523 [5]	0.230 [10]
Eval. time reduction (%)	55.77	54.45	45.41	55.77
Network size (MB)	12	30	29	38
Pruned network size (MB)	5.6	14.2	13.6	13.4
Compressing ratio (%)	46.67	47.30	46.89	35.20

original model and Slim Model. From Table 1, for 2d Smoke Plume data sample, the model size has been reduced from the original 12 MB to 5.6MB by 53.32%. The inference speed has also been improved about 2×, and the evaluation time for batch size 100 has been reduced by 55.77%. For the larger 3D SmokeObstacle and SmokeInlow data samples, our pruned model can reduce more parameters. The size of the SmokeObstacle model is reduced by 52.7%, the size of the Smoke-Inflow model is reduced by 53.11%, and the corresponding evaluation time for batch size 5 is also reduced by 54.45% and 45.41% respectively. In addition, we also calculated the corresponding FLOPS and latency. We compared the calculation amount of the model before and after pruning. From this perspective, it proves that the model calculation amount is indeed greatly reduced.

4.3   Qualitative Result

In the following, our results shows the fluid reconstruction effects from our slim model on smoke plume. On the plume data set, we employ the model to predict series of frames of smoke development from scratch, from which we sample 10 frames, as shown in the Fig. 3. As can be seen from the display effect of Fig. 3, the smoke source has evolved reasonably well over time, with considerable authenticity and superior visual effects.

In addition, we also compared our fluid reconstruciton, interpolation and inference effects with original model. For the reconstruction effect on the same position parameter p from slim model and original model is also compared. Slim model can almost reproduce the visual effect of the original model. We compare

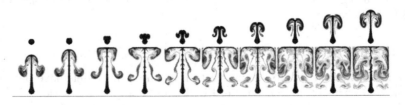

Fig. 3. Snapshots showing advected densities sampled 10 out of 200 frames

it with the interpolation effect on SmokeObstacle dataset between slim model and original model. It can be proved that the interpolating ability of our Slim model is comparable to original model.

5   Discussion and Conclusions

In this paper, we propose a pruned fluid neural network model after structured weight pruning using ADMM. We perform structured pruning on convolutional layers in auto-Encoder and fully connected layers in Latent Space Network, respectively. Through pruning, the 2-D smoke model size is 46.67% of original model and the inference speed becomes about 2×, and the 3-D smoke model size is about 40% and the inference speed becomes 2–3×. Since fluid simulation requires both real-time and high precision, we have confirmed the feasibility of pruning a high-precision fluid neural network model to reduce the model size, improve the model inference speed, and enhance the model's real-time performance by our experiments. Since our work performs pruning on two sub-module separately and then combines them together to infer, we are planning to prune larger-scale end-to-end complex models in the fluid field in the future. In addition, we expect to establish a unified fluid reconstruction neural network model for input data of 2d, 3d and different sizes.

Acknowledgements. This work was supported in part by the National Natural Science Foundation of China under Grants 62272298, 61872241 and 62077037, in part by Shanghai Municipal Science and Technology Major Project under Grant 2021SHZDZX0102.

References

1. Yang, S., He, X., Zhu, B.: Learning physical constraints with neural projections. Adv. Neural. Inf. Process. Syst. **33**, 5178–5189 (2020)
2. Wiewel, S., Kim, B., Azevedo, V.C., Solenthaler, B., Thuerey, N.: Latent space subdivision: stable and controllable time predictions for fluid flow. In: Computer Graphics Forum, vol. 39, pp. 15–25. Wiley Online Library (2020)
3. Xie, Y., Franz, E., Chu, M., Thuerey, N.: tempoGAN: a temporally coherent, volumetric GAN for super-resolution fluid flow. ACM Trans. Graph. (TOG) **37**(4), 1–15 (2018)
4. Ummenhofer, B., Prantl, L., Thuerey, N., Koltun, V.: Lagrangian fluid simulation with continuous convolutions. In: International Conference on Learning Representations (2020)
5. Kim, B., Azevedo, V.C., Thuerey, N., Kim, T., Gross, M., Solenthaler, B.: Deep fluids: a generative network for parameterized fluid simulations (2018)
6. Chu, M., Thuerey, N., Seidel, H.P., Theobalt, C., Zayer, R.: Learning meaningful controls for fluids. ACM Trans. Graph. **40**(4), 1–13 (2021)
7. Zhang, T., Ye, S., Zhang, Y., Wang, Y., Fardad, M.: Systematic weight pruning of DNNs using alternating direction method of multipliers (2018)
8. Bridson, R.: Fluid Simulation for Computer Graphics. AK Peters/CRC Press (2015)

9. Foster, N., Metaxas, D.N.: Controlling fluid animation. In: Computer Graphics International Conference, CGI 1997, Hasselt and Diepenbeek, Belgium, 23–27 June 1997, pp. 178–188. IEEE Computer Society (1997). https://doi.org/10.1109/CGI.1997.601299

10. Stam, J.: Stable fluids. In: Proceedings of the 26th Annual Conference on Computer Graphics and Interactive Techniques, pp. 121–128 (1999)

11. Harlow, F.H., Welch, J.E.: Numerical calculation of time-dependent viscous incompressible flow of fluid with free surface. phys. Fluids 8(12), 2182–2189 (1965)

12. Chentanez, N., Müller, M.: Real-time Eulerian water simulation using a restricted tall cell grid. In: ACM Siggraph 2011 Papers, pp. 1–10 (2011)

13. Zhu, B., Lu, W., Cong, M., Kim, B., Fedkiw, R.: A new grid structure for domain extension. ACM Trans. Graph. (TOG) 32(4), 1–12 (2013)

14. Xiao, Y., Chan, S., Wang, S., Zhu, B., Yang, X.: An adaptive staggered-tilted grid for incompressible flow simulation. ACM Trans. Graph. (TOG) 39(6), 1–15 (2020)

15. Macklin, M., Müller, M.: Position based fluids. ACM Trans. Graph. (TOG) 32(4), 1–12 (2013)

16. Müller, M., Charypar, D., Gross, M.: Particle-based fluid simulation for interactive applications. In: Proceedings of the 2003 ACM SIGGRAPH/Eurographics symposium on Computer animation, pp. 154–159. Citeseer (2003)

17. Cornelis, J., Ihmsen, M., Peer, A., Teschner, M.: IISPH-FLIP for incompressible fluids. In: Computer Graphics Forum, vol. 33, pp. 255–262. Wiley Online Library (2014)

18. Bender, J., Koschier, D.: Divergence-free SPH for incompressible and viscous fluids. IEEE Trans. Visual Comput. Graph. 23(3), 1193–1206 (2016)

19. Zhu, Y., Bridson, R.: Animating sand as a fluid. ACM Trans. Graph. (TOG) 24(3), 965–972 (2005)

20. Harlow, F.H.: The particle-in-cell method for numerical solution of problems in fluid dynamics. Technical report, Los Alamos National Lab. (LANL), Los Alamos, NM (United States) (1962)

21. Brackbill, J.U., Ruppel, H.M.: FLIP: a method for adaptively zoned, particle-in-cell calculations of fluid flows in two dimensions. J. Comput. Phys. 65(2), 314–343 (1986)

22. Jiang, C., Schroeder, C., Selle, A., Teran, J., Stomakhin, A.: The affine particle-in-cell method. ACM Trans. Graph. (TOG) 34(4), 1–10 (2015)

23. Fu, C., Guo, Q., Gast, T., Jiang, C., Teran, J.: A polynomial particle-in-cell method. ACM Trans. Graph. (TOG) 36(6), 1–12 (2017)

24. Chen, Q., Wang, Y., Wang, H., Yang, X.: Data-driven simulation in fluids animation: a survey. Virtual Reality Intell. Hardw. 3(2), 87–104 (2021)

25. Chu, M., Thuerey, N.: Data-driven synthesis of smoke flows with CNN-based feature descriptors. ACM Trans. Graph. (TOG) 36(4), 1–14 (2017)

26. Ladický, L., Jeong, S., Solenthaler, B., Pollefeys, M., Gross, M.: Data-driven fluid simulations using regression forests. ACM Trans. Graph. (TOG) 34(6), 1–9 (2015)

27. Stanton, M., Humberston, B., Kase, B., O'Brien, J.F., Fatahalian, K., Treuille, A.: Self-refining games using player analytics. ACM Trans. Graph. (TOG) 33(4), 1–9 (2014)

28. Li, Y., Wu, J., Tedrake, R., Tenenbaum, J.B., Torralba, A.: Learning particle dynamics for manipulating rigid bodies, deformable objects, and fluids. arXiv preprint arXiv:1810.01566 (2018)

29. Sanchez-Gonzalez, A., Godwin, J., Pfaff, T., Ying, R., Leskovec, J., Battaglia, P.: Learning to simulate complex physics with graph networks. In: International Conference on Machine Learning, pp. 8459–8468. PMLR (2020)

30. Schenck, C., Fox, D.: SPNets: differentiable fluid dynamics for deep neural networks. In: Conference on Robot Learning, pp. 317–335. PMLR (2018)
31. Yang, C., Yang, X., Xiao, X.: Data-driven projection method in fluid simulation. Comput. Animat. Virtual Worlds **27**(3–4), 415–424 (2016)
32. Tompson, J., Schlachter, K., Sprechmann, P., Perlin, K.: Accelerating Eulerian fluid simulation with convolutional networks. In: International Conference on Machine Learning, pp. 3424–3433. PMLR (2017)
33. Chu, J., Zafar, N.B., Yang, X.: A schur complement preconditioner for scalable parallel fluid simulation. ACM Trans. Graph. (TOG) **36**(4), 1 (2017)
34. Gao, M., et al.: GPU optimization of material point methods. ACM Trans. Graph. (TOG) **37**(6), 1–12 (2018)
35. Cui, H., Zhang, H., Ganger, G.R., Gibbons, P.B., Xing, E.P.: GeePS: scalable deep learning on distributed GPUs with a GPU-specialized parameter server. In: Proceedings of the Eleventh European Conference on Computer Systems, pp. 1–16 (2016)
36. McAdams, A., Sifakis, E., Teran, J.: A parallel multigrid poisson solver for fluids simulation on large grids. In: Symposium on Computer Animation, pp. 65–73 (2010)
37. Liu, H., Mitchell, N., Aanjaneya, M., Sifakis, E.: A scalable Schur-complement fluids solver for heterogeneous compute platforms. ACM Trans. Graph. (TOG) **35**(6), 1–12 (2016)
38. Jung, H.R., Kim, S.T., Noh, J., Hong, J.M.: A heterogeneous CPU-GPU parallel approach to a multigrid poisson solver for incompressible fluid simulation. Comput. Animat. Virtual Worlds **24**(3–4), 185–193 (2013)
39. Lentine, M., Zheng, W., Fedkiw, R.: A novel algorithm for incompressible flow using only a coarse grid projection. ACM Trans. Graph. (TOG) **29**(4), 1–9 (2010)
40. Hu, Y., Li, T.M., Anderson, L., Ragan-Kelley, J., Durand, F.: Taichi: a language for high-performance computation on spatially sparse data structures. ACM Trans. Graph. (TOG) **38**(6), 1–16 (2019)
41. Hu, Y., et al.: DiffTaichi: differentiable programming for physical simulation. arXiv preprint arXiv:1910.00935 (2019)
42. Treuille, A., Lewis, A., Popović, Z.: Model reduction for real-time fluids. ACM Trans. Graph. (TOG) **25**(3), 826–834 (2006)
43. Li, H., Kadav, A., Durdanovic, I., Samet, H., Graf, H.P.: Pruning filters for efficient convnets. arXiv preprint arXiv:1608.08710 (2016)
44. He, Y., Kang, G., Dong, X., Fu, Y., Yang, Y.: Soft filter pruning for accelerating deep convolutional neural networks. In: Proceedings of the Twenty-Seventh International Joint Conference on Artificial Intelligence, IJCAI-18, pp. 2234–2240. International Joint Conferences on Artificial Intelligence Organization (2018). https://doi.org/10.24963/ijcai.2018/309

Author Index

Abdallah, Asma Ben   451

Bao, Yongtang   330
Bedoui, Mohamed Hedi   451
Benvenuti, Davide   239
Boeckers, Judith   345
Boukadida, Rahma   451

Cai, Jinghan   477
Chen, Hui   79
Chen, Jia   503
Chen, Jin   53
Chen, Jun   53
Chen, Ningxin   395
Chen, Wenjie   554
Chen, Xinzhou   503
Cui, Jinrong   290
Cui, Xiao   477

Deng, Yaoyu   515

Ekeland, Ivar   170
Elloumi, Yaroub   451

Fan, Keyue   305
Fan, Yachun   395
Fei, Lunke   290
Feibush, Eliot   67
Fischer, Roland   345

Gai, Wei   424
Gao, Shiyu   157
Guha, Anshul   67
Gui, Xiuxiu   117
Guo, Lijun   41
Guo, Mengsi   145

Han, Zhen   53
Hao, Huaying   41
Hlavacs, Helmut   199
Hu, Xinrong   503
Huang, Dongjin   465
Huang, Jin   145, 503

Huang, Xiaoting   554
Huang, Yu   424

Ikkala, Julius   211

Jääskeläinen, Pekka   211
Ji, Xiaohui   477
Jiang, Xinghao   278
Jiang, Zhenbang   527
Jin, Xiaogang   227

Kachouri, Rostom   451
Kuang, Jinhui   477

Leria, Erwan   211
Li, Haipeng   569
Li, Lin   318
Li, Ping   582
Li, Shuyi   290
Li, Weiguang   582
Li, Xiangxian   424
Li, Xiaoxuan   381
Li, Zhaoxin   157
Liang, Chao   53
Liang, Jiajia   92
Liang, Yanxing   129
Liao, Yihui   92
Lin, Chia-Wen   53
Lin, Gang   129, 439
Liu, Hanlin   41
Liu, Hao   424
Liu, Jinhua   465
Liu, Shiguang   305
Liu, Shu   15, 266
Liu, Xiaoping   318
Liu, Xueting   554
Liu, Yonghuai   41
Liu, Yuhao   541
Liu, Yuqi   489
Long, Wei   489
Lu, Feixiang   369
Lu, Ping   145

Lu, Wenhuan 305
Lu, Zheng 395
Lv, Yushan 465

Ma, Jiaxing 439
Ma, Junxia 477
Ma, Lizhuang 357
Mäkitalo, Markku 211
Mani, Anamitra 407
Meng, Min 79
Meng, Ziyao 145
Miao, Hui 369
Muraleedharan, Lakshmi Priya 407

Nan, Bin 129

Peng, Tao 503

Qi, Fu 554
Qi, Yue 330
Qian, Pengjiang 129, 439
Qiao, Yu 541
Qin, Wenhu 28

Raut, Chinmay 407
Ren, Luqian 107

Sen, Liu 145
Shao, Wenhao 79
Sheng, Bin 92, 145, 582
Shi, Weipeng 28
Shu, Zhenyu 489
Song, Chunying 183
Sun, Libo 28
Sun, Tanfeng 278
Sun, Tao 3
Sun, Wenxin 227
Sun, Yuzhou 357
Suta, Anton 199

Tan, Taizhe 515
Temam, Roger 170

Velappan, Raghavan 407

Wang, Chongwen 255
Wang, He 227
Wang, Jingzhao 183
Wang, Kai 183

Wang, Min 15
Wang, Rui 107
Wang, Sen 357
Wang, Shuang 3
Wang, Shuning 227
Wang, Xiang 318
Wang, Xiaoyu 266
Wang, Yangjun 227
Wang, Yinghui 129, 439
Wang, Yuxin 541
Wang, Zepeng 278
Wang, Zhaoqi 157
Wang, Zhaosheng 357
Wang, Zhen 381
Wang, Zheng 53
Wei, Jianxiong 290
Wei, Ziqi 541
Wen, Jie 290
Wu, Di 465
Wu, Enhua 582
Wu, Huisi 554
Wu, Jigang 79
Wu, Min 129
Wu, Wenyan 107

Xiang, Hao 582
Xiao, Xinfei 330
Xie, Jianyang 41
Xie, Zhifeng 92, 357
Xin, Shiqing 489
Xiong, Zhaoyu 569
Xu, Dan 569
Xu, Hengshuo 381
Xu, Ke 278
Xu, Peisen 239
Xu, Pengfei 395
Xu, Tiancheng 369

Yang, Chenglei 424
Yang, Liuming 395
Yang, Xin 541
Yang, Yukun 28
Yang, Zhuo 107
Yao, Xinran 227
Yi, Shun 489
Yu, Chunpeng 92
Yu, Jipeng 515
Yu, Songyang 582

Yu, Xinhui   395
Yun, Nan   183

Zachmann, Gabriel   345
Zhang, Han   145
Zhang, Hao   569
Zhang, Jiong   41
Zhang, Kun   183
Zhang, Liangjun   369
Zhang, Qiang   541
Zhang, Xinyu   117
Zhang, Yi   255
Zhang, Yue   15
Zhang, Zhifeng   477

Zhao, Shuaiqiang   527
Zhao, Shuping   290
Zhao, Wenqing   145
Zhao, Yitian   41
Zhao, Zhe   477
Zheng, Zude   318
Zhong, Shenjie   3
Zhou, Bin   369
Zhou, Dongsheng   541
Zhou, Jingbo   424
Zhu, Chengzhang   266
Zhu, Jian   107
Zou, Beiji   15, 266
Zou, Kuansheng   527

Printed in the United States
by Baker & Taylor Publisher Services